CIVIL PROCEDURE
2014
Fourth Cumulative Supplement
to the
2014 Edition

Up–to–date generally to October 1, 2014

SWEET & MAXWELL THOMSON REUTERS

Published in 2014 by Sweet & Maxwell, 100 Avenue Road, London NW3 3PF
part of Thomson Reuters (Professional) UK Limited
(Registered in England & Wales, Company No. 1679046.
Registered Office and address for service:
Aldgate House, 33 Aldgate High Street, London EC3N 1DL)
All typesetting by Sweet & Maxwell electronic publishing system.
Printed and bound in the UK by CPI Group (UK) Ltd, Croydon, CR0 4YY.
For further information on our products and services, visit
http://www.sweetandmaxwell.co.uk.

*No natural forests were destroyed to make this product; only farmed timber was used
and replanted.*

British Library Cataloguing in Publication Data
A catalogue record for this book is available from the British Library

ISBN–978–0–41403–708–3

PUBLISHER'S NOTE

Civil Procedure 2014 published on March 27, 2014. This Supplement contains updating material for both Volumes of *Civil Procedure 2014* and brings the work up–to–date to October 1, 2014. It is a cumulative supplement so it includes the text of the previous three Supplements.

The Fourth Supplement is published to take account of amendments made to the Civil Procedure Rules introduced by the Civil Procedure (Amendment No.6) Rules (SI 2014/2044) and the 74th and 75th Updates to the Practice Directions.

The 74th Update brings into force a new Practice Direction (PD2C) which assists court users in deciding where to start proceedings following the introduction of the Single County Court.

The 75th Update brings into force a wealth of amendments, including changes made to the CPR in respect of Low Value Personal Injury Claims in Road Traffic Accidents and the introduction of a new Practice Direction allowing the automatic transfer of certain cases issued in the County Court Money Claims Centre and the County Court Business Centre to the County Court at Central London. Changes are also made to Part 52 on Appeals, Part 57 on Probate and Inheritance, Part 65 on Proceedings Relating to Anti–Social Behaviour and Harassment, Part 81 on Contempt and Committal and Part 83 on Writs and Warrants.

In addition, a revised Insolvency Practice Direction is published.

The 2015 edition of Civil Procedure will publish in Spring 2015. *Civil Procedure News* and the *White Book* Updating Service will continue to keep you abreast of developments.

For further updates see **http://www.sweetandmaxwell.co.uk/whitebook** and click on "White Book Updating Service". You will need to enter your subscriber password: **WB2014**. This site contains the latest Civil Procedure Rules and Practice Directions. Changes which have been introduced since the *White Book* published are highlighted in red. Court forms are also published here.

We welcome feedback from subscribers—please email *whitebook@sweetandmaxwell.co.uk* with any comments or suggestions.

The White Book Team
September 2014

MASTER R. EASTMAN
A Master of the Senior Courts, Queen's Bench Division

M. GIBBON Q.C.
Barrister, Maitland Chambers

MASTER A. GORDON–SAKER
A Master of the Senior Courts Costs Office

JOAN GOULBOURN
Of the Public Guardianship Office

DISTRICT JUDGE MICHAEL HOVINGTON
Manchester County Court; Member of the Civil Procedure Rule Committee

R. JAY
Solicitor

E. JEARY
Of the Court Funds Office

MASTER JERVIS KAY
Admiralty Registrar and a Master of the Senior Courts, Queen's Bench Division; One of Her Majesty's Counsel

DISTRICT JUDGE M. LANGLEY
A District Judge of the Central London County Court; Chair of the London Association of District Judges

THE HONOURABLE MR JUSTICE LEWIS
Judge of the Queen's Bench Division of the High Court

HIS HONOUR JUDGE MACKIE C.B.E., Q.C.
London Mercantile Court

SARA MASTERS Q.C.
One of Her Majesty's Counsel

MASTER VICTORIA MCCLOUD
A Master of the Senior Courts, Queen's Bench Division

DISTRICT JUDGE SIMON MIDDLETON
Truro Courts of Justice and Bodmin County Court

KARON MONAGHAN Q.C.
One of Her Majesty's Counsel

HELEN MOUNTFIELD Q.C.
One of Her Majesty's Counsel

MASTER J. O'HARE
A Master of the Senior Courts Costs Office

HIS HONOUR JUDGE RICHARD PARKES Q.C.
A Circuit Judge on the South Eastern Circuit

HER HONOUR JUDGE PATRICIA PEARL
A Circuit Judge on the South Eastern Circuit

MASTER ROBERTS
A Master of the Senior Courts, Queen's Bench Division

DISTRICT JUDGE RICHARD ROBINSON
Principal Registry of the Family Division

C. SANDERS
Solicitor

IAN SEWELL
Costs Clerk, Supreme Court of the United Kingdom

K. TALBOT
Barrister, Member of the New York Bar

MASTER TEVERSON
A Master of the Senior Courts, Chancery Division

RICHARD WALFORD
Barrister, Serle Court Chambers

CONTENTS

Section C—Pre-Action Conduct and Protocols

Section A1—Procedural Guides

Section 1—Court Guides

Section 2—Specialist Proceedings

Section 3—Other Proceedings

TABLE OF CASES

TABLE OF STATUTES

Table of International and European Legislation, Treaties and Conventions

*All references to material in **Volume 2** are enclosed within square parentheses.*

VOLUME 1

CIVIL PROCEDURE RULES

SECTION A

CIVIL PROCEDURE RULES 1998

PART 1

OVERRIDING OBJECTIVE

Editorial introduction

In the first paragraph, in the first instance it occurs, after "High Court" add:
(except in relation to its jurisdiction under the Extradition Act 2003)   **1.0.2**

Amendments to CPR

Add at end:

    Civil Procedure (Amendment) Rules 2014 (SI 2014/407)—April 1, 6 & 22, **1.0.3**
    2014
    Civil Procedure (Amendment No. 2) Rules 2014 (SI 2014/482)—April 6,
    2014
    Civil Procedure (Amendment No. 3) Rules 2014 (SI 2014/610)—April 6,
    2014
    Civil Procedure (Amendment No. 4) Rules 2014 (SI 2014/867)—April 22,
    2014
    Civil Procedure (Amendment No. 5) Rules 2014 (SI 2014/1233)—June 5,
    2014
    Civil Procedure (Amendment No. 6) Rules 2014 (SI 2014/2044)—October 1,
    2014

Identification, clarification and ordering of issues

*In the second paragraph, after "making full allowance for the implications of a possible appeal.",
add:*

    In Section 8 of the Technology and Construction Court Guide the matters which **1.4.5**
the court should take into account in deciding in any particular civil proceedings
whether or not to order a preliminary issue are listed (Vol.2 para.2C–90). See also
Steele v Steele [2001] C.P. Rep 106 (Neuberger J.) (listing ten factors to be considered),
and *Lexi Holdings Plc v Pannone & Partners* [2009] EWHC 3607 (Ch), December 14,
2009, unrep. (Briggs J.) (referring to factors relevant to trial as a preliminary issue of
an ex turpi causa defence).

PART 2

APPLICATION AND INTERPRETATION OF THE RULES

In the Contents, after the entry for Practice Direction 2B, add:

Contents   **2.0.1**

3

Practice Direction 2D—References in the Rules to
actions done by the court   2DPD.1

Editorial introduction

Add new paragraphs at end:

2.0.2   By CPR Update 74 (July 2014), Part 2 was further supplemented by Practice Direction 2C—Starting Proceedings in the County Court (see para.2CPD.1 below). This Practice Direction came into force on July 31, 2014, and (as para.1.1 states) applies to proceedings in the County Court. It provides an overview (together with references to relevant rules, practice directions and enactments) of those claims or applications which must be started, or, in some cases, heard, in particular County Court hearing centres, or which may be sent or transferred to another hearing centre if started elsewhere. Parties should always refer to the relevant provisions in the Rules and related Practice Directions and other enactments referred to in this Practice Direction. It also includes a directory which identifies each County Court hearing centre and, where appropriate, provides additional information about them.

By CPR Update 75 (July 2014), Part 2 was further supplemented by Practice Direction 2D—References in the rules to actions done by the court (see para.2DPD.1 below). This Practice Direction came into effect on October 1, 2014.

General note on application of rules (r.2.1)

In the third paragraph, for "county courts" substitute:

2.1.1   the County Court

Proceedings to which CPR do not apply

In the first paragraph, for "a county court" substitute:

2.1.3   the County Court

Add new paragraph at end:

Although (as r.2.1 states) the CPR apply to "all proceedings" in the High Court, as result of amendments made by s.174 of the Anti–social Behaviour, Crime and Policing Act 2014, to the Civil Procedure Act 1997 s.1 and to the Courts Act 2003 s.68, with effect from October 1, 2014, Civil Procedure Rules do not govern the practice and procedure to be followed in the High Court "in relation to its jurisdiction under the Extradition Act 2003". From that date such practice and procedure is governed by provisions in Part 17 of the Criminal Procedure Rules 2014 (SI 2014/1610) (see further para.52.1.1.1 below).

"the court"

In the first paragraph, for "a particular county court" substitute:
the County Court

2.3.11   *In the first paragraph, for "county courts" substitute:*
the County Court

Delete the second paragraph (beginning "The county courts,") and substitute:
The County Court, on the other hand, is an inferior court with limited legal jurisdiction. Over the years, the limits on the legal jurisdiction of the County Court has been relaxed and the problems inherent in the former territorial limits on jurisdiction have been largely overcome, mainly by rules enabling the easy movement of cases from court to court. The introduction, with effect from April 22, 2014, of the single County Court, means that what were previously separate county courts are now re–designated as local hearing centres of the unified County Court. The CPR contain rules of court applicable to proceedings both in the High Court and in the County Court. In various contexts it is convenient if the expression "the court" can be taken to mean, not only the County Court and the High Court, but also the High Court either at the RCJ or at a location where a district registry of the High Court is situated (see, particularly, Pt 30 (Transfer)). However, in particular circumstances, when applying a CPR provision, care has to be taken to be clear about whether "the court" is the High Court or the County Court; see e.g. *Osuji v Holmes* [2011] EWCA Civ 476, March 14, 2011, CA, unrep. (court's permission under r.38.2 to discontinue a claim).

4

Specialist lists (r.2.3(2))

In the first paragraph, for the sentence beginning "Rule 63.3 is more" substitute:

The Intellectual Property Enterprise Court is a specialist list established within the **2.3.14** Chancery Division of the High Court (r.63.2(9)). Rule 63.3 states that claims in the Patents Court form a specialist list "for the purposes of rule 30.5". Planning Court claims also form a specialist list (r.54.22(1)).

Effect of rule

Delete the first paragraph and substitute:

This rule distinguishes High Court proceedings from County Court proceedings. **2.4.1** Since the 1990s. especially following the implementation of the Access to Justice reforms and the bringing into effect of the CPR, there has been increasing integration between the operations of the High Court on the one hand and the County Court on the other. Nevertheless the two levels of court remain quite distinct. The High Court is a superior Court, the County Court is an inferior court. The Senior Courts Act 1981 s.4(1) states that the High Court "consists of" certain ex officio judges and puisne judges. The judges are the court and the court is the judges. The judges exercise the jurisdiction of the court (see Vol.2, para.9A–16+). Generally the jurisdiction of the court may be exercised by a single judge sitting alone. The County Court (as it is not a superior court) does not "consist of" judges at all. The County Courts Act 1984 (as amended by s.17 of The Crime and Courts Act 2013) states in place of the former network of county courts, there is to be, as of April 22, 2014, a single court of record in England and Wales, called the county court, for the purpose of exercising the jurisdiction and powers conferred on it by the County Courts Act 1984 or any other Act. Schedule 9 of the 2013 Act inserts a new s.5 in the County Courts Act 1984 which provides that in addition to circuit judges and district judges every judge from the Lord Chief Justice downwards is a judge of the County Court and the former requirement for a district judge to be assigned to one or more specific districts has been abolished.

In the second paragraph, for "an (inferior) county court" substitute:

the (inferior) County Court

In the second paragraph, in the first instance, for "county courts" substitute:

certain County Court hearing Centres

In the second paragraph, in the second instance, for "county courts" substitute:

County Court

Delete the seventh paragraph (beginning "By virtue of their office,") and substitute:

By virtue of their office, every judge of the Court of Appeal, every judge of the High Court and every Recorder, is capable of sitting as a judge of the County Court in the circumstances provided for by the County Courts Act 1984 s.5(3) as amended by sch.9 of the Crime and Courts Act 2013 (see Vol.2, para.9A–419+). There is nothing to prevent a High Court judge with Administrative Court experience from sitting in the County Court for the purpose of trying a claim in which the claimant claimed (1) a declaration that a public body had acted incompatibly with their Convention rights, and (2) damages for false imprisonment (*D. v Home Office* [2005] EWCA Civ 38; [2006] 1 W.L.R. 1003, CA (where held that the bringing of such an action in a county court, rather than by way of proceedings under Pt 54, is not an abuse of process)).

Delete the eighth paragraph (beginning "Throughout the CPR, references") and substitute:

Throughout the CPR, references are made to the "court", rather than to a judge or to a particular court (whether the High Court, the County Court, or the Court of Appeal) except where it is necessary to do otherwise (e.g. r.29.9 (Powers of "trial judge" in relation to orders previously made), r.30.2 (Transfer between County Courts hearing centres and within the High Court), r.34.13 (High Court's power to order letter of request) and r.44.1(1) (defining "costs judge")). Where the context requires, a reference to "the court" means a reference to the County Court, a district registry or the Royal Courts of Justice (r.2.3(2)). Rule 2.3 states that "judge" means, unless the context otherwise requires, a judge, Master or district judge or a person authorised to act as such. Rule 2.4 states the general rule that where "the court" may perform any act then that act may be performed, not only by the judges of the court, but also by lesser judicial officers. Rule 2.4 draws a clear distinction between proceedings in the High Court and proceedings in the County Court. The rule is confined to circumstances in which these Rules refer to the performance of an "act" by the court. The general principle is that Masters and district judges should have power to act. It should be noted that the rule speaks, not of "any act" that the court may perform, but of "any act" which "these Rules provide for the court to perform". Where the court performs an "act" not provided for by the CPR (e.g. tries a claim) the rule has no application.

In the tenth paragraph, for "a county court" substitute:
the County Court

In the tenth paragraph, for "a county" substitute:
the County Court

In the tenth paragraph, for "a county court or on the judge of a county court" substitute:
the County Court or on the judge of the County Court

In the thirteenth paragraph, in each place it occurs, for "a county court" substitute:
the County Court

In the fourteenth paragraph, for "a county court" substitute:
the County Court

In the sixteenth paragraph, for "a county court" substitute:
the County Court

In the seventeenth paragraph, for "a county court" substitute:
the County Court

"district judge of that Court"

2.4.2 *After "one district judge" delete "for a county court district".*

"act of a formal or administrative character"

After the first paragraph, add as a new paragraph:
2.5.3   Certain provisions, whilst not conferring powers on court staff expressly, would appear to do so by implication for obvious practical reasons. For example, the notification of the parties by the court of the appointment of a person as an assessor under the statutory provisions referred to in r.35.15 (in accordance with Practice Direction 35 para.10(1)) would appear to constitute a formal or administrative act within the meaning of r.2.5(1), but the appointment of an assessor is not and requires a decision by a judge (*Cary v Commissioner of Police of the Metropolis* [2014] EWCA Civ 987, July 17, 2014, CA, unrep.).

Effect of rule

In the third paragraph, for "county court" substitute:
2.7.1   County Court hearing Centre

In the fourth paragraph, for the sentence beginning "In any county court" substitute:
Section 3(2A) of the County Courts Act 1984 (inserted by Sch.9 to the Crime and Courts Act 2013 states that the places at which the County Court sits, and the days and times at which it sits in any place, are to be determined in accordance with directions given by the Lord Chancellor after consulting the Lord Chief Justice.

Specified period ending on day on which court office closed

2.8.4 *Delete the last paragraph beginning "In terms,".*

Documents filed under Electronic Working Scheme

Delete the second sentence (beginning "Paragraph 7.2") and substitute:
2.8.6   By CPR Update 75, this Practice Direction was omitted from October 1, 2014.

Effect of rule

In the second paragraph, add at end:
2.9.1   See further r.40.2(2)(a), and commentary thereon in para.40.2.6 below.

Insert Practice Directions 2C and 2D:

PRACTICE DIRECTION 2C—STARTING PROCEEDINGS IN THE COUNTY COURT

This Practice Direction supplements CPR Part 2   **2CPD.1**

Scope

1.1 This Practice Direction applies to proceedings in the County Court. It provides an overview (together with references to relevant rules, practice directions and enactments) of those claims or applications which must be started, or, in some cases, heard, in particular County Court hearing centres, or which may be sent or transferred to another hearing centre if started elsewhere. Parties should always refer to the relevant provisions in the Rules and related Practice Directions and other enactments referred to in this Practice Direction.

1.2 This Practice Direction also includes a directory which identifies each County Court hearing centre and, where appropriate, provides additional information about them.

Starting proceedings—general

2. In the County Court, a claim or application may be started in any County Court hearing centre, unless any rule, practice direction or enactment provides otherwise.

Proceedings and claims which must be started in a particular County Court hearing centre or County Court Office

3.1(1) If any rule, practice direction or enactment provides that a claim or application must be started at a particular County Court hearing centre and that claim or application is started at the wrong hearing centre, a court officer will send it to the correct hearing centre before it is issued.

(2) A party should consider the potential delay which may result if a claim or application is not made at the correct County Court hearing centre in the first instance.

(3) In the following cases, proceedings must be started in a designated County Court hearing centre—

  (a) probate claims (designated by rule 57.2 and Practice Direction 57, paragraph 2.2(3));

  (b) Technology and Construction Court claims (designated by Practice Direction 60, paragraphs 3.1 and 3.4);

  (c) intellectual property claims (designated by rule 63.13 and Practice Direction 63, paragraphs 16.3 and 21.1);

  (d) proceedings under Parts 1 to 11 of the Insolvency Act 1986 (designated by the Insolvency (Commencement of Proceedings) and Insolvency Rules (Amendment) Rules 2014 (S.I. 2014/817)); and

  (e) proceedings under section 67(1) and (2) of the Race Relations Act 1976 (designated by the Civil Courts Order 1983 (S.I. 1983/713), which has been revoked, subject to savings, by the Crime and Courts Act 2013 (Consequential, Transitional and Saving Provisions) Order 2014 (S.I. 2014/820). The effect of this provision is that, for the time being, only those County Court hearing centres which correspond to the county courts designated in the 1983 Order will hear these proceedings).

3.2(1) Subject to subparagraphs (2) and (3), the claim form in respect of a claim for an amount of money started under Part 7 of the Civil Procedure Rules must be sent to the County Court Money Claims Centre, unless it is a claim for which special procedures are provided in Rules or in practice directions (Practice Direction 7 A, paragraph 4A.1).

(2) A person who is permitted to start a Part 7 claim through the Production Centre pursuant to Practice Direction 7C must send the claim form to the Production Centre at the County Court Business Centre, St Katharine's House, 21–27 St Katharine's Street, Northampton, NN1 2LH. DX 702885 Northampton 7. Fax no. 0845 4085311.

(3) An application for a Part 7 claim to be issued through the Money Claim Online scheme pursuant to Practice Direction 7E, must be sent electronically. Any other document, application or request, other than one which is filed electronically must be sent to the County Court Business Centre at the address in subparagraph (2) (Practice Direction 7E, paragraph 1.4).

3.3(1) Proceedings under the Companies Acts or the Limited Liability Partnerships Act 2000, in respect of which the County Court has jurisdiction, must be started in a County Court hearing centre which is specified in the Insolvency (Commencement of Proceedings) and Insolvency Rules (Amendment) Rules 2014 as one in which proceedings under Parts 1 to 11 of the Insolvency Act 1986 may be commenced, unless subparagraph (2) applies.

(2) Proceedings within the London insolvency district may be started in the High Court.

(3) In this paragraph—

    (a) "Companies Acts" means the enactments specified in section 2 of the Companies Act 2006; and

    (b) "the London insolvency district" means the area specified in article 3 of the London Insolvency District (County Court at Central London) Order 2014 (S.I. 2014/818).

3.4 A claim of a debtor or hirer for an order under section 129(1)(b) or 129(1)(ba) of the Consumer Credit Act 2006 (known as a "time order") must be made at the County Court hearing centre where the claimant debtor or hirer resides or carries on business (Practice Direction 7B, paragraph 4.3).

3.5 The claim form in respect of an application under the Mental Health Act 1983 must be filed—

    (a) in the County Court hearing centre serving the address where the patient's place of residence is situated; or

    (b) in the case of an application under section 30, in the court or County Court hearing centre that made the order under section 29 which the application seeks to discharge or vary (Practice Direction 8A, paragraph 18.2).

3.6 Applications for certification of enforcement agents under section 64 of the Tribunals Courts and Enforcement Act 2007 must be made to one of the County Court hearing centres listed in Practice Direction 84 at Paragraph 2.2.

Claims and applications that may be started in any County Court hearing centre, but which will be sent or transferred to another County Court hearing centre following issue

4(1) In the following cases, a claim or application may be started or made at any County Court hearing centre. However, if it has not been started or made in an appropriate County Court hearing centre then, following issue, the claim or application will be sent or transferred to the appropriate hearing centre in accordance with the following rules and practice directions—

Claim or application	Rule or Practice Direction
Certain Consumer Credit Act 2006 claims	Practice Direction 7B, paragraphs 4.1, 4.2 and 5.1A
Possession claims	Rules 55.3 and 55.5(1A)
Accelerated possession claims	Rules 55.16(1A)
Landlord and tenant claims	Rule 56.2
Applications for an injunction—	Rule 65.3
(a) Housing Act 1986 injunctions	Rule 65.4 Rule 65.28(1)(b)(ii) and (2)
(b) demotion or suspension claims which are not made in the alternative to a possession claim	Rule 65.43 (Practice Direction 65, paragraph 1.2 provides that, unless the court otherwise orders, an
(c) claims under section 3 of the Protection from Harassment Act 1997	application on notice for an injunction under rule 65.43 or any other hearing
(d) applications for an injunction under the Policing and Crime Act 2009	requiring the respondent's attendance must be heard at one of the County Court hearing centres listed in that paragraph.)

(2) A party should consider the potential delay which may result if a claim or application is not made at the appropriate County Court hearing centre in the first instance.

Part 8 claims (CPR 8.1(2A) and Practice Direction 8, paragraphs 4.1 and 4.2)

6. A claim under the Part 8 procedure may be made at any County Court hearing centre unless a rule, practice direction or enactment provides otherwise. However, when a claim is given a hearing date, the court may direct that proceedings should be transferred to another hearing centre if appropriate to do so.

Part 23 applications (CPR 23.2 and Practice Direction 23, paragraphs 5A.1 and 5A.2)

7.1 The general rule is that an application must be made to the County Court hearing centre where the claim was started.

7.2 If a claim has been transferred to another court or transferred or sent to another County Court hearing centre since it was started, an application must be made to the court to or County Court hearing centre to which the claim has been transferred or sent, unless there is good reason to make the application to a different court.

7.3 If the parties have been notified of a fixed date for the trial, an application must be made to the court where the trial is to take place.

7.4 If an application is made before a claim has been started, it must be made to the court where it is likely that the claim to which the application relates will be started unless there is good reason to make the application to a different court. An application made in the County Court before a claim has been started may be made at any County Court hearing centre, unless any enactment, rule or practice direction provides otherwise.

7.5 If an application is made after proceedings to enforce judgment have begun, it must be made to the court, or County Court hearing centre which is dealing with the enforcement of the judgment unless any enactment rule or practice direction provides otherwise.

7.6 If the claim is started in the County Court Money Claims Centre, an application made after the claim has been started must be made to the County Court hearing centre to which the claim has been sent, or, if the claim has not been sent to a County Court hearing centre, to the County Court Money Claims Centre.

County Court Directory

8(1) The County Court Directory identifies—

    (a) in column 1, each County Court hearing centre;

    (b) in column 2—

        (i) those hearing centres which are co–located at District Registries, Chancery District Registries or Mercantile Courts; and

        (ii) those hearing centres which are designated as Civil Trial Centres;

    (c) in column 3, the Civil Trial Centre to which cases allocated to the multi–track, pursuant to Practice Direction 26, paragraph 10, may be transferred;

    (d) in column 4—

        (i) those hearing centres at which certain proceedings are must be started such, as insolvency proceedings;

        (ii) those hearing centres which are designated to hear certain proceedings, such as race relations proceedings and applications on notice for an injunction under the Policing and Crime Act 2009; and

        (iii) those hearing centres which are designated as Technology and Construction Courts; and

    (e) in column 5, the feeder courts for those hearing centres designated as Civil Trial Centres which are specified in the schedule to Practice Direction 26.

(A feeder court is a hearing centre which is not a Civil Trial

Centre, and from which proceedings may be transferred to a specified Civil Trial Centre.)

(2) The address and contact details for each County Court hearing centre can be found by using the Court Finder tool available at: *courttribunalfinder.service.gov.uk/*

Schedule: County Court Directory

Key	Proceedings and co-located courts	Relevant provisions
I	Insolvency	The Insolvency (Commencement of Proceedings) and Insolvency Rules (Amendment) Rules 2014, S.I. 2014/817
C/LLP	Company and Limited Liability Partnerships	Practice Direction 2C, paragraph 3
CDR	Chancery District Registry	The Civil Courts Order 2014, S.I. 2014/819
CEA	Certification of Enforcement Agents	Practice Direction 84 – Enforcement by Taking Control of Goods
CTC	Civil Trial Centre	Practice Direction 26 – Case Management – Preliminary Stage: Allocation and Re-allocation
DR	District Registry	The Civil Courts Order 2014, S.I. 2014/819
GVI	Application on notice for an injunction under the Policing and Crime Act 2009	Practice Direction 65 – Proceedings Relating to Anti-social Behaviour and Harassment
MC	Mercantile Court	Practice Direction 59 – Mercantile Courts
RR	Race Relations	The Civil Courts Order 1981, S.I. 1983/713
TCC	Technology and Construction Court	Practice Direction 63 – Technology and Construction Courts

Column 1 County Court Hearing Centre	Column 2 District Registry, Chancery District Registry, Mercantile Court Or Civil Trial Centre	Column 3 Civil Trial Centre to Which Cases Allocated to the Multi-Track Will Be Transferred	Column 4 Additional Proceedings	Column 5 Civil Trial Centres – Feeder Courts
Aberystwyth	DR	Swansea	I C/LLP	
Accrington		Burnley		
Aldershot & Farnham		Winchester		
Altrincham		Manchester		
Aylesbury		Oxford	I C/LLP	
Banbury		Oxford	I C/LLP	
Barnet		Central London	Part of the London Insolvency District (High Court for Parts 1 to 7, County Court at Central London for Parts 7A to 11) (C/LLP should be started in the High Court)	
Barnsley	DR	Sheffield	I C/LLP	
Barnstaple	DR	Exeter	I C/LLP	
Barrow-in-Furness	DR	Carlisle	I C/LLP	
Basildon		Southend		
Basingstoke	DR	Winchester		
Bath	DR	Bristol	I C/LLP	
Bedford	DR	Luton	I C/LLP	
Birkenhead	DR	Liverpool	I C/LLP CEA	

12

Column 1	Column 2	Column 3	Column 4	Column 5
Birmingham	DR CDR MC CTC		I C/LLP CEA GVI RR TCC	Dudley
Blackburn	DR	Preston	I C/LLP	
Blackpool	DR		I C/LLP	
Blackwood	DR	Cardiff	I C/LLP	
Bodmin		Truro		
Bolton	DR	Manchester	I C/LLP	
Boston	DR	Lincoln	I C/LLP	
Bournemouth & Poole	DR CTC		I C/LLP	Weymouth
Bow		Central London	Part of the London Insolvency District (High Court for Parts 1 to 7, County Court at Central London for Parts 7A to 11) (C/LLP should be started in the High Court)	
Bradford	DR CTC		I C/LLP GVI	Skipton
Brecon (hearings only – all administration is undertaken at Merthyr Tydfil)	DR (to be called Brecknock District Registry)	Cardiff		
Brentford		Central London	Part of the London Insolvency District (High Court for Parts 1 to 7, County Court at Central London for Parts 7A to 11) (C/LLP should be started in the High Court)	

Column 1	Column 2	Column 3	Column 4	Column 5
Bridgend	DR		I C/LLP	
Brighton	DR CTC	Cardiff	I C/LLP CEA	Chichester, Eastbourne, Hastings, Horsham, Lewes, Worthing
Bristol	DR CDR MC CTC		I C/LLP CEA GVI RR TCC	Bath, Weston-super-Mare
Bromley		Central London		
Burnley	DR CTC		I C/LLP CEA	Accrington
Bury	DR	Manchester	I C/LLP	
Bury St Edmunds	DR	Cambridge	I C/LLP	
Buxton		Derby		
Caernarfon	DR CDR CTC		I C/LLP CEA	Llangefni
Cambridge	DR CTC		I C/LLP RR	Bury St Edmunds, Chelmsford, Peterborough
Canterbury	DR CTC		I C/LLP RR	Maidstone, Medway, Thanet
Cardiff	DR CDR MC CTC		I C/LLP CEA GVI TCC RR	Blackwood, Bridgend, Newport (Gwent)
Carlisle	DR CTC		I C/LLP RR	Barrow-in-Furness, Kendal, West Cumbria
Carmarthen (hearings only)	DR	Swansea	I C/LLP	

Column 1	Column 2	Column 3	Column 4	Column 5
Central London (the building will closed in May 2014, after which the hearing centre will be relocated to the Royal Courts of Justice)	CTC		Part of the London insolvency district (High Court for Parts 1 to 7, County Court at Central London for Parts 7A to 11) (C/LLP should be started in the High Court) CEA RR	Barnet, Bow, Brentford, Bromley, Clerkenwell & Shoreditch, Croydon, Edmonton, Kingston–upon–Thames, Lambeth, Mayor's & City of London, Romford, Wandsworth, Hammersmith (formerly known as "West London"), Willesden, Woolwich, Uxbridge
Chelmsford	DR	Southend		
Chester	DR MC CTC		I C/LLP CEA I C/LLP TCC	Crewe, Macclesfield, Warrington
Chesterfield	DR	Derby	I C/LLP	
Chichester	DR	Brighton		
Chippenham and Trowbridge		Winchester		
Clerkenwell and Shoreditch		Central London	Part of the London Insolvency District (High Court for Parts 1 to 7, County Court at Central London for Parts 7A to 11) (C/LLP should be started in the High Court)	
Colchester	DR CTC	Southend	I C/LLP	

Column 1	Column 2	Column 3	Column 4	Column 5
Conwy & Colwyn (the building has closed – hearings are listed in Llandudno Magistrates Court; all administration is undertaken at Rhyl)		Caernarfon		
Coventry	DR CTC		I C/LLP	Nuneaton, Warwick
Crewe	DR		I C/LLP	
Croydon	DR CTC	Chester	I C/LLP GVI	
Darlington	DR	Central London	I C/LLP	
Dartford	CTC	Middlesbrough	CEA	
Derby	DR CTC	Central London	I C/LLP	Buxton, Chesterfield
Doncaster	DR	Sheffield	I C/LLP	
Dudley (hearings take place at Dudley Magistrates' Court)	DR	Birmingham	I C/LLP	
Durham	DR	Newcastle–upon–Tyne	I C/LLP	
Eastbourne	DR	Brighton	I C/LLP	
Edmonton		Central London	Part of the London Insolvency District (High Court for Parts 1 to 7, County Court at Central London for Parts 7A to 11) (C/LLP should be started in the High Court)	
Exeter	DR CTC		I C/LLP RR TCC	Barnstaple, Torquay & Newton Abbott

Column 1	Column 2	Column 3	Column 4	Column 5
Gateshead		Newcastle–upon–Tyne	CEA	
Gloucester and Cheltenham	DR CTC		I C/LLP	Cheltenham
Great Grimsby	DR CTC		I C/LLP	Scunthorpe
Guildford	DR		I C/LLP	Reigate, Staines
Halifax	DR	Huddersfield	I C/LLP	
Harrogate	DR	York	I C/LLP	
Hartlepool	DR	Middlesbrough		
Hastings	DR	Brighton	I C/LLP	
Haverfordwest	DR	Swansea	I C/LLP	
Hereford	DR	Worcester	I C/LLP	
Hertford		Luton	I C/LLP CEA	
High Wycombe		Reading		
Horsham		Brighton		
Huddersfield	DR CTC		I C/LLP	Halifax
Ipswich	DR	Norwich or Southend	I C/LLP	
Kendal	DR	Carlisle	I C/LLP	
Kettering		Northampton		
King's Lynn	DR	Norwich	I C/LLP	
Kingston-upon-Hull	DR CTC		I C/LLP CEA	Grimsby and Scunthorpe
Kingston-upon-Thames		Central London	I C/LLP	

Column 1	Column 2	Column 3 Central London	Column 4 Part of the London Insolvency District (High Court for Parts 1 to 7, County Court at Central London for Parts 7A to 11) (C/LLP should be started in the High Court)	Column 5
Lambeth				
Lancaster	DR CTC		I C/LLP	None
Leeds	DR CDR MC CTC		I C/LLP TCC RR	Wakefield
Leicester	DR CTC		I C/LLP GVI	
Lewes		Brighton		
Lincoln	DR CTC		I C/LLP	Boston
Liverpool	DR CDR MC CTC		I C/LLP GVI TCC	Birkenhead, St Helens, Wigan
Llanelli		Swansea		
Llangefni (hearings only, all administration is undertaken at Caernarfon)	DR	Caernarfon	I C/LLP	
Lowestoft		Norwich		
Luton	DR CTC		I C/LLP	Bedford, Hertford, St Albans, Watford
Macclesfield	DR	Chester		
Maidstone	DR	Canterbury	I C/LLP	

Column 1	Column 2	Column 3	Column 4	Column 5
Manchester	DR CDR MC CTC		I C/LLP GVI RR TCC	Altrincham, Bolton, Bury, Oldham, Stockport, Tameside
Mansfield	DR	Nottingham		
Mayor's & City of London	CTC	Central London	Part of the London Insolvency District (High Court for Parts 1 to 7, County Court at Central London for Parts 7A to 11) (C/LLP should be started in the High Court)	
Medway	DR	Canterbury	I C/LLP	
Merthyr Tydfil	DR	Swansea	I C/LLP CEA	
Middlesbrough	DR CTC		I C/LLP	Darlington, Hartlepool
Milton Keynes	DR	Oxford		
Mold (hearings only – all administration is undertaken at Wrexham)	DR CDR MC	Wrexham		
Morpeth & Berwick		Newcastle-upon-Tyne		
Neath & Port Talbot		Swansea	I C/LLP	
Newcastle-upon-Tyne	DR CDR MC CTC		I C/LLP GVI RR TCC	Durham, Gateshead, Morpeth, North Shields, South Shields, Sunderland
Newport (Gwent)	DR	Cardiff	I C/LLP	
Newport (Isle of Wight)	DR	Portsmouth	I C/LLP	

Column 1	Column 2	Column 3	Column 4	Column 5
Northampton	DR CTC		I C/LLP CEA	Kettering, Peterborough
North Shields		Newcastle-upon-Tyne		
Norwich	DR CTC		I C/LLP CEA	Ipswich, King's Lynn, Lowestoft
Nottingham	DR CTC		I C/LLP CEA GVI RR TCC	Mansfield
Nuneaton		Coventry		
Oldham	DR	Manchester	I C/LLP CEA	
Oxford	DR CTC		I C/LLP CEA RR	Aylesbury, Banbury, Milton Keynes
Peterborough	DR	Cambridge	I C/LLP GVI	
Plymouth	DR CTC		I C/LLP CEA RR	None
Pontypridd	DR	Swansea	I C/LLP	
Portsmouth	DR CTC		I C/LLP GVI	Newport (Isle of Wight)
Preston	DR CDR CTC		I C/LLP GVI	Blackburn
Reading	DR CTC		I C/LLP	High Wycombe, Slough
Reigate		Guildford		
Rhyl	DR	Contact the Rhyl hearing centre for information regarding the CTC	I C/LLP	
Romford	DR	Central London	I C/LLP	
Rotherham		Sheffield		
Salisbury	DR	Swindon	I C/LLP	
Scarborough	DR	York	I C/LLP	

Column 1	Column 2	Column 3	Column 4	Column 5
Scunthorpe	DR	Great Grimsby	I C/LLP	
Sheffield	DR CTC		I C/LLP GVI	Barnsley, Doncaster, Rotherham
Skipton	DR	Bradford	I C/LLP	
Slough		Reading	I C/LLP	
Southampton	DR CTC		I C/LLP CEA RR	None
Southend	DR CTC		I C/LLP	Basildon, Chelmsford, Colchester, Ipswich
South Shields	DR	Newcastle–upon–Tyne		
St Albans		Luton	I C/LLP	
St Helens	DR	Liverpool		
Stafford	DR	Stoke–on–Trent	I C/LLP	
Staines		Guildford		
Stockport	DR	Manchester	I C/LLP	
Stoke–on–Trent	DR CTC		I C/LLP	Stafford, Walsall
Sunderland	DR	Newcastle–upon–Tyne	I C/LLP	
Swansea	DR CTC		I C/LLP CEA	Aberystwyth, Brecon, Carmarthen, Haverfordwest, Llanelli, Merthyr Tydfil, Neath, Pontypridd
Swindon	DR CTC		I C/LLP	Trowbridge, Salisbury
Tameside	CTC	Manchester	I C/LLP	
Taunton	DR CTC		I C/LLP	Yeovil
Telford	DR CTC		I C/LLP	Wolverhampton

Column 1	Column 2	Column 3	Column 4	Column 5
Thanet	DR	Canterbury		
Torquay & Newton Abbot	DR	Exeter		Bodmin
Truro	DR CTC		I C/LLP	
Tunbridge Wells	DR	Canterbury	I C/LLP	
Uxbridge		Central London		
Wakefield	DR	Leeds	I C/LLP	
Walsall	DR	Stoke-on-Trent	I C/LLP	
Wandsworth		Central London	Part of the London Insolvency District (High Court for Parts 1 to 7, County Court at Central London for Parts 7A to 11) (C/LLP should be started in the High Court)	
Warrington	DR	Chester	I C/LLP	
Warwick	DR	Coventry	I C/LLP	
Watford		Luton		
Welshpool & Newtown (hearings only – all administration is undertaken at Wrexham)	DR	Wrexham	I C/LLP	
West Cumbria	DR (to be called Workington District Registry)	Carlisle	I C/LLP	

Column 1	Column 2	Column 3	Column 4	Column 5
Hammersmith (formerly known as "West London")		Central London	Part of the London Insolvency District (High Court for Parts 1 to 7, County Court at Central London for Parts 7A to 11) (C/LLP should be started in the High Court) GVI	
Weston-super-Mare		Bristol		
Weymouth	DR	Bournemouth	I C/LLP	
Wigan	DR	Liverpool	I C/LLP	
Willesden		Central London	Part of the London Insolvency District (High Court for Parts 1 to 7, County Court at Central London for Parts 7A to 11) (C/LLP should be started in the High Court)	
Winchester	DR CTC		I C/LLP	Aldershot & Farnham, Basingstoke
Wolverhampton	DR	Telford	I C/LLP	
Woolwich		Central London		
Worcester	DR CTC		I C/LLP CEA	Hereford
Worthing	DR	Brighton		
Wrexham	DR CTC	Wrexham	I C/LLP RR CEA	Mold, Rhyl, Welshpool and Newton
Yeovil	DR	Taunton	I C/LLP	
York	DR CTC		I C/LLP CEA	Harrogate, Scarborough

PRACTICE DIRECTION 2D—REFERENCES IN THE RULES TO ACTIONS DONE BY THE COURT

2DPD.1   *This Practice Direction supplements CPR Part 2*

In the past, where the Rules have provided for an action to be done by the court, they have provided that the court "will" do that action.

From and including 1 October 2014, and including amendments coming into force on that date, where an amendment is made to these Rules to insert a new provision or alter an existing one, and that amendment provides for an action to be done by the court, the Rules will generally provide that the court "must" do the action, rather than "will". This is to make it clearer where an obligation lies with the court to do something. Occasionally in the future, it may still be appropriate to use the word "will", for example in a statement of future intent, and on those occasions, "will" will be used.

This does not affect the meaning of "will" and "must" in the Rules before 1 October 2014.

PART 3

THE COURT'S CASE AND COSTS MANAGEMENT POWERS

Extending or shortening time limits

After the fourth paragraph (ending "in exceptional circumstances".) add as a new paragraph:

3.1.2   In *Webb Resolutions Ltd v E–Surv Ltd* [2014] EWHC 49 (QB) Turner J. it was held that an applicant making an out of time request for reconsideration of refusal of permission to appeal at an oral hearing under r.52.3(5) must satisfy the tests applicable to applications for relief from sanctions under r.3.9; see para.3.9.3 below.

In the fifth paragraph, before the sentence beginning "In the matter of Atrium Training" add:

In *Mitchell v News Group Newspapers Ltd* [2013] EWCA Civ 1537; [2014] 1 W.L.R. 795 and *Denton v TH White* [2014] EWCA Civ 906 the Court of Appeal has given new guidance as to the robust approach the courts should take to the importance of complying with time limits. see paras 3.9.3 and 3.9.4 below.

Making orders subject to conditions

After the third paragraph, add as a new paragraph:

3.1.4   *Huscroft v P&O Ferries* (above) was applied in *Shagang Shipping Co Ltd v HNA Group Co Ltd* [2014] EWHC 2241 (Comm). In respect of an application to amend a defence in a charterparty dispute, in which the charterer sought to add a new defence relating to newly discovered evidence of bribery, the claimant failed in its contention that the defendants should only be given permission to amend if, as a condition of doing so, they paid into court the claimant's estimated costs in dealing with the bribery defence. The claimant's contention that the evidence had been obtained by untoward means was not supported by evidence, and the aim of securing its costs was not a proper purpose when considering applications under CPR r.3.1(3). The defence was arguable and the defendants had acted as quickly as they possibly could and entirely properly in only putting forward any allegations of bribery when they were in a position properly to do so.

Court's power to vary or revoke an order (r.3.1(7))

3.1.9   *In the fifth paragraph, insert full stop after "para.3.1.9.1" and delete the remaining text.*

After the fifth paragraph add:

In *Thevarajah v Riordan and Others* [2014] EWCA Civ 14; [2014] 1 Costs L.R.163; it was held that the *Tibbles* criteria apply where it is sought to set aside by a second application under r.3.1(7) the provisions of a previous order refusing relief under r.3.9. For further consideration of *Thevarajah*, see 3.9.5.

Attempts to re–litigate decided issues

Before the last paragraph, add as a new paragraph:

In *Virgin Atlantic Airways Ltd v Zodiac Seats UK Ltd* [2013] UKSC 46; [2014] A.C.160; **3.4.3.2**
[2013] 3 W.L.R. 299; a patent infringement case, Lord Sumption set out the principles
of *res judicata*. He stated that *Arnold v National Westminster Bank plc* [1991] 2 AC 93
(above) was authority for the following propositions. (1) Cause of action estoppel is
absolute in relation to all points which had to be and were decided in order to establish the existence or non–existence of a cause of action. (2) Cause of action estoppel
also bars the raising in subsequent proceedings of points essential to the existence or
non–existence of a cause of action which were not decided because they were not
raised in the earlier proceedings, if they could with reasonable diligence and should in
all the circumstances have been raised. (3) Except in special circumstances where this
would cause injustice, issue estoppel bars the raising in subsequent proceedings of
points which (i) were not raised in the earlier proceedings or (ii) were raised but
unsuccessfully. If the relevant point was not raised, the bar will usually be absolute if it
could with reasonable diligence and should in all the circumstances have been raised.
Lord Sumption rejected the proposition that recent case law had re–categorised
Henderson v Henderson so as to treat it as concerned with abuse of process and not *res
judicata*. He said that the principle in *Henderson v Henderson* has always been thought to
be directed against the abuse of process involved in seeking to raise in subsequent litigation points which could and should have been raised before but that was an application of the law of *res judicata*. The focus in *Johnson v Gore–Wood* (above) was inevitably
on abuse of process because the parties to the two actions were different, and neither
issue estoppel nor cause of action estoppel could therefore run.

In *Gaydamak v Leview* [2014] EWHC 1167 (Ch); Mann J., the claimant in earlier
proceedings sued the defendant to enforce obligations under an agreement. It was
held that a later settlement agreement had released the defendant from any liability.
The claimant's attempt at allege that the settlement agreement had been brought
about by fraudulent misrepresentations failed. The claimant then brought the present
proceedings alleging breach of trust and seeking to impeach the settlement agreement.
It was held, following *Virgin Atlantic*, that the correct starting point was to consider
cause of action estoppel rather than whether there was an abuse of process. The trust
argument should have been raised at the first trial and plainly fell within Lord Sumption's second category of cause of action estoppel. The new claim was also an abuse of
process. The claim was struck out.

In *OMV Petrom v Glencore International AG* [2014] EWHC 242 (Comm); Blair J., it
was held that in a claim for damages for conspiracy and/or deceit, on the basis of an
agreement to defraud by the delivery of cargoes of crude oil which purported to be
the contracted cargoes but were in fact blends made up of cheaper and heavier crude
oils, it would not be an abuse of process for the defendant supplier to relitigate findings made against it in arbitral proceedings. The question was whether it was more
unfair on the claimant to require it to prove very serious charges of fraud than it was
unfair on the defendant to prevent it from defending itself in the new proceedings.

Pointless and wasteful litigation

Add new paragraph at end:

In *Lilley v DMG Events Ltd* [2014] EWHC 610 (IPEC); *Jameel* was applied. A claim **3.4.3.4**
for copyright infringement was struck out where the holder of intellectual property
rights had adopted the wrong approach to calculating the damages to which he would
be entitled were his claim for infringement to be successful. He was unable to show
that he would be entitled to more than about £83, and allocating court resources to
such a claim would amount to an abuse of process.

Other forms of abuse

After the first paragraph, add as new paragraphs:

With effect from November 1, 2013 by direction of the Lord Chief Justice, most ap- **3.4.3.6**
plications for judicial review of immigration and asylum decisions had been transferred
from the Administrative Court to the Upper Tribunal. One of the excluded categories
was challenge to the lawfulness of detention. In *Ashraf v Secretary of State for the Home
Department* [2013] EWHC 4028 (Admin); Cranston J., it was stated that the inclusion of
an unmeritorious unlawful detention claim to avoid such transfer could be an abuse of
process by the lawyers involved.

In *Vaughan v Lewisham LBC* [2013] EWHC 4118 (QB); Sir David Eady held that it had been an abuse of process for the claimant to withdraw proceedings in the employment tribunal, which represented the appropriate forum for the adjudication of her claims, and to proceed instead with a defamation claim against her former employer in the High Court. The judge stated that it could not be right that the claimant could decide for herself that such large sums of public money already spent should simply be written off and the defendants required, from now on, to commit even more to the current action. If that were permitted, the court would be abdicating its duty of case management and abandoning the interests of one party to the untutored whims of the other. That would be quite contrary to the principles underlying the CPR and, in particular, inconsistent with the overriding objective. There was a further ground for striking the action out. The claimant could not demonstrate a "real and substantial tort", given the limited publications relied on. Insofar as there was any vindication required, it could have been achieved much earlier by means of the tribunal proceedings. It was neither necessary nor proportionate for the claimant to press ahead, come what may, for the purpose of achieving either compensation or vindication.

Claim "totally without merit"

After the second paragraph, add as a new paragraph:

3.4.10   In *R (Grace) v Secretary of State for the Home Department* [2014] EWCA Civ 1091, June 9, 2014, CA, unrep., the Court of Appeal stated that the proper meaning of "totally without merit" is simply "bound to fail". The court made the point that no judge would certify an application as totally without merit unless he was confident that the case was truly bound to fail.

Effect of rule (as inserted April 2014)

In the first sentence, for "substituted" substitute:

3.6A.1   inserted

Sanctions have effect unless defaulting party obtains relief

Delete rule 3.8(3)(b) and substitute:

3.8   **(b) specifies the consequence of failure to comply,
the time for doing the act in question may not be
extended by agreement between the parties except as
provided in paragraph (4).**

Add new rule 3.8(4):

**(4) In the circumstances referred to in paragraph (3) and unless
the court orders otherwise, the time for doing the act in question
may be extended by prior written agreement of the parties for up to
a maximum of 28 days, provided always that any such extension
does not put at risk any hearing date.**

Effect of rule

Add new paragraph at beginning:

3.8.1   In this and other rules the term "sanction" refers to any adverse consequence imposed upon a party because of his failure to comply with a rule, practice direction or court order (see *Summit Navigation Ltd v Generali Romania Assigurare Reasigurare SA* [2014] EWHC 398 (Comm) at [27]). Many rules, practice directions and orders specify a sanction which will come into operation in the case of non–compliance. If no sanction is specified, one may be imposed by an order obtained by the non–defaulting party on an application under r.3.4(2)(c) ("failure to comply with a rule, practice direction or court order"; and see para.3.4.4, above and 3.9.5.14, below).

Add at end:

In *Nelson & Ors v Circle Thirty Three Housing Trust Ltd* [2014] EWCA Civ 106, the

Court of Appeal confirmed that the court could consider relief from sanctions of its own motion under r.3.9.

The case of *Mitchell v News Group Newspapers Ltd* [2013] EWCA Civ 1537; [2014] 1 W.L.R. 795 (as to which see paras.3.9.3 to 3.9.5.14, below) resulted in a large number of applications to the court for orders recording the parties' agreement for extensions of time to serve witness statements or other documents. Busy courts, with limited resources, could not cope with this influx. The applications themselves resulted in costs being needlessly incurred. In the Queen's Bench Division, Central Office, the designated clinical negligence Masters introduced what has become widely known as a "buffer" direction and this was adopted in many other courts. The standard direction is as follows:

> "The Parties may, by prior agreement in writing, extend time for a Direction in this Order by up to 28 days and without the need to apply to Court. Beyond that 28–day period, any agreed extensions of time must be submitted to the Court by email including a brief explanation of the reasons, confirmation that it will not prejudice any hearing date and with the draft Consent Order in Word format. The Court will then consider whether a formal application and hearing is necessary. Any retrospective agreement to extend time is to submitted to the Court in like manner."

The Civil Procedure (Amendment No. 5) Rules 2014, which came into force on June 5, 2014, sanctions this approach at least in relation to prospective agreements.

Although the new r.3.8(4) does not relate to retrospective agreements to extend time, it is submitted that the standard direction (which does include retrospective agreements) may sensibly be adopted given the judicial scrutiny involved.

Formulation of rule since April 2013

Delete paragraph 3.9.3 and substitute:

Under the new r.3.9(1) the court is required to consider "all the circumstances of **3.9.3** the case, so as to enable it to deal justly with the application". Two circumstances are specifically mentioned (factors (a) the need for litigation to be conducted efficiently and at proportionate cost and (b) the need to enforce compliance with rules, practice directions and court orders).

In *Biffa Waste Services Ltd v Ali Dinler* [2013] EWHC 3582 (QB); October 10, 2013, Swift J. unrep. Swift J. allowed an appeal against the decision of a judge who had given relief from sanctions. The case involved a flagrant disregard of court orders in the face of an unless order and without any explanation for significant delays. Swift J., stated that the decision whether or not to grant relief from sanctions involved a balancing exercise including consideration of proportionality and the overriding objective. All the circumstances had to be considered including the waste of court time and resources and the lack of explanation.

In *Mitchell v News Group Newspapers Ltd* [2013] EWHC 2355 (QB) Master McCloud; the claimant had failed to lodge a cost budget within seven days prior to the date of first hearing of his defamation claim as required under PD51D para.4.2; (see now r.3.13). The Master limited his budget to court fees. At a subsequent hearing the Master, on the facts, refused relief from sanctions under r.3.9 but gave permission to appeal on the question of whether the court was adopting too strict an approach. The appeal went directly to the Court of Appeal.

In the landmark decision *Mitchell v News Group Newspapers Ltd* [2013] EWCA Civ 1537; [2014] 1 W.L.R. 795, the Court of Appeal, dismissing the appeal from the Master, considered the application of r.3.9 and endeavoured to answer the question: how strictly should the courts now enforce compliance with rules, practice directions and court orders? The guidance given by the Court of Appeal may be summarised as follows:

(1) If a breach is trivial, the court will usually grant relief provided that an application is made promptly. Thus, the court will usually grant relief if there has been no more than an insignificant failure to comply with an order: for example, where there has been a failure of form rather than substance; or where the party has narrowly missed the deadline imposed by the order, but has otherwise fully complied with its terms.

(2) If the non–compliance cannot be characterised as trivial, then the burden is on the defaulting party to persuade the court to grant relief. The court will want to consider why the default occurred. If there is a good reason for it, the court

will be likely to decide that relief should be granted. For example, if the reason why a document was not filed with the court was that the party or his solicitor suffered from a debilitating illness or was involved in an accident, then, depending on the circumstances, that may constitute a good reason.

(3) Later developments in the course of the litigation process are likely to be a good reason if they show that the period for compliance originally imposed was unreasonable, although the period seemed to be reasonable at the time and could not realistically have been the subject of an appeal (and see also, *Tarn Insurance Services Ltd v Kirby* [2009] EWCA Civ 19).

(4) Mere overlooking a deadline, whether on account of overwork or otherwise, is unlikely to be a good reason.

(5) Solicitors may be under pressure and have too much work. That will rarely be a good reason. Solicitors cannot take on too much work and expect to be able to persuade a court that this is a good reason for their failure to meet deadlines. They should either delegate the work to others in their firm or, if they are unable to do this, they should not take on the work at all.

(6) Applications for an extension of time made before time has expired will be looked upon more favourably than applications for relief from sanction made after the event.

(7) If there is a very good reason for the failure then relief will usually be granted. The weaker the reason, the more likely the court will be to refuse to grant relief. (Adopting the approach taken in *Hashtroodi v Hancock* [2004] EWCA Civ 652, [2004] 1 WLR 3206 in the context of applications for an extension to the period of validity of a claim form under r.7.6)

(8) An application for relief from a sanction presupposes that the sanction has in principle been properly imposed. If a party wishes to contend that it was not appropriate to make the order, that should be by way of appeal or, exceptionally, by asking the court which imposed the order to vary or revoke it under r.3.1(7). The circumstances in which the latter discretion can be exercised were considered in *Tibbles v SIG Plc (trading as Asphaltic Roofing Supplies)* [2012] EWCA Civ 518, [2012] 1 WLR 2591. In that case the court held that considerations of finality, the undesirability of allowing litigants to have two bites at the cherry and the need to avoid undermining the concept of appeal all required a principled curtailment of an otherwise apparently open discretion. The discretion might be appropriately exercised normally only (i) where there had been a material change of circumstances since the order was made; (ii) where the facts on which the original decision was made had been misstated; or (iii) where there had been a manifest mistake on the part of the judge in formulating the order. Moreover, as the court emphasised, the application must be made promptly. This reasoning has equal validity in the context of an application under r.3.9.

(9) Rule 3.14 sets out a stark and simple default sanction which will usually apply unless the breach in question is trivial or there was good reason for it. The grant of partial relief from the sanction will not often be appropriate. If partial relief were to be encouraged, that would give rise to uncertainty and complexity and stimulate satellite litigation.

The Court of Appeal decision in *Mitchell* explains the substantial change to the law and practice relating to applications for relief from sanctions which has been made by the re-formulation of r.3.9: although the court is still required to consider "all the circumstances of the case, so as to enable it to deal justly with the application", circumstances other than the two considerations which are specifically mentioned (factors (a) the need for litigation to be conducted efficiently and at proportionate cost and (b) the need to enforce compliance with rules, practice directions and court orders) should now be given less weight. This makes it necessary for the court to treat with caution some of the guidance given in cases interpreting the pre–April 2013 formulation of the rule.

The *Mitchell* decision led to an avalanche of new cases on the principles it laid down and substantial criticism and debate among practitioners and academics. In *Denton v TH White Ltd* [2014] EWCA Civ 906, the Court of Appeal, dealing with three appeals, with the Bar Council and the Law Society intervening, clarified and further explained the guidance given in *Mitchell*. The guidance was very much needed. As the Court of Appeal itself stated, the judgment in *Mitchell* has been misunderstood and misapplied by some courts. The result has been to encourage uncooperative behaviour by litigants, unreasonable satellite litigation and an increase in costs. The most important decisions since *Mitchell* are referred to in *Denton*. *Mitchell* itself must be read with *Denton* if further misunderstanding is to be avoided. The Court of Appeal expressed the hope that the further guidance will avoid the need in future to resort to the earlier decisions.

Summary of guidance given in Denton

Delete paragraph 3.9.4 and substitute:

The guidance given in *Denton* may be summarised as follows: a judge should address an application for relief from sanctions in three stages. The first stage is to identify and assess the seriousness and significance of the "failure to comply with any rule, practice direction or court order" which engages r.3.9(1). If the breach is neither serious nor significant, the court is unlikely to need to spend much time on the second and third stages. The second stage is to consider why the default occurred. The third stage is to evaluate all the circumstances of the case, so as to enable the court to deal justly with the application including r.3.9 (1)(a)(b). The court also gave guidance as to the importance of penalising parties who unreasonably oppose applications for relief from sanctions. **3.9.4**

Add new paragraphs 3.9.4.1 to 3.9.4.4:

The First Stage: assess seriousness and significance of breach

As far as the first stage is concerned, the Court of Appeal recognised that the use of the word "trivial" in *Mitchell* had given rise to some difficulty and semantic disputes. The court said that it would be preferable if in future the focus of the enquiry at the first stage should not be on whether the breach has been trivial. Rather, it should be on whether the breach has been serious or significant. The court stated that in many circumstances whether or not a breach imperilled future hearing dates or otherwise disrupts the conduct of litigation (including litigation generally) would be the most useful measure of whether a breach has been serious or significant. However, the court added that there were breaches which are serious although they are incapable of affecting the efficient progress of the litigation: e.g., the failure to pay court fees. The court stated that the concepts of seriousness and significance are not hard-edged and that there are degrees of seriousness and significance. The court expressed the hope that, assisted by the guidance given and its application in individual cases over time, courts will deal with these applications in a consistent manner. **3.9.4.1**

At the first stage, the assessment of the seriousness or significance of the breach should concentrate on the very breach in respect of which relief from sanction is sought. Considerations of the defaulter's previous conduct in the litigation (for example, if the breach is the latest in a series of failures to comply) should be left to the third stage.

If a judge concludes that a breach is not serious or significant, then relief from sanctions will usually be granted and it will usually be unnecessary to spend much time on the second or third stages. If, however, the court decides that the breach is serious or significant, then the second and third stages assume greater importance.

The Second Stage: why the default occurred

The second stage is particularly important where the breach is serious or significant. The court declined to give any examples of good and bad reasons for a failure to comply with rules, practice directions or court orders. *Mitehell* gave examples, at [41], but they are no more than examples. **3.9.4.2**

The Third Stage: all the circumstances of the case, including r.3.9 (1)(a) and (b)

The Court of Appeal highlighted what had been an important misunderstanding of *Mitchell*: i.e., that, if (i) there is a non-trivial (now serious or significant) breach and (ii) there is no good reason for the breach, the application for relief from sanctions will automatically fail. That is not so. Rule 3.9(1) requires that, in every case, the court will consider "all the circumstances of the case, so as to enable it to deal justly with the application". The Court of Appeal regard this as the third stage. **3.9.4.3**

Two circumstances which are specifically mentioned in r.3.9 are (a) the need for litigation to be conducted efficiently and at proportionate cost and (b) the need to enforce compliance with rules, practice directions and court orders and are referred to in *Denton* as factors (a) and (b). The court stated that factor (a) makes it clear that the court must consider the effect of the breach in every case. If the breach has prevented the court or the parties from conducting the litigation (or other litigation) efficiently and at proportionate cost, that will be a factor weighing in favour of refusing relief. Factor (b) emphasises the importance of complying with rules, practice directions and orders. The court observed that this factor received insufficient attention in the past. However, the old lax culture of non–compliance is no longer tolerated.

Other factors or circumstances mentioned in *Denton* are the need to consider whether the sanction imposed is proportionate to the breach in question (see the ruling given in *Decadent Vapours Ltd v Bevan* a case which was heard with *Denton*), whether the application for relief from sanctions was made promptly, and whether the defaulting party has a poor record as to compliance with proper court procedures: other past or current breaches of the rules, practice directions and court orders may also be taken into account as a relevant circumstance.

The majority of the Court of Appeal (The Master of the Rolls; Vos LJ) expressed the view that, whilst factors (a) and (b) may not be of paramount importance, they are of particular importance and should be given particular weight at the third stage when all the circumstances of the case are considered. However, this is not what the rule actually says. Jackson LJ dissented on this point and expressed the view that the rule does not require the courts to give factors (a) and (b) any greater weight than any other circumstances. All that the rule requires is that they are specifically considered in every case. Some commentators have expressed a fear that this controversy as to the importance of factors (a) and (b) may become a cause of uncertainty and satellite litigation.

The more serious or significant the breach the less likely it is that relief will be granted unless there is a good reason for it. Where there is a good reason for a serious or significant breach, relief is likely to be granted. Where the breach is not serious or significant, relief is also likely to be granted.

The importance of discouraging opportunism by the non–defaulting party

3.9.4.4   The Court of Appeal went on to state that litigation cannot be conducted efficiently and at proportionate cost without fostering a culture of compliance with rules, practice directions and court orders, and cooperation between the parties and their lawyers. Rule 1.3 provides that "the parties are required to help the court to further the overriding objective". Parties who opportunistically and unreasonably oppose applications for relief from sanctions take up court time and act in breach of this obligation. The court made it plain that it is wholly inappropriate for litigants or their lawyers to take advantage of mistakes made by opposing parties in the hope that relief from sanctions will be denied and that they will obtain a windfall strike out or other litigation advantage. In a case where (a) the failure can be seen to be neither serious nor significant, (b) where a good reason is demonstrated, or (c) where it is otherwise obvious that relief from sanctions is appropriate, parties should agree that relief from sanctions be granted without the need for further costs to be expended in satellite litigation. The parties should in any event be ready to agree limited but reasonable extensions of time up to 28 days as envisaged by the new r.3.8(4). The court will be more ready in the future to penalise opportunism. It is as unacceptable for a party to try to take advantage of a minor inadvertent error, as it is for rules, orders and practice directions to be breached in the first place. Heavy costs sanctions should, therefore, be imposed on parties who behave unreasonably in refusing to agree extensions of time or unreasonably oppose applications for relief from sanctions.

Relief from sanctions cases decided after Mitchell

Delete paragraph 3.9.5 and substitute:

3.9.5   The Court of Appeal's decision in *Mitchell v News Group Newspapers Ltd* [2013] EWCA Civ 1537; [2014] 1 W.L.R. 795 has led to an avalanche of new cases on the scope and application of the principles it laid down. Summaries of the decisions in several post *Mitchell* cases are set out in the rest of this paragraph. In the sub–paragraphs which follow them, these cases and several others are grouped together under various headings. The titles to these sub–paragraphs are provided for convenience only and should not be treated as a rigid classification: many cases could properly be placed under more than one heading.

In *Durrant v Chief Constable of Avon & Somerset* [2013] EWCA Civ 1624, the Court of Appeal held that a judge's decision to grant relief from sanction for non–compliance with a court order was not justified on a proper application of r.3.9. It was said that decisions under r.3.9 which failed to follow the robust approach laid down in *Mitchell* should not be allowed to stand. The case concerned an unless order relating to the service of witness statements. Through incompetence, the defendant failed to comply with the order and served two witness statements one day late; four statements about three months late and two further statements about one month later which was just a few days before trial. In reaching his decision (which resulted in the adjournment of the trial), the judge placed particular weight on the potential effect on the careers and reputations of individuals and the police force if the officers concerned were unable to give evidence, and on the public interest in scrutinising the actions of police officers in the light of all of the evidence from both sides. The Court of Appeal stated that considerations of that kind have only a limited role to play in the context of relief from sanction. They may be relevant to the question of how much time should be allowed for service of witness statements in the first place, and even to the question of what sanction should be imposed for failure to meet the deadline; but once the court has determined both the deadline and the sanction applicable for failure to comply, such considerations cannot properly carry much weight in determining whether to grant relief from the sanction for non–compliance. The Court of Appeal, exercising the r.3.9 discretion afresh, refused relief from the sanction of the unless order. In relation to the two witness statements which had been served one day late, relief from sanction was refused on the basis that the application for relief from sanction had not been made promptly: it having been made some two months after the deadline for service of the statements.

In *Thevarajah v Riordan and Others* [2014] EWCA Civ 14; [2014] 1 Costs L.R.163; the defendants were in breach of an unless order relating to disclosure and their defence and counterclaim was struck out. The defendants applied for relief from sanction which was refused by the judge (Hildyard J.). There was no appeal against that order. A second application for relief from sanction was made about two months after relief had been refused and just two days before the trial date. By this time the defendants had complied with the order. The deputy judge granted relief from sanction under r.3.9. The order of Hildyard J. was set aside. The claimant appealed to the Court of Appeal. The appeal was allowed. It was held that the deputy judge had been wrong to rely on the decision in *Woodhouse v Consignia Plc* [2002] EWCA Civ 275; [2002] 1 W.L.R. 2558 as clear authority that a second application for relief was permissible. *Woodhouse* was not to be read as displacing the normal operation of r.3.1(7) in a case involving r.3.9. The defendants' "second bite" application was in substance an application under r.3.1(7) for the setting aside of the provisions of the earlier order refusing relief under r.3.9, and had first to satisfy the criteria in *Tibbles v SIG Plc (t/a Asphaltic Roofing Supplies)* [2012] EWCA Civ 518; [2012] 1 W.L.R. 2591 which it manifestly did not. The *Tibbles* criteria apply where it is sought to set aside by a second application the provisions of a previous order refusing relief under r.3.9. The deputy judge had been wrong to hold that defendants' subsequent compliance with the unless order amounted to "a material change of circumstances" for the purposes of an application under r.3.1(7). It could not alter the fact of non–compliance with the unless order or amount to a good reason for that non–compliance, nor would it undermine the reasoning that led Hildyard J to refuse relief from sanction. Even if the deputy judge had been entitled to give fresh consideration to the question of relief from sanction, his general approach to the application of r.3.9 in its current form was wrong in principle. It lacked the robustness called for by the guidance subsequently given in *Mitchell*. Further, the deputy judge had paid insufficient attention to the defendants' lack of promptness in bringing the second application.

In *Adlington v ELS International Lawyers LLP (In administration)* [2013] EWHC B29 (QB), it was held that non–compliance with an unless order stipulating a deadline for the service of particulars of claim by seven out of 132 claimants in a group action because they were out of the country on holiday and therefore unavailable to sign the statements of truth was a failure of form not substance and could properly be characterised as "trivial" within the meaning of *Mitchell* so as to justify the grant of relief from sanction under r.3.9. The judge stated that even if the non–compliance could not have been characterised as trivial, relief would still have been granted as the claimants' solicitor had not realised that his clients would be unavailable to sign the papers. His clients' holiday arrangements were outside his control.

In *Re Guidezone Ltd* [2014] EWHC 1165 (Ch); Nugee J. held that the guidelines in *Mitchell* did not apply to an "in–time" application for an extension of time; instead, such an application was to be decided by reference to the overriding objective. *Robert v Momentum Services Ltd* [2003] EWCA Civ 299; [2003] 1 W.L.R. 1577 remained good law and was authority for the proposition that an in–time application should not be treated as if it were an application for relief from sanctions. (This decision was later approved by the Court of Appeal in *Hallam Estates v Baker* [2014] EWCA Civ 661 (see below).) In applying the overriding objective, the court now has to have regard to the fact that it had been reformulated to add explicit reference to "enforcing compliance with rules, practice directions and orders". However, unlike in the case of relief from sanctions, that consideration was not to be given paramount status. The judge said:

> "49. The consistent message from these authorities is that a party who needs more time for a procedural step in existing proceedings should not just ignore the problem but should ask the other side for consent, and if consent is not forthcoming, should make an in–time application for an extension; and conversely that the other side should respond positively and in a spirit of co–operation to reasonable requests for consent rather than 'cry foul' and seek to take opportunistic advantage of the other party's difficulties."

In *Summit Navigation Ltd v Generali Romania Asigurare Reasigurare SA* [2014] EWHC 398 (Comm); [2014] 2 Costs L.R 367; Leggatt J., a consent order had been made under which the claimant agreed to provide security for the defendants costs by a specified time, failing which the claim would be stayed. It was held that such a stay was a sanction within the meaning of r.3.9. The term "sanction" included any consequence adverse to the party to whom it applied. However, it was said that not all sanctions are equal and are to be treated as equivalent to one another for the purposes of CPR 3.9. The sanction here was not intended to be permanent and therefore could be approached differently under r.3.9 so that Mitchell did not apply. There is a significant difference between an order which specifies the consequence that proceedings are to be stayed if security for costs is not provided by a specified date and an order that, unless security is provided by a specified date, the claim will be struck out. The difference is that the former stay is not intended to be permanent whereas the latter is intended to be permanent subject to relief being granted.

In case he was wrong in finding that *Mitchell* did not apply, the learned judge proceeded to apply that case and granted relief from sanction on the basis that the non–compliance was trivial: the deadline had been missed by a very narrow margin (one day) and there had otherwise been full compliance with the terms of the order; and the failure did not have any impact on the efficient conduct of the proceedings, or on the wider public interest of ensuring that litigants could obtain justice efficiently and proportionately. In case he was wrong in finding that the breach was trivial, the judge found that there was good reason for the delay in that it was caused by a third party underwriter who had no responsibility for the conduct of the litigation.

The judge found that the defendant's stance in refusing to lift the stay was unreasonable and disregarded the duty of the parties and their representatives to co–operate with each other in the conduct of proceedings and the need for litigation to be conducted efficiently and at a proportionate cost. Save for the claimant's costs in issuing the application, the defendant was ordered to pay the costs. The judge said this:

> "63. Save for the costs incurred by the claimants in issuing their application, which were necessitated by their default, I also ordered the defendants to pay the claimants' costs of both applications. The defendants seem to have viewed their opposition to the stay being lifted as a potentially free ride whereby, if successful, they would obtain a fortuitous dismissal of the claim without a trial and, if unsuccessful, would still have their costs paid by the claimants as the defaulting party. It is important to discourage that approach. Quite apart from the fact that the claimants are the successful party, I think it right that the order for costs should reflect the defendants' unreasonable conduct in refusing to agree to the stay being lifted and the waste of time and money which that entailed."

In *Rattan v UBS AG* [2014] EWHC 665 (Comm); Males J., it was made clear that the Commercial Court would firmly discourage the taking of futile and time wasting procedural points. The claimant was ordered to pay costs on an indemnity basis where, after agreeing with the defendant that costs budgets should be filed "on" or "by" February 28, the claimant served his on February 27 and asserted that the defendant's budget, which was served the next day, should be disallowed because February 28 was six days before the case management conference, not seven days as required by r.3.13. It was said that if relief from sanctions had been necessary, which is was not, the case for relief would have been overwhelming.

In *Lakatamia Shipping Co Ltd v Nobu SU and Others* [2014] EWHC 275 (Comm); [2014] 2 Costs L.R. 307, a defendant served its disclosure list 46 minutes late thereby failing to comply with an unless order striking out its defence and counterclaim. Hamblen J granted relief from sanction under r.3.9: the breach was trivial and, in addition, there were good reasons why the default occurred. The fact that the defendant had a history of default did not convert a trivial default into a serious default. The learned judge regarded the breach as de minimis and this was borne out by its effect: it had caused no prejudice. As to the list itself, the judge applied *Realkredit Danmark A/S v York Montague Ltd* [1999] C.P.L.R. 272 in which the Court of Appeal indicated that an order to provide disclosure was complied with for the purposes of an unless order as long as a list was provided and that list was not "illusory". It would be "illusory" if the court could infer "lack of good faith where it is obvious from patent deficiencies in the list that it had been prepared in apparent but not real compliance with the obligation to give discovery". It was not contended that the list in the instant case was "illusory" in that sense, nor was it found to be so. See also: *Global Marine Drillships Ltd v La Bella* [2014] EWHC 1230 (Ch); disclosure under unless order; inept compliance rather than non–compliance.

In the subsequent hearing in *Lakatamia*, reported at [2014] EWHC 796 (Comm), on the question of the costs relating to the application for relief from sanctions, the defendant was ordered to pay the costs of preparing its application and the witness statements and a proportion of the costs of the hearing. However, the respondent to the application was ordered to pay the bulk of the costs of the hearing. The judge took the view that opposition at the hearing was unreasonable:

> [7] "I also consider that it is important that the message goes out that when a party applies for relief from sanctions, the other party should not assume that it is going to get a free costs ride in opposing that application. If the court considers that it was unreasonable to do so, then there will be cost consequences, and I consider that that is what should occur in this case. The Mitchell guidance was provided in order to help to avoid endless satellite litigation. If parties consider that they can always come to court to oppose any application for relief, then there will be no end to that satellite litigation."

In *Mitchell* the retrospective application in *Raayan al Iraq Co Ltd v Trans Victory Marine Inc*, [2013] EWHC 2696 (Comm) for a two days extension for service of particulars of claim was described as "in substance" being for relief from sanctions under r.3.9. In *Associated Electrical Industries Ltd v Alstom UK* [2014] EWHC 430 (Comm); Andrew Smith J., there was a delay of 20 days in serving particulars of claim and no good reason was shown for the late service. The defendant applied to strike the claim out under r.3.4(2)(c) and the claimant belatedly applied for an extension of time to serve the particulars of claim. It was held that although, as between the parties, it was disproportionate to strike out a claim for late service of the particulars, the emphasis given by decisions of the Court of Appeal to enforcement of the CPR to encourage procedural discipline led to the conclusion that the claim should be struck out, on the defendant's application, and the application for an extension of time refused.

In *Primus Telecommunications Netherlands BV v Pan European Limited* [2005] EWCA Civ 273, the Court of Appeal stated that the wording of r.32.10 (consequences of failure to serve witness statement or summary) amounts to a sanction and that, accordingly, r.3.9 falls to be applied. This may not have been widely appreciated by practitioners. In *M A Lloyd & Sons Ltd v PPC International Ltd* [2014] EWHC 41 (QB); [2014] 2 Costs L.R. 256; Turner J., a claimant who had failed who comply with an order for the sequential exchange of witness statements on a particular issue was debarred from producing evidence on that issue at trial. The claimant's delay (nearly three months) was substantial and there was no good reason for it. The judge famously stated; "This case provides yet another example of a litigant treating an order of the court as if compliance were an optional indulgence." The case highlighted the fact that not only did r.3.9 apply but that, given the wording of r.3.8(3) as it was then, the time for service of witness statements could not be extended by agreement between the parties. There had to be a court order endorsing the parties' agreement. The judge made the point that the court should not passively rubber stamp such orders. The judge observed that in the light of the *Mitchell* decision the courts have taken a consistently robust approach to the late service of witness statements.

In *Chartwell Estate Agents Ltd v Fergies Properties SA and Another* [2014] EWCA Civ 506, it was held that the first instance judge had been entitled to grant a claimant relief from sanctions for failing to serve witness statements within the specified time where both parties had been in default and refusal of relief would have had the disproportionate effect of ending the claim. The burden of proof was on the claimant and it would have no claim. The learned judge and the Court of Appeal regarded it as significant that the trial date would not be lost if relief were granted and a fair trial could still be had; and the fact that no significant extra cost would be occasioned if relief were granted. Davis LJ made the point that r.32.10 does not provide, as the stipulated sanction, that failure to serve a witness statement by the specified time results in the pursuit of the claim or the defence, as the case may be, being struck out or debarred (unless the court grants permission). Rather, the sanction is that that particular witness may not be called (unless the court gives permission). Thus by no means in every case would the sanction for failure to serve a witness statement by the specified date result in the effective termination of the claim or defence, as the case may be. But in this case it would. It is to be noted that counsel for the claimant did not seek to rely in argument on Article 6 of the Convention or on any of the case law arising thereunder and the Court of Appeal therefore expressed no view on any possible implications of that jurisprudence. Davis LJ emphasised that the courts in considering applications under r.3.9 do not have and should not have as their sole objective a display of judicial musculature. The objective under r.3.9 is to achieve a just result, having regard not simply to the interests of the parties but also to the wider interests of justice. Davis LJ concluded:

"63. Accordingly, the enjoinder that the Court of Appeal will not lightly interfere with a case management decision and will support robust and fair case management decisions should not be taken as applying, when CPR 3.9 is in point, only to decisions where relief from sanction has been refused. It does not. It likewise applies to robust and fair case management decisions where relief from sanction has been granted. If parties understand this then at least satellite interlocutory appeals should be avoided and at all events will get no encouragement from the appellate court."

In *Newland Shipping & Forwarding Ltd v Toba Trading FZC* [2014] EWHC 210 (Comm); [2014] 2 Costs L.R 279; Hamblen J. held that the loss of legal representation as a result of a dispute over fees which were due to its solicitors was not a good reason for the defendant's failure to comply with an order requiring disclosure and the exchange of witness statements. Accordingly, the defendant was not entitled to relief from sanctions under r.3.9 in respect of an order entering judgment against it. It should be noted that the judge found that any difficulties that arose as a result of loss of representation were foreseeable consequences of the defendant not being prepared to pay fees which it was able to pay, but chose not to.

In *Hallam Estates v Baker* [2014] EWCA Civ 661; the costs judge had granted the claimants an extension of time for serving points of dispute in a detailed assessment. A judge reversed that decision and ordered the issue of a default costs certificate under r.47.9(4). The background was that the defendant served her bill of costs eight months late. Six days before the claimants were required to serve their points of dispute, they asked the defendant for a 21 day extension of time. The defendant did not agree and on the day that the claimants should have served their points of dispute they applied for an extension of time and their application was issued by the court on the next day. The costs judge dealt with the application without notice on the papers and granted the extension. The defendant unsuccessfully applied for the order to be set aside. The claimants served their points of dispute within the extended time for doing so. The defendant appealed. Allowing the defendant's appeal, the judge found that claimant's application for an extension of time was issued out of time and therefore they were seeking relief from sanctions which the costs judge should not have granted as rules should be complied with. The Court of Appeal (Jackson, Lewison, and Christopher Clarke, LLJ) allowed the appeal. The claimant's application for an extension was made before the expiry of the time allowed for filing the points of dispute. The fact that the court staff did not date stamp the application until the following day was immaterial (see r.23.5). An application for an extension of the time to take any particular step in litigation was not an application for relief from sanctions, provided that the applicant filed his application notice before expiry of the permitted time period. That was the case even if the court dealt with the application after the expiry of the relevant period, *Robert v Momentum Services Ltd* [2003] EWCA Civ 299; [2003] 1 W.L.R. 1577 applied. That remained the case following the recent civil justice reforms, *Guidezone Ltd, Re* [2014] EWHC 1165 (Ch)approved. It followed that the costs judge was dealing with a straightforward application to extend time under r.3.1(2)(a) and the principles concerning relief from sanctions in *Mitchell* did not apply. It was incumbent on the costs judge to deal with the application in accordance with the recently amended over-riding objective, which he had. The claimants had made a reasonable application for an extension of time, which did not imperil any future hearing dates or otherwise disrupt the proceedings. The costs judge's decision to grant an extension was a proper exercise of his case management discretion. His rejection of her application to set aside, for which he gave sensible reasons, was also a proper exercise of his case manage-ment powers. Accordingly the judge had erred in reversing that decision.

The Court of Appeal stated that when the claimants asked the defendant to agree an extension of time, the defendant should have agreed; given her own delays, she could hardly complain about that modest extension. Under r.1.3 parties had a duty to help the court in furthering the overriding objective, which included allotting an ap-propriate share of the court's resources to an individual case. Therefore legal representatives were not in breach of any duty to their client when they agreed to a reasonable extension of time which neither imperilled future hearing dates nor otherwise disrupted the conduct of the litigation. On the contrary, by avoiding the need for a contested application they were furthering the overriding objective and also saving costs. Similarly, the courts should not refuse, and r.1.1(2)(f) did not require them to refuse, to grant reasonable extensions of time in such circumstances.

Referring to his report on civil justice in which he had recommended that the court should be less tolerant of unjustified delays and breaches of court orders, Lord Justice Jackson said:

> "Nevertheless it was no part of my recommendations that parties should refrain from agreeing reasonable extensions of time, which neither imperil hearing dates nor otherwise disrupt the proceedings. The contrary is the case. . . Nor was it any part of my recommendations that the court should refuse to grant rea-sonable extensions of time in those circumstances.[30]
>
> The Rule Committee has inserted a new sub–paragraph 1.1(2)(f) into the over-riding objective. In my view this new provision (which was not one of my recom-mendations) does not require courts to refuse reasonable extensions of time, which neither imperil hearing dates nor otherwise disrupt the proceedings.[31]"

For the most important case since *Mitchell*, see: *Denton v TH White Ltd* [2014] EWCA Civ 906. The guidance given in *Denton* is summarised in para.3.9.4 above. The report in fact covers three appeals. The *Denton* case itself concerned a 10 day trial involving six experts and numerous factual witnesses due to attend the trial. A month or so before trial the claimants served six witnesses statements. At the pre–trial review, the judge granted relief from the sanction contained in r.32.10 and permitted the claim-ants to rely on the further witness statements. The trial was adjourned so that the defendant could answer that evidence. Adopting the three stage approach (see above para.3.9.4) the breach was significant in that it caused the trial to be vacated. Under the second stage, there was no good reason for the breach. Notwithstanding the answers to the first and second stage, the third stage had to be undertaken. Sub paragraphs (a) and (b) each militated heavily in favour of refusing relief. There was little to weigh in the balance under "all the circumstances of the case" and the need to deal with cases justly. The claimants had had ample opportunity to serve their ad-ditional evidence long before they did and it was their own fault that they had not done so. An adjournment would result in the protraction of proceedings which had al-ready dragged on for far too long. It would cause a waste of court resources and generate substantial extra costs for the parties. The order of the judge was set aside.

Decadent Vapours Ltd v Bevan (one of the two other cases heard with *Denton*), concerned the late payment of court fees under an unless order by the claimant. The non payment was only discovered at the pre–trial review. The solicitors' cheque had been sent in the DX and should have arrived the next day (a day outside the unless order) but it never reached its destination. The claim was automatically struck out given that the claimant had not complied with the unless order. The judge refused the claimant's application for relief from sanctions. The Court of Appeal's view was that the judge had fallen into error. His first task was to consider the seriousness and sig-nificance of the claimant's failure to pay the fees. All failures to pay court fees are seri-ous, because it is important that litigants pay court fees on time. But some failures to pay fees are more serious than others. The failure in this case was near the bottom of the range of seriousness. At the second stage, the judge ought to have considered whether there was good reason for the breach. There was not, since the solicitor knew in advance that his method of payment would inevitably give rise to a breach of the court order. At the third stage, however, the judge should have concluded that r.3.9(1)(a) pointed in favour of relief, since the late payment of the fees did not prevent the litigation being conducted efficiently and at proportionate cost. Rule 3.9(1)(b) also pointed in favour of the grant of relief since the breach was near the bottom of the range of seriousness: there was a delay of only one day in sending the cheque and the breach was promptly remedied when the loss of the cheque came to light. It only affected the orderly conduct of the litigation, because of the approach adopted by the defendants and the court. On a consideration of all the circumstances of the case, the only reasonable conclusion in this case was to grant relief. This was not a case where, in all the circumstances of the case, it was proportionate to strike out the entire claim. The reference of proportionality as a factor to be taken into account at the third stage is to be noted.

In *Utilise TDS Ltd v Davies* (another case heard with *Denton*) two breaches were under consideration. First, the claimant filed a costs budget some 45 minutes late in breach of an order which specifically made reference to the automatic sanctions in r.3.14 which provides that: "…unless the court otherwise orders, any party which fails to file a budget despite being required to do so will be treated as having filed a budget comprising only the applicable court fees". Secondly, the claimant was 13 days late in complying with an order requiring it to notify the court of the outcome of negotiations. The District Judge declined to grant relief from the sanctions in r.3.14, holding that the second breach rendered the first breach, which would otherwise have been trivial, a non–trivial one. The judge on the first appeal held that, despite the fact that the District Judge had been wrong to think that there had been a previous default in filing a costs budget, there was no good reason for him to interfere with the exercise of her case management discretion. The judge held that, viewed in isolation, the 45 minute delay was a trivial breach, but the court was entitled to have regard to other breaches. The cumulative effect was that the 45 minute delay was not trivial. There was no good reason for the non–compliance. It was held that both the district judge and the judge were wrong. At the first stage, the district judge ought to have considered that the delay in filing the costs budget in breach of the October order was neither serious nor significant. On any view, the 45 minute delay was trivial. The breach did not imperil any future hearing date or otherwise disrupt the conduct of this or other litigation. The Court of Appeal stated that having regard to this assessment of the breach, the district judge did not need to spend much time on either of the second or third stages in the case. There was, however, no good reason demonstrated for the delay in filing a costs budget. As regards the third stage, neither r.3.9(1)(a) nor r.3.9(1) (b) pointed towards a refusal of relief for the simple reason that, as we have said, the breach did not prevent the litigation from being conducted efficiently and at proportionate cost, and did not imperil any future hearing date or otherwise disrupt the conduct of this or any other litigation. At the third stage, the district judge would also have considered the fact the claimant's solicitor applied for relief as soon as he became aware of the position. It was also at the third stage that the district judge and the judge ought to have considered the effect of the additional breach the failure to notify the court timeously of the outcome of negotiations. The court stated that the district judge and Judge were wrong to think that the later breach of the order, which was itself neither serious nor significant, turned what was neither a serious nor a significant breach into something worse.

Add new paragraphs 3.9.5.1 to 3.9.5.14:

No sanction

3.9.5.1   Non–compliance with an order does not always involve the imposition of a sanction upon the defaulting party. For example, no sanction is imposed by an order for security for costs if the security is ordered on terms that "all further proceedings be stayed until security is given". In such a case the stay will be lifted upon compliance with the order; it is not imposed as a consequence of non–compliance (contrast the order for security made in *Summit Navigation Ltd v Generali Romania Assigurare Reasigurare SA* [2014] EWHC 398 which did impose a sanction in the following terms: "In the event that such security is not provided by the said date the action be stayed"; and see further para.3.9.5, above).

Many rules, practice directions and orders specify the time limits by which certain steps must be taken. Even though no sanction is specified for failure to comply with the time limit, the courts regularly apply the *Mitchell/Denton* principles to any application for an extension of the time limit if that application is made after the time limit has expired (see further, para.3.9.5.8, below).

Many rules and practice directions impose requirements on parties without specifying any time limit or any sanction for non–compliance (for example, requirements as to how service of a document is to be effected and requirements that applications for a particular order must be supported by evidence). Non–compliance with these requirements will not necessitate an application under r.3.9. In these instances, failure to comply is treated as an irregularity; it does not invalidate the step taken or any document, judgment or order obtained thereon unless the court so orders (see further r.3.10 and the commentary thereon). However, the non–defaulting party may make an application under r.3.4(2)(c) for an order striking out the defaulting party's statement of case for "failure to comply with a rule, practice direction or court order" (as to which, see para.3.4.4, above and 3.9.5.14, below).

Given the stringency with which the courts now treat applications for relief from sanctions and out–of–time applications for an extension of time, parties agreeing time-table directions should be extremely careful not to under–estimate the amount of time which may be reasonably needed to complete each stage in the timetable. Similarly, a party against whom an order is sought should be cautious when considering what if any sanction he should consent to or advocate for (and see further, note (8) in para.3.9.4, above *Denton v TH White* [2014] EWCA Civ 906 at [44]). In *Porter Capital Corpn v Zulfikar Masters*, March 19, 2014, unrep., Mr N. Strauss QC (sitting as a deputy judge of the High Court) stated that the court should adopt a cautious approach when making an order imposing a sanction, especially where the order requires the payment of money as opposed to compliance with a procedural direction (refusal to impose a sanction in an order for an interim payment).

Conduct complained of did not bring sanction into operation

Filing a costs budget which, although signed by the solicitor, did not contain the full **3.9.5.2** words of the required statement of truth did not amount to a breach of the requirement in r.3.13 to "file a budget as required by the rules" (*Bank of Ireland v Philip Pank Partnership* [2014] EWHC 284 (TCC). Similarly, serving a list of documents which was deficient did not by itself amount to a failure to comply with an unless order to give standard disclosure provided that the list was not illusory (*Lakatamia Shipping Co Ltd v Nobu Su* [2014] EWHC 275 (Comm); a list would be illusory if the court could infer lack of good faith where it was obvious, from deficiencies in the list that it had been prepared in apparent but not real compliance with the obligation to give disclosure; as to the failure to serve the list in time in *Lakatamia*, see further, para.3.9.5, above).

Filing a costs budget one day later than the time prescribed by r.3.13 did not bring into operation the sanction imposed by r.3.14 where the budget was filed in accordance with a written agreement by which the parties had extended the time for filing (*Rattan v UBS* [2014] EWHC 665 (Comm): as to written agreements extending certain time limits, see r.2.11; however, it is difficult to reconcile this decision with r.3.8(3) in the form it had before the June 2014 amendment and the inclusion of r.3.8(4)).

Filing a costs budget which was not signed the party's senior legal representative as required by Practice Direction 3E, para.1 (see 3EPD.1) did not bring into operation the sanction imposed by r.3.14 where the budget was signed by a costs draftsman; the document suffered only from an irregularity (as to which, see r.3.10) and r.3.14 was not applicable (*Americhem Europe Ltd v Rakem Ltd* [2014] EWHC 1881 (TCC)).

Breach avoided by an in–time application for extension of time which was granted

An in–time application for extension of time refers to an application which is **3.9.5.3** received by the court office before the relevant time limit has been reached. In *In the matter of Guidezone Ltd* [2014] EWHC 1165 (Ch) Nugee J. adopted this term as a clearer alternative to "a prospective application for extension of time" because it often happens that, if such applications proceed to a hearing, that hearing will not take place until after the relevant time limit has expired and, therefore, the extension sought is to that extent retrospective. Subsequently, the term was adopted and used by the Court of Appeal (see *Hallam Estates v Baker* [2014] EWCA Civ 661). In that case, the Court of Appeal held that the *Mitchell* principles do not apply to an in–time application: instead the guidance given by the Court of Appeal in *Robert v Momentum Services Ltd* [2003] EWCA Civ 299; [2003] 1 W.L.R. 1577 (as to which, see para.3.1.2, above) remains good law. In such cases the court's discretion to vary a time limit or deadline is to be exercised having regard to the overriding objective (as to which, see r.1.1) and without reference to r.3.9(1)(a) and (b) (i.e., the two considerations which are to be treated as having paramount importance). The addition of sub–paragraph

1.1(2)(f) into the overriding objective ("enforcing compliance with rules, practice directions and orders") does not require courts to refuse reasonable extensions of time, which neither imperil hearing dates nor otherwise disrupt the proceedings.

The decision in *Kagalovsky v Balmore Investment Ltd and Others* [2014] EWHC 108 (QB), Turner J, provides a post–*Mitchell* example of an in–time application for an extension of time which was refused. In that case the eighth defendant had been found to be in contempt of court. He applied for an extension of time to file an appellant's notice on the last day on which the notice should have been filed. The application was refused. It was held that it was not appropriate to grant an extension of time despite the potential seriousness of the consequences for him and the absence of prejudice to the claimants. It should also be noted that the judge exercised a discretion taking a number of factors adverse to the application into account. The case is not authority for the proposition that extensions of time should never be granted.

Breach trivial: matter of form, not substance

3.9.5.4   A mistake of form rather than substance is one of the examples given in *Mitchell* (at [40]) of a case where the non–compliance can be regarded as "trivial" so that the court will usually grant relief. In *Denton v TH White* [2014] EWCA Civ 906 the Court of Appeal re–stated the approach the courts should take by replacing the reference to "trivial" with the words "neither serious nor significant" (see [24]). In*Forstater v Monty Python Pictures Ltd* [2013] EWHC 3759 (Ch) the receiving party failed to serve a notice of funding pursuant to the old r.44.3B (see para.44x.3B, below) the sanction for which is the loss of most of the recoverable success fees otherwise payable. Although there was no good reason for this failure the receiving party did belatedly give some of the required information to its opponent by letter. Norris J held that, from the date of the informal notice by letter, the receiving party's breach was largely a matter of form not substance and so granted relief from sanctions from that date onwards.

In *Adlington v ELS International Lawyers LLP* [2013] EWHC B29 (QB) seven out of 132 claimants applied for relief from an Unless order striking out their claims because of their failure to meet a deadline for the filing and serving of individual particulars of claim. His Honour Judge Oliver–Jones QC considered the non–compliance to be a matter of form not substance: the names of the seven claimants could easily be moved into a different schedule of claimants in respect of whom the Unless order did not apply. (Other reasons included the fact that the non–compliance was trivial, having regard to the absence of any harm caused (as to which, see para.3.9.5.5, below) and the fact that the deadline had been only narrowly missed (as to which, see para.3.9.5.6, below).)

In *Bank of Ireland v Philip Pank Partnership* [2014] EWHC 284 (TCC) Phillips J. held that the filing a costs budget which did not contain the full words of the required statement of truth did not amount to a breach of the requirement in r.3.13 to "file a budget as required by the rules" (see para.3.9.5.2, above) or in the alternative, amounted to a mistake of form only, not substance and therefore suitable for relief from the sanction imposed by r.3.14.

Breach trivial: no harm caused to the non–defaulting party, to the court's timetable for this case or to other court users

3.9.5.5   Considerations of the type summarised in the heading to this sub–paragraph are not expressly mentioned in *Mitchell* but are frequently mentioned in subsequent cases in which relief from sanctions is given, often as part of a finding that the breach complained of is trivial, insignificant or immaterial because it has not harmed the interests of the non–defaulting party or the wider interests of justice referred to in *Mitchell* (see for example, *Adlington v ELS International Lawyers LLP* [2013] EWHC B29 (QB) at [32(b)]; *Wain v Gloucester County Council* [2014] EWHC 1274 (TCC) at [7]); *Warner v Merrett*, June 12, 2014, HH Judge Mackie QC (QBD, Merc) unrep.). In *Summit Navigation Ltd v Generali Romania Assigurare Reasigurare SA* [2014] EWHC 398 (Comm) Leggatt J. treated the absence of harm as part of "all the circumstances" the court is required to consider (see further, para.3.9.5.12, below) even if the breach in question was not trivial and there was no good reason for it (see [48]–[53]). In *Denton v TH White* [2014] EWCA Civ 906 the Court of Appeal stated that arguments on these points amounted merely to semantic disputes which "do not promote the conduct of litigation efficiently and at proportionate cost. In these circumstances we think it would be preferable if in future the focus of the enquiry should not be on whether the breach has been trivial. Rather, it should be on whether the breach has been serious or significant" (see [26]).

It sometimes happens that an application for relief from sanctions which is strongly opposed causes heavy delay and expense to the parties and also uses up considerable amounts of the court's resources which would otherwise have been available for other court users. In the matter of *Guidezone Ltd* [2014] EWHC 1165 (Ch) Nugee J. held (at [71]) that the court should not treat strong opposition as a reason, by itself, for refusing the application. To do so would simply increase the temptation for the respondents to refuse to negotiate and to argue at length why relief or any extension of time should not be granted (and see also, *AEI v Alstom* [2014] EWHC 430 (Comm) at [26]).

In *Decadent Vapours Ltd v Bevan* [2014] EWCA Civ 906, an appeal heard at the same time as *Denton* and reported with it, the claimant failed to comply with an Unless order by sending a cheque for a court fee one day late. The cheque went astray, either before or after delivery to the court office but the claimant's solicitor remedied the breach promptly once the loss of the cheque came to light. The Court of Appeal set aside the lower court's refusal to grant relief: (i) the failure in this case was near the bottom of the range of seriousness, (ii) there was no good reason for the breach but (iii) both factor (a) (the need for litigation to be conducted efficiently and at proportionate cost) and (b) (the need to enforce compliance with rules, practice directions and court orders) pointed in favour of the grant of relief. The breach only affected the orderly conduct of the litigation because of the approach adopted by the defendants' failure to consent to relief being given, and by the approach taken by the lower courts (see at [58] to [66]).

In *Utilise TDS Limited v Davies* [2014] EWCA Civ 906, another appeal heard at the same time as *Denton* and reported with it, the claimant failed to comply with an Unless order by filing a costs budget 45 minutes late and, subsequently, failed to comply with another order (in respect of which no sanction applied) by notifying the court of the outcome of certain negotiations 13 days late. The claimant's solicitor promptly applied for relief in respect of the Unless order but was refused on the basis of the cumulative effect of the breaches. The Court of Appeal set aside the lower court's refusal to grant relief: (i) the 45 minute delay was trivial: it did not imperil any future hearing date or otherwise disrupt the conduct of this or other litigation. In the circumstances there was no need for the district judge to spend much time on either of the second or third stages, (ii) there was no good reason for the breach but (iii) both factor (a) (the need for litigation to be conducted efficiently and at proportionate cost) and (b) (the need to enforce compliance with rules, practice directions and court orders) pointed in favour of the grant of relief. It was only at the third stage that the courts should have considered the subsequent breach (as to which there was no specified sanction); this subsequent breach was of itself neither serious nor significant and so did not outweigh the other factors. The Court of Appeal considered that the defendants ought to have consented to the grant of relief from sanctions (see at [67] to [80]).

Breach trivial: deadline only narrowly missed

Another example of what might amount to a trivial non–compliance given in *Mitch-* **3.9.5.6** *ell* (at [40]) is that the defaulting party has only narrowly missed a deadline imposed by an order, but has otherwise fully complied with its terms. For example, delay measured in minutes or hours in providing security for costs (*Summit Navigation Ltd v Generali Romania Assigurare Reasigurare SA* [2014] EWHC 398 (Comm)), or in providing standard disclosure in compliance with an unless order (*Lakatamia Shipping Co Ltd v Nobu Su* [2014] EWHC 275 (Comm)) or delay in filing a costs budget not exceeding one day ((*Rattan v UBS* [2014] EWHC 665 (Comm); *Wain v Gloucester County Council* [2014] EWHC 1274 (TCC)). In *Denton v White* [2014] EWCA Civ 906 the Court of Appeal re–stated the approach the courts should take by replacing the reference to "trivial" with the words "neither serious nor significant" (see [24]). In *Utilise TDS Limited v Davies* [2014] EWCA Civ 906, an appeal heard at the same time as *Denton*, the Court of Appeal held that a delay of 45 minutes in filing a costs budget was neither serious nor significant and, indeed, was trivial (see further, para.3.9.5.5, above).

Substantial breach of a deadline

This sub–paragraph deals with cases in which in a rule, practice direction or order **3.9.5.7** requires a party to perform a procedural direction by a stated deadline and also states a sanction which will take effect in the case of non–compliance and the defaulting party cannot show that the deadline was narrowly missed (as to which, see para.3.9.5.6, above) and cannot show some good reason for the non–compliance (as to which, see para.3.9.5.9, below).

In *Durrant v Chief Constable of Avon & Somerset* [2013] EWCA Civ 1624 an order was made specifying the deadline for filing and service of any witness statements the defendant wished to rely upon at trial on terms that the defendant would not be permitted to rely upon any witness evidence "other than that of witnesses whose statements have been so served". The defendant did not make an in–time application for an extension of time (as to which, see para.3.9.5.3, above) and without good reason failed to serve all but two witness statements until 6 weeks after the expiry of the deadline; the Court of Appeal held that no relief from that sanction should be allowed (as to the other two witness statements, see also, para.3.9.5.11, below).

In *AEI v Alstom* [2014] EWHC 430 (Comm) a delay of 20 days in serving particulars of claim was held to be substantial (see further, para.3.9.5, above).

In *Denton v TH White* [2014] EWCA Civ 906 the deadline for serving witness statements expired in June 2013 and the trial was fixed for ten days starting in mid–January 2014. In late November and early December 2013 the claimants served six further witness statements. At the pre–trial review on 23 December 2013 the judge granted relief from the sanction contained in r.32.10 and adjourned the trial. The Court of Appeal set aside that order and directed the trial be listed for trial at the earliest practicable date: (i) the service of witness statements so long after the deadline was serious and significant because it caused the trial date to be vacated and therefore disrupted the conduct of the litigation; (ii) there was no good reason for the breach; the issues dealt with in the new evidence had been known about since August 2013 at the latest, with most of the information being available since 2012; (iii) both factor (a) (the need for litigation to be conducted efficiently and at proportionate cost) and (b) (the need to enforce compliance with rules, practice directions and court orders) militated heavily or strongly in favour of refusing relief and there was very little to weigh in the balance in favour of granting relief. The adjournment of the proceedings caused a waste of court resources and generated substantial extra costs for the parties. It caused inconvenience to a large number of busy people (including six experts and numerous factual witnesses) who had carved out space in their diaries for the anticipated trial (see at [46] to [57]).

Extension of time: out–of–time application

3.9.5.8   The term "out–of–time application" refers to an application for an extension of a time limit specified by a rule, practice direction or order which is not made until after the relevant time limit has expired. Rule 3.9 does not apply to such applications if the rule, practice direction or order did not specify a sanction for non–compliance. Nevertheless, the law and practice as to r.3.9 are often applied to such cases by analogy. A party's inability to take the procedural step in question once the time limit has expired does not amount to an express sanction. However, for the applicant seeking an extension of the time limit, the consequences are exactly the same as if it did (see further, *Sayers v Clarke Walker* [2002] 1 W.L.R. 3095; [2002] 3 All E.R. 490, CA, noted in para.3.1.2, above). Accordingly, an out–of–time application for an extension of time is often treated as an application for relief from sanctions. For a contrary view, see *Associated Electrical Industries Ltd v Alstom UK* [2014] EWHC 430 (Comm) at [45]–[47]; however, in that case, the learned judge applied the recently amended definition of the Overriding Objective (r.1.1(2)) and reached the same result as he would have done had r.3.9 applied.

In each of the following cases, an extension of time was refused on the grounds that the delay in question was not trivial and the applicant could give no good reason explaining it: *Associated Electrical Industries Ltd v Alstom UK* [2014] EWHC 430 (Comm); Andrew Smith J. (a delay of 20 days in serving particulars of claim); *M A Lloyd & Sons Ltd v PPC International Ltd* [2014] EWHC 41 (QB), [2014] 2 Costs L.R. 256; Turner J. (nearly 3 months' delay in serving witness statements); *Webb Resolutions Ltd v E–Surv Ltd* [2014] EWHC 49(QB) Turner J. (request for reconsideration of a refusal of permission to appeal made over 8 weeks late).

Good reason for breach

3.9.5.9   If some good reason is shown for the failure to comply with a rule, practice direction or order, the court will usually grant relief from any sanction imposed because of it (*Mitchell*, see note (2) in para.3.9.3, above). The court gave several examples of what might, depending upon the circumstances, amount to good reasons: the fact that the defaulting party or his solicitor suffered from a debilitating illness or was involved in an accident ([41]); later developments in the course of the litigation process if they show that the period for compliance originally imposed was unreasonable, although the period seemed to be reasonable at the time and could not realistically have been the subject of an appeal ([41]) "...good reasons are likely to arise from circumstances outside the control of the party in default..." ([43]). See also: *Summit Navigation Ltd v Generali Romania Assigurare Reasigurare SA* [2014] EWHC 398 (Comm) at [27] (failure to deliver an insurance bond in time caused by the difficulties encountered in getting the underwriter's signature to the bond); *Cranford Community College v Cranford College Ltd*, June 6, 2014, HH Judge Bacon (IPEC), unrep. (one of the defaulting party's key witnesses had been pre–occupied with caring for and visiting his very ill wife in hospital); *Swinden v Grima* June 18, 2014, Nicol J, (QBD) unrep. (failure to serve a witness statement in time caused by the difficulties locating the witness having done everything in their power to do so); *Service Insurance Company Ltd v Beackon*, 25 June 2014, Andrews J, (QBD) unrep. (non–compliance with a consent order to issue a new claim form by September 21, 2013; although the claimant had delivered the new claim form to the court office in good time, the court office had not issued it until September 25, 2013, i.e., nine days after receipt and four days after the deadline; if the conduct complained of brought a sanction into operation, the delay was outside the control of the claimant).

No good reason for breach

Case examples of reasons held not to be good reasons explaining a failure to comply **3.9.5.10** with a rule, practice direction or order include the following: "...overlooking a deadline will rarely be a good reason" ([41]); "...well–intentioned incompetence, for which there is no good reason, should not usually attract relief from a sanction unless the default is trivial" ([48]). See also *Newland Shipping & Forwarding Ltd v Toba Trading FZC* [2014] EWHC 210 (Comm); [2014] 2 Costs L.R 279; Hamblen J. (the loss of legal representation as a result of a dispute over fees payable in respect of it).

Even if the breach in question is non–trivial (now serious or significant), the absence of any good reason explaining why it occurred need not be fatal to an application for relief from sanctions. Although the court will not usually grant relief in such a case, in some circumstances it may do (see further, *Decadent Vapours Ltd v Bevan*, an appeal heard at the same time as *Denton* and reported with it, noted in para.3.9.5.5, above and see also para.3.9.5.12, below). However, the weaker the reason, the more likely the court will be to refuse to grant relief (see *Mitchell* [42]).

Failure to apply for relief promptly

"Every application should be made as soon as it becomes apparent that it is neces- **3.9.5.11** sary or desirable to make it" (PD23A, para.2.7; see 23APD.2, below). The need for promptitude in applying for relief from sanctions was particularly mentioned in *Mitchell* in the context of granting relief in respect of a breach held to be trivial (see note (1) in para.3.9.4, above). A simplistic reading of that guidance would suggest that promptitude was a pre–requisite to the grant of relief but only in cases where the breach in question was held to be trivial. The guidance given in a subsequent Court of Appeal decision make plain that promptitude of application is a material factor in all relief from sanctions hearing but is never a pre–requisite to the grant of relief (*Chartwell Estate Agents Ltd v Fergies Properties SA and Another* [2014] EWCA Civ 506 at [34])]; *Denton v White* [2014] EWCA Civ 906 at [36], [64] and [72]). In a case in which the relevant breach is neither serious nor significant, promptitude of application, and the other circumstances and the question why the breach occurred, are matters which the court is unlikely to need to spend much time considering (*Denton* at [24]).

In some cases the need for any application will be overtaken by steps taken by the non–defaulting party (*AEI v Alstom* [2014] EWHC 430 (Comm)). However, the fact that the non–defaulting party could have made an application but did not does not excuse the defaulting party's obligation to apply promptly (*Medical Supplies & Services International Ltd v Acies Engineering Ltd* [2014] EWHC 1032 (QB)).

In *Durrant v Chief Constable of Avon & Somerset* [2013] EWCA Civ 1624; [2014] 2 All E.R.757, the Court of Appeal held reversed a judge's decision to grant relief from sanctions in respect of the late service of witness statements in breach of an order akin to an Unless order. The deadline for exchange was March 12, 2013 and the trial date was set for June 10, 2013. The defendant served two witness statements one day late and, six weeks later, in May 2013, made an application for relief from sanctions. The defendant then served four further witness statements and, five days before the trial was due to start, made a further application for relief from sanctions in respect of two further witness statements. In respect of most of the witness statements the period of delay was substantial. In relation to the two witness statements which had been served one day late, relief from sanction was refused on the basis that the application for relief from sanctions had not been made promptly.

In *Clarke v Barclays Bank Plc* [2014] EWHC 505 (Ch) the requirement the claimant had failed to comply with was PD23A, para.2.7 itself (i.e., the need to make applications promptly, see the text of para.2.7 quoted above). In that case the claimant's chosen expert informed the claimant that he was going to retire and so did not wish to participate further in the litigation. That information was given to the claimant's solicitor a few weeks after timetable directions for expert evidence had been given but no application for permission to call a different expert was made until another six months had elapsed by which time, if permission had been granted, the trial would have had to have been adjourned. Applying *Mitchell* principles to what was, essentially, an out-of-time application, Mr R Hollington QC (sitting as a Deputy Judge of the High Court) held that permission to rely upon the evidence of a replacement expert should be refused.

In *Integral Petroleum SA v SCU–Finanz AG* [2014] EWHC 702 (Comm), the claimant obtained a default judgment on July 17, 2013 and the defendant's application to set it aside was issued more than 5 months later, on December 30, 2013. Popplewell J. held that the relevant period to consider in respect of delay in this case was under 3 months, from September 13, 2013 (the date the defendant first had notice of the judgment) to December 6, 2013 (the date upon which the defendant's solicitors wrote to the claimant's solicitors setting out the grounds on which the application would be made and inviting consent). As to further details of this case, see para.3.9.5.14, below.

Relevance of "all the circumstances"

3.9.5.12   On an application for relief from sanctions, all the circumstances have to be considered but the rule makes express reference to (a) the need for litigation to be conducted efficiently and at proportionate cost and (b) the need to enforce compliance with rules, practice directions and court orders. In *Denton v TH White* [2014] EWCA Civ 906 the Court of Appeal decided by a majority (Lord Dyson MR and Vos L.J.) that these two factors "are of particular importance and should be given particular weight at the third stage when all the circumstances of the case are considered" (see [32]; Jackson L.J., dissenting on this point: "What the rule requires is that the two factors be specifically considered in every case. The weight to be attached to those two factors is a matter for the court having regard to all the circumstances" (see [85])). Nevertheless, the Court of Appeal in *Denton* was unanimous in its desire to discourage courts from taking an unduly draconian approach to r.3.9(1) and (at [37]) repeated the passage from the 18th Implementation Lecture on the Jackson reforms which is also referred to in *Mitchell* (at [38]):

> "It [the relationship between justice and procedure] has changed not by transforming rules and rule compliance into trip wires. Nor has it changed it by turning the rules and rule compliance into the mistress rather than the handmaid of justice. If that were the case then we would have, quite impermissibly, rendered compliance an end in itself and one superior to doing justice in any case" (Lord Dyson MR, 22 March 2013).

Decisions as to whether or not to grant relief from sanctions are always discretionary and are highly case–sensitive. Appeal courts will not interfere with a lower court's decision on such matters unless satisfied that the lower court erred in law, erred in fact or reached a conclusion which falls outside the generous ambit within which reasonable disagreement is possible (see para.52.11.4, below). The fact that "other circumstances" may influence the court's decision even where the two specified factors militate in favour of refusing relief may be taken as an indication that the court's new policy in respect of non–compliance with rules, practice directions and orders is one of low tolerance rather than no tolerance. "My understanding of *Mitchell* is that the court should strive to be a tough but wise, not an officious or pointlessly strict, disciplinarian" (Mr R Hollington QC, sitting as a Deputy Judge of the High Court, in *Clarke v Barclays Bank Plc* [2014] EWHC 505 (Ch).

In *Summit Navigation Ltd v Generali Romania Assigurare Reasigurare SA* [2014] EWHC 398 (Comm) Leggatt J. held, obiter, that the absence of any impact on the efficient conduct of that case or on the wider public interest of the needs and interests of all court users, would have justified an order granting relief from sanctions even if the breach in question had been substantial and there had been no good reason for it (see [48]–[53]).

In *Chartwell Estate Agents Ltd v Fergies Properties SA and Another* [2014] EWCA Civ 506, the "other circumstances" which justified relief in that case were the fact that both parties had been in default, the refusal of relief would have had the disproportionate effect of ending the claim, its grant would not lead to an adjournment of the trial date and would not cause any significant extra cost (see further, para.3.9.5, above).

Orders granting partial relief from sanctions

As an alternative to seeking full relief from a sanction imposed upon him, an applicant may invite the court to allow partial relief, such as, for example: permission to rely upon some if not all the new witness statements served late; or a disallowance of some rather than all future costs in excess of court fees; or to grant relief on terms: for example, terms as to costs payable by the defaulting party; or interest, whether payable by or to the defaulting party; or terms requiring a payment into court to secure a claim for compensation, or to secure the non–defaulting party's costs.   **3.9.5.13**

In *Mitchell* the Court of Appeal accepted that the court has power to grant of partial relief from sanctions but did not consider that the grant of partial relief from CPR 3.14 will often be appropriate (see [58] and see note (9) in para.3.9.3, above). That guidance may make some courts generally reluctant to grant partial relief from sanctions in any case. Whilst is arguable that the guidance applies only to the sanction imposed by r.3.14 ("Failure to file a budget") the reasons given for it appear to apply equally to most if not all sanctions: most of them are simple and stark and, if partial relief were to be encouraged, that would give rise to uncertainty and complexity and stimulate satellite litigation. An unwillingness to grant partial relief is consistent with the assumption which the court should make, that the sanction in question was properly imposed (see note (8) in para.3.9.3, above). Granting partial relief from sanctions may, depending upon the circumstances, simply amount to a watering down of the sanction which would otherwise have applied.

In *Denton* the Court of Appeal did not give any specific guidance on this topic. Although it stated that the guidance given at [40] and [41] of *Mitchell* remains "substantially sound" (see [24]) no mention was made of para.[58] of *Mitchell*. However, the more nuanced approach advocated in *Denton* (see [36] and [37]) may lessen any reluctance the courts might otherwise have had on this topic. A consideration of all the circumstances, including factors (a) and (b), may sometimes make it appropriate to grant partial relief, or to grant relief on terms.

In *Riff Trading Ltd (in liquidation) v Saunders (deceased)* [2014] EWHC 2116 (Ch) (Edward Bartley Jones QC) defendants who had failed to file evidence in time in compliance with an Unless order were given relief from sanctions and allowed further time to serve evidence conditional upon the following terms: (a) in respect of the new time limit for serving their evidence, time was to be of the essence; (b) they were to pay the claimant's costs of the application for relief within a defined period, time being of the essence; (c) even if they were successful at trial, they would not be able to recover any costs from the claimant or its liquidator.

Non–compliance cases not governed by Mitchell/Denton principles

The *Mitchell/Denton* principles apply to applications made pursuant to r.3.9, out–of–time applications for an extension of time (see para.3.9.5.8, above) and applications to set aside judgments obtained under r.3.5 ("Judgment without trial after striking out" and see further r.3.6(4)). The *Mitchell* principles do not apply in cases in which the non–compliance does not result in the imposition of a sanction (see para.3.9.5.1, above) or in which non–compliance is avoided by means of an in–time application for an extension of time (see para.3.9.5.3, above).   **3.9.5.14**

In *Summit Navigation Ltd v Generali Romania Asigurare Reasigurare SA* [2014] EWHC 398 (Comm); [2014] 2 Costs L.R 367; Leggatt J., the claimant failed to comply with a consent order under which it agreed to provide security for the defendant's costs by a specified time, failing which the claim would be stayed. The learned judge held that sanction here was not intended to be permanent and therefore could be approached differently under r.3.9 so that *Mitchell* did not apply. This was because there is a significant difference between an order which specifies the consequence that proceedings are to be stayed if security for costs is not provided by a specified date and an order that, unless security is provided by a specified date, the claim will be struck out. The difference is that a stay is not intended to be permanent whereas a strike out is intended to be permanent unless relief is granted (and see further, para.3.9.5, above).

It is arguable that the *Mitchell/Denton* principles do not apply at all in applications under r.3.4(2)(c) ("failure to comply with a rule, practice direction or court order") where the non–compliance complained of does not relate to a breach of a time limit; for example, a failure to serve a document in the correct manner (as to which see r.3.10 and *Stoute v LTA Operations Ltd* [2014] EWCA Civ 657) or serving Points of Dispute without an accompanying open offer to settle (as to which, see Practice Direction 47, para.8.3). In these cases the court is being asked to impose a sanction, rather than asked to grant relief against a sanction already imposed.

There is controversy as to the extent to which *Mitchell/Denton* principles apply to non–compliance issues in respect of which there are express rules or practice directions governing the effect of non–compliance. The most important examples of such rules are r.13.3, which relates to the setting aside of a default judgment (other than a judgment wrongly entered, which can be set aside as of right under r.13.2) and r.47.12(2), which relates to the setting aside of a default costs certificate (other than a certificate wrongly issued, which can be set aside as of right under r.47.12(1)). Under both rules the court must approach the application to set aside as follows: (i) determine whether there is some good reason why the proceedings should be permitted to continue; (ii) if there is, determine whether the court should exercise its discretionary power to set aside or vary the judgment or certificate; and (iii) in addressing that question, consider whether the applicant has acted promptly in seeking to have the judgment or certificate set aside (as to (iii), see r.13.3(2) and Practice Direction 47, para.11.2(2) which are set out at paras.13.3 and 47PD.11, below). It is argued that, if the applicant prevails on each of those points, the judgment or certificate may be set aside even if there was no good reason for failing to serve a defence or points of dispute in time. As to step (i) the court's consideration is upon future events, not past misdemeanours (cf. *Henry v News Group Newspapers Ltd* [2011] EWCA Civ 1364).

In two cases it has been held that the "new regime", which is explained in *Mitchell* and is based upon and underpinned by the changes to the overriding objective, also applies to applications to set aside default judgments: *Samara v MBI & Partners UK Ltd* [2014] EWHC 563 (QB) Silber J; and *Mid–East Sales Ltd v United Engineering & Trading Co (PVT) Ltd* [2014] EWHC 1457 (Comm), Burton J. However, it is arguable that, in both cases, these remarks were directed to the requirement to make applications promptly (r.13.3(2), step (iii) in the list given above): in *Samara*, see [23], [27], [38], [50] and [58]; in *Mid–East Sales*, see [83], [88] and [89]. In both cases the defendants showed some good reason why the proceedings should be permitted to continue (step (i) in the list given above). In neither case were the defendants called upon to give a good reason for their failure to file an acknowledgment of service or serve a defence within the times allowed. However, as these cases show, the courts will treat non–compliance with an obligation to make an application "promptly" in the same way as they treat non–compliance with a time limit (as to which, see para.3.9.5.8, above). For a contrary authority, see Newland Shipping & Forwarding Ltd v *Toba Trading FZC* [2014] EWHC 864 (Comm) (Males J) in which it was stated that, at least at first instance, it is established that an application to set aside a default judgment pursuant to r.13.3 is an application for relief from sanctions.

In *Integral Petroleum SA v SCU–Finanz AG* [2014] EWHC 702 (Comm), Popplewell J. heard an application to set aside a default judgment under rr.13.2 or 13.3. As to the application under r.13.2 it was held that the claimant's error of procedure in serving particulars of claim by e–mail was "a failure to comply with a rule or practice direction" under r.3.10 and therefore the defendant's request that the judgment be set aside as of right was refused (see [42]). As to the application under r.13.3 it was held, after referring to *Mitchell* (at [77]) that the application had not been promptly made (see [78]) but having regard to the strong prospects of success shown by the defendant and other factors (see [79]) the default judgment should be set aside.

Non–compliance with unless orders

Delete paragraph 3.9.6 and substitute:

3.9.6   See *Durrant v Chief Constable of Avon & Somerset* [2013] EWCA Civ 1624; [2014] 2 All E.R.757, noted in paras. 3.9.5 and 3.9.5.11, above and *Adlington v ELS International Lawyers LLP* [2013] EWHC B29 (QB), noted in paras. 3.9.5, 3.9.5.4 and 3.9.5.5, above.

Add new paragraph 3.9.13:

Consequence if relief from sanctions is refused

3.9.13   If an application for relief from sanctions fails, the sanction in question "has effect" (see r.3.8(1)). Subsequent compliance with the obligation which led to it will not, by itself, amount to "a material change of circumstances" for the purposes of an application under r.3.1(7) (*Thevarajah v Riordan and Others* [2014] EWCA Civ 14; [2014] 1 Costs L.R.163, as to which, see para.3.9.5, above).

Where a sanction has effect which makes it impossible or impracticable for a claimant to continue the proceedings, it is open to him to discontinue them, pay the defendant's costs to date and, if the relevant limitation period has not expired, issue a new claim. The question then arises whether that new claim could be struck out as an abuse of the court's process (see r.3.4(2)(b)). In *Wahab v Khan* [2011] EWHC 908 (Ch), Briggs J. held that on such an application the court should consider all the circumstances of the particular case, including the questions as to whether a claimant would actually use a disproportionate share of court's resources, justice between the parties and also any unfairness to them (see further, para.3.4.8, above and the discussion of these points by Andrew Smith J. in *Associated Electrical Industries Ltd v Alstom UK* [2014] EWHC 430 (Comm), paras.[36] to [40]).

Meaning of "procedural error"

After the third paragraph (ending "and the commentary thereto".) add as a new paragraph:

In *Stoute v LTA Operations Ltd* [2014] EWCA Civ 657; it was held, applying *Steele* **3.10.3** (above) and considering *Phillips* (above), that service of the claim form by the court, in disregard of the claimant's notification under r.6.4(1)(b) that he wished to effect service himself, was an error of procedure under r.3.10. There was no reason why the rule should not apply to an error of the court. Service of the claim form by the court was not a nullity but, if there was an some important reason why in a particular case service had to be effected by a claimant, an order could be made under r.3.10(a) invalidating the court's service.

In *Integral Petroleum SA v SCU–Finanz AG* [2014] EWHC 702 (Comm), Popplewell J., on an application to set aside a default judgment, it was held that the claimant's error of procedure in serving particulars of claim by e–mail was "a failure to comply with a rule or practice direction" under r.3.10. Accordingly, under r.3.10(a), service was to be treated as valid. The judge indicated that a narrower approach to r.3.10 would be justified in relation to originating documents. It was said that *Phillips v Nussberger* (reported sub nom *Phillips & Another v Symes & Others* (No 3)) establishes that r.3.10 is to be construed as of wide effect so as to be available to be used beneficially wherever the defect has had no prejudicial effect on the other party.

II. Costs Management

Application of this Section and the purpose of costs management

In rule 3.12, for paragraph (1) substitute:

(1) **This Section and Practice Direction 3E apply to all Part 7** **3.12** **multi–track cases, except—**

> (a) **where the claim is commenced on or after 22nd April 2014 and the amount of money claimed as stated on the claim form is £10 million or more; or**
>
> (b) **where the claim is commenced on or after 22nd April 2014 and is for a monetary claim which is not quantified or not fully quantified or is for a non–monetary claim and in any such case the claim form contains a statement that the claim is valued at £10 million or more; or**
>
> (c) **where the proceedings are the subject of fixed costs or scale costs or where the court otherwise orders.**

(1A) **This Section and Practice Direction 3E will apply to any other proceedings (including applications) where the court so orders.**

Effect of Section II and Practice Direction 3E

Delete the third paragraph (beginning "The provisions of Section II and Practice Direction 3E") and substitute:

3.12.1   As originally enacted, r.3.12 applied to all multi–track cases commenced on or after April 1, 2013 except cases in the Admiralty and Commercial Courts unless the proceedings were the subject of fixed costs or scale costs or unless the court otherwise ordered (see SI 2013/262). Before the rule came into force it was amended so as to give powers to the Chancellor of the High Court and to the President of the Queen's Bench Division to create further exceptions, which powers the Chancellor and President exercised so as to exclude cases in the Chancery Division, the Technology and Construction Courts and the Mercantile Courts "where, at the date of the first case management conference, the sums in dispute in the proceedings exceed £2,000,000, excluding interest and costs except where the court so orders".

As a result of amendments made to r.3.12 by the Civil Procedure (Amendment No.4) Rules 2014 (SI 2014/867) (which came into force on April 22, 2014) the powers granted to the Chancellor of the High Court and the President of the Queen's Bench Division to create exceptions were revoked and the number of cases in which legally represented parties are required to file and exchange costs budgets before the first CMC has been widened so as to apply to virtually all Pt 7 multi–track cases (i.e. including cases assigned to the Admiralty and Commercial Courts). Under the amended rule, the primary exceptions from the costs management provisions are Pt 7 multi–track cases where the amount of the money claimed or value of the claim as stated on the claim form is £10 million or more, and all Pt 8 claims.

Transitional provision in respect of this change was made by r.25(1) of SI 2014/867. On April 4, 2014, the Rule Committee announced that the plain intention of r.25(1) was that the un–amended version of r.3.12(1) should govern proceedings commenced before April 22, 2014, and that the amended version should govern proceedings commenced on or after that date. On that basis, the words "to which that rule applied and" included in r.25(1) were unnecessary and potentially misleading. Subsequently a further statutory instrument deleted those words from r.25(1) of SI 2014/867 (see r.6 of the Civil Procedure (Amendment No. 5) Rules 2014 (SI 2014/1233), which came into force on June 5, 2014).

Practice Direction 3E (as amended from April 22, 2014) provides for case management in other cases where the parties are not required by rules 3.12 and 3.13 to file and exchange costs budgets. In these other cases the court has a discretion to make an order requiring the parties to do so. The court may exercise the power on its own initiative or on the application of a party. Paragraph 5 of the amended Practice Direction gives examples of the types of case in which the provision of costs budgets may be particularly appropriate.

"file and exchange budgets"

Add at end:

3.13.1   See also: *Rattan v UBS AG* [2014] EWHC 665 (Comm), noted in para.3.9.4 above.

Statement of truth for use in Precedent H

Add new paragraphs at end:

3.13.2   As from April 22, 2014 the form of Precedent H was revised so as to include within it the full text of the prescribed statement of truth. Previously, the form merely sign–posted the need for such a statement using the words "[Statement of Truth]". In *Bank of Ireland v Philip Pank Partnership* [2014] 2 Costs L.R. 301 one litigant relied upon a budget which, although signed by its solicitor, did not include the full text of the required statement of truth. Stuart–Smith J held that the failure to include the full text did not expose the litigant to the sanction imposed by r.3.14 (disallowance of all future costs in excess of court fees); alternatively he held that the error was an error of form only, not of substance, and so merited the grant of relief from the sanction of r.3.14. This revision of the prescribed form is likely to reduce the number of cases in which this error occurs. That said, the reliance upon a budget which is unsigned may well lead to the imposition of some sanction unless the statement is signed at, if not before, the case management conference by someone who has authority to sign it (see above, r.3.4(2)(c) and the commentary thereto).

In *Americhem Europe Ltd v Rakem Ltd* [2014] EWHC 1881 (TCC), Stuart–Smith J., a solicitor had served and filed a costs budget in the form of Precedent H in time, but it was signed by a costs draftsman and not by a senior legal representative within the meaning of PD3E. It was held that the error did not render the budget a nullity. The document suffered only from an irregularity and CPR r.3.14 was not applicable. The learned judge stated that while CPR 3.14 provides a sanction in the event that a party "fails to provide a budget", it does not include the additional words "complying in all respects with the formal requirements laid down by PD3E".

Costs management orders

In rule 3.15(2), for "By such order the court will—" substitute:

Where costs budgets have been filed and exchanged the court will make a costs management order unless it is satisfied that the litigation can be conducted justly and at proportionate cost in accordance with the overriding objective without such an order being made. By a costs management order the court will— 3.15

Effect of Section III

Add new paragraph at end:

For the proper approach to the operation of r.3.19, see: *Tidal Energy Ltd v Bank of Scotland Plc* [2014] EWCA Civ 847. The case suggests that given the terms of r.3.19(5)(c), the rule may be limited to the rare cases in which there is evidence that the cost judge could not adequately distinguish between costs reasonably incurred and costs unreasonably incurred, for instance, of very extensive and detailed litigation on a technical matter. 3.19.1

PRACTICE DIRECTION 3D—MESOTHELOMIA CLAIMS

"Mesothelioma"

In the fourth paragraph, after "supervised by" add:
Master Whitaker 3DPD.1.1

Delete the fifth paragraph and substitute:

In 2007 the Civil Justice Council brought together Master Whitaker and other judges from courts where these claims are issued and representative claimant and defendant lawyers, to establish by consensus a standard method of resolving these claims based on the system in use at the RCJ. This Practice Direction, in force from April 6, 2008 is the result. For an up to date description of the procedure in the asbestos disease court at the RCJ see the judgment of Master McCloud in *Yates v Commissioners for Her Majesty's Revenue & Customs* [2014] EWCH 2311 (QB) unrep. paras 10 to 21.

Add new paragraph 3DPD.1.3:

The Mesothelioma Act 2014

This Act received Royal Assent on January 30, 2014. Its purpose is to establish a payment scheme for victims of mesothelioma (and their eligible dependants) where their employer or employers' liability insurance company cannot be traced, and to make provision about the resolution of certain insurance disputes. The scheme is to be funded by a levy on insurance companies that are currently active in the employers' liability insurance market. The provisions of the Act resulted from a prior public consultation, which also led to a government decision not to introduce a dedicated protocol for Mesothelioma claims. The diseases protocol and this PD therefore remain the primary sources of procedural guidance. 3DPD.1.3

Delete Practice Direction 3E and Precedent H and substitute:

PRACTICE DIRECTION 3E—COSTS MANAGEMENT

This Practice Direction supplements Section II of CPR Part 3 3EPD.1

A.   Production of Costs Budgets

1. Part 7 multi–track claims with a value of less than £10 million

The Rules require the parties in Part 7 multi–track claims with a value of less than £10 million to file and exchange costs budgets: see rules 3.12 and 3.13.

2. Other cases

In any case where the parties are not required by rules 3.12 and 3.13 to file and exchange costs budgets, the court has a discretion to make an order requiring them to do so. That power may be exercised by the court on its own initiative or on the application of a party. Where costs budgets are filed and exchanged, the court will be in a position to consider making a costs management order: see Section C below. In all cases the court will have regard to the need for litigation to be conducted justly and at proportionate cost in accordance with the overriding objective.

3. At an early stage in the litigation the parties should consider and, where practicable, discuss whether to apply for an order for the provision of costs budgets, with a view to a costs management order being made.

4. If all parties consent to an application for an order for provision of costs budgets, the court will (other than in exceptional cases) make such an order.

5. An order for the provision of costs budgets with a view to a costs management order being made may be particularly appropriate in the following cases:

(a) unfair prejudice petitions under section 994 of the Companies Act 2006;

(b) disqualification proceedings pursuant to the Company Directors Disqualification Act 1986;

(c) applications under the Trusts of Land and Appointment of Trustees Act 1996;

(d) claims pursuant to the Inheritance (Provision for Family and Dependants) Act 1975;

(e) any Part 8 claims or other applications involving a substantial dispute of fact and/or likely to require oral evidence and/or extensive disclosure; and

(f) personal injury and clinical negligence cases where the value of the claim is £10 million or more.

B.   Budget format

3EPD.2   **6.** Unless the court otherwise orders, a budget must be in the form of Precedent H annexed to this Practice Direction. It must be in landscape format with an easily legible typeface. In substantial cases, the court may direct that budgets be limited initially to part only of the proceedings and subsequently extended to cover the whole proceedings. A budget must be dated and verified by a statement of truth signed by a senior legal representative of the party. In cases where a party's budgeted costs do not exceed £25,000, there is no obligation on that party to complete more than the first page of Precedent H.

(The wording for a statement of truth verifying a budget is set out in Practice Direction 22.)

C.   Costs management orders

7.1 Where costs budgets are filed and exchanged, the court will **3EPD.3** generally make a costs management order under rule rule 3.15. If the court makes a costs management order under rule 3.15, the following paragraphs shall apply.

7.2 Save in exceptional circumstances—

(a) the recoverable costs of initially completing Precedent H shall not exceed the higher of £1,000 or 1% of the approved or agreed budget; and

(b) all other recoverable costs of the budgeting and costs management process shall not exceed 2% of the approved or agreed budget.

7.3 If the budgets or parts of the budgets are agreed between all parties, the court will record the extent of such agreement. In so far as the budgets are not agreed, the court will review them and, after making any appropriate revisions, record its approval of those budgets. The court's approval will relate only to the total figures for each phase of the proceedings, although in the course of its review the court may have regard to the constituent elements of each total figure. When reviewing budgets, the court will not undertake a detailed assessment in advance, but rather will consider whether the budgeted costs fall within the range of reasonable and proportionate costs.

7.4 As part of the costs management process the court may not approve costs incurred before the date of any budget. The court may, however, record its comments on those costs and will take those costs into account when considering the reasonableness and proportionality of all subsequent costs.

7.5 The court may set a timetable or give other directions for future reviews of budgets.

7.6 Each party shall revise its budget in respect of future costs upwards or downwards, if significant developments in the litigation warrant such revisions. Such amended budgets shall be submitted to the other parties for agreement. In default of agreement, the amended budgets shall be submitted to the court, together with a note of (a) the changes made and the reasons for those changes and (b) the objections of any other party. The court may approve, vary or disapprove the revisions, having regard to any significant developments which have occurred since the date when the previous budget was approved or agreed.

7.7 After its budget has been approved or agreed, each party shall re-file and re-serve the budget in the form approved or agreed with re-cast figures, annexed to the order approving it or recording its agreement.

7.8 A litigant in person, even though not required to prepare a budget, shall nevertheless be provided with a copy of the budget of any other party.

7.9 If interim applications are made which, reasonably, were not included in a budget, then the costs of such interim applications shall be treated as additional to the approved budgets.

Precedent H—Costs budget

Please refer to *http://www.justice.gov.uk/courts/procedure–rules/civil* for future versions of **3EPD.4** Precedent H.

In the: [to be completed]
Parties: [to be completed]
Claim number: [to be completed]

Costs budget of [Claimant / Defendant] dated [ ]

PRECEDENT H (wef: 22 April 2014)

Work done / to be done	Assumptions	Incurred			Estimated		
		Disbursements (£)	Time costs (£)		Disbursements (£)	Time costs (£)	Total (£)
Pre-action costs		£0.00	£0.00		£0.00	£0.00	£0.00
Issue /statements of case		£0.00	£0.00		£0.00	£0.00	£0.00
CMC		£0.00	£0.00		£0.00	£0.00	£0.00
Disclosure		£0.00	£0.00		£0.00	£0.00	£0.00
Witness statements		£0.00	£0.00		£0.00	£0.00	£0.00
Expert reports		£0.00	£0.00		£0.00	£0.00	£0.00
PTR		£0.00	£0.00		£0.00	£0.00	£0.00
Trial preparation		£0.00	£0.00		£0.00	£0.00	£0.00
Trial		£0.00	£0.00		£0.00	£0.00	£0.00
ADR / Settlement discussions		£0.00	£0.00		£0.00	£0.00	£0.00
Contingent cost A: [explanation]		£0.00	£0.00		£0.00	£0.00	£0.00
Contingent cost B: [explanation]		£0.00	£0.00		£0.00	£0.00	£0.00
GRAND TOTAL (including both incurred costs and estimated costs)		£0.00	£0.00		£0.00	£0.00	£0.00

This estimate excludes VAT (if applicable), success fees and ATE insurance premiums (if applicable), costs of detailed assessment, costs of any appeals, costs of enforcing any judgment and [complete as appropriate]

Statement of Truth

This budget is a fair and accurate statement of incurred and estimated costs which it would be reasonable and proportionate for my client to incur in this litigation.

Signed

Position   Date

Page 1 of 5

50

In the: [to be completed]
Parties: [to be completed]
Claim number: [to be completed]

	RATE (per hour)	PRE-ACTION COSTS				ISSUE / STATEMENTS OF CASE				CMC			
		Incurred costs	Estimated costs		TOTAL	Incurred costs	Estimated costs		TOTAL	Incurred costs	Estimated costs		TOTAL
		£	Hours	£	£	£	Hours	£	£	£	Hours	£	£
Fee earners' time costs [fee earner description]													
1	£0.00			£0.00	£0.00			£0.00	£0.00			£0.00	£0.00
2	£0.00			£0.00	£0.00			£0.00	£0.00			£0.00	£0.00
3	£0.00			£0.00	£0.00			£0.00	£0.00			£0.00	£0.00
4	£0.00			£0.00	£0.00			£0.00	£0.00			£0.00	£0.00
5 Total Profit Costs (1 to 4)		£0.00		£0.00	£0.00	£0.00		£0.00	£0.00	£0.00		£0.00	£0.00
Expert's costs													
6 Fees					£0.00				£0.00				£0.00
7 Disbursements					£0.00				£0.00				£0.00
Counsel's fees [indicate seniority]													
8 Leading counsel					£0.00				£0.00				£0.00
9 Junior counsel					£0.00				£0.00				£0.00
10 Court fees					£0.00				£0.00				£0.00
11 Other Disbursements					£0.00				£0.00				£0.00
12 Explanation of disbursements [details to be completed]													
13 Total Disbursements (6 to 11)		£0.00			£0.00	£0.00			£0.00	£0.00			£0.00
14 Total (5 + 13)		0			£0.00	0			£0.00	0			£0.00

Page 2 of 5

In the: [to be completed]
Parties: [to be completed]
Claim number: [to be completed]

	RATE (per hour)	DISCLOSURE				WITNESS STATEMENTS				EXPERT REPORTS			
		Incurred costs	Estimated costs		TOTAL	Incurred costs	Estimated costs		TOTAL	Incurred costs	Estimated costs		TOTAL
		£	Hours	£	£	£	Hours	£	£	£	Hours	£	£
Fee earners' time costs (fee earner description)													
1	£0.00			£0.00	£0.00			£0.00	£0.00			£0.00	£0.00
2	£0.00			£0.00	£0.00			£0.00	£0.00			£0.00	£0.00
3	£0.00			£0.00	£0.00			£0.00	£0.00			£0.00	£0.00
4	£0.00			£0.00	£0.00			£0.00	£0.00			£0.00	£0.00
5 Total Profit Costs (1 to 4)		£0.00	0	£0.00	£0.00	£0.00		£0.00	£0.00	£0.00		£0.00	£0.00
6 Expert's costs / Fees	£0.00			£0.00	£0.00				£0.00				£0.00
7 Disbursements				£0.00	£0.00				£0.00				£0.00
8 Counsel's fees [indicate seniority] / Leading counsel				£0.00	£0.00				£0.00				£0.00
9 Junior counsel					£0.00				£0.00				£0.00
10 Court fees					£0.00				£0.00				£0.00
11 Other Disbursements													
12 Explanation of disbursements [details to be completed]													
13 Total Disbursements (6 to 11)		£0.00		£0.00	£0.00	£0.00		£0.00	£0.00	£0.00		£0.00	£0.00
14 Total (5 + 13)		0		£0.00	£0.00	0		£0.00	£0.00	0		£0.00	£0.00

In the: [to be completed]
Parties: [to be completed]
Claim number: [to be completed]

	RATE (per hour)	PTR				TRIAL PREPARATION				TRIAL			
		Incurred costs	Estimated costs		TOTAL	Incurred costs	Estimated costs		TOTAL	Incurred costs	Estimated costs		TOTAL
	£	£	Hours	£	£	£	Hours	£	£	£	Hours	£	£
Fee earners' time costs (fee earner description)													
1	£0.00			£0.00	£0.00			£0.00	£0.00			£0.00	£0.00
2	£0.00			£0.00	£0.00			£0.00	£0.00			£0.00	£0.00
3	£0.00			£0.00	£0.00			£0.00	£0.00			£0.00	£0.00
4	£0.00			£0.00	£0.00			£0.00	£0.00			£0.00	£0.00
5 **Total Profit Costs (1 to 4)**		£0.00	0	£0.00	£0.00	£0.00		£0.00	£0.00	£0.00		£0.00	£0.00
Expert's costs													
6 Fees	£0.00				£0.00				£0.00				£0.00
7 Disbursements					£0.00				£0.00				£0.00
Counsel's fees [indicate seniority]													
8 Leading counsel					£0.00				£0.00				£0.00
9 Junior counsel					£0.00				£0.00				£0.00
10 Court fees					£0.00				£0.00				£0.00
11 Other Disbursements					£0.00				£0.00				£0.00
12 Explanation of disbursements [details to be completed]													
13 **Total Disbursements (6 to 11)**		£0.00		£0.00	£0.00	£0.00			£0.00	£0.00		£0.00	£0.00
14 **Total (5 + 13)**		0		£0.00	£0.00	0			£0.00	0			£0.00

In the: [to be completed]
Parties: [to be completed]
Claim number: [to be completed]

	RATE (per hour)	SETTLEMENT / ADR				CONTINGENT COST A: [EXPLAIN]				CONTINGENT COST B: [EXPLAIN]			
		Incurred costs £	Estimated costs Hours	Estimated costs £	TOTAL £	Incurred costs £	Estimated costs Hours	Estimated costs £	TOTAL £	Incurred costs £	Estimated costs Hours	Estimated costs £	TOTAL £
Fee earners' time costs (fee earner description)													
1	£0.00				£0.00			£0.00	£0.00			£0.00	£0.00
2	£0.00				£0.00			£0.00	£0.00			£0.00	£0.00
3	£0.00				£0.00			£0.00	£0.00			£0.00	£0.00
4	£0.00				£0.00			£0.00	£0.00			£0.00	£0.00
5 Total Profit Costs (1 to 4)	£0.00	£0.00			£0.00	£0.00		£0.00	£0.00	£0.00		£0.00	£0.00
6 Expert's costs — Fees	£0.00				£0.00				£0.00				£0.00
7 Disbursements — Counsel's fees [indicate seniority]:					£0.00				£0.00			£0.00	£0.00
8 Leading counsel					£0.00				£0.00			£0.00	£0.00
9 Junior counsel													
10 Court fees					£0.00				£0.00			£0.00	£0.00
11 Other Disbursements													
12 Explanation of disbursements [details to be completed]													
13 Total Disbursements (6 to 11)	£0.00	£0.00			£0.00	£0.00			£0.00	£0.00		£0.00	£0.00
14 Total (5 + 13)	0	0			£0.00	0			£0.00	0		£0.00	£0.00

PRACTICE DIRECTION 3F—COSTS CAPPING

Section II of this Practice Direction—Costs Capping in Relation to Trust Funds

Costs capping orders in relation to trust funds

Delete paragraph 5.3 and substitute:

3FPD.5   **5.3** This Section supplements rules 3.19 to 3.21 and Section I of this Practice Direction.

PART 5

Court Documents

In Contents, delete the entry for "Practice Direction 5C—Electronic Working Scheme".

Editorial introduction

In the last paragraph, for the last sentence (beginning "Rule 5.5 (and r.7.12)") substitute:

Rule 5.5 (and r.7.12) were supplemented by Practice Direction 5C (Electronic **5.0.2**
Working Scheme), but that practice direction was omitted by CPR Update 75 with effect from October 1, 2014.

Related sources

Delete the entry for Practice Direction 5C. **5.0.3**

Preparation of documents

Delete rule 5.2(1) and substitute:

**5.2—(1) Where under these Rules, a document is to be prepared 5.2
by the court, the document may be prepared by the party whose
document it is, unless—**

(a) a court officer otherwise directs; or
(b) it is a document to which—
(i) [Revoked]
(ii) [Revoked]
(iii) CCR Order 28, rule 11(1) (issue of warrant of committal), applies.

Effect of rule

Delete the third paragraph beginning "Paragraph 9.1". **5.3.1**

Viewing the case record

Delete the last sentence beginning "Practice Direction 5C". **5.4B.9**

Open justice—availability of documents to non–parties

Add at end:

Toulson L.J. said (at para.85) that where documents have been placed before a **5.4C.10**
judge and referred to in the course of proceedings, the "default position" should be
that access should be permitted on the open justice principle and where access is
sought "for a proper journalistic purpose" the case for allowing it "will be particularly
strong". The significance of this decision of the Court of Appeal in the context of
r.5.4C (and of r.31.22) was stressed in *NAB v Serco Ltd* [2014] EWHC 1225 (QB), April
16, 2014, unrep. (Bean J.).

Filing by electronic means

Delete the last two paragraphs. **5.5.1**

PRACTICE DIRECTION 5C—ELECTRONIC WORKING SCHEME

Delete Practice Direction 5C—Electronic Working Scheme. **5CPD.1**

PART 6

Service of Documents

"claim" "claim form"

*In the second paragraph, for "Hills Contractors and Construction Ltd v Struth [2013] EWHC
1693 (TCC)" substitute:*

6.2.3   *Hills Contractors and Construction Ltd v Struth* [2013] EWHC 1693 (TCC), [2014] 1 W.L.R.1 (Ramsey J.)

Add new paragraph at end:

CPR r.81.10(2) states that, where a committal application is made against a person who is not an existing party to the proceedings, it is made against that person by an application notice under Part 23. Such a notice is "a document in which the applicant states his intention to seek a court order" (r.23.1). By operation of r.6.2(c), it is also it a "claim form" and in appropriate circumstances could be within the meaning of r.6.36 (Service of the claim form out of the jurisdiction where the permission of the court is required) (*Dar Al Arkan Real Estate Development Co v Al Refai* [2013] EWHC 4112 (Comm), December 20, 2013, unrep. (Andrew Smith J.) paras.70 to 73.

Effect of rule (r.6.4)

In the first paragraph, after the first sentence add:

6.4.1   Service by the court is to be read in appropriate cases as the taking of the step required of the claimant for service by r.7.5(1). See para.7 of *Stoute v LTA Operations Ltd (t/a Lawn Tennis Association)* [2014] EWCA Civ 657.

In the second sentence, for the first "it" substitute:

the general rule

Delete the last sentence (beginning "(Failure to notify") and substitute:

(See para.16.2.10 below. In certain circumstances failure to notify the other party of a funding arrangement may mean that all or part of a success fee or insurance premium will not be recoverable.) Where the court serves the claim form in error, having been notified under r.6.4(1)(b) that the claimant wishes to serve it, this will amount to an error of procedure within r.3.10(a) and service will automatically be valid unless the court orders otherwise. See *Stoute v LTA Operations Ltd (t/a Lawn Tennis Association)* [2014] EWCA Civ 657 following *Steele v Mooney* [2005] EWCA Civ 96; [2005] 1 W.L.R. 2819 and *Phillips v Nussberger* (reported sub. nom. *Phillips v Symes (No.3)* [2008] UKHL 1; [2008] 1 W.L.R. 180).

Duty to take "reasonable steps" to ascertain current address and consequences thereof

After the second paragraph, add as a new paragraph:

6.9.5   In *MB Garden Buildings Limited v Mark Burton Construction Limited and another* [2014] EWHC 431 (IPEC) Hacon J ruled that the claimant is not required by the rule to conduct his enquiries in order to take "reasonable steps", on the day on which the step required for service within the meaning of r.7.5(1) is carried out, for example, the posting of the claim form. If the claimant has carried out inquiries with reasonable diligence as to the defendant's last known residence before that date and on that date it is still objectively reasonable for the claimant to believe that the defendant's residence has remained unchanged, even if it has in fact changed, then on that date the residence last known to the claimant is effective for service.

Add new paragraph 6.9.6:

Individual being sued in the name of a business

6.9.6   Where a claim form is to be served on an individual within the jurisdiction the first question to be addressed under this rule is whether the defendant is to be served at his usual or last known residence or is an individual being sued in the name of a business and hence to be served at his principal or last known place of business. It has been held by the C of A in *Murrills v Berlanda and another* [2014] EWCA Civ 6, that a defendant, for example, practicing medicine, may be carrying on a business for the purpose of this rule but not if he is an employee or self employed working in someone else's business. An individual is sued in the name of a business when he is sued in the name of a business which is not his personal name. See further CPR PD7A.5C. Thus the first defendant medical practitioner who resided in Italy and carried on his business there but who worked from time to time in the second defendants business in the jurisdiction was not within r.6.9 and should be served under the provisions of r.6.41.

Renumber existing paragraph 6.9.6 as 6.9.7.

Effect of rule (r.6.11)

At the end of the fifth paragraph, add:

This interpretation is supported by the decision in *Ageas (UK) Ltd v Kwik–Fit (GB)* **6.11.1**
Ltd [2013] EWHC 3261 (Green J.) in which the claimant was required to give notice of
any warranty claims within a specified period and to serve proceedings in respect of a
notified claim within six months of the notice. The contract did not provide a specific
mechanism for the service of legal proceedings. The defendant argued that because
the contract referred to the claimant "validly issuing and serving legal process" the
deemed service provisions in r.6.14 should be applied to decide whether the
contractual deadline for service had been met. Green J. disagreed and held that, in
the absence of any express provisions to the contrary, in this context the word "serving" should be given its ordinary meaning, that is delivery in a form which brings the
contents of the document being served to the attention of the recipient. It was common ground that the claim form had in fact been delivered and received by the
defendant before the contractual deadline had passed, and the judge held that the
claim form had been validly served and was in time under the contact though it would
not have been regarded as served in time if the deemed service provisions in r.6.14
had applied.

However, since the decision in *T & L Sugars Ltd v Tate & Lyle Industries Ltd* [2014]
EWHC 1066 (Comm.) Flaux J. (April 10, 2014) there appear to be conflicting first
instance decisions on the meaning of the word "served" in a contract and whether it
means served in accordance with the CPR. Flaux J. decided that the word "served" in
the contract meant service in accordance with the CPR and that the claims in that case
had been "issued and served" within the meaning of the contractual provision when
the claimant's solicitors delivered the claim form and particulars of claim to the
defendant's solicitors within the 12 month time limit provided. The judge stated that
he disagreed with Green J's reasoning in *Ageas*, that the word service in a similar
contractual provision did not mean service in accordance with the CPR. However, he
agreed with Green J's obiter comment that if service did mean service in accordance
with the CPR, it was CPR r.7.5 and not CPR r.6.14 which prevailed for the purpose of
determining when actual service took place. Therefore the effect of the decision is the
same as that in Ageas, that a technical point cannot be taken that service under a
contract is not effective because although physically served in time, rr.6.14 and 6.26
would deem the documents served at a later date outside the time limit in the contract.

Add new paragraph at end:

In *DVB Bank SE v Isim Amin Ltd and another* [2014] EWCH 2156 (Comm) May 9,
2014 unrep. the Court ruled that in a case where the contractual provision allowed
each party to serve on a nominated agent for service, that provision constituted an irrevocable holding out as to the authority of the nominated agent to accept service so
that when the nominated agent entered creditor's voluntary liquidation so that actual
authority to accept service lapsed, service could still be effected as if actual authority
had not lapsed. In this case, service had been effected by post and courier on the
agent and a default judgment was not set aside.

"good reason to authorise"

At the end of the first paragraph, add:

The Court of Appeal applied this guidance and made an order under r.6.15(2) in **6.15.3**
Power v Meloy White Robinson Solicitors [2014] EWCA Civ 898, July 7, 2014 unrep. a case
in which, after there had been pre–action case management, the court served the
claim form on the defendant firm though they had been requested to return the service copies for solicitor service on the defendant's solicitors in order to effect valid service on them at their business address under r.6.7(1). There was good reason to order
that there had been good service by an alternative means because as well as there having been pre–action case management, there was after the purported service, correspondence between the parties proceeding on the clear understanding that the claimant was pursuing the claim and consistent with the claim form being accepted as
having been served and further the defendants knew all they needed to know about
the claim, hence there was something more than the mere fact that the defendant had
learned of the existence and contents of the claim form.

After the third paragraph, add as a new paragraph:

Deutsche Bank AG v Sebastian Holdings Inc and another [2014] EWHC 112 (Comm) January 30, 2014, unrep. (Cooke J.), was a case in which an order for alternative service on a defendant served in Conneticut by a method valid under the law of that State and which had come to his notice, was set aside on the grounds that there was no good reason not to use the method of service available under the Hague Convention. The judge found that the fact that in Abela there was no service convention involved but that in Cecil there was, was a critically important distinction and that while in Abela the Supreme Court considered that in Cecil, to talk of "interference with the sovereignty of a foreign state" was to overstate the position, the fact remains that where there is an applicable convention, the two states in question have specifically agreed to the service of foreign process in accordance with it. In such circumstances this must represent the prime way of service in such a contracting state. There must be good reason for allowing service by a means other than provided by r.6.40(3)(b). There was no evidence that service under the Hague Convention would cause substantial delay or of attempts to avoid service.

Retrospective operation—"steps already taken"

After the first paragraph, add as a new paragraph:

6.15.5   The rule is concerned with giving retrospective validation to an event which has already happened and it is not engaged unless some event such as purported service at some place or by some method as could be deemed to be service at or by an alternative place or method has occurred. See *Astrazenica UK Limited v Vincent and others* [2014] EWHC 1637 (QB).

Effect of rule (r.6.16)

Add at end:

6.16.1   However, in appropriate cases r.3.10 can be relied on to regard a procedural step in service of a claim form or other document as not invalidated, so that an order under r.6.16 need not be made. In *Integral Petroleum SA v SCU–Finanz AG* [2014] EWHC 702(Comm) March 11, 2014 unrep. Poppelwell J, the judge, relying on the decision of the House of Lords in *Phillips v Nussberger* (reported sub nom *Phillips & Another v Symes & Others (No.3)* [2008] 1 W.L.R.180. Held that a failure to fulfill the conditions in Practice Direction 6A (because the email address of the EEA lawyer to whom the Particulars of Claim was transmitted was not contained in the Acknowledgement of Service nor was it on the writing paper of the lawyer and he had not indicated in writing that an email address might be used for service) was an error of procedure in serving the Particulars of Claim by email and was a failure to comply with a rule of Practice Direction which fell within CPR r.3.10. It should be noted, however, (1) that while the view that the failure of procedure in the *Phillips* case was within the CPR r.3.10 was very powerful obiter (the decision was in fact about whether in the circumstances the first instance judge was right to invoke not r.3.10 but the then r.6.9 (now r.6.16) to dispense with service), the judge, had difficulty with the view that an error of procedure in CPR r.3.10 could encompass circumstances where there is no purported service of any document of any kind. He reinforced this by stating "I can envisage circumstances in which purported service by a method which is not permitted by the rules at all is sufficiently distant from what is required by the rules as arguably to fall outside CPR r.3.10. Moreover I should not be thought to be endorsing any proposition that CPR r.3.10 can be used as a matter of course to circumvent service out of the jurisdiction on a firm of solicitors or other lawyers as a matter of practical convenience without seeking an order for service by an alternative method". (2) The judge also opined that a narrower approach to CPR r.3.10 is justified when it is sought to be applied to the service of originating process, because such service is what establishes in personam jurisdiction over the defendant. (3) the logic of r.3.10(a) is that it treats as valid, steps which fall within the rule automatically without need of an order remedying the error under r.3.10(b).

The decision in *Integral Petroleum SA*, together with the dicta in the *Phillips* case (see in particular Lord Brown at para.33) suggest that the particular question to be asked is whether the attempt to serve the Claim Form or other document was or was not ineffective so that it could be said that there has been an "error of procedure" within r.3.10(a) which does not invalidate the step taken in the proceedings, that is, in this case, attempted service. Read in that way, r.3.10 prevents triumph of form over substance and does not readily apply where there has been no attempt at a procedural step or such step is one which is not permitted by or within the rules at all where an order under r.6.16 might be appropriate.

Service of claim form by electronic method (r.6.3(1)(b))

In the first paragraph, after "to dispense with service." add:

However, in *Integral Petroleum SA v SCU–Finanz AG* [2014] EWHC 702 (Comm) **6.20.4**
March 11, 2014 unrep. Poppelwell J, the judge, relying on the decision of the House
of Lords in *Phillips v Nussberger* (reported sub nom *Phillips & Another v Symes & Others
(no 3)* [2008] 1 WLR 180 held that a failure to fulfill the conditions in PD6A (because
the email address of the EEA lawyer to whom the Particulars of Claim was transmitted
was not contained in the Acknowledgement of Service nor was it on the writing paper
of the lawyer and he had not indicated in writing that an email address might be used
for service) was an error of procedure in serving the Particulars of Claim by email and
was a failure to comply with a rule of Practice Direction which fell within CPR r.3.10.
It should be noted, however, (1) that while the view of the H of L that the failure of
procedure in the *Phillips* case was within CPR r.3.10 was very powerful obiter (the decision was in fact about whether in the circumstances the first instance judge was right
to invoke not r.3.10 but the then r.6.9 (now r.6.16) to dispense with service), the judge
in Integral Petroleum, had difficulty with the view that an error of procedure in CPR
r.3.10 could encompass circumstances where there is no purported service of any document of any kind. He reinforced this by stating "I can envisage circumstances in
which purported service by a method which is not permitted by the rules at all is sufficiently distant from what is required by the rules as arguably to fall outside CPR
r.3.10. Moreover I should not be thought to be endorsing any proposition that CPR
r.3.10 can be used as a matter of course to circumvent service out of the jurisdiction
on a firm of solicitors or other lawyers as a matter of practical convenience without
seeking an order for service by an alternative method" (2) The judge also opined that
a narrower approach to CPR r.3.10 is justified when it is sought to be applied to the
service of originating process, because such service is what establishes in personam jurisdiction over the defendant. (3) the logic of r.3.10(a) is that it treats as valid, steps
which fall within the rule automatically without need of an order remedying the error
under r.3.10(b).

The decision in *Integral Petroleum SA*, together with the dicta in the *Phillips* case (see
in particular Lord Brown at para.33) suggest that the question to be asked is whether
the attempt to serve the Claim Form or other document was or was not ineffective so
that it could be said that there has been an "error of procedure" within r.3.10(a) which
does not invalidate the step taken in the proceedings, that is, in this case, attempted
service. Read in that way, r.3.10 prevents triumph of form over substance and does
not readily apply where there has been no attempt at a procedural step or such step is
one which is not permitted by or within the rules at all.

Address for service where service by means of electronic communication

At the end of the second paragraph, add:

(And see *Integral Petroleum SA v SCU–Finanz AG* [2014] EWHC 702 (Comm) March **6.23.3**
11, 2014 unrep. Poppelwell J, in respect of a failure to comply with the conditions of
para.4.)

Matters relating to a contract

After the eighteenth paragraph (ending "disposal over the goods") add as a new paragraph:

In *Krejci Lager & Umschlagbetriebs GMBH v Olbrich Transport und Logistik GMBH (C–* **6.33.13**
469/12) [2014] I.L.Pr.8, the ECJ held that a warehousing contract was a contract for
the "provision of services" and therefore a claim for payment of fees due had to be
made at the place where the warehouse was situated.

In the nineteenth paragraph (beginning "In the case of documentary") add at end:

In *Corman v Collins SA v La Maison du Whisky SA* (Case C–9/12) [2014] Q.B. 431, the
ECJ considered that a framework cross–border distribution agreement was a contract
for the provision of services falling within article 5(1)(b).

Matters relating to tort, delict or quasi–delict

At the end of the fifth paragraph (ending "[2009] 2 Lloyd's Rep. 123.") add:

Where the tort or delict was based upon the claimant being deprived of a contractual **6.33.14** benefit (viz. the right to enforce an exclusive jurisdiction clause in favour of the English Courts) damage was likely to have been suffered in the place where the benefit should have been received, see *AMT Futures v Marziller and others* [2014] EWHC 1085 (Comm), judgment of April 11, 2014 (Popplewell J).

At the end of the ninth paragraph (ending "The English court had no jurisdiction.") add:

In *Melzer v MF Global UK Ltd (C–228/11)* [2013] QB 1112, the ECJ considered that it was not permissible to define where the harmful event occurred by reference to a rule of national law which permitted a party to be sued in a place where one of the participants had taken part in committing the tort even if that party had committed no act within the jurisdiction of the court seised.

At the end of the eleventh paragraph (ending "[2012] I.L.Pr.23") add:

and in the case of an action for copyright infringement by publication on the internet, see *Pinckney v KDG Mediatech AG (C–170/12)* [2013] Bus LR 1313.

Same cause of action

In the last paragraph, add at end:

6.33.22   ; [2014] 1 Lloyd's Rep 725.

Add new paragraph at end:

In *SET Select Energy GmbH v F&M Bunkering Ltd* [2014] EWHC 192 (Comm), judgment of April 6, 2014 (Blair J), it was held that a claim for the costs of bunkers supplied had a different "object" and "cause" from a claim for an injunction to prevent payment to the claimant under a bank guarantee.

Degree to which proceedings must be "related"

In the fifth paragraph, after "February 6, 2013 (Walker J.)" add:

6.33.23   and *Nomura International Plc v Banca Monte Dei Paschi Di Siena SpA* [2013] EWHC 3187 (Comm), judgement of October 24, 2013 (Eden J.).

Exclusive jurisdiction in relation to particular subject matter

In the last paragraph, for the last sentence (beginning "However, and for the") substitute:

6.33.25   However, in *Dar Al Arkan Real Estate Development Co v Al–Refai* [2013] EWHC 4122 (Comm), judgment of December 20, 2013, Andrew Smith J. extensively criticised the decision in *Choudhary v Bhattar*. On appeal ([2014] EWCA Civ 715 (CA), judgment of May 23, 2014) the Court of Appeal did not consider it necessary to decide the point but considered Andrew Smith J.'s reasoning that the case had been decided per incuriam to be compelling. For the reflective application of art.22 in a dispute regarding the ownership of shares in a Ukranian mining company, see *Ferrexpo AG v Giltson Investments Ltd* [2012] EWHC 721 (Comm); [2012] Lloyd's Rep. 588.

Jurisdiction agreements

After the fourteenth paragraph (ending "[2008] 2 C.L.C. 520.") add as a new paragraph:

6.33.26   However, an exclusive jurisdiction clause contained in a contract for the supply of jet fuel did not cover a claim based on a finding that the vendor had breached EU competition rules, see *Ryanair Ltd v Esso Italiana SrL* [2013] EWCA Civ 1450, judgment of November 19, 2013 (CA).

Service "out of the jurisdiction" (rr.6.36 and 6.37)

Add at end:

6.37.1   CPR r.81.10(2) states that, where a committal application is made against a person who is not an existing party to the proceedings, it is made against that person by an application notice under Part 23. Such a notice is "a document in which the applicant states his intention to seek a court order" (r.23.1). By operation of r.6.2(c), it is also a "claim form" and in appropriate circumstances could be within the meaning of r.6.36 (service of the claim form out of the jurisdiction where the permission of the court is required) (*Dar Al Arkan Real Estate Development Co v Al Refai* [2013] EWHC 4112 (Comm), December 20, 2013, unrep. (Andrew Smith J.) paras 70 to 73, where permission to serve the committal application on an individual out of the jurisdiction under r.6.36 and Practice Direction 6B para.3.1(3)(b) on ground that he was a necessary and proper party to the contempt proceedings was granted). This decision was upheld on appeal ([2014] EWCA Civ 715 (CA), judgment of May 23, 2014).

Rule 6.36 and para.3.1 of 6BPD

At the end of the second paragraph, add:

For the applicable test where the Claimant puts his claim in the alternative that one **6.37.15.1** or other of the Defendants must be liable, see *Virgin Atlantic Airways Limited v H. I. Holdings* [2014] EWHC 1671 (Comm), judgment of May 22, 2014, where Burton J. held at [18] that it was sufficient to demonstrate a good arguable case that one or other of the Defendants was liable.

Paragraph 3.1(2) of 6BPD: Injunction

Add at end:

; see also *Conductive Inkjet Technology Ltd v Uni–Pixel Displays Inc* [2013] EWHC 2968 **6.37.27** (ch); [2014] 1 ALL E.R. (comm) 654.

Service on a defendant out of the United Kingdom (r.6.40(3) and (4))

In the fifth paragraph, for "Hills Contractors and Construction Ltd v Struth [2013] EWHC 1693 (TCC)" substitute:

Hills Contractors and Construction Ltd v Struth [2013] EWHC 1693 (TCC); [2014] 1 **6.40.5** W.L.R. 1 (Ramsay J.).

PART 7

HOW TO START PROCEEDINGS—THE CLAIM FORM

Practice Directions

In the second paragraph, for "the commencement date for those provisions" substitute:
from April 22, 2014 **7.0.8**

Interest on debts

(f) Late Payment of Commercial Debts (Interest) Act 1998

Add at end:

For a discussion as to what amounts to a "qualifying debt" under this Act as opposed **7.0.11** to common law damages for breach of contract see *National Museums and Galleries on Merseyside Board of Trustees v AEW Architects and Designers Ltd* [2013] EWHC 3025 (TCC); [2014] 1 Costs L.O. 39.

Starting a claim in the County Court Money Claims Centre

In the first paragraph, for the sentence beginning "The claimant must specify" substitute:
The claimant must specify the preferred County Court hearing centre (that is to say **7.2.2** the hearing centre to which the claimant wishes the claim to be sent if it becomes defended or if a hearing is required) in the practice form **N1**.

Add at end:

References in the guidance note to "any county court" should now be read as references to "any County Court hearing centre".

Service of particulars of claim

At the end of the third paragraph, add:

This is illustrated by the comments of the *C of A in Mitchell v News Group Newspapers* **7.4.3** *Ltd* 2014 1 WLR 795 (paras 49 to 51) on the decision of the judge in the case of *Raayan Al Iraq Co Ltd v Trans Victory Marine Inc* [2013] EWCH 2696. In that case the claimant applied for a two day extension of time to serve particulars of claim which application was properly dealt with as in substance an application for relief from sanctions under r.3.9. The judge had had regard to all the factors set out in the old pre-

Jackson version of r.3.9 and did not accept that "the change in the rule or a change in the attitude or approach of the court to applications of this kind means that relief from sanctions will be refused even where injustice would result" The C of A felt that the judge was focusing exclusively on doing justice between the parties and not applying the new stricter approach by having regard to a wider range of interests and giving first place to considerations of the need for litigation to be conducted efficiently and at proportionate cost and to enforce compliance with rules, practice directions and orders. And see *Associated Electrical Industries Ltd v Alstom UK* [2014] EWHC 430 (Comm), following the new approach.

Effect of rule

In the first paragraph, after the third sentence (ending "in that time") add:

7.5.1   The rule refers to "the claimant" completing the step required for service. This includes, where appropriate, the step being taken by the Court under r.6.4(1). See para.7 of *Stoute v LTA Operations Ltd (t/a Lawn Tennis Association)* [2014] EWCA Civ 657.

At the end of the fifth paragraph, add:

    ; [2014] 1 W.L.R. 1 (Ramsey J.)

At the end of the sixth paragraph, add:

Where there is a dispute as to whether a document has been posted, it may be necessary for evidence to be given about this and in some circumstances for there to be cross–examination. See the judgment of *Underhill LJ in Price v Price* [2014] EWCA Civ 655.

At the end of the ninth paragraph, add:

However, a claim form on which addresses for service of the Defendant both inside and outside the jurisdiction have been given is still only for service in the jurisdiction unless permission to serve out has been given. So the regime under r.7.5(2) applies to it and it is out of time if the relevant step for service within the jurisdiction is taken more than 4 months from issue. See *American Leisure Group Ltd v Garrard and others* [2014] EWCH 2101(Ch), June 26, 2014 unrep. where the claim form contained an address for service outside the jurisdiction and one inside but where the was no permission to serve out, was served in the jurisdiction outside the four month limit but inside the six month limit. CPR r.7.5(2) is concerned exclusively with service out of the jurisdiction and it cannot be argued that where a claim form is one that is intended to be served out of the jurisdiction, the time for service is six months from the date of issue even if service is purported to be effected in the jurisdiction. Rules 6.40(3)(c) and 6.15 did not assist because the former is concerned only with service out and the latter with whether service should be deemed good at an alternative place or by an alternative method and not as in this case, whether service had been effected in time. The case is otherwise an unremarkable example of a refusal to extend time for service where the claimant had taken insufficient steps to ascertain if the defendant was resident in the jurisdiction or out of it.

Applications under 7.6(2)

In the first paragraph, after "para.7.6.5 below)" add:

7.6.2   (The similarity of the approach in *Hashtroodi* and the approach to relief from sanctions under the post Jackson version of r.3.9 was commented on by the C of A in *Mitchell v News Group Newspapers Ltd* 2014 1 WLR 795 (paras 42 and 43)). For a case applying the approach post Jackson see *Lincolnshire County Council v Mouchel Business Services Ltd and another* [2014] EWHC 352 (TCC). But see the decision in *Kaneria v Kaneria and others* [2014] EWHC 1165 (Ch), in respect of an in time application for an extension of time to serve a defence.

Applications under 7.6(3)

Add at end:

7.6.3   In *MB Garden Buildings Limited v Mark Burton Construction Limited and another* [2014] EWHC 431 (IPEC) Hacon.J the judge ruled that a retrospective extension of time under r.7.6(3) cannot be regarded as having been made by implication. An extension is not a trivial matter and must be made after an application supported by evidence. The logic of this decision would seem to apply equally to other applications under this rule. It should be noted that in this case the District Judge seems to have made an "own volition" order under r.3.3(5)(a). The case of *Haley v Siddiqui and others* [2014] EWHC 835 shows that an application to set aside such an order is not an application for relief from sanctions and r.3.9 is not engaged. Care should be taken in such cases not to present such an application as one for relief.

In *American Leisure Group Ltd v Garrard and others* [2014] EWCH 2101 (Ch), June 26, 2014 unrep. an extension applied for after the 4 month period for service had expired was refused where the claimants had put an address for service for the defendant both in and out of the jurisdiction on the claim form but had failed to take elementary steps to discover that he had in fact been residing in the jurisdiction for 3 years.

Extension of time for serving particulars of claim

At the end of the second paragraph, add:

(See 7.4.3 above and the comments of the C of A in *Mitchell v News Group Newspapers* **7.6.8** *Ltd* 2014 1 WLR 795 (paras.49 to 51) on the decision of the judge in the case of *Raayan Al Iraq Co Ltd v Trans Victory Marine Inc* [2013] EWCH 2696. And see *Associated Electrical Industries Ltd v Alstom UK* [2014] EWHC 430 (Comm), following the new approach in respect of an out of time application.)

Add new paragraph at end:

In *Stoute v LTA Operations Limited* [2014] EWCA Civ 657 the court considered the position where, contrary to a request from the claimant's solicitor to the County Court Money Claims Centre (CCMCC) in accordance with r.6.4(1)(b) to issue the claim but return the claim form unserved, the claim form is inadvertently sent by the staff at the CCMCC to the defendant. The Court of Appeal held that service of the claim form in such circumstances amounted to an "error of procedure" within the meaning of r.3.10 and that the claim form had been validly served. At para.41 of his judgment Underhill L.J. observed:

> "In so far as the claimant has suffered some tactical prejudice by the cat being let out of the bag early the damage will have been done whether or not it is a nullity, so that service has to be effected afresh, or not. In so far as there is procedural prejudice, e.g. because he is not ready to serve particulars of claim, that can be addressed by the grant of an appropriate extension."

This lends support to the view that in such circumstances the appropriate order to be made is one which extends time for service of the particulars of claim up to the latest date on which the claimant could have served them had the claim form been retained and only served immediately prior to the expiry of the time limit provided by r.7.5.

PRACTICE DIRECTION 7A—HOW TO START PROCEEDINGS—THE CLAIM FORM

Notes on Practice Direction supplementing CPR Pt 7 (see PD 1 para.7 et seq.)

In paragraph 3.3, in the list, delete entry for "Interpleader Proceedings Ord.17". **7APD.9**

PRACTICE DIRECTION 7D—CLAIMS FOR THE RECOVERY OF TAXES AND DUTIES

Note on Practice Direction—Claims for the Recovery of Taxes and Duties

In the fourth paragraph, delete the first sentence ending "County Court hearing centre." and substitute:

Paragraph 4A.1(2) of PD7A provides that for the purposes of that Practice Direction **7DPD.3.1** the obligation under para.2.2 of PD7D to fix a hearing date upon the filing of a defence does not constitute a "special procedure". This resolves the former uncertainty as to whether it was necessary for claims to which this Practice Direction applies to be issued through the County Court Money Claims Centre. It is now clear that such claims are to be issued at the CCMCC in the same way as any other Pt 7 money claim. On the filing of a defence the file will be sent to the appropriate County Court hearing centre for a hearing to be fixed.

PRACTICE DIRECTION 7E—MONEY CLAIM ONLINE

Request for judgment or issue of warrant

In paragraph 11.2(2), in each place it occurs, for "execution" substitute:

control **7EPD.11**

PART 8

ALTERNATIVE PROCEDURE FOR CLAIMS

Part 8 Practice Direction

At the end of the first paragraph, add:

8.0.4   Section C contains special provisions relating to applications and proceedings under a variety of statutes indicating whether the appropriate originating process is by way of Part 8 claim or Part 23 application or by some other method, and in some instances indicating the person or body upon whom service of such process should be effected. Additions are made to this Section C according to need. A special provision relating to applications under the Anti–social Behaviour, Crime and Policing Act 2013 s.66 was added by CPR Update 75 (July 2014).

Managing the claim

In the first paragraph, delete from the sentence beginning "The court can order" to the end and substitute:

8.0.5   The court can order a directions hearing if appropriate. Part 29 is not specified in CPR r.8.9 as not applying, subject to modifications, to Pt 8 claims. In *Kershaw v Roberts* [2014] EWHC 1037 (Ch) the court held however that Pt 29 does not apply to Pt 8 claims that are not specifically allocated by the court to the multi–track, that CPR r.8.9(c) does not automatically allocate Pt 8 claims to the multi–track but merely provides that such claims are treated as so allocated, and that the express power in CPR r.29.3(l) to fix a case management conference is triggered by the court's allocation to the multi–track.

Costs Management

Delete paragraph 8.0.5.1 and substitute:

8.0.5.1   In *Kershaw v Roberts* ante the court (dealing with a claim issued before April 22, 2014) held that in the case of Pt 8 claims, the requirement to serve a costs budget was only triggered by the fixing of a case management conference following specific allocation to the multi–track.

On and after April 22, 2014 (by the Civil Procedure (Amendment No.4) Rules 2014) it is expressly provided that CPR r.3.12 and PD 3E applies, with exceptions, to all Pt 7 multi–track cases. The effect of this clarification is that Pt 8 claims will not be subject to costs management unless there is a specific direction. It is to be noted that examples of types of non Pt 7 claims where the parties and the court should consider whether a costs management order should be sought or made include applications under the Trusts of Land and Appointment of Trustees Act 1996 and claims under the Inheritance (Provision for Family and Dependants) Act 1975 and, importantly, Part 8 claims or applications involving a substantial dispute of fact and/or likely to require oral evidence and/or extensive disclosure. The Civil Procedure Rule Committee's note of clarification of April 4 advises that the unamended version of CPR r.3.12 will continue to govern claims commenced before April 22, 2014. Paragraph 5 of Practice Direction 3F contains detailed provisions in relation to costs capping orders in relation to trust funds and provides that in the case of a Pt 8 claim any party who intends to apply for costs out of a trust fund must serve written notice together with a budget in the form of Precedent H of the costs likely to be incurred by that party. See commentary at Vol.1 para.57.16.5.

Agreed Directions

Delete paragraph 8.4.3 and substitute:

8.4.3   Although in *Kershaw v Roberts* ante the court held that CPR Pt 29 does not apply to Pt 8 claims that are not specifically allocated to the multi track, nonetheless it is sensible practice for the parties to seek to agree directions and submit them to the court immediately after the time limited for filing an acknowledgment by the defendant. At the latest the parties will be expected to have tried to agree directions by the time of any directions hearing and produced a draft order for consideration by the court.

PRACTICE DIRECTION 8A—ALTERNATIVE PROCEDURE FOR CLAIMS

In the table in paragraph 9.4, for the entry "Interpleader (Mode of application)" substitute:

Stakeholder applications—mode of application, unless there are existing proceedings (Rule 86.2(3))		Chancery or Queen's Bench		**8APD.9**

In the table in paragraph 9.4, add new entry at end:

Application under section 66 of the Anti–Social Behaviour, Crime and Policing Act 2014 to question the validity of a public spaces protection order or variation of such an order	Paragraph 22	Administrative Court	

Application to quash certain orders, schemes, etc

Add new paragraph 22.12:

22.12 Where an application is made under section 66 of the Anti– **8APD.22** Social Behaviour, Crime and Policing Act 2014 to question the validity of a public spaces protection order or of a variation of such an order—

    (a) the claim form must be served on the local authority by which the order or variation was made or varied; and

    (b) paragraphs 22.2, 22.3 and 22.7 to 22.11 apply.

PRACTICE DIRECTION 8B—THE PRE-ACTION PROTOCOLS FOR LOW VALUE PERSONAL INJURY CLAIMS IN ROAD TRAFFIC ACCIDENTS AND LOW VALUE PERSON INJURY (EMPLOYERS' LIABILITY AND PUBLIC LIABILITY) CLAIMS—STAGE 3 PROCEDURE

Editorial introduction

Add new paragraph at end:

This Practice Direction was amended as from October 1, 2014, by CPR Update 75 **8BPD.0** (July 2014). The amendments apply to a "whiplash" claim (referred to as a "soft tissue injury claim") (see para.6.1A). Paragraph 3.5 refers to the fixed fee now allowed for a medical report in such cases. The fee is £180 (see rr.45.1 and 45.29I, as amended). These amendments to the Practice Direction apply only to soft tissue personal injury claims where the Claim Notification Form is sent in accordance with that Protocol on or after October 1, 2014.

Definitions

Add new paragraph 3.5:

3.5 "Fixed cost medical report" and "soft tissue injury claim" have **8BPD.3** the same meaning as in para.1.1 (10A) and (16A), respectively, of the RTA Protocol.

Note

Add at end:

Paragraph 3.5 was inserted by CPR Update 75 (July 2014) and came into effect on **8BPD.3.1** October 1, 2014.

Filing and serving written evidence

Add new paragraph 6.1A:

6.1A In a soft tissue injury claim, the claimant may not proceed **8BPD.6** unless the medical report is a fixed cost medical report. Where the claimant includes more than one medical report, the first report obtained must be a fixed cost medical report and any further report from an expert in any of the following disciplines must also be a fixed cost medical report—

(a) Consultant Orthopaedic Surgeon;
(b) Consultant in Accident and Emergency Medicine;
(c) General Practitioner registered with the General Medical Council;
(d) Physiotherapist registered with the Health and Care Professions Council.

Note

Add new paragraph at end:

8BPD.6.1   Paragraph 6.1A was inserted by CPR Update 75 (July 2014) and came into effect on October 1, 2014. This amendment was one of several made to the RTA Protocol and related rules and practice directions as part of a new regime for the recovery of costs allowed for medical reports in "soft tissue injury" claims. Paragraph 6.1A applies where the Claim Notification Form is sent in accordance with that Protocol on or after October 1, 2014.

PART 12

Default Judgment

"judgment in default of an acknowledgment of service"

In the first paragraph, for "county courts" substitute:

12.3.1   County Court

"judgment in default of defence"

Add at end:

12.3.3   In *Mole v Hunter* [2014] EWHC 658 (QB) it was held that a claimant was not in default of defence within CPR r.12.3 in circumstances where she had failed to serve a defence to a counterclaim in defamation in proceedings in the County Court as the County Court had no jurisdiction to entertain such a counterclaim.

Effect of rule (as substituted April 2014)

For "the commencement date for those provisions" substitute:

12.5A.1   April 22, 2014

Effect of rule

Add at end:

12.9.1   If the application for judgment is made under r.12.9(2) in relation to a claim proceeding in the CCMCC the claim will be sent to the preferred court in accordance with r.12.5A.

PART 13

Setting Aside or Varying Default Judgment

Add new paragraph 13.3.5:

Effects of court's approach following implementation of Jackson

13.3.5   In *Samara v MBI & Partners Uk Ltd* [2014] EWHC 563 (QB); (2014) 164(7598) N.L.J. 18 at [34] to [39], Silber J. held that although the 15th and 18th Lectures in the Implementation Programme on the Application of the Amendments to the Civil Procedure Rules do not deal specifically with the approach to CPR r.13.3, that as Rule 1.1 applied to all the CPR, the effect of that rule, as amended from April 1, 2013, must be taken into account in considering the requirement to act promptly.

In contrast, in *Integral Petroleum SA v SCU-Finanz AG* [2014] EWHC 702 (Comm) the court adopted a generous interpretation of Rule 3.10, and held that electronic service of particulars of claim 5 days late and failing to comply with Practice Direction 6A governing service by electronic means could be treated as valid by CPR 3.10 and refused to set aside a default judgment on the basis of invalid service of the particulars of claim.

PART 14

Admissions

"admission by notice in writing"

Add at end:

In *Akhtar v Boland* [2014] EWCA Civ 872 it was held that where a defendant had **14.3.1**
made an admission of part of two heads of damages, the claimant is entitled to judgment on that admission. If the admission was equivocal or inconsistent with other
parts of the defence, the claimant could seek clarification by way of a Part 18 request
or the judge could ask for clarification at a hearing. Here the judgment was entered at
a hearing it was not open to the defendant to continue to challenge those items so as
to bring the case within the financial limit of the fast track, as opposed to the small
claims track to which it had been allocated.

Scope of provision

Add new paragraph at beginning:

Paragraph (3) and (3A) of this rule were amended by r.10(m) of the Civil Procedure **14.13.1**
(Amendment) Rules 2014 (SI 2014/407) with effect from the date of the commencement of legislation creating the single County Court (April 22, 2014). The instruction
in r.10(m) relating to para.(3A) is not wholly clear. The text of that provision has been
rendered above in the manner in which White Book editors believe was intended.

"defendant's home court"

In the second sentence, for "transferred" substitute:

sent **14.13.3**

PART 15

Defence and Reply

"a copy of the defence must be served"

At the end of the paragraph, for "form N152" substitute:

a notice of proposed allocation **15.6.1**

PART 16

Statements of Case

Providing information about a funding arrangement

For "48n.0.1" substitute:
48.0.2 below **16.2.10**

For "defined in the r.43.2 which is set out in Vol.1" substitute:
defined in the old r.43.2, see para.43x.2, below

For "see generally Vol. 1, rr.44.3B, 44.15" substitute:
see generally, paras 44x.3B, 44x.15

Statement of value to be included in the claim form

Delete rule 16.3(2) and substitute:

(2) The claimant must, in the claim form, state— **16.3**
    (a) the amount of money claimed;

    (b) that the claimant expects to recover—
        (i) not more than £10,000;
        (ii) more than £10,000 but not more than £25,000; or
        (iii) more than £25,000; or
    (c) that the claimant cannot say how much is likely to be recovered.

Effect of rule (as amended April 2014)

In the first paragraph, for the third sentence beginning "In paras (2) and (5) of this rule ...", substitute:

16.3.1   In para.(5) of this rule the figure of £100,000 was substituted for the figure of £25,000 by the Civil Procedure (Amendment) Rules 2014 (SI 2014/407), as a consequence of the coming into force of provisions in the Crime and Courts Act 2013 s.17 and Sch.9 creating the single County Court, with effect from the commencement date for those provisions.

"such other matters as may be set out in a practice direction"

After the first paragraph, add as a new paragraph:

16.4.4   Paragraph 4.3A was added to the Practice Direction by CPR Update 75 (July 2014) and came into effect on October 1, 2014. This amendment was one of several made to CPR rules and practice directions (in particular those related to the RTA Protocol) as part of a new regime for the recovery of costs allowed for medical reports in "soft tissue injury" claims (as defined in para.1.1(16A) of the RTA Protocol). Paragraph 4.3A(1) states that the claimant in such a claim may not proceed unless the medical report attached to or served with his particulars of claim is a "fixed costs medical report" (as defined in para.1.1(10A) of the RTA Protocol).

PRACTICE DIRECTION 16—STATMENTS OF CASE

Matters which must be included in the particulars of claim in certain types of claim

Personal injury claims

Add new paragraph 4.3A:

16PD.4   **4.3A**(1) In a soft tissue injury claim, the claimant may not proceed unless the medical report is a fixed cost medical report. Where the claimant files more than one medical report, the first report obtained must be a fixed cost medical report and any further report from an expert in any of the following disciplines must also be a fixed cost medical report:
    (a) Consultant Orthopaedic Surgeon;
    (b) Consultant in Accident and Emergency Medicine;
    (c) General Practitioner registered with the General Medical Council;
    (d) Physiotherapist registered with the Health and Care Professions Council.
    (2) In this paragraph, "fixed cost medical report" and "soft tissue injury claim" have the same meaning as in para.1.1 (10A) and (16A), respectively, of the RTA Protocol.

PART 17

AMENDMENTS TO STATEMENTS OF CASE

Late amendments

At the end of the fourth paragraph, add:

However, in *Cutting v Islam* [2014] EWHC 1515 (QB) the re–amendment of a **17.3.7** personal injury claim on the first day of trial had not substantially altered the case which the defendant had to meet, and accordingly the general rule that a defendant was entitled to his costs up to the late amendment of a claim did not apply.

At the end of the fifth paragraph, after "reports served pre–trial" add:

In *Dany Lions Ltd v Bristol Cars Ltd* [2014] EWHC 928 (QB) (amendment sought two days before trial) Andrews J refused to allow amendments prompted by a reappraisal of the merits of the case by newly instructed counsel and stated that the practice on late amendments should also take account of the stricter views as to defaults in compliance with rules which were indicated by the Court of Appeal in *Mitchell v News Group Newspapers Ltd* [2013] EWCA Civ 1537; [2014] 1 WLR 795; [2014] 2 All ER 430.

Costs of amendments

Delete first sentence and substitute:

Applicants who obtain permission to amend are often ordered to pay the other par- **17.3.10** ties' costs of and caused by the application (*Taylor v Burton* [2014] EWCA Civ 21; and as to the meaning of "costs of and caused by", see Practice Direction 44, para.4.2 (44PD.4).

PART 18

FURTHER INFORMATION

Effect of rule

In the fourth paragraph, for "Secretary of State for Health v Servier Laboratories Ltd [2013] EWCA Civ 1234", substitute:

Secretary of State for Health v Servier Laboratories Ltd [2014] U.K.C.L.R. 263; [2014] **18.1.2** Lloyd's Rep. F.C.175

In the sixth paragraph, for "XYZ v Various sub nom Re Breast Implant Litigation [2013] EWHC 3643 (QB)", substitute:

XYZ v Various sub nom Re Breast Implant Litigation [2014] 2 Costs L.O.197

Judicial review

For "R. (Bredenkamp) v Secretary of State for Foreign and Commonwealth Affairs [2013] EWHC 2480 (Admin)", substitute:

R. (Bredenkamp) v Secretary of State for Foreign and Commonwealth Affairs [2013] Lloyd's **18.1.2.2** Rep F.C. 690

PART 19

PARTIES AND GROUP LITIGATION

"claim cannot properly be carried on" (r.19.5(3)(b) and s.35(6)(b))

In the sixth paragraph, for "Nemeti v Sabre Insurance Co Ltd [2013] EWCA Civ 1555", substitute:

Nemeti v Sabre Insurance Co Ltd [2013] EWCA Civ 1555; [2014] CP Rep 16; [2014] **19.5.8** CP Rep 16

Editorial note

Add new paragraph at end.

However, in *Holloway v Transport Medical Group* [2014] EWHC 1641 (QB) the judge **19.13.1** ruled that the need to apply to join the register after the cut off date was a sanction that engaged CPR r.3.9 and that consequently the guidance given in *Mitchell v News Group Newspapers Ltd* 2014 1 WLR 795 was in point.

PART 21

CHILDREN AND PROTECTED PARTIES

The protected party

Before the last paragraph (beginning "It should be noted"), add as a new paragraph:

21.0.3   The defendant's appeals in *Dunhill* were dismissed by the Supreme Court; see [2014] UKSC 18; [2014] 1 W.L.R. 933. The Supreme Court confirmed that capacity is to be judged in relation to the decision or activity in question and not globally. Hence, as was concluded in the *Masterman–Lister* case, capacity for this purpose meant capacity to conduct the proceedings. Rule 21.2(1) and r.21.4(3) suggest a focus on proceedings in general rather than on the proceedings as framed. Part 21 posits a person with a cause of action who must have the capacity to bring and conduct proceedings in respect of that cause of action. Accordingly, the Supreme Court held that the test of capacity to conduct proceedings for the purpose of Part 21 is the capacity to conduct the claim which the claimant in fact has, rather than to conduct the claim as formulated by lawyers. Judged by that test, it was common ground that the claimant did not have the capacity to conduct the claim. The claimant should have had a litigation friend. Accordingly, the settlement order was invalid. The Supreme Court accepted that a court has the power to retrospectively validate any step under r.21.3(4) but stated that, of course, everything must depend on the particular facts. It might be appropriate retrospectively to validate some steps but not others. In the instant case, the settlement finally disposing of the claim could not be retrospectively validated. The purpose of r.21.10 was to impose an external check on the propriety of the settlement. Following, *Dietz v Lennin Chemicals Ltd* [1969] 1 A.C. 170; [1967] 3 W.L.R. 165, the Supreme Court held that r.21.10 was intra vires and, in the case of both children and protected parties, prevailed over the general rule of contract that a contract would be binding if the incapacity of a party was not known to the other party. The court observed that the policy underlying the CPR is clear: that children and protected parties require and deserve protection, not only from themselves but also from their legal advisers.

At the end of the last paragraph, add:

This was confirmed by the Supreme Court in *Dunhill* (above).

Effect of rule

In the fourth paragraph, delete "and" then after "EWHC 3163 (QB)" add:

21.3.1   and *Dunhill v Burgin* [2014] UKSC 18; [2014] 1 W.L.R. 933

Effect of rule

In the second paragraph, delete "and" then after "EWHC 3163 (QB)" add:

21.10.2   and *Dunhill v Burgin* [2014] UKSC 18; [2014] 1 W.L.R. 933

PRACTICE DIRECTION 21—CHILDREN AND PROTECTED PARTIES

Settlement or compromise by or on behalf of a child or protected party before the issue of proceedings

Delete paragraph 5.1(6)(b) and substitute:

21PD.5   (b) medical and quantum reports and joint statements material to the opinion required by paragraph 5.2,

Settlement or compromise by or on behalf of a child or protected party after proceedings have been issued

Delete paragraph 6.4 and substitute:

21PD.6   **6.4**

The court must be supplied with—

(1) an opinion on the merits of the settlement or compromise given by counsel or solicitor acting for the child or protected party, except in very clear cases;

(2) a copy of any financial advice; and

(3) documentary evidence material to the opinion referred to at paragraph 6.4(1).

PART 22

Statements of Truth

Related sources

Delete the last entry for Practice Direction 5C.   **22.0.3**

Statement of case

Delete the last paragraph starting "Practice Direction 5C".   **22.1.2**

PART 23

General Rules about Applications for Court Orders

Effect of rule

In the first paragraph, for "a particular county court" substitute:
the County Court   **23.2.1**

In the second paragraph, in the first place it occurs, for "county courts" substitute:
County Court hearing centres

Delete third paragraph and substitute:
Proceedings arising on an application may be transferred from one court or County Court hearing centre in accordance with r.30.2(1). The County Court may order proceedings before it, or any part of them (such as an application made in the proceedings), to be sent to another County Court hearing centre. An application for an order to transfer such proceedings must be made to the court where the claim in which the application arises is proceeding and, presumably, should be made in accordance with Pt 23.

Delete the last paragraph and substitute:
Any application in relation to a claim which has been started at the County Court Money Claims Centre (CCMCC) and has not yet been sent to a County Court hearing centre must be sent to the CCMCC. If it is considered appropriate so to do, the application may be dealt with by a District Judge at the CCMCC without a hearing. If the application requires a hearing the claim will be sent to the appropriate County Court hearing centre.

Effect of rule

In the ninth paragraph, for "Hills Contractors and Construction Ltd v Struth [2013] EWHC 1693 (TCC), June 17, 2013, unrep. (Ramsey J.)", substitute:
Hills Contractors and Construction Ltd v Struth [2013] EWHC 1693 (TCC); [2014] 1 **23.8.1**
W.L.R.1 (Ramsey J.),

Effect of rule

In the first paragraph, delete the last sentence (beginning "Other provisions").   **23.12.1**

Delete the second paragraph and substitute:
Other provisions to similar effect (and also enacted by SI 2004/2072) are para.(7) of r.3.3 (Court's power to make an order of its own initiative), and para.(6) of r.3.4 (Power to strike out a statement of case) (see para.3.4.10 above) and paras (5) and (6) of r.52.10 (see para.52.10.7.3 below). Certain provisions (subsequently enacted) provide

that where, in dismissing a particular application the court has recorded the fact that the application was totally without merit, any reconsideration of or appeal against (as the case may be) that dismissal will be determined on paper without an oral hearing; e.g. para.(4A) of r.52.3 (Permission) (see para.52.3.8.1 below), para.(1A) of r.52.15 (Judicial review appeals) (see para.52.15.1 below), and para.(7) of r.54.12 (Permission decision without a hearing) (see para.54.12.1 below).

Application "totally without merit"

In the second paragraph, for the first sentence (beginning "Rule 23.12 applies") substitute:

23.12.2   Rule 23.12 applies to applications generally and is not confined to applications of the type referred to therein or made under r.3.4.

After the second paragraph, add as a new paragraph:

Under r.23.12, consideration by the court of the question whether it is appropriate to make a civil restraint order (CRO) is triggered by a finding that the application was totally without merit (TWM). The least severe of the several forms of CRO may not be made unless at least two applications made by the party have been found to be TWM. The questions (1) whether the court should record a finding of TWM and (2) whether it is appropriate to make a CRO are distinct and raise different considerations. In *R. (Drake) v Secretary of State for the Home Department* [2014] EWCA Civ 1091, *The Times* July 14, 2014, CA, a High Court judge on paper dealt with and dismissed an application under r.54.4 for permission to proceed with a judicial review claim and, in accordance with r.23.12(a), recorded the fact that the application was totally without merit with the result that, by operation of r.54.12(7), the applicant was barred from requesting that the dismissal of the application be re–considered at a hearing. (No question of whether it was appropriate to make a CRO arose.) The Court of Appeal held that, in these circumstances, the proper test for determining whether an application is totally without merit was whether it was "bound to fail"; it was not necessary for it to be shown that the application was abusive or vexatious.

PART 24

SUMMARY JUDGMENT

An order dealing with costs

24.6.7   *In the first paragraph, delete "(see para.44n.1)".*

In the third paragraph, delete "(see para.44n10)".

PART 25

INTERIM REMEDIES AND SECURITY FOR COSTS

Court Guides and interim remedies procedure

In the first paragraph, for "Queen's Bench Guide, para.7.13 (Vol. 2, para.1B–53)" substitute:

25.0.6   Queen's Bench Guide, para.7.12 (Vol.2, para.1B–54)

In the second paragraph, for "Queen's Bench Guide, para.7.13 (Vol. 2, para.1B–53)" substitute:

Queen's Bench Guide, para.7.12(Vol.2, para.1B–54)

In the third paragraph, for "Queen's Bench Guide, Sections 6 and 9 (Vol.2 paras 1B–29 and 1B–60)" substitute:

Queen's Bench Guide Sections 6 and 9 (Vol.2 paras 1B–30 and 1B–62)

Powers of Masters and district judges in relation to interim remedies

Delete the last paragraph and substitute:

25.0.8   Paragraphs 8.1 to 8.4 of Practice Direction 2B (Allocation of Cases to Level of Judiciary) make it clear that applications for injunctions which the County Court has jurisdiction to make will be allocated to a Circuit Judge, save for specific instances, when

District Judges have jurisdiction (see para.2BPD.8 above). Generally, the granting of such jurisdiction is based on express statutory provisions. Circuit Judges have jurisdiction to grant freezing orders (see para.2BPD.8.4 above) but not search orders.

Jurisdiction of county courts to grant interim relief

In the second sentence beginning "The circumstances in", for "paras 25.1.23 and 25.1.25" substitute:

paras. 25.1.25 and 25.1.27 **25.1.2**

How to make the application

Delete the second paragraph and substitute:

In Queen's Bench proceedings at the RCJ, an application notice for an interim **25.1.12** injunction should be filed in accordance with the practice outlined in para.7.12 of the Queen's Bench Guide (see Vol.2, para.1B–54).

Practice

In the first paragraph, for "paras 25.1.20 and 25.1.22" substitute:

paras. 25.1.25 and 25.1.27 **25.1.12.1**

Interim non–disclosure orders—restraining freedom of expression

After the second paragraph (ending "(Tugendhat J.)") add as a new paragraph:

For an explanation of the distinctions between interim non–disclosure orders and **25.1.12.5** anonymity orders (under r.39.2(4)) and their respective functions, see *CVB v MGN Ltd* [2012] EWHC 1148 (QB); [2012] E.M.L.R. 29 (Tugendhat J.).

Delete the title and substitute:

Defendant consenting to continuation, or offering undertakings pending return date or trial

Add new paragraph at end:

The same applies where a defendant consents to the continuation of an order made **25.1.12.7** without notice. In *Stephens McBride Piercy Taylor Ltd v McBride* [2014] EWHC 1231 (QB), April 16, 2014, unrep. (Slade J.), the defendant applied to discharge a without notice order that had been made 6 months earlier. It was held that, having consented, the defendant could only succeed in his application to discharge if there had been a material change of relevant circumstances. Nor was any reason tendered for the delay in applying.

Interim declaration (r.25.1(1)(b))

In the fifth paragraph (ending "the police powers") add:

In *Bank St Petersburg v Arkhangelsky* [2014] EWHC 574 (Ch), March 5, 2014, unrep. **25.1.15** (Hildyard J.) the claimants applied for an interim declaration that the defendants had dealt with certain assets in breach of the freezing order. The application was refused as a matter of the court's discretion because of the risk that it would be used as a stepping stone to a committal for contempt, without such alleged contempt having been proved to the requisite criminal standard.

Inspection of relevant property (r.25.1(1)(c)(ii))

Add new paragraph at end:

In *CBS Butler Ltd v Brown* [2013] EWHC 3944 (QB), December 16, 2013, unrep. **25.1.18** (Tugendhat J.) the claimant obtained a without notice order to allow images of the defendant's computer hard drives to be made, but the court did not order inspection without notice. An on notice application for the right to inspect was refused.

Jurisdiction—County Court

Delete paragraph 25.1.25.2 and substitute:

In the County Court Remedies Regulations 1991 the orders of a prescribed kind **25.1.25.2** which the County Court did not have power to make included freezing injunctions and search orders. The County Court Remedies Regulations 2014 (SI 2014/982), which revoked and replaced the 1991 Regulations with effect from April 22, 2014, make no provision for freezing injunctions; consequently, that remedy is no longer prescribed and the County Court has unrestricted jurisdiction to make orders for that form of injunctive relief. An application in the County Court for a freezing order must be made to a Circuit Judge.

Applicant's duties

In the third paragraph, for "Thane Investments Ltd v Tomlinson, The Times, December 10, 2002 (Neuberger J.)" substitute:

25.1.25.4   *Thane Investments Ltd v Tomlinson* [2002] EWHC 2972 (Ch); *The Times*, December 10, 2002 (Neuberger J.).

In the fourth paragraph, for "UL v BK [2013] EWHC 1735 (Fam); [2013] Fam. Law 1379, June 24, 2013, unrep. (Moystyn J.)", substitute:

L v K (Freezing Orders: Principles and Safeguards) [2013] EWHC 1735(Fam); [2014] 1 W.L.R. 914 (Mostyn J.).

Evidence

After the fourth paragraph (ending "(discussed below)"), add as a new paragraph:

25.1.25.5   The test to be met by an applicant seeking a freezing order is that they must show a "good arguable case." The test of "much the better of the argument" (used on applications for permission to serve out of the jurisdiction) is a higher hurdle and does not apply (*Kazakhstan Kagazy Plc v Arip* [2014] EWCA Civ 381, April 2, 2014, CA, unrep.).

Example of order to restrain disposal of assets

After the third paragraph (ending "para.15–87"), add as a new paragraph:

25.1.25.6   A freezing order prohibits the respondent from removing, disposing of, dealing with, or diminishing the value of his "assets", and the respondent is to be regarded as having such power if a third party holds or controls the asset in accordance with his direct or indirect instructions. Paragraph 6 of the example of a freezing order as contained in Appendix 5 of the Admiralty and Commercial Courts Guide (see Vol. 2 para.2A–162) states that the injunction applies to all of the respondent's assets whether or not they are in his own name, and whether they are solely or jointly owned. Further, the order may state that the order applies to assets in which the respondent is interested "legally, beneficially or otherwise". Determining what is and what is not an "asset" caught by a freezing order is matter for legal analysis. Generally there will be no difficulty. Problems that have arisen in decided cases were explained by the Court of Appeal in *JSC BTA Bank v Ablyazov* [2013] EWCA Civ 928, [2014] 1 Lloyd's Rep. 195, CA, where the Court held (allowing the respondent's appeal) that his contractual right to draw down under a loan facility agreement (a chose in action) was not an "asset" for these purposes, and his exercise of that right by directing the lender to pay the sum drawn down to a third party did not constitute "disposing of" or "dealing with" an asset. See further Vol. 2 para.15–55.

After the fourth paragraph (ending "(ibid)"), add as a new paragraph:

In *Bank St Petersburg v Arkhangelsky* [2014] EWHC 574 (Ch), March 5, 2014, unrep. (Hildyard J.) the court declined to tighten a freezing order so as to prevent the defendants using frozen funds for their legal and living expenses. The court held that, substantial disclosure having been given (even if belatedly), the burden was on the claimants to show that the defendants' evidence of disclosure was incredible or obviously incomplete.

After the fifth paragraph (ending "amount expended"), add as a new paragraph:

It is for the party seeking to pay legal expenses out of frozen funds to persuade the court that it would be just to permit it in all the circumstances. If it is clear that the defendant has assets which are not restrained assets, the court will normally not vary the order to permit payment from frozen funds as it would not be consistent with the underlying purpose of the order (*Fortress Value Recovery Fund I LLC v Blue Skye Special Opportunities Fund LP* [2014] EWHC 551 (Comm), February 4, 2014, unrep. (Andrew Smith J.)).

Add new paragraph at end:

The example wording for a freezing order does not restrain disposal of the assets of a company in respect of which the claimant cannot demonstrate that the defendant is beneficial owner (*Lakatamia Shipping Co Ltd v Su* [2014] EWCA Civ 636, May 14, 2014, CA, unrep.) In such a case, and assuming good reason can be shown, it is necessary to amend the standard wording to prohibit the defendant from causing or procuring the relevant company from disposing of or dissipating its assets other than in the normal course of business. In *Group Seven Ltd v Allied Investment Corp Ltd* [2013] EWHC 1509 (QB), [2014] 1 W.L.R. 735 (Hildyard J.) the judge expressed the opinion that suggested that, where the evidence suggests that a company is a mere receptacle for assets of the respondent, the standard form freezing order may need to be modified, e.g. by restraining at least until the return date or after assets disclosure, transactions diminishing the value of the respondent's shares (paras.80 & 81).

Term requiring respondent to provide information about assets

In the second paragraph, add at end:
Note also para.31.6.7 below (Disclosure and inspection of documents subject to search order). **25.1.25.7**

Search order (formerly Anton Piller order) (r.25.1(1)(h))

In the fourth paragraph, add at end:
Note also para.31.6.7 below (Disclosure and inspection of documents subject to search order). **25.1.27**

Jurisdiction—county courts

Add at end:
The County Court Remedies Regulations 1991 were revoked and replaced by the County Court Remedies Regulations 2014 (SI 2014/982) with effect from April 9, 2014. The restriction on the County Court's powers is retained by the 2014 Regulations. **25.1.27.2**

Applications to set aside for material non–disclosure not to be made without proper reason

In the second paragraph, add at end:
In *Kazakhstan Kagazy Plc v Arip* [2014] EWCA Civ 381, April 2, 2014, CA, unrep., the Court of Appeal stressed that issues of non–disclosure or abuse of process in relation to the operation of a freezing order ought to be capable of being dealt with quite concisely, and stated that the duty to disclose does not mean that the applicant must rehearse before the judge at the without notice application a detailed analysis of possible inferences the defendant may seek to rely on, especially when both the existence and relevance of the underlying facts are disputed. **25.3.7**

Duty to provide notes of the without notice hearing

For "Thane Investments Ltd v Tomlinson [2003] EWHC 2972 (Ch), December 6, 2002, unrep., at [18] (Neuberger J.)" substitute:
Thane Investments Ltd v Tomlinson [2003] EWHC 2972 (Ch); *The Times*, December 10, 2002, at [18] (Neuberger J.) **25.3.10**

Application for an order for interim payment

Delete the second paragraph and substitute:
In Queen's Bench proceedings at the RCJ, the application notices for an interim payment should be filed in the Masters' Support Unit, Room E07 in accordance with the practice stated in para.7.12.6 of the Queen's Bench Guide (see Vol.2, para.1B–54). **25.6.2**

"A defendant to any claim may apply"

In the second paragraph, for "Thistle Hotels Ltd v Gamma Four Ltd [2004] EWHC 322; [2004] B.C.L.C 174" substitute:
Thistle Hotels Ltd v Orb Estates Ltd [2004] EWHC 322; [2004] B.C.L.C. 174 **25.12.4**

PART 26

Case Management—Preliminary Stage

Effect of rule
Delete last sentence beginning "Note too CPR r.30.2". **26.2.1**

Specialist list

Delete paragraph 26.2.2 and substitute:

26.2.2   In the CPR, a reference to a "specialist list" is a reference to a list that has been designated as such by a rule or practice direction (r.2.3(2)). Among the lists designated as "specialist" are the lists for claims proceeding in the Commercial Court, in the Intellectual Property and Enterprise Court, in the Planning Court, in a Mercantile Court, and in a Technology and Construction Court (see further para.2.3.14 above). The general rule is that an application for the transfer of proceedings to or from a specialist list must be made to the judge dealing with claims in that list (r.30.5(3)).

Transfer of money claims within the County Court

In rule 26.2A(6)(c)(ii), for "execution" substitute:

26.2A   **control**

Add new paragraph 26.2A.2:

County Court at Central London Multi–Track Pilot Scheme

26.2A.2   By CPR Update 75 (July 2014) Practice Direction 51I (The County Court at Central London Multi–Track Pilot Scheme), made under Pt 51 was introduced. It provides for a pilot scheme in respect of money claims issued at the County Court Business Centre and the County Court Money Claims Centre for a period of 12 months from October 1, 2014, to September 30, 2015 (see para.51IPD.1 below). It applies in the circumstances stated in para.2.2 and, where it applies, modifies the effects of certain provisions in r.26.2A (see paras 2.3 to 2.5).

Each party must file the completed questionnaire no later than the date specified

Delete the second paragraph, (starting "On filing a directions questionnaire") and substitute:

26.3.3   No fee is now payable on the filing of a directions questionnaire or receipt of a notice of allocation. (The Civil Proceedings Fees (Amendment) Order 2014 (SI 2014/874) (L.17)).

Estimate of costs

Add new paragraph at end:

26.3.4   In r.26.3(1)(b)(i) "any matter to be complied with" includes the requirement (pursuant to r.3.13) to exchange and file costs budgets in any case in which the notice of provisional allocation indicates that he case is suitable for allocation to the multi track. Form **N149C** has been amended with effect from April 2014 to include a specific reference to costs budgets. The form in use at the CCMCC prior to April 2014 omitted any reference to costs budgets. In *Porbanderwalla v Daybridge Limited* (unreported: County Court at Birmingham 30 January 2014) HHJ Worster held that a failure to file and exchange a costs budget in a case in which the old version of the form had been served did not amount to a breach of r.3.13. The form has since been amended to include an express reference to the filing and exchange of costs budgets by the date specified in the notice.

Multi–track

In the second paragraph, in each place it occurs, for "a county court" substitute:

the County Court

In the third paragraph, for "at 9B 935", substitute:

as amended by the High Court and County Court Jurisdiction (Amendment) Order 2014 (SI 2014/821) – see Vol.2 para.9B–935.

In the third paragraph, for "county courts" and "a county court", substitute:

the County Court

PART 27

THE SMALL CLAIMS TRACK

Editorial introduction

In the last paragraph, for "Patents County Court" substitute:
intellectual property enterprise court (formerly the patents county court) **27.0.2**

Features of the small claims track

Delete subsection (xviii) and substitute:
The court fees on the small claims track are lower than those on the fast track and **27.0.3** multitrack but the fees are still significant. Fees to issue are on a sliding scale starting at £25 and rising to £455 depending on the amount of the claim. A hearing fee is charged for all cases also calculated on a sliding scale depending on the amount of the claim starting at £25 and rising to £335. The hearing fee will be refunded in whole or in part if the hearing is vacated more than 7 days before the final hearing.

Delete subsection (xix).

Renumber subsection xx as xix.

Effect of rule

In the first bullet point, for "£5000" substitute:
£10,000 **27.1.1**

Add at end:
The small claims track is the normal track for claims with a financial limit of not more than £10,000.

Costs on appeal

Delete the first paragraph and substitute:
Rule 27.14(2) applies the "no costs" rule to small claims appeals. This includes not **27.14.1.1** only "first" appeals to the circuit judge but also "second" appeals to the court of appeal: *Akhtar v Boland* [2014] EWCA Civ 943, July 8, 2014 CA unrep. Generally, the effect of r.52.9A does not empower the appeal court to award costs where there is no power so to do in the court below; for a full discussion of the meaning and effect of that rule please refer to the commentary in para.52.9A.1.

Routine award for costs

Delete the second paragraph starting "Court fees". **27.14.2**

In the fifth paragraph, for "£250" substitute:
£750

PART 28

THE FAST TRACK

Scope of provision

Delete the third sentence ("Disclosure will be "standard disclosure" (see r.31.6) or less.") and substitute:
Disclosure will be limited to what is required in each case having regard to what is **28.3.1** proportionate. Standard disclosure now only applies where the claim includes a claim for damages for personal injury. Otherwise the court is likely to order a limited form of disclosure and leave it to the parties to seek specific disclosure if required.

Agreed directions

In the second sentence, for "allocation" substitute:

28.3.4   directions

Effect of rule

After the third sentence (ending "...any such agreement must be in writing.") add:

28.4.1   It should be noted that the order for directions will now have the warning on the top of it as to compliance with its terms and the imposition of sanctions if the event of default. The rules have been amended so as to provide that the parties may agree to vary the dates for compliance with the directions given (apart from any variation of any hearing dates and the dates for filing pre–trial check lists) by up to 28 days. This should be used when the parties are negotiating and it should be included in the order. The court must be notified of any such agreement.

PRACTICE DIRECTION 28—THE FAST TRACK

Variation of Directions

In paragraph 4.5(1), after "other than those stated in the note to that rule)" add:

28PD.4   , rule 3.8(4) (extensions of time by written agreement in circumstances within rule 3.8(3))

PART 29

THE MULTI–TRACK

Filing costs estimates

For "44nPD.3" substitute:

29.6.3   44PD.3

Case Management in the Royal Courts of Justice

In paragraph 2.2, for "£50,000" substitute:

29PD.2   £100,000

In paragraph 2.3, for "£50,000" substitute:

£100,000

PRACTICE DIRECTION 29—THE MULTI-TRACK

Variation of Directions

In paragraph 6.5(1), after "court for doing any act other than those stated in the note to that rule)" add:

29PD.6   , rule 3.8(4) (extensions of time by written agreement in circumstances within rule 3.8(3))

PART 30

TRANSFER

Editorial introduction

In the first paragraph, for "between county courts;" substitute:

30.0.2   within the County Court;

Related sources

For "(Vol.2, Section 9B, paras 9B–928 to 9B–953)" substitute:

   as amended by the High Court and County Court Jurisdiction (Amendment) Order **30.0.3**
2014 (SI 2014/821)

" the county court" (r.30.2(1))

Delete paragraph 30.2.1 and substitute:

   The power may be exercised by a judge or district judge— CPR r.2.4.   **30.2.1**

Delete paragraph 30.2.7.

"transfer between the High Court and the county court" (r.30.3(1)(a))

Delete paragraph 30.3.1 and substitute:

   See High Court and County Court Jurisdiction Order 1991 (SI 1991/724)   **30.3.1**
as amended by the High Court and County Court Jurisdiction (Amendment) Order
2014 (SI 2014/821).

   If proceedings are commenced in the High Court when they should have been
commenced in the county court, the High Court must transfer to the county court,
but if the person bringing the proceedings knew, or ought to have known, that they
should have been brought in the county court, there is a residual jurisdiction to strike
out—see *Restick v Crickmore* [1994] 1 W.L.R. 420, CA. However, in view of the overriding objective (r.1.1(1) and (2)(b)) the power to strike out is only likely to be exercised
in extreme cases.

   See too Practice Direction to Pt 29 para.2 which provides that cases with an
estimated value of less than £50,000 issued in the High Court will generally be
transferred to the county court unless they are required by an enactment to be tried in
the High Court, fall within a specialist list (see CPR Pt 49) or come with Practice Direction to Pt 29 para.2.6 (*viz.* claims involving professional negligence, Fatal Accident Act,
fraud or undue influence, defamation, malicious prosecution or false imprisonment,
claims against the police and contentious probate claims).

   The High Court's power of transfer to the county court under County Courts Act
1984 s.40(2) is not limited to cases which would otherwise be within the county court's
jurisdiction (*National Westminster Bank v King* [2008] EWHC 280 (Ch); *The Times*, April
14, 2008 —transfer of proceedings to enforce a charging order where it appears that
the value exceeded the county court's £30,000 limit for such cases).

"the financial value" (r.30.3(2)(a))

For "(Vol.2, Section 9B, paras 9B–928 to 9B–953)" substitute:

   as amended by the High Court and County Court Jurisdiction (Amendment) Order **30.3.3**
2014 (SI 2014/821)

"the availability of a judge specialising" (r.30.3(2)(c))

For "county courts" substitute:

   County Court hearing centres   **30.3.4**

Transfer from county court to High Court

For "county courts" substitute:

   the County Court   **30.3.13**

Transfer between Divisions and to and from a specialist list

Add new rule 30.5(4):

   (4) An order for transfer of proceedings between the Chancery **30.5**
Division and a Queen's Bench Division specialist list may only be
made with the consent of the Chancellor of the High Court.

Specialist list

Add new paragraph at beginning:

30.5.1   Paragraph (4) was added to this rule by the Civil Procedure (Amendment No.2) Rules 2014 (SI 2014/2044) with effect from October 1, 2014. That provision is restricted to the transfer of proceedings between (1) the Chancery Division and (2) a Queen's Bench specialist list (see below). Although an application for an order transferring proceedings from or to the Chancery Division may be made to a judge, no order may be made without the consent of the Chancellor (the head of that Division). For practical reasons it was seen fit to make the Chancellor the arbiter. In a given case, various reasons may motivate a party's desire to have proceedings transferred from or to the Chancery Division. One may well be the effect that transfer would have on the application to the proceedings of the costs management provisions in Section II of Part 3.

In the second paragraph, for "a county court" and "country courts" substitute:
     the county court

PART 31

DISCLOSURE AND INSPECTION OF DOCUMENTS

"... under any Act for disclosure before proceedings have started"

Add new paragraph at end:

31.16.1   The court has jurisdiction to order pre–action disclosure in relation to contemplated judicial review proceedings, though the court will only exercise this jurisdiction in very rare cases: *British Union for the Abolition of Vivisection (BUAV) v Secretary of State for the Home Department* [2014] EWHC 43, paras.32, 34 per Ouseley J.

"... under any Act for disclosure by a person who is not a party to the proceedings"

At end of last paragraph, for "Flatman v Germany [2011] EWHC 2945 (QB), paras.28–29", substitute:

31.17.1   *Germany v Flatman* [2011] EWHC 2945 (QB), paras.28–29; appeal upheld on different grounds, [2013] EWCA Civ 278; [2013] 1 W.L.R. 2676, CA

Add new paragraph at end:
     For the approach to an application for disclosure of statements given to police, see *Mitchell v News Group Newspapers Ltd* [2014] EWHC 879 (QB).

Add new paragraph 31.17.2.1:

"The court may make an order . . ."

31.17.2.1   Even where the criteria of relevance and necessity in r.31.17(3) are satisfied, the court still has a discretion from the opening words of the paragraph ("the court may make an order"), to decide whether it ought to order disclosure: *Mitchell v News Group Newspapers Ltd* [2014] EWHC 1885 (QB), paras 14–15. In exercising discretion to order third party disclosure in that case the judge took into account the strong public interest in the court having before it all the relevant evidence and documents, that while the third parties had legitimate concerns about becoming involved in an action they were all police officers and the events in question arise out of their official duties, the public interest in disclosure outweighed the interests of the individual third parties, and in so far as the third parties had raised issues, their concerns could be addressed by the conditions under which the order for disclosure was made.
     Where the material is sought not, at present at least, for use in specific proceedings, but for the taking of preliminary steps to enable a party to receive legal advice and, if so advised, to make an appropriate application in the proceedings, the court will take into account that to refuse permission in respect of such a course of action would be to deny the applicant the opportunity of making an application in the present proceedings, and that may be contrary to ordinary principles of justice and fairness: *Tchenguiz and others v Director of the Serious Fraud Office* [2014] EWHC 2379 (Comm).

Rule 31.17(3)(a)

Add new paragraph at end:

Before a defendant can apply for disclosure against a third party the defendant will **31.17.3** probably need to plead the defence, in order to show that the disclosure sought may support his or her "case", otherwise the CPR r.31.17 application may be premature: *Abbas v Yousuf* [2014] EWHC 662 (QB).

Subsequent use of disclosed documents

After the first paragraph, add as a new paragraph:

A similar approach will probably be taken in applications under CPR 31.22 (2) to **31.22.1** restrict the use of documents referred to at public hearings, and applications under CPR 31.22 (1)(b) for permission to use disclosed documents not referred to in public, the difference between the two probably only going to the burden of proof: *NAB v Serco Ltd* [2014] EWHC 1225 (QB), para.27. In exercising its discretion under CPR 31.22(2) to decide whether to restrict or prohibit the use of a document which has been referred to at a hearing which has been held in public, the default position will be one of open access, and the open justice principle will be central to the court's evaluation: *NAB v Serco Ltd* [2014] EWHC 1225 (QB), paras 28–38.

At the end of the second paragraph, add:

A document mentioned briefly in oral evidence and exhibited to a witness statement which was before the judge was held to be "referred to" for the purpose of CPR r.31.22(1)(a): *NAB v Serco Ltd* [2014] EWHC 1225 (QB), para.27.

Add new paragraphs at end:

The judgment of Eder J. in *Tchenguiz v Director of the Serious Fraud Office* [2014] EWHC 1315 (Comm) paras.19–25 contains useful indicators to the circumstances in which permission is likely to be granted pursuant to CPR r.31.22(1)(b). The fact that the use that is sought for documents is only for the obtaining of legal advice rather than for the purpose of deploying the documents or information contained therein in proceedings renders it more likely that permission will be granted: *Tchenguiz*, para.19. If the documents may reveal criminality such as perjury or bribery then this would be a strong factor in favour of the grant of permission for the purposes of CPR r.31.22(1)(b): *Tchenguiz*, para.22.

In *Cosmetic Warriors Ltd v Amazon.co.uk Ltd* [2014] EWHC 1316 (Ch), [2014] IP & T 519 Amazon sought an order under r.31.22 to keep private documents relating to its corporate structure and a section of the transcript of the proceedings, detailing a change to the way in which products might be prioritised. The court declined to make such an order under 31.22, holding that there was no sufficient justification for maintaining confidentiality over the evidence, and insufficient justification for the application: see paras 71–79.

Proceedings for Contempt

Add at end:

An application for committal is the commencement of proceedings: *Dar Al Arkan* **31.23.1** *Real Estate Development Co v Al Refai* [2014] EWCA Civ 715, *The Times* June 30, 2014. For an example of an application under r.31.23 being brought against a party out of the jurisdiction see *Dar Al Arkan Real Estate Development Co*, ibid.

PART 32

EVIDENCE

Add new paragraph 32.1.4.3:

Exclusion of witnesses from the court

CPR r.32.2(1) states that the general rule is that any fact which needs to be proved **32.1.4.3** by the evidence of witnesses is to be proved at trial by their oral evidence given in public. In civil trials the witnesses as to fact of both parties are normally allowed to remain in court throughout the hearing. But, for the purpose of preventing the evidence of such witnesses from being influenced by what they have heard and seen of witnesses called to testify before them, the judge has power on his or her own initiative or on the application of a party to exclude them from the hearing until they are called, and also to require them to remain in court after they have testified. No rule of law requires that in a trial witnesses must remain out of court until their turn to give testimony arises; it is purely a matter within the discretion of the court (*Moore v Lambeth County Court Registrar* [1969] 1 W.L.R. 141, CA; In *re Nightingale, Green v Nightingale* [1975] 1 W.L.R. 80; and *R (Elvington Park Ltd) v York Crown Court* [2011] EWHC 2213 (Admin), August 26, 2011, and authorities referred to there). In *Luckwell v Limata* [2014] EWHC 536 (Fam), February 13, 2014, unrep. (Holman J.), it was stated that a judge should only exclude witnesses if satisfied, on the facts and in the circumstances of the particular situation, that it would, for good reasons, be an appropriate step to take. The power to exclude witnesses does not extend to parties themselves, who have a right to remain in court throughout, or to their solicitors, or to the parties' expert witnesses (*Tomlinson v Tomlinson* [1980] 1 W.L.R. 322, DC).

"court may give directions" (r.32.2(3))

Add at end:

32.2.3.1 The significance of the addition of para.(3) is that the ability to restrict evidence no longer depends on whether it is characterised as expert evidence or not; it is now clear that evidence can be controlled, however it is characterised (*Fenty v Arcadia Group Bands Ltd* [2013] EWHC 1945 (Ch), July 5, 2013, urep. (Birss J.) at para.37). In *Maclennan v Morgan Sindall (Infrastructure) Plc* [2013] EWHC 4044 (QB), December 17, 2013, unrep. (Green J.), where the provenance and purpose of sub–rule (3) were explained, it was stated that (1) the court will ordinarily consider its powers under the provision after less intrusive measures for ensuring the fair and efficient conduct of the trial have been considered and rejected, (2) the powers are best exercised before any witness statements have been prepared, but may be exercised subsequently, and (3) in order to minimise the risk that any directions made by a court in exercise of the powers may be seen, with the benefit of hindsight, to cause unfairness, parties should ensure that the court has the fullest possible information available to it and should co-operate in a pragmatic and sensible manner.

Witness immunity

Add new paragraph at end:

32.2.6 The authorities on the extent to which the immunity applies to out of court statements, for example, statements made by a person to the police instigating or as part of a criminal investigation has been explained and applied by the Court of Appeal in several cases: e.g. *Westcott v Westcott* [2008] EWCA Civ 818; [2009] Q.B. 407, CA (where the privilege was relied on in a defamation claim); *Crawford v Jenkins* [2014] EWCA Civ 1035, July 24, 2014, CA, unrep. (where the privilege was relied on in an harassment claim). See also the review and analysis of the authorities in *Singh v Reading BC* [2013] EWCA Civ 909; [2013] 1 W.L.R. 3052, CA (where held that a claimant in a constructive and unfair dismissal case was not precluded by the privilege from alleging that the defendant employers had exercised undue pressure in order to procure the making of a false witness statement by another employee).

Time limits

Delete from "Where a party (C)" to the end of the paragraph and substitute as new paragraphs:

32.4.9 In *Karbhari v Ahmed* [2013] EWHC 4042 (QB), [2014] 1 Costs L.R. 151 (Turner J.) it was explained that, when the court gives directions that witness statements are to be served by a specified date, and it is anticipated by the parties and the court at that time that there is a realistic possibility that there will be developments between that date and the trial date, being developments relating to issues arising in the case as to which a party may wish to give evidence, the court's directions may provide for that, thereby obviating the need for the party to apply to the court after the specified date for permission to serve a supplemental or additional witness statement. In effect the court would give two directions. The first would provide for a date which would give a realistic opportunity for all sides to comply with in respect to matters which have arisen beforehand, and the second would provide a later "backstop" date for the service of further witness statements limited in content to matters which occurred, or were reasonably discoverable, only after the first date.

For consequences of failure to serve a witness statement within the time specified by the court, see r.32.10 and commentary thereon.

"witness may not be called ... unless the court gives permission"

In the third paragraph, delete the sentence beginning "However, where before trial" and substitute:

    In *Chartwell Estate Agents Ltd v Fergies Properties SA*, [2014] EWCA Civ 506, April 16, **32.10.2** 2014, CA, unrep., the Court of Appeal explained that, on an application for relief from the sanction imposed under r.32.10, the question is not whether the sanction is of itself disproportionate or unjust, but whether the sanction should be disapplied in the particular case, a matter to be determined in accordance with r.3.9 (as revised with effect from April 1, 2013) and the authorities thereon (see further para.3.9.1 above et seq.). The phrase "unless the court gives permission" as contained in r.32.10 cannot be applied in a free–standing way (leaving the exercise of judicial discretion at large) (ibid). In *Durrant v Chief Constable of Somerset & Avon* [2013] EWCA Civ 1624, [2014] C.P. Rep. 11, CA, on the application of the defendants (D), a judge extended the time for service of their witness statements specified by the court and in doing so imposed the condition that D should not be permitted to rely on any witness evidence other than that of witnesses whose statements were served within the extended time. D failed to serve their witnesses statement within the extended time and the condition, a "sanction" within r.3.8, took effect. The Court of Appeal held that (1) that the condition was properly imposed and complied with the overriding objective, and (2) that D's application for relief from sanction under r.3.9 should have been refused (see further para.3.9.6 above).

Delete the fourth paragraph (beginning "Where a witness statement") and substitute:

    A court may direct that the parties exchange witness statements on or by a particular date, or may direct that statements (or some of them) be exchanged sequentially (r.32.4(3)). Since the amendment of r.3.9 (and r.1.1) taking effect on April 1, 2013, the courts have been less willing than previously to grant relief from procedural sanctions in all contexts, including where the sanction takes effect by operation of r.32.10. Where, within the time specified by the court for exchange, one party is ready and willing to serve their witness statements but the other party is not, the wise course for the former party to adopt is to serve their statements rather than risk falling into default. It has been held that, where the court has directed sequential exchange, with one party (A) required to serve their statements by (say) May 1 and the other party (B) theirs by May 14, and A defaults, putting B at risk of defaulting also, there was no need (in the circumstances) for B to apply to the court for an extension of time (*M A Lloyd & Sons Ltd v PPC International Ltd* [2014] EWHC 41 (Ch), [2014] 2 Costs L.R. 2456 (Turner J.)). See further para.32.4.9 above.

    In the circumstances provided for in para.(4) of r.3.8 (which was inserted by the Civil Procedure (Amendment No. 5) Rules 2014 (SI 2014/1233) and came into effect on June 5, 2014) and subject to the conditions imposed thereby, the time specified for service of a witness statement or witness summary may be extended by prior written agreement of the parties.

Effect of rule

After the fourth paragraph, add as a new paragraph:

    For subsequent use of disclosed documents, including circumstance where such use **32.13.1** involves making such documents available for inspection, see powers exercisable by parties and by the court under r.31.22.

PART 35

EXPERTS AND ASSESSORS

In the Contents, for the entry "Protocol for the Instruction of Experts to give Evidence in Civil Claims" substitute:

Contents   **35.0.1**

Expert evidence at trial

Add new paragraph at end:

35.0.6   In *Hatton and Hatton v Connew and Connew* [2013] EWCA Civ 1560 a judge determining a boundary dispute had discussions with the parties' expert surveyors at a site visit, of which no note was made. The experts did not give oral evidence at trial. The judge relied upon what had been said at the site visit in reaching his conclusions. It was held this was wrong, as there had been no opportunity for the parties to cross–examine the experts on the critical issue in open court. That aspect of the case was remitted for retrial before a different judge.

Effect of rule

Add new paragraph at end:

35.1.1   In *Rich v Hull and East Yorkshire Hospitals Trust*, April 4, 2014, unrep., the claimant alleged failure to administer ante–natal steroids prior to delivery had caused cerebral palsy. The issue revolved around the word "likely". C wished to call the Professor who had been on the committee formulating guidelines. The Judge held that the meaning of "likely" was factual evidence. Justice required the evidence to be admitted. When a case management decision could potentially tie the hands of a trial judge, that had to be treated cautiously.

When an expert fails to comply with their duty

Add at end:

35.3.4   *David Rowley v Brian Dunlop and others* 2014 EWHC 1995 (Ch) was an application to strike out a claim, because the claimant's expert had failed to disclose he had a conflict of interest, as he was a partner in a firm owned by the sole director of the claimant case management company (who were instructed on a contingency arrangement). It was alleged, therefore, that his report was fundamentally flawed. But it was held that there was no conflict of interest because there was no evidence that the expert would benefit from the litigation, therefore, the report was admissible, and the wider issues about the conflict of interest were matters for cross—examination at trial.

Court's power to restrict expert evidence

Add new rules 35.4(3B) and 3(C):

35.4   **(3B) In a soft tissue injury claim, permission—**
   (a) may normally only be given for one expert medical report;
   (b) may not be given initially unless the medical report is a fixed cost medical report. Where the claimant seeks permission to obtain a further medical report, if the report is from a medical expert in any of the following disciplines—
      (i) Consultant Orthopaedic Surgeon;
      (ii) Consultant in Accident and Emergency Medicine;
      (iii) General Practitioner registered with the General Medical Council; or
      (iv) Physiotherapist registered with the Health and Care Professions Council,
   the report must be a fixed cost medical report.

   (3C) In this rule, 'fixed cost medical report' and 'soft tissue injury claim' have the same meaning as in paragraph 1.1(10A) and (16A), respectively, of the RTA Protocol.

Effect of rule

After the first paragraph, add as a new paragraph:

35.4.1   Paragraph (3B) was inserted in r.35.4 by Civil Procedure (Amendment No.6) Rules

2014 (SI 2014/2044) as one of several amendments made to the CPR to effect certain reforms in relation to the handling of claims that are subject to, or which cease to be subject to, the RTA Protocol. The RTA Protocol contains bespoke provisions for medical reports (see para.35.4.3 below), including provisions imposing a fixed costs regime for such reports in "soft tissue" injury claims. Paragraph (3B) of r.35.4 imposes a similar regime on claims that cease to be subject to the Protocol and proceed as claims under the CPR. Paragraph (3B) applies to claims started under the RTA Protocol where the claim notification form was sent in accordance with that Protocol on or after October 1, 2014.

Court's permission

Add at end:

In *Lalvinder Dass v Satish Dass* [2013] EWHC 2520 (QB), a personal injury claim, **35.4.2** arising from a road traffic accident, a High Court Master was entitled to exercise case management powers to exclude the defendant's expert medical evidence when the insurers had deliberately and tactically decided not to comply with court directions for the exchange of expert evidence until two years after the directions were given.

Effect of rule

At the end of the ninth paragraph (beginning "In Beck v Ministry of Defence"), add:

In *BMG (Mansfield) Ltd v Galliford Try Construction Ltd* [2013] EWHC 3183 TCC, a **35.5.1** building dispute concerning the adequacy of fire protection in the roof space of a shopping centre following a serious fire, where proceedings were issued six years after the investigation into the fire, the claimant sought to change their expert architect, then aged 70, after an unsuccessful mediation, and were accused by the defendants of expert shopping. It was held this was not shopping as no permission for experts had yet been sought under CPR r.35.4, the previous expert's report of 2005 had been disclosed, it was reasonable for the expert to want to retire at 70, and the defendant's application for the disclosure of the claimant's solicitor's notes of discussions with the expert was refused.

Effect of rule

In the third paragraph, for "Practice Direction (Committal Applications), para.10 (see para.scpd52.6 below)" substitute:

Paragraph 14.3 of Practice Direction 81 (Applications and Proceedings in Relation **35.9.1** to Contempt of Court) (see para.81PD.15 below)

Appointment of assessor

Add at end:

Cary v Commissioner of Police for the Metropolis [2014] EWCA Civ 987, July 17, 2014, **35.15.2** CA, unrep., was a claim for discrimination, on the ground of same sex orientation, in the way that the Police had dealt with complaints by the claimant about a neighbour. Five months before the trial in September 2013, in a Consent Order, the parties provided for two assessors to sit with the trial judge. Only 6 days before the trial the court released one name to the parties, with no CV, or any explanation as to how the person had been selected. A CV was provided a few days later. At trial the judge overruled the claimant's objections that the assessor did not have specialist expertise. The Court of Appeal upheld that decision, because in most discrimination cases the skill required of an assessor was in evaluation and analysis, and not necessarily particular experience. But they criticised the non–transparent and late process that had been followed by the court, and gave guidance on the steps to be taken, including, as required by PD 35, that a judge (not court staff) must decide who to propose, provide a CV and explanation, and, after giving the parties 21 days to object, make an appointment.

Delete paragraphs 35.16 to 35.38 and substitute:

Guidance for the instruction of experts to give evidence in civil claims 2014

Introduction

1. The purpose of this guidance is to assist litigants, those instruct- **35.16** ing experts and experts to understand best practice in complying with Part 35 of the Civil Procedure Rules (CPR) and court orders. Experts and those who instruct them should ensure they are familiar with CPR 35 and the Practice Direction (PD35). This guidance replaces the Protocol for the instruction of experts in civil claims (2007).

2. Those instructing experts, and the experts, must also have regard to the objectives underpinning the Pre–Action Protocols to:

    a. encourage the exchange of early and full information about the expert issues involved in the prospective claim;

    b. enable the parties to avoid or reduce the scope of the litigation by agreeing the whole or part of an expert issue before proceedings are started; and

    c. support the efficient management of proceedings where litigation cannot be avoided.

3. Additionally, experts and those instructing them should be aware that some cases will be governed by the specific pre–action protocols and some may be "specialist proceedings" (CPR 49) where specific rules may apply.

Selecting and Instructing experts

The need for experts

35.17   **4.** Those intending to instruct experts to give or prepare evidence for the purpose of civil proceedings should consider whether expert evidence is necessary, taking account of the principles set out in CPR Parts 1 and 35, and in particular whether "it is required to resolve the proceedings" (CPR 35.1).

5. Although the court's permission is not generally required to instruct an expert, the court's permission is required before an expert's report can be relied upon or an expert can be called to give oral evidence (CPR 35.4).

6. Advice from an expert before proceedings are started which the parties do not intend to rely upon in litigation is likely to be confidential; this guidance does not apply then. The same applies where, after the commencement of proceedings, experts are instructed only to advise (e.g. to comment upon a single joint expert's report) and not to prepare evidence for the proceedings. The expert's role then is that of an expert advisor.

7. However this guidance does apply if experts who were formerly instructed only to advise, are later instructed as an expert witness to prepare or give evidence in the proceedings.

8. In the remainder of this guidance, a reference to an expert means an expert witness to whom Part 35 applies.

Duties and obligations of experts

35.18   **9.** Experts always owe a duty to exercise reasonable skill and care to those instructing them, and to comply with any relevant professional code. However when they are instructed to give or prepare evidence for civil proceedings they have an overriding duty to help the court on matters within their expertise (CPR 35.3). This duty overrides any obligation to the person instructing or paying them. Experts must not serve the exclusive interest of those who retain them.

10. Experts should be aware of the overriding objective that courts deal with cases justly and that they are under an obligation to assist the court in this respect. This includes dealing with cases proportionately (keeping the work and costs in proportion to the value and importance of the case to the parties), expeditiously and fairly (CPR 1.1).

11. Experts must provide opinions that are independent, regardless of the pressures of litigation. A useful test of 'independence' is that the expert would express the same opinion if given the same instructions by another party. Experts should not take it upon themselves to promote the point of view of the party instructing them or engage in the role of advocates or mediators.

12. Experts should confine their opinions to matters which are material to the disputes and provide opinions only in relation to matters which lie within their expertise. Experts should indicate without delay where particular questions or issues fall outside their expertise.

13. Experts should take into account all material facts before them. Their reports should set out those facts and any literature or material on which they have relied in forming their opinions. They should indicate if an opinion is provisional, or qualified, or where they consider that further information is required or if, for any other reason, they are not satisfied that an opinion can be expressed finally and without qualification.

14. Experts should inform those instructing them without delay of any change in their opinions on any material matter and the reasons for this (see also paragraphs 62–64).

15. Experts should be aware that any failure to comply with the rules or court orders, or any excessive delay for which they are responsible, may result in the parties who instructed them being penalised in costs, or debarred from relying upon the expert evidence (see also paragraphs 86–88).

The appointment of experts

16. Before experts are instructed or the court's permission to ap- **35.19** point named experts is sought, it should be established whether the experts:

 a. have the appropriate expertise and experience for the particular instruction;
 b. are familiar with the general duties of an expert;
 c. can produce a report, deal with questions and have discussions with other experts within a reasonable time, and at a cost proportionate to the matters in issue;
 d. are available to attend the trial, if attendance is required; and
 e. have no potential conflict of interest.

17. Terms of appointment should be agreed at the outset and should normally include:

 a. the capacity in which the expert is to be appointed (e.g. party appointed expert or single joint expert);
 b. the services required of the expert (e.g. provision of an expert's report, answering questions in writing, attendance at meetings and attendance at court);
 c. time for delivery of the report;

    d. the basis of the expert's charges (e.g. daily or hourly rates and an estimate of the time likely to be required, or a fixed fee for the services). Parties must provide an estimate to the court of the costs of the proposed expert evidence and for each stage of the proceedings (R.35.4(2));

    e. travelling expenses and disbursements;

    f. cancellation charges;

    g. any fees for attending court;

    h. time for making the payment;

    i. whether fees are to be paid by a third party;

    j. if a party is publicly funded, whether the expert's charges will be subject to assessment; and

    k. guidance that the expert's fees and expenses may be limited by the court (note expert's recoverable fees in the small claims track cannot exceed £750: see PD 27 paragraph 7).

18. When necessary, arrangements should be made for dealing with questions to experts and discussions between experts, including any directions given by the court.

19. Experts should be kept informed about deadlines for all matters concerning them. Those instructing experts should send them promptly copies of all court orders and directions that may affect the preparation of their reports or any other matters concerning their obligations.

Instructions

35.20 **20.** Those instructing experts should ensure that they give clear instructions (and attach relevant documents), including the following:

    a. basic information, such as names, addresses, telephone numbers, dates of incidents and any relevant claim reference numbers;

    b. the nature of the expertise required;

    c. the purpose of the advice or report, a description of the matter(s) to be investigated, the issues to be addressed and the identity of all parties;

    d. the statement(s) of case (if any), those documents which form part of disclosure and witness statements that are relevant to the advice or report;

    e. where proceedings have not been started, whether they are contemplated and, if so, whether the expert is being asked only for advice;

    f. an outline programme, consistent with good case management and the expert's availability, for the completion and delivery of each stage of the expert's work; and

    g. where proceedings have been started, the dates of any hearings (including any case/costs management conferences and/or pre–trial reviews), the dates fixed by the court or agreed between the parties for the exchange of experts' reports and any other relevant deadlines to be adhered to, the name of the court, the claim number, the track to which the claim has been allocated and whether there is a specific budget for the experts' fees.

21. Those instructing experts should seek to agree, where practicable, the instructions for the experts, and that they receive the same factual material.

Acceptance of instructions

22. Experts should confirm without delay whether they accept **35.21** their instructions.

23. They should also inform those instructing them (whether on initial instruction or at any later stage) without delay if:

a. instructions are not acceptable because, for example, they require work that falls outside their expertise, impose unrealistic deadlines, or are insufficiently clear. Experts who do not receive clear instructions should request clarification and may indicate that they are not prepared to act unless and until such clear instructions are received;

b. they consider that instructions are insufficient to complete the work;

c. they become aware that they may not be able to fulfil any of the terms of appointment;

d. the instructions and/or work have, for any reason, placed them in conflict with their duties as an expert. Where an expert advisor is approached to act as an expert witness they will need to consider carefully whether they can accept a role as expert witness; or

e. they are not satisfied that they can comply with any orders that have been made.

24. Experts must neither express an opinion outside the scope of their field of expertise, nor accept any instructions to do so.

25. Where an expert identifies that the basis of his instruction differs from that of another expert, he should inform those instructing him.

26. Experts should agree the terms on which they are to be paid with those instructing them. Experts should be aware that they will be required to provide estimates for the court and that the court may limit the amount to be paid as part of any order for budgeted costs (CPR 35.4–5).

Experts' Withdrawal

27. Where experts' instructions are incompatible with their duties, **35.22** through incompleteness, a conflict between their duty to the court and their instructions, or for any other reason, the experts may consider withdrawing from the case. However, experts should not do so without first discussing the position with those who instruct them and considering whether it would be more appropriate to make a written request for directions from the court. If experts do withdraw, they must give formal written notice to those instructing them.

Experts' right to ask court for directions

28. Experts may request directions from the court to assist them in **35.23** carrying out their functions (CPR 35.14), for example, if experts consider that they have not been provided with information they require. Experts should normally discuss this with those who instruct them before making a request. Unless the court otherwise orders, any proposed request for directions should be sent to the party instructing the expert at least seven days before filing any request with the court, and to all other parties at least four days before filing it.

29. Requests to the court for directions should be made by letter clearly marked "expert's request for directions" containing:

    a. the title of the claim;

    b. the claim number;

    c. the name of the expert;

    d. why directions are sought; and

    e. copies of any relevant documentation.

Experts' access to information held by the parties

35.24   **30.** Experts should try to ensure that they have access to all relevant information held by the parties, and that the same information has been disclosed to each expert in the same discipline. Experts should seek to confirm this soon after accepting instructions, notifying instructing solicitors of any omissions.

31. Experts should be specifically aware of CPR 35.9. This provides that, where one party has access to information that is not readily available to the other party, the court may direct the party who has access to the information to prepare, file and copy to the other party a document recording the information. If experts require such information which has not been disclosed, they should discuss the position with those instructing them without delay, so that a request for the information can be made, and, if not forthcoming, an application can be made to the court.

32. Any request for further information from the other party made by an expert should be in a letter to the expert's instructing party and should state why the information is necessary and the significance in relation to the expert issues in the case.

Single joint experts

35.25   **33.** CPR 35.7–8 and PD 35 paragraph 5 deal with the instruction and use of joint experts by the parties and the powers of the court to order their use. The CPR encourage the use of joint experts. Wherever possible a joint report should be obtained. Single joint experts are the norm in cases allocated to the small claims track and the fast track.

34. In the early stages of a dispute, when investigations, tests, site inspections, photographs, plans or other similar preliminary expert tasks are necessary, consideration should be given to the instruction of a single joint expert, especially where such matters are not expected to be contentious. The objective should be to agree or to narrow issues.

35. Experts who have previously advised a party (whether in the same case or otherwise) should only be proposed as single joint experts if the other parties are given all relevant information about the previous involvement.

36. The appointment of a single joint expert does not prevent parties from instructing their own experts to advise (but the cost of such expert advisors will not be recoverable from another party).

Joint instructions

37. The parties should try to agree joint instructions to single joint **35.26** experts, but in default of agreement, each party may give instructions. In particular, all parties should try to agree what documents should be included with instructions and what assumptions single joint experts should make.

38. Where the parties fail to agree joint instructions, they should try to agree where the areas of disagreement lie and their instructions should make this clear. If separate instructions are given, they should be copied to the other instructing parties.

39. Where experts are instructed by two or more parties, the terms of appointment should, unless the court has directed otherwise, or the parties have agreed otherwise, include:

a. a statement that all the instructing parties are jointly and severally liable to pay the experts' fees and, accordingly, that experts' invoices should be sent simultaneously to all instructing parties or their solicitors (as appropriate); and

b. a copy of any order limiting experts' fees and expenses (CPR 35.8(4)(a)).

40. Where instructions have not been received by the expert from one or more of the instructing parties, the expert should give notice (normally at least 7 days) of a deadline for their receipt. Unless the instructions are received within the deadline the expert may begin work. If instructions are received after the deadline but before the completion of the report the expert should consider whether it is practicable to comply without adversely affecting the timetable for delivery of the report and without greatly increasing the costs and exceeding any court approved budget. An expert who decides to issue a report without taking into account instructions received after the deadline must inform the parties, who may apply to the court for directions. In either event the report must show clearly that the expert did not receive instructions within the deadline, or, as the case may be, at all.

Conduct of the single joint expert

41. Single joint experts should keep all instructing parties informed **35.27** of any material steps that they may be taking by, for example, copying all correspondence to those instructing them.

42. Single joint experts are Part 35 experts and so have an overriding duty to the court. They are the parties' appointed experts and therefore owe an equal duty to all parties. They should maintain independence, impartiality and transparency at all times.

43. Single joint experts should not attend a meeting or conference that is not a joint one, unless all the parties have agreed in writing or the court has directed that such a meeting may be held. There also needs to be agreement about who is to pay the experts' fees for the meeting.

44. Single joint experts may request directions from the court (see paragraphs 28–29).

45. Single joint experts should serve their reports simultaneously on all instructing parties. They should provide a single report even though they may have received instructions that contain conflicts. If conflicting instructions lead to different opinions (for example, because the instructions require the expert to make different assumptions of fact), reports may need to contain more than one set of opinions on any issue. It is for the court to determine the facts.

Cross–examination of the single joint expert

35.28   46. Single joint experts do not normally give oral evidence at trial but if they do, all parties may ask questions. In general, written questions (CPR 35.6) should be put to single joint experts before requests are made for them to attend court for the purpose of cross–examination.

Experts' reports

35.29   47. The content of experts' reports should be governed by their instructions and general obligations, any court directions, CPR 35 and PD35, and the experts' overriding duty to the court.

48. In preparing reports, experts should maintain professional objectivity and impartiality at all times.

49. PD 35, paragraph 2 provides that experts' reports should be addressed to the court and gives detailed directions about their form and content. All experts and those who instruct them should ensure that they are familiar with these requirements.

50. Model forms of experts' reports are available from bodies such as the Academy of Experts and the Expert Witness Institute and a template for medical reports has been created by the Ministry of Justice.

51. Experts' reports must contain statements that they:
   a. understand their duty to the court and have complied and will continue to comply with it; and
   b. are aware of and have complied with the requirements of CPR 35 and PD 35 and this guidance.

52. Experts' reports must also be verified by a statement of truth. The form of the statement of truth is:

> *"I confirm that I have made clear which facts and matters referred to in this report are within my own knowledge and which are not. Those that are within my own knowledge I confirm to be true. The opinions I have expressed represent my true and complete professional opinions on the matters to which they refer."*

53. The details of experts' qualifications in reports should be commensurate with the nature and complexity of the case. It may be sufficient to state any academic and professional qualifications. However, where highly specialised expertise is called for, experts should include the detail of particular training and/or experience that qualifies them to provide that specialised evidence.

54. The mandatory statement of the substance of all material instructions should not be incomplete or otherwise tend to mislead. The imperative is transparency. The term "instructions" includes all material that solicitors send to experts. The omission from the state-

ment of 'off–the–record' oral instructions is not permitted. Courts may allow cross–examination about the instructions if there are reasonable grounds to consider that the statement may be inaccurate or incomplete.

55. Where tests of a scientific or technical nature have been carried out, experts should state:

a. the methodology used; and

b. by whom the tests were undertaken and under whose supervision, summarising their respective qualifications and experience.

56. When addressing questions of fact and opinion, experts should keep the two separate. Experts must state those facts (whether assumed or otherwise) upon which their opinions are based; experts should have primary regard to their instructions (paragraphs 20–25 above). Experts must distinguish clearly between those facts that they know to be true and those facts which they assume.

57. Where there are material facts in dispute experts should express separate opinions on each hypothesis put forward. They should not express a view in favour of one or other disputed version of the facts unless, as a result of particular expertise and experience, they consider one set of facts as being improbable or less probable, in which case they may express that view and should give reasons for holding it.

58. If the mandatory summary of the range of opinion is based on published sources, experts should explain those sources and, where appropriate, state the qualifications of the originator(s) of the opinions from which they differ, particularly if such opinions represent a well–established school of thought.

59. Where there is no available source for the range of opinion, experts may need to express opinions on what they believe to be the range that other experts would arrive at if asked. In those circumstances, experts should make it clear that the range that they summarise is based on their own judgement and explain the basis of that judgement.

Conclusions of reports

60. A summary of conclusions is mandatory. Generally the summary should be at the end of the report after the reasoning. There may be cases, however, where the court would find it helpful to have a short summary at the beginning, with the full conclusions at the end. For example, in cases involving highly complex matters which fall outside the general knowledge of the court the judge may be assisted in the comprehension of the facts and analysis if the report explains at the outset the basis of the reasoning. **35.30**

Sequential exchange of experts' reports

61. Where there is to be sequential exchange of reports then the defendant's expert's report usually will be produced in response to the claimant's. The defendant's report should then: **35.31**

a. confirm whether the background set out in the claimant's expert report is agreed, or identify those parts that in the defendant's expert's view require revision, setting out the necessary revisions. The defendant's expert need not repeat information that is adequately dealt with in the claimant's expert report;

b. focus only on those material areas of difference with the claimant's expert's opinion. The defendant's report should identify those assumptions of the claimant's expert that they consider reasonable (and agree with) and those that they do not; and

c. in particular where the experts are addressing the financial value of heads of claim (for example, the costs of a care regime or loss of profits), the defendant's report should contain a reconciliation between the claimant's expert's loss assessment and the defendant's, identifying for each assumption any different conclusion to the claimant's expert.

Amendment of reports

35.32 **62.** It may become necessary for experts to amend their reports:

a. as a result of an exchange of questions and answers;

a. following agreements reached at meetings between experts; or

a. where further evidence or documentation is disclosed.

63. Experts should not be asked to amend, expand or alter any parts of reports in a manner which distorts their true opinion, but may be invited to do so to ensure accuracy, clarity, internal consistency, completeness and relevance to the issues. Although experts should generally follow the recommendations of solicitors with regard to the form of reports, they should form their own independent views on the opinions and contents of their reports and not include any suggestions that do not accord with their views.

64. Where experts change their opinion following a meeting of experts, a signed and dated note to that effect is generally sufficient. Where experts significantly alter their opinion, as a result of new evidence or for any other reason, they must inform those who instruct them and amend their reports explaining the reasons. Those instructing experts should inform other parties as soon as possible of any change of opinion.

Written questions to experts

35.33 **65.** Experts have a duty to provide answers to questions properly put. Where they fail to do so, the court may impose sanctions against the party instructing the expert, and, if there is continued non–compliance, debar a party from relying on the report. Experts should copy their answers to those instructing them.

66. Experts' answers to questions become part of their reports. They are covered by the statement of truth, and form part of the expert evidence.

67. Where experts believe that questions put are not properly directed to the clarification of the report, or have been asked out of time, they should discuss the questions with those instructing them and, if appropriate, those asking the questions. Attempts should be made to resolve such problems without the need for an application to the court for directions, but in the absence of agreement or application for directions by the party or parties, experts may themselves file a written request to court for directions (see paragraphs 28–29).

Discussions between experts

68. The court has the power to direct discussions between experts **35.34** for the purposes set out in the Rules (CPR 35.12). Parties may also agree that discussions take place between their experts at any stage.

69. The purpose of discussions between experts should be, wherever possible, to:

a. identify and discuss the expert issues in the proceedings;

b. reach agreed opinions on those issues, and, if that is not possible, narrow the issues;

c. identify those issues on which they agree and disagree and summarise their reasons for disagreement on any issue; and

d. identify what action, if any, may be taken to resolve any of the outstanding issues between the parties.

They are not to seek to settle the proceedings.

70. Where single joint experts have been instructed but parties have, with the permission of the court, instructed their own additional Part 35 experts, there may, if the court so orders or the parties agree, be discussions between the single joint experts and the additional Part 35 experts. Such discussions should be confined to those matters within the remit of the additional Part 35 experts or as ordered by the court.

71. Where there is sequential exchange of expert reports, with the defendant's expert's report prepared in accordance with the guidance at paragraph 61 above, the joint statement should focus upon the areas of disagreement, save for the need for the claimant's expert to consider and respond to material, information and commentary included within the defendant's expert's report.

72. Arrangements for discussions between experts should be proportionate to the value of cases. In small claims and fast–tracks cases there should not normally be face to face meetings between experts: telephone discussion or an exchange of letters should usually suffice. In multi–track cases discussion may be face to face but the practicalities or the proportionality principle may require discussions to be by telephone or video–conference.

73. In multi–track cases the parties, their lawyers and experts should cooperate to produce an agenda for any discussion between experts, although primary responsibility for preparation of the agenda should normally lie with the parties' solicitors.

74. The agenda should indicate what has been agreed and summarise concisely matters that are in dispute. It is often helpful to include questions to be answered by the experts. If agreement cannot be reached promptly or a party is unrepresented, the court may give directions for the drawing up of the agenda. The agenda should be circulated to experts and those instructing them to allow sufficient time for the experts to prepare for the discussion.

75. Those instructing experts must not instruct experts to avoid reaching agreement (or to defer doing so) on any matter within the experts' competence. Experts are not permitted to accept such instructions.

76. The content of discussions between experts should not be referred to at trial unless the parties agree (CPR 35.12(4)). It is good practice for any such agreement to be in writing.

77. At the conclusion of any discussion between experts, a joint statement should be prepared setting out:

a. issues that have been agreed and the basis of that agreement;

b. issues that have not been agreed and the basis of the disagreement;

c. any further issues that have arisen that were not included in the original agenda for discussion; and

d. a record of further action, if any, to be taken or recommended, including if appropriate a further discussion between experts.

78. The joint statement should include a brief re–statement that the experts recognise their duties (or a cross–reference to the relevant statements in their respective reports). The joint statement should also include an express statement that the experts have not been instructed to avoid reaching agreement (or otherwise defer from doing so) on any matter within the experts' competence.

79. The joint statement should be agreed and signed by all the parties to the discussion as soon as practicable.

80. Agreements between experts during discussions do not bind the parties unless the parties expressly agree to be bound (CPR 35.12(5)). However, parties should give careful consideration before refusing to be bound by such an agreement and be able to explain their refusal should it become relevant to the issue of costs.

81. Since April 2013 the court has had the power to order at any stage that experts of like disciplines give their evidence at trial concurrently, not sequentially with their party's evidence as has been the norm hitherto: PD 35 paragraphs 11.1–11.4 (this is often known as "hot–tubbing"). The experts will then be questioned together, firstly by the judge based upon disagreements in the joint statement, and then by the parties' advocates. Concurrent evidence can save time and costs, and assist the judge in assessing the difference of views between experts. Experts need to be told in advance of the trial if the court has made an order for concurrent evidence.

Attendance of experts at court

35.35   **82.** Those instructing experts should ascertain the availability of experts before trial dates are fixed; keep experts updated with timetables (including the dates and times experts are to attend), the location of the court and court orders; consider, where appropriate, whether experts might give evidence via video–link; and inform experts immediately if trial dates are vacated or adjourned.

83. Experts have an obligation to attend court and should ensure that those instructing them are aware of their dates to avoid and that they take all reasonable steps to be available.

84. Experts should normally attend court without the need for a witness summons, but on occasion they may be served to require their attendance (CPR 34). The use of witness summonses does not affect the contractual or other obligations of the parties to pay experts' fees.

Experts and conditional and contingency fees

85. Payment of experts' fees contingent upon the nature of the **35.36** expert evidence or upon the outcome of the case is strongly discouraged. In *ex parte Factortame (no8)* [2008] QB 381 at [73], the court said 'we consider that it will be a rare case indeed that the court will be prepared to consent to an expert being instructed under a contingency fee agreement'.

Sanctions

86. Solicitors and experts should be aware that sanctions might ap- **35.37** ply because of a failure to comply with CPR 35, the PD or court orders.

87. Whether or not court proceedings have been commenced a professional instructing an expert, or an expert, may be subject to sanction for misconduct by their professional body/regulator.

88. If proceedings have been started the court has the power under CPR 44 to impose sanctions:

    a. cost penalties against those instructing the expert (including a wasted costs order) or the expert (such as disallowance or reduction of the expert fee) (CPR 35.4(4) and CPR 44).

    b. that an expert's report/evidence be inadmissible.

89. Experts should also be aware of other possible sanctions

    a. In more extreme cases, if the court has been misled it may invoke general powers for contempt in the face of the court. The court would then have the power to fine or imprison the wrongdoer.

    b. If an expert commits perjury, criminal sanctions may follow.

    c. If an expert has been negligent there may be a claim on their professional indemnity insurance.

Civil Justice Council
August 2014

PART 36

OFFERS TO SETTLE

Add new paragraph 36.10.1.1:

Costs in "soft tissue injury claim"

By CPR Update 75 the RTA Pre–Action Protocol was amended in various respects **36.10.1.1** for the purpose of ensuring that in personal injury claims to which the Protocol applies that are defined as "soft tissue injury claims" (1) the use and cost of medical reports is controlled, (2) in most cases only one medical report is obtained, (3) the medical expert is normally independent of any medical treatment, and (4) offers are made only after a fixed cost medical report has been obtained and disclosed. (See further para.45.16.4 below.) The introduction of this special regime involved the amendment of several CPR rules and practice directions whose provisions interact with the RTA Pre–Action Protocol, including (in Part 36), r.36.10A (adding paras (5A) and (5B)) and r.36.14A (adding para. (3A) and (3B)). Paragraph (2) of r.36.14 does not apply to a soft tissue injury claim to which r.36.14A applies (r.36.14(7)). These amendments were effected by the Civil Procedure (Amendment No.6) Rules 2014 (SI 2014/2044) and came into effect on October 1, 2014. (The transitional provision in SI 2014/2044 states that the amendments made to r.36.10A, r.36.14 and r.36.14A apply only to soft tissue injury claims started under the RTA Pre–Action Protocol where the claim notification form is sent in accordance with that Protocol on or after October 1, 2014.)

Costs consequences of acceptance of a Part 36 offer where Section IIIA of Part 45 applies

In rule 36.10A(4), for "paragraph (5)" substitute:

36.10A   **paragraphs (5), (5A) and (5B)**

In rule 36.10(A)(5), for "Where" substitute:

Subject to paragraphs (5A) and (5B), where

Add new rules 36.10A(5A) and (5B):

(5A)   In a soft tissue injury claim, if the defendant makes a Part 36 offer before the defendant receives a fixed cost medical report, paragraphs (4) and (5) will only have effect if the claimant accepts the offer more than 21 days after the defendant received the report.

(5B)   In this rule, 'fixed cost medical report' and 'soft tissue injury claim' have the same meaning as in paragraph 1.1(10A) and (16A), respectively, of the RTA Protocol.

Costs consequences following judgment

In rule 36.14(2), for "paragraph (6)" substitute:

36.14   **paragraphs (6) and (7)**

Add new rule 36.14(7):

(7) Paragraph (2) of this rule does not apply to a soft tissue injury claim to which rule 36.14A applies.

Unless it considers it unjust (r.36.14(2) and (3))

Add new paragraph at beginning:
36.14.4   Paragraph (7), which was added to this rule by SI 2014/2044 states that para.(2) of the rule does not apply to a "soft tissue injury claim"; see further para.36.10.1.1 above.

Costs consequences following judgment where Section IIIA of Part 45 applies

In rule 36.14A(2), for "paragraph (3)" substitute:

36.14A   **paragraphs (3), (3A) and (3B)**

In rule 36.14A(3), for "Where" substitute:

Subject to paragraphs (3A) and (3B), where

Add new rules 36.14A(3A) and (3B) (after the words in parentheses following rule 36.14A(3)):

(3A) In a soft tissue injury claim, if the defendant makes a Part 36 offer or Protocol offer before the defendant receives a fixed cost medical report, paragraphs (2) and (3) will only have effect in respect of costs incurred by either party more than 21 days after the defendant received the report.

(3B) In this rule, "fixed cost medical report" and "soft tissue injury claim" have the same meaning as in paragraph 1.1(10A) and (16A), respectively, of the RTA Protocol.

Costs in "soft tissue injury claim"

Add new paragraph 36.14A.2:
36.14A.2   See para.36.10.1.1 above.

PART 38

Discontinuance

Effect of rule

In the seventh paragraph, for "and Nelson's Yard Management Co v Eziefula [2013] EWCA Civ 235, March 21, 2013." substitute:

, *Nelson's Yard Management Co v Eziefula* [2013] EWCA Civ 235, March 21, 2013 and **38.6.1** *Norbrook Laboratories Ltd v Vetplus Ltd* [2013] EWHC 4032 QBD (Simon J.), 7 October 2013 noted in Lawtel.

At end of last paragraph, add:

As to the particular rules governing discontinuance of applications for permission to apply for judicial review and the rule that the general provisions of CPR r.38.6(1) should yield to them, see *R. (Smoke Club) v Network Rail Infrastructure Ltd* [2013] EWHC 3830 (Admin), October 29, 2013, *R. (Mount Cook Land Ltd) v Westminster City Council* [2003] EWCA Civ 1346; [2004] C.P. Rep. 12, and *R. (Davey) v Aylesbury Vale DC (Practice Note)* [2007] EWCA Civ 1166; [2008] 1 W.L.R. 878.

PART 39

Miscellaneous Provisions Relating to Hearings

Practice Directions

Add at end:

The Practice Directions repay careful reading. In particular paragraph 3 of 39APD **39.0.4** sets out a code for the preparation and supply of bundles for trial. Additional guidelines, which are of general assistance, are set out in appendix 6 of the Chancery Guide (vol.2 para.1A–223) and appendix 10 of the Admiralty and Commercial Courts Guide (vol.2 para.2A–168).

Add new paragraph 39.2.7.1:

Order following a hearing in private

The order must include the words after the name of the judge, "sitting in private" **39.2.7.1** (see CPR 39APD32 para.1.13). The words are important. Their inclusion means that the court's permission is required before a transcript of judgment or a copy of an order can be obtained by a non party (CPR PD 39A para.1.12).

Transcripts and orders

Delete paragraph 39.2.8 and substitute:

See Practice Direction, paras.1.11 and 1.12 (para.39APD.1). When a hearing takes **39.2.8** place in public a non party may obtain a transcript of judgment on payment of the appropriate fee. If the hearing takes place in private, the permission of the judge is required. The right to obtain from court records a copy of a court order made in public is limited by CPR 5.4C(1)(b), (1B) and (3). As to the fee payable and application process see CPR 5.4D.

Add new paragraph 39.2.12:

The exclusion of witnesses until called

If a court is sitting in public and if an application is made to exclude a witness until **39.2.12** the witness is called to give evidence, the court has the power to exclude. The power should only be exercised if in the circumstances of the particular case there is good reason for the exclusion (see *Luckwell v Limata* [2014] EWHC 536 (Fam) a decision of Holman J.). The test is perhaps that a witness should be excluded where exclusion is in the interest of justice. The decision concerned a non party. It seems unlikely that the power should be exercised if the witness is an active party to the proceedings. Where a witness is excluded, the court should be astute (as was Holman J. in *Luckwell*) to ensure that the period of exclusion is no more than is necessary to serve the interests of justice.

"a relevant practice direction" (r.39.5(1)(a))

In the sixth paragraph, for "para.28PD.13" substitute:

39.5.3   para.28PD.18

For title "Chancery Division and Queen's Bench Division" substitute:

Court Guides

For "1A–65" substitute:

39.5.5   1A–68 and *St Albans Court Ltd v Daldorch Estates Ltd*, *The Times*, May 24, 1999, Ch D and for guidance on the preparation of bundles in the Queen's Bench Division, see The Queen's Bench Guide, para.7.11.7 onwards at 1B–51.

Add at end:

See also Appendix 10 of the Admiralty and Commercial Courts Guide (Vol.2 para.2A–168).

Add new paragraph 39.7.6:

Contact details update

39.7.6   The memorandum as printed remains in place. The contact details of the Attorney General's office have changed and are now:

20 Victoria Street
London
SW1H ONF

The present address of the Bar Pro Bono Unit is:

The National Pro Bono Centre
48 Chancery Lane
London
WC2A 1JF
Email: enquiries@nationalprobonocentre.org.uk

PRACTICE DIRECTION 39A—MISCELLANEOUS PROVISIONS RELATING TO HEARINGS

Hearings

In paragraph 1.5(3), for "warrant of execution" substitute:

39APD.1   warrant of control

PRACTICE DIRECTION 39B—COURT SITTINGS

VACATIONS

The High Court

In paragraph 2.3(2), for "RSC Order 113 (Schedule 1 to the CPR)" substitute:

39BPD.2   rule 83.13(3)

PART 40

JUDGMENTS, ORDERS, SALE OF LAND ETC.

Judgments and orders to be dated

Add new paragraph at end:

40.2.6   Rule 2.9(1) states that where the court gives a judgment, order or direction which imposes a time limit for doing any act, the last date for compliance must, wherever practicable, (a) be expressed as a calendar date, and (b) include the time of day by which the act must be done. Paragraph 8.2 of Practice Direction 40B gives two examples of appropriate terms to be inserted in orders for these purposes. The first of them (which should be used "wherever possible") says the time of day should be stated as 4.00 pm (see para40BP.8 below). In the Admiralty and Commercial Courts Guide, para.D19.2 states that, absent any specific provision in an order, the latest time for compliance is 4:30 pm on the day in question (see Vol. 2 para.2A–79).

Statutory rate of interest

Add new paragraph at end:

Once judgment on an arbitral award has been entered under the Arbitration Act **40.8.3** 1996 s.66, that judgment has the same characteristics as any other judgment of the court and interest will run under s.17 from the date of the judgment, as the obligation to honour the award has then merged into the judgment debt (*La Societe pour la Recherche, la Production, le Transport, la Transformation et la Commercialisatio v Statoil Natural Gas LLC (Statoil)* [2014] EWHC 875 (Comm), April 2, 2014, unrep. (Flaux J)).

General power to vary or revoke orders

Add new paragraph at end:

In *Mitchell v News Group Newspapers Ltd (Practice Note)* [2013] EWCA 1537; [2014] 1 **40.9.3** W.L.R. 795 CA, the Court of Appeal emphasised the distinction between an application under r.3.9 for relief from sanction and an application under r.3.1(7) to vary or revoke the order imposing the sanction in the first place. The Court stated (para.45) that if the application for relief under r.3.9 is combined with an application to vary or revoke under r.3.1(7), then that should be considered first and the *Tibbles* criteria applied. See also *Thevarajah v Riordan* [2014] EWCA Civ 14; [2014] 1 Costs L.R. 163, CA, and *Newland Shipping and Forwarding Ltd v Toba Trading FZC* [2014] EWHC 210 (Comm), February 6, 2014, unrep. (Hamblen J.) (where defendants applied under r.3.9 for relief from procedural sanction imposed for their failure to comply with various orders and judge granted their application to amend the application to include an application under r.3.1(7) to vary or revoke the order, allowed it in part but dismissed their application under r.3.9).

The slip rule

Add at end:

In the case of *In re A. (A Child)* [2014] EWCA Civ 871, June 26, 2014, CA, unrep., **40.12.1** where the Court of Appeal held (following earlier authority relevant to r.52.10) that if a judge's findings of fact are of the kind which are not to be regarded as forming part of his judgment so as to be amenable to appeal in themselves then the Court has no jurisdiction to entertain an appeal from a judge's refusal to amend such findings in accordance with the criticisms of the affected party, the Court further held that findings of that kind do not fall into the category of errors in a judgment or order that may be corrected by a court under r.40.12.

Effect of rule

Add at end:

Rule 83.19 (Creditor's request for transfer to the High Court for enforcement) ap- **40.14A.1** plies where the creditor makes a request for a certificate of judgment under r.40.14A(1) in the circumstances provided for in that rule.

PART 44

GENERAL RULES ABOUT COSTS

Orders displacing the general—"a different order"

Add new paragraphs at end:

In judicial review proceedings concerning the uncertain immigration status of the **44.2.6** interested party, the claimant was unsuccessful against the first defendant, but made an application for the costs of the proceedings against both defendants. The court held that the general rule, r.44.3(2)(a) (now r.44.2(2)(a)) meant that the claimant was not entitled to its costs against the first defendant. The claimant was not the successful party as against that defendant. The basis upon which the claimant had put its case had the effect of going behind the decision of the Judge on the judicial review, which was that there was no case in law against the first defendant. The court held that it was not legitimate to go behind that underlying judgment on the merits, much less endeavour to contradict it, in order to argue about costs. The court commented that whilst reliance on the conduct provisions of rr.44.3(4)(a) and (5), (44.2(4)(a) and (5)) might reduce and sometimes eliminate an unsuccessful party's obligations to pay costs to a successful party, and could lead to orders in favour of the unsuccessful party on certain issues, there was no case in which conduct alone had led to an order by which the unsuccessful party recovered the totality of its costs from the successful party: *R (Royal Free London NHS Foundation Trust) v Secretary of State for the Home Department (1) Brent Borough Council (2) Samhir Saker–interested party* [2013] EWHC 4101 (Admin) Coulson J.

In litigation over a construction dispute the claimant sought to recover £23,572 in respect of unpaid invoices, retentions and VAT. Following submissions to the Adjudicator the claimant was awarded £23,440, which was paid by the defendant. The defendant, however, counterclaimed damages in respect of defects, delay and additional preliminaries totalling £169,138. Various offers were made by both parties to settle the matter, but the defendant was awarded a net figure of £10,885. The Judge awarded the defendant the majority of its costs of the action. The Court of Appeal overturned the Judge's decision, stating that the Judge, when considering the history of the matter and assessing the various offers, had failed adequately to take into account the commercial reality of the litigation, how it was conducted on each side, its ultimate outcome and who, on an objective basis, was the more successful party. By failing to take into account these relevant matters, and simply focusing on the various offers the Judge had adopted too mechanistic an approach and failed to address the costs issues in their proper commercial context (paragraph 73). The court also found that the Judge had failed adequately to consider the respective conduct of the parties to the litigation and the adjudication processes and that the Judge should have approached the question of costs on the basis that the very best that the defendant could do was to secure an order that the claimant should pay a proportion of its costs and that approach should then have governed the Judge's approach to the Calderbank offers when he came to consider them. In considering the relevant Calderbank offer the Judge did not appear to have given appropriate weight to the fact that the claimant could not realistically have made a Part 36 offer, because that would have had the automatic consequence that, if the offer were accepted, the defendant would have been entitled to all its costs of the proceedings to date. On the facts the court found that the defendant had not beaten the Calderbank offer. The court went on to order the claimant to pay 50% of the defendant's costs, up to the date by which the defendant should have responded to the claimant's Calderbank offer. The defendant was ordered to pay the claimant's costs from that date until judgment: *Walker Construction (UK) Ltd v Quayside Homes Ltd & Peter Brett Associates LLP* [2014] EWCA Civ 90.

Additional commentary on basis of assessment

Add new paragraph at end:

44.3.2 In proceedings which the court described as a "relatively uncomplicated leasehold dilapidations dispute" which had been settled by acceptance of the Part 36 offer, the parties could not agree the issue of costs which resulted in a one day hearing and in excess of five hours judicial reading time. The costs of that exercise alone were nearly £100,000 inclusive of VAT. The court stated that, whilst the claimant was entitled to come to court to seek indemnity costs, what it could not be allowed to do was to act in a disproportionate way when it came to present its application. The application for costs on the indemnity basis was refused, but the court added that had the application succeeded the Judge would have been minded to reduce its costs to reflect the serious concerns about the proportionality of the costs bill:

> "In cases where the parties have settled through the Part 36 procedure or otherwise but leave the Judge to decide costs, particularly where indemnity costs are claimed, parties must act in a proportionate way. There can be few if any

cases in which there should in effect be a trial of all or some of the settled issues in the case. Where the indemnity costs application depends on evidence which is likely to involve material conflicts of evidence the applicant party needs to think long and hard about whether it is appropriate to pursue the application."

Courtwell Properties Ltd v Greencore PF (UK) Ltd [2014] EWHC 184 (TCC) Akenhead J.

Rule 44.9(1)(b) Part 36

Add new paragraph at end:

A claimant who had been exposed to asbestos during his working life sued his ten **44.9.2** previous employers. After his death the action was carried on by his widow who accepted a Part 36 offer from one defendant, in settlement of her claim against that defendant, plus costs on the standard basis. The claims against the other nine defendants were abandoned and the claimant lodged a bill seeking all the costs incurred in suing all the defendants, relying on CPR r.36.10(1) to establish that she was entitled to "the costs of the proceedings". The court held that the meaning of the rule was that the recoverable costs were those in respect of the proceedings against the defendant in respect of whom the deemed order had been made. Any broader definition would achieve obvious injustice and violate the language of the rule. With regard to common costs these fell into two categories: non specific costs which would have been incurred in any event, regardless of the number of defendants; and specific costs, which were in principle capable of identification and division: *Haynes v Department for Business Innovation Skills* [2014] EWHC 643 (QB) Jay J.

PART 45

Fixed Costs

Fixed enforcement costs

In rule 45.8, for Table 5, substitute:

Table 5

For an application under rule 70.5(4) that an award may be enforced as if payable under a court order, where the amount outstanding under the award:		**45.8**
exceeds £25 but does not exceed £250	£30.75	
exceeds £250 but does not exceed £600	£41.00	
exceeds £600 but does not exceed £2,000	£69.50	
exceeds £2,000	£75.50	
On attendance to question a judgment debtor (or officer of a company or other corporation) who has been ordered to attend court under rule 71.2 where the questioning takes place before a court officer, including attendance by a responsible representative of the legal representative	for each half hour or part, £15.00	
On the making of a final third party debt order under rule 72.8(6)(a) or an order for the payment to the judgment creditor of money in court under rule 72.10(1)(b):		
if the amount recovered is less than £150	one–half of the amount recovered	
otherwise	£98.50	

On the making of a final charging order under rule 73.8(2)(a):	£110.00
	The court may also allow reasonable disbursements in respect of search fees and the registration of the order.
Where a certificate is issued and registered under Schedule 6 to the Civil Jurisdiction and Judgments Act 1982, the costs of registration	£39.00
Where permission is given under rule 83.13 to enforce a judgment or order giving possession of land and costs are allowed on the judgment or order, the amount to be added to the judgment or order for costs—	
(a) basic costs	£42.50
(b) where notice of the proceedings is to be to more than one person, for each additional person	£2.75
Where a writ of control as defined in rule 83.1(2)(k) is issued against any party	£51.75
Where a writ of execution as defined in rule 83.1(2)(1) is issued against any party	£51.75
Fixed Enforcement Costs	
Where a request is filed for the issue of a warrant of control under rule 83.15 for a sum exceeding £25	£2.25
Where a request is filed for the issue of a warrant of delivery under rule 83.15 for a sum exceeding £25	£2.25
Where an application for an attachment of earnings order is made and costs are allowed under CCR Order 27, rule 9 or CCR Order 28, rule 10, for each attendance on the hearing of the application	£8.50

Add new paragraph 45.16.4:

"fixed cost medical report" in "soft tissue injury claim"

45.16.4   By CPR Update 75 the RTA Pre–Action Protocol was amended for the purpose of ensuring that in personal injury claims to which the Protocol applies that are defined as "soft tissue injury claims" (1) the use and cost of medical reports is controlled; (2) in most cases only one medical report is obtained; (3) the medical expert is normally independent of any medical treatment; and (4) offers are made only after a fixed cost medical report has been obtained and disclosed.

A "soft tissue injury claim" is a claim "brought by an occupant of a motor vehicle where the significant physical injury caused is a soft tissue injury and includes claims where there is a minor psychological injury secondary in significance to the physical injury" (para.1.1(16A)). (Injuries popularly described as "whiplash" injuries fall into the category.) The use and costs of medical reports in such claims is controlled by various means, including by provisions that enable the claimant to obtain and deploy in accordance with the provisions in the several Stages of the Protocol scheme (and to recover the costs of as appropriate) a medical report from a medical expert who (save in exceptional circumstances) (1) has not provided treatment to the claimant, (2) is not associated with any person who has provided treatment, and (3) does not propose or recommend that they or an associate provide treatment (para.1.1(10A)). Because the recoverable cost (as a disbursement) of obtaining such a report is fixed (by CPR r. 45.19(2A)(a), at £180) it is described as a "fixed cost medical report" (para.1.1(10A)). The use of further reports (in addition to a fixed cost medical report) is possible in controlled circumstances (see paras 7.1A and 7.8A) and the costs recoverable for them are fixed (by CPR r.45.19(2A)).

The implementation of these special arrangements for the handling of "soft tissue injury claims" has involved the amendment of CPR rules and practice directions, in particular of r.45.19 (as already indicated) and of r.45.29I (which is the rule in Section IIIA of Part 45 fixing the costs of disbursements in claims which cease to continue under the RTA Protocol). (Other CPR provisions affected include r.36.10A (Costs consequences of acceptance of a Part 36 offer where Section IIIA of Part 45 applies) and r.36.14A (Costs consequences following judgment where Section IIIA of Part 45 applies).)

Disbursements

In rule 45.19(1), for "The Court" substitute:

Subject to paragraphs (2A) to (2E), the court   **45.19**

Add new rules 45.19(2A) to (2E):

(2A) In a soft tissue injury claim to which the RTA Protocol applies, the only sums (exclusive of VAT) that are recoverable in respect of the cost of obtaining a fixed cost medical report or medical records are as follows—

- **(a) obtaining the first report from any expert permitted under 1.1(12) of the RTA Protocol: £180;**
- **(b) obtaining a further report where justified from one of the following disciplines—**
  - **(i) Consultant Orthopaedic Surgeon (inclusive of a review of medical records where applicable): £420;**
  - **(ii) Consultant in Accident and Emergency Medicine: £360;**
  - **(iii) General Practitioner registered with the General Medical Council: £180; or**
  - **(iv) Physiotherapist registered with the Health and Care Professions Council: £180;**
- **(c) obtaining medical records: no more than £30 plus the direct cost from the holder of the records, and limited to £80 in total for each set of records required. Where relevant records are required from more than one holder of records, the fixed fee applies to each set of records required;**
- **(d) addendum report on medical records (except by Consultant Orthopaedic Surgeon): £50; and**
- **(e) answer to questions under Part 35: £80.**

(2B) Save in exceptional circumstances, no fee may be allowed for the cost of obtaining a report from a medical expert who—

- **(a) has provided treatment to the claimant;**
- **(b) is associated with any person who has provided treatment; or**
- **(c) proposes or recommends that they or an associate provide treatment.**

(2C) The cost of obtaining a further report from an expert not listed in paragraph (2A)(b) is not fixed, but the use of that expert and the cost must be justified.

(2D) Where appropriate, VAT may be recovered in addition to the cost of obtaining a fixed cost medical report or medical records.

(2E) In this rule, "associate", "associated with", "fixed cost medical report" and "soft tissue injury claim" have the same meaning as in paragraph 1.1(1A), (10A) and (16A), respectively, of the RTA Protocol.

Add new paragraph 45.19.2:

Costs in "soft tissue injury claim"

45.19.2 Paragraphs (2A) to (2E) were added to this rule by the Civil Procedure (Amendment No.6) Rules (SI 2014/2044) with effect from October 1, 2014, for the purposes explained in para.45.16.4 above. See also r.45.29I.

Defendants' costs

In rule 45.29F(9), for "claimant's" substitute:

45.29F defendant's

Disbursements

In rule 45.29I(1), for "The Court" substitute:

45.29I Subject to paragraphs (2A) to (2E), the court

Add new rules 45.29I(2A) to (2E):

(2A) In a soft tissue injury claim to which the RTA Protocol applies, the only sums (exclusive of VAT) that are recoverable in respect of the cost of obtaining a fixed cost medical report or medical records are as follows—

    (a) obtaining the first report from any expert permitted under 1.1(12) of the RTA Protocol: £180;

    (b) obtaining a further report where justified from one of the following disciplines—

        (i) Consultant Orthopaedic Surgeon (inclusive of a review of medical records where applicable): £420;

        (ii) Consultant in Accident and Emergency Medicine: £360;

        (iii) General Practitioner registered with the General Medical Council: £180; or

        (iv) Physiotherapist registered with the Health and Care Professions Council: £180;

    (c) obtaining medical records: no more than £30 plus the direct cost from the holder of the records, and limited to £80 in total for each set of records required. Where relevant records are required from more than one holder of records, the fixed fee applies to each set of records required;

    (d) addendum report on medical records (except by Consultant Orthopaedic Surgeon): £50; and

    (e) answer to questions under Part 35: £80.

(2B) Save in exceptional circumstances, no fee may be allowed for the cost of obtaining a report from a medical expert who—

(a) has provided treatment to the claimant;

(b) is associated with any person who has provided treatment; or

(c) proposes or recommends that they or an associate provide treatment.

(2C) The cost of obtaining a further report from an expert not listed in paragraph (2A)(b) is not fixed, but the use of that expert and the cost must be justified.

(2D) Where appropriate, VAT may be recovered in addition to the cost of obtaining a fixed cost medical report or medical records.

(2E) In this rule, "associate", "associated with", "fixed cost medical report" and "soft tissue injury claim" have the same meaning as in paragraph 1.1(1A), (10A) and (16A), respectively, of the RTA Protocol.

Add new paragraph 45.29I.2:

Costs in "soft tissue injury claim"

Paragraphs (2A) to (2E) were added to this rule by the Civil Procedure (Amendment No.6) Rules (SI 2014/2044) with effect from October 1, 2014, for the purposes explained in para.45.16.4 above. See also r.45.19. **45.29I.2**

Effect of Section

Add new paragraph at end:

The Intellectual Property Enterprise Court could only depart from the overall caps **45.30.1** on costs and scale costs in truly exceptional circumstances. It was, however, possible not to apply scale costs for one or more of earlier stages of the claim provided the total award remained within the overall cap: *Brumdle v Perry & Ors* [2014] EWHC 979 (IPEC) Judge Hacon.

Effect of rule

Add new paragraph at end:

A party has the opportunity to proceed in the Patents County Court (now the Intel- **45.31.1** lectual Property Enterprise Court) in an appropriate case if it so wished, but if a claimant wished to proceed in the High Court, and the case merited it, that option should not lightly be taken away. In the instant case, because an earlier CFA had been properly entered into, the claimant was entitled to expect his case to be dealt with under the old costs regime in the High Court. Transfer to the PCC would result in capping which would be unfair when the claimant had chosen the benefits of proceeding in the High Court under a CFA: *Crocuer Enterprises Ltd v Giordano Poultry – Plast SPA* [2013] EWHC 2491 (Ch); [2013] FSR 44, Mann J.

Effect of Section

Add new paragraph at end:

The Court of Justice of the European Union found that the costs regime in the UK **45.41.1** did not properly implement the requirements in the Aarhus Convention that access to environmental justice must not be prohibitively expensive. The judgment was given before amendments to the rules concerning protective costs orders and new guidance on costs undertakings in interim injunctions in environmental judicial review cases were introduced in April 2013: *European Commission v United Kingdom* [2014] EUECJ C/530/11.

PART 46

COSTS—SPECIAL CASES

Solicitors acting on own account

Add new paragraph at end:

Where the Bar Standards Board brought proceedings against a non–practicing **46.5.6** barrister before the Disciplinary Tribunal of the Council of the Inns of Courts the barrister successfully defended the proceedings in person. The Administrative Court expressed the view that the principle in London Scottish Benefit Society that a solicitor litigant acting in person was entitled to costs incurred in the expenditure of his own professional skill had been overturned by r.46.5(6) (formerly r.48.6(6)). Neither a solicitor nor a barrister acting in person could include in his proof of financial loss under r.46.5(4)(a) the cost of the provision of his own professional skill. Since a barrister was not a solicitor coming within the exception in PD 46(3) there was no means by which a barrister could avoid that conclusion and claim costs unless she employed someone else on her behalf. The Civil Procedure Rules did not apply, and were not even persuasive authority. If the Bar Standards Board wished to avoid having the pay the costs of a barrister's time when that barrister had successfully defended proceedings it was open to it to provide in its rules that the CPR should apply but it had not done so. The correct basis of assessing the cost was in accordance with the Board's own rules, namely to award such costs as the tribunal thought fit. There was no basis for saying that the expenditure of a barrister's own time and skills should not be compensated where that barrister was successful: *R (Bar Standards Board) v Disciplinary Tribunal of the Council of the Inns of Court and Sivanandan (interested party)* [2014] EWHC 1570 (Admin).

Editorial note

Add new paragraph at end:

46.10.2   The claimant company sought detailed assessment of its solicitors' bills and was ordered to serve Points of Dispute. During the hearing of the assessment it became clear that the client was seeking to raise points which had not been mentioned in the Points of Dispute and to go through the bill on a line by line basis. The Master directed the claimant to "set out as briefly as possible in a schedule" the items which remained in dispute. The schedule which was lodged identified the items by reference to the solicitors' time sheets, each item being described either as "excessive" or having "no supporting evidence". The Master ruled that the schedule was inadmissible, since it did not comply with his order and he decided that it would be unjust to allow the client a third opportunity to put its case and accordingly stayed the assessment. The claimant appealed and the Appeal Court found that the Master was entitled to find that both the original Points of Dispute and the later schedule were defective because neither adequately stated the claimant's case. Whilst the decision to stay was certainly a robust one, in all the circumstances the Master was not in error in taking the view, for good reason, that the assessment which the claimant wished to carry out could not be done at proportionate cost. The appeal was dismissed: *Mount Eden Land Ltd v Speechly Bircham LLP* [2014] EWHC 169 (QB) Teare J.

Offers to settle in costs–only proceedings

In the fourth paragraph, for "Tasleem v Beverley [2013] EWCA Civ 6 November" substitute:

46.14.2   *Tasleem v Beverley* [2013] EWCA Civ 1805

PART 47

PROCEDURE FOR DETAILED ASSESSMENT OF COSTS AND DEFAULT PROVISIONS

Editorial Note

Delete paragraph 47.9.2 and substitute:

47.9.2   Claimant appellants appealed against a decision reversing a Costs Judge's decision to grant them an extension of time for serving points of dispute in a detailed costs assessment thereby entitling the respondent to a default costs certificate. The Court of Appeal found that the paying parties had applied for a reasonable extension of time in which to serve their points of dispute. That extension of time would not imperil any hearing dates or otherwise disrupt the proceedings. The Costs Judge granted that extension and subsequently rejected an application to set it aside. The receiving party appealed to the High Court against that decision and the Judge allowed the appeal on the ground that there had been (1) non–disclosure and (2) the Costs Judge had impermissibly granted relief from sanction. On appeal the allegations of non–disclosure were withdrawn. The Court of Appeal found that the Costs Judge was not dealing with an application for a relief from sanction but making a case management decision about extension of time. The judge ought not to have interfered with the Costs Judge's exercise of his discretion: *Hallam Estates Ltd v Baker* [2014] EWCA Civ 661.

Effect of rule

Add at end:

    The Court of Appeal recalled its order refusing permission to an appellant to ap- **47.12.1** peal when it found that there was a procedural irregularity in the wording of the costs order issued by the Judge below which stated that a third party should be liable for the costs "in accordance with the costs certificate". There was a real prospect of success on appeal in arguing that the third party could only challenge, by means of the instant appeal, the determination by the Judge that the costs payable by him should be those for which the costs certificate had been issued against the respondent party. The Judge below had failed to consider the extent to which the third party should pay the costs of the action or how the amount of those costs should be established. The judge had overlooked the need to provide the third party with an opportunity to be heard on the costs: *Salekipour v Parmar* [2013] EWCA Civ 1376 [2014] 1 Cost LR 81.

Effect of rule

In the second paragraph, for "Supreme Court Costs Office", substitute:

    Senior Courts Costs Office **47.22.1**

PART 48

Part 2 of the Legal Aid, Sentencing and Punishment of Offenders Act 2012 Relating to Civil Litigation Funding and Costs: Transitional Provision in Relation to Pre-Commencement Funding Arrangements

PRACTICE DIRECTION 28A—COSTS (FPR PT 28)

Add new paragraph 48BPD.4.1:

Note

    The Legal Aid Sentencing and Punishment of Offenders Act 2002 put the powers of **48BPD.4.1** the court to award a costs allowance in divorce proceedings onto a statutory footing. New ss.22ZA and 22ZB of the Matrimonial Causes Act 1973 set out the principles where the court is considering making a legal services payment order. The court gave guidance on the application of the new sections: *Rubin v Rubin* [2014] EWHC 611 (Fam) Mostyn J.

PART 44

[Before April 1, 2013] General Rules about Costs

Rule 44.3(6)—types of order

After the seventh paragraph, add as a new paragraph:

    The purpose of the power of the court to order interest on costs including pre- **44x.3.22** judgment interest is to compensate a party who has been deprived of the use of his money and who has had to borrow money to pay for legal fees. The court's discretion is not fettered by the statutory rate of interest but is at large. In exercising the discretion the court conducts a general appraisal of the position having regard to what is reasonable for both the paying and the receiving parties. The claimant's solicitors had fulfilled the role of a bank but on terms more advantageous to the claimants than those which would have been offered by a bank. The agreement between the client and the solicitors was a genuine agreement which gave rise to a real liability on the part of the claimants to pay interest in the event that they won their claims. The argument that the arrangements were unreal or notional was rejected. The judge was incorrect to have regard to the means of the clients rather than the solicitors when making the order: *Jones v Secretary of State for Energy and Climate Change* [2014] EWCA Civ 363.

Rule 44.4(2)—proportionality

After the eleventh paragraph, insert as a new paragraph:

44x.4.2   When conducting a detailed assessment under old rule 44.4(2) the court could consider on an item by item basis whether the particular cost was proportionate and necessary even if, on a global basis, the costs appeared proportionate. During the course of the assessment the District Judge had used the terms "necessary" and "need" indiscriminately. This was not, however, fatal to his decision. The court held that the terms had been used in their ordinary sense to convey a notion of justification when enquiring whether the costs were proportionate. The judge was not to be taken as having applied the test of necessity but, even if he had done so, he would not have been wrong to do so. *Finglands Coachways Ltd v O'Hare* [2014] EWHC 1513 (QB) Cranston J.

Rule 44.4(3)—costs on the indemnity basis

After the first paragraph, add as a new paragraph:

44x.4.3   When considering whether to make an order for costs on the indemnity basis the trial judge has a wide discretion but it is critical that there be some conduct or circumstance that takes a case out of the norm. Such factors include the high–risk situation where a claim is speculative, weak, opportunistic or thin, and where a claimant commenced and pursued large–scale and expensive litigation in circumstances calculated to exert unfair and commercial pressure on a defendant to renegotiate what had become a commercially unattractive contract. The fact that one party lost resoundingly, did not automatically mean that the other should be awarded costs on the indemnity basis. On the facts, an order for costs on the indemnity basis was not made although it had not been unreasonable for the successful party to seek such an order: *Obrascon Huarte Lain SA v Government of Gibraltar* [2014] EWHC 2291 (TCC) Akenhead J.

PART 48

[BEFORE APRIL 1, 2013] COSTS—SPECIAL CASES

GENERAL PRINCIPLES AND GUIDANCE ON COSTS

GENERAL PRINCIPLES AND CASE LAW RELATING TO COSTS AND THEIR ASSESSMENT

1. Costs in specific courts and other tribunals

The Upper Tribunal (Tax Chamber)

Add new paragraphs at end:

48GP.71   It is within the power of the Upper Tribunal to order a respondent to pay an appellants' costs of obtaining permission to appeal. The Tribunal also has the power to award the costs of resisting an application for permission to a respondent if those costs have been reasonably incurred. The Tribunal indicated that the Upper Tribunal should lean towards refusing a costs direction in favour of a respondent to an application for permission, although that presumption should not be excessively hard to displace: *Softhouse Consulting Ltd v Revenue & Customs Commissioners*, February 19, 2014, UT (TAX) Judge Colin Bishopp.

Although rule 10 of the Tribunal Procedure (First–Tier Tribunal) (TAX Chamber) Rules 2009 excluded the First Tier Tribunal's jurisdiction to make costs orders, the Tribunal was able to make case management decisions which would have the result that the costs of, for example, preparing trial bundles would be shared. The Tribunal did not, however, have the power to order that the cost of preparing bundles should be shared equally between the parties: *Revenue & Customs Commissioners v Eclipse Film Partners* No.35 LLP [2014] EWCA Civ 184.

4. Costs relating to particular types of parties and miscellaneous

Protective Costs Orders

In the first paragraph, for "rr.44.18 to 44.20 and commentary in para.43.2.1.2 above", substitute:

rr. 3.19 to 3.21.   **48GP.96**

PART 51

TRANSITIONAL ARRANGEMENTS AND PILOT SCHEMES

In Contents, after the entry for Practice Direction 51A add:

Contents   **51.0.1**

Add new paragraph 51.2.11:

County Court at Central London Multi–Track Pilot Scheme

By CPR Update 75 (July 2014) Practice Direction 51I (The County Court at Central **51.2.11** London Multi–Track Pilot Scheme), made under Pt 51 and supplementing Pt 26, was introduced. It provides for a pilot scheme in respect of money claims issued at the County Court Business Centre and the County Court Money Claims Centre for a period of 12 months from October 1, 2014 to September 30, 2015. (See para.51IPD.1 below.)

Add new Practice Direction 51I:

PRACTICE DIRECTION 51I—THE COUNTY COURT AT CENTRAL LONDON MULTI–TRACK PILOT SCHEME

This Practice Direction supplements CPR Part 26   **51IPD.1**

1. Scope and interpretation

   1.1 This Practice Direction is made under rule 51.2. It provides **51IPD.2** for a pilot scheme ("the County Court at Central London Multi–Track Pilot Scheme") in respect of money claims issued at the County Court Business Centre ("CCBC") and the County Court Money Claims Centre ("CCMCC") for a period of 12 months from 1 October 2014 to 30 September 2015.

   1.2 In this Practice Direction "the County Court Business Centre" means the Production Centre and Money Claims Online.

2. Certain money claims in the CCBC and CCMCC to be sent to the County Court at Central London: modification of rule 26.2A

   2.1 In the circumstances set out in paragraph 2.2, rule 26.2A ap- **51IPD.3** plies with the modifications in paragraphs 2.3 to 2.5.

2.2 The circumstances are that—

(a) a money claim is started at the CCBC or CCMCC;

(b) a court officer provisionally decides pursuant to rule 26.3 that the track which appears to be most suitable for the claim is the multi–track; and

(c) either—

(i) the defendant's home court or the preferred court specified on the defendant's directions questionnaire (where the defendant is an individual); or

(ii) the claimant's preferred court (where the defendant is not an individual),

is one of the following County Court hearing centres— Barnet, Bow, Brentford, Bromley, Central London, Clerkenwell and Shoreditch, Croydon, Edmonton, Kingston, Lambeth, Mayors and City of London, Romford, Uxbridge, Wandsworth, Hammersmith, Willesden and Woolwich (a "London hearing centre").

2.3 Rule 26.2A(3) is modified to provide that—

(a) if there is a single defendant who is an individual, at the relevant time the claim will be sent to the County Court at Central London; and

(b) where there are two or more defendants, at least one of whom is an individual, the claim will be sent to the County Court at Central London if the home court of the first defendant to file a defence is a London hearing centre.

2.4 Rule 26.2A(4) is modified to provide that, if the preferred court is a London hearing centre, at the relevant time the claim will be sent to the County Court at Central London.

2.5 Rule 26.2A(5) is modified to provide that if the preferred court specified on the relevant directions questionnaire is a London hearing centre, the claim will be sent to the County Court at Central London.

PART 52

APPEALS

In the Contents, add new entries 52.5A and 52.15A and amend the entry for 52.15:

52.0.1 Contents

The Court of Appeal

Add new paragraph at end:

52.0.12 Where a judge at first instance dismisses a claim for breach of a Convention right on ground that he was bound by a decision of the House of Lords, being a decision in conflict with a later decision of the European Court of Human Rights, and the claimant appeals to the Court of Appeal, the Court, in dismissing the appeal (also following the House of Lords' decision) but giving permission to appeal to the Supreme Court, is not bound to hear substantive argument and to give a judgment considering the issues in detail (*R. (Kaiyam) v Secretary of State for Justice* [2013] EWCA Civ 1587, [2014] 1 W.L.R. 1208, CA).

Scope of Part 52

In the quotation following the first paragraph, for "paragraph 17.1 (4)" substitute:
paragraph 17.1(2)
52.1.1

In the last paragraph, for "but that Section is not exhaustive" substitute:
but the list of special provisions about appeals in the table in Section 4 of the Practice Direction is not exhaustive

Add new paragraph 52.1.1.1:

High Court's jurisdiction under the Extradition Act 2003

Until October 1, 2014, the rules for appeals to the High Court against orders ap- **52.1.1.1**
proving or refusing extradition made in the magistrates' courts or by the Secretary of State under the Extradition Act 2003 were the normal rules for appeals to the High Court as stated in Pt 52 and supplemented by para.21.1 of Practice Direction 52D. As a result of amendments made by s.174 of the Anti–social Behaviour, Crime and Policing Act 2014 to the Civil Procedure Act 1997 s.1 and to the Courts Act 2003 s.68, with effect from that date appeals to the High Court in extradition cases were made subject to the Criminal Procedure Rules 2014 (SI 2014/1610) (in particular Part 17 thereof), with the result that appeal provisions in the CPR no longer apply in relation to the High Court's exercise of such jurisdiction. (Accordingly, para.21.1 was removed from Practice Direction 52D by CPR Update 75 (July 2014); the change entailed no amendment to rules in Part 52.) Extradition hearings in magistrates' courts are conducted before District Judges in accordance with rules in the Criminal Procedure Rules 2014. The advantage of the changes triggered by s.174 of the 2014 Act is that the whole extradition process including appeals to the High Court (albeit a civil and not a criminal process) is governed by the same set of procedural rules.

Appeals in contempt proceedings

After the second paragraph (ending "r.52.3 below.") add as a new paragraph:
In *Thursfield v Thursfield* [2013] EWCA Civ 840, [2013] C.P. Rep. 44, CA, Court of **52.1.2**
Appeal suggested that consideration should be given to imposing on an appellant contemnor who had not submitted to the court's jurisdiction and had deliberately absented himself from the committal proceedings, a requirement to apply for permission to appeal.

Permission

In rule 52.3(1)(a), for "the County Court or the High Court" substitute:
the County Court, family court or the High Court
52.3

In the second set of words in parentheses after rule 52.3(2), for "the County Court or the High Court" substitute:
the County Court, family court or the High Court

In rule 52.3(4), after "paragraph (4A)" add:
and except where a rule or practice direction provides otherwise

How the appeal court deals with such applications

In the second paragraph, delete the first sentence (beginning "If the appeal court") and the second sentence (ending "Practice Direction 52B") and substitute:
Rule 52.3(4) states that if the appeal court refuses permission on paper, then **52.3.6**
subject to exceptions (see below) the appellant is entitled to have the matter reconsidered at an oral hearing (see also r.52.16(6), para.7.2 of Practice Direction 52B and para.15(2) of Practice Direction 52C). For application of (and possible extension

of) the time limit in r.52.3(5) where, without a hearing, the Court of Appeal grants permission to appeal on some issues, but refuses it on others, see para.18 of Practice Direction 52C.

At the end of the second paragraph, add:

In r.52.3, para.(4) is expressed as subject to para.(4A); see para.52.3.8.1 below. And, by an amendment made by SI 2014/2044, it is also made subject to any rule or practice direction which "provides otherwise".

The effect of refusal of permission

After the second paragraph (ending "refused permission") add as a new paragraph:

52.3.8   Where an appeal court without a hearing refuses permission to appeal, the person seeking permission may request the decision to be reconsidered at a hearing (r.52.3(4)); the request must be filed within seven days after service of the notice that permission has been refused (r.52.3(5)). That seven–day time limit is unequivocally expressed in mandatory terms and, although the rule does not in terms provide for a specific procedural sanction for non–compliance, applications to extend it are to be determined in accordance with r.3.9 (as amended with effect from April 1, 2013) and the authorities thereon (*Webb Resolutions Ltd v E Surv Ltd* [2014] EWHC 49 (QB), January 20, 2014, unrep. (Turner J.).

Before the last paragraph, add as a new paragraph:

Rule 23.12 states that, if the court dismisses an application for permission to appeal and it considers that the application is totally without merit, the court's order must record that fact (see para.52.3.8.1 below) and "at the same time" consider whether it is appropriate to make a civil restraint order (see further r.3.11 (Power of the court to make a civil restraint order)).

Application for permission to appeal "totally without merit"–reconsideration

Add new paragraph at beginning:

52.3.8.1   Rule 23.12(a) states that, if the court dismisses an application for permission to appeal and it considers that the application is "totally without merit", the court's order must record that fact. See further paras 23.12.1 and 23.12.2 above.

Time for filing appellant's notice

After the second paragraph (ending "can be prepared.") add as a new paragraph:

52.4.1   It is particularly important that time limits in respect of appeals against judgment are observed so that the parties and the court know when the matters adjudicated have been put beyond the reach of appellate review. Generally, the fact that a potential appellant has reasons for wanting to delay filing a notice of appeal until the full consequences of the judgment against him are apparent is not a good reason for deferring the filing of an appellant's notice (*Kagalovsky v Balmore Invest Limited*, [2014] EWHC 108 (QB), January 27, 2014, unrep. (Turner J.), where the judgment committed the potential appellant for contempt and his reasons for seeking an extension included his desire to await the imposing of penalty).

Statutory time limits for filing notice of appeal

Before the fifth sentence (beginning "Further, where,") add:

52.4.1.1   Paragraph 3.5 of PD52D states that, where any statute prescribes a period within which an appeal must be filed then, unless the statute otherwise provides, the appeal court may not extend that period.

For "R. (Adesina) v Nursing & Midwifery Council [2013] EWCA Civ 818, July 9, 2013, CA" substitute:

R. (Adesina) v Nursing & Midwifery Council [2013] EWCA Civ 818; [2013] W.L.R. 3156, CA.

Add new paragraph at end:

In relation to appeals under s.26(4) of the Extradition Act 2003, para.21.1(c) of PD52D states that the appellant must serve a copy of the notice of appeal on the CPS, if they are not a party to the appeal, in addition to the persons to be served under r.52.4(3) "and in accordance with that rule". The court has no general discretion to extend the 7 day time limit for service on the CPS (*R (Bajorek Sawczuk) v Poland* [2014] EWHC 1108 (Admin), March 21, 2014, unrep. (Collins J.)).

Add new rule 52.5A:

Transcripts at public expense[1]

52.5A—(1) Subject to paragraph (2), the lower court or the ap-   **52.5A**
peal court may direct, on the application of a party to the proceed-
ings, that an official transcript of the judgment of the lower court,
or of any part of the evidence or the proceedings in the lower court,
be obtained at public expense for the purposes of an appeal.

(2) Before making a direction under paragraph (1), the court
must be satisfied that—

    (a) the applicant qualifies for fee remission or is otherwise
        in such poor financial circumstances that the cost of
        obtaining a transcript would be an excessive burden; and

    (b) it is necessary in the interests of justice for such a
        transcript to be obtained.

Add new paragraph 52.5A.1:

Effect of rule

This rule was enacted by r.8(c) of the Civil Procedure (Amendment No.6) Rules   **52.5A.1**
2014 (SI 2014/2044) and came into effect on October 1, 2014. It is designed to ensure
a uniform practice for the providing of transcripts at public expense in appeals to the
Civil Division of the Court of Appeal, the High Court and the County Court. Any application for a transcript at public expense should be made in the appellant's notice
(Practice Direction 52B para.4.3 and Practice Direction 52C para.6.2).

Criteria to be applied on applications to extend time

At the end of the third paragraph (ending "[2003] 2 All E.R. 74") add:

In *Kagalovsky v Balmore Invest Limited*, [2014] EWHC 108 (QB), January 27, 2014,   **52.6.2**
unrep. (Turner J.), the judge noted that, with effect from April 1, 2013, the overriding
objective, which figured prominently in the reasoning in the *Robert* case, was reformulated to include considerations calculated to achieve the enforcement of and
compliance with rules, practice directions and orders.

General approach

Add at end:

For summaries of the principles and examples of their application, see *Mahtani v*   **52.7.1**
Sippy [2013] EWCA Civ 1820, September 26, 2013, CA, unrep. (Aikens LJ), and *Otkritie*
International Investment Management Ltd v Urumov [2014] EWHC 755 (Comm), March
14, 2014, unrep. (Eder J).

Striking out appeal notices and setting aside or imposing condi-tions on permission to appeal

In rule 52.9(3), for "he" substitute:

they   **52.9**

Imposition of conditions

At the end of the first paragraph, add:

In *McLeod v Gold Harp Properties Ltd* [2014] EWCA Civ 532, April 9, 2014, CA,   **52.9.4**
unrep., an interim costs order was made in the proceedings in the court below against
a corporate defendant (D1) and an individual co–defendant (D2) behind and associated with D1 and on D1's appeal the claimants applied for the satisfaction of that order, either by payment to them or by payment into court, to be imposed as a condi-

---

[1] Introduced by the Civil Procedure (Amendment No.6) Rules (SI 2014/2044).

tion for the bringing of D1's appeal. The Court of Appeal stated that, although such condition could formally only be imposed on D1 (D2 not being an appellant), in considering whether it ought to be imposed it was relevant for the appeal court to have regard to the ability of D2 to satisfy the order.

After the second paragraph, insert as new paragraphs:

Where a respondent applies for the satisfaction by the appellant of an order for payment of costs on account made against him by the court below to be imposed as a condition upon which the appeal may be brought, the fact that the appellant was not facing any consequences as a result of his failure to comply with that order does not constitute a "compelling reason" for imposing such condition (*McLeod v Gold Harp Properties Ltd* [2014] EWCA Civ 532, April 9, 2014, CA, unrep.).

Although a good deal may be said in favour of a principle to the effect that a defendant who wishes to appeal and obtains permission to appeal, but who has not complied with a judgment of the court below and has obtained no stay of execution of it, must as a matter of course be required to comply with and satisfy that judgment as a condition of being permitted to pursue an appeal, that is not the law (*McLeod v Gold Harp Properties Ltd* above; see also *Mahtani v Sippy* [2013] EWCA Civ 1820, September 26, 2013, CA, unrep.).

Effect of rule

After the first paragraph, insert as a new paragraph:

52.9A.1   The phrase "the recoverable costs of an appeal" means the costs recoverable by the winning party on the appeal, whoever the winner may turn out to be; the rule does not contemplate an order in favour of just one party, win or lose (*JE (Jamaica) v Secretary of State for the Home Department* [2014] EWCA Civ 192; [2014] C.P. Rep. 24, CA, where an application under the rule by an appellant appealing against an order of the Upper Tribunal for a one–way costs shifting order was rejected).

Delete the last paragraph (beginning "Rule 27.14(2) states that") and substitute:

Rule 27.14(2) states that, in any case which has been allocated to the small claims track, the court may not order a party to pay a sum to another in respect of that party's costs, fees and expenses "including those relating to an appeal", except to the limited extent provided by that rule. The extension of that rule to include, not only the costs of original small claims proceedings, but also costs "relating to an appeal", was effected by the Civil Procedure (Amendment) Rules 2006 (SI 2006/1689) r.5, and followed upon responses received to a consultation paper issued by the Department of Constitutional Affairs ("Proposed Changes to Civil Appeals Rules" (CP 20/05, September 9, 2005)). The consultation paper included, amongst other things, the proposals (1) that the costs rules in Pt 27 which apply to claims should apply to appeals also, and (2) that costs may be ordered (as in Pt 27) "where a party behaves unreasonably" (see now r.27.14(2)(g)). The consultation paper did not suggest that a distinction might or should be drawn between "first" and "second" appeals, and, in terms, r.27.14(2) draws no such distinction. The statement in para.3.3 of Ch.34 of the Review of Litigation Costs, above, to the effect that appeals in small claims proceedings which reached the Court of Appeal (as second appeals) "are subject to full costs shifting" gave currency to the inference that, on such appeals, the provision recommended in that Review and enacted as r.52.9A would in those circumstances come into play. However, in *Akhtar v Boland* [2014] EWCA Civ 943, July 8, 2014, CA, unrep., the Court of Appeal held that r.27.14(2) applies to both "first" and "second" appeals and explained that, although r.52.9A confers power on an appeal court to limit costs of an appeal, it does not confer power to award costs where there is a provision in the CPR, such as r.27.14(2), precluding a costs order. Rule 27.14(2) covers first instance and appeal costs in small claims proceedings. Generally, the costs which a court may award under r.27.14(2) are not apposite to appeal proceedings, but some are, e.g. costs ordered to be paid by a party who has behaved unreasonably (r.27.14(2)(g)). See further para.27.14.1.1 above.

Add new paragraph 52.10.7.3:

Application, appellant's notice or appeal "totally without merit"

52.10.7.3   By the Civil Procedure (Amendment No.2) Rules 2004 (SI 2004/2072), paras (5) and (6) were inserted in r.52.10 as part of a number of amendments accompanying the enactment of r.3.11 (Power of the court to make civil restraint orders). See also r.23.12 (Dismissal of totally without merit applications). Consideration by the appeal court of the question whether it is appropriate to make a civil restraint order (CRO) is triggered by a finding that the application, the appellant's notice or appeal was totally without merit (TWM). The questions (1) whether the appeal court should record a finding of TWM and (2) whether it is appropriate to make a CRO are distinct and raise different considerations. The proper test for determining whether an application is totally without merit is whether it is "bound to fail"; it is not necessary for it to be shown that the application was abusive or vexatious (*R. (Drake) v Secretary of State for the Home Department* [2014] EWCA Civ 1091, *The Times* July 14, 2014, CA); see further paras 23.12.2 and 52.3.8.1 above.

Grounds for allowing appeal

After the sixth paragraph (ending "disagreement is possible.") add as a new paragraph:

Reasons for judgment will always be capable of having been better expressed. A judge's reasons should be read on the assumption that the judge knew (unless he has demonstrated to the contrary) how he should perform his functions and which matters he should take into account (In *re C (A Child) (Adoption: Placement order) (Practice Note)* [2013] EWCA Civ 431, [2013] 1 W.L.R. 3720, CA, at para.39 per Sir James Munby P.; *Piglowska v Piglowska* [1999] 1 W.L.R. 1360, HL, at p 1372 per Lord Hoffmann). An appellate court should resist the temptation to subvert the principle that they should not substitute their own discretion for that of the judge by a narrow textual analysis which enables them to claim that he misdirected himself (ibid). **52.11.4**

Failure to give reasons

At the end of the first paragraph (ending "to this decision.") add:

The duty to give reasons is a function of due process and therefore justice, both at common law and under Art 6 of the Human Rights Convention; justice will not be done if it is not apparent to the parties why one has lost and the other has won; fairness requires that the parties, especially the losing party, should be left in no doubt why they have won or lost; want of reasons may be a good self–standing ground of appeal (*Bassano v Battista* [2007] EWCA Civ 370, February 8, 2007, CA, where the Court of Appeal referred to the authorities on the duty of a judge to give adequate reasons, particularly in a case which turns on the credibility of witnesses, and on the power of the Court to review judgments based on credibility). **52.11.5**

Add new paragraph 52.11.7:

Reasons for dismissing appeal

In the case of In *re Portsmouth Football Club*; *Neumans LLP v Andronikou*, [2013] EWCA Civ 916, [2014] 1 All E.R. 12, CA, the Court of Appeal stated (at para.38), that an appeal court does not have to produce a detailed judgment on matters that the court believes have been dealt with correctly and indetail in the judgment under appeal. If the judgment in the court below is correct, the appeal court can legitimately adopt and affirm it without any obligation to say the same things over again in different words. The losing party will be told exactly why the appeal has been dismissed, that is because there was nothing wrong with the decision below or the reasons for it. **52.11.7**

II. Special Provisions Applying to the Court of Appeal

Filing documents

Add new paragraph at end:

The Court of Appeal is dependent on the papers filed by the parties. In the case of *R (A Child), Re* [2014] EWCA Civ 597, May 8, 2014, CA, unrep., the Court explained the increasing difficulties caused for the Court by the failures of unrepresented appellants to comply with the requirements of Practice Direction 52C, particularly in care proceedings appeals where local authorities are respondents and particularly the requirements as to the filing of bundles of documents. The Court stated that if it is to be able to deal properly with such an appeal, and to do so speedily, then the respondent local authority involved will have to expect to assist by ensuring that the Court is provided with appeal bundles. **52.12.1.2**

Second appeals to the Court

In rule 52.13(1), for "the County Court or the High Court" substitute:

the County Court, family court or the High Court **52.13**

What constitute "first" and "second" appeals for these purposes

Add new paragraph at end:

52.13.2   In *Dillard v F&C Commercial Property Holdings Ltd* [2014] EWHC 1219 (QB), April 16, 2014, unrep. (Akenhead J), where a dispute between a householder (C) and a property developer (D) was submitted to the dispute resolution procedure provided for by the Party Wall etc Act 1996 s.10, C exercised his right to appeal to the County Court granted by that section against an award made under that procedure and, on the appeal, unsuccessfully contended that the award was a nullity. A High Court judge granted C permission to appeal to the High Court and at the hearing of the appeal the Court rejected D's submission that C's appeal was a "second" appeal which ought to have been made to the Court of Appeal and for which permission under r.52.13 was required.

Appeals from the Upper Tribunal to the Court of Appeal

Add new paragraph at end:

52.13.6   In *Samuda v Secretary of State for Work & Pensions* [2014] EWCA Civ 1; [2014] 3 All E.R. 201, CA, the Upper Tribunal refused a party to proceedings in the First–tier Tribunal (Social Entitlement Chamber) permission to appeal to it from a decision of the First–tier Tribunal and subsequently dismissed that party's application to reconsider and set aside the refusal. On the party's application to the Court of Appeal for permission to appeal against the Upper Tribunal's refusal of his application to reconsider and set aside the Court held that by virtue of provisions in the Tribunals, Courts and Enforcement Act 2007 ss.10 and 13 the Upper Tribunal had no jurisdiction to entertain such an application. (The party's only remedy lay by way of judicial review.) Accordingly, the Court of Appeal held that there could be no appeal to it from a refusal of the Upper Tribunal to review its decision to refuse permission to appeal, and the Court could not grant permission to appeal from that refusal.

Judicial review appeals from the High Court[1]

Delete rule 52.15 and substitute:

52.15   **52.15—(1) Where permission to apply for judicial review has been refused at a hearing in the High Court, the person seeking that permission may apply to the Court of Appeal for permission to appeal.**

(1A) Where permission to apply for judicial review of a decision of the Upper Tribunal has been refused by the High Court or where permission to apply for judicial review has been refused and recorded as totally without merit in accordance with rule 23.12—

> **(a) the applicant may apply to the Court of Appeal for permission to appeal;**
>
> **(b) the application will be determined on paper without an oral hearing.**

(2) An application in accordance with paragraphs (1) or (1A) must be made within 7 days of the decision of the High Court to refuse to give permission to apply for judicial review or, in the case of an application under paragraph (1A), within 7 days of service of the order of the High Court refusing permission to apply for judicial review.

(3) On an application under paragraph (1) or (1A), the Court of Appeal may, instead of giving permission to appeal, give permission to apply for judicial review.

---

[1] Introduced by the Civil Procedure (Amendment) Rules 2000 (SI 2000/221) and amended by the Civil Procedure (Amendment No.2) Rules 2012 (SI 2012/2208), the Civil Procedure (Amendment No.4) Rules 2013 (SI 2013/1412) and the Civil Procedure (Amendment No.6) Rules (SI 2014/2044).

(4) Where the Court of Appeal gives permission to apply for judicial review in accordance with paragraph (3), the case will proceed in the High Court unless the Court of Appeal orders otherwise.

Application for permission to appeal against refusal of permission below

In the first paragraph, delete the first sentence (beginning "Where a claimant") and substitute:

The court's permission to proceed is required in a claim for judicial review (r.54.4). **52.15.1** Where permission to apply for judicial review has been refused at a hearing in the High Court, the person seeking that permission may apply to the Court of Appeal for permission to appeal (r.52.15(1)). (Where the court, without a hearing, refuses permission to proceed the provisions of r.54.12 apply.)

At the end of the second paragraph add:

For meaning of "totally without merit", see para.23.12.2 above and para.54.12.1 below.

Time limit for application to Court of Appeal

Delete paragraph 52.15.6 and substitute:

The time limits for applying to the Court of Appeal for permission to appeal are as **52.15.6** stated in r.52.15(2). That provision was clarified by amendments made by the Civil Procedure (Amendment No.6) Rules 2014 (SI 2014/2044). Depending on the circumstances, the seven day period runs either from the date of the decision of the High Court or from the date of service of the order of the High Court. The principles governing the grant of any extension of time are as set out in the notes to r.52.6 above.

Add new rule 52.15A:

Judicial review appeals from the Upper Tribunal[1]

52.15A—(1) Where permission to bring judicial review proceed- **52.15A** **ings has been refused by the Upper Tribunal and permission to appeal has been refused by the Upper Tribunal, an application for permission to appeal may be made to the Court of Appeal.**

(2) Where an application for permission to bring judicial review proceedings has been recorded by the Upper Tribunal as being completely without merit and an application for permission to appeal is made to the Court of Appeal in accordance with paragraph (1) above, the application will be determined on paper without an oral hearing.

(The time limits for filing an appellant's notice under rule 52.15A(1) are set out in Practice Direction 52D.)

Add new paragraph 52.15A.1:

Effect of rule

This rule was inserted by the Civil Procedure (Amendment No.6) Rules 2014 (SI **52.15A.1** 2014/2044) and came into effect on October 1, 2014.

Paragraph 3.3 of Practice Direction 52D (substituted by CPR Update 75 (July 2014), with effect from October 1, 2014) states that, where the appellant wishes to appeal against a decision of the Upper Tribunal, the appellant's notice must be filed within 28 days of the date on which notice of the Upper Tribunal's decision on permission to appeal to the Court of Appeal is sent to the appellant.

An application for permission to appeal may be considered by an appeal court at an oral hearing or on paper. Paragraph (2) of this rule states, categorically, that in the circumstances provided for therein "the application will be determined on paper without an oral hearing". In this respect, r.2.15A accords with r.52.15.

---

[1] Introduced by the Civil Procedure (Amendment No.6) Rules (SI 2014/2044).

Rule 30 of the Tribunal Procedure (Upper Tribunal) Rules 2008 states that where that rule applies and the Upper Tribunal refuses permission to bring judicial review proceedings and considers the application to be totally without merit, it shall record that fact in its decision notice.

Scope of the rule

After the second paragraph, add as a new paragraph:

52.17.2   In *McWilliams v Norton Finance (UK) Ltd* [2014] EWCA Civ 818, May 15, 2014, CA, unrep., the claimants' appeal to the Court of Appeal (for which permission had been granted) against the trial judge's dismissal of their claim against a company for mis–selling of payment protection insurance was dismissed by consent. The Court of Appeal expressed the opinion that there had been no "final determination" (no final adjudication on the merits) and doubted whether an application by the claimants under r.52.17 could succeed. In any event, there was an "alternative effective remedy" open to the claimants, and that was an application under r.3.1(7) to revoke the Court's order dismissing the appeal by consent which the Court could entertain and which, in the circumstances, it was prepared to grant.

PRACTICE DIRECTION 52B—APPEALS IN THE COUNTY COURT AND HIGH COURT

Section 4

Initiating an appeal

In paragraph 4.3, for the last sentence (beginning "Where the applicant") substitute:

52BPD.5   Any application for a transcript at public expense should be made within the appellant's notice.

PRACTICE DIRECTION 52C—APPEALS TO THE COURT OF APPEAL

Non–availability of documents

Delete paragraph 6 and substitute:

52CPD.6   6(1) If the appellant is unable to provide any of the necessary documents in time, the appellant must complete the appeal notice on the basis of the available documents. The notice may be amended subsequently with the permission of the court (see paragraph 30).

(2) Any application for a transcript at public expense should be made within the appellant's notice.

Service on the respondent

In paragraph 7.1A, after "skeleton argument" add:

52CPD.7   in respect of an application for permission to appeal

Determination of applications for permission to appeal

In paragraph 15(2), for "except where rule 52.3(4A) (applications totally without merit) applies" substitute:

52CPD.15   except where the rules otherwise provide.

PRACTICE DIRECTION 52D—STATUTORY APPEALS AND APPEALS SUBJECT TO SPECIAL PROVISION

Section 3

General provisions about statutory appeals

Delete paragraph 3.3 and substitute:

52DPD.4   **3.3** Where the appellant wishes to appeal against a decision of the Upper Tribunal, the appellant's notice must be filed within 28 days of the date on which notice of the Upper Tribunal's decision on permission to appeal to the Court of Appearl is sent to the appellant.

In paragraph 3.3A, for "received by" substitute:

sent to

Appeals under the Extradition Act 2003

Delete paragraph 21.1 and substitute:

21.1 [Omitted by CPR Update 75 (July 2014) with effect from October 1, 2014.] **52DPD.22**

PART 53

DEFAMATION CLAIMS

PRACTICE DIRECTION 53—DEFAMATION CLAIMS

Honest comment or opinion

After the second paragraph, add as a new paragraph:

The bounds of acceptable criticism are probably wider, and honest comment or opinion more easily established, where the claimant is a public figure or the words complained of are part of a political debate: see *Mughal v Telegraph Media Group Ltd* [2014] EWHC 1371 (QB). **53PD.15**

The section 3 procedure

In the first paragraph, after " [2010] E.M.L.R. 11." add:

An application to make a statement should normally be dealt with on paper: *Murray v Associated Newspapers Ltd* [2014] EWHC 1170 (QB). **53PD.29**

Ruling on meaning

Add at end:

For the advantages in terms of both speed and cost, of determining the actual meaning by way of preliminary issue, see *RBS Shareholders Action Group v News Group Newspapers Ltd* [2014] EWHC 130 (QB); [2014] E.M.L.R. 15. **53PD.32**

Where a statement is opposed

Add new paragraph at end:

It should be the norm for applications to read unilateral statements, even if opposed, to be dealt with on paper: *Murray v Associated Newspapers Ltd* [2014] EWHC 1170 (QB). **53PD.44**

PART 54

JUDICIAL REVIEW AND STATUTORY REVIEW

In the Contents, after the entry for rule 54.20, add:

Contents

54.0.1

II. Planning Court

In the contents, after the entry for Practice Direction 54D, add:

Practice Direction 54E—Planning Court Claims   para.54PDE.1

Reconsideration of a refusal of permission

Add at end:

54.12.1   The Court of Appeal has held that the proper test for determining whether an application is totally without merit was whether it was bound to fail. It was not necessary to show that the application was abusive or vexatious: *R (Grace) v Secretary of State for the Home Department* [2014] EWCA Civ 1091, *The Times*, July 14, 2014, CA.

Add new Section II to Part 54:

II. Planning Court

General

54.21   **54.21—(1) This Section applies to Planning Court claims.**

(2) In this Section, "Planning Court claim" means a judicial review or statutory challenge which—

    (a) involves any of the following matters—

        (i) planning permission, other development consents, the enforcement of planning control and the enforcement of other statutory schemes;

        (ii) applications under the Transport and Works Act 1992;

        (iii) wayleaves;

        (iv) highways and other rights of way;

        (v) compulsory purchase orders;

        (vi) village greens;

        (vii) European Union environmental legislation and domestic transpositions, including assessments for development consents, habitats, waste and pollution control;

        (viii) national, regional or other planning policy documents, statutory or otherwise; or

        (ix) any other matter the judge appointed under rule 54.22(2) considers appropriate; and

    (b) has been issued or transferred to the Planning Court.

(Part 30 (Transfer) applies to transfers to and from the Planning Court.)

Effect of rule

54.21.1   This rule establishes a new Planning Court. It does so by establishing a specialist list comprising judicial reviews and statutory challenges in planning–related matters. The rule applies to all claims issued on or after April 6, 2014 or transferred to the Planning Court after that date. The principal areas of its work will include challenges to decisions involving the grant of planning permissions or those based on rights derived from EU environmental legislation. A Planning Liaison Judge will be appointed to be in charge of the list. Practice Direction 54E—Planning Court Claims (made by CPR Update 71) provides target timescales for significant Planning Court claims. These include claims which relate to commercial, residential or other developments having a significant economic impact or which raise important points of law or generate significant public interest or require judges with significant planning experience. The Planning Liaison Judge will determine whether a case is a significant planning case and parties wishing to make representations on that issue must do so within the time scales within paragraph 3.3 of Practice Direction 54E. The target is to deal with such cases within very short timescales. Applications for permission are intended to be dealt with within three weeks of the expiry of the time for lodging an acknowledgement of service in judicial review claims. Oral renewals for permission, following a refusal on the papers, are intended to be heard within one month of the issue of the application. Substantive judicial reviews are intended to be heard within 10 weeks of the expiry of the time for service of detailed grounds. Applications for permission in cases involving statutory applications to quash under s.289 of the Town and Country Planning Act 1990 are intended to be heard within one month. Substantive statutory applications and appeals are to be heard within six months of the claim being issued. The Planning Liaison Judge may also direct the expedition of any Planning Court claim if he considers it necessary to deal with the case justly.

Specialist list

54.22—(1) The Planning Court claims form a specialist list.   54.22
(2) A judge nominated by the President of the Queen's Bench Division will be in charge of the Planning Court specialist list and will be known as the Planning Liaison Judge.
(3) The President of the Queen's Bench Division will be responsible for the nomination of specialist planning judges to deal with Planning Court claims which are significant within the meaning of Practice Direction 54E, and of other judges to deal with other Planning Court claims.

Application of the Civil Procedure Rules

54.23   These Rules and their practice directions will apply to 54.23 **Planning Court claims unless this section or a practice direction provides otherwise.**

Further provision about Planning Court claims

54.24   Practice Direction 54E makes further provision about 54.24 **Planning Court claims, in particular about the timescales for determining such claims.**

Add new Practice Direction 54E:

PRACTICE DIRECTION 54E—PLANNING COURT CLAIMS
This Practice Direction supplements Part 54   **54EPD.1**

General
1.1 This Practice Direction applies to Planning Court claims.

How to start a Planning Court claim
2.1 Planning Court claims must be issued or lodged in the **54EPD.2** Administrative Court Office of the High Court in accordance with Practice Direction 54D.
2.2 The form must be marked the "Planning Court".

Categorisation of Planning Court claims
3.1 Planning Court claims may be categorised as "significant" by **54EPD.3** the Planning Liaison Judge.
3.2 Significant Planning Court claims include claims which—

(a) relate to commercial, residential, or other developments which have significant economic impact either at a local level or beyond their immediate locality;

(b) raise important points of law;

(c) generate significant public interest; or

(d) by virtue of the volume or nature of technical material, are best dealt with by judges with significant experience of handling such matters.

3.3 A party wishing to make representations in respect of the categorisation of a Planning Court claim must do so in writing, on issuing the claim or lodging an acknowledgment of service as appropriate.

3.4 The target timescales for the hearing of significant (as defined by paragraph 3.2) Planning Court claims, which the parties should prepare to meet, are as follows, subject to the overriding objective of the interests of justice—

(a) applications for permission to apply for judicial review are to be determined within three weeks of the expiry of the time limit for filing of the acknowledgment of service;

(b) oral renewals of applications for permission to apply for judicial review are to be heard within one month of receipt of request for renewal;

(c) applications for permission under section 289 of the Town and Country Planning Act 1990 are to be determined within one month of issue;

(d) substantive statutory applications, including applications under section 288 of the Town and Country Planning Act 1990, are to be heard within six months of issue; and

(e) judicial reviews are to be heard within ten weeks of the expiry of the period for the submission of detailed grounds by the defendant or any other party as provided in Rule 54.14.

3.5 The Planning Court may make case management directions, including a direction to any party intending to contest the claim to file and serve a summary of his grounds for doing so.

3.6 Notwithstanding the categorisation under paragraph 3.1 of a Planning Court claim as significant or otherwise, the Planning Liaison Judge may direct the expedition of any Planning Court claim if he considers it to be necessary to deal with the case justly.

PART 55

POSSESSION CLAIMS

Editorial introduction

Add at end:

55.0.2 For enforcement of possession orders, see CPR rr.83.13 and 83.26.

Related sources

For "CCR Ord.24 r.6 (warrants of possession and restitution)" substitute:

55.0.3 CPR r.83.13 (High Court writ of possession)

For "CCR Ord.26 r.17 (warrants of possession)" substitute:
CPR r.83.26 (county court warrant of possession)

Which court?

In the first paragraph, for "The basic rule is that possession claims must be started in the county court for the district where the property is situated (CPR r.55.3(1))." substitute:
The basic rule is that possession claims must be started in the hearing centre for the **55.3.3** district where the property is situated (CPR r.55.3(1)).

Add at end:
For examples of possession claims started in the High Court which should have been started in the county court, see *Crompton v Woodford Scrap Metal* [2014] EWHC 1260 (QB) noted on LAWTEL; March 17, 2014 and *Enfield LBC v Phoenix* [2013] EWHC 4286 (QB), March 19, 2013 in which HHJ Reddihough, sitting as a judge of the High Court, stated that in so far as Civil Procedure Rules (CPR) Practice Direction 55A para.1.3(3) refers to "a substantial risk of public disturbance or of serious harm to persons or property which properly require immediate determination", it is clearly referring to "a present substantial risk . . . of a nature that is such that immediate determination of the possession claim is required". Simply to argue that at some time in the future there may be problems about enforcing any possession order that is made is not sufficient to come within this paragraph in the Practice Direction (para.12).

Applications by unauthorised tenants to apply for suspension of warrant

For "CCR Order 26 r.17(2A)" substitute:
CPR r.83.26(5)   **55.10.4**

Accelerated possession procedure

For "Such claims must be started in the county court for the district in which the property is situated." substitute:
Such claims must be started in the hearing centre for the district in which the prop- **55.11.2** erty is situated.

Service and enforcement of the IPO

In rule 55.26(3), for "CCR Order 26, rule 17 does" substitute:
Rules 83.2, 83.3 and 83.26(1) to (9) do   **55.26**

Delete paragraph 55.26.2.

After IPO made

In rule 55.27(5), for "CCR Order 24, rule 6" substitute:
Rule 83.26(10) to (12)   **55.27**

Delete paragraph 55.27.2.

PRACTICE DIRECTION 55B—POSSESSION CLAIMS ONLINE

Request for Issue of Warrant

Following paragraph 12.2(2), for the words in parentheses, substitute:
(Rule 83.2 sets out certain circumstances in which a warrant of possession may not **55BPD.12** be issued without the permission of the court.)

PART 56

LANDLORD AND TENANT CLAIMS AND MISCELLANEOUS PROVISIONS ABOUT LAND

Protocols

Delete paragraph 56.0.5 and substitute:
There is no specific Protocol for use in connection with landlord and tenant claims. **56.0.5**

However, the "Practice Direction—Pre–Action Conduct" provides that unless the circumstances make it inappropriate the parties should exchange sufficient information about the matter to allow them to understand each other's position and make informed decisions about settlement and how to proceed, and make appropriate attempts to resolve the matter without starting proceedings, and in particular to consider the use of an appropriate form of ADR in order to do so (para.6—see Vol. 2 para.C3–18). In applications under Pt II of the Landlord and Tenant Act 1954 there are of course time limits for bringing proceedings where notices have been served unless the time has been extended (see Vol. 2 para.3B–165). However, the general principles apply especially as there is the ability to extend those time limits before commencement.

Which court?

Delete paragraph 56.2.1 and substitute:

56.2.1   Both the High Court and the County Court have jurisdiction to hear a claim for a new tenancy (Landlord and Tenant Act 1954 s.63). However, the basic rule is that the claim should be started in the County Court hearing centre that serves the address. If it is not, then there is likely to be a delay in proceedings whilst the matter is transferred to the appropriate hearing centre (CPR 56, 2.2 and CPR 56 PD para.2.2 (2)).

Only exceptional circumstances justify starting the claim in the High Court. (CPR 56 PD para.2.2.) If the claim is started in the High Court and the court decides that it should have been started in the County Court, the court will normally either strike out the claim or transfer it to the county court on its own initiative. Circumstances that may, in an appropriate case, justify starting a claim in the High Court are if there are complicated disputes of fact or there are points of law of general importance. The value of the property and the amount of any financial claim may be relevant circumstances but these factors alone will not normally justify starting the claim in the High Court. (PD 56.2.) The best policy is therefore almost invariably to start the claim in the County Court and if it is thought appropriate to ask that court to transfer the claim to the High Court. If the claim is begun in the High Court, it must be brought in the Chancery Division. (PD 56 para.2.6.) If the claim is begun in the High Court, it must be brought in the Chancery Division. (PD 56 para.2.6.)

PART 57

Delete title "Probate and Inheritance" and substitute:

PROBATE, INHERITANCE AND PRESUMPTION OF DEATH

In the Contents, after the entry for 57.16 add:

57.0.1 Contents

V. Proceedings under the Presumption of Death Act 2013

Editorial introduction

Delete paragraph 57.0.2 and substitute:

57.0.2   Part 57 is in five Sections. The first Section deals with contentious probate. The second and third Sections are concerned with matters other than contentious probate, namely rectification of wills and the removal or substitution of personal representatives. The fourth deals with claims under the Inheritance (Provision for Family and Dependants) Act 1975, and the fifth with applications for declarations of death and related matters, under the Presumption of Death Act 2013. The five sections are all contained within one CPR Part because they share an underlying theme: death. Directions in Practice Direction 57 (Probate) supplement rules in the first four Sections (para.57PD.1 below). Directions in Practice Direction 57B (Proceedings Under the Presumption of Death Act 2013) supplement rules in the fifth Section (para.57BPD.1 below).

Scope of this Part and definitions

In rule 57.1(c)(ii), delete "and".   **57.1**

In rule 57.1(d), for "." substitute:
  ; and

Add new rule 57.1(e):

(e) proceedings under the Presumption of Death Act 2013.

Procedure for claims under section 1 of the Act

In rule 57.16(3), after "must" add:

, except in the circumstances specified in paragraph (3A),   **57.16**

Add new rules 57.16(3A) and (3B):

(3A) Where no grant has been obtained, the claimant may make a claim without naming a defendant and may apply for directions as to the representation of the estate. The written evidence must—

> **(a) explain the reasons why it has not been possible for a grant to be obtained;**
>
> **(b) be accompanied by the original or a copy (if either is available) of the will or other testamentary document in respect of which probate or letters of administration are to be granted; and**
>
> **(c) contain the following information, so far as known to the claimant—**
>> **(i) brief details of the property comprised in the estate, with an approximate estimate of its capital value and any income that is received from it;**
>>
>> **(ii) brief details of the liabilities of the estate;**
>>
>> **(iii) the names and addresses of the persons who are in possession of the documents relating to the estate; and**
>>
>> **(iv) the names of the beneficiaries and their respective interests in the estate.**

(3B) Where a claim is made in accordance with paragraph (3A), the court may give directions as to the parties to the claim and as to the representation of the estate either on the claimant's application or on its own initiative.

(Section 4 of the 1975 Act as amended confirms that nothing prevents the making of an application under the Act before representation with respect to the estate of the deceased person is taken out.)

Procedure

After the sixth paragraph (ending "s.25 of the Act") add as a new paragraph:

57.16.0   Paragraphs (3A) and (3B) were inserted in r.57.16 by the Civil Procedure (Amendment No.6) Rules 2014 (SI 2014/2044), with effect from October 1, 2014. Amendments made to s.4 of the 1975 Act (by provisions in the Inheritance and Trustees' Powers Act 2014, implementing a Law Commission recommendation) enable proceedings to be commenced before a grant of representation has been obtained. Paragraphs. (3A) and (3B) provide rules for the handling of claims made in those circumstances. The insertion of these paragraphs has not been attended by any amendments to Practice Direction 57.

Time–limit for applications

Delete paragraph 57.16.0.1 and substitute:

57.16.0.1   By s.4 of the Act an application under s.2 shall not, except with the permission of the court, be made after the end of the period of six months from the date on which a grant of representation to the estate of the deceased is first taken out. Section 4 as amended by s.6 and para.6 of sch.2 of the Inheritance and Trustees' Powers Act 2014 enables an application under s.2 to be made before a grant of representation is taken out. Provision is made for this in the rules by the insertion in r.57.16 of new paras (3A) and (3B). Section 23 of the Act (as amended by s.7 and para.2 of sch.3 of the 2014 Act) clarifies the date when representation is first taken out for the purposes of s.4. The amendments to ss 4 and 23 of the Act apply to deaths occurring after the coming into force of the relevant provisions of the 2014 Act.

Add new paragraphs 57.16.4 and 57.16.5:

Costs management

57.16.4   Claims under the Act are expressly referred to as one of the categories of other cases (non Pt 7 multi–track) in which an order for the provision of costs budgets with a view to a costs management order being made may be particularly appropriate: see Practice Direction 3E (as amended from April 22, 2014) at para.5(d). It is to be expected in view of their specific identification as being "particularly appropriate" for costs management that in proceedings under the Act costs management orders will often be made.

The requirement to file a costs budget in claims under the Act

57.16.5   The requirement to file a costs budget under Pt 3 Section II and Practice Direction 3E does not arise in the case of a Part 8 claim commenced on or after April 22, 2014 until an order has been made under r.3.12(1A) by the court. In Part 8 proceedings commenced before April 22, 2014 the requirement to file a costs budget under Pt 3 Section II and Practice Direction 3E does not automatically apply and is only triggered by an order or direction of the court: see *Kershaw v Roberts* [2014] EWHC 1037 (Ch) itself a claim under the Act.

Paragraph 5.4 of Section II provides that any party to "such proceedings" (a reference back to "proceedings relating to trust funds" in para.5.2) who intends to apply for an order for the payment of costs out of the trust fund must file and serve on all other parties written notice of that intention together with a budget of the costs likely to be incurred by that party. Paragraph 5.5 provides that the documents mentioned in para.5.4 must be filed and served, in a Part 8 claim, with the evidence (or if a defendant does not intend to serve and file evidence, with the acknowledgement of service).

The effect of these provisions (which have been in force since April 1, 2013) has been widely overlooked, perhaps not surprisingly given their location. They would appear to apply to most, if not all, claims under the Act where it is common for a party to seek to recover costs out of the deceased's estate. The provisions do not fit easily with the recent amendments made to r.3.12 to exclude Pt 8 claims from costs management unless the court orders Section II of Pt 3 and Practice Direction 3E to apply. It is to be hoped that these provisions will be looked at again by the rules committee.

After rule 57.16, insert new Section V to Part 57:

V. Proceedings under the Presumption of Death Act 2013

Scope and interpretation[1]

57.17—(1) This Section contains rules about proceedings under **57.17** the Presumption of Death Act 2013.

(2) In this Section, terms used in the Presumption of Death Act 2013 Act have the meaning given by that Act, and—

 (a) "the 2013 Act" means the Presumption of Death Act 2013;

 (b) "a claim for a declaration of presumed death" means a claim under section 1 of the 2013 Act for a declaration that a missing person is presumed to be dead;

 (c) "a claim for a variation order" means a claim for an order under section 5 of the 2013 Act varying or revoking a declaration of presumed death.

Editorial Note

Section V was added to Part 57 by the Civil Procedure (Amendment No.6) Rules **57.17.1** 2014 (SI 2014/2044) and came into effect on October 1, 2014. The rules in this Section are supplemented by directions in Practice Direction 57B (Proceedings Under the Presumption of Death Act 2013), see para.57BPD.1 et seq below. The rules in Section V specifically engage rules in other CPR Parts, in particular Part 6, Part 8 and Part 40, and to an extent modify the effects of some of those rules.

Proceedings to be in the High Court[2]

57.18—(1) Proceedings under the 2013 Act must be issued in the **57.18** High Court in either—

 (a) the Chancery Division; or

 (b) the Family Division.

(2) The Civil Procedure Rules apply to proceedings under the 2013 Act which are brought in the Family Division, except that the provisions of the Family Procedure Rules 2010(1) relating to the drawing up and service of orders apply instead of the provisions in Part 40 and Practice Direction 40B.

Procedure for claims for a declaration of presumed death or a variation order[3]

57.19—(1) A claim for a declaration of presumed death or for a **57.19** variation order must be made by issuing a claim form in accordance with Part 8.

(2) In addition to the matters set out in rule 8.2 (contents of the claim form), the claim form must also include or be accompanied by the information required by Practice Direction 57B.

(3) Rules 8.2A, 8.3, 8.4 and 8.5 apply as modified by paragraphs (4) to (7) of this rule (and references elsewhere in these Rules to a

---

[1] Introduced by the Civil Procedure (Amendment No.6) Rules 2014 (SI 2014/2044).
[2] Introduced by the Civil Procedure (Amendment No.6) Rules 2014 (SI 2014/2044).
[3] Introduced by the Civil Procedure (Amendment No.6) Rules 2014 (SI 2014/2044).

defendant and to an acknowledgment of service are, where relevant, to be read as references to the substitute terms in rules 8.2A, 8.3, 8.4 and 8.5 as so modified).

(4) Rule 8.2A (issue of claim form without naming defendants) applies as if for "without naming a defendant" in paragraph (1) there were substituted "without serving notice on any person".

(5) Rule 8.3 (acknowledgment of service) applies—

(a) as if, instead of referring to a defendant, it referred to a person giving notice of intention to intervene or applying for permission to intervene, as the case may be;

(b) as if, instead of referring to an acknowledgment of service, it referred to a notice of intention to intervene or an application for permission to intervene, as the case may be; and

(c) subject to paragraph (7), with the substitution of 21 days for 14 days as the time within which the notice of intention to intervene or application for permission to intervene must be filed and served.

(6) Rules 8.4 (consequence of not filing an acknowledgment of service) and 8.5 (filing and serving written evidence) apply—

(a) as if, instead of referring to a defendant, they referred to a person giving notice of intention to intervene or applying for permission to intervene, as the case may be; and

(b) as if, instead of referring to an acknowledgment of service, they referred to a notice of intention to intervene or an application for permission to intervene, as the case may be.

(7) If the claim form is served out of the jurisdiction under rule 6.32 or 6.33, the period for filing notice of intention to intervene or an application for permission to intervene, as the case may be, and any written evidence, is 7 days longer than the relevant period for serving an acknowledgement of service specified in rule 6.35 or Practice Direction 6B.

Effect of rule

57.19.1   For directions supplementing this rule, see paras 1.1 to 1.5 of Practice Direction 57B.

Giving notice of claim[1]

57.20   57.20—(1) Where the claim is for a declaration of presumed death, the claimant must give notice of the claim by serving a copy of it on the following persons (where not the claimant)—

(a) the spouse or civil partner of the missing person;

(b) any parent of the missing person;

(c) any child of the missing person;

(d) any sibling of the missing person;

(e) if there are no persons within sub–paragraphs (a) to (d), the nearest relative of the missing person known to the claimant; and

(f) any other person (including in particular any insurance

---

[1] Introduced by the Civil Procedure (Amendment No.6) Rules 2014 (SI 2014/2044).

company) appearing to the claimant to have an interest in the claim.

(2) Where the claim is for a variation order, the claimant must give notice of the claim by serving a copy of it on the following persons (where not the claimant)—

    (a) the person who was the claimant for the declaration of presumed death or (as the case may be) previous variation order which it is sought to have varied or revoked;

    (b) the spouse or civil partner of the missing person;

    (c) any parent of the missing person;

    (d) any child of the missing person;

    (e) any sibling of the missing person;

    (f) if there are no persons within sub–paragraphs (b) to (e), the nearest relative of the missing person known to the claimant; and

    (g) any other person (including in particular any insurance company) appearing to the claimant to have an interest in the claim.

(3) Notice under paragraph (1)(a) to (f) or paragraph (2)(a) to (g) must be given within 7 days after the claim is issued.

Advertisement of claim[1]

57.21—(1) The claimant (whether the claim is for a declaration of presumed death or for a variation order) must, within 7 days of issue of the claim, ensure that notice of the claim is published—   **57.21**

    (a) in a form which meets the requirements set out in Practice Direction 57B; and

    (b) in at least one newspaper circulating in the vicinity of the last known address of the missing person.

(2) The claimant must, at least 5 days before the hearing, file a copy of the page of the newspaper bearing the advertisement of notice of the claim required by paragraph (1) and the date on which it was published.

Effect of rule

The advertisement of the claim required by s.9(2) of the 2013 Act and r.57.21(1)(a) is set out in para.2.1 of Practice Direction 57B.   **57.21.1**

Interveners[2]

57.22—(1) The Attorney General, or a person who is entitled to intervene in proceedings under section 11(1), must first notify the court of the intention to intervene in accordance with the requirements of Practice Direction 57B.   **57.22**

(2) Any other person who wishes to intervene in such proceedings must submit an application for permission to intervene in accordance with the requirements of Practice Direction 57B.

(3) Where the court grants permission to intervene, it may do so on conditions and may give case management directions.

---

[1] Introduced by the Civil Procedure (Amendment No.6) Rules 2014 (SI 2014/2044).
[2] Introduced by the Civil Procedure (Amendment No.6) Rules 2014 (SI 2014/2044).

(4) The court may direct that a person who intervenes in proceedings, other than the Attorney General, be joined as a claimant or defendant.

Effect of rule

57.22.1 For directions supplementing this rule, see paras 3.1 and 3.2 of Practice Direction 57B.

Requirement to provide information[1]

57.23 **57.23—(1) An application for an order under section 12(1) of the 2013 Act must be supported by evidence and must in particular—**

> **(a) specify or describe the information in respect of which the order is sought;**
>
> **(b) set out the reasons why the person making the application believes that the person against whom the order is sought is likely to have such information; and**
>
> **(c) include any further details, where known, of the missing person which are likely to assist in providing the information sought.**

(2) The person making the application must serve a copy of the application notice on the person against whom the order is sought, and on every other party to the proceedings (within the meaning of section 20(2) of the 2013 Act), at least 14 days before the date fixed for the hearing of the application.

(3) An application for discharge or variation under section 12(6) of an order made under section 12(1) may be made without notice unless the court directs otherwise.

Add new Practice Direction 57B:

PRACTICE DIRECTION 57B—PROCEEDINGS UNDER THE PRESUMPTION OF DEATH ACT 2013

57BPD.1 *This Practice Direction supplements CPR Part 57*

Procedure for claims—Rule 57.19

1.1 Claim for declaration of presumed death—claim form

The claim form for a claim for a declaration of presumed death must include or be accompanied by the following (where known)—

> (1) *Information about the claimant*
>> (a) the claimant's name and address;
>> (b) the relationship of the claimant to the missing person; and
>> (c) if the claimant is not the missing person's spouse, civil partner, parent, child or sibling, details of the claimant's interest in the determination of the application;
>
> (2) *Information about the missing person*
>> (a) the missing person's name and surname, and any other names by which the missing person is or has formerly been known;
>> (b) the missing person's gender;

---

[1] Introduced by the Civil Procedure (Amendment No. 6) Rules 2014 (SI 2014/2044).

(c) if the claimant is not the missing person's spouse, civil partner, parent, child or sibling, details of the claimant's interest in the determination of the application;

(c) the missing person's maiden surname (if any);

(d) the missing person's date and place of birth;

(e) the occupation of the missing person;

(f) the occupation, name and surname of—

    (i) the missing person's spouse or civil partner (or late spouse or civil partner if the marriage or civil partnership ended on death);

    (ii) where the missing person was under 16 years of age, the missing person's parents;

(g) the missing person's National Insurance number;

(h) the date on which missing person is thought to have died, or on which the missing person was last known have been alive;

(i) on which of the grounds in section 1(4) of the 2013 Act the court is considered to have jurisdiction to entertain the claim; and

(j) the name and address of the spouse or civil partner, parents, children or siblings of the missing person (if any, and if not the claimant);

(3) *Information about steps taken to trace the missing person*

(a) details of any enquiries made or other steps taken to trace the missing person or confirm when the missing person was last known to be alive; and

(b) details of the results of such enquiries or other steps;

(4) *Information about the missing person's property*

(a) an estimate of the total value of the assets of the missing person;

(b) details of property owned by the missing person; and

(c) details of the interest of any other person in the missing person's property which it is sought to have determined by the court; and

(5) *Information about advertisement and recipients of notice of the claim*

(a) details of the newspaper in which the claimant proposes to advertise the claim; and

(b) details of the persons to whom the claimant is giving notice of the claim and, where notice is being given to a person under rule 57.20(1)(f), the nature of that person's interest in the claim.

1.2 Claim for variation order

The claim form for a variation order must include or be accompanied by the following (where known)—

(1) *Information about the claimant*

(a) the claimant's name and address;

(b) the relationship of the claimant to the missing person; and

(c) details of the claimant's interest in the determination of the application;

(2) *Information about previous claim and missing person's property*

(a) details of the declaration of presumed death or (as the

case may be) previous variation order which it is sought to have varied or revoked;

(b) details of the circumstances which are claimed to justify a variation order, and evidence of the enquiries made and other steps taken to verify them and their outcomes; and

(c) details of any interest in property acquired as a result of the declaration of presumed death or (as the case may be) previous variation order which it is sought to have varied or revoked; and

(3) *Information about advertisement and recipients of notice of the claim*

(a) details of the newspaper in which the claimant proposes to advertise the claim; and

(b) details of the persons to whom the claimant is giving notice of the claim and, where notice is being given to a person under rule 57.20(2)(g), the nature of that person's interest in the claim.

1.3 Issue of claim form without serving notice on any person

For the purposes of rule 8.2A as modified by rule 57.19, an application for permission to issue a claim form, whether the claim is for a declaration or presumed death or for a variation order, may be made only where the claimant believes there to be no person within paragraph (1)(a) to (f) or paragraph (2)(a) to (g) of rule 57.20. The application must explain why the claimant believes that there is no such person.

1.4 Case management—first directions hearing

A claim (whether for a declaration of presumed death or for a variation order) must be listed for case management directions either—

(a) more than 28 days (but where practicable no more than 56 days) after issue; or

(b) where the claim form has been served outside the jurisdiction, more than 7 days (but where practicable no more than 35 days) after the period for filing provided for by rule 57.19(7),

to allow for time for those served with notice of the claim or who respond to the advertisement of the claim to file notice of intention to intervene or an application for permission to intervene as the case may be.

1.5 The court must notify all those who have filed notice of intention to intervene or an application for permission to intervene of the date of the directions hearing.

Advertisement of claim—Rule 57.21

57BPD.2 **2.1** The advertisement of the claim required by section 9(2) of the 2013 Act and rule 57.21(1)(a) must be in the form set out below, or contain the equivalent information about the claim and the possibility of applying, and where and by when to apply, to the Court—

IN THE HIGH COURT OF JUSTICE [CHANCERY] [FAMILY] DIVISION

Case Number . . .

IN THE MATTER OF AN APPLICATION FOR A DECLARA-
TION OF THE PRESUMED DEATH OF (*INSERT NAME*)

A claim has been issued in the High Court of Justice, for a [declara-
tion] [variation of a declaration] that (insert name), whose last
known address was (insert address) is presumed to be dead. Any
person having an interest may apply to the Court to intervene in
the matter.

If you wish to apply to the Court, you should do so at [Court ad-
dress] as soon as possible, and if possible within 21 days of the date
of this notice. Delay may harm your prospects of being able to
intervene.

[*If the claimant is legally represented*]

(Name)

Claimant's Legal Representative

(Address)

[*If the claimant is not legally represented*]

(Claimant's address for service)

Interveners—Rule 57.22

3.1 The Attorney General, or a person who is entitled to intervene **57BPD.3**
in the proceedings by virtue of section 11(1) (the missing person's
spouse, civil partner, parent, child or sibling) should notify the intention to intervene as early as possible by filing, and serving on the
claimant, notice in writing, specifying—

(a) the intervener's name and address;
(b) the intervener's relationship to the missing person (where the
intervener is not the Attorney General);
(c) the reasons for intervening; and
(d) particulars of any determination or order sought under section 11(4)(b) or (c) of the 2013 Act.

3.2 An application under rule 57.22(2) for permission to intervene
must be served on the claimant and must specify—

(a) the applicant's relationship to the missing person or other
interest in the proceedings;
(b) the reasons for seeking to intervene; and
(c) particulars of any determination or order sought under section 11(4)(b) or (c) of the 2013 Act.

PART 64

ESTATES, TRUSTS AND CHARITIES

Related sources

In the sixth bullet point delete "2009" after "Chancery Guide"   **64.0.3**

Prospective Costs Orders in relation to applications under r.64.2(a)

Costs capping

Add at end as new paragraph:

Attention is drawn to PD3F para.5 which provides for costs capping orders in rela- **64.2.2**
tion to trust funds. Paragraph 5.4 provides that any party who intends to apply for

costs out of a trust fund mustfile and serve on all parties notice of that intention together with a costs budget.

PART 65

PROCEEDINGS RELATING TO ANTI–SOCIAL BEHAVIOUR AND HARASSMENT

In the Contents, for the entry "VIII. Injunctions under the Policing and Crime Act 2009" substitute:

65.0.1 Contents

VIII. Injunctions under the Policing and Crime Act 2009 and under Part 1 of the Anti–Social Behaviour, Crime and Policing Act 2014

In the Contents for the entry for rule 65.46, substitute:

Editorial introduction

In the fourth paragraph beginning "Section VIII" add at end:

65.0.2 Section VIII was amended by the Civil Procedure (Amendment No.6) Rules 2014 (SI 2014/2044) with effect from October 1, 2014, so as to make provision for (in addition to applications for injunctions and other related proceedings under Pt 4 of the 2009 Act), applications for injunctions and other related proceedings under Pt 1 of the Anti–social Behaviour, Crime and Policing Act 2014 (see Vol.2 para.3A–1776).

Related sources

Add new entry at end:

65.0.3 Anti–social Behaviour, Crime and Policing Act 2014, Pt 1.

Editorial introduction

Add new paragraph at beginning:

65.3.1 Paragraphs (2) and (2A) of this rule were amended by r.28(a) of the Civil Procedure (Amendment) Rules 2014 (SI 2014/407) with effect from the date of the commencement of legislation creating the single County Court (April 22, 2014). The instruction in r.28(a) relating to para.(2) is not wholly comprehensible. The text of that provision has been rendered above in the manner in which White Book editors believe was intended.

Starting a demotion or suspension claim

Delete rule 65.14(1) and substitute:

65.14 **(1) (a) The claim may be made at any County Court hearing centre;**

(b) the claim will be issued by the hearing centre where the claim is made; and

(c) if the claim is not made at the County Court hearing centre which serves the address where the property is situated, the claim, when it is issued, will be sent to that hearing centre.

(Practice Direction 65 makes further provision in respect of claims which are not made at the County Court hearing centre which serves the address where the property is situated.)

Delete Section VIII title and substitute:

VIII. Injunctions under the Policing and Crime Act 2009 and under Part 1 of the Anti–social Behaviour, Crime and Policing Act 2014

Scope of this Section and interpretation

In rule 65.42(1) add at end:

and under Part 1 of the Anti–social Behaviour, Crime and **65.42**
Policing Act 2014 (Injunctions)

Delete rule 65.42(2) and substitute:

(2) In this Section—
    (a) "the 2009 Act" means the Policing and Crime Act 2009; and
    (b) "the 2014 Act" means the Anti–Social Behaviour, Crime and Policing Act 2014.

Effect of rule

Delete paragraph 65.42.1 and substitute:

Section VIII (rr.65.42 to 65.49) was inserted by the Civil Procedure (Amendment **65.42.1** No.2) Rules 2010 (SI 2010/1953). The Section was amended by the Civil Procedure (Amendment No.6) Rules 2014 (SI 2014/2044) with effect from October 1, 2014, so as to make provision for, in addition to applications for injunctions and other related proceedings under Pt 4 of the Policing and Crime Act 2009, similar proceedings under Pt 1 of the Anti–social Behaviour, Crime and Policing Act 2014 (see further para.65.0.2 above). In some respects the rules in Section VIII of Pt 65 and the statutory provisions in Pt 4 of the 2009 Act (see Vol 2 para.3A–1719) and in Pt 1 of the 2014 Act (see Vol.2 para.3A–1776) are closely connected and should be read together. In the 2009 Act Schedule 5 (Injunctions: powers to remand) and Schedule 5A (Breach of injunction: powers of court in respect of under–18s) are incorporated in Pt 4 (see Vol 2 para.3A–1737). In the 2014 Act Schedule 1 (Remands under ss.9 and 10) and Sch.2 (Breach of injunction: powers of court in respect of under–18s) are incorporated in Pt 1.

Provisions supplementing Section VIII are found in Section I of Practice Direction 65, as amended by CPR Update 75 (July 2014) to take account of the application of rules in Section VIII of Part 65 to proceedings under Pt I of the 2014 Act (see para.65PD.1 below). The most substantial of the 2014 amendments is para.1A which comes into force together with s.18 of the 2014 Act (see below) and which states the practice to be followed where proceedings under Pt 4 of the 2009 Act or Pt 1 of the 2014 Act which were commenced in a youth court are transferred to the High Court or the County Court after the respondent attained the age of 18.

Section 48(1) of the 2009 Act states that rules of court may provide that any power conferred on the County Court to grant, vary or discharge an injunction under Pt 4 may be exercised by a judge or a district judge. Accordingly, paras 8.1 and 8.3 of Practice Direction 2B (Allocation of Cases to Levels of Judiciary) provide that a district judge has jurisdiction to grant an injunction under Pt 4, to attach a power of arrest to such an injunction, and to make an order remanding or committing to prison a person as provided by that Part (see para.2BPD.8 above).

Section 18(1) of the 2014 Act states that rules of court may provide that an appeal from a decision of the High Court, the County Court or a youth court (a) to dismiss an application for a injunction under s.1 of the Act made without notice being given to the respondent, or (b) to refuse to grant an interim injunction when adjourning proceedings following such an application, may be made without notice being given to the respondent. Section 18(3) states that rules of court may provide for the transfer of proceedings from the youth court to the High Court or the County Court (see further para.1A of Practice Direction 65 referred to above).

Where an application is made in the County Court to commit a person to prison for breach of an injunction in the circumstances provided for by r.65.47, Sections 2 and 8 of Part 81 apply as if references in that rule to the judge include references to a district judge (r.65.47(5)).

Applications for an injunction

In rule 65.43(1), after "the 2009 Act" add:

65.43 **or Part 1 of the 2014 Act**

Injunction containing provisions to which a power of arrest is attached

In the words in parentheses after rule 65.44(1), after "2009 Act" add:

65.44 **and section 4(1)(a) and (b) and (2) of the 2014 Act**

Application to vary or discharge an injunction

In rule 65.45(1), after "2009 Act" add:

65.45 **or section 8(1)(a) and (b) of the 2014 Act**

Delete the title to rule 65.46 and substitute:

Application for warrant of arrest under section 44(2) of the 2009 Act or section 10 of the 2014 Act

In rule 65.46(1), after "2009 Act" add:

65.46 **or section 10 of the 2014 Act**

In rule 65.46(2), after "2009 Act" add:

or section 10 of the 2014 Act

Proceedings following arrest under the 2009 Act

In rule 65.47(3), after "2009 Act" add:

65.47 **or section 9 or 10 of the 2014 Act**

Recognizance

In rule 65.48(1), after "2009 Act" add:

65.48 **or paragraph 2(3)(b) of Schedule 1 to the 2014 Act**

Applications for a power of arrest to be attached to any provision of an injunction

In rule 65.49(1), after "2009 Act" add:

65.49 **or section 5 or 6 of the 2014 Act**

PRACTICE DIRECTION 65—ANTI-SOCIAL BEHAVIOUR AND HARASSMENT

Delete title "I. Housing Act 1996..." and substitute:

I. Housing Act 1996, Policing and Crime Act 2009 and Anti–Social Behaviour, Crime and Policing Act 2014

Issuing the Claim

In paragraph 1.1(1), for "1996 Act or Part 4 of the 2009 Act" substitute:

65PD.1 1996 Act, Part 4 of the 2009 Act or Part 1 of the 2014 Act

Proceedings transferred from youth court, or breach of injunction made by youth court

Delete paragraph 1A.1 and substitute:

1A.1 Where proceedings under Part 4 of the 2009 Act or Part 1 of the 2014 Act which were commenced in a youth court have been transferred to the High Court or County Court after the respondent attained the age of 18, anything done in the youth court in or in relation to those proceedings will have effect, for the purposes of continuing the proceedings in the High Court or County Court, as if it had been done in the High Court or County Court as the case may be.

1A.2 Proceedings transferred to the County Court will be sent to the County Court hearing centre which serves the address where the respondent resides.

1A.3 Where a person aged 18 or over is brought before a judge following arrest for a breach of an injunction granted by a youth court (whether pursuant to a power of arrest attached to the injunction or to a warrant issued for that person's arrest under section 44 of the 2009 Act or section 10 of the 2014 Act), it is the responsibility of the injunction applicant (within the meaning of paragraph 1(9) of Schedule 5A to the 2009 Act) or original applicant (within the meaning of paragraph 1(2) of Schedule 2 to the 2014 Act) to provide the judge with the information necessary to determine whether to deal with the matter or adjourn the proceedings under rule 65.47.

Hearings—Part 4 of the 2009 Act

Delete paragraph 1.2 and substitute:

1.2 Unless the court otherwise orders, an application on notice for an injunction under Part 4 of the 2009 Act under rule 65.43 or any other hearing in relation to such an injunction requiring the respondent's attendance must be heard at one of the following County Court hearing centres—

  (a) Birmingham
  (b) Bradford
  (c) Brighton
  (d) Bristol
  (e) Cardiff
  (f) Chelmsford
  (g) Croydon
  (h) Hammersmith (formerly known as West London)
  (i) Leicester
  (j) Liverpool
  (k) Luton
  (l) Manchester
  (m) Newcastle
  (n) Norwich
  (o) Nottingham
  (p) Oxford

(q) Peterborough

(r) Portsmouth

(s) Preston

(t) Sheffield.

(Attention is drawn to the statutory guidance on listing for hearings. These hearings will take place in courts which have been identified as having suitable facilities if special measures are needed for potential witnesses or security.)

Warrant of Arrest on an Application under Section 155(3) of the 1996 Act, Section 44(2) of the 2009 Act and Section 10 of the 2014 Act

Delete paragraph 2.1 and substitute:

65PD.2 **2.1** In accordance with section 155(4) of the 1996 Act, section 44(3) of the 2009 Act and section 10 of the 2014 Act, a warrant of arrest on an application under section 155(3) of the 1996 Act, section 44(2) of the 2009 Act or section 10 of the 2014 Act shall not be issued unless—

(1) the application is substantiated on oath; and

(2) in any proceedings under the 1996 Act or the 2014 Act the judge has reasonable grounds for believing that the defendant has failed to comply with the injunction.

Application for Bail

In paragraph 3.1(1), for "1996 Act or Part 4 of the 2009 Act" substitute:

65PD.3 1996 Act, Part 4 of the 2009 Act or Part 1 of the 2014 Act

In paragraph 3.1(2), for "1996 Act or Part 4 of the 2009 Act" substitute:

1996 Act, Part 4 of the 2009 Act or Part 1 of the 2014 Act

Remand for Medical Examination and Report

In paragraph 4.1, for "1996 Act and section 45(5) of the 2009 Act" substitute:

65PD.4 1996 Act, section 45(5) of the 2009 Act and Paragraph 6 of Schedule 1 to the 2014 Act

PART 66

CROWN PROCEEDINGS

Enforcement against the Crown

Delete rule 66.6(1)(a) and substitute:

66.6 **(a) Rules 40.8A and 70.2A and Parts 69 to 73, 81, 83 and 84; and**

Omit rule 66.6(1)(b).

Delete rule 66.6(1)(c) and substitute:

(c) CCR Orders 27 and 28

PART 67

PROCEEDINGS RELATING TO SOLICITORS

Note

Add new paragraph at end:

Claimants were represented in litigation by a firm of lawyers registered in the Brit- **67.3.1** ish Virgin Islands of whom two were British qualified solicitors. When a dispute arose over the lawyers' bill the claimants sought relief in relation to those bills under Part III of the Solicitors Act 1974. The purpose of Part III of the 1974 Act was to protect clients of solicitors and provide them with a mechanism for the assessment of fees. There was nothing to suggest that it was intended to protect clients from delinquents masquerading as solicitors. Neither estoppel nor contract could create a Part III jurisdiction where it would not otherwise exist. The application was struck out and the previous order staying arbitration between the parties was set aside: *Assaubayev & Ors v Michael Wilson & Partners Ltd* [2014] EWHC March 21 (QB) Walker J.

PRACTICE DIRECTION 67—PROCEEDINGS RELATING TO SOLICITORS

Proceedings in the Costs Office

Delete paragraph 2.2A and substitute:

2.2A Where a claim under section 70 or 71 of the Act is made by **67PD.2** Part 8 claim form in the Costs Office, the court will fix a date for a hearing at which directions will be given, unless the claim is not contested, when an order for detailed assessment will be made. Evidence need not be filed or served by either party before that hearing.

PART 68

REFERENCES TO THE EUROPEAN COURT

Editorial introduction

Add at end:

On January 31, 2014, new practice directions for parties concerning cases brought **68.0.2** before the European Court of Justice (ECJ) were published in the Official Journal (OJ 2014 L31/1). They apply to all categories of cases brought before the ECJ. They deal in detail with the conduct of proceedings before the Court and the constraints on the Court, particularly those associated with the processing and translation of procedural documents or the simultaneous interpretation of the observations submitted in the course of a hearing. They also include certain provisions previously included in Notes for the Guidance of Counsel, the Instructions to the Registrar of the Court relating to the lodging and service of procedural documents and to the actual conduct of the oral part of the procedure. They entered into force on February 1, 2014. [*http://eur–lex.europa.eu/LexUriServ/LexUriServ.do?uri=OJ:L:2014:031:0001:0013:EN:PDF*].

Effect of rule

Add at end:

And see the new practice directions in force from February 1, 2014 at [*http://eur–* **68.2.1** *lex.europa.eu/LexUriServ/LexUriServ.do?uri=OJ:L:2014:031:0001:0013:EN:PDF*].

Add new paragraph 68.3.1:

Applications for a preliminary ruling

In *Antonio Gramsci Shipping and others* (Order of the Court) (Case C–350/13__CO) **68.3.1** [2014] EUECJ (June 5, 2014) the ECJ, refusing an application from the English High Court, gave guidance on when it is required to give a preliminary ruling. The application to the ECJ related to a freezing injunction granted in the High Court but by the time the ECJ came to consider the questions put to it, the injunction had been set aside. The ECJ set out the following guidance: In exceptional circumstances the ECJ can examine the conditions of a request for a preliminary ruling, to establish whether it has jurisdiction. However, there are a number of circumstances in which it may refuse to provide a ruling, including where the problem is hypothetical (*Di Donna v Societa Imballaggi Metallici Salerno srl* (SIMSA) (Case C–492/11) [2013] EUECJ). A national court or tribunal cannot make a request for a preliminary ruling unless it is dealing with a pending case in which it is required to give a decision that is capable of taking account of the preliminary ruling and the fact that similar cases are pending before that national court is irrelevant. In the *Antonio Gramsci* case the High Court's order had been set aside and so it was no longer dealing with a pending case. Consequently the questions referred to the ECJ had become hypothetical and so the ECJ was not required to provide a ruling.

PART 70

General Rules about Enforcement of Judgments and Orders

Related sources

Delete the entries for RSC Orders 45, 46, 47, and CCR Orders 25 and 26 and substitute:
70.0.3   • Parts 83 & 84—Writs and Warrants of Control

Designated money claims

Delete paragraph 70.0.7 and substitute:
70.0.7   With effect from March 19, 2012, Practice Direction 70 was substantially amended by TSO CPR Update 58 by which it was divided into two Sections with paras 8 to 11 added as Section 2 (see para.70PD.8 below). The provisions in Section 2 deal with the automatic transfer for enforcement of judgments in "designated money claims". A designated money claim is a claim which (a) is started in the County Court under Pt 7, (b) is only a claim for either or both a specified amount of money or an unspecified amount of money, and (c) is not a claim for which special procedures are provided in the CPR (see r.2.3(1)). Such claims are issued in the National Civil Business Centre (generally known as "the Business Centre") situated at Salford. (A party commences such a claim by sending the appropriate practice form to the Business Centre; see para.7.2.2 above.) Provisions inserted in the CPR by the Civil Procedure (Amendment No.4) Rules 2011 (SI 2011/3103) and related amendments to practice directions made by TSO CPR Update 58 provide for the transfer of designated money claim cases to other hearing centres for particular purposes before judgment (see rr.3.5A, 12.5A, 14.7A, 26.2A). Further provisions inserted in Pts 71 to 73 and CCR Ord.27 by the Civil Procedure (Amendment) Rules 2012 (SI 2012/505) deal with the transfer of designated money claims for enforcement purposes. The automatic transfer provisions in Section 2 of PD70 follow from those rule amendments and come into play where applications are made for orders to obtain information, for third party debt orders, charging orders and attachment of earnings orders. See, further, commentary in paras 71.2.3, 72.3.3, 73.3.3 and cc27.3.1 below.

Methods of enforcement

For the entry "Writ of fieri" substitute:
70.2.1   Writ of control (Parts 83 & 84)

For the entry "Warrant of execution" substitute:
Warrant of control (Parts 83 & 84)

For the entry, "Sequestration…"substitute:
Sequestration (Pt 81 rr.19 to 27)

PART 71

Orders to Obtain Information from Judgment Debtors

Foreign companies

Add new paragraph at end:
71.2.7   In *CIMC Raffles Offshore (Singapore) Pte Ltd v Schahin Holdings SA* [2014] EWHC 1742

(Comm) Field J, setting aside orders made against Brazilian citizens living in Brazil said "In my judgment it is clear that the House of Lorda held in Masri that the court has no power to entertain an application or to make an order in respect of an individual who was outside the jurisdiction. In my view that means that if the individual is not within the jurisdiction at the time the application was made and at the time the order is made there is no power in the court to make an order against him."

"unless the court otherwise orders"

Delete "r.6.8" and substitute:

r.6.27 applying r.6.15   **71.3.2**

PART 74

ENFORCEMENT OF JUDGMENTS IN DIFFERENT JURISDICTIONS

Public policy

Add at end:

Note also *Joint Stock Company (Aeroflot–Russian Airlines) v Berezovsky* [2014] EWCA Civ **74.7.3**
20 at [56] to [60] where it was held that on a claim for enforcement of a foreign judgment there is a presumption that the foreign judgment is in compliance with article 6 unless the contrary is shown.

Add new paragraph 74.33.1:

Enforcement costs following rescission of EEO in court of origin

Lothschutz v Vogel [2014] EWHC 473 (QB) (24 January 2014) concerned the **74.33.1**
defendant's liability for the costs of resisting enforcement of the EEO in England. The claimant had obtained an EEO certificate in Germany upon an authentic instrument and obtained a registration order in respect of the EEO in England. The defendant lost his appeal against the registration order but shortly afterwards; the German Notary rescinded the EEO certificate. The defendant argued that the rescission of the EEO certificate entitled him to have the English court enforcement orders set aside, together with all of the costs previously ordered against him. That submission was rejected. HHJ Seymour QC stated that the law of the member state of origin (as defined by Council Regulation (EC) 805/2004) applied to the rectification or withdrawal of an EEO certificate (Article 10.2). However, enforcement procedures were governed by the law of the member state of enforcement (Article 20.1). It was held that, once an EEO certificate had been delivered to the English court, the court had no option but to permit enforcement and could not review its substance. There is no mechanism for a challenge in this court to the validity of the EEO certificate (Article 21). The court's powers if an EEO certificate is withdrawn are limited to exercising its powers under Article 23. The court had no power to allow the defendant a further appeal and, if it did, it should not exercise its power to do so. The orders for costs were not dependent on the validity of the EEO certificate, but on the validity of English court orders which could not be challenged further.

PART 81

APPLICATIONS AND PROCEEDINGS IN RELATION TO CONTEMPT OF COURT

Structure of Part 81

Delete the last paragraph and substitute:

In the Family Procedure Rules 2014 (SI 2010/2955), Part 37 contains rules compa- **81.0.3**
rable to those found in CPR Pt 81. Part 37 was inserted in the FPR when the Family

Court was established on April 22, 2014. At the same time, the Contempt of Court Act 1984 s.14 was amended for the purpose of enabling Regulations to be made specifying the contempt powers exercisable by judges of different levels sitting in the Family Court (see further Vol. 2 para.3C–88).

Enforcement against body corporate

Add new paragraph at end:

81.4.5   In *Dar Al Arkan Real Estate Development Co v Al Refai* [2014] EWCA Civ 715, May 23, 2014, CA, the Court of Appeal rejected the submission that the principle against the extra–territorial effect of legislation meant that r.81.4(3) cannot be properly construed to enable a committal order to be made against a foreign director who is not within the jurisdiction and cannot be served in England. In that case, a foreign company instituted proceedings within the jurisdiction but failed to comply with orders of the court and the defendants applied for a declaration that they were in contempt, for orders that they be fined and that a director, being a foreign national not within the jurisdiction, be imprisoned. The Court upheld the judge's decision that the proceedings against the director were within the scope of r.81.4(1) and (3).

Corporation required "to do or not do the act in question"

For "r.81.3(5)" substitute:

81.5.2   r.81.3(c)

Add new paragraph at end:

In *Dar Al Arkan Real Estate Development Co v Al Refai* [2014] EWCA Civ 715, May 23, 2014, CA, where the defendants made an application for permission to serve committal proceedings on a director of a foreign claimant company who was a foreign national and outside the jurisdiction, the Court of Appeal upheld the judge's ruling that permission to effect service on the director could and should be granted under r.6.36 and Practice Direction 6B para.3.1(3)(b).

Effect of rule

At the end of the second paragraph, add:

81.11.1   See further commentary in Vol.2 para.3C–24 ("Enforcement by committal order of solicitor's undertaking").

Court to which application for permission under this Section is to be made

In rule 81.13(1)(d), for "Queen's Bench Division" substitute:

81.13   High Court

Certifications of conduct, and applications under section 336 of the Charities Act 2011, to the High Court under this Section

In rule 81.15(1), after "tribunal" add:

81.15   , body

Scope of Section

After the third paragraph, add as a new paragraph:

81.15.1   By an amendment made by the Civil Procedure (Amendment No.6) Rules 2014 (SI 2014/2044) and taking effect on October 1, 2014, r.81.15(1) was extended to apply to acts or omission done, not only in relation to "a court, tribunal or person", but also in relation to a "body". This was done to accommodate the granting to the Independent Police Complaints Commission of the power to "certify in writing to the High Court" that a person had failed to comply with an "information notice", thereby invoking the High Court's jurisdiction to "deal with the person as if the person had committed a contempt of court" (Police Reform Act 2002 s.19ZB).

Committal application in relation to a false statement of truth or disclosure statement

In rule 81.18(3)(a), for "Queen's Bench Division" substitute:

High Court
81.18

Hearing date—adjournment or stay

Add new paragraph at end:

Where it arises, the question whether a committal application should be heard **81.28.2** before or after the trial is a decision for the judge's case management discretion and there is certainly no rule of law as to the timetable to be adopted (*Dar Al Arkan Real Estate Development Co v Al Refai* [2014] EWHC 1055 (Comm), April 1, 2014, unrep. (Andrew Smith J.), where held that, in the circumstances, the committal application should be heard well before trial because that timetable was preferable in order to uphold the court's authority and to work fairness between the parties).

Offences under section 124 of the Act

In rule 81.35, for "an officer of the court" substitute:

a person
81.35

Non–payment of fine

In rule 81.37(3), for "execution", substitute:

control
81.37

PART 82

Closed Material Procedure

Editorial Introduction

In the last paragraph, for "CF v Security Service [2013] EWHC 3401 (QB), November 7, 2013, unrep. (Irwin J.)" substitute:

F v Security Service [2013] EWHC 3402 (QB); [2014] 1 W.L.R. 1699 (Irwin J.) **82.0.2**

PART 83

Writs and Warrants—General Provisions

In the Contents, after the entry for rule 83.2, add:

Contents
83.0.1

83.2A	Application for permission to issue a writ of sequestration	para.83.2A

Editorial introduction

Delete the third paragraph and substitute:

These new Parts were effected by the Civil Procedure (Amendment) Rules 2014 (SI **83.0.2** 2014/407) and are in force from April 6, 2014. The transitional arrangements are set out below.

Transitional arrangements

Delete the first sentence and substitute:

83.0.3 The transitional arrangements for Pts 83 and 84 (up to 84.16) are set out at para.41(1)–(3) of the Civil Procedure (Amendment) Rules 2014 (SI 2014/407).

Add at end:

Separate transitional arrangements apply in respect of enforcement agents certificates and these are set out in the Certification of Enforcement Agents Regulations at reg.14.

Enforcement Agent

Add at end:

83.0.8 The Certification of Enforcement Agent Regulations 2014 (see SI 2014/421) and r.84.18 set out the procedure for obtaining a certificate to operate as an enforcement agent. For text of SI 2014/421, see Vol. 2, para.9B–1432 et seq.

Exempt goods

After "regs 4 and 5 of the Taking Control of Goods Regulations 2013" add:

83.0.12 , see Vol.2 paras 9A–1237 and 9A–1238 for the full detail

Add at end:

The procedure for a debtor to make a claim to exempt goods is set out in r.85.8.

Goods owned by debtor and third person

Add at end:

83.0.16 See Part 85 generally in respect of claims on controlled goods.

Related Sources

Add at end:

83.0.20 ● The Certification of Enforcement Agents Regulations 2014 (2014/421)

Forms

Delete paragraph 83.0.21 and substitute:

83.0.21
● **Form 53** Writ of control
● **Form 54** Writ of control on order for costs
● **Form 56** Writ of control (of Part)
● **Form 58** Writ of fieri facias de bonis ecclesiasticis
● **Form 59** Writ of sequestrari de bonis ecclesiasticis
● **Form 62** Writ of control to enforce Northern Irish or Scottish judgment
● **Form 63** Writ of control to enforce foreign registered judgment
● **Form 64** Writ of specific delivery: delivery of goods, damages and costs
● **Form 65** Writ of delivery of goods or value, damages and costs
● **Form 66** Combined writ of possession and control
● **Form 66A** Combined writ of possession and control for costs of action
● **Form 67** Writ of sequestration
● **Form 68** Writ of restitution
● **Form 69** Writ of assistance
● **Form 71** Notice of the extension of a writ of execution
● **N42** Warrant of control
● **N46** Warrant of delivery and of control for damages and costs
● **N49** Warrant for possession of land
● **N50** Warrant of restitution
● **N51** Warrant of Restitution (trespass)
● **N52** Warrant for Possession of Land (Trespassers)
● **N244** Application notice
● **N245** Application for suspension of warrant (and for variation of an instalment)
● **N246** Claimant's reply to defendant's application to vary instalment order

- **N246A** Claimant's reply to defendant's application to suspend warrant
- **N322** Order for recovery of money awarded by tribunal
- **N322A** Application for order to recover money awarded by tribunal or other body
- **N322H** Request to register a High Court judgment or order for enforcement
- **N323** Request for a warrant of control
- **N324** Request for warrant of delivery of goods
- **N325** Request for warrant of possession
- **N326** Notice of issue of warrant of control
- **N327** Notice of issue of warrant of control to enforce a judgment or order
- **N328** Notice of transfer of proceedings to the High Court
- **N444** Details of sale under a warrant of control

II. Writs and Warrants

Writs and warrants of control, writs of execution, warrants of delivery and warrants of possession—permission to issue certain writs or warrants

In rule 83.2, after paragraph (7), insert:

(7A) Where— **83.2**
  (a) **the court grants permission, under this rule or otherwise, for the issue of a writ of execution or writ of control ("the permission order"); and**
  (b) **the writ is not issued within one year after the date of the permission order,**
the permission order will cease to have effect.
(7B) Where a permission order has ceased to have effect, the court may grant a fresh permission order.

Effect of rule

In the second paragraph, for "para.2E–252", substitute:
  para. 2E–241 **83.2.1**

Add new rule 83.2A:

Application for permission to issue a writ of sequestration

83.2A Notwithstanding anything in rule 83.2, an application for 83.2A permission to issue a writ of sequestration must be made in accordance with Part 81 and in particular Section 7 of that Part.

Writs and warrants— levying execution on certain days[1]

Delete rule 83.6 and substitute:

83.6—(1) This rule applies to writs and warrants other than— 83.6
  (a) **writs of control;**
  (b) **warrants of control; and**
  (c) **writs or warrants in relation to an Admiralty claim in rem.**
(2) Where a writ or warrant is not a writ of control or warrant of control but nevertheless confers the power to use the TCG proce-

---

[1] Amended by the Civil Procedure (Amendment No. 6) Rules (SI 2014/2044).

dure, this rule applies to the parts of the writ or warrant that do not confer the power to use the TCG Procedure.

(3) Unless the court orders otherwise, a writ or warrant to enforce a judgment or order must not be executed on a Sunday, Good Friday or Christmas Day.

Effect of the rule

Delete the first sentence and substitute:

83.6.1   This rule was substituted by the Civil Procedure (Amendment No.6) Rules 2014 (SI 2014/2044), with effect from October 1, 2014, for the purpose of correcting an unintended consequence inherent in the rule as originally enacted. The necessary correction is made by what is now para.(2) in the rule. As originally enacted, para.(1) stated that the rule did not apply, not only to the writs or warrants now listed in paras (a) to (c) therefore, but also to any other writs or warrants "that confer a power to use the TCG procedure". The unintended consequence was that, where a writ or warrant contained both taking control of goods elements and non–taking control of goods elements, an Enforcement Officer could levy on certain elements of a hybrid writ or warrant at any time. This rule provides that writs and warrants, other than those set out in r.83.6(1)(a)–(c), but including those covered by para.(2) must not be executed on a Sunday, Good Friday or Christmas Day.

III. Writs

Issue of writs of execution and writs of control

Add new rule 83.9(1)(ca):

83.9   (ca) where the proceedings are in the Chancery Division, Chancery Chambers;

Effect of the rule

For "Although only concerned with writs, this" substitute:

83.18.1   This

Restrictions

For "writs", in each place it occurs, substitute:

83.18.2   warrants

Add new paragraph 83.22.1.1:

r.22(2)(a)

83.22.1.1   The enforcement agent must then issue a Notice of Abandonment of Goods—see the appropriate form appended to the Certification of Enforcement Agents Regulations 2014.

Failure to supply an inventory

Add at end:

83.24.4   The form of inventory is appended to the Certification of Enforcement Agents Regulations 2014.

PART 84

ENFORCEMENT BY TAKING CONTROL OF GOODS

In the Contents, after the entry for rule 84.16, add:

84.0.1 Contents

IV. Proceedings in relation to certificates under section 64 of the 2007 Act

Editorial information

In the first paragraph delete from "Part 84 needs to be read" to the end and substitute:

Rules 84.17 to 84.20 deal with the certification of and complaints against enforce- **84.0.2** ment agents. The certification procedure is dealt with in the Certification of Enforcement Agents Regulations 2014 (2014/421). Part 84 needs to be read in conjunction with s.64 and Sch.12 to the Tribunals, Courts and Enforcement Act 2007 and the three sets of regulations as the detailed provisions to which the applications relate are to be found in the statute and the regulations. Web links to the provisions of Sch.12 and the first two mentioned regulations are set out in 84PD 1.1.

Overview

Add at end:

Rules 84.17 to 84.20 deal exclusively with applications for enforcement agent certi- **84.0.3** fication and complaints against enforcement agents. Relevant documentation and information required in support of these procedures is set out in Section 2 of the Practice Direction to this part.

Controlled goods agreements

After "written controlled goods agreement." add:

A form of Controlled Goods Agreement is appended to the Certification of Enforce- **84.0.4** ment Agents Regulations 2014.

Add new paragraph 84.0.5.1:

Proceedings relating to certificates to act as an enforcement agent

Section IV (rr.84.17 to 84.20) was added to this Part by the Civil Procedure (Amend- **84.0.5.1** ment No.2) Rules 2014 (SI 2014/482) with effect from April 6, 2014 (subject to transitional provisions in r.5, see further below).

Under the Tribunals, Courts and Enforcement Act 2007 s.64 (1) (as amended by the Crime and Courts Act 2013) a certificate to act as an enforcement agent may be issued by a judge of the County Court. Power to make regulations about enforcement agent certificates is granted to the Lord Chancellor by s.64(2). Regulations made in exercise of that power are the Certification of Enforcement Agents Regulations 2014 (SI 2014/421). Those Regulations (the Certification Regulations) came into effect on April 6, 2014, and make provision for the process by which persons who may, by virtue of s.63 of the 2007 Act, require a certificate in order to act as enforcement agents are issued with a certificate. (For text of these Regulations, see Vol. 2, para.9B–1432 et seq.) They also provide for the issue of replacement certificates and the surrender of certificates, and for complaints as to fitness to hold a certificate. All of those matters may involve applications to the County Court. Necessary rules of court for the handling of such applications are provided in Section IV of Part 84 and are supplemented by directions in para.2 of Practice Direction 84 made by CPR Update 70 (see para.84PD.3 below).

A certificate under the Law of Distress Amendment Act 1888 s.7 which is in force on April 6, 2014, has effect as a certificate under s.64 effect for the period provided for when it was granted (s.64(4) and reg.15).

Paragraph (1) of reg.14 of the Certification Regulations states that the Distress for Rent Rules 1988 (see Vol. 2 para.9B–1365) continue to apply in relation to (a) an application for the grant of a certificate which was made before April 6, 2014, by a person who does not hold a certificate but was not determined before that date; (b) an application for the grant of a certificate to replace an existing certificate which ceases to have effect on or before August 6, 2014. Paragraph (2) states that a certificate granted on or after April 6, 2014, pursuant to an application referred to in para.(1)(a) or (b) has effect as a certificate under s.64 of the 2007 Act in the same way as a certificate under s.7 of the 1888 Act which is in force on that date.

Rule 5 of the Civil Procedure (Amendment No.2) Rules 2014 (SI 2014/482) recognises that, as the rules in Section IV come into effect on April 6, 2014, they will apply before the establishment of the "single" County Court on April 22, 2014, and therefore will apply in the existing several county courts during the intervening period. Between the two dates, rr.84.18, 84.19 and 84.20 have effect has provided in r.5.

Related sources

Add at end:

84.0.6   ● The Certification of Enforcement Agents Regulations 2014 (2014/421)

Forms

Add at end:

84.0.7   ● **EAC 1** Application for certificate to act as an enforcement agent
            ● **EAC 2** Complaint against a certificated person

Effect of rule

In first paragraph, after "control of the debtor's goods." add:

84.4.1   The form of notice is appended to the Certification of Enforcement Agents Regulations 2014.

Effect of rule

Add at end:

84.8.1   A form of notice to re–enter premises is appended to the Certification of Enforcement Agents Regulations 2014.

Effect of rule

For "final" substitute:

84.14.1   next

After rule 84.16, insert new Section IV to Part 84:

IV. Proceedings in relation to certificates under section 64 of the 2007 Act

Interpretation
84.17   **84.17 In this Section—**
            (a) "Certification Regulations" means the Certification of Enforcement Agents Regulations 2014;
            (b) "applicant", "certificate", "certificated person" and "complainant" have the meanings given in regulation 2 of the Certification Regulations.

Effect of Section

84.17.1   This Section was added to Part 84 by the Civil Procedure (Amendment No.2) Rules 2014 (SI 2014/482). See further para.84.0.5.1 above.

Application for issue of a certificate under section 64 of the 2007 Act
84.18   **84.18—(1) This rule applies to an application for the issue of a certificate under section 64 of the 2007 Act.**
            (2) The application must be made to the County Court Business Centre, using the relevant form prescribed in Practice Direction 4.
            (3) The application must specify one of the County Court hearing centres listed in Practice Direction 84 as the centre at which the application is to be heard.

(4) The application must, in addition to the matters specified in rule 23.6, provide evidence that the applicant fulfils the requirements of regulation 3(b) of the Certification Regulations, and in particular—

    (a) the application must be accompanied by the documents specified in Practice Direction 84; and

    (b) the additional documents specified in Practice Direction 84 must be produced to the court on the day of the hearing.

(5) If any reasons have been submitted to the court in response to the notice of the application required by regulation 4(5) of the Certification Regulations, a copy of those reasons must be sent to the applicant at least 7 days before the hearing, and the applicant may respond both in writing and at the hearing.

(6) The applicant must also file such further evidence as the court may direct.

(7) The applicant must attend for examination on the day of the hearing.

(8) Rules 23.2, 23.4, 23.7, 23.8, 23.9 and 23.10 do not apply to an application to which this rule applies.

r.84.18(2)

Note that the application must be made to the "business centre" rather than to one **84.18.1** of the local hearing centre, even though the applicant must specify at which of the local hearing centres the application should be heard.

"using the relevant form"

Form **EAC 1**.   **84.18.2**

r.84.18(4)

Note that the application must provide the information and documentation referred **84.18.3** to in both the PD to this part and in the Certification of Enforcement Agents Regulations 2014.

Issue of replacement certificates and surrender of certificates

84.19—(1) Where changes are required to be notified and the cer- 84.19 tificate produced under regulation 8 of the Certification Regulations, the changes must be notified to, and the certificate produced at, the County Court hearing centre at which the certificate was issued.

(2) Where a certificate is required to be surrendered under regulation 12 of the Certification Regulations, the certificate must be surrendered to the County Court hearing centre at which the certificate was issued.

Complaints as to fitness to hold a certificate

84.20—(1) This rule applies to a complaint under regulation 9(1) 84.20 of the Certification Regulations.

(2) The complaint must be submitted to the County Court hearing centre at which the certificate was issued, using the relevant form prescribed in Practice Direction 4.

(3) A copy of the complaint must be sent to the applicant at least

14 days before the hearing, and the applicant may respond both in writing and at the hearing.

(4) The complainant is not liable for any costs incurred by the certificated person in responding to the complaint, unless paragraph (5) applies.

(5) The court may order the complainant to pay such costs as it considers reasonable if it is satisfied that the complaint—

> **(a) discloses no reasonable grounds for considering that the certificated person is not a fit person to hold a certificate; and**
>
> **(b) amounts to an abuse of the court's process.**

"using the relevant form"

84.20.1   Form **EAC 2**.

PRACTICE DIRECTION 84—ENFORCEMENT BY TAKING CONTROL OF GOODS

After paragraph 1.3, insert:

Part 84—Section IV—Proceedings in relation to certificates under section 64 of the 2007 Act

84PD.3 Rule 84.18—Documents to accompany application for issue of a certificate

> **2.1**(1) The application for the issue of a certificate must state the applicant's name (and employer, if any), and be accompanied by the following—
>
> (a) two references, of which—
>
>> (i) one may be from the applicant's employer or an approved officer of the Civil Enforcement Association or of the High Court Enforcement Officers' Association; and
>>
>> (ii) one must deal with the applicant's knowledge of the law and procedure relating to powers of enforcement by taking control of goods and commercial rent arrears recovery, and the applicant's experience of, and conduct in, exercising such powers;
>
> (b) a certified copy of the result of a search (which must be no more than one month old) of the Register of judgments, orders, fines and tribunal decisions against—
>
>> (i) the applicant's full name; and
>>
>> (ii) the applicant's home and business addresses for the last six years;
>
> (c) two passport–sized photographs of the applicant (one to be retained on the court file and the other to be affixed to the certificate if issued);
>
> (d) a copy (which must conform to the design and layout prescribed in the Schedule to the Certification Regulations and be on paper of durable quality and in a clear and legible printed or typewritten form with a font size no less than 10 point) of each of the following forms required by the TCG Regulations and intended to be used by the applicant when exercising powers of taking control of goods or commercial rent arrears recovery—
>
>> (i) notice of enforcement (required by Regulation 7);
>>
>> (ii) controlled goods agreement (required by Regulation 15);

    (iii) warning of immobilisation (required by Regulation 16(3));

    (iv) notice of re–entry (required by Regulation 26);

    (v) notice after entry or taking control of goods on a highway and inventory of goods taken into control (required by Regulation 30);

    (vi) notice of removal for storage or sale (required by Regulation 32);

    (vii) inventory of goods (required by Regulation 33);

    (viii) notice of sale (required by Regulation 39);

    (ix) notice of abandonment (required by Regulation 47(3));

  (e) proof that the applicant—

    (i) has achieved at least a qualification on Taking Control of Goods at (or above) Level 2 of the Qualifications and Credit Framework or equivalent as determined by a nationally accredited awarding body; or

    (ii) has been authorised to act as an enforcement officer in accordance with the High Court Enforcement Officers Regulations 2004.

(2) In addition, the applicant must produce to the court on the date of the hearing—

  (a) a certified copy of a—

    (i) criminal conviction certificate;

    (ii) criminal record certificate; or

    (iii) enhanced criminal record certificate

issued pursuant to Part V of the Police Act 1997 and which is not more than one month old;

  (b) written evidence of the lodging by way of bond of the security required by regulation 6 of the Certification Regulations.

Rule 84.18—Application for issue of a certificate

2.2 The County Court hearing centres referred to in rule 84.18(3) are—

London
Central London
Midlands
Birmingham
Northampton
Nottingham
Worcester
North–East
Gateshead
Kingston Upon Hull
Middlesbrough
York
North–West
Birkenhead
Burnley
Oldham
South–East
Brighton

Chelmsford
Dartford
Hertford
Norwich
Oxford
South–West
Bristol
Plymouth
Southampton
Wales
Caernarfon
Cardiff
Swansea
Wrexham

PART 85

CLAIMS ON CONTROLLED GOODS AND EXECUTED GOODS

Commencement date and transitional provisions

Delete paragraph 85.0.4 and substitute:

85.0.4   Rule 85 takes effect on April 6, 2014 and applies to disputes relating to writs or warrants issued on or after that date (Civil Procedure Amendment Rules 2014 (SI 2014/407), r.41).

Add new paragraph 85.0.6:

Claim made by the debtor that goods are exempt from execution

85.0.6   The Taking Control of Goods Regulations 2013 (regs.4 and 5) sets out a lengthy and non exclusive list of goods which are protected against execution. In summary these are the items needed by the debtor to work or study up to a total value of £1350 plus personal and domestic items used by the debtor and his family.

Part 85 sets out a step by step process for the debtor making a claim that goods are exempt and thus protected from removal and provide a strict timetable to be followed by the debtor, the enforcement officer/relevant enforcement officer, the creditor/any other claimants to the goods.

>**Step 1**: The debtor must make his claim in writing to the enforcement agent as soon as practicable and in any event within 7 days of the removal of the goods. Rule 85.8(1) sets out the information which the claim must set out which includes not only the grounds for the claim but a full list of the items claimed.
>**Step 2**: The enforcement agent then notifies the judgment creditor and any other claimants to the goods of the debtors claim; this must be done within 3 days of the debtors claim (rule 85.8(2)).
>**Step 3**: Those notified under step 2 must respond within 7 days stating if they contest or accept the debtors claim. The next steps depend on whether the claim is contested or accepted.
>**Step 4 If the debtors claim is accepted within 7 days under step 3**: If the creditor accepts the claim within this time limit of 7 days this affords protection not only to the creditor but also to the debtors goods ; the creditor is protected against any costs and fees and expenses incurred by the enforcement officer after the receipt of the notice (rule 85.8(5)) plus the debtors goods are protected against enforcement action and the enforcement officer must make the goods available ,if removed, for collection by the debtor as soon as reasonably practicable, or
>**Step 4 If the creditor does not respond under step 3 within 7 days**: If the creditor or other claimants do not respond within 7 days the enforcement

agent may seek directions from the court and an order protecting them from a claim made if they seize the goods.

Add new paragraph 85.0.7:

Debtors application to the court

If the creditor maintains the claim to the goods which the debtor says are exempt the procedures set out in r.85.9 apply; the burden falling upon the debtor to make a claim to the court by application within 7 days. **85.0.7**

Add new paragraph 85.0.8:

Related sources

- The Taking Control of Goods Regulations Volume 2, Section 9A, 9A–1233. **85.0.8**
- The Taking Control of Goods (Fees) Regulations Volume 2, Section 9A, 9A–1289.

PART 86

STAKEHOLDER CLAIMS AND APPLICATIONS

Commencement date and transitional provisions

Delete paragraph 86.0.4 and substitute:

These new rules were effected by the Civil Procedure (Amendment) Rules 2014 (SI 2014/407) and come into force on April 6, 2014. **86.0.4**

SCHEDULE 1

RSC ORDER 115—CONFISCATION AND FORFEITURE IN CONNECTION WITH CRIMINAL PROCEEDINGS

"restraint order ... charging order"

1988 Act

For "For an explanation of the provisions see R. v Benjafield, R. v Rezvi [2003] 1 A.C. 1099, HL and [2008] 1 A.C. 1028." substitute:

For an explanation of the provisions see *R. v Benjafield; R. v Rezvi* [2003] 1 A.C. 1099, HL, *May* [2008] 1 A.C. 1028 and *R. v Ahmad (Shakeel)* [2014] UKSC 36; [2014] 3 W.L.R. 23. **sc115.3.1**

In the last paragraph, after "Whether to make such an order is a question of judicial discretion.", add:

The prosecutor should carefully consider whether a restraint order is justified as, if it is not, it is liable to cause more harm than good. Even if the statutory conditions for grant are made out, the court must analyse the potential adverse consequences to the defendant (*CPS v Eastenders Group* [2014] 2 W.L.R. 1269).

The principles which govern that discretion are similar to those applicable to CPR Pt 25 freezing orders (*SFO v X* [2005] EWCA Vic 1564). In particular, the applicant must demonstrate a risk of dissipation of assets, otherwise the restraint order has no proper purpose and would amount to a disproportionate interference with property rights conferred by art.1 of protocol 1 of the European Convention on Human Rights (see *Jennings v CPS* [2006] 1 W.L.R. 182; *R v B* [2008] EWCA Crim 1374). If there has been a breach of the duty of full and frank disclosure, the Court should not discharge the order, unless the failure to comply with the duty is appalling; instead the failure should be marked by an order for costs against the prosecutor (*Jennings* (above) and see *Director of Serious Fraud Office v A* [2007] EWCA Crim 1947.).

Restraint order

After the eighth paragraph, add as a new paragraph:

sc115.4.4 As with a civil freezing order, incurring legal fees whilst subject to a restraint order does not amount to a dealing with assets so is not a breach of a restraint order (*Revell–Reade v Serious Fraud Office* [2013] EWHC 1483 (Admin)).

"application ... under section 29"

After the fourth paragraph, add as a new paragraph:

sc115.7.1 It is an abuse of process or otherwise impermissible for the defendant against whom the confiscation order was made to claim in receivership proceedings a lesser interest in property than that found by the Crown Court when the confiscation order was made (*Price, Re* [2013 EWHC 2859 (Admin)).

"where a receiver is appointed"

Delete the third paragraph and substitute:

sc115.8.3 *Hughes* and *Capewell* were approved in general terms by the Supreme Court in *CPS v Eastenders Group* [2014] 2 W.L.R. 1269. The Court explained that where a management receivership order was set aside, the receiver was generally entitled to remuneration out of the assets at common law. Generally, receivership orders made under the confiscation legislation were compatible with the ECHR, article 1 protocol 1. However, where there was no reasonable cause to believe benefit from crime (a statutory requirement for grant of a receivership order) then there could be a breach of an innocent person's A1 P1 rights if assets became subject to a receivership order from which receivership costs would normally be paid. This did not mean that the receiver could not recover his remuneration and expenses for the period when in office. This should be paid for by the CPS on contractual principles. Further, when granting a receivership order in the first place, even if the statutory conditions for an order are made out, the court must consider carefully the potential adverse consequences to the respondents. It may be that the court should direct when appointing a receiver that if the assets turn out to be belong to a third party, the receivership costs should be paid by the prosecutor.

Following a receiver's formal discharge by the court, he continues to be an officer of the court and subject to its jurisdiction. He continues to be entitled to charge remuneration for post–discharge services *Glatt v Sinclair* [2013] 1 W.L.R. 3602.

"certificate under section 17(1)"

After the third paragraph (ending "EWHC 1231 (Admin)" add as a new paragraph:

sc115.9.1 Where the prosecution and defence agreed the extent of the defendant's assets at the confiscation hearing, the prosecution is not bound by that finding on an application for a certificate of inadequacy if it is apparent that the defendant misled the prosecutor and the court as to the limit of his assets when the order was made (*Adams, Re* [2014] EWHC 2639 (Admin)).

SCHEDULE 2

Please note the following general amendments made by the Civil Procedure (Amendment No.4) Rules 2014 (SI 2014/867): In CCR Orders 1, 28, 39, 44 and 49—unless amended elsewhere in these rules—(i) for "a county court", in each place, substitute "the County Court"; (ii) for "county court", in each place, substitute "County Court"; (iii) for "county courts", in each place, substitute "the County Court"; and (iv) for "district judge", in each place, substitute "District Judge".

CCR ORDER 1—CITATION, APPLICATION AND INTERPRETATION

Application of RSC to County Court proceedings

cc1.6 *In CCR Order 1, rule 6(b), for "registrar" substitute:*

Registrar

In CCR Order 1, rule 6(b), for "taxing officer" substitute:

Taxing Officer

In CCR Order 1, rule 6(d), for "County Court office" substitute:

office of a County Court hearing centre

CCR ORDER 16—TRANSFER OF PROCEEDINGS

Omit CCR Order 16.

CCR ORDER 27—ATTACHMENT OF EARNINGS

Venue

Add new paragraph at end:

Paragraph (4) of this rule was amended by r.39(d) of the Civil Procedure (Amend- **cc27.3.1** ment) Rules 2014 (SI 2014/407) with effect from the date of the commencement of legislation creating the single County Court. The instruction in r.39(d) relating to para.(4) is not wholly comprehensible. The text of that provision has been rendered above in the manner in which White Book editors believe was intended.

Mode of applying

Delete paragraph (1)(b) and substitute:

(b) a witness statement or affidavit verifying the amount due **cc27.4** under the order or, if payments under the order are required to be made to the designated officer for the magistrates' court, a certificate by that designated officer to the same effect.

Omit Order 27, rule 4(2) (omitted by the Crime and Courts Act 2013 (Family Court: Consequential Provision) (No.2) Order 2014, (SI 2014/879) reg.77, with effect from April 22, 2014).

Add new paragraph cc27.4.1:

Enforcing order of magistrates' court

Rule 39(e) of the Civil Procedure (Amendment) Rules 2014 (SI 2014/407) purported **cc27.4.1** to amend sub–paragraph (b) of para.(1) of this rule but that amendment was misconceived because it failed to take account of the amendment made to that provision by para.176 of the Courts Act 2003 (Consequential Provisions) (No.2) Order 2005 (SI 2005/617), substituting "designated officer" for "justices' chief executive". Paragraph (2) of this rule was revoked by SI 2014/879, with effect from April 22, 2014.

Forms

Add at end:

Rule 39(k) of the Civil Procedure (Amendment) Rules 2014 (SI 2014/407) purported **cc27.10.1** to amend para.(3) of this rule but that amendment was misconceived because it failed to take account of the amendment made to that provision by para.176 of the Courts Act 2003 (Consequential Provisions) (No.2) Order 2005 (SI 2005/617), substituting "designated officer" for "justices' chief executive".

CCR ORDER 28—JUDGMENT SUMMONSES

In the Contents, delete the entry for rule 12.

Application for judgment summons

In CCR Order 28, for rule 1(1), substitute:

(1) An application for the issue of a judgment summons may be **cc28.1** made to the County Court hearing centre which serves the address where the debtor resides or carries on business or, if the summons is to issue against two or more persons jointly liable under the judgment or order sought to be enforced, in the County Court hear-

ing centre which serves the address where any of the debtors resides or carries on business.

In CCR Order 28, rule 1(2), for "his" substitute:

the

In CCR Order 28, rule 1(3), for "he" substitute:

the judgment creditor

Mode of service

In CCR Order 28, rule 2(2), for "within the district of the court" substitute:

cc28.2   at an address which is served by the County Court hearing centre

In CCR Order 28, rule 2(3), for "him" substitute:

the debtor

In CCR Order 28, rule 2(3)(a), for "he" substitute:

the debtor

Enforcement of debtor's attendance

In CCR Order 28, rule 4(2), for "his" substitute:

cc28.4   the debtor's

In CCR Order 28, rule 4(2), delete "to him".

Evidence

In CCR Order 28, rule 5(1)(b)(i), for "he has made default" substitute:

cc28.5   default has been made

Suspension of committal order

In CCR Order 28, rule 7(1), for "judge" substitute:

cc28.7   court

In CCR Order 28, rule 7(3), for "judge" substitute:

court

In CCR Order 28, rule 7(4), for "he desires" substitute:

desired

In CCR Order 28, rule 7(4), for "his" substitute:

the debtor's

In CCR Order 28, rule 7(4), for "judge" substitute:

court

New order on judgment summons

In CCR Order 28, rule 8(1), for "judge" substitute:

cc28.8   court

Costs on judgment summons

cc28.10 *In CCR Order 28, rule 10(2)(a)(i), for "judge" substitute:*

court

Issue of warrant of committal

cc28.11 *Omit CCR Order 28, rule 11(3).*

Omit CCR Order 28, rule 12.

Payment after debtor lodged in prison

In CCR Order 28, rule 13(1)(a), delete "responsible for the execution of the warrant".   **cc28.13**

Omit CCR Order 28, rule 13(1)(b).

In CCR Order 28, rule 13(1)(c), for "he" substitute:

the gaoler

Discharge of debtor otherwise than on payment

In CCR Order 28, rule 14(1), for "the district judge", both times it appears, substitute:

the court   **cc28.14**

For CCR Order 28, rule 14(2) substitute:

(2) Where a debtor who has been lodged in prison under a warrant of committal desires to apply for discharge under section 121 of the Act, the application shall be made to the judge in writing and without notice showing the reasons why the debtor alleges that the debtor is unable to pay the sum in respect of which the debtor has been committed and ought to be discharged and stating any offer which the debtor desires to make as to the terms on which discharge is to be ordered, and, Order 27 rule 8(3) and (4), shall apply, with the necessary modifications, as it applies to an application by a debtor for discharge from custody under section 23(7) of the Attachment of Earnings Act 1971.

In CCR Order 28, rule 14(3), for "judge" substitute:

court

CCR ORDER 39—ADMINISTRATION ORDERS

In the Contents in the entry for rule 1, delete "by district judge".

In CCR Order 39, rule 1, for the title, substitute:

Exercise of powers

In CCR Order 39, rule 1, for "the district judge" substitute:

a judge of the County Court   **cc39.1**

Request and list of creditors

In CCR Order 39, rule 2(1), for "in the court for the district in which he" substitute:

at the County Court hearing centre which serves the address where **cc39.2**
the debtor

In CCR Order 39, rule 2(2) substitute:

(2) Where on examination under CPR Part 71, or otherwise, a debtor furnishes to the court on oath a list of creditors and the amounts owed to them respectively and sufficient particulars of the debtor's resources and needs, the court may proceed as if the debtor has filed a request under paragraph (1).

Orders made by the court officer

In CCR Order 39, rule 5(2), for "he" substitute:

the court officer   **cc39.5**

In CCR Order 39, rule 5(2)(a), for "him", in the first place it appears, substitute:

the debtor

In CCR Order 39, rule 5(2)(a), delete "he may have".

In CCR Order 39, rule 5(2)(a), for "notification upon him" substitute:

that notification

In CCR Order 39, rule 5(2)(c), for "he" substitute:

the creditor

In CCR Order 39, rule 5(2)(c), for "him" substitute:

the creditor

In CCR Order 39, rule 5(4), for "district judge" substitute:

court

In CCR Order 39, rule 5(5), for "he", in the first place it appears, substitute:

the court officer

In CCR Order 39, rule 5(5), for "he shall refer the request to the district judge" substitute:

the request shall be referred to the court

In CCR Order 39, rule 5(6), for "district judge considers that he is" substitute:

the court considers that it is

In CCR Order 39, rule 5(6), after "in the list" add:

may be fixed

For CCR Order 39, rule 5(8), substitute:

Where the court does not fix the proposed rate under paragraph (6), it will direct the court officer to fix a day for a hearing at which the court will decide whether an administration order should be made and the court officer shall give not less than 14 days' notice of the day so fixed to the debtor and to each creditor mentioned in the list provided by the debtor.

Notice of objection by creditor

In CCR Order 39, rule 6(1) for "his" substitute:

cc39.6   that

In CCR Order 39, rule 6(1) for "he objects" substitute:

the objection is made.

In CCR Order 39, rule 6(2) for "he has given notice of his" substitute:

that creditor has given notice of the

Procedure on day of hearing

cc39.7   *In CCR Order 39, rule 7(a), delete "he is".*

In CCR Order 39, rule 7(a) for "his" substitute:

their

In CCR Order 39, rule 7(c) for "his" substitute:

that

Service of order

cc39.9   *In CCR Order 39, rule 9(c) for "his" substitute:*

their

In CCR Order 39, rule 9(d) for "district judge" substitute:

court

Subsequent objection by creditor

In CCR Order 39, rule 10(1) for "his" substitute:

cc39.10   that

In CCR Order 39, rule 10(3) for "his" substitute:

the creditor

Subsequent proof by creditor

For CCR Order 39, rule 11(1) substitute:

(1) Any creditor whose debt is not scheduled to an administration **cc39.11**
order, and any person who after the date of the order became a
creditor of the debtor, shall, if that creditor wishes to prove that
debt, send particulars of the claim to the court officer, who shall give
notice of it to the debtor and to every creditor whose debt is so
scheduled.

In CCR Order 39, rule 11(2) for "he objects" substitute:

they object

Review by court officer in default of payment

In CCR Order 39, rule 13A(1) for "his", in the first place it appears, substitute:

the court officer's   **cc39.13A**

In CCR Order 39, rule 13A(1)(a) for "him" substitute:

the debtor

In CCR Order 39, rule 13A(1)(b) for "him", in each place, substitute:

the debtor

In CCR Order 39, rule 13A(1)(b)(ii) for "his" substitute:

the

For CCR Order 39, rule 13A(3) substitute:

(3) If a debtor gives notice under paragraph (1)(b)(ii), (iii) or (iv),
the court may—

    (a) without requiring the attendance of the parties—

        (i) revoke the administration order or vary it so as to
provide for payment of the debts included in the order in full or to such extent and within such a period
as appears practicable in the circumstances of the case;
or

        (ii) suspend the operation of the administration order for
such time and on such terms as it thinks fit; or

    (b) require the court officer to fix a day for the review of the
administration order and to give to the debtor and to every
creditor whose debt is scheduled to the administration order not less than 8 days' notice of the day so fixed.

For CCR Order 39, rule 13A(4) substitute:

(4) Any party affected by an order made under paragraph (2) or
(3)(a) may, within 14 days of service of the order on them and giving
their reasons, apply on notice for the court to consider the matter
afresh and the court officer shall fix a day for the hearing of the application and give to the debtor and to every creditor whose debt is
scheduled to the administration order not less than 8 days' notice of
the day so fixed.

In CCR Order 39, rule 13A(5) for "district judge" substitute:

court

In CCR Order 39, rule 13A(5) for "he" substitute:

it

Change of debtor's address

cc39.19   *In CCR Order 39, rule 19(1), delete, in the first instance, "his".*

In CCR Order 39, rule 19(1) for "his", in the second instance, substitute:

their

CCR ORDER 44—THE AGRICULTURAL HOLDINGS ACT 1986

Enforcement of order imposing penalty

For CCR Order 44, rule 4(2) substitute:

cc44.4   (2) Where it is desired to enforce the order by warrant of control, the proceedings may be taken in the County Court hearing centre serving the address where execution is to be levied.

CCR ORDER 49—MISCELLANEOUS STATUTES

Trade Union and Labour Relations Consolidation Act 1992

In CCR Order 49, rule 19(1), for "he" substitute:

cc49.19   the complainant

In CCR Order 49, rule 19(1), for "court for the district in which he" substitute:

County Court hearing centre which serves the address where the complainant

SECTION C

PRE–ACTION CONDUCT AND PROTOCOLS

SECTION C

PRE–ACTION CONDUCT AND PROTOCOLS

Compliance with the Practice Direction and Protocols: The Court's Role

Add new paragraph at end:

C1A–010   In *Nelson's Yard Management Co v Eziefula* 2013 EWCA Civ 235 the claimant was not ordered to pay the defendant's costs under r.38.6(1) when the claim was discontinued, because of the defendant's unreasonable conduct pre–action, particularly in failing to respond to several letters from the claimant who was objecting to the defendant's excavations very close to the retaining wall and foundations of the claimant's properties.

The more pertinent case law

Add new paragraphs at end:

C1A–012.2   In *Smith v Secretary of State for the Environment and Climate Change* [2013] EWCA Civ 1585 the claimant had worked for the National Coal Board for 30 years and claimed to have suffered hearing loss through working in a noisy environment. The defendant refused his request for pre–action disclosure of the noise surveys at the pits as too onerous in a speculative claim, where there was no expert evidence of the hearing loss. The claimant's application was granted as it passed the basic threshold test (likely parties to proceedings, documents within standard disclosure, disclosure could dispose fairly or assist with settlement), there was no minimum arguability level and the claimant knew that his hearing had deteriorated.

In *British Union for the Abolition of Vivisection (BUAV) v Secretary of State for the Home*

Department [2014] EWHC 43 it was held that neither r.31.16 nor Pt 54 precluded pre-action disclosure from the range of powers available in judicial review proceedings. However it was not normal procedure, Pt 54 worked well without it and this case was not sufficiently exceptional to permit a departure.

The Construction and Engineering Protocol

Add new paragraph at end:

In *Lincolnshire CC v Mouchel Business Services Ltd* [2014] EWHC 352 TCC a claim was **C5A–001** struck out for failure to serve within four months of issue, because the claimant had failed to follow the Construction and Engineering Protocol before issue because the claim might become time–barred, or to apply to the court on notice for an extension of time to do so, but had merely sought and obtained extensions of time for service without notice. Part 6 of the protocol and para.2.3.2 of the TCC Guide, in these circumstances, required a claimant to bring the case before the court on notice.

Pre–Action Protocol for Low Value Personal Injury Claims in Road Traffic Accidents

Add new paragraph C13A–010:

The 2014 Amendments

Several amendments have been made to the Protocol itself, to its supporting PD **C13A–010** (PD8B) and to its supporting rules (CPR rules 35.4, 36.10A, 36.14, 36.14A, 45.19, 45.29I) by Civil Procedure (Amendment No. 6) Rules 2014 (SI 2014/2044) and Update 75. All changes come into force on October 1, 2014. They are principally concerned with "whiplash claims" (referred to as "soft tissue injury claims").

Fixed fees for medical reports are prescribed. The fee for a first report is £180. There will normally be this one report only. However, exceptionally, if a second report is justified the amended Part 45 fixes the costs for these too. Reports must be obtained from a medical expert who has not treated the claimant, is not associated with any person who has provided treatment and who does not propose or recommend that they or an associate provide treatment. Fixed fees are also set for the provision of medical records.

Amendments are intended to deter a defendant from making an offer to settle a claim, and the claimant from accepting it, before the defendant receives the fixed cost medical report. The amendments apply only to soft tissue injury claims where the Claim Notification Form is sent in accordance with the Protocol on or after that date.

PRE-ACTION PROTOCOL FOR LOW VALUE PERSONAL INJURY CLAIMS IN ROAD TRAFFIC ACCIDENTS

In the Contents, after the entry for Paragraph 6.18 add:

SECTION I—INTRODUCTION

Definitions

Add new paragraph 1.1(1A):

(1A) 'associate' means, in respect of a medical expert, any person **C13–002** whose business is linked to that expert or to any intermediary who commissions either the expert's report or any proposed medical treatment and 'associated with' has the equivalent meaning;

Add new paragraph 1.1(10A):

(10A) 'fixed cost medical report' means a report in a soft tissue injury claim which is from a medical expert who, save in exceptional circumstances—
(a) has not provided treatment to the claimant;
(b) is not associated with any person who has provided treatment; and

(c) does not propose or recommend that they or an associate provide treatment;

In paragraph 1.1(12)(c), after "Health" add:

and Care

Add new paragraph 1.1(16A):

(16A) 'soft tissue injury claim' means a claim brought by an occupant of a motor vehicle where the significant physical injury caused is a soft tissue injury and includes claims where there is a minor psychological injury secondary in significance to the physical injury;

Aims

Add new paragraph 3.2:

C13–004 **3.2** In soft tissue injury claims, the additional aim of this Protocol is to ensure that—

(1) the use and cost of medical reports is controlled;

(2) in most cases only one medical report is obtained;

(3) the medical expert is normally independent of any medical treatment; and

(4) offers are made only after a fixed cost medical report has been obtained and disclosed.

Scope

Add new paragraph 4.7:

C13–005 **4.7** The provisions for soft tissue injury claims apply to any such claim for damages which arises from a road traffic accident where the CNF is submitted on or after 1 October 2014.

SECTION III—THE STAGES OF THE PROCESS
Stage 1

Stage 1 fixed costs

Delete paragraph 6.18 and substitute:

C13–007 **6.18** Except where the claimant is a child, the defendant must pay the Stage 1 fixed costs in rule 45.18 and, in a soft tissue injury claim, the cost of obtaining the fixed cost medical report and any cost for obtaining medical records in rule 45.19(2A) (collectively the "Stage 1 fixed recoverable costs") where—

(1) liability is admitted; or

(2) liability is admitted and contributory negligence is alleged only in relation to the claimant's admitted failure to wear a seat belt,

within 10 days after receiving the Stage 2 Settlement Pack, provided that invoices for the cost of obtaining the medical report and any medical records in a soft tissue injury claim have been included in the Stage 2 Settlement Pack.

In paragraph 6.19, after "the Stage 1 fixed" add:

recoverable

Add new paragraphs 6.19A and 6.19B:

Defendant's account in soft tissue injury claims

6.19A Where liability is admitted in a soft tissue injury claim, it is expected that in most cases the defendant's account will not be relevant to the procedure in Stage 2. In the limited cases where it is considered appropriate, the defendant may send their account to the claimant electronically at the same time as the CNF response. The defendant's insurer must have the defendant's written authority to provide this account and, in sending it, is certifying that it has that authority. For the purposes of this paragraph, the defendant's written authority may be provided electronically.

6.19B The procedure in paragraph 6.19A applies to the MIB, save that the MIB is certifying that the defendant user of the vehicle has provided such authority.

Stage 2

Medical Reports

Add new paragraph 7.1A:

7.1A Subject to paragraph 7.8A, in a soft tissue injury claim—   C13–008
  (1) the claimant should obtain a medical report and if the claimant does so, the report must be a fixed cost medical report;
  (2) subject to the restriction on further reports in paragraph 7.8A, any further report must also be a fixed cost medical report; and
  (3) where the defendant provides a different account under paragraph 6.19A, the claimant must provide this as part of the instructions to the medical expert for the sole purpose of asking the expert to comment on the impact, if any, on diagnosis and prognosis if—
  (a) the claimant's account is found to be true; or
  (b) the defendant's account is found to be true.

Subsequent medical reports

Add new paragraph 7.8A:

7.8A In a soft tissue injury claim—
  (1) it is expected that only one medical report will be required; and
  (2) a further medical report, whether from the first expert instructed or from an expert in another discipline, will only be justified where—
  (a) it is recommended in the first expert's report; and
  (b) that report has first been disclosed to the defendant.

Submitting the Stage 2 Settlement Pack to the defendant

Add new paragraph 7.32(4A):

  (4A) in a soft tissue injury claim, the invoice for the cost of obtaining the fixed cost medical report and any invoice for the cost of obtaining medical records;

Add new paragraph 7.32A:

7.32A In a soft tissue injury claim, the Stage 2 Settlement Pack is of no effect unless the medical report is a fixed cost medical report. Where the claimant includes more than one medical report, the first report obtained must be a fixed cost medical report and any further report from an expert in any of the following disciplines must also be a fixed cost medical report—

    (1) Consultant Orthopaedic Surgeon;

    (2) Consultant in Accident and Emergency Medicine;

    (3) General Practitioner registered with the General Medical Council;

    (4) Physiotherapist registered with the Health and Care Professions Council.

Defendant accepts offer or makes counter–offer

Delete paragraph 7.44(3) and substitute:

    (3) an agreement in principle to pay relevant disbursements allowed in accordance with rule 45.19;

    (3A) in a soft tissue injury claim, the cost of obtaining a medical report in rule 45.19(2A)(a); or

Add new paragraph 7.44A:

7.44A In a soft tissue injury claim, an offer to settle made by either party before a fixed cost medical report has been obtained and disclosed will have no adverse costs consequences until after the report has been disclosed.

Settlement

In paragraph 7.47(5), for "; and" substitute:

including any disbursements fixed under rule 45.19(2A); and

Settlement after claim for additional damages

In paragraph 7.62(5), for "; and" substitute:

including any disbursements fixed under rule 45.19(2A); and

Non–settlement payment by the defendant at the end of Stage 2

In paragraph 7.70(4), add at end:

including any disbursements fixed under rule 45.19(2A).

VOLUME 2

CIVIL PROCEDURE RULES

SECTION A1

PROCEDURAL GUIDES

9. EXECUTION

9.1. Execution: Application to Obtain Information from Judgment Debtors

In Guide 9.1, delete the first entry under "Making the application" and substitute:

Form **N316** *Form* **N316A**	The application may be made without notice to the debtor and must be issued in the court which made the judgment or order which it is sought to enforce, except that if the proceedings have since been transferred to a different court, it must be issued in that court or, subject to the foregoing, if it is to enforce a judgment made in County Court Money Claims Centre in respect of a designated money claim, it must be issued in accordance with section 2 of PD 70.	**A1.9–001**

In Guide 9.1, delete the third entry under "Making the application" and substitute:

CPR r.71.2	An order containing a penal notice will be made requiring the debtor to attend court and to produce any documents stated in the order and answer on oath any questions the court may require.

In Guide 9.1, delete the first entry under "Debtor's failure to comply" and substitute:

CPR r.71.8	If the judgment debtor fails to attend court or refuses to take the oath or answer any question, or otherwise fails to comply the court will refer the matter to a High Court judge or a circuit judge who may make a committal order provided the rules at r.71.8 concerning expenses and evidence have been complied with by the creditor.

9.2. Execution: Applications for Attachment of Earnings Orders

In Guide 9.2, delete the fifth entry under "Application for attachment of earnings order" and substitute:

CCR 0.27, r.3(4)	Where the judgment was made in County Court Money Claims Centre in respect of a designated money claim and the proceedings have not since been transferred to a different court, the application must be made in accordance with section 2 of PD 70.	**A1.9–002**

In guide 9.2, delete the entry for "Failures by debtors under maintenance orders".

9.3. Execution: Third Party Debt Orders

In Guide 9.3, delete the first entry under "The Application" and substitute:

A1.9–003   *CPR r.72.3*   The application must be issued in the court which made the judgment or order which it is sought to enforce, except that if the proceedings have since been transferred to a different court, it must be issued in that court or, subject to the foregoing, if it is to enforce a judgment made in County Court Money Claims Centre in respect of a designated money claim, it must be issued in accordance with section 2 of PD 70.

In guide 9.3, delete the first entry under Hardship payments orders during interim period and substitute:

     CPR r.72.7   A judgment debtor who is an individual may seek discretionary relief from the effects of an interim third party debtor order, in the form of an order (a "hardship payments order") allowing payments to him out of a bank or building society account, if he is prevented by the interim order from withdrawing money from his account, provided the court is satisfied that the debtor or his family is suffering hardship in meeting ordinary living expenses.

Application is made to the Royal Courts of Justice or any District Registry (in the case of High Court claims) and to any County Court hearing centre, in County Court hearing centre proceedings.

The application must:
- be made to only one court; and
- be supported by evidence and a statement of truth; and
- be served on the creditor no later than two days before the date fixed for hearing; and
- need *not* be served on the third party.

9.4. Execution: Charging Orders

In Guide 9.4, delete the first and second entries under "Procedure" and substitute:

A1.9–004   *CPR r.73.3(1)*   The application may be made without notice, and the creditor may apply for a single charging order in respect of more than one judgment or order against the same debtor (subject to what follows).

It should be made to the court which made the judgment or order which it is sought to enforce *unless*:
- the proceedings have since been transferred to a different court, in which case the application must be issued in that court; or
- the application is made under the Council Tax (Administration and Enforcement) Regulations 1992, in which case it must be issued in the county court for the district in which the relevant dwelling (as defined in reg.50(3)(b)of those Regulations) is situated; or
- the application is for a charging order over an interest in a fund in court, in which case it must be issued in the court in which the claim relating to that fund is or was proceeding; or
- the application is for a charging order over an interest in a fund in court, in which case it must be issued in the court in which the claim relating to that fund is or was proceeding; or

the application must be issued in the court which made the judgment or order which it is sought to enforce, except that if the proceedings have since been transferred to a different court, it must be issued in that court or, subject to the foregoing, if it is to enforce a judgment made inCounty Court Money Claims Centrein respect of a designated money claim, it must be issued in accordance with section 2 of PD 70.

Charging Orders Act 1979 s.1(2) — the application is to enforce a judgment or order of the High Court and it is required by s.1(2) of the 1979 Act to be made to the county court.

Delete Guide 9.5 and substitute:

9.5. Enforcement by Taking Control of Goods

Scope of CPR Pt 84   **A1.9–005**

Enforcement by taking control of goods is governed by Sch.12 to the Tribunals, Courts and Enforcement Act 2007 and Regulations under that Schedule (Taking Control of Goods Regulations 2013) CPR r.84 governs the procedure to be adopted.

Where to apply

r.84.3 — If no proceedings have been begun: County Court. Otherwise: County Court or High Court using CPR Part 23.

Applications for short notice enforcement

r.48.4 — Applications to enforce on abridged notice to the debtor may be made without notice but must be accompanied by evidence demonstrating that if the order is not made, it is likely that goods of the debtor will be moved or otherwise disposed of, in order to avoid the enforcement agent taking control of the goods.

Applications to extend the time within which enforcement must take place

r.84.5 — Evidence in support of application must confirm that no previous application under regulation 9(4) has been made to extend that period and must give grounds why enforcement has not taken place within the original period specified by Reg.9(1).

Applications by debtor for remedies in relation to goods taken into control

r.84.13 Para.66, Sch.12 TCA 2007 — Apply under r.84.13 where the debtor seeks remedies of any of the following types:
breach of a provision of Schedule 12 (use CPR Part 23); or
(b) enforcement action taken under a defective instrument (use CPR Part 23).
In each such application the applicant must provide evidence of how the provisions of Sch.12 have been breached and in what ways the instrument is said to be defective.

Delete Guide 9.7 and substitute:

9.7. Claims on Controlled Goods and Executed Goods

Scope   **A1.9–007**

r.85 — CPR 85 applies where a person makes an application to the court claiming that goods of which control has been taken belong to that person and not to the debtor or makes an application to the court claiming that goods, money or chattels taken or intended to be taken under a writ of execution or the proceeds or value of such goods or chattels belong to that person and not to the debtor or a debtor, whose goods have been made subject to an enforcement power under an enactment, writ or warrant of control or have been taken or are intended to be taken under a writ of execution, claims that such goods or any of them are exempt goods.

Procedure (Claims on Controlled goods)

r.85.4

Any person making a claim in relation to disputed goods under para.60(1) of Sch.12 to the Tribunals Courts and Enforcement Act 2007 must, as soon as practicable but in any event **within 7 days of the goods being removed** under the exercise of an enforcement power, give notice in writing of their claim to the enforcement agent who has taken control of the goods.

Evidence

r.85.4(1)

The notice to the enforcement agent must list the disputed goods and give grounds for the claim in respect of each of them.

Notice to Creditor

r.85.4(2)

The enforcement agent must within 3 days of receipt of notice under r.85.4(1) give notice to the judgment creditor and to anyone else making a claim to the goods, of the dispute.

Response by Creditor

r.85.4(3)

Within 7 days of receipt of the enforcement agent's notice under r.85.4(3) the creditor, and any other claimant to the controlled goods, must give notice in writing to the enforcement agent informing them whether the claim to controlled goods is admitted or disputed in whole or in part.

Further notice to debtor

r.85.4(4)

The enforcement agent must notify the claimant to the controlled goods in writing within 3 days of receiving the notice in r.85.4(3) whether the claim to controlled goods is admitted or disputed in whole or in part.

Commencing the claim

Where a creditor, or any other claimant to controlled goods to whom a notice of claim to the disputed goods was given, gives notice under r.85.4(3) that the claim to controlled goods, r.85.5 is disputed, and wishes to maintain their claim in court then the claimant to controlled goods must make an application supported by witness statement specifying any money; describing any goods claimed; and setting out the grounds upon which their claim to the controlled goods is based, and must provide copies of any supporting documents that will assist the court to determine the claim.
High Court: Claimant to controlled goods must serve creditor, any other claimant to the goods, and the enforcement agent. County Court: Claimant to controlled goods must provide the County Court with addresses for service.

Procedure

r.85.5(5),(6)

The application must be made to the court which issued the writ or warrant conferring power to take control of the controlled goods, or, if the power was conferred under an enactment, to the debtor's home court.
The claimant to controlled goods **must** make the required payments on issue of the application in accordance with paragraph 60(4)(a) of unless such claimant

seeks a direction from the court that the required payment be a proportion of the value of the goods, in which case they must seek such a direction **immediately**after issue of the application, on notice to the creditor and to the enforcement agent.

Court's powers

r.85.5(7)

The court may give directions for further evidence from any party, list a hearing to give directions; list a hearing of the application; determine the amount of the required payments, make directions or list a hearing to determine any issue relating to the amount of the required payments or the value of the controlled goods; stay, or dismiss, the application if the required payments have not been made; make directions for the retention, sale or disposal of the controlled goods; or give directions for determination of any issue raised by a claim to controlled goods.

Procedure (Claims on Executed goods)

r.85.6, r.85.7

The Notice, and claim procedure is anglogous to that for claims on controlled goods, and is set out in rr.85.6 and 85.7. However in addition, where the creditor, or any other claimant to executed goods to whom a notice of claim to executed goods was given, fails, within the period in r.85.6(3), ie within 7 days of receipt of notice of the dispute, to give the required notice of wither admitting or disputing the claim then the enforcement officer may seek the directions of the court by way of an application and may seek an order preventing the bringing of any claim against them for, or in respect of, the seizure of the executed goods or their having failed so to do.

Delete Guides 9.9 and 9.10 and substitute:

9.9. Enforcement of orders for possession of land

High Court

A1.9–009

r.83.13

Permission of the court is required to enforce orders for possession of land in the High Court other than where the order is against trespassers and enforcement is by Writ of Possession, in which case no permission is required. If the order was made no more than 3 months before issue of the Writ. Orders for possession of land may be enforced by committal, by sequestration or by Writ of Possession.

Writs of restitution

r.83.13(5)

The courts' permission to issue a writ of restitution in aid of a writ of possession is required whether or not permission was required for the writ of possession.

County Court

An application for a warrant of possession must be made to the County Court hearing centre where the judgment or order which it is sought to enforce was made, or the County Court hearing centre to which the proceedings have since been transferred.

The person applying for a warrant of possession must file a certificate that the land which is subject of the judgment or order has not been vacated.

When applying for a warrant of possession of a dwelling–house subject to a mortgage, the claimant must certify that notice has been given in accordance with the Dwelling Houses (Execution of Possession Orders by Mortgagees) Regulations 2010.

Where a warrant of possession is issued, the creditor will be entitled, by the same or a separate warrant, to execution against the debtor's goods for any money payable under the judgment or order.

Breaches of suspended possession orders

r.83.26(7)   Where an order for possession has been suspended on terms as to payment of a sum of money by instalments, the creditor must certify the amount of money remaining due under the judgment or order and that the whole or part of any instalment due remains unpaid.

Warrants of Restitution

r.83.26(8)   A warrant of restitution may be issued, with the permission of the court, in aid of any warrant of possession.

Time limit

r.83.26(11)   No warrant of possession against a trespasser may be issued after the expiry of 3 months from the date of the order without the permission of the court.

Renumber Guide 9.11 as 9.10.

9.10. Enforcement of decisions of bodies other than the High Court and county courts and compromises enforceable by enactment

In renumbered Guide 9.10, delete the first entry and substitute:

A1.9–010

Where an Act or SI governs the decision of a court or tribunal which is neither a County Court nor the High Court, and provides that a decision of the court or tribunal or a compromise of proceedings before that court or tribunal may enforced as if it were a court order (or as if payable under a court order)	The procedure to be adopted is that a party may enforce the decision or compromise by applying for a specific method of enforcement under CPR Pts 71 to 73 or RSC (whichever is relevant to the case).

SECTION 1

COURT GUIDES

1B   QUEEN'S BENCH GUIDE

Delete Queen's Bench Guide and substitute:

Editorial note

1B–1   This Guide has been prepared under the direction of the Senior Master, acting under the authority of the President of the Queen's Bench Division, and provides a general explanation of the work and practice of the Queen's Bench Division with particular regard to proceedings started in the Central Office, and is designed to make it easier for parties to use and proceed in the Queen's Bench Division.

The Guide will be updated at regular intervals as the need arises.

SECTION 1

INTRODUCTION

1.1 The Guide:

1.1.1 This Guide has been prepared under the direction of the Senior Master, acting **1B–2** under the authority of the President of the Queen's Bench Division, and provides a general explanation of the work and practice of the Queen's Bench Division with particular regard to proceedings started in the Central Office, and is designed to make it easier for parties to use and proceed in the Queen's Bench Division.

1.1.2 The Guide must be read with the Civil Procedure Rules ("CPR") and the supporting Practice Directions. Litigants and their advisers are responsible for acquainting themselves with the CPR; it is not the task of this Guide to summarise the CPR, nor should anyone regard it as a substitute for the CPR. It is intended to bring the Guide up to date at regular intervals as necessary.

1.1.3 The Guide does not have the force of law, but parties using the Queen's Bench Division will be expected to act in accordance with this Guide. Further guidance as to the practice of the Queen's Bench Division may be obtained from the Practice Master (see paragraph 6.1 below).

1.1.4 It is assumed throughout the Guide that the litigant intends to proceed in the Royal Courts of Justice. For all essential purposes, though, the Guide is equally applicable to the work of the District Registries, which deal with the work of the Queen's Bench Division outside London, but it should be borne in mind that there are some differences.

1.1.5 The telephone numbers and room numbers quoted in the Guide are correct at the time of going to press.

1.2 The Civil Procedure Rules:

1.2.1 The Overriding Objective set out in Part 1 of CPR is central to civil proceedings **1B–3** and enables the court to deal with cases justly and at proportionate cost. To further this aim the work is allocated to one of three tracks – the small claims track, the fast track and the multi–track – so as to dispose of the work in the most appropriate and effective way combined with active case management by the court. Whilst the track regime is of everyday concern in the County Courts, it should be noted that, by a combination of the Rules, both as to jurisdiction and as to procedure, and of practice, all cases proceeding in the Central Office of the Queen's Bench Division at the Royal Courts of Justice, and in the District Registries of the Queen's Bench Division outside London, will necessarily be allocated to the multi–track.

1.2.2 The CPR are divided into Parts. A particular Part is referred to in the Guide as Part 7, etc., as the case may be. Any particular rule within a Part is referred to as rule 6.4(2), and so on.

1.3 The Practice Directions:

1.3.1 Each Part—or almost each Part—has an accompanying Practice Direction or **1B–4** Directions, and other Practice Directions deal with matters such as the Pre–Action Protocols. Such of the former Rules of the Supreme Court and of the former County Court Rules as are still applicable are scheduled to Part 50.

1.3.2 The Practice Directions are made pursuant to statute, and have the same authority as do the CPR themselves. However, in case of any conflict between a Rule and a Practice Direction, the Rule will prevail. Each Practice Direction is referred to in the Guide with the number of any Part that it supplements preceding it; for example, the Practice Direction supplementing Part 6 is referred to as the Part 6 Practice Direction. But where there is more than one Practice Direction supplementing a Part it will also be described either by topic, for example, the Part 25 Practice Direction—Interim Payments or, where appropriate, the Part 40B Practice Direction. A convenient abbreviated reference to a particular sub–paragraph of (for example) the Part 40B Practice Direction would be PD40B, Para.1.1.

1.4 The Forms:

1B–5 1.4.1 The Practice Direction supplementing Part 4 lists the forms generally required to be used under the CPR.

1.4.2 The Practice Direction contains 3 tables.

Table 1 contains the "N forms" that are referred to and required by the Rules (i.e. CPR 1 to 81) and the Practice Direction. There are also Court Funds Office forms referred to but not listed in Table 1.

Table 2 lists the Practice Forms that may be used. It contains forms that were previously:–
   (a) Prescribed Forms contained in Appendix A to the Rules of the Supreme Court 1965
   (b) Queen's Bench Masters' Practice Forms
   (c) Chancery Masters' Practice Forms

Table 3 lists County Court forms.

1.4.3 The forms contained in the 3 lists above are not, for reasons of space, reproduced as an Annex in this Guide. They are however available in the various practitioners' textbooks, and on Her Majesty's Courts and Tribunals website at **www.hmcourts–service.gov.uk**. Users may access the forms at **http://hmctsformfinder.justice.gov.uk** and at **www.justice.gov.uk/forms**.

1.4.4 The forms may be modified as circumstances in individual cases require, but it is essential that a modified form contains at least as full information or guidance as would have been given if the original form had been used.

1.4.5 Where the Royal Arms appear on any listed form they must appear on any modification of that form. The same format for the Royal Arms as is used on the listed forms need not be used. All that is necessary is that there is a complete Royal Arms.

1.5 The Queen's Bench Division:

1B–6 1.5.1 The Queen's Bench Division is one of the three divisions of the High Court, together with the Chancery Division and Family Division. The President of the Queen's Bench Division (Sir Brian Leveson) assisted by the Vice President (who is appointed by the Lord Chief Justice and is currently Lord Justice Davis) are responsible for its overall management. A High Court Judge is appointed as Judge in charge of the Lists and is currently Mr Justice Tugendhat.

1.5.2 Outside London, the work of the Queen's Bench Division is administered in provincial offices known as District Registries. In London, the work is administered in the Central Office at the Royal Courts of Justice. The work in the Central Office of the Queen's Bench Division is the responsibility of the Senior Master, acting under the authority of the President of the Queen's Bench Division.

1.5.3 The work of the Queen's Bench Division is (with certain exceptions) governed by the CPR. The Administrative Court, the Admiralty Court, the Commercial Court, the Mercantile Courts and the Technology and Construction Court are all part of the Queen's Bench Division. However, each does specialised work requiring a distinct procedure that to some extent modifies the CPR. For that reason each has an individual Part of the CPR, its own Practice Direction and (except for the Administrative Court) its own Guide, to which reference should be made by parties wishing to proceed in these specialist courts.

1.5.4 The work of the Queen's Bench Division consists mainly of claims for:
   (1) damages and/or an injunction in respect of:
      (a) personal injury,
      (b) negligence,(including professional negligence)
      (c) breach of statutory duty,
      (d) libel and slander (defamation),

(e) other tortious conduct,

(f) breach of contract

(g) breaches of the Human Rights Act 1998

and (2) non–payment of a debt.

Proceedings retained to be dealt with in the Central Office will almost invariably be multi–track claims.

1.5.5 In many types of claim—for example claims in respect of negligence by solicitors, accountants, etc., or claims for possession of land—the claimant has a choice whether to bring the claim in the Queen's Bench Division or in the Chancery Division. However, there are certain matters that may be brought only in the Queen's Bench Division, namely:

(1) High Court Enforcement Officer's interpleader proceedings,

(2) applications for the enrolment of deeds,

(3) applications under Part 74 for the registration of foreign judgments for enforcement in England and Wales under the Administration of Justice Act 1920, the Foreign Judgments (Reciprocal Enforcement) Act 1933, the Civil Jurisdiction Act 1982, the Judgments Regulation, or the Lugano Convention,

(4) applications for bail in criminal proceedings,

(5) registration and satisfaction of Bills of Sale,

(6) Election Petitions,

(7) applications for orders to obtain evidence for foreign courts.

1.5.6 Regard should also be had to paragraphs 1 and 2 of Schedule 1 to the Senior Courts Act 1981 under which certain matters are assigned respectively to the Chancery Division and the Queen's Bench Division.

1.6 The Central Office:

1.6.1 The information in this and the following sub–paragraph is to be found in **1B–7** Practice Direction 2A para.2; it is reproduced here for the convenience of litigants. The Central Office is open for business from 10 a.m. to 4.30 p.m. on every day of the year except;

(a) Saturdays and Sundays,

(b) Good Friday,

(c) Christmas Day,

(d) A further day over the Christmas period determined in accordance with the table specifically annexed to the Practice Direction. This will depend on which day of the week Christmas Day falls.

(e) Bank holidays in England and Wales

(f) Such other days as the Lord Chancellor, with the concurrence of the Lord Chief Justice, the Master of the Rolls, the President of the Queen's Bench Division, the President of the Family Division and the Chancellor of the High Court ("the Heads of Division") may direct.

1.6.2 One of the Masters of the Queen's Bench Division (the "Practice Master") is present on every day on which the Central Office is open, for the purpose of superintending the business performed there and giving any directions which may be required on questions of practice and procedure. (See Paragraph 6.1 below for further information about the Practice Master).

1.6.3 The Central Office consists of the Action Department, the Queen's Bench Associates' Department, the High Court Judges' Listing Office, the Registry of the Technology and Construction Court, and the Admiralty and Commercial Registry.

1.6.4 The Action Department, which is located as shown by Annex 1 at the end of this Guide, deals with the issue of claims, responses to claims, admissions, undefended and summary judgments, the issue of application notices, drawing up orders, enforcement of judgments and orders, public searches, provision of copies of court documents, enrolment of deeds, the registration of foreign judgments, and the provision of certificates for enforcement abroad of judgments of the Queen's Bench Division.

1.6.5 For these purposes, the Action Department is divided into sections as follows:–

(1) the Masters' Support Unit, which provides support (a) to the Masters, including assistance on all aspects of case management, and (b) to the Senior Master. There is a Queen's Bench Masters' Secretary, whose office is located within the Masters' Support Unit.

(2) the Foreign Process Section, which deals with all aspects of service abroad of proceedings brought here, and of service here of proceedings brought abroad.

(3) the Enforcement Section which deals with enforcement of judgments obtained in the Queen's Bench Division and of foreign judgments which may be enforced here: see Section 12 below. It also deals with Writs, Bills of Sale and changes of name by Deeds Poll.

(4) the Children's Funds Section which deals in particular with investment of children's funds made pursuant to an order of a Judge or a Master: see paragraphs 10.3.10 to 10.3.12 below.

Also one of the staff acts as the Chief Clerk to the Prescribed Officer for Election Petitions, namely the Senior Master: see Paragraph 13.2 below.

1.6.6 The Queen's Bench Associates sit in court with the Judges during trials and certain interim hearings. The Associates draw up the orders made in court at trial and those interim orders that are directed to be drawn by the Court rather than (as is more usual) by the parties themselves. The Associates Delivery Manager manages the Queen's Bench Associates and also provides support to the Senior Master as the Queen's Remembrancer.

1.6.7 The High Court Judges' Listing office lists all trials and matters before the Judges (see Section 9 below).

1.6.8 The Commercial Court (being a constituent part of the Queen's Bench Division) deals with commercial claims, i.e any claim arising out of the transaction of trade and commerce. Its proceedings are subject to Part 58 of the Rules and to the Part 58 Practice Direction. The types of claim which may be brought in the Commercial Court are expanded upon in rule 58.1 (2). The commercial list is a specialist list for all claims proceeding in the Commercial Court and one of the judges of that Court is in charge of the commercial list. By PD58 Paras.1.4 and 2.1 the Admiralty and Commercial Registry is the administrative office of the court for all proceedings in the commercial list; and all claims in the Commercial Court must be issued in the Admiralty and Commercial Registry. The address of the registry is 7 Rolls Building, Fetter Lane, London EC4A 1NL. Extensive guidance on proceedings both in the Commercial Court and in the Admiralty Court is found in a single guide, entitled "The Admiralty and Commercial Courts Guide"

1.6.9 Mercantile Courts are established, again as constituent parts of the Q.B.D., to deal with claims relating to "a commercial or business–matter in a broad sense": see rule 59.1. Such courts are established in the following district registries of the High Court, namely Birmingham, Bristol, Cardiff, Chester, Leeds, Liverpool, Manchester, Mold and Newcastle–upon–Tyne; and in the Commercial Court at the Royal Courts of Justice (called "The London Mercantile Court"). Their proceedings are governed by Part 59 and the Part 59 Practice Direction. They decide business disputes of all kinds apart from those which, because of their size, value or complexity, will be dealt with in the Commercial Court. Extensive guidance on the conduct of proceedings there is found in the Mercantile Court Guide. It is available on–line at:– *www.justice.gov.uk/downloads/courts/mercantile–court/mercantile–court–guide*.

1.6.10 The Technology and Construction Court deals with claims which involve issues or questions which are technically complex or for which a trial by a Judge of that court is desirable: see rule 60.1 (3), and the Practice Direction to Part 60, in particular PD60 para.2.1 which lists examples of claims which it may be appropriate to bring in that Court. Extensive guidance on proceedings in the TCC is found in the Technology and Construction Court Guide.

1.6.11 The Admiralty Court is defined as the Admiralty Court of the Queen's Bench Division of the High Court of Justice, and deals with claims within the Admiralty jurisdiction of the High Court as set out in Section 20 of the Senior Courts Act 1981: see rules 61.1 and 61.2 which themselves make reference to the particular types of claim which may, or must, be brought in the Admiralty Court. Such claims are subject to Part 61 of the Rules and the Part 61 Practice Direction. The Registrar of the Admiralty Court means the Queen's Bench Master with responsibility for Admiralty claims, and he has all the powers of the Admiralty judge except where a rule or practice direction provides otherwise. Extensive guidance on proceedings in the Admiralty Court is found in the Admiralty and Commercial Courts Guide at Section N thereof.

1.6.12 Arbitration claims and proceedings are the subject of Part 62 and the Part 62 Practice Direction. These provide for the allocation of those courts in which arbitration claims and proceedings may, or must, be issued: see in particular PD62, Paras.2, 14 and 16. Extensive guidance on arbitration claims is found at Section 0 of the Admiralty and Commercial Courts Guide.

1.7 The Judiciary:

1.7.1 The judiciary in the Queen's Bench Division consists of the High Court Judges **1B–8** (The Honourable Mr/Mrs Justice .... and addressed in court as my Lord/my Lady) and, in the Royal Courts of Justice, the Masters (addressed in court as Master). They include two female Masters (Master Fontaine and Master McCloud) who are addressed as Master. In the District Registries the work of the Masters is conducted by District Judges (addressed in court as Sir or Madam).

1.7.2 Trials normally take place before a High Court Judge (or a Deputy High Court Judge or a Circuit Judge sitting as a Judge of the High Court) who may also hear pre–trial reviews and other interim applications. Wherever possible the judge before whom a trial has been fixed will hear any pre–trial review. A High Court Judge will hear applications to commit for contempt of court, applications for injunctions and most appeals from Masters' orders. (See the Part 2B Practice Direction: Allocation of cases to levels of Judiciary; and see Paragraphs 7.10 and 7.11 below for more information on hearings and applications.)

1.7.3 The Masters deal with interim and pre–action applications, and manage the claims so that they proceed without delay. The Masters' rooms are situated in the Masters' corridor on the first floor of the East Block of the Royal Courts of Justice: see Plan B at the end of this Guide. Hearings take place in these rooms or (for chambers applications) in Room E102 in the Bear Garden, or, in certain circumstances, in a court.

1.7.4 Cases are assigned on issue by a court officer in the Masters' Support Unit to Masters on a rota basis, and that Master is then known as the assigned Master in relation to that case. (See Paragraphs 6.2 and 6.3 below for more information about assignment and the Masters' lists.)

1.7.5 General enquiries about the business dealt with by the Masters should initially be made in writing to the Masters' Support Unit in Room E107.

Section 2

General

2.1 Essential matters:

2.1.1 Before bringing any proceedings, the intending claimant should think carefully **1B–9** about the implications of so doing. (See Section 3 below about steps to be taken before issuing a claim form.)

2.1.2 A litigant who is acting in person faces a heavier burden in terms of time and effort than does a litigant who is legally represented, but all litigation calls for a high level of commitment from the parties. No intending claimant should underestimate this.

2.1.3 The Overriding Objective of the CPR is to deal with cases justly and at proportionate cost. This means dealing with the claim in a way which is proportionate (amongst other things) to the amount of money involved. However, in all proceedings there are winners and losers; the loser is generally ordered to pay the costs of the winner and the costs of litigation can still be large. The risk of large costs is particularly acute in cases involving expert witnesses, barristers and solicitors. Also, the costs of an interim hearing are almost always summarily assessed and made payable by the unsuccessful party, usually within 14 days after the order for costs is made. There may be a number of interim hearings before the trial itself is reached, so the costs must be paid as the claim progresses. (See also Paragraph 2.5 below as to costs which includes reference to important new provisions of the Rules dealing (a) with the court's powers of managing the costs of a case, and (b) making specific costs capping orders).

2.1.4 The intending claimant should also keep in mind that every claim must be proved, unless of course the defendant admits the allegations. There is little point in incurring the risks and expense of litigating if the claim cannot be proved. An intending claimant should therefore be taking steps to obtain statements from his prospective witnesses before starting the claim; if he delays until later, it may turn out that he is in fact unable to obtain the evidence that he needs to prove his claim. A defendant faces a similar task.

2.1.5 Any party may, if he is to succeed, need an opinion from one or more expert witnesses, such as medical practitioners, engineers, accountants, or as the case may be. However he must remember that no expert evidence may be given at trial without the permission of the court. The services of such experts are in great demand, especially as, in some fields of expertise, there are few of them. It may take many months to obtain an opinion, and the cost may be high. (See Paragraph 7.8 below for information about experts' evidence.) If the claim is for compensation for personal injuries and the claimant is relying on medical evidence he must produce a medical report with his particulars of claim.

2.1.6 The claimant must remember also not to allow the time limit for starting his claim to pass (see Paragraph 2.3 below for information about time limits).

2.1.7 Any intending claimant should also have in mind that he will usually be required to give disclosure of documents which are or have been in his control. In complex cases it may still be necessary to disclose relatively large quantities of documents, and this invariably involves much time, effort and expense. (See Paragraph 7.7 below for information about disclosure.)

2.1.8 In many cases the parties will need legal assistance, whether by way of advice, drafting, representation at hearings or otherwise. It is not the function of court staff to give legal advice; however, subject to that, they will do their best to assist any litigant. Litigants in person who are enquiring as to the possibility of obtaining legal assistance or representation may contact Civil Legal Advice at 0845 345 4345 (9.00am to 8.00pm Mondays to Fridays and 9.00am to 12.30pm on Saturdays) or on the website at **https://cladvice.justice.gov.uk.** In general, while the availability of legal aid has become very restricted under the Legal Aid, Sentencing and Punishment of Offenders Act 2012, applicants will probably be directed to pursue their enquiries via firms of solicitors practising in areas of legal aid.

2.1.9 There is an RCJ Advice Bureau off the Main Hall at the RCJ. The Bureau runs an appointment–based service. Applicants should contact 0844 856 3534 from a landline or (from a mobile) 0300 456 8341 between 10.00am and 1.00pm on Mondays to Fridays. Also, enquiries for an appointment can be made in person at the Bureau between 2.00pm and 4.00pm on Mondays to Fridays. In addition to the above, advice can be sought on the telephone at 0207 288 7678 between 10.00am and 1.00pm and 2.00pm and 4.30pm on Mondays to Fridays.

2.1.10 The Personal Support Unit (PSU) is an independent charity which supports litigants in person, witnesses, victims, their family members and other supporters attending the Royal Courts of Justice and other courts across the country including Birmingham, Cardiff, Leeds, Liverpool and Manchester. There are now just over 100 fully trained and experienced volunteers in the Royal Courts of Justice. Requests vary from the very simple to the complex. Some people just require directions or advice about procedures. Others need to unburden themselves, while others request the moral and emotional support of being accompanied in court. The PSU can be particularly helpful for clients with special needs. Its address is:–

The PSU
Room M104
Royal Courts of Justice
Strand
WC2A 2LL Tel: 0207 947 7701/3 Fax: 0207 947 7702
email: **rcj@thepsu.co.uk** or: **www.thepsu.co.uk**

2.2 Inspection and copies of documents:

2.2.1 Intending claimants must not expect to be able to keep the details of a claim **1B–10**
away from public scrutiny. In addition to the right of a party to obtain copies of
certain specified documents in the proceedings to which he is a party from the court
record (on payment of the prescribed fee: see CPR 5.4B and 5.4D), any person may
obtain from the court records a copy of a statement of case, but not of any documents
filed with it or attached to it: see CPR 5.4C. Any judgment or order made in public
(whether made at a hearing or without a hearing) may also, subject to CPR 5.4C
(1B), be obtained from the records of the court on payment of the appropriate fee.
Additionally, under CPR 5.4B, 5.4C and 5.4D, other documents, including
communications between the court and a party or another person, may be obtained
with the permission of the court, upon making an application in accordance with Part
23.

2.2.2 Witness statements used at trial are open to inspection during the course of the
trial, unless the court directs otherwise.

2.2.3 CPR 5.4C(5) sets out how the court may, on application by a party or any
person identified in a statement of case, restrict inspection and obtaining of copies.

2.3 Time Limits:

2.3.1 There are strict time limits that apply to every claim. These will arise, **1B–11**
principally, under the Limitation Act 1980 or the Human Rights Act 1996, which lay
down time limits within which the proceedings must be brought. There are
circumstances in which the court may disapply the time limits, but such disapplication
is to be regarded as exceptional and the burden is on the claimant to persuade the
court that it is right to do so. In all other cases, once the relevant time limit has
expired, it is rarely possible to start a claim.

2.3.2 Secondly, in order to try and bring the proceedings to an early trial date, a
timetable will be set with which all parties must comply. Unless the CPR or a Practice
Direction provides otherwise, or the court orders otherwise, the timetable may be
varied by the written agreement of the parties. However, there are certain
"milestone" events in the timetable in respect of which the parties may not vary the
time limits. Examples of these are;
  (1) filing a Defence more than 28 days after the period required by the Rules: see
      CPR 15.5
  (2) return of the Directions Questionnaire, or the Reply to Defence which should
      be returned together with the Directions Questionnaire: see CPR 26.3 (6A)
  (3) date(s) for the case management conference(s)
  (4) return of the Pre–Trial Checklists
  (5) date fixed for trial: see CPR 29.5(2)

Where parties have extended a time limit by agreement, the party for whom the time
has been extended must notify the Registry Section in writing of the appropriate
event in the proceedings for which the time has been extended and the new date by
which it must take place. For example, if an extension is agreed for the filing of the
defence, it is for the defendant to inform the Registry Section.

2.3.3 The court has power to impose a sanction on any party who fails to comply with
a time limit. If the court considers that a prior warning should be given before a
sanction is imposed, it will make an 'unless' order; in other words, the court will
order that, unless that party performs his obligation by the time specified, he will be
penalised in the manner set out in the order. This may involve the party in default
having his claim or statement of case struck out and judgment given against him. An

order striking out a claim or statement of case must be applied for after the time specified has expired, as this is not automatic unless the Unless Order so provides.

2.4 Legal Representation:

1B–12 2.4.1 A party may act in person or be represented by a lawyer. A party who is acting in person may be assisted at any hearing by an unqualified person (often referred to as a McKenzie friend) subject to the discretion of the court. The McKenzie friend is allowed to help by taking notes, quietly prompting the litigant and offering advice and suggestions. The litigant however must conduct his own case; the McKenzie friend may not represent him and may only in very exceptional circumstances be allowed to address the court on behalf of the litigant.

2.4.2 A written statement should be provided to the court at any hearing concerning the representation of the parties in accordance with Paragraph 5.1 of Practice Direction 39A (the Court Record Form, found outside the Masters' Rooms or in the Bear Garden). Note particularly the information required by Paragraph 5.2 where a company or other corporation is to be represented at the hearing by an employee.

2.4.3 At a trial, a company or corporation may be represented by an employee if the company or corporation authorises him to do so and the court gives permission. Where this is to be the case, the permission of the Judge who is to hear the case may be sought informally; Paragraph 5 of PD39A describes what is needed to obtain permission from the court for this purpose and mentions some of the considerations relevant to the grant or refusal of permission. As stated above, a statement concerning representation should be provided in accordance with Paragraph 5.2 of the Practice Direction.

2.4.4 Experienced outdoor clerks from solicitors' firms are permitted to appear before the Masters. Barristers' clerks may attend before a Master to fix a hearing date for Counsel.

2.5 Costs:

1B–13 2.5.1 Costs (i.e the right of one party to recover costs from another party) are dealt with in the admirably clear new provisions of CPR 44 to 48 and of the Practice Direction to each of those Parts. Detailed treatment of the subject of costs may be found in the Senior Courts Costs Office Guide 2006.

2.5.2 The layout of the new rules is as follows:–

Part 44 deals with general rules about costs and includes new rules on qualified one–way costs shifting and damages–based agreements.

Part 45 deals with fixed costs.

Part 46 deals with costs in special cases

Part 47 deals with the procedure for detailed assessment of costs and default provisions.

Part 48 deals with transitional provisions.

2.5.3 Before turning to those Parts it is right to say that new rules have provided in particular for two important matters (a) costs management by the court: see CPR 3.12 to 3.18 and Practice Direction 3E; and (b) costs capping by the court: see CPR 3.19 to 3.21.

2.5.4 Costs management. The purpose of costs management is that the court should manage both the steps to be taken in the proceedings and the costs to be incurred so as to further the overriding objective: see rule 13.12(2). The overriding objective has been re–defined in rule 1.1(1) so as to enable the court to deal with cases justly and at proportionate cost. That now includes enforcing compliance with rules, practice directions and orders: see the new rule 1.1(2)(f). All parties except litigants in person are to exchange costs budgets (in Form Precedent H) by a certain time: rule 3.13. And, by rule 3.14, unless the court otherwise orders, any party which fails to file a budget despite being required to do so will be treated as having filed a budget comprising only the applicable court fees. Any party in breach of such rules may find, upon application for relief from the sanction in rule 3.14, that the availability of relief has become more restricted by the new wording of rule 3.9 (relief from sanctions) and the new definition of the overriding objective in rule1.1 And see Paragraph 7.15 below under the heading "Relief from sanctions"

The court may make costs management orders. This will include recording the extent to which budgets are agreed, or approving after appropriate revisions budgets which are not agreed. The court may hold costs management conferences, for example to approve revised budgets. In any case where a costs management order has been made, when it comes to assessing costs that are actually to be recovered, the court will have regard to the receiving party's last approved or agreed budget, and not depart from that unless satisfied that there is good reason to do so.

2.5.5 Costs capping orders. The court may make a costs capping order at any stage of the proceedings if (a) it is in the interests of justice to do so, (b) there is a substantial risk that without such an order costs will be disproportionately incurred, and (c) the court is not satisfied that such risk can be adequately controlled by case management directions or orders and by detailed assessment of costs: see CPR 3.19(5). A costs capping order will limit the costs recoverable by the party in question unless a successful application is made to vary the order; and no variation will be made unless there has been a material and substantial change of circumstances since the order was made, or there is some other compelling reason why a variation should be made. An application for a costs capping order must be made on notice under Part 23. It must set out in particular why a costs capping order should be made and must contain a budget setting out the applicant's own costs to date and likely costs in the future.

2.5.6 Part 44. The court has an overall discretion as to costs. This is described in rule 44.2(1) as a discretion as to:
    (a) whether costs are payable by one party to another
    (b) the amount of those costs; and
    (c) when they are to be paid

2.5.7 There are certain costs orders which the court will commonly make in proceedings before trial. These, and the precise effect of such orders, are very usefully set out in the table to para.4.2 of the PD to Part 44. They include:–
    Costs in any event
    Costs in the case
    Costs in the application
    Costs reserved
    Claimant's/Defendant's costs in case/application
    Costs thrown away
    Costs of and caused by
    Costs here and below
    No order as to costs
    Each party to pay own costs

2.5.8 The general rule is that the unsuccessful party will be ordered to pay the costs of the successful party but the court may make a different order.

2.5.9 In deciding what order to make the court will have regard to all the circumstances of the case including the specific matters set out in CPR 44.2(4) and (5).

2.5.10 Orders that the court may make include payment of a proportion of costs or costs from or until a certain date only: rule 44.2(6).

2.5.11 Interest on costs. Under rule 44.3(6) the court has a discretion to order interest on costs from or until a certain date, including a date before judgment.

2.5.12 Where there is an order for costs subject to detailed assessment the court will order payment of a reasonable sum on account unless there is good reason not to do so: rule 44.2(8).

2.5.13 Where costs are to be assessed (whether by summary or detailed assessment) they will be assessed either on the standard basis or on the indemnity basis. If on the standard basis, then, in relation to cases commenced on or after 1st April 2013, the costs allowed must be proportionate to the matters in issue. Disproportionate costs may be disallowed or reduced even if reasonably or necessarily incurred. The test of proportionality is laid down in rule 44.3(5).

2.5.14 The essential distinction between the standard basis and the indemnity basis is that in the former case doubt as to reasonableness is resolved in favour of the paying party; in the latter case in favour of the receiving party.

2.5.15 The court will have regard to all the circumstances in deciding the amount of costs. It will have regard to the specific matters set out in rule 44.4(3), which include the conduct of the parties (including efforts to try to resolve the dispute), and the receiving party's last approved or agreed budget.

2.5.16 As to the procedure for assessing costs, the court may (unless prevented by rule, practice direction or other enactment) make a summary assessment (i.e an assessment at the conclusion of the hearing by the judge who heard the matter) or order detailed assessment by a costs judge or officer. PD44 sets out the factors which will guide the court's decision as to which process is adopted.

2.5.17 Summary assessment. Paragraph 9 of the PD to Part 44 deals in particular with this subject. The court shall consider in all cases where fixed costs do not arise whether to make a summary assessment. It should do so at the conclusion of a hearing which has lasted not more than one day, in which case the assessment will deal with the costs of the application. If the hearing disposes of the whole claim the court may make an assessment of the costs of the whole claim. These provisions apply unless there is good reason not to make a summary assessment e.g. where there is a substantial dispute as to costs. In order to assist the court in making a summary assessment the parties must provide, usually in schedule form in Form N260, the information, such as number of hours and rate claimed, set out in para.9.5 of the PD. And such schedule should be filed and served not less than 24 hours before the hearing. Note however that summary assessment will not take place of the costs of a receiving party who is legally aided (see para.9.8), or who is a child or protected party unless his legal representative has waived the right to further costs (see para.9.9).

2.5.18 The time for complying with an order for costs is laid down in rule 44.7.

2.5.19 A legal representative for a party has a duty within 7 days to notify the party (which includes the client, or a trade union or insurer or the Legal Aid Agency or the Lord Chancellor if instructions have been received from such source) of an order for costs made in the absence of the party: see rule 44.8 and PD44 Paras.10.1 to 10.3.

2.5.20 No order for costs. Specific provision is made under rule 44.10 in cases where the court's order does not mention costs. Reference should be made to the rule for its precise terms, including the question of costs on an application made without notice.

2.5.21 Misconduct. The court has power to disallow the costs of a party being assessed where that party's conduct or his legal representative's conduct was unreasonable or improper; or, for like reason, to order that the costs of any other party be paid by the party at fault or by his legal representative. This rule should be read together with rule 46.8 (wasted costs orders against a legal representative) whereby a reasonable opportunity must be given to the legal representative to make written submissions or attend a hearing before making such an order.

2.5.22 Costs against a claimant. Qualified one–way costs shifting (QOCS). Protection against costs is given to claimants who have failed in personal injury and fatal accident cases by the new regime introduced by CPR 44.13 to 44.16. Orders against a claimant may be enforced without permission only to the extent that the amount of such orders does not exceed damages awarded to the claimant. But such orders may be enforced in full without permission where the proceedings have been struck out on the grounds, for example, that the claimant has shown no reasonable grounds for bringing them. And such orders may be enforced in full with the permission of the court where the claim is found on the balance of probabilities to be fundamentally dishonest; or (to the extent that the court considers just) where the claim is brought for the financial benefit of another person (as defined). These new provisions do not apply to cases in which the funding arrangement for the claimant was entered into before April 1, 2013: see rule 44.17.

2.5.23 Costs recoverable by a claimant. Conditional fee agreements. Defendants are no longer to be liable, on arrangements made on or after April 1, 2013, for either

    (i) a success fee, i.e a percentage uplift in the fees payable by the claimant to his legal representatives, or

    (ii) after–the–event insurance premiums payable by the claimant

These reforms are introduced by Part II of the Legal Aid, Sentencing and Punishment of Offenders Act 2012, but are subject to exceptions still presently available for mesothelioma claims, insolvency proceedings, and defamation and privacy claims, and exceptions in relation to experts' fees in clinical negligence claims. See in particular the Practice Direction to CPR Part 48.

As to damages–based agreements between claimants and their lawyers, lawyers may recover from their client under the agreement subject to strict caps laid down by the Act and by the Damages–Based Agreements Regulations 2013; but recoverability against the defendant is governed by CPR 44.18 whereby, if costs are to be assessed in favour of a party who has entered into a DBA, the recoverable costs will be assessed in the normal way (i.e. on the standard or indemnity basis) under rule 44.3; and the party may not recover more than the total amount that he has to pay for legal services under his DBA. Thus in some cases a party may recover less by way of costs from his opponent than he is liable to pay under his DBA.

The statutory reforms have included, in part as compensation to claimants for loss of recoverability of success fees, a 10% uplift in the level of general damages awarded against the defendant; see *Simmons v Castle* [2012]EWCA Civ 1039;1288.

2.5.24 The reforms set out in Paragraph 2.5.23 above take effect in relation to cases where the funding arrangement was made on or after April 1, 2013. The old rules as to recoverability of costs by a funded claimant continue to apply where the funding arrangement (called a "pre–commencement funding arrangement") was made before that date: see CPR 48.1 and 48.2. A valuable explanation of these transitional provisions is contained in the Practice Direction to Part 48. And see para.2.5.31 below.

2.5.25 Fixed Costs. Fixed costs are stipulated in Part 45 and are recoverable in the various situations there set out. These include, particularly in relation to proceedings in the Queen's Bench Division, the entry of judgment in default under Part 12, or on admission under Part 14, and on summary judgment under Part 24. They also include enforcement proceedings such as charging orders under Part 73. As may be expected, the court has power to order costs otherwise than by way of the fixed amounts, e.g. by way of summary or detailed assessment: see rule 45.1(1).

2.5.26 Part 46 and the Practice Direction to that Part deal with costs in special cases. These include:–

    (a) costs of pre–commencement disclosure applications

    (b) costs of applications for disclosure to be made by a non–party.

    (c) costs orders in favour of or against non–parties

    (d) limitations on the court's power to award costs in favour of a trustee or personal representative. The general rule is that his costs, in so far as they are not recovered from or paid by any other person, are to be paid out of the trust fund or estate.

    (e) costs where money is payable by or to a child or protected party. The general rule is that the court must order a detailed assessment of the costs. A particular exception, which frequently arises, is where another party has agreed to pay a specific sum in respect of costs and the legal representative of the child or protected party has waived the right to claim further costs.

    (f) the costs recoverable by litigants in person: see rule 46.5. Note the definition of a litigant in person in rule 46.5(6); and the amount of costs to be allowed for any item of work claimed in rule 46.5(4).

    (g) costs where the court has made a group litigation order: rule 46.6.

(h) orders in respect of pro bono representation, including orders for payment of a sum representing costs by the paying party to a specified charity.

(i) wasted costs orders against a legal representative personally: see rule 46.8, and also para.2.5.21 above.

(j) basis of detailed assessment of costs between solicitors and client: rules 46.9 and 46.10, and

(k) rules applicable in claims for the recovery of costs only i.e. where all other issues have been agreed: rule 46.14.

2.5.27 Part 47. Detailed assessment. The court may in its discretion order detailed assessment of the costs of proceedings or part of the proceedings. If it does so the provisions of Part 47 lay down the necessary procedure for assessment. An authorised costs officer may carry out the assessment in all save specified cases, subject to a right of appeal to a costs judge or a district judge of the High Court: rules 47.3 and 47.22.

2.5.28 At the outset however in relation to detailed assessment a new rule has been enacted, following pilot schemes. This relates to provisional assessment – see rule 47.15.

2.5.29 As from April 1, 2013, in cases where the costs claimed are £75,000 or less, the parties must comply with the procedure laid down for provisional assessment. The court will undertake a provisional assessment of the receiving party's costs on receipt of the required documents: rule 47.15(3). It may at any time decide that the matter is unsuitable for provisional assessment and direct an oral hearing, but subject to this the court will send a copy of the bill as provisionally assessed to all parties. If no request is then received, within 21 days, for an oral hearing the provisional assessment is binding save in exceptional circumstances. The rule then provides for the procedure for challenge at an oral hearing and states that any party who has requested an oral hearing will pay the costs of that hearing unless he achieves an adjustment in his own favour of 20% or more of the sum provisionally assessed.

2.5.30 Subject to provisional assessment, the rules as to detailed assessment generally are laid down by 47.1 to 47.14. These include particularly the following:

(a) the time when the assessment may be carried out. In general the assessment is not to be carried out until the conclusion of the proceedings, but the court may and often does order an immediate assessment at the end of a hearing.

(b) the power of authorised court officer to make a detailed assessment

(c) the venue for the assessment

(d) the commencement of the assessment (by the receiving party serving notice of commencement and a copy of the bill of costs)

(e) the time limited for commencement

(f) the sanctions for failing to commence assessment proceedings. In particular, the court has power, on application by a paying party, to make an unless order, in default of compliance with which all or part of the costs to which the receiving party would otherwise be entitled will be disallowed: see rule 47.8. Even if no such application is made, the court may disallow interest otherwise payable to the receiving party

(g) points of dispute by the paying party. The Practice Direction to Part 47 sets out the form of points of dispute. If points of dispute are not served within the required time (21 days after commencement) the receiving party may file a request for a default costs certificate. Such certificate when issued will include an order to pay the costs

(h) if points of dispute are served, rule 47.14 lays down a clear timetable, including provisions for the filing of a request for an oral hearing, the documents which must be lodged with the request, and the fixing of the hearing

(i) as noted above, in cases where the costs claimed are £75,000 or less, the rules introduce a mandatory procedure for provisional assessment: see rule 47.15 and para.14 of the PD to Part 47

(j) the court has power at any time after a request for detailed assessment has been filed to issue an interim certificate "for such sum as it considers appropriate"

(k) at the conclusion of the assessment, upon the filing of a completed bill following the assessment, the court will issue and serve a final certificate. This will include an order to pay the costs to which it relates unless the court orders otherwise: rule 47.17(5)

(l) rule 47.20 provides for the costs of the detailed assessment proceedings themselves.

2.5.31 Part 48 and the Practice Direction to that Part contain necessary saving provisions to allow the rules as to costs as they were in force up to 1st April 2013 to continue to apply to pre–commencement funding arrangements. Accordingly, in those cases, success fees, or after–the–event insurance premiums, may still be recoverable against the defendant where the funding arrangement was made before that date. However, in mesothelioma claims, certain insolvency proceedings, and publication and privacy proceedings, the new reforms preventing recovery of such fees or premiums under arrangements made on or after that date have still yet to be implemented. Accordingly, such fees or premiums continue to be recoverable against a defendant whenever the funding arrangement was made.

2.6 Court fees:

2.6.1 The court fees payable in the High Court are set out in detail in Schedule 1 to **1B–14** the Civil Proceedings Fees Order 2008 (S.I 2008 No. 1053), as amended by subsequent statutory instruments. Remissions and part remissions are dealt with in Schedule 2, as also amended. Information as to fees and remissions can be obtained from the Fees Office in Room E01 (see Plan A at the end of this Guide) or from the website at: **www.justice.gov.uk/guidance/courts–and–tribunals/courts/fees**.

2.6.2 In the Royal Courts of Justice fees are paid in the Fees Office and, by way of receipt, the fee is usually stamped on the document to which it relates.

2.7 Information Technology:

2.7.1 To support the work of the Central Office in operating the provisions of the **1B–15** CPR, and to facilitate effective case management, there is a computerised court system which is able to provide a brief log or index of documents filed in court, for example:–

(a) the claim form (with date of issue)
(b) the acknowledgement of service (with date of receipt)
(c) affidavits filed (with date of receipt)
(d) statements of case filed
(e) letters and e–mails received
(f) application notices (with date of receipt)
(g) orders (with date of the making of the order and date of sealing of the order)
(h) an order made, for example, under CPR 5.4C(4) that a non–party may not obtain a copy of a statement of case
(i) details of the parties or their legal representatives, including their addresses for service.

2.7.2 In relation to the filing of documents by electronic means the position is governed by CPR 5.5 and Practice Direction 5B. Communication of specified documents may be sent by e–mail or by the on–line forms service. Such communication is particularly useful in relation to filing application notices, (subject to payment of the fee therefor), case summaries, skeleton arguments, costs summaries (for summary assessment of costs) and draft orders. Once an order has been made, the Master will frequently direct that the party with responsibility for drawing up the order is to send him a draft by e–mail so that the Master may then give permission to seal the order in those terms.

2.7.3 Parties should note that a transmission received after 4pm is treated as received on the next day the court office is open; and that filing of a document by e–mail where a fee is payable is not permitted: see PD 5B para.3.3. Also note that the subject line of an e–mail must contain the case number, the parties' names (abbreviated if necessary) and the date and time of any forthcoming hearing. Any emails that do not comply will not be processed.

2.7.4 Parties should not file by electronic means where the number of pages of such documents renders that inconvenient. A limit of one attachment consisting of a maximum ten pages is prescribed by the Court. **Also, where one method of filing is chosen, it will not be appropriate to burden the court by filing by other means as well.**

2.7.5 As to service of documents (as opposed to filing), the position as to service of the claim form by fax or other electronic means is governed by CPR 6.3(1)(d); and the position as to service of other documents by fax or other electronic means is governed by CPR 6.20(1)(d). In either case the provisions of PD 6A apply. Parties should note the closely written terms of para.4 of that PD with which they must comply.

2.7.6 Video conferencing and telephone hearings. Under CPR 32.3 the court may allow a witness to give evidence through a video link or by other means. The Practice Direction to Part 32 contains, as Annex 3, extensive guidance on the use of video conferencing. Under PD 23A para.7, where parties wish to use video conferencing facilities for an application, they should apply to the Master for directions. Telephone hearings, which are now very frequent before the Masters, are dealt with under Paragraph 6 of PD 23A.

Section 3

Steps before the Issue of a Claim Form

3.1 Settlement:

1B–16 3.1.1 So far as reasonably possible, a claimant should try to resolve his claim without litigation. The court is increasingly taking the view that litigation should be a last resort and parties may wish to consider the use of Alternative Dispute Resolution ("ADR"): see Paragraph 6.6 below.

3.1.2 There are codes of practice for preliminary negotiations in certain types of claim. These codes of practice are called "Protocols" and are set out in Para.5.2 of the Protocols Practice Direction to the CPR. Even if there is no protocol that applies to the claim, the parties will nonetheless be expected to comply with principles governing their conduct. Those principles are set out in Section III of the Practice Direction. Where a protocol does apply litigants should refer to its detailed terms.

3.1.3 An offer to settle a claim may be made by either party whether before or after a claim is brought. The court will take account of any offer to settle made before proceedings are started when making any order as to costs after proceedings have started.

3.2 Disclosure before proceedings are started:

1B–17 3.2.1 An intending claimant may need documents to which he does not yet have access. If the documents are not disclosed voluntarily, in accordance with the Pre Action Protocols, then rule 31.16 sets out the provisions for making an application for disclosure of documents before proceedings have started. An application notice under Part 23 is required together with the appropriate fee. This may be issued in the Registry Section, Room E07, and will be assigned to a Master for hearing.

3.2.2 Essentially, the court must be satisfied that the applicant and respondent to the application are likely to be parties when proceedings are brought, that the required documents are those that the respondent would be required to disclose by way of standard disclosure under rule 31.6 when proceedings are brought, and that their early disclosure is desirable to dispose of or assist the disposal of anticipated proceedings or to save costs.

3.3 Defamation proceedings: Offer of Amends

1B–18 3.3.1 Application may be made to the court before a claim is brought for the court's assistance in accepting an offer of amends under section 3 of the Defamation Act 1996. The application is made by a Part 8 Claim Form. For more information see Paragraph 4.3 (Part 8 procedure) and Paragraph 8.1 (defamation) below.

Section 4

Starting Proceedings in the Central Office

4.1 Issuing and serving the Claim Form:

4.1.1 All claims must be started by issuing a claim form. The great majority of claims **1B–19** involve a dispute of fact, and the claim form should be issued in accordance with Part 7 of the CPR. The Part 8 procedure may be followed in the types of claim described in Paragraphs 4.3.1 to 4.3.3 below.

4.1.2 The requirements for issuing a claim form are set out in Part 7 and in Practice Direction 7A, the main points of which are summarised in the following paragraphs.

4.1.3 The Practice Direction, at Paragraphs 2, 3 and 4 thereof, provides information as to;
1. where a claim should be started,
2. certain matters that must be included in the claim form, and
3. how the heading of the claim should be set out in the claim form.

Parties should note that rule 16.2 and PD 16 para.2 also set out specific matters that must be included in the claim form. In defamation cases, the Part 53 Practice Direction sets out matters that must, in addition in such cases, be included in the claim form and particulars of claim.

4.1.4 Proceedings are started when the court issues a claim form. A claim form is issued on the date sealed on the claim form by the court. However, where a claim form is received in the court office on an earlier date than the date of issue, then, for the purposes of the Limitation Act 1980, the claim is brought on the earlier date (see Paragraphs 5.1 to 5.4 of the Practice Direction).

4.1.5 To start proceedings in the Action Department, a claimant must use form N1 (or form N208 for a Part 8 claim) (or a form suitably modified as permitted by Part 4), and should take or send the claim form to Room E07, Masters' Support Unit, Queen's Bench Action Department, Royal Courts of Justice, Strand, London WC2A 2LL. If the court is to serve the claim form, the claimant must provide sufficient copies for each defendant. The claimant will be required to provide a court copy, a claimant's copy and one copy for each named defendant. Copies of forms relevant to the work of the Action Department (including the claim form and response pack) are available from that office. Alternatively, claimants may produce their own forms, which may be modified as the circumstances require, provided that all essential information, especially any information or guidance which the form gives to the recipient, is included: see PD4–Forms, Para.1.2.

4.1.6 On issuing the claim form, the court will give or send the claimant a notice of issue endorsed with the date of issue of the claim form. If the claimant requires the court to serve the claim form, the date of posting and deemed date of service will also be endorsed on the notice of issue. Claimants and especially their solicitors who use the Action Department, are encouraged to serve their own documents but must inform the court when service has been effected (see Paragraph 4.4 below in relation to service by the claimant and the certificate of service). For certain types of claims, the notice of issue contains a request for judgment. (See Paragraph 5.5 below for information about default judgments.)

4.1.7 A claim form must be served within 4 months after the date of issue. rule 7.5 (1) sets out in precise terms, with reference to the mode of service employed, how the period of 4 months is calculated. Where the claim form is to be served out of the jurisdiction the period allowed is 6 months: see rule 7.5(2). Paragraph 4.4 below provides information about service.

4.1.8 Extension of time for service. Rule 7.6 and paragraph 8 of Practice Direction 7A set out how and on what grounds an extension of time for service of the claim form may be sought. Good reason must always be shown. In particular, the evidence should state a full explanation as to why the claim form has not been served: see Para 8.2(4). It has been emphasized that the reason for the failure to serve the claim form in time is highly material. The weaker the reason, the more likely the court will be to refuse to grant the extension. Furthermore, the general rule is that an application must be made within the time limited for service (either by rule 7.5 or by any earlier order extending time). If the application is made after that time the court may grant an extension only if the conditions in rule 7.6(3) are satisfied. These include the condition that the claimant has acted promptly in making the application.

4.2 Particulars of Claim

1B–20   4.2.1 Under rule 7.4, and under the Part 16 Practice Direction para.3.1, the particulars of claim must be contained in or served with the claim form; or must be served within 14 days after service of the claim form provided nonetheless that they are served within the latest time for serving the claim form.

4.2.2 A claim form that does not include particulars of claim must nevertheless include a concise statement of the nature of the claim: rule 16.2. And, when the particulars of claim are served, they must comply with rule 16.4 by setting out a concise statement of the facts on which the claimant relies. This last requirement is very important in practice.

4.2.3 Any claim form or particulars of claim that
   1. does not comply with rules 16.2 or 16.4, or
   2. is garbled or abusive

will be referred to a Master and is likely to be struck out by the court.

4.2.4 Where it is the claimant who serves the claim form, he must within 21 days after service of the particulars of claim, file a certificate of service (unless all defendants have filed an acknowledgement of service). He may not obtain judgment in default unless he does so. And, where the particulars of claim are served separately from the claim form, the claimant must also within 7 days file a copy of the particulars of claim (so that they are on the court record): compare rules 6.17 and 7.4.

4.2.5 Certain forms must accompany the particulars of claim when they are served on the defendant. These are listed in rule 7.8 and are included in a response pack which is available from the Masters' Support Unit.

4.2.6 A party who has entered into a funding arrangement and who wishes (subject to the new legislation as to recoverability: see Paragraphs 2.5.23, 2.5. 24 and 2.5.31 above) to claim an additional liability must give the court and any other party information about the claim if he is to recover the additional liability. Where the funding arrangement has been entered into before proceedings are commenced the claimant should file notice of funding in Form N251 when the claim form is issued.

4.2.7 Part 22 and the PD to Part 22 require the claim form and particulars of claim to be verified by a statement of truth. Where the particulars of claim are not included in the claim form itself they are to be separately verified by a statement of truth; see para.7 of PD 7A.

4.2.8 The requirements as to filing and service of particulars of claim do not apply where the claimant uses the Part 8 procedure: see rule 16.1.

4.3 Part 8 Procedure

1B–21   4.3.1 A claimant may use the Part 8 procedure where;
   (1) he seeks the court's decision on a question that is unlikely to involve a substantial dispute of fact, or
   (2) a rule or practice direction requires or permits the use of the Part 8 procedure.

However, the court may at any stage order the claim to continue as if the claimant had not used the Part 8 procedure: rule 8.1(3).

4.3.2 Certain matters that must be included on the claim form when the Part 8 procedure is being used are set out in rule 8.2. The types of claim, among many others, for which the Part 8 procedure may be used include;
   1. a claim by or against a child or protected party that has been settled before the commencement of proceedings, the sole purpose of the claim being to obtain the approval of the court to the settlement,
   2. a claim for provisional damages that has been settled before the commencement of proceedings, the sole purpose of the claim being to obtain a judgment by consent,
   3. a claim under S. 3 of the Defamation Act 1996 made other than in existing proceedings: see para.3.2 of the Part 53 Practice Direction; and

4. a claim under rule 46.14 where the parties have agreed all issues before the commencement of proceedings except the amount of costs and an order for costs is required.

4.3.3 In addition to the provisions of rule 8.1, attention is drawn also to Practice Direction 8A which deals with proceedings brought under "the Schedule Rules".

See Paragraph 6.7 below for more information regarding the Part 8 procedure.

4.4 Service:

4.4.1 Service of documents is dealt with in Part 6. This is split into sections. Section I **1B–22** (rules 6.1 and 6.2) deals with scope and interpretation. Section II (rules 6.3 to 6.19) deals with service of the claim form within the jurisdiction or, in specified circumstances, within the EEA. Section III (rules 6.20 to 6.29) deals with service of documents other than the claim form in the United Kingdom or, in specified circumstances, within the EEA. Section IV (rules 6.30 to 6.47) deals with service of the claim form and other documents out of the jurisdiction. Section V (rules 6.48 to 6.52) deals with service from foreign courts or tribunals. Some of the more important provisions are described below.

Within the jurisdiction Service of the claim form

4.4.2 The methods by which a claim form may be served are found in rule 6.3. Under rule 6.4, the court will serve the claim form except where
  (a) a rule or practice direction provides that the claimant must serve it
  (b) the claimant notifies the court that the claimant wishes to serve it, or
  (c) the court orders otherwise

It is anticipated that practitioners familiar with Central Office procedures will wish to continue to serve their own documents.

4.4.3 Where the court has undertaken service of the claim form it will send the claimant a notice including the date on which the claim form is deemed served: rule 6.17 (1). If however the court has attempted service by post and the claim form is returned, the court will send notification of that to the claimant: rule 6.18. Note however that, even in that case, the claim form will be deemed served unless the address for the defendant is not the correct address to comply with rules 6.7 to 6.10. The court will not try to serve the claim form again: rule 6.4(4).

4.4.4 Where the claimant has served the claim form, he must file a certificate of service within 21 days of service of the particulars of claim (unless all defendants have filed acknowledgements of service). He may not obtain judgment in default unless he has done so. rule 6.17, which must be carefully followed, sets out the contents of the certificate of service according to which method of service has been adopted; and it sets out the date of the relevant step taken by the claimant in the case of each such method.

4.4.5 Rule 6.5 applies to personal service. It describes what personal service is, and states when personal service must (in some cases) and may (in other cases) be effected.

4.4.6 The claimant must state on the claim form an address at which the defendant may be served, including a full postcode or its equivalent in any EEA state.

4.4.7 Where the defendant has given the business address within the jurisdiction of a solicitor as an address at which the defendant may be served, or has given the business address of a European lawyer in any EEA state as an address at which the defendant may be served, or such solicitors or lawyers have notified the claimant that they are instructed to accept service of the claim form at such an address, then the claim form must be served at such address: rule 6.7.

4.4.8 Subject to the defendant not having given before proceedings an address at which he may be served, rule 6.9 sets out, in well–known terms, the places where any particular defendant must be served, e.g in the case of an individual at his usual or last known residence. By recent amending legislation however, where the claimant has reason to believe that the address of the defendant is one at which he no longer resides, he must take reasonable steps to ascertain the defendant's current residence. Rule 6.9 goes on to provide a framework to cater for the results of such enquiries including, importantly, a provision for the claimant to apply for permission to serve by an alternative method under rule 6.15 where he cannot ascertain the defendant's current address: and see para.4.4.11 below.

4.4.9 Rule 6.13 deals with service of the claim form on children and protected parties.

4.4.10 The day of deemed service. In all cases of service within the jurisdiction this is the second business day after completion of the relevant step under rule 7.5 (1): see rule 6.14. "Business day" means any day except Saturday, Sunday, a bank holiday, Good Friday or Christmas Day: rule 6.2. Thus, the day of deemed service which affects, for example, the time for filing an acknowledgement of service or a defence by the defendant is always different from, and later than, the date of the relevant step which must be taken by the claimant.

4.4.11 Alternative service. Where there is good reason to authorise service of the claim form by a method or at a place not otherwise permitted, the court may, and quite often does, make an order: see rule 6.15. An application (which may be made without notice) must be made by application notice. It must be supported by evidence. The court will consider in its discretion whether to make an order and if so in what terms; and, if an order is made, the order must specify the method or place of service, the date of deemed service, and the period for filing an acknowledgement of service, an admission or a defence.

4.4.12 In exceptional circumstances the court may, either prospectively or retrospectively, dispense with service of a claim form: rule 6.16.

Service of documents other than the claim form

4.4.13 This is dealt with by the specific provisions of rules 6.20 to 6.29.

4.4.14 Rule 6.20 sets out the methods by which such other documents, which may of course be many and various in nature, may be served. Note the availability of service by fax or other electronic means, in which case the strictly regulatory provisions of Paragraph 4 of Practice Direction 6A must be followed.

4.4.15 Rule 6.21 provides for who is to serve such documents. In general a party will serve a document prepared by him, whereas the court will serve a document prepared by the court.

4.4.16 Rule 6.23 contains important provisions as to the duty on a party to provide an address for service of documents on him in the proceedings. This applies as much to the claimant, who will give an address in the claim form, as to the defendant. A party's address must be the business address of a solicitor or European lawyer acting for him or instructed to accept service for him; or, if none, an address in the United Kingdom or any other EEA state at which the party resides or carries on business; and, if that does not apply, an address for service in the United Kingdom. Occasions arise where the Master will be required to consider what order to make (e.g. an order to strike out) where a party fails or refuses to comply with this rule. Likewise, there is a duty on a party to give notice of change of address to the court and to every party as soon as it occurs: rule 6.24.

4.4.17 Service of documents other than the claim form on children and protected parties is dealt with by rule 6.25. In general, a child or protected party will have a litigation friend (see the detailed provisions of CPR 21.1 to 21.9), and the document in question will be served on him or, under the provisions of 6.23, on the solicitor acting in the litigation.

4.4.18 The date of deemed service is dealt with by rule 6.26 and the provisions of paras.10.1 to 10.7 of PD 6A. The provisions are detailed in accordance with the type of service adopted, and should be consulted in each case. For example, in the case of service by e–mail, if the e–mail is sent on a business day before 4.30 pm, service is deemed on that day; otherwise on the next business day after it was sent.

4.4.19 As with the claim form, an alternative method or place of service may be ordered: rule 6.27.

4.4.20 And, as with the claim form, a certificate of service must (where so required) be filed by the party serving the document setting out the method of service and date when the relevant step in effecting service took place: rule 6.29.

Out of the jurisdiction

4.4.21 The legislation is set out in Section IV of Part 6, which contains rules 6.30 to 6.47, and Practice Direction 6B.

4.4.22 Essentially, these relate to service of the claim form and other documents out of the jurisdiction; to the question of whether permission is or is not required to serve out and, if it is, how to obtain such permission; and to the procedure for such service.

4.4.23 It should be noted that a claimant may issue a claim form against a defendant who appears to be out of the jurisdiction, without first having obtained permission for service, provided that, if the case is not one where service may be effected without permission, the claim form is endorsed by the court "Not for service out of the Jurisdiction"

Without permission

4.4.24 Rules 6.32 and 6.33 deal with cases where the claimant may, without permission, serve a defendant in Scotland or Northern Ireland (rule 6.32); or out of the United Kingdom (rule 6.33). The rules are detailed and should be consulted in each case. If proceedings are served where they do not fall within the rules, they risk being struck out or stayed, e.g. for want of jurisdiction under CPR 11.

4.4.25 As a corollary to exercising his right to serve without permission, the claimant must comply with rule 6.34, i.e. he must file with the claim form a notice containing a statement of the grounds on which he is so entitled and serve a copy of that notice with the claim form. The form of the notice is found in Practice Form 510. And see PD 6B para.2.1. If the claimant fails to file such notice, the sanction contained in rule 6.34(2) is that the claim form may only be served once the claimant files the notice, or if the court gives permission. Again, proceedings which fall foul of this rule will stand the risk of being struck out or stayed.

4.4.26 The period for the defendant to file an acknowledgement of service, an admission, or a defence is set out in rule 6.35. The periods vary according to the country in which service took place. In each case the period will run from the date of service of the particulars of claim. In many cases, where service is in a foreign country falling under rule 6.35(5), resort will be had to the table contained in PD 6B (and referred to specifically in PD 6B paras.6.3 and 6.4) which sets out the country concerned and the period, in terms of days, for compliance.

With permission

4.4.27 Rule 6.36 governs the position. In any proceedings where permission is required, (i.e. where the "without permission" provisions of rules 6.32 and 6.33 do not apply) the claimant may serve the claim form out of the jurisdiction with the permission of the court if any of the grounds set out in para.3.1 of PD 6B apply. Those grounds are clearly set out and must be consulted in each case. It must be noted straight away however that the court will not give permission unless it is satisfied that England and Wales is the proper place in which to bring the claim: rule 6.37(3). And in this respect there are added qualifications for service in Scotland or Northern Ireland: 6.37(4).

4.4.28 Application for permission is made under rule 6.37. That rule requires an application notice complying with Part 23. The application must set out which ground in para.3.1 of the Practice Direction is relied on. The proper practice is to support the application with a witness statement verified by a statement of truth, or to verify the contents of the application notice itself by a statement of truth, in each case stating the facts relied on and stating specifically (by number) the sub–paragraph of para.3.1 relied on. Furthermore, the application must state that the claimant believes that the claim has a reasonable prospect of success: see 6.37 (1)(b); and must state the defendant's address or, if not known, in what place the defendant is, or is likely, to be found. Applications which do not comply with these requirements will not be granted.

4.4.29 In the event that permission is granted, the court order will specify the periods for acknowledgement of service, admission or defence. Again, resort will be had to the table set out in Practice Direction 6B for the number of days required. The court may also, and often does, give directions about the method of service.

4.4.30 Under rule 6.38, where permission is required to serve the claim form out of the jurisdiction, permission is likewise required to serve any other document in the proceedings. Separate permission for the particulars of claim is not however required where the court gives permission for the claim form to be served and the claim form itself states that particulars of claim are to follow.

Methods of service out of the jurisdiction

4.4.31 The various methods of service available are set out in rules 6.40(2) and (3). Where service is to take place in Scotland or Northern Ireland the method must be one permitted by sections II or III of Part 6. Where service is to take place out of the UK the method may be one of those referred to in rule 6.40(3). These include particularly:

(1) service through a Receiving Agency under the Service Regulation, i.e. Council Regulation (EC) No 1393/2007. This is printed as an annex to PD 6B. Rule 6.41 sets out the documents which the claimant must file when he proposes service under the Regulation. He files them in the Foreign Process Section in Room E10, and

(2) service through the authority designated under the Hague Convention or any other Civil Procedure Convention or Treaty in respect of the country concerned. The procedure in that case is fully laid out in rule 6.43.

4.4.32 The remaining methods of service, and the procedure to be followed if they are adopted, are set out in rules 6.42 to 6.45. These include service on a State as defined in rule 6.44.

4.4.33 It should be noted that service out of the UK may be achieved by any method permitted by the law of the country in which service is to take place; but that nothing in rule 6.40(3) or in any court order authorises or requires any person to do anything which is contrary to the law of the country where the document is to be served: rule 6.40(4).

4.4.34 There is jurisdiction in an appropriate case to make an order permitting service out of the jurisdiction by an alternative method or at an alternative place but an order cannot be made if its effect would be contrary to the law of the country concerned. The jurisdiction to make such an order and the circumstances in which discretion may be exercised to make such an order are the subject of the decision of the Supreme Court in *Abela v Baadarani* [2013] UKSC 44, per Lord Clarke of Stone–cum–Ebony JSC. As to alternative service see Paragraph 4.4.11 above.

4.4.35 Further advice on service out of the jurisdiction may be obtained from the Foreign Process Section in Room E10.

Service of documents from Foreign Courts or Tribunals

4.4.36 Section V of Part 6 (containing rules 6.48 to 6.52) deals with incoming service from a foreign court or tribunal. Such rules do not apply where the Service Regulation, which has its own in–built provisions, applies. Service is by request from the foreign court to the Senior Master, who will determine the method of service. This is usually by a process server. Once service is effected the process server must send to the Senior Master a copy of the document and proof of service (or a statement why the document could not be served); and the Senior Master will send to the person requesting service a certificate stating when and how the document was served (or the reason why it has not been served) and a copy of the document.

Section 5

Response to a Part 7 Claim

5.1 General:

5.1.1 Responding to particulars of claim is dealt with in Part 9. A defendant may **1B–23** respond to the service of particulars of claim by;
1. filing or serving an admission in accordance with Part 14,
2. filing a defence in accordance with Part 15,
3. doing both (if part only of the claim is admitted), or
4. filing an acknowledgement of service in accordance with Part 10.

5.1.2 Where a defendant receives a claim form that states that particulars of claim are to follow, he need not respond to the claim until the particulars of claim have been served on him.

5.1.3 Where a defendant fails to file an acknowledgement of service within the time specified in rule 10.3 or to file a defence within the time specified in rule 15.4 the claimant may obtain default judgment if Part 12 allows it. (See Paragraph 5.5 below for information about default judgments.)

5.2 Acknowledgement of service:

5.2.1 Acknowledgements of service are dealt with in Part 10. A defendant may file an **1B–24** acknowledgement of service if;
    (a) he is unable to file a defence within the period specified in rule 15.4; or
    (b) he wishes to dispute the court's jurisdiction under Part 11. Indeed, under rule 11(2) a defendant who wishes to dispute jurisdiction must first file an acknowledgement of service. The rules concerning an application to dispute jurisdiction and the results of any such application, depending on whether an order is or is not made declaring that the court has no jurisdiction, are set out in detail in Part 11.

Filing an acknowledgement of service has, in general, the effect of extending the time for filing the defence by 14 days; see rule 15.4.

5.2.2 A defendant who wishes to acknowledge service of a claim form should do so by using form N9.

5.2.3. Rule 10.5 states that the acknowledgement of service must;
    (a) be signed by the defendant or his legal representative, and
    (b) include the defendant's address for service, as to which see para.4.4.16 above.

The Part 10 Practice Direction contains further information relating to the acknowledgement of service and how it may be signed.

5.3 Admissions:

5.3.1 The manner in which, and the time within which, a defendant may make an **1B–25** admission of a claim or part of a claim are set out in rules 14.1 to 14.2.

5.3.2 As to admission made after the commencement of proceedings, the position is laid down by rule 14.1. The defendant may admit the claim in writing such as by a statement of case or by letter. If the only remedy sought by the claimant is the payment of money, the defendant may also make his admission as follows:
    (a) under rule 14.4 (admission of whole claim for specified amount)
    (b) under rule 14.5 (admission of part of claim for specified amount)
    (c) under rule 14.6 (admission of liability to pay whole of claim for unspecified amount)
    (d) under rule 14.7 (admission of liability to pay claim for unspecified amount where defendant offers a sum in satisfaction.

5.3.3 It is these forms of admission as above which will govern the procedure to be then followed, and the right of the claimant to obtain judgment.

5.3.4 If the admission is made in writing under rule 14.1(2), application may be made for judgment. Judgment shall be such "as it appears to the court that the applicant is entitled to on the admission": rule 14.3.

5.3.5 If admission is made of the whole claim for a specified amount of money, the position is governed by rule 14.4. The defendant will return the relevant practice form (in form N9A included in the response pack accompanying the claim form) to the claimant. The claimant may then file a request for judgment in form N225A. At that stage, matters will depend on whether the defendant has in his admission requested time to pay. If he has not, the claimant may request judgment payable by a certain date or at a certain rate. Judgment will be entered for the amount of the claim and costs payable at that time or rate; or, if the claimant has not specified a time or rate, immediately: rule 14.4(6). If, as is more usual, the defendant has requested time to pay, the procedure in rules 14.9 and 14.10 will apply, namely that the claimant may accept the defendant's request. If he does, judgment will be entered for payment at the time and rate specified in the defendant's request. If he does not, judgment will be entered for the amount admitted at a time and rate determined by the court: rule 14.10(4). Determination may be by a court officer without a hearing where the amount outstanding is not more than £50,000: rule 14.11. This is subject to a right of re-determination by a judge: rule 14.13. The question whether such re-determination takes place at a hearing or without a hearing is governed by para.5 of the Part 14 Practice Direction.

5.3.6 Admission of part of a claim for a specified amount of money is governed by rule 14.5. On receipt of such an admission the court will serve notice on the claimant requiring him to state:
    (a) that he accepts the amount admitted in satisfaction,
    (b) that he does not so accept and wishes the proceedings to continue, or
    (c) that if the defendant has requested time to pay, he accepts the amount admitted but not the defendant's proposals as to payment.

The procedure then for entering judgment and determining the time and rate of payment is similar to that described under para.5.3.5 above. If the claimant wishes the proceedings to continue, the procedure in Part 26 will operate: see para.6.5 below.

5.3.7 Where the defendant admits liability to pay the whole claim for an unspecified amount the position is governed by rule 14.6. After the necessary steps judgment will be entered for an amount to be decided by the court. The amount may then be decided by a Master at a disposal hearing. For the procedure, see para.12 of the Practice Direction to Part 26. Note that directions may be given: para.12.2.

5.3.8 If the defendant admits liability to pay a claim for an unspecified amount of money and offers a sum in satisfaction the position is governed by rule 14.7. If the claimant accepts the offer he may obtain judgment; and the position as to payment by instalments if requested will be that laid down in rule 14.9. If the claimant does not accept the offer he may obtain judgment for an amount to be decided by the court and costs.

5.3.9 It should be noted that where determination of the time and rate of payment under judgment for a specified sum is to be by a judge at a hearing, the proceedings will, if the defendant is an individual, be transferred to the defendant's home court: rule 14.12.

5.3.10 The factors to be taken into account by the court in deciding time and rate of payment are set out in para.5.1 of the PD to Part 14, including the defendant's statement of means.

5.3.11 An admission may be made before the commencement of proceedings. The circumstances in which this may be done are laid down in rule 14.1A. Application may be made by the claimant for judgment on the pre-action admission. And application may be made by the person who made it for permission to withdraw it: see rule 14.1A(5).

5.3.12 Applications for permission to withdraw an admission under Part 14, whether an admission made after commencement of proceedings under rule 14.1 or a pre–action admission under rule 14.1A, are governed by the PD to Part 14. In deciding whether to give permission the court will have regard to all the circumstances, including the particular matters under para.7.2. One of those matters, but not the only one, is whether new evidence has come to light. The interests of the administration of justice are also engaged: para.7.2(g).

5.3.13 Interest. The right to enter judgment for an amount of interest claimed is governed by rule 14.14. If the closely defined conditions of that rule are not satisfied, judgment will be for interest to be decided by the court.

5.3.14 Judgment will not be entered on an admission where;
1. the defendant is a child or protected party, or
2. the claimant is a child or protected party and the admission is made in respect of
    (a) part of a claim for a specified amount of money, or
    (b) by way of a sum offered in satisfaction of a claim for an unspecified amount of money.

See Part 21 and the Part 21 Practice Direction, and in particular rule 21.10 which provides that, where a claim is made by or on behalf of a child or protected party or against a child or protected party, no settlement, compromise or payment shall be valid, so far as it relates to such claim, without the approval of the court.

5.4 Defence:

5.4.1 A defendant who wishes to defend all or part of a claim must file a defence, and **1B–26** if he fails to do so the claimant may obtain default judgment if Part 12 allows it. The time for filing a defence is set out in rule 15.4. As to the contents of the defence, see para.5.7 below.

5.4.2 A form for defending the claim is included in the response pack. The form for defending the claim also contains provision for making a counterclaim. Part 22 requires a defence to be verified by a statement of truth (see the Part 15 Practice Direction, paragraph 2; and see also Part 22 and the Part 22 Practice Direction). The court may, amongst its other powers, strike out a defence which is not verified by a statement of truth.

5.4.3 The parties may, by agreement, extend the period specified in rule 15.4 for filing a defence by up to 28 days. If the parties do so, the defendant must notify the court in writing of the date by which the defence must be filed. If the claimant will not agree to extend time for filing of the defence, or if a defendant seeks further time beyond 28 days, the defendant must issue an application under Part 23 to obtain a court order for further time. The claimant may consent to such an application. The Master has a very wide discretion when considering applications to extend time and may, if he sees fit, impose terms when granting an order.

5.5 Default judgment:

5.5.1 CPR Part 12 governs the position. A claimant may obtain default judgment, i.e. **1B–27** judgment without trial where the defendant has failed to file an acknowledgment of service or has failed to file a defence. The conditions to be satisfied in either case are clearly laid down in rules 12.3.(1) and (2). Judgment in default is not however permitted in the cases set out in rule 12.2 (among which are cases using the Part 8 procedure), and in rule 12.3(3) (among which are, importantly, cases where the defendant has applied to strike out the claim or for summary judgment on the claim and the application has not been disposed of). See also paras.1.2 and 1.3 of the Part 12 Practice Direction.

5.5.2 To obtain default judgment in the circumstances set out in rule 12.4(1) (i.e on a claim for a specified amount of money, an amount of money to be decided by the court, or for delivery of goods where the claim gives the option for the defendant to pay their value) the claimant may file a request for judgment. The limits of this rule are often overlooked in practice. If the claimant seeks default judgment where the claim consists of or includes a claim for any other remedy he must make an application for that purpose: rule 12.4(2)(a). He may however obtain a default judgment on request if he abandons the claim for any other remedy in his request: rule 12.4(3).

5.5.3 The request is made in forms N205A or N225 for specified amounts or, in the case of claims where the amount of money or the amount representing the value of goods is to decided by the court, in forms 205B or 227. A court officer deals with the request and will require to be satisfied that the provisions of PD12 para.4.1 are complied with before entering judgment.

5.5.4 Default judgment in respect of claims specified in rule 12.4(2)(a) as described above, or rules 12.9 or 12.10, must be obtained by making an application to a Master. rule 12.9 is concerned with claims for costs only (other than fixed costs). rule 12.10 is concerned, importantly, with claims against a child or protected party, and (inter alia) claims in tort by a spouse or civil partner against the other, claims against a defendant served without permission out of the jurisdiction under the Civil Jurisdiction and Judgments Act 1982, claims against a defendant domiciled in Scotland or Northern Ireland and claims against a State. Procedural provisions are contained in rule 12.11 and the Part 12 Practice Direction.

5.5.5 Where application is made, judgment is to be such judgment as it appears to the court that the claimant is entitled to on his statement of case: rule 12.11 (1).

5.5.6 The Crown. Special provisions apply in proceedings against the Crown. Under rule 12.4(4), a request for default judgment must be considered by a Master or District Judge, who must in particular be satisfied that the proceedings have been properly served on the Crown in accordance with Section 18 of the Crown Proceedings Act 1947 and rule 6.10.

5.5.7 Where default judgment has been obtained for an amount to be decided by the court, the matter will be referred to a Master for directions and a date to be fixed for the disposal hearing.

5.6 Setting aside default judgment

1B–28 5.6.1 It is open to the court to set aside a default judgment under rules 13.2 or 13.3. In the former case the judgment must be set aside if the judgment was wrongly entered because any of the conditions referred to in the rule have not been satisfied, or if the whole of the claim was satisfied before judgment was entered. In the latter case, the judgment may be set aside or varied if (a) the defendant has a real prospect of successfully defending the claim, or (b) there is some other good reason why the judgment should be set aside or varied or why the defendant should be allowed to defend the claim. The court must have regard to whether the applicant made the application promptly. Close attention is always paid to this rule. Further, in deciding whether to set aside or vary the court has wide discretionary powers to impose terms (such as payment into court) on the applicant.

5.7 Statements of Case:

1B–29 5.7.1 Statements of case are defined in rule 2.3(1) They include the claim form, the particulars of claim where not included in the claim form, the defence and any reply. They also include any further information in relation to them, whether given voluntarily or under court order. Part 16 deals specifically with statements of case. Note that Part 16 does not apply to cases proceeding under Part 8.

5.7.2 The particulars of claim, whether contained in the claim form or served separately, should set out the claim clearly and fully. The same principle applies to the defence.

5.7.3 Part 16 sets out certain matters that must be included in a statement of case. Paras.4 to 7 of the Practice Direction contain matters that must be included in specific types of claim; and para.8 contains matters that must be specifically set out in the particulars of claim if relied upon. These include, but are not limited to, any allegation of fraud, and details of any misrepresentation. As to the defence, rule 16.5 deals with the matter. At the forefront of the defendant's obligations are the requirement to state which of the claimant's allegations he denies; which he is unable to admit or deny but which he requires the claimant to prove; and which he admits. If the defendant denies an allegation he must state his reasons for doing so; and if he intends to put forward a different version of events from that given by the claimant he must state his own version. Points of law may be set out in any statement of case. For information in respect of statements of case in defamation claims see the Part 53 Practice Direction.

5.7.4 In addition to the requirements contained in Part 16 and the Part 16 Practice Direction, the following guidelines on preparing a statement of case should be followed;

    (1) a statement of case must be as brief and concise as possible and confined to setting out the bald facts and not the evidence of them,

    (2) a statement of case should be set out in separate consecutively numbered paragraphs and sub–paragraphs,

    (3) so far as possible each paragraph or sub–paragraph should contain no more than one allegation,

    (4) the facts and other matters alleged should be set out as far as reasonably possible in chronological order,

    (5) the statement of case should deal with the claim on a point–by–point basis, to allow a point–by–point response,

    (6) where a party is required to give reasons, the allegation should be stated first and then the reasons listed one by one in separate numbered sub–paragraphs,

    (7) a party wishing to advance a positive claim must identify that claim in the statement of case,

    (8) any matter which, if not stated, might take another party by surprise should be stated,

    (9) where they will assist, headings, abbreviations and definitions should be used and a glossary annexed; contentious headings, abbreviations, paraphrasing and definitions should not be used and every effort should be made to ensure that they are in a form acceptable to the other parties,

    (10) particulars of primary allegations should be stated as particulars and not as primary allegations,

    (11) schedules or appendices should be used if this would be helpful, for example where lengthy particulars are necessary, and any response should also be stated in a schedule or appendix,

    (12) any lengthy extracts from documents should be placed in a schedule.

5.7.5 A statement of case should be verified by a statement of truth. If a party fails to verify his statement of case, it will remain effective unless struck out, but that party may not rely on the statement of case as evidence of any of the matters contained in it. A statement of case verified by a statement of truth is advisable so as to constitute evidence at hearings other than the trial: see rule 32.6(2). Any party may apply to the court for an order to strike out a statement of case which has not been verified.

Section 6

Preliminary Case Management

6.1 The Practice Master:

6.1.1 On every working day, the Practice Master is available from 10.30a.m. to **1B–30** 1.00p.m. and from 2.00p.m. to 4.30p.m. to deal with questions about the practice of the Queen's Bench Division. Usually, one Master takes the Morning Practice, and another Master takes the Afternoon Practice. This will be shown on the Daily Cause List, on the notice boards in the Masters' corridor, and on the Listing Notice board outside the Foreign Process Section, Room E16. Also, a board is placed on the door of the Master who is sitting as Practice Master.

6.1.2 The Practice Master is there to deal with urgent applications which do not require notice to be given to the Respondent and to deal with any Consent Orders notwithstanding that the claim in which it is to be made has been assigned to another Master. Furthermore he may grant urgent stays of execution on terms considered appropriate by him. The Practice Master is also there to give guidance on the many questions of practice and procedure which will arise on a daily basis in litigation in the Queen's Bench Division. It is unnecessary to make an appointment to see the Practice Master and litigants are generally seen in order of arrival. However, the Practice Master cannot give advice whether about a given case or about the law generally.

6.2 Assignment to Masters:

1B–31 6.2.1 A claim issued in the Central Office will normally be assigned upon issue to a particular Master as the procedural judge responsible for managing the claim. The Masters' Support Unit will endorse the name of the assigned Master on the claim form. However, assignment may be triggered at an earlier stage, for example, in one of the following events:

    1. an application for pre–action disclosure under rule 31.16,

    2. an application for an interim remedy before the commencement of a claim or where there is no relevant claim (Part 25).

It occasionally happens that a claim is assigned to a Master who may have an "interest" in the claim. In such cases the Senior Master will re–assign the claim to another Master.

6.2.2 Where either an application notice or a Part 8 Claim Form is issued which requires a hearing date to be given immediately, the Registry will assign a Master and the Masters' Support Unit will give a hearing date.

6.2.3 The Senior Master may assign a particular Master to a class/group of claims or may re–assign work generally. At present clinical negligence claims are assigned to Master Roberts and Master Cook. Claims for mesothelioma are assigned to Master Eastman and Master McCloud. In the event of an assigned Master being on leave or for any other reason temporarily absent from the Royal Courts of Justice then the Masters' Support Unit may endorse on the appropriate document the name of another Master.

6.2.4 A court file will be opened when a claim form is issued. The name of the assigned Master will be endorsed on the court file and entered on the claim form. Any application notice in an assigned claim for hearing before a Master should have the name of the assigned Master entered on it by the solicitors/litigant making the application.

6.3 Listing before Masters:

1B–32 6.3.1 The Masters' lists consist of:

    1. the Chambers List – short applications of not more than half an hour in Room E102 ("the Bear Garden list"). The Masters take this list by rotation on each morning of the week. Cases are listed at 10.30am; 11am; 11.30am; and 12 noon. There is an additional list on some days at 2pm.

    2. Private Room Appointments, (using the prescribed PRA form to obtain the appointment) and

    3. the High Court Enforcement Officer's Interpleader applications (formerly Sheriffs' Interpleader applications): and see Paragraph 12.5 below.

6.3.2 Parties attending on all applications before the Masters are requested to complete the Court Record Sheet (form PF48), which will be used to record details of the parties' names, representation and the nature of the application. Copies of this form may be found on the writing desks in the Masters' corridor and the Bear Garden. The form will be placed on the file when the hearing is concluded.

6.3.3 Solicitors and Counsel may attend any application in the Bear Garden although the costs of being represented by Counsel may be disallowed if not fully justified. As a matter of courtesy parties should inform the other side in advance if Counsel is being retained. If the Master considers that the application is likely to take longer than 30 minutes he may adjourn it to a private room appointment. The applicant must then complete the PRA form giving details of the parties' availability as fully as possible. Failure to do so may result in the form being returned for further information thereby delaying the hearing date. The PRA form is available in the Masters' Support Unit, Room E07 and from the Court Service Website.

6.3.4 Hearing dates for the Chambers Lists (Bear Garden lists) are given by the Masters' Support Unit. The assigned Master gives hearing dates for private room appointments personally. The parties or their legal representatives must inform the Masters' Support Unit of any settlements as soon as possible. All time estimates must be updated as necessary. Any order made which results in a hearing not being required must be notified to the Master by using the Notice of Cancellation form available from the Masters' Support Unit Room E07. This should be completed by the parties, and will be sent to the assigned Master as soon as possible for him to note in his diary accordingly.

6.3.5 Applications in the Chambers Lists (Bear Garden lists) may, by agreement or where the application notice has not been served, be transferred to a private room appointment on a date to be specified by the Master, or may be re–listed for another date in the Chambers List. In all other cases an application for a postponement of the hearing date must be made to the Master to whom the claim has been assigned. An application may be re–listed in the Chambers List (Bear Garden list) without permission of a Master if for any reason the application has not been heard or has not been fully disposed of.

6.3.6 When an application in the Bear Garden list is adjourned by a Master he will specify the date to which it is adjourned.

6.3.7 An application for the adjournment of a private room appointment must be made to the Master who gave the appointment unless the application is by agreement of all parties and the Master approves. The Master will usually require details of parties' availability. Any adjournment will normally be to a new hearing date.

6.3.8 If the application for an adjournment is opposed by any other party, the party seeking the adjournment must issue an application for an adjournment, if time permits, and must give the court and all other parties as much notice as possible of such application. Where possible, it is preferable that such application is heard before the date for the hearing. The Master will not grant an adjournment readily where it is opposed by any other party. Good reason will need to be shown, and if the reason is illness of a party, an original (not a photocopy) medical certificate signed and dated by a medical practitioner should be produced, setting out the reasons why attendance at court is not possible.

6.3.9 If an adjournment of a hearing is granted, the Master will usually require details of parties' availability in order to fix the new date.

6.3.10 Where an application for which a Master has given a private room appointment has been settled, it is the duty of the parties or their legal representatives, particularly those who obtained that appointment, to notify the Master immediately.

6.3.11 If the Master hearing an application considers that the result of the application might affect the date fixed for a trial, he may refer the application to the Judge in Charge of the Lists. This possibility should be considered when making an application, and a request should if appropriate be included in the application notice asking the Master to refer the application to the Judge.

6.3.12 If the Master considers that an application should more properly be heard by a Judge, he may either during the hearing or before it takes place refer the application to the Interim Applications Judge. See in particular PD 2B para.1.2. Among the circumstances that may make this appropriate are;
   1. that the time required for the hearing is longer than a Master could ordinarily make available,
   2. that the application raises issues of unusual difficulty or importance etc., or
   3. that the outcome is likely to affect the trial date or window (in which case the referral will be to the Judge in Charge of the Lists).

However, it is emphasised that no single factor or combination of factors is necessarily decisive, and the Master has a complete discretion.

6.3.13 The High Court Enforcement Officer's first return applications are interpleader applications (see Paragraph 6.3.1 above). The jurisdiction of the Master, who may make a variety of orders on such applications, is found at RSC Order 17 in Schedule 1 to the CPR. These applications are listed before a Master at 10.30am or 2pm, usually on alternate Mondays in each month. Any enquiries about such applications should be made to the Enforcement Section in Room E17.

6.4 Automatic Transfer:

1B–33 6.4.1 Part 26 requires certain claims to be transferred automatically. Where:

1. the claim is for a specified amount of money,
2. the claim has not been issued in a specialist list,
3. the defendant, or one of the defendants, is an individual,
4. the claim has not been issued in the individual defendant's home court, and
5. the claim has not already been transferred to another individual defendant's home court, the claim will, on receipt of the defence, be transferred to the individual defendant's home court.

6.4.2 The defendant's home court will be the district registry for the district in which the defendant resides or carries on business or where (as in London) there is no such district registry, the Royal Courts of Justice. Accordingly, in such cases, where proceedings are started in the Royal Courts of Justice, they will remain there. If the claim is against more than one individual defendant, the claim will be transferred to the home court of the defendant who first files a defence.

6.4.3 In relation to court orders for transfer (as opposed to automatic transfer) see Paragraph 6.9 below.

6.5 Allocation and directions:

1B–34 6.5.1 As previously observed (para.1.2.1 above) the allocation of cases in the High Court is necessarily to the multi–track. Accordingly, the provisions of the new CPR 26.3 (taking effect from 1ˢᵗ April 2013) as to provisional allocation by a court officer are unlikely to be of great significance in the High Court. What is required is, once a defence has been filed, for the court to serve a notice of proposed allocation which will require the parties to file a completed Directions Questionnaire by the date specified in the notice: rule 26.3(1)(b). If the notice does not contain a provision requiring a costs budget to be filed and exchanged by a particular date the budget must be filed and exchanged at least 7 days before the first case management conference or as otherwise directed. The form of the Directions questionnaire is in form N181. A party must serve a copy of his DQ on all other parties. The court will in the case of an unrepresented litigant provide a copy of the form for completion by that party. Where there are two or more defendants, and at least one of them files a defence, the notice from the court will be served when all defendants have filed a defence or (if sooner) when the time for filing the last defence has expired.

6.5.2 Of particular importance when completing the DQ are the obligations on a party:–

(1) to give the court further information if believed to be relevant to costs and case management, and to copy this to the other parties. In particular the cost of any proposed expert report should be given at section E and if it is thought that the claim should not be subjected to costs budgeting reasons should be given: PD 26, para.2.2 (1),

(2) to consult the other parties and to co–operate in completing the questionnaire: PD26, para.2.3(1),

(3) to try to agree case management directions with the other parties: PD 26, para.2.3(2). Specimen directions are available on the Justice website as now referred to in that paragraph.

6.5.3 It should be noted that in multi–track cases a costs budget need not be filed with the DQ but must be filed in accordance with rule 3.13. it should also be noted that failure by a party to file a costs budget as required may result in that party's recoverable costs being limited to the applicable court fees only: see rule 3.14.

6.5.4 In cases of automatic transfer under rule 26.2 the court will not transfer the claim until all parties have complied with the notice to file a DQ or the time for doing so has expired.

6.5.5 Stay to allow for settlement of the case. A party may when filing his completed DQ make a written request for the proceedings to be stayed while the parties try to settle the case by ADR or other means. If all parties request a stay, the proceedings will be stayed for one month and the court will notify the parties accordingly. In addition, if the court considers that such a stay would be appropriate it will direct that the proceedings, either in whole or in part, be stayed for one month or such other period as it considers appropriate: see rule 26.4.

6.5.6 Assuming compliance by the parties with the obligation to file a DQ the court will allocate the claim to the multi-track unless it proposes to order (as the circumstances of the claim may warrant) transfer to the county court, or unless it has stayed the proceedings under rule 26.4: see rule 26.5.

6.5.7 In the event of default, however, by a party of his obligation to file a DQ the court has wide and varied powers. rule 26.3(8) provides that the court will make such order as it considers appropriate, including:–

(a) an order for directions
(b) an order to strike out the claim
(c) an order to strike out the defence and enter judgment, or
(d) an order to list the case for a CMC

Costs consequences are likely to arise against a party in default under rule 26.3(10).

6.6 Alternative Dispute Resolution ("ADR"):

6.6.1 Parties are encouraged to use ADR (such as, but not confined to, mediation, **1B–35** conciliation and early neutral evaluation) to try to resolve their disputes or particular issues. Legal representatives should consider with their clients and the other parties the possibility of attempting to resolve the dispute or particular issues by ADR and they should ensure that their clients are fully informed as to the most cost effective means of resolving the dispute.

6.6.2 The settlement of disputes by ADR can:

(1) significantly reduce parties' costs,
(2) save parties the delay of litigation in resolving their disputes,
(3) assist parties to preserve their existing commercial relationships while resolving their disputes, and
(4) provide a wider range of remedies than those available through litigation.

The Master will, in an appropriate case, invite the parties to consider whether their dispute, or particular issues in it, could be resolved by ADR. The Master may also either stay proceedings for a specified period of time or extend the time for compliance with an order, a rule or practice direction so as to encourage and enable the parties to use ADR. Parties may apply for directions seeking a stay for ADR at any time.

6.6.3 Valuable information concerning the availability of ADR may be obtained, among other sources, from the Advice Guide published by the Citizens Advice Bureau at **www.adviceguide.org.uk**

6.7 Part 8—Alternative procedure for claims:

6.7.1 Paragraph 4.3 above refers to the availability of an alternative means of making **1B–36** a claim, namely by using the Part 8 procedure. Rule 8.1(2) lays down the types of claim where the procedure may be used, notably where no significant dispute of fact will be involved. It will be noted also that a rule or practice direction may, in relation to a specified type of proceedings, "require or permit" the use of the Part 8 procedure. Thus, Practice Direction 8A sets out, in para.3.1, examples of cases where it <u>may</u> be used. And, importantly, in para.3.2, certain proceedings where it <u>must</u> be used. Those latter proceedings include the claims, petitions and applications listed in the table in Section B of the Practice Direction. That table usefully sets out the jurisdictional origin of the application in question, with a reference, where applicable, to the Rule of the former Rules of the Supreme Court under which the jurisdiction was exercised. An example, frequently arising in practice, is an application for interpleader relief by the High Court Enforcement Officer (formerly the Sheriff) under RSC Order 17, rule 3(1).

6.7.2 A rule or practice direction may disapply or modify the rules set out in Part 8 so far as they relate to particular types of proceedings. Thus, Section C of PD8A lays down its own procedural regime for each of the particular applications referred to in section C.

6.7.3 The main features of the Part 8 procedure are:–
   (a) the claim form is issued in Form N208
   (b) it must state that Part 8 applies
   (c) it must state the question which the claimant wants the court to decide; or the remedy which the claimant is seeking and the legal basis for the claim to that remedy.
   (d) if the claim is made under an enactment, it must state what that enactment is
   (e) Part 16 (statements of case) does not apply, but the claimant may be required to file details when issuing, for example as may be required by Section C of PD8A relating to the application in question.
   (f) Part 15 (defence and reply) does not apply
   (g) judgment in default may not be obtained: see CPR 12.2 and 8.1(5)
   (h) the claimant may not obtain judgment by request on an admission and therefore rules 14.4 to 14.7 do not apply
   (i) the claim shall be treated as allocated to the multi–track (see however PD8A, para.8.2 under which directions may be given specifically allocating to track).

6.7.4 All Part 8 claim forms will be referred to a Master for directions as soon as issued. These may include fixing a hearing date. Where a hearing date is fixed, notice of the hearing date must be served with the claim form. Where the Master does not fix a hearing date when the claim form is issued he will give directions for the disposal of the claim as soon as practicable after the receipt of the acknowledgement of service or, as the case may be, the expiry of the period for acknowledging service. The court may, and often does, convene a directions hearing under PD6A para.6.4 before giving directions.

6.7.5 Where a Part 8 claim form has been issued for the purpose of approving and giving effect to a consent order for an award of damages to a child or protected party or an award of provisional damages as in Paragraph 4.3.2 above, a draft of the order sought should be attached to the claim form. For more information see Paragraphs 6.8.1 to 6.8.15 and 10.3.10 to 10.3.12 about children and protected parties, and 6.8.16 and 10.3.13 and 10.3.14 about provisional damages.

6.7.6 A defendant who wishes to respond to a Part 8 claim form should acknowledge service of it and may do so either by using form N210 or otherwise in writing giving the following information:
   (1) whether he contests the claim, and
   (2) where he is seeking a different remedy from that set out in the claim form, what that remedy is.

If a defendant does not acknowledge service of the claim form within the specified time he may attend the hearing of the claim but may not take part in the hearing unless the court gives permission.

6.7.7 Rules 8.5 and 8.6 and paragraph 7 of the Part 8 Practice Direction deal with evidence to be relied on in Part 8 proceedings. The claimant's evidence must be filed and served with the claim form, and the defendant's evidence (if any) must be filed with his acknowledgement of service. If the defendant files written evidence he must at the same time serve it on the other parties. It is helpful to the court if, where the defendant does not intend to rely on written evidence, he notifies the court in writing to that effect.

6.7.8 Where a defendant contends that the Part 8 procedure should not be used, he may state his reasons when he files an acknowledgement of service: rule 8.8(1). If he objects to the use of the Part 8 procedure and (as may well be the case) his reasons include matters of evidence, his acknowledgment of service must be verified by a statement of truth: PD8A, para.5.3.

6.7.9 Furthermore, the court itself has wide powers as to the continuation of a claim under the Part 8 procedure. It may, under rule 8.1(3), at any stage order the claim to continue as if the claimant had not used the Part 8 procedure, and where it does so it may give any directions it considers appropriate.

6.8 Specific matters which may be dealt with under the procedure:

Settlements on behalf of children and protected parties

6.8.1 Part 21 of the CPR and the Practice Direction to Part 21 set out the **1B–37** requirements for litigation by or against children and protected parties. Part 21 contains its own definitions.

Thus:–

    (1) "child" means a person under 18, and

    (2) "protected party" means a party, or an intended party, who lacks capacity to conduct the proceedings.

6.8.2 "Lacks capacity" means lacks capacity within the meaning of the Mental Capacity Act 2005. That Act supplies the meaning by enacting, in Section 2(1), that a person lacks capacity in relation to a matter if at the material time he is unable to make a decision for himself in relation to the matter because of an impairment of, or a disturbance in the functioning of, the mind or brain. Reference should be made to the specific provisions of Sections 1, 2 and 3 of the Act which relate to that definition; and judicial assistance is found in the decision in *V v R* [2001] EWHC 822 (QB) when considering whether or not a claimant has capacity to conduct litigation with reference to the above tests.

6.8.3 No settlement or compromise of a claim by or against a child or protected party will be valid, so far as it relates to the claim by or against the child or protected party, unless and until the court has approved it: CPR 21.10 (1). Furthermore, a settlement of a claim by a child includes an agreement on a sum to be apportioned to a dependent child under the Fatal Accidents Act 1976: see para.1.3 of the Practice Direction. It should be noted also that the approval of the court is required to sanction any interim payment, including any voluntary interim payment, under the claim.

6.8.4 A protected party must have a litigation friend to conduct proceedings on his behalf. So must a child, unless the court makes an order permitting the child to act without one. A litigation friend is, under rule 21.4(3), someone who can fairly and competently conduct proceedings on behalf of the child or protected party, has no interest adverse to that of the child or protected party, and (where the child or protected party is a claimant) undertakes to pay any costs which the child or protected party may be ordered to pay in relation to the proceedings. Such person must file a certificate of suitability stating that he satisfies those requirements. Rules 21.4 to 21.8, and Paragraphs 2 and 3 of the Practice Direction, set out how a person may become a litigation friend.

6.8.5 Applications for the approval of settlements or compromises of claims by or against a child or protected party proceeding in the Central Office are heard by a Master. If the purpose of starting the claim is to obtain approval, a Part 8 claim form must be issued in Form N208 and must include a request to the court for approval of the settlement or compromise. The claim form must, in addition to satisfying the requirements of rule 21.10(2), include all the information set out in paragraph 5 of the Practice Direction. Thus, the terms of the settlement or compromise must be set out or (as is usually required by the Master) a draft consent order in Form N292 should be provided. Amongst the other requirements, the information should contain the litigation friend's approval of the proposed settlement or compromise and, under para.5.2(1), an opinion on the merits of the settlement given by counsel or solicitor acting for the child or protected party. Where, in any personal injury case, a claim for future pecuniary loss is settled the court must be satisfied that the parties have considered whether the damages should take the form of periodical payments. And, if the settlement does include provision for periodical payments the draft order should comply with rules 41.8 and 41.9 setting out the details of such payments: see para.5 of the Practice Direction. The Part 8 claim form must, of course, be served on the opposing party and, in accordance with the procedure under Part 8, the Master will give a hearing, for an appropriate date and length of time, to consider the question of approval.

6.8.6 Where parties reach a settlement or compromise in proceedings already started by the issue of Part 7 claim form (where the trial has not started) an application must be made to the Master for approval. Such application is by application notice in Form N244 and should follow the terms of form PF170(B). A draft consent order should be provided in Form N292. The application notice is lodged in Room E07.

6.8.7 As in the case of settlements before proceedings have started (Paragraph 6.8.5 above), where in any personal injury case a claim for future pecuniary loss is settled the court must be satisfied, on an application for approval, that the parties have considered whether the award should take the form of periodical payments; and, if the settlement does include provision for periodical payments, the requirements of rules 41.8 and 41.9 must be satisfied: see para.6 of the Practice Direction.

6.8.8 The procedure for obtaining approval in cases involving dependent children under the Fatal Accidents Act 1976 are as described above, depending on whether proceedings have or have not already been started. (see paras.6.8.5 and 6.8.6). Since settlement of a claim under the Act may well involve the apportionment to children of part of the total sum awarded, approval will be required. Paragraph 7.4 of the Practice Direction sets out the matters of which the court must particularly be informed. It should be remembered that approval proceedings in such cases will require the court's consideration of the appropriateness of the whole sum agreed, in order then to consider the appropriateness of the amount apportioned to each child.

6.8.9 Approval hearings will normally be held in public unless the Judge or Master orders otherwise. The court may however make an anonymity order, namely that the identity of any party must not be disclosed if it considers non–disclosure necessary to protect the interest of that party: CPR 39.2(4).

6.8.10 Investment of the approved sum. CPR 21.11 requires that money recovered by or on behalf of or for the benefit of a child or protected party will be dealt with in accordance with directions under that rule and not otherwise.

6.8.11 Protected parties. The court is required to consider whether the protected party is also a protected beneficiary. If that is the case, directions will be given in accordance with para.10 of the Part 21 Practice Direction which should be consulted for its terms. In cases of £50,000 or more the order will, unless a power of attorney is in place or a deputy has already been appointed by the Court of Protection, be that the litigation friend is to apply to the Court of Protection for the appointment of a deputy after which the fund will be dealt with as directed by that Court. A form of order transferring the fund to the Court of Protection is set out in form N292. If the fund is under £50,000 it may be retained in court and invested in the same way as the fund of a child. By an amendment to para.10 of the Practice Direction the Court of Protection now has jurisdiction to make such an order even in the case of a fund of £50,000 or more, either of its own initiative or at the request of the judge giving directions on approval of the settlement.

6.8.12 Children. Paragraph 9 of the Practice Direction applies. At the approval hearing the litigation friend or his legal representative must provide the court with the child's birth certificate and form CFO 320 (initial application for investment of damages) for completion by the Judge or Master. Also, any evidence or information which the litigation friend wishes the court to consider in relation to investment must be provided. Following the hearing and making of the court order, the court will forward to the Court Funds Office a request for investment decision in Form 212 and the Court Funds Office will make the appropriate investment.

6.8.13 If the court has approved periodical payments by way of the whole or part of an award (whether in the case of a child or a protected party) it will, in accordance with CPR 41.8 and 41.9, include in its order the specific terms that are required to be embodied by those two rules. Such terms frequently require complex drafting and the court will expect to be provided in advance with a draft order considered by both parties to the litigation.

6.8.14 An approved order for investment may include liberty to apply to vary the form of investment. And, as a separate matter, the Master may hear applications by the litigation friend from time to time to direct payments out of the fund in order to defray proper expenditure on the child's behalf. Good reason must be shown to support such applications, particularly in Fatal Accident Act cases where a parent of the child has himself or herself been awarded damages on his or her own behalf which may be expected to include provision for the day to day maintenance of the child.

6.8.15 When a child reaches full age control of his fund must (provided he is not also a protected beneficiary) pass to him. If the fund is in the form of money it will, on his application be paid out to him. If in the form of investments, they will either be sold and the proceeds paid out to him, or transferred into his name: see para.13 of the Practice Direction.

Settlement of a provisional damages claim

6.8.16 A claim for provisional damages may proceed under Part 8 where the claim form is issued solely for the purposes of obtaining a consent judgment. The claimant must state in his claim form, in addition to the matters set out in Paragraph 4.4 of the Part 16 Practice Direction, that the parties have reached agreement and request a consent judgment. A draft order in accordance with Paragraph 4.2 of the Part 41 Practice Direction should be attached to the claim form. The claimant or his legal representative must lodge the case file documents (set out in the draft order) in Room E07. Once the provisional damages claim has been approved the documents lodged will be compiled into a file and preserved by the court. For more information about provisional damages claims and orders, see Part 41 and the Part 41 Practice Direction, and Paragraphs 10.3.13 and 10.3.14 below.

Costs only proceedings

6.8.17 Proceedings may be brought under Part 8 where the parties to a dispute have reached an agreement on all issues (including which party is to pay the costs) which is made or confirmed in writing but have failed to agree the amount of those costs, and no proceedings have been started. The position is governed by the new CPR 46.14 and para.9 of the Part 46 PD. A Part 8 claim form may be issued to determine the amount of such costs but should not be issued in the High Court unless the dispute to which the agreement relates was of such a value or type that proceedings would have been commenced in the High Court. A claim form which is to be issued in the High Court at the Royal Courts of Justice will be issued in the Senior Courts Costs Office at Thomas More Building, Royal Courts of Justice, Strand, London WC2A 2LL. Paragraphs 9.3 to 9.12 of the PD helpfully set out the procedure to be followed.

6.9 Transfer:

6.9.1 The Queen's Bench Division has power, and in some cases an obligation, to **1B–38** order transfer of a case proceeding in such Division.

6.9.2 Thus, under Section 40(1) of the County Courts Act 1984, where the High Court is satisfied that any proceedings before it are required by an enactment to be in a county court, it shall order transfer of the proceedings to a county court. Under the same subsection, if the court is satisfied that the person bringing the proceedings knew, or ought to have known, of that requirement, it shall order that the proceedings be struck out. The court is however not bound to strike out in such cases but may, and should normally, order transfer to a county court.

6.9.3 Important financial limits in relation to starting proceedings in the High Court are found in the High Court and County Courts Jurisdiction Order 1991 (S.I 1991 No724) as amended, and in Practice Direction 7A to Part 7 of the CPR.

6.9.4 Thus, under para.2.1 of the Practice Direction a claim for money in which the county courts have jurisdiction may only be commenced in the High Court if the value of the claim is more than £100,000. Article 4A of the Jurisdiction Order has been amended accordingly. And, under Article 5, proceedings (other than claims for clinical negligence) which include a claim for damages in respect of personal injuries may only be commenced in the High Court if the value of the claim is £50,000 or more.

6.9.5 Subject to the requirements of Section 40(1), the High Court has a wide discretion as to whether or not a case should be transferred to the county court: see Section 40(2). Such an order, if made, may be made of the court's own motion or on the application of a party. Rule 30.2 of the CPR specifically sets out the criteria to which the court should have regard when considering whether or not to make an order under S.40(2). These include amongst other considerations the financial value of the claim, and whether the facts, legal issues, remedies or procedures involved are simple or complex.

6.9.6 Guidance is also given by the Part 29 Practice Direction, which applies to claims begun by claim form issued in the Central Office. By para.2.2 of this PD, a claim with an estimated value of less than £100,000 will generally be transferred to a county court unless

(a) it is required by an enactment to be tried in the High Court

(b) it falls within a specialist list

(c) it falls within one of the categories set out in para.2.6, which include:–

   (1) professional negligence claims

   (2) Fatal Accident Act claims

   (3) fraud or undue influence claims

   (4) defamation claims

   (5) claims for malicious prosecution or false imprisonment

   (6) claims against the police

6.9.7 If proceedings are transferred under the discretionary power under Section 40(2), they are to be transferred to such county court as the High Court considers appropriate, having regard (inter alia) to the convenience of the parties.

6.9.8 Section 41 of the County Courts Act 1984 contains provisions for the High Court to order transfer <u>from</u> a county court to the High Court; and Section 42(2) contains provisions for a county court to order such transfer. The criteria already referred to in CPR 30.3(2) are again applicable when the court is considering the matter.

6.9.9 Transfers <u>within</u> the High Court

(A) Transfers from the Royal Courts of Justice to a district registry; or from a district registry to the Royal Courts of Justice or to another district registry. CPR 30.2(4) governs the position; and again the criteria in rule 30.3 are applicable. It should be noted that an application to transfer <u>from</u> a district registry must be made to the district registry in which the claim is proceeding.

(B) Transfers between Divisions of the High Court and to and from a specialist list. CPR 30.5 governs the position. There is a wide discretion to order transfer from one Division to another. Recourse in practice is often had to Schedule 1 to the Senior Courts Act 1981 under which certain causes and matters are specifically assigned to the Chancery Division and, respectively, the Queen's Bench Division. The Master's order for transfer may refer to such schedule. In the case of transfer to a specialist list, it should not be overlooked that application is made, not to the Master, but to the Judge dealing with claims in that list: rule 30.5(3).

6.9.10 An order for transfer takes effect from the date on which it is made. When the order is sealed the court officer will immediately send the file to the receiving court. At the same time the court officer will notify the parties of the transfer.

6.9.11 An order for transfer to the Queen's Bench Division of the High Court at the Royal Courts of Justice should, in order to avoid any ambiguity, state "transfer to the Queen's Bench Action Department, Central Office, Queen's Bench Division, Royal Courts of Justice"

6.9.12 An order for transfer may be made without notice to a party. If so made, any application to set aside the order should be made in accordance with the procedure in Part 23 (in particular rule 23.10) and the Part 23 Practice Direction; and it should be made to the court which made the order: PD30, para.6.1.

6.10 Part 20 proceedings: counterclaims and other additional claims

6.10.1 The regime for making counterclaims or other additional claims is laid down **1B–39** in Part 20 and the Part 20 Practice Direction.

6.10.2 Thus Part 20 deals with (a) counterclaims, i.e. counterclaims by a defendant against the claimant or against the claimant and some other person, (b) an additional claim by the defendant against any person (whether or not already a party) for contribution or indemnity, or some other remedy and (c) where an additional claim has been made against a person who is not already a party, any additional claim made by that person against any other person (whether or not already a party).

6.10.3 A defendant may make a counterclaim against a claimant by filing particulars of the counterclaim. He will do so by completing the defence and counterclaim form provided in the response pack. He must also pay the relevant fee payable on the counterclaim. He may counterclaim without the permission of the court when filing his defence. Otherwise he must apply for permission. The matters which the court will consider on an application for permission are laid down in rule 20.9. And Paragraph 2 of the Practice Direction requires that the application for permission must be supported by evidence stating (inter alia) the stage which the proceedings have reached and the nature of the additional claim to be made or details of the question or issue to be decided. Particulars of claim under the proposed counterclaim should be provided.

6.10.4 Where a counterclaim seeks to bring in a new party the defendant must apply for permission: rule 20.5. He should apply in Form PF21A adding the new party as defendant; and the provisions of para.2 of the Practice Direction will again apply.

6.10.5 A defendant claiming contribution or indemnity from another defendant may do so by filing notice in Form PF22 and serving it on the other defendant. He may do so without permission if he files and serves it with his defence. Otherwise he must apply for permission: rule 20.6.

6.10.6 Any other additional claim may be brought by the issue of a Part 20 claim form in Form N211. Again, no permission is required if the additional claim form is issued before or at the same time as the defendant files his defence: rule 20.7. Otherwise permission must be applied for by application notice in Form N244.

6.10.7 Rule 20.8 deals with service of a Part 20 claim form and rule 20.12 sets out the forms which must accompany the claim form on such service. It should be noted that where the court gives permission to make an additional claim it will give directions as to its service (rule 20.8 (3)); and where the court makes an order giving permission to add an additional party it will give directions as to the management of the case (rule 20.5 (3)). Thus, parties on an application for permission should be alert to such directions as may be required and may wish to provide the Master with a draft order.

6.10.8 As to nomenclature in relation to the parties in a case which involves additional claims, the Practice Direction gives very clear guidance. Thus, for example, under para.7.4, where a defendant makes separate additional claims against two additional parties, the additional parties are referred to in the title of the proceedings as "Third Party" and "Fourth Party". Whereas, under para.7.5, if an additional claim is made against more than one party jointly, the additional parties are referred to in the title as "First Named Third Party" and "Second Named Third Party"

6.10.9 Where a defence is filed to an additional claim the court must consider the future conduct of the proceedings and give appropriate directions. So far as practicable these will ensure that the original claim and the additional claims are managed together: rule 20.13.

6.11 Striking Out

6.11.1 The court has wide powers, both under its inherent jurisdiction and under the **1B–40** CPR, to strike out proceedings or part of them. A sizeable proportion of the Masters' and District Judges' work concerns applications to strike out a statement of case, whether by a defendant to strike out a claim form or particulars of claim, or by a claimant to strike out a defence.

6.11.2 Statements of case must be intelligible. If they are garbled or incoherent or abusive they may be struck out without further order. The court has a discretion under rule 3.4(2)(b) to strike out a statement of case that is an abuse of the Court's process or is otherwise likely to obstruct the just disposal of the proceedings.

6.11.3 Though a statement of case may be properly presented it may nonetheless show no case on its merits. Thus an application may be brought by a party to strike out his opponent's case on the ground that it discloses no reasonable grounds for bringing or defending the claim: rule 3.4(2)(a). This may, for example, be because, assuming the facts stated to be true, the claim form or particulars of claim does not disclose a claim known to the law.

6.11.4 Parties should consult Practice Direction 3A which gives useful examples. A party applying to strike out may combine his application with an application for summary judgment under Part 24 (see para.6.12 below). Thus, as referred to in para.1.7 of the PD, a party may believe that he can show without trial that an opponent's case has no real prospect of success on the facts, or that the case is bound to succeed or fail, as the case may be, because of a point of law, including the construction (or interpretation) of a document. In such a case the party concerned may make an application under rule 3.4 (striking out) or Part 24 (summary judgment) or both as he thinks appropriate,

6.11.5 Evidence is admissible by witness statement in applications to strike out and is usually tendered. An applicant must however show that there is no valid answer to his application. The hearing is not in substitution for a trial. If there are material facts which are truly in issue and which should be determined at trial (for example by cross–examination of witnesses) the court will not strike out.

6.11.6 The power to strike out a statement of case extends to cases where there has been a failure to comply with a rule, practice direction or court order: rule 3.4 (2)(c). This power is frequently exercised, particularly in cases of failure to comply with a time limit in the rules, though in practice the court in some cases may in the first instance make an "unless order" including (typically) an order that unless he complies with a certain requirement by a certain time on a certain day, his statement of case will be struck out. Parties must nonetheless beware of the fact that a stricter approach is now applied to granting relief from sanctions imposed for a failure to comply with any rule, practice direction or court order: see para.7.15 below.

6.11.7 A statement of case which is defective and liable to be struck out may be curable by amendment. In such cases the Master may impose terms such as an order that, unless an application be made and served by (date) for permission to amend the statement of case, the same will be struck out; and that, upon the making of any such application for permission to amend, the application to strike out be adjourned for further consideration together with the application to amend. It frequently occurs that a claim is on the face of it barred by a statutory lime limit. In order to preserve the claimant's right to apply to exclude the time limit (as for example under Section 33 of the Limitation Act 1980) the court may order that, unless such an application is made and served by a certain date, the claim be struck out; and that, upon the making of any such application, the case be listed for further directions to be given so that the application can appropriately be dealt with in the proceedings.

6.11.8 Striking out may well arise, not upon an application by a party, but by order of the court's own initiative: see the court's powers under rule 3.3 (and see para.7.16 below). Thus, as frequently happens, a court officer may be asked to issue a claim form which he believes to fall within rule 3.4 (2)(a) or (b). In that case PD3A para.2.1 gives guidance. It provides that the court officer should issue the claim form but may then consult a judge (who is likely to be a Master or District Judge) before returning the claim form to the claimant or taking any other step to serve it. The judge may then of his own initiative make an immediate order designed to ensure that the claim is disposed of or (as the case may be) proceeds in a way that accords with the rules. Paragraph 2.4 of the PD then gives an example of an order that is frequently adopted by the Master or District Judge. The fact, if it be the case, that a claim is allowed to proceed in such circumstances does not prejudice the right of any party to apply for an order against the claimant: para 2.6.

6.11.9 Claimant's cases that are totally without merit are the subject of special treatment under rule 3.4(6). If appropriate, the court may make a civil restraint order against the claimant: see para.7.14 below.

6.12 Summary Judgment:

6.12.1 The court may give summary judgment under Part 24 against a claimant or **1B–41** defendant on the whole of a claim or on a particular issue if
- (a) it considers that (i) the claimant has no real prospect of succeeding on the claim or issue, or (ii) the defendant has no real prospect of successfully defending the claim or issue; and
- (b) there is no other compelling reason why the claim or issue should be disposed of at a trial.

6.12.2 The court may give summary judgment against a claimant in any type of proceedings; and against a defendant in any type of proceedings except (a) proceedings for possession of residential premises against a mortgagor, or a tenant or person holding over after the end of his tenancy whose occupancy is protected within the meaning of the Rent Act 1977 or the Housing Act 1988, and (b) proceedings for an admiralty claim in rem. For information about summary disposal of defamation claims see Part 53, the Part 53 Practice Direction and paragraph 8.3 below.

6.12.3 Parties should note that a claimant may not apply for summary judgment against a defendant who has not filed an acknowledgment or service or a defence unless the court gives permission or a practice direction provides otherwise. Such permission may be given in very clear cases where it is appropriate that the claimant should have the opportunity to apply for judgment on the merits rather than entering judgment in default.

6.12.4 An application for summary judgment should be made in accordance with Part 23. The application notice must comply with the requirements of Paragraph 2 of the Part 24 Practice Direction. Particular attention is drawn to the requirements of para.2(3), failure to comply with which may result in the application notice being rejected. The application notice should be filed and served on the respondent giving at least 14 days notice of the date fixed for the hearing and the issues to be decided at the hearing. Unless the application notice itself contains all the evidence on which the applicant relies, the application notice should identify that evidence.

6.12.5 The application will normally be listed before a Master unless, for example, an injunction is also sought: see PD2 para.2.2. In that case the application notice should state that the application is intended to be made to a Judge. The Master may also, in an appropriate case, direct that the application be referred to a Judge for hearing: see PD2 para.1.2.

6.12.6 . The orders which the court may make on a summary judgment application are concisely set out in PD24 para.5. Where an order made on an application for summary judgment does not dispose of the claim or issue, the court will give case management directions in respect of the claim or issue.

6.13 Offers to settle and payments into and out of court:

6.13.1 Part 36 deals with offers to settle. The rules in this Part came into force on 6 **1B–42** April 2007. As to offers made before that date, transitional provisions are found in Practice Direction 36B and should be consulted if necessary.

6.13.2 A party may offer to settle a claim in whatever way he chooses. But if the offer is not made in accordance with Part 36 it will not have the costs consequences which Part 36 specifies. Where an admissible offer to settle is made which does not accord with Part 36, rule 44.2 should be consulted. See in particular rule 44.2 (4)(c).

6.13.3 An offer to settle made in accordance with Part 36 will have the costs and other consequences specified in that Part. It must, under rule 36.2:–
- (a) be in writing
- (b) state on the face of it that it is intended to have the consequences of Section I of Part 36
- (c) specify a period of not less than 21 days within which the defendant will be li-

able for the claimant's costs in accordance with rule 36.10 if the offer is accepted (not applicable if the offer is made less than 21 days before the start of the trial)

(d) state whether it relates to the whole claim or to part of it or to an issue that arises in it and if so which part or issue

(e) state whether it takes into account any counterclaim

6.13.4 A Part 36 offer may be an offer to settle solely in relation to liability: rule 36.2(5),

6.13.5 The offer may be made at any time, including before the commencement of proceedings. It will be treated as inclusive of all interest until the specified period of not less than 21 days has expired. It may be withdrawn before the expiry of that period only with the permission of the court; but without permission after the expiry of such period. Notice of withdrawal or change of terms of an offer is served by written notice on the offeree: rule 36.3.

6.13.6 In personal injury claims which include a claim for future pecuniary loss, attention must be paid when making a Part 36 offer to the requirements of rule 36.5. In particular, if the offer or part of the offer is for periodical payments, the amount and duration of such payments, and the way in which the continuity of such payments will be secured must (among other requirements) be spelt out. And, if such an offer is accepted, the claimant must within 7 days of the acceptance, <u>apply</u> to the court for an order under rule 41.8.

6.13.7 Again, where a Part 36 offeror proposes that a settlement shall include an award of provisional damages, there are special provisions in rule 36.6 as to what the offer must state. And, if such offer is accepted, the claimant must apply for an order for provisional damages under rule 41.2.

6.13.8 A Part 36 offer is made on the date when it is served on the offeree.

6.13.9 Clarification of a Part 36 offer may be, and often is in practice, called for under rule 36.8. There is a time limit of 7 days to seek such clarification. If it is not given, application to the court may be made. If the court makes an order it will then specify the date on which the offer is treated as having been made.

6.13.10 A Part 36 offer may be accepted by serving notice in writing at any time unless the offer has been withdrawn: rule 36.9(1) and (2). Permission to accept is however required in specified cases, including (as set out in rule 36.12(1) those where the offer is made by one or more but not all of multiple defendants, and those where the trial has started. The notice of acceptance must be filed with the court. It has been held that a Part 36 offer no longer remains open for acceptance where the claim has been struck out or there has been failure to comply with an unless order: *Joyce v West Bus Coach Services Ltd* [2012] EWHC 404.

6.13.11 If permission is required to accept a Part 36 offer, application must be made in accordance with Part 23. Such application must be dealt with by a judge other than the judge allocated to conduct the trial, unless the parties agree otherwise: see PD 36 para.3.2.

6.13.12 Cost consequences. If the offer is accepted within the relevant period (as defined in rule 36.3) the claimant will be entitled to the costs of the proceedings up to the date of service of the notice of acceptance: see rule 36.10(1). Such costs will be assessed on the standard basis if not agreed. Special provision is made in cases where a defendant's offer relates to part only of the claim: rule 36.10(2).

6.13.13 Where however (a) a Part 36 offer that was made less than 21 days before trial is accepted, or (b) a Part 36 offer is accepted after the expiry of the relevant period, the court will (unless the parties agree) be called on to make an order as to costs. And, in the latter case, unless the court orders otherwise,

(i) the claimant will be entitled to costs up to the date on which the relevant period expired, and

(ii) the offeree will be liable for the offeror's costs for the period from the date of expiry to the date of acceptance: see rule 36.10(4) and (5).

6.13.14 The effect of acceptance is to stay the claim upon the terms of the offer. If the offer relates to part of the claim, however, special provisions apply: rule 36.11. A stay does not affect the power of the court to enforce the terms of the offer under its general jurisdiction; nor does it affect the power of the court to deal with any question of costs. As to enforcement generally, see rule 36.11(6) and (7).

6.13.15 Rule 36.12 deals with offers by one or more, but not all, of multiple defendants.

6.13.16 Rule 36.13 provides that a Part 36 offer is to be treated as without prejudice save as to costs, and deals with questions that may arise as to the communication of such offer to the trial judge.

6.13.17 Rule 36.14 deals with the costs consequences where judgment is entered on a claim, namely:–

    (a) If the claimant fails to beat the defendant's Part 36 offer, the court will, unless it considers it unjust to do so, order the defendant's costs from the date of expiry of the relevant period under rule 36.2, and interest on those costs.

    (b) If, on the other hand, the claimant obtains judgment at least as advantageous as contained in his own Part 36 offer, he will be entitled to interest on the sum awarded, and costs on the indemnity basis plus interest on those costs. Furthermore, by the addition of a new Paragraph 36.14(3)(d) to the rule, the claimant's reward for making an adequate Part 36 offer is increased by an uplift, calculated on the amount of money awarded by the judgment or (in the case of a non–monetary claim) on the sum awarded in respect of costs. Reference should be made to the terms of the new rule and to the statutory instrument which introduced it, namely the Offers to Settle in Civil Proceedings Order 2013 (S.I 2013 No.93). The amendment does not apply to a claimant's offer which was made before April 1, 2013.

6.13.18 Deduction of benefits. Rule 36.15 governs the position where payment to a claimant following a Part 36 offer would be a compensation payment as defined in the Social Security (Recovery of Benefits) Act 1977. A defendant making a Part 36 offer should state (a) whether the offer is made without regard to any liability for recoverable amounts, or (b), on the contrary, that it is intended to include any deductible amounts. If the latter, a regime is set out in rules 36.15(5) to (9) for specifying the net amount of compensation and for ascertaining whether on judgment being entered the claimant has or has not beaten the Part 36 offer. Care should be taken to ensure that the amount of benefit to be set off is set off only against the appropriate head of damage in respect of which the benefit has been paid (e.g past loss of earnings) and is not being brought generally into account.

6.13.19 Part 37 deals with payments into and out of court, which are now confined to certain limited circumstances:

    1. Money paid into court under a court order—a party making such a payment must serve notice of this on every other party and file a certificate of service in respect of each such notice.

    2. Where a defendant wishes to rely on a defence of tender before claim he must make a payment into court of the amount which he says was tendered.

    3. Payments into court under enactments—see the Part 37 Practice Direction, paragraphs 4 to 8.

6.13.20 Money paid into court should be paid by cheque payable to the Accountant General of the Senior Courts. It must be accompanied by a sealed copy of the order providing for the payment in, or an copy of the defence, whichever is applicable, and the Court Funds Office form 100.

6.13.21 Money paid into court under a court order or in support of a defence of tender may not be paid out without the court's permission except where a Part 36 offer is accepted without needing the permission of the court and the defendant agrees that a sum paid into court by him should be used to satisfy the offer in whole or in part.

6.13.22 Where permission is required to take funds out of court an application must be made in accordance with Part 23. If the court's permission is not required, the requesting party should file a request for payment in Court Funds Office form 201 with the Court Funds Office, accompanied by a statement that the defendant agrees that the money should be used to satisfy the Part 36 offer in Court Funds Office form 202: see the Part 37 Practice Direction, para.3.5 for the details required to be provided on the form. A party is obliged to notify the court whether he is or has been in receipt of legal funding by the Legal Services Commission.

SECTION 7

CASE MANAGEMENT AND INTERIM REMEDIES

7.1 Case management—general:

1B–43 7.1.1 The CPR require the court to provide a high degree of case and costs management. Case management includes; identifying disputed issues at an early stage; fixing timetables; dealing with as many aspects of the claim as possible on the same occasion; controlling costs; disposing of proceedings summarily (including striking out) where appropriate; dealing with applications without a hearing where appropriate; and giving directions to ensure that the trial of a claim proceeds quickly and efficiently. The court will expect the parties to co–operate with each other and, where appropriate, will encourage the parties to use ADR or otherwise help them settle the case.

7.1.2 Costs management requires the court to manage both the steps to be taken and the costs to be incurred by a party so as to further the overriding objective: rule 3.12(2). The task of the court when reviewing budgets is not to carry out a detailed assessment but to consider whether the budgeted costs fall within the range of reasonable and proportionate costs, see Practice Direction 3E paragraph 2.3.

7.1.3 Paragraph 6.5 above deals with the parties' obligations when filing Directions Questionnaires under Part 26. Assuming that the claim is to remain in the High Court and is to be allocated to the multi–track, Part 29 and the Practice Direction to Part 29 lay down comprehensive provisions as to the management of the claim.

7.1.4 Parties and their legal representatives will be expected to do all that they can to agree proposals for the management of the claim in accordance with rule 29.4 and paragraphs 4.6 to 4.8 of the Part 29 Practice Direction. They must submit agreed directions, or their respective proposals, to the court at least 7 days before any case management conference. Attention should be paid to para.5 of the PD which spells out particular matters which the court will consider at any such CMC. There is provision in the Directions Questionnaire for proposing certain directions to be made; otherwise parties may use form PF 50 for making the application (attaching to it the draft form of order in form PF 52) and file it for the Master's approval. If the Master approves the proposals he will give directions accordingly. It should be noted that when drafting case management directions both the parties and the court should take as their starting point any relevant model directions and standard directions which can be found on the website referred to in rule 29.1(2) and adapt them as appropriate to the circumstances of the particular case.

7.1.5 Case management and costs management are interrelated. The court will usually wish to consider making a costs management order at the first case management hearing. The parties should file their respective costs budgets at least 7 days before the hearing unless otherwise ordered. The Master will expect the parties to have discussed the budgets before they are prepared so that the parties are working on the same assumptions and the budgets are prepared so that the work included in each stage of proceedings can easily be compared.

7.2 The Costs and Case Management Conference:

1B–44 7.2.1 Parties who are unable to agree proposals for the management of the case should notify the court of the matters which they are unable to agree.

7.2.2 Where:
   1. the parties' proposed directions and/or budgets are not approved, or
   2. parties are unable to agree proposed directions and/or budgets, or

3. the Master wishes to make further directions,

the Master will generally either consult the parties or direct that a costs and/or case management conference be held.

7.2.3 In relatively straightforward claims and provided the parties have agreed their respective budgets the court may give directions without holding a case management conference.

7.2.4 Any party who considers that a case management conference should be held before any directions are given should so state in his Directions Questionnaire, (or in a Part 8 claim should notify the Master in writing), giving his reasons and supplying a realistic time estimate for the case management conference, with a list of any dates or times convenient to all parties, in form PF 49.

7.2.5 Where a case management conference has been fixed, parties should ensure that any other suitable applications are listed or made at that hearing. A party applying for directions at the case management conference should use form PF 50 for making the application and attach to it the draft order for directions (form PF 52).

7.2.6 Parties should consider whether a case summary would assist the Master at the case management conference in dealing with the issues. Paragraph 5.7 of the Part 29 Practice Direction sets out the provisions for preparation of a case summary which should be prepared by the claimant and agreed with the other parties if possible.

7.2.7 Where the parties have not agreed their budgets they should prepare a summary of the costs issues arising between them and a composite summary of their respective costs budgets.

7.2.8 It will usually be appropriate for the advocates instructed or expected to be instructed to appear at the trial to attend any hearing at which costs and case management directions are likely to be given. In any event, the legal representatives who attend the case management conference must be familiar with the case and have sufficient authority to deal with any issues which may arise. Where necessary, the court may order the attendance of a party.

7.3 Preliminary issues:

7.3.1 Costs can sometimes be saved by identifying decisive issues, or potentially **1B–45** decisive issues, and by the court ordering that they be tried first. The decision of one issue, although not necessarily itself decisive of the claim as a whole, may enable the parties to settle the remainder of the dispute. In such a case, the trial of a preliminary issue may be appropriate. The power so to order arises, for example, under CPR 3.1(1)(i). In the Queen's Bench Division, in personal injury cases, the Master may often, after hearing the parties, order separate trial of the issue of liability. Care should be taken however in all cases where the possibility of trial of a separate issue arises to consider precisely what that issue is and to draft the terms of the issue to be incorporated in any order accordingly. In some cases, while a separate issue to determine a point of law may have its attractions, an order should not be made where the facts can be shortly found and these may determine the case: see *Tilling v Whiteman* [1980] A.C.1 H.L, where at p.25C Lord Scarman held "Preliminary points of law are too often treacherous short cuts"

7.3.2 At the directions stage, at any case management conference and again at any pre–trial review, the court will consider whether the trial of a preliminary issue may be helpful. Where such an order is made, the parties and the court should consider whether the costs of the issue should be in the issue or in the claim as a whole.

7.3.3 Where there is an application for summary judgment, and issues of law or construction may be determined in the respondent's favour, it will usually be in the interests of the parties for such issues to be determined conclusively, rather than that the application should simply be dismissed.

7.4 Trial directions and trial timetable:

7.4.1 The Master will at the earliest practicable opportunity give directions for trial: **1B–46** see CPR 29.2(2). These will, typically, include:

(a) the trial window, i.e the period of time (often coinciding with a Law Term) during which the trial date or period to be fixed will occur,

(b) the venue for trial. If in London, at the Royal Courts of Justice. If outside London, a trial centre will be specified,

(c) an order for trial by Judge alone; or, in cases where trial by a Judge sitting with a jury is required under Section 69 of the Senior Courts Act 1981 and application therefor is duly made, trial by Judge and jury. See para.9.3.1 below.

(d) the listing category. As an additional aid to listing, when making an order, the Master will give a provisional estimate of the substance, difficulty or public importance of the case. This is done by giving cases a listing category according to whether they are:

    A. cases of great substance or great difficulty or of public importance

    B. cases of substance or difficulty

    C. other cases

    Cases in category A will be heard by a High Court Judge; in category B the case will be heard by a High Court Judge if available, a deputy High Court Judge or a Circuit Judge sitting as a Judge of the High Court; and in category C by a deputy High Court Judge or a Circuit Judge sitting as a High Court Judge.

(e) a direction as to the estimated length of the trial. The parties must be prepared to assist the Master as to such length,

(f) a direction that the parties apply to the High Court Listing Officer by a certain date for the fixing of a trial date or period as in (a) above and

(g) that the parties file pre–trial check lists in Form N170 as may be directed by the High Court Listing Officer: see CPR 29.6 and PD29, para.8.1. Pre–trial check lists will not be dispensed with save in exceptional circumstances.

7.4.2 As to the trial timetable, in order to assist the court a draft timetable should be prepared by the claimant's advocate(s) after consulting the other party's advocate(s). If there are differing views, those differences should be clearly indicated in the timetable. The draft timetable should be filed with the trial bundle.

7.4.3 The trial timetable will normally include times for giving evidence (whether of fact or opinion) and for oral submissions during the trial.

7.4.4 Under CPR 29.8, as soon as practicable after (a) each party has filed a completed pre–trial checklist, (b) the court has held a listing hearing under rule 29.6(4), or (c) the court has held a pre–trial review under rule 29.7 the court will:–

    (i) set a timetable for the trial unless a timetable has already been fixed, or the court considers that it would be inappropriate to do so;

    (ii) confirm the date for the trial or the week in which the trial is to begin, and

    (iii) notify the parties of the trial timetable (where one is fixed under this rule) and the date or trial period.

7.5 Pre–trial review:

1B–47 7.5.1 Where the trial of a claim is in the jury list or estimated to last more than 10 days, or where the circumstances require it, the Master may direct that a pre–trial review ("PTR") should be held. The PTR may be heard by a Master, but more usually is heard by a Judge.

7.5.2 Application should normally be made to the Queen's Bench Listing Officer for the PTR to be heard by the trial Judge (if known), and the applicant should do all that he can to ensure that it is heard between 4 and 8 weeks before the trial date, and in any event long enough before the trial date to allow a realistic time in which to complete any outstanding matters.

7.5.3 The PTR should be attended by the advocates who are to represent the parties at the trial.

7.5.4 At least 7 days before the date fixed for the PTR, the applicant must serve the other parties with a list of matters to be considered at the PTR, and those other parties must serve their responses at least 2 days before the PTR. Account must be taken of the answers in any pre–trial checklists filed. Realistic proposals must be put forward and if possible agreed as to the time likely to be required for each stage of the trial and as to the order in which witnesses are to be called.

7.5.5 The applicant should lodge a properly indexed bundle containing the pre–trial check lists (if directed to be filed) and the lists of matters to be considered and the proposals, together with the results of discussions between the parties, and any other relevant material, in the Queen's Bench Listing Office, Room WG08, by no later than 10.30am on the day before the day fixed for the hearing of the PTR. If the PTR is to take place before a Master and he asks for the bundle in advance, it should be lodged in the Masters' Support Unit, Room E07. Otherwise it should be lodged at the hearing.

7.5.6 At the PTR, the court will review the parties' state of preparation, deal with any outstanding matters, and give any directions or further directions that may be necessary.

7.6 Requests for further information:

7.6.1 A party seeking further information or clarification under Part 18 should serve **1B–48** a written request on the party from whom the information is sought before making an application to the court. Paragraph 1 of the Part 18 Practice Direction deals with how the request should be made, and Paragraph 2 deals with the response. A statement of truth should verify a response. Parties may use form PF 56 for a combined request and reply, if they so wish. Note that under CPR 18.1 clarification or further information may be sought in relation to any matter in dispute in the proceedings whether or not that matter is contained in a statement of case.

7.6.2 If a party who has been asked to provide further information or clarification objects or is unable to do so, he must notify the party making the request in writing.

7.6.3 Where it is necessary to apply for an order for further information or clarification the party making the application should set out in or attach to his application notice:
1. the text of the order sought specifying the matters on which further informa-tion or clarification is sought, and
2. whether a request has been made and, if so, the result of that request.

Applicants may refer to form PF 57 for the contents of their application notice.

7.7 Disclosure and Inspection of Documents:

7.7.1 Disclosure and inspection of documents involves two stages. First, disclosure of **1B–49** the existence of documents and claiming privilege from inspection for such documents as may attract privilege (e.g. those to which 'legal advice' privilege applies); and secondly, offering facilities to the opposing party for inspection of certain of those documents. The distinction between disclosure on the one hand and inspection on the other hand is important. The Master may make orders which require for example that a party do by a certain time give inspection of those documents which he has disclosed and to the inspection of which he does not object.

7.7.2 Part 31 provides for various orders as to disclosure that may be made. Upon the making of any such order a party falls under a duty to disclose. It should be noted in any event that a party is prevented from relying on any document that he has not disclosed, and is required to give inspection of any document to which he refers in his statement of case or in any witness statement.

7.7.3 If an order for disclosure is made, unless the contrary is stated, the order will be for standard disclosure, namely disclosure requiring a party to disclose only:–
(a) the documents on which he relies, and
(b) the documents which
    (i) adversely affect his own case;
    (ii) adversely affect another party's case; or
    (iii) support another party's case; and
(c) the documents which he is required to disclose by a relevant practice direction.

The intention is that disclosure should be proportionate to the value of the claim. Parties should give standard disclosure by completing form N265 and may list the documents by category.

7.7.4 Furthermore, new provisions have been enacted, in seeking to reduce costs, relating to disclosure in all multi–track cases other than those which include a claim for personal injuries. Those provisions are contained in rule 31.5(3) to (8). In short, unless the court orders otherwise, the parties are not less than 14 days before the first CMC to file and serve a report verified by a statement of truth describing briefly what documents exist or may exist that are or may be relevant to the matters in issue; estimating the broad range of costs that could be involved in giving standard disclosure; and stating what directions as to disclosure will be sought from the court. Not less than 7 days before the first CMC the parties are to discuss and seek to agree a proposal as to disclosure that meets the overriding objective. The court's position is laid down in 31.5(7) and (8). It will at the first or any subsequent CMC decide what appropriate orders it should make. These include:

    (1) an order dispensing with disclosure
    (2) an order that a party disclose the documents on which he relies and at the same time request any specific disclosure he requires from any other party
    (3) an order for disclosure on an issue by issue basis
    (4) an order that each party disclose documents which may enable that party to advance its own case or damage that of any other party, or which leads to an enquiry having either of those consequences and
    (5) an order that a party give standard disclosure.

Directions may be given at any point as to the form of disclosure. And, to the extent that any of the documents to be disclosed are electronic, Practice Direction 31B (Disclosure of Electronic Documents) is to apply. Parties should consult the full terms of that PD.

7.7.5 The procedure for giving standard disclosure, including
    (1) the service of lists of documents
    (2) the inclusion in the lists of those documents in respect of which the party claims a right or duty to withhold inspection, and
    (3) the making of disclosure statements

is closely laid down in rule 31.10.

7.7.6 The court may either limit or dispense with disclosure (and the parties may agree to do likewise). The court may also order disclosure of specified documents or specified classes of documents. In deciding whether to make any such order for specific disclosure, the court will want to be satisfied that the disclosure is necessary, that the cost of disclosure will not outweigh the benefits of disclosure and that a party's ability to continue the litigation would not be impaired by any such order.

7.7.7 The court will therefore seek to ensure that any specific disclosure ordered is appropriate to the particular case, taking into account the financial position of the parties, the importance of the case and the complexity of the issues.

7.7.8 If specific disclosure is sought, a separate application for specific disclosure should be made in accordance with Part 23; it is not a matter that would be routinely dealt with at the CMC. The parties should give careful thought to ways of limiting the burdens of such disclosure, whether by giving disclosure in stages, by dispensing with the need to produce copies of the same document, by requiring disclosure of documents sufficient merely for a limited purpose, or otherwise. They should also consider whether the need for disclosure could be reduced or eliminated by a request for further information.

7.7.9 A party who has the right to inspect a document should give written notice of his wish to inspect to the party disclosing the document. That party must permit inspection not more than 7 days after receipt of the notice. Copies must also be supplied on undertaking by the requesting party to pay reasonable copying costs.

7.7.10 An order for disclosure before proceedings have started may be made under rule 31.16. And an order for disclosure by a non–party may be made under rule 31.17 (as to which see Paragraphs 7.9.11 to 7.9.13 below).

7.8 Experts and Assessors:

7.8.1 The parties to a claim must bear in mind that under Part 35 no party may call **1B–50** an expert or put in evidence an expert's report without the court's express permission. The court is under a duty to restrict such evidence to that which is reasonably required to resolve the proceedings.

7.8.2 The duty of an expert called to give evidence is to assist the court. This duty overrides any obligation to the party instructing him or by whom he is being paid: see rule 35.3(2) and para.4.1 of the Protocol for the instruction of experts to give evidence in civil claims. In fulfilment of this duty, an expert must for instance make it clear if a particular question or issue falls outside his expertise or if he considers that insufficient information is available on which to express an opinion.

7.8.3 Before the Master gives permission, he must be told the field of expertise of the expert on whose evidence a party wishes to rely and where practicable the identity of the expert and in all cases an estimate of the cost of the evidence must be provided. The Master may, before giving permission, impose a limit on the extent to which the cost of such evidence may be recovered from the other parties in the claim.

7.8.4 Parties should always consider whether a single expert could be appointed in a particular claim or to deal with a particular issue. Before giving permission for the parties to call separate experts, the Master will always consider whether a single joint expert ought to be used, whether in relation to the issues as a whole or to a particular issue.

7.8.5 In many cases it is possible for the question of expert evidence, or one or more of the areas of expert evidence, to be dealt with by a single expert. Single experts are, for example, often appropriate to deal with questions of quantum in cases where the primary issues are as to liability. Likewise, where expert evidence is required in order to acquaint the court with matters of fact, as opposed to opinion, a single expert will usually be appropriate. There remain however, a body of cases where liability will turn upon expert opinion evidence and where it will be appropriate for the parties to instruct their own experts. For example, in cases where the issue for determination is as to whether a party acted in accordance with proper professional standards, it will usually be of value to the court to hear the opinions of more than one expert as to the proper standard in order that the court becomes acquainted with a range of views existing upon the question and in order that the evidence can be tested in cross–examination.

7.8.6 It will not be a sufficient ground for objecting to an order for a single joint expert that the parties have already chosen their own experts. An order for a single joint expert does not prevent a party from having his own expert to advise him, though that is likely to be at his own cost, regardless of the outcome.

7.8.7 When the use of a single joint expert is being considered, the Master will expect the parties to co–operate in agreeing terms of reference for and instructions to the expert. In most cases, such terms of reference/instructions will include a statement of what the expert is asked to do, will identify any documents that he will be asked to consider and will specify any assumptions that he is asked to make.

7.8.8 Where the Master has given permission for separate experts to be engaged for the claimant and the defendant (or other parties) he is likely to make a structured order as to their evidence, such as
(1) permission to each party to rely on (one) expert (naming the experts if practicable) in each of the following fields (naming such fields)
(2) that the parties do exchange the reports of such experts by (naming the dates in respect of each field). Or, alternatively, the Master may wish to order that reports in a particular field are served sequentially (e.g the claimant's report by (date) and the defendant's report by (date)). This latter alternative may commend itself particularly where the nature of the case requires that the claimant should disclose his position first; or in cases where it is possible that the defendant's expert, having seen the claimant's expert's report, may be able to agree all or much of it. Thus costs may be saved. See also PD29 para.4.11 which refers to exchange of reports on liability and sequential service of reports on quantum.

(3) that (reports having been served) the experts in like fields do by (date) confer with each other without prejudice as to the matters in issue between them and do by (date) file a joint statement as to the matters agreed and not agreed between them, and a summary of their reasons for any continuing disagreement.

(4) that the parties have permission to call their experts to give oral evidence at trial limited to the matters remaining in disagreement between them.

7.8.9 The direction to 'confer' gives the experts the choice of discussing the matter by telephone or in any other convenient way, as an alternative to attending an actual meeting.

7.8.10 The Master may, in his discretion, make an order as to the costs of obtaining or giving expert evidence, such as that they be reserved to the trial judge; and/or that such costs be limited to a certain amount.

7.8.11 Any material change of view of an expert should be communicated in writing to the other parties through their legal representatives and, where appropriate, to the court.

7.8.12 Change of expert. Good reason is required to obtain permission to rely on an expert in substitution for an expert for whom permission has been earlier obtained. "Expert shopping" is to be discouraged. And the court may, depending on the circumstances, require disclosure of an earlier expert's report as a condition of giving permission for a subsequent expert.

7.8.13 Written questions (which must be proportionate) may be put once only to an expert within 28 days after service of his report, but must be for purposes only of clarification of the report. Questions going beyond this can be put only with the agreement of the parties or the Master's permission. The procedure of putting written questions to experts is not intended to interfere with the procedure for an exchange of professional opinion in discussions between experts or to inhibit that exchange of professional opinion. If questions that are oppressive in number or content are put, the court is likely to disallow the questions and make an appropriate order for costs against the party putting them. (See Paragraph 6.2 of the Part 35 Practice Direction with respect to payment of an expert's fees for answering questions under Rule 35.6.) The experts themselves may seek the directions of the court in relation to their functions, including the answering of written questions: see rule 35.14, and PD35 para.16.4. Experts should guard against accidentally informing the court about, or about matters connected with, communications or potential communications between the parties that are without prejudice or privileged. An expert may properly be asked to be privy to the content of these communications because he has been asked to assist the party instructing him to evaluate them.

7.8.14 The experts' evidence at trial. Where oral evidence is required experts have in the past always given their evidence separately from the witness box and this may continue to be the practice in many cases. Important new provisions have however been introduced enabling the court to direct that some or all of the experts of like discipline shall give their evidence concurrently: see PD35 paras.11.1 to 11.4. Thus, the parties may be directed that an agenda for the taking of concurrent evidence be agreed; at the appropriate time the relevant experts are to take the oath or affirm; and, subject to the Judge's discretion to modify the procedure in any particular case, a practical form of procedure for taking their evidence is laid down.

7.8.15 Under rule 35.15 the court may appoint an assessor to assist it in relation to any matter in which he has skill and experience. He will take such part in the proceedings as the court may direct. His report is made available to the parties. His remuneration is decided by the court and forms part of the costs of the proceedings.

7.9 Evidence:

1B–51 7.9.1 Evidence is dealt with in the CPR in Parts 32, 33 and 34.

7.9.2 The most common form of written evidence is a witness statement. The Part 32 Practice Direction at Paragraphs 17, 18 and 19 contains information about the heading, body (what it must contain) and format of a witness statement. The witness must sign a statement of truth to verify the witness statement; the wording of the statement of truth is set out in Paragraph 20.2 of the Practice Direction.

7.9.3 A witness statement may be used as evidence of fact in support of an interim application: see rule 32.2(1)(b).

7.9.4 At trial, the general rule is that evidence of fact is given orally: rule 32.2(1)(a). The court will however have ordered each party to serve witness statements in respect of evidence of fact to be relied on at trial: see rule 32.4(2). The Master will have given directions as to such service, usually by way of exchange of witness statements. It should be noted that under the new rule 32.2(3) the court may give directions identifying or limiting the issues to which factual evidence may be directed; identifying the witnesses who may be called or whose evidence may be read; and limiting the length or format of witness statements. Part 33 contains provisions relating to the use of hearsay evidence in a witness statement at trial.

7.9.5 In addition to the requirements for making a witness statement mentioned in Paragraph 7.9.2, the following matters should be borne in mind;
   1. a witness statement must contain the truth, the whole truth and nothing but the truth on the issues it covers,
   2. those issues should consist only of the issues on which the party serving the witness statement wishes that witness to give evidence in chief and should not include commentary on the trial bundle or other matters which may arise during the trial or may have arisen during the proceedings,
   3. a witness statement should be as concise as the circumstances allow; inadmissible or irrelevant material should not be included. Application may be made by an opposing party to strike out inadmissible or irrelevant material.
   4. the cost of preparation of an over–elaborate witness statement may not be allowed,
   5. Rule 32.10 states that if a witness statement for use at trial is not served within the time specified by the court, then the witness may not be called to give oral evidence unless the court gives permission.
   6. Rule 32.14 states that proceedings for contempt of court may be brought against a person if he makes, or causes to be made, a false statement in a document verified by a statement of truth without an honest belief in its truth. Part 81 and the Practice Direction to that part govern the procedure which applies to proceedings for contempt,
   7. if a party discovers that a witness statement which he has served is incorrect he must inform the other parties immediately.

7.9.6 Evidence may also be given by affidavit; but unless an affidavit is specifically required either in compliance with a court order, a rule or practice direction, or an enactment, the party putting forward the affidavit may not recover from another party the cost of making it unless the court so orders.

7.9.7 The Part 32 Practice Direction, at Paragraphs 3 to 6, contains information about the heading, body, jurat (the sworn statement which authenticates the affidavit) and the format of an affidavit. The court will normally give directions as to whether a witness statement or, where appropriate, an affidavit is to be filed.

7.9.8 A statement of case which has been verified by a statement of truth and an application notice containing facts which have been verified by a statement of truth may also stand as evidence other than at the trial.

7.9.9 Evidence by deposition is dealt with in Part 34. A party may apply to a Master for an order for a person to be examined before a hearing takes place: rule 34.8. Evidence obtained on an examination under that rule is referred to as a deposition. The Master may order the person to be examined before either a Judge, an examiner of the court or such other person as the court appoints. PD34A, at Paragraph 4, sets out in detail how the examination should take place. A deposition taken under this rule may be given in evidence at a hearing unless the court orders otherwise.

7.9.10 Provisions relating to applications for evidence to be taken by deposition either;
   (1) abroad for use in proceedings within the jurisdiction; or
   (2) in this country for use in a foreign court,

are set out in detail in PD34A, at Paragraphs 5 and 6. The position as to taking of evidence by deposition between EU member states is governed by Paragraphs 7 to 11.

7.9.11 Witness summonses. The procedure for issuing a witness summons is also dealt with in Part 34 and Practice Direction 34A. A witness summons may require a witness to

1. attend court to give evidence
2. produce documents to the court, or
3. both

See rule 34.2 and PD 34A para.1. The summons may require the witness to produce documents on a date fixed for a hearing or on such date as the court may direct. But the only documents that a summons under this rule can require a witness to produce before a hearing are those which he could be required to produce at the hearing: rule 34.2(5). The summons must be in the relevant practice form which is Form N20.

7.9.12 The summons may be issued without permission of the court save in those cases specified in rule 34.3(2).

7.9.13 The court may set aside or vary a witness summons issued under this rule. It should be borne in mind that the object of a witness summons requiring a witness to produce documents is to obtain production at trial of specified documents; accordingly it must specifically identify the documents sought, it must not be used as an instrument to obtain disclosure and it must not be of a fishing or speculative nature: *South Tyneside BC v Wickes Building Supplies Ltd* [2004] EWHC 2428 (Comm). A procedure to obtain disclosure of documents by a non–party, rather than to obtain production of documents by witness summons, is available under CPR 31.17. If a party seeks to avail himself of that rule he should observe its requirements, which are specifically laid out, and be careful to follow them. On the other hand it will be seen that, as a matter of discretion, the court may give permission under rule 34.3(2)(b) to issue a witness summons for production of documents on any date except the date fixed for trial. If the court sees fit to give that permission, and if the production of the documents is not opposed by the witness, that may result in a less costly and more expeditious outcome than would be likely to be the case on an application for disclosure under rule 31.17.

7.9.14 The court may also issue a witness summons in aid of a court or tribunal which does not have the power to issue a witness summons in relation to the proceedings before it: see rule 34.4 and PD34A, para.2.

7.9.15 To issue a witness summons, two copies should be filed in the Masters' Support Unit, Action Department, in Room E07 for sealing; one copy will be retained on the court file.

7.9.16 A witness summons must be served at least 7 days before the date upon which the witness is required to attend. If this is not possible for any reason, an order must be sought from a Master that the summons is binding although it will be served less than 7 days before the date when the witness is required to attend. The Practice Master will usually be prepared to deal with this in Practice, without notice.

7.9.17 A witness summons will be served by the court unless the party on whose behalf it is issued indicates in writing that he wishes to serve it himself. If time is a critical factor, it may be preferable for the party to serve the witness summons. And, if service is to be on a reluctant witness, it may be better to effect personal service.

7.9.18 At the time of service of the witness summons the witness must be offered or paid

(a) conduct money, i.e a reasonable sum sufficient to cover his expenses in travel-ling to or from the court, and
(b) compensation for loss of time. The sum referred to in this respect in PD34A paras.3.2 and 3.3 is based on the sums payable to witnesses attending the Crown Court, as to which see the Guide to Allowances under Part V of the Costs in Criminal Cases (General) Regulations 1986 (S.1.1986 No.1335) which can be found at *www.legislation.gov.uk/ukji/1986/1335/made*.

7.10 Hearings:

Hearings generally

7.10.1

Hearings in public/private

All hearings are in principle open to the public, even though in practice most of the hearings until the trial itself will be attended only by the parties and their representatives: see rule 39.2(1). The requirement for a public hearing does not however require the court to make special arrangements for accommodating members of the public: rule 39.2(2). Thus, many hearings, whilst in public, are held in the Masters' own rooms or in chambers in the Bear Garden which are relatively small. In an appropriate case the court may decide to hold a hearing, or part of it, in private. rule 39.2(3) lists the circumstances where it may be appropriate to hold a hearing, whether of interim proceedings or of the trial itself, in private. The fact that a case falls under one or more of such circumstances does not give a right to a hearing in private. An application will usually have to be made, and be made to the Judge holding the hearing, and he will reach his decision on considering the rules and the arguments put to him. In some cases it may be appropriate for the hearing to be in private, but for the order reached and a reasoned judgment in support of the order to be made public.

7.10.2 Paragraph 1.5 of the Part 39 Practice Direction lists certain matters falling under rule 39.3(2)(c), which relates particularly to confidential information on personal financial matters, which are in the first instance to be listed in private.

7.10.3 The court also has power under section 11 of the Contempt of Court Act 1981 to make an order forbidding publication of any details that might identify one or more of the parties. Such orders are granted only in exceptional cases.

7.10.4 References in the CPR and the Practice Directions to hearings being in public or private do not restrict any existing rights of audience or confer any new rights of audience in respect of applications or proceedings which under the rules previously in force would have been heard in court or chambers respectively. Nor is it intended that the new routes of appeal should restrict the advocate's right of audience, in that a solicitor who appeared in a county court matter which is the subject of an appeal to a High Court Judge would normally be allowed to appear at the appeal hearing. Advocates (and judges) do not wear robes at interim hearings before High Court Judges. Robes are worn for trials and certain other proceedings such as preliminary issues, committals etc.

7.10.5

Conduct of the parties

Parties are reminded that they are expected to act with courtesy and respect for the other parties present and for the proceedings of the court. Punctuality is particularly important; being late for hearings, even by a few minutes, is unfair to the other parties and other court users, as well as being discourteous to them and to the court and being disruptive of court business. An apology and explanation for lateness ought always to be given.

Preparation for hearings

7.10.6 To ensure that court time is used efficiently there must be adequate preparation prior to the hearing. This includes the preparation and exchange of skeleton arguments, the compilation of bundles of documents and the giving of realistic time estimates. Where estimates prove inaccurate, a hearing may have to be adjourned to a later date, and the party responsible for the adjournment is likely to be ordered to pay the costs thrown away. For the obligations of the parties and of the court in relation to the trial timetable, see Paragraphs 7.4.2 to 7.4.4 above.

7.10.7 The parties should use their best endeavours to agree beforehand the issues, or main issues between them, and must co–operate with the court and each other to enable the court to deal with claims justly and at proportionate cost; parties may expect to be penalised for failing to do so.

7.10.8 A bundle of documents must be compiled for the court's use at the trial, and also for hearings before the Interim Applications Judge or a Master where the documents to be referred to total 25 pages or more. The party lodging a trial or hearing bundle should supply identical bundles to all parties and for the use of witnesses. The efficient preparation of bundles is very important. Where bundles have been properly prepared, the claim will be easier to understand and present, and time and costs are likely to be saved. Where documents are copied unnecessarily or bundled incompetently, the costs may be disallowed. Paragraph 3 of the Part 39 Practice Direction sets out in full the requirements for compiling bundles of documents for hearings or trial. Under para.3.9 the contents of the bundle should be agreed where possible. If it is not possible to agree, a summary of the points of disagreement should be included. Furthermore, the parties should agree if possible

(1) that the documents are authentic even if not disclosed under Part 31, and

(2) that the documents may be treated as evidence of the facts stated in them even if no notice under the Civil Evidence Act 1995 has been served.

7.10.9 The trial bundle must be filed not more than 7 and not less than 3 days before the start of the trial. Bundles for a Master's hearing should be brought to the hearing unless it is likely to assist the Master to read the bundle in advance in which case it should be lodged with the Masters' Support Unit or with the Master directly 1–3 days in advance. If the trial/hearing bundles are extensive and either party wishes the judge to read certain documents in advance of the hearing, a reading list should be provided.

7.10.10 Lists of authorities for use at trial or at substantial hearings before a Judge should be provided to the usher by 9.00am on the first day of the hearing. For other applications before a Judge, or applications before a Master, copies of the authorities should be included in the bundle or in a separate bundle.

7.10.11 For trial and most hearings before a Judge, and substantial hearings before a Master, a chronology, a list of the persons involved and a list of the issues should be prepared and filed with the skeleton argument. A chronology should be non–contentious and agreed with the other parties if possible. If there is a material dispute about any event stated in the chronology, that should be stated.

7.10.12 Skeleton arguments should be prepared, filed and served;

1. for trials, not less than 2 days before the trial in the Listing Office, and

2. for substantial applications or appeals, not later than 1 day before the hearing in the Listing Office and, where the Master has requested papers in advance of a hearing before him, in the Masters' Support Unit Room E16 or directly with the Master. Parties should avoid handing skeleton arguments to the other party at the door of the court even for less substantial hearings, so that each party has time to consider the other party's case.

7.10.13 A skeleton argument should;

1. concisely summarise the party's submissions in relation to each of the issues (where appropriate by reference to the relevant paragraphs in the statements of case),

2. cite the main authorities relied on, which may be attached,

3. contain a reading list and an estimate of the time it will take the Judge to read,

4. be as brief as the issues allow and not normally be longer than 20 pages of double–spaced A4 paper,

5. be divided into numbered paragraphs and paged consecutively,

6. avoid formality and use understandable abbreviations, and

7. identify any core documents which it would be helpful to read beforehand.

7.10.14 Where a party decides not to call a witness whose witness statement has been served to give oral evidence at trial, prompt notice of this decision should be given to all other parties. The party should also indicate whether he proposes to put, or seek to put, the witness statement in as hearsay evidence. If he does not, any other party may do so.

Recording of proceedings

7.10.15 The recording of proceedings in the High Court, whether before a Judge or a Master, is now governed by Paragraphs 6.1 to 6.5 of Practice Direction 39A. All hearings will be tape recorded unless the Judge or Master orders otherwise. Any party or person may require a transcript of the recording of a hearing to be supplied to him on payment of the appropriate charges. He should apply for that purpose to the Courts Recording and Transcription Unit in room WB14. A person who is not a party may not however obtain a transcript of a hearing which took place in private unless the court so orders.

7.10.16 No party or member of the public may use unofficial recording equipment in any court or judge's room without the permission of the court. To do so without permission constitutes a contempt of court.

7.11 Applications:

7.11.1 Applications for court orders are governed by Part 23 and Practice Direction **1B–53** 23A. Rule 23.6 and paragraph 2 of the Practice Direction set out the matters an application notice must include. The Practice Direction states that form N244 may be used; however, parties may prefer to use form PF244 which is available for use in the Royal Courts of Justice only. To make an application the applicant must file an application notice unless a rule or practice direction permits otherwise or the court dispenses with the requirement for an application notice. A Master will not normally make an order on the basis of correspondence alone.

7.11.2 An application notice must be served on every party (and generally not less than 3 days before the hearing) unless the application is permitted to be made without service by a rule, practice direction or court order: see rule 23.4. PD23A para.3(1) refers to cases (including cases of exceptional urgency) where service may not be required. These may include for example applications for search orders. See also for further examples those cases referred to in Paragraph 7.11.4 below.

7.11.3 Applications for remedies which a Master has jurisdiction to grant should ordinarily be made to a Master. The Part 2 Practice Direction 2B (Allocation of Cases to Levels of Judiciary) contains information about the types of applications which may be dealt with by Masters and Judges. An application notice for hearing by a Judge should be issued in the Queen's Bench Listing Office Room WG08. An application for hearing by a Master should be issued in the Masters' Support Unit, Room E07. All applications should be accompanied by a draft in double spacing of the order sought.

7.11.4 The following are examples of applications which may be heard by a Master where service of the application notice is not required:—
   (1) service by an alternative method under rule 6.15,
   (2) service of a claim form out of the jurisdiction under section IV of Part 6,
   (3) default judgment under rule 12.11(4) or (5),
   (4) substituting a party under rule 19.2(4): see PD 19A, para.1.4,
   (5) permission to issue a witness summons under rule 34.3(2),
   (6) deposition for use in a foreign court under rule 34.17,
   (7) interim charging order under rule 73.3(1), and
   (8) interim third party debt order under rule 72.3(1).

7.11.5 Where an application is heard in the absence of one or more of the parties, it is the duty of the party attending to disclose fully all matters relevant to the application, even those matters adverse to the applicant. Failure to do so may result in the order being set aside. In addition rule 23.9 requires that, where the court has made an order on an application which it permitted to be made without notice, a copy of the application notice and any evidence in support of it must, unless the court orders otherwise, be served with the order on any party or other person against whom the order was made or sought. The order must contain a statement of the right to apply to set aside or vary the order. Applications under rule 23.10 to set aside or vary such orders, which must be made within 7 days after service of the order, frequently arise in practice.

7.11.6 Where notice of an application is to be given, the application notice should be served as soon as practicable after issue and, if there is to be a hearing, at least 3 clear days before the hearing date, unless the rules or a practice direction specify another time limit or permission for shorter service is obtained from a Master. Where there is insufficient time to serve an application notice before a proposed hearing date, informal notice of the application should be given.

7.11.7 The court may and often does deal with an application without a hearing if:—
(1) the parties agree the terms of the order sought,
(2) the parties agree that the application should be dealt with without a hearing, or
(3) the court does not consider that a hearing would be appropriate.

7.11.8 Under para.6.2 of PD23A certain hearings, including interim applications, case management conferences and pre–trial reviews lasting not more than one hour are to held by telephone unless the court orders otherwise In practice, the Master will be likely to hold short CMCs and other short applications where there are few contested issues by telephone. The order listing the hearing will always indicate whether the parties are to attend, or whether the matter is to be dealt with on the telephone. The actual procedure for conducting a telephone hearing is laid down by para.10 of the PD. The Master will often direct after reaching his decision on the telephone that one party is to draw the order, send the draft to the other party for agreement, and then to the Master to give permission to seal the order. The order is to be dated as at the date when it was orally made, and such date will appear on the face of the order, although the date of sealing may well be a subsequent date.

7.11.9

Urgent applications

Applications of extreme urgency may be made out of hours and will be dealt with by the duty Judge. An explanation will be required as to why it was not made or could not be made during normal court hours.

7.11.10 Initial contact should be made through the Security Office on 0207 947 6260 who will require the applicant's phone number. The clerk to the duty Judge will then contact the applicant and will require the following information;
(1) the name of the party on whose behalf the application is to be made,
(2) the name and status of the person making the application,
(3) the nature of the application,
(4) the degree of urgency, and
(5) the contact telephone number(s).

7.11.11 The duty Judge will indicate to the Judge's clerk whether it is appropriate for the application to be dealt with by telephone or in court. The clerk will inform the applicant and make the necessary arrangements. Where the duty Judge decides to deal with the application by telephone, and the facility is available, it is likely that the Judge will require a draft order to be faxed to him. An application for an injunction will be dealt with by telephone only where counsel or solicitors represent the applicant.

7.11.12 It is not normally possible to seal an order out of hours. The Judge is likely to order the applicant to file the application notice and evidence in support on the same or next working day, together with two copies of the order for sealing.

7.12 Interim remedies:

1B–54   7.12.1 Interim remedies which the court may grant are listed in rule 25.1(1). They are many and various in nature and it should be noted that the fact that a particular remedy is not listed does not affect any power that the court may have to grant that remedy. An order for an interim remedy may be made at any time including before proceedings are started and after judgment has been given. Some of the most commonly sought remedies are injunctions, many of which are heard by the Interim Applications Judge.

7.12.2 Where a claim has been started, an application on notice for an injunction should be filed in the Listing Office, Room WG08 for a hearing to be listed. If the application is to be made without giving notice to the other parties in the first instance, the application notice stamped with the appropriate fee should be brought to the Interim Applications Court, Court 37, together with the evidence in support, a skeleton argument (where appropriate) and two copies of the order sought. Applications without notice are heard in Court 37 at 10.00am and 2.00pm, and at such other times as the urgency of the application dictates.

7.12.3 Where an injunction is granted without the other party being present it will normally be for a limited period with a return date 1 to 2 weeks ahead. If the injunction order contains an undertaking to issue a claim form, this should be issued before the application notice for the return date is filed in Room WG08 prior to service. Furthermore, service of particulars of claim should not be deferred pending the return date.

7.12.4 Practice Direction 25A—interim injunctions—deals fully with the procedure for making an application for an injunction. Paragraph 2 states what the application notice must contain. In general it must be served not less than 3 days before the court is due to hear the application. Paragraph 3 requires any application for an injunction to be supported by evidence (in the case of application for search orders or freezing injunctions by affidavit evidence). Paragraph 4 deals with urgent applications and applications without notice. These fall specifically into two categories, according as to whether a claim form has or has not already been issued. The procedure for making urgent applications by telephone (already referred to in Paragraphs 7.11.9 to 7.11.12 above) is set out in para.4.5 of the PD. Orders for injunctions must, unless the court otherwise orders, contain an undertaking by the applicant to the court to pay damages and, if the application is made without notice, to serve the application and evidence in support as soon as practicable: see para.5.1. Paragraphs 6 and 7 contain important provisions as to freezing orders and search orders respectively; examples of both such orders are annexed to the PD.

7.12.5 Certain applications may be heard in private if the judge thinks it appropriate to do so (rule 39.2(3)). An application to hear in private should be made at the outset of the hearing. Certain applications for search orders and freezing injunctions might be appropriate for hearing in private.

7.12.6 Applications for interim payments fall under rules 25.6 to 25.9 and are heard by a Master. Rule 25.7 sets out the conditions which must be satisfied if an order for interim payment is to be made. These include (as often arises in practice) the conditions which apply where the claimant is seeking an order against one or more of the defendants and the court is satisfied that judgment for a substantial sum of money would be obtained at trial against at least one of the defendants but the court cannot determine which. The application notice should be filed in the Masters' Support Unit, Room E07. The procedural requirements for obtaining an order are fully dealt with in Practice Direction 25B – Interim Payments.

7.13 Interlocutory Orders:

Orders made by the Masters

7.13.1 In the majority of cases orders by Masters in the Queen's Bench Division are **1B–55** drawn up by one of the parties, who must then arrange to have the order sealed in the Masters' Support Unit (Room E07) and effect service on all other parties. In a limited number of circumstances, e.g. where an order is made of the court's own initiative, the court will draw up, seal and serve an order. Reference should be made to CPR 40.3 in this respect.

7.13.2 Where an application notice has been issued, and there has been a hearing, the Master will endorse the order in handwriting upon the original application notice. (If the original is not at the hearing, the party drawing up the order will have to ask the Master's permission to treat a photocopy as an original). If the parties have provided a draft order, the Master will endorse this, with or without amendment. The application notice will then be endorsed "Order in form initialled". The Masters habitually use their initials, rather than their full signatures, when making orders. Parties should familiarise themselves with these initials. The date when the order is made is inserted below the initials. If the hearing is one where there is no application notice, for example a case management conference, then the Master will endorse the order on any notice of the hearing sent by the court, or will use a draft order provided by one of the parties to endorse the order.

7.13.3 The Master will usually direct which party should be responsible for drawing up the order. In the absence of such direction, this will be the party who issued the application to which the order relates, or the claimant where the order was made at a case management conference. The Master will also direct a date by which the order should be drawn up, filed for sealing and served. If a party fails in his obligation to draw an order for filing, any other party may do so: see PD40B, para.1.2. An order, when sealed, should always state the name and judicial title of the person who made it save in those cases set out in rule 40.2.

7.13.4 The party responsible for drawing up the order should lodge with the Masters' Support Unit:
  i. The application notice (or other document) endorsed by the Master;
  ii. Clean copies for sealing, one for each party and one for the court file;
  iii. Evidence of payment of the court fee

7.13.5 That party should serve the sealed order upon each other party to the claim by the date specified. If not sealed and served by that date, a party will have to obtain the court's permission to file the order out of time, which should be sought from the Practice Master.

7.13.6 If an order is made without a hearing, the party making the application must likewise draw up, file and serve the order in accordance with the procedure set out above.

7.13.7 Accidental slips or omissions are dealt with under rule 40.12 and PD40B para.4. A party may apply informally (by letter) to correct an order even after it has been sealed. The Master may deal with such application without notice if the slip or omission is obvious. Or he may direct notice to be given to the other parties. If corrected the order will be re–sealed with a printed endorsement at the top stating that it is corrected and re–sealed under rule 40.12.

Orders made by a High Court Judge

7.13.8 Orders made by a Judge on an interim application will, where the parties have legal representation, generally be drawn up in the same way as orders made by the Masters. However, the court will draw, seal and serve orders on behalf of litigants in person, and also orders made in appeal proceedings.

7.14 Civil Restraint Orders:

1B–56 7.14.1 The power of the court to make civil restraint orders ("CROs") is governed by CPR 3.11. However, Practice Direction 3C—Civil Restraint Orders—sets out the procedure in detail.

7.14.2 There are 3 types of CRO—limited civil restraint orders, extended civil restraint orders and general civil restraint orders. These may be made against a party who has issued claims or made applications which are totally without merit. An application for a civil restraint order may be made by any of the other parties to the proceedings.

7.14.3 For a limited CRO ("LCRO") to be made the court must have found that two or more applications made by the litigant are totally without merit. An LCRO may be made by a Judge of any court, which includes a Master of District Judge. An LCRO restrains the litigant from making any further applications in the proceedings in which the order is made without first obtaining the permission of a judge identified in the order. The order will usually remain in effect for the duration of those proceedings. Paragraph 2 of PD3C sets out in detail (amongst other matters) how permission is to be applied for, including service of notice on the other parties; and the effect of making any further application in the proceedings without obtaining such permission.

7.14.4 An extended CRO ("ECRO") may be made where a litigant has persistently issued claims or made applications which are totally without merit. An ECRO may be made (a) in relation to proceedings in any court if the order is made by a judge of the Court of Appeal; (b) in relation to proceedings in the High Court or any county court if made by a judge of the High Court; and (c) in relation to proceedings in any county court identified in the order if made by a designated civil judge or his appointed deputy. An ECRO usually restrains the litigant from issuing claims or making applications "concerning any matter involving or relating to or touching upon or leading to the proceedings in which the order is made" without first obtaining the permission of a judge identified in the order. Again, under para.3 of the PD, detailed provisions are set out as to how permission may be applied for, including service of notice on the other parties; and the effect of issuing claims or making applications without first obtaining such permission. An ECRO will be made for a specified period not exceeding 2 years with the possibility of an extension not exceeding 2 years on any given occasion. If a Master or District Judge in the High Court considers that it would be appropriate to make an ECRO he must transfer the proceedings to a High Court Judge.

7.14.5 A general CRO ("GCRO") may be made where a litigant has persistently issued claims or made applications which are totally without merit in circumstances where an ECRO would not be sufficient or appropriate. A GCRO may be made (a) in relation to proceedings in any court if made by a judge of the Court of Appeal; (b) in relation to proceedings in the High Court or any county court if made by a judge of the High Court; and (c) in relation to proceedings in any county court identified in the order if made by a designated civil judge or his appointed deputy. A GCRO usually restrains the litigant from making any claim or making any application without first obtaining the permission of a judge identified in the order. Again, under para.4 of the PD, provisions are set out as to how permission may be applied for, including service of notice on the other parties and the effect of issuing claims or making applications without first obtaining permission. A GCRO will be made for a specified period not exceeding 2 years with the possibility of an extension not exceeding 2 years on any given occasion. If a Master or District Judge considers that it would be appropriate to make a GCRO he must transfer the proceedings to a High Court Judge.

7.15 Relief from sanctions

7.15.1 The court has power under rule 3.9 to order relief from any sanction imposed **1B–57** for a failure to comply with any rule, practice direction or court order.

7.15.2 Litigants should note that the rule, as recently amended, requires the court to consider all the circumstances of the case, so as to enable it to deal justly with the application, including the need:
(a) for litigation to be conducted efficiently and at proportionate cost; and
(b) to enforce compliance with rules, practice directions and orders.

A stricter test is now applied than under the former rule. The most important factors are the two specifically referred to in (a) and (b) above: see *Mitchell v News Group Newspapers Ltd* [2013] EWCA Civ 1537, including particularly the guidance given by the judgment of the Court of Appeal at Paragraphs 40 and onwards of the judgment in relation to any application for relief from sanctions.

7.16 Orders of the court's own initiative

7.16.1 The court has power to make an order of its own initiative. The power is **1B–58** exercised under rule 3.3. Such order may be made after considering representations about the proposed order (rule 3.3(2)); after notice of a hearing to consider the proposed order (rule 3.3(3)); or without a hearing or opportunity to make representations (rule 3.3(4)). In the last case any party affected by the order may apply to have it set aside, varied or stayed; and the order must contain a statement of that right. The right must be exercised within such period as may be specified; or, if no period is specified, within 7 days after service of the order on the party making the application.

7.16.2 It frequently happens that upon reading an application notice the Master is minded to make an order, not as asked by the applicant, but of his own initiative. He may do so, and in such case it is very desirable that the order should make the position clear. Thus, the order should be drawn "Upon reading an application notice by the (party) dated...., and of the court's own initiative under CPR 3.3(4), it is ordered" etc. Of course in such case the order must contain the statement of the right to apply to set aside, vary or stay.

SECTION 8

DEFAMATION CLAIMS

1B–59   Defamation claims are governed by Part 53 and the Part 53 Practice Direction. Paragraph 2 of the Practice Direction sets out the information which should be included in a statement of case.

8.1 Offer to make amends

8.1.1 Under section 2 of the Defamation Act 1996 a person who has published a statement alleged to be defamatory of another may offer to make amends ("a section 2 offer"). The section 2 offer must;

1. be in writing,
2. be expressed to be an offer to make amends under section 2 of the Act, and
3. state whether it is a qualified offer, (i.e limited to a specific defamatory meaning which the offeror accepts that the statement conveys) and, if so, set out that meaning

A section 2 offer is an offer;

1. to make a suitable correction of the statement complained of and a sufficient apology,
2. to publish the correction and apology in a manner that is reasonable and practicable in the circumstances, and
3. to pay to the aggrieved party such compensation (if any), and such costs, as may be agreed or determined to be payable.

8.1.2 The defendant may not make use of the offer of amends procedure after service of a defence in defamation proceedings brought in respect of the publication. He should accordingly make up his mind whether or not to make an offer by the time limited for serving a defence.

8.1.3 Where a section 2 offer is accepted by an aggrieved person he may not bring or continue defamation proceedings, but he is entitled to enforce the offer as follows:—

(a) if the parties are agreed on the steps to be taken in the fulfilment of the offer he may apply to the court for an order accordingly

(b) if the parties are not agreed on the steps to be taken by way of correction apology and publication the offeror may take such steps as he thinks appropriate, including making a statement in open court in terms approved by the court. He may also give an undertaking to the court as to the manner of publication.

(c) if the parties are not agreed on the amount of compensation to be paid the amount is to be determined by the court on the same principles as damages in defamation proceedings. The aggrieved party may apply for that purpose.

8.1.4 The application to invoke the court's assistance under Paragraph 8.1.3 above should, in existing proceedings, be made by application notice under Part 23; otherwise a Part 8 claim form should be issued. Such application or claim form must comply with para.3 of the Practice Direction to Part 53. It must, in particular, be supported by written evidence and must contain all the material set out in para.3.3(2) and (3). The application notice or claim form will be filed or issued in the Masters' Support Unit (Room E07). It will be laid before a Master or, if the application or claim seeks approval of a statement to be read in open court, the Senior Master. In either case the Master may direct that the matter be referred to the Judge in charge of the jury list for his consideration.

8.1.5 If the offer to make amends is not accepted the fact that it was made will, under the terms of section 4 of the Defamation 1996, constitute a defence to defamation proceedings in respect of the publication. Such a defence will not however avail the person making the offer if he knew or had reason to believe that the statement

(a) referred to the aggrieved party or was likely to be understood as referring to him, and

(b) was both false and defamatory of that party.

8.2 Ruling on meaning

8.2.1 An application for a ruling by a Judge on meaning may have a valuable effect in determining critical questions in defamation actions before trial. Any such ruling will bind the trial Judge; and following a ruling on meaning the court may, if appropriate, exercise its power to strike out a statement of case: see the Practice Direction to Part 53, para.4.4.

8.2.2 It should be noted that, under section 7 of the Defamation Act 1996, the court is not to be asked to rule whether a statement is arguably capable, as opposed to capable, of bearing a particular meaning or meanings attributed to it.

8.2.3 An application for an order determining whether or not a statement complained of is capable of:—
    (1) having any meaning attributed to it is a statement of case,
    (2) being defamatory of the claimant, or
    (3) bearing any other meaning defamatory of the claimant

may be made by the claimant or the defendant and may be made at any time after service of the particulars of claim. It should however be made promptly: PD53 para.4.2. It is commonplace for a claimant so to apply in order to determine whether a meaning which the defendant attributes and seeks to justify is one which the words are capable of bearing. Paragraphs 4.3 and 4.4 set out the matters which the application notice and/or the evidence in support of it must contain; in particular the precise identification of the statement, and the meaning attributed to it, which the court is being asked to consider.

8.2.4 The application notice should be filed in the Listing Office, Room WG08, for hearing by a Judge, usually the Judge in charge of the Jury List, or another designated Judge.

8.3 Summary disposal

8.3.1 Section 8 of the Defamation Act 1996 gives the court power to dispose **1B–60** summarily of the claimant's claim. The court may;
    1. dismiss the claim if it appears that it has no realistic prospect of success and there is no reason why it should be tried, or
    2. give judgment for the claimant and grant him summary relief if it appears that there is no defence to the claim which has a realistic prospect of success and there is no reason why it should be tried.

    In considering whether the claim should be tried the court must have regard to the matters set out in section 8(4).

8.3.2 Summary relief includes the following;
    (1) a declaration that the statement was false and defamatory of the claimant,
    (2) an order that the defendant publish or cause to be published a suitable correction and apology,
    (3) damages not exceeding £10,000,
    (4) an order restraining the defendant from publishing or further publishing the matter complained of.

8.3.3 Applications for summary disposal are dealt with in rule 53.2 and paragraphs 5.1 to 5.3 of the Part 53 Practice Direction. Substantial claims and those involving the police authorities or the media, or those seeking an order restraining publication, will be dealt with by the Judge in charge of the Jury List or another designated Judge, and the application notice should be filed in the Listing Office, Room WG08. Applications for summary disposal in other defamation claims may be made at first instance to a Master.

8.3.4 Whilst combined applications have in practice been made under Section 8 for summary disposal and under Part 24 for summary judgment, the restrictions imposed by rule 52.2(3) on hearing an application for summary judgment until an application for summary disposal has been disposed of should be noted.

8.3.5 An application notice for summary disposal must state;
    1. that it is an application for summary disposal made in accordance with section 8 of the Act,

2. the matters set out in paragraph 2(3) of the Part 24 Practice Direction, and
3. whether or not the defendant has made an offer to make amends under section 2 of the Act, and whether or not it has been withdrawn.

When providing evidence in support of an application for summary disposal, in accordance with para.2(3) of the Part 24 Practice Direction, a claimant should as a matter of practice specifically deal with the points set out in section 8(4) of the Act. The application may be made at any time after service of the particulars of claim and the provisions of rule 24.4(1)(a) and (b) do not apply.

8.3.6 Where the court has made an order for summary relief as in 8.3.2(2) above (specifying the date by which the parties should agree the content, time, manner, form and place of publication of the correction and apology) and the parties are unable to comply within the specified time, the claimant must prepare a summary of the court's judgment and serve it on the other parties within 3 days following the date specified in the order for the content to be agreed by the parties.

8.3.7 If the parties are unable to agree the summary, they must within 3 days of its receipt, apply to the court to settle the summary by:—
1. filing an application notice, and
2. filing and serving on all the other parties a copy of the summary showing the revisions they wish to make to it.

The court (normally the Judge who delivered the judgment) will then settle the summary.

8.4 Statements read in Open Court

1B–61 8.4.1 Paragraph 6 of the Part 53 Practice Direction only applies where a party wishes to accept a Part 36 offer or other offer of settlement. For Part 36 offers, see Paragraph 6.12 above.

8.4.2 An application for permission to make a statement before a Judge in open court may be made before or after acceptance of a Part 36 offer, or other offer to settle, and should be made in accordance with Part 23 to the Senior Master or, if not available, to the Practice Master. The application notice, together with a copy of the proposed statement, should be filed in the Masters' Support Unit, Room E07.

8.4.3 The statement may be bilateral in that both parties may wish to join in it, or it may be unilateral in which case it may be opposed or not opposed.

8.4.4 Where permission is given, the parties may take a copy of the order to the Listing Office, Room WG08 for the matter to be listed before the Judge in charge of the Jury List for mention. Otherwise, (as in cases where the statement is opposed) the Action Department will send the court file to the Listing Office for the matter of permission to be listed before the Judge.

Section 9

Listing Before Judges

9.1 Responsibility for Listing:

1B–62 9.1.1 At the case management conference the Master will order a "trial window", i.e. a period of time within which the Queen's Bench Judges' Listing Officer (formerly known as the Clerk of the Lists) is to arrange for the trial to take place. The window may be a period defined by reference to certain named dates or months, or defined by reference to a stated Law Term. In some cases, to allow flexibility, the Master will give merely an opening date for the window. The parties (usually by counsel's clerks) then attend before the Listing officer at the Listing office in room WG08 to agree either a trial date (i.e. a fixed date for commencement of the trial) or, more usually, a trial period (being a 5 day period or a 3 day period) within the trial window on which or during which the trial will commence. The Master will not generally order a fixed trial date without first consulting the Listing Officer.

9.1.2 The Listing officer is in general responsible for listing. All applications relating to listing should in the first instance be made to him. Any party dissatisfied with any decision by him may, on one day's notice to all other parties, apply to the Judge in charge of the relevant list.

9.1.3 Any such application should be made within 7 days of the decision of the Listing Officer and should be arranged through the Listing Office in room WG08.

9.2 The Lists:

9.2 There are three Lists, namely: **1B–63**
  (1) the Jury List
  (2) the Non–Jury List, and
  (3) the Interim Hearings List.

These Lists are described below.

9.3 The Jury List:

9.3.1 Claims for damages for fraud, malicious prosecution and false imprisonment **1B–64** will, upon proper application by the party entitled made in accordance with CPR 26.11(1), be tried by a Judge and jury unless the court orders trial by a Judge alone: see Section 69(1) of the Senior Courts Act 1981. The application must be made within 28 days of the service of the defence. By section 11 of the Defamation Act 2013 however (enacted on 25 April 2013 and brought into force on 1 January 2014) section 69(1) no longer applies to claims for libel or slander. Thus, in such cases, the action will be tried without a jury unless the court in its discretion orders it to be tried with a jury. Application for trial with a jury will thus have to be made for that purpose, and made in accordance with CPR 26.11(2) which requires the application to be made at the first case management conference.

9.3.2 Where a claim is being tried by a Judge and jury it is vitally important that the jury should not suffer hardship and inconvenience by having been misled by an incorrect time estimate. It is therefore essential that time estimates given to the court are accurate and realistic.

9.3.3 Dates for the trial of substantial claims will be fixed by the Listing Office within the trial window after consideration of the parties' views.

9.3.4 Furthermore, in substantial claims likely to take more than 10 days to try, the Master will probably have directed a pre–trial review to be heard. The parties will thus be required to obtain from the Listing Officer an appointment for such PTR on a suitable date to be fixed, and to be heard if practicable by the Judge allocated to conduct the trial.

9.3.5 Jury applications (i.e applications in jury actions other than the trial itself) will enter the Interim Warned List not less than two weeks from the date the application notice is filed. Parties may "offer" a date for hearing the application either within or outside the week for which they are warned. Subject to court availability, the application will be listed on the offered date. Any application not reached on the offered date will return to the current Warned List and will be taken from that List as and when required.

9.3.6 Applications in defamation claims in respect of "meaning" (see Paragraph 8.2 above) may be listed for hearing on a specific day allocated for such matters.

9.3.7 Applications for directions and other applications in jury actions within the Master's jurisdiction should firstly be made to a Master unless:
  (1) a direction has been given for the arranging of a trial date or period, or
  (2) a date has been fixed or a period given for the trial.

Interim applications made after (1) or (2) above should (because they may have the effect of impacting on the trial date) be made to the Judge. In other circumstances the Master will use his or her discretion to refer a matter to the Judge if it is right to do so.

9.3.8 If a party believes that the Master is very likely to refer the application to the

Judge, for example where there is a substantial application to strike out, the matter should first be referred to the Master or Practice Master on notice to the other parties without waiting for a private room appointment. The Master will then decide whether the application should be referred to the Judge.

9.4 The Non–Jury List:

1B–65 9.4.1 This List consists of trials (other than Jury trials), preliminary questions or issues ordered to be tried (for example under CPR 3.1(2)(i)) and proceedings to commit for contempt of court.

9.4.2 The Royal Courts of Justice present unique problems in terms of fixing trial dates. The number of Judges involved and their geographical location has caused, for the time being at least, a different approach to the fixing of trials in the Chancery and Queen's Bench Divisions.

9.4.3 The requirement of Judges in the Queen's Bench Division to go on Circuit, sit in the Criminal Division of the Court of Appeal, and to deal with cases in the Administrative Court and other lists makes it difficult to fix dates for trials before particular Judges. Accordingly the following will only apply to the Queen's Bench Listing Office in the Royal Courts of Justice.

9.4.4 At as early an interim stage as practicable, the court will give directions identifying the trial window (see Paragraph 9.1.1 above).

9.4.5 The Master will usually direct that the claimant do by a certain date obtain a listing appointment from the Listing Officer to fix a trial date or period within that window and give notice of the appointment to the other parties. The Master may also in appropriate cases give specific directions, for example that the trial do not begin earlier than a specific date to provide the parties enough time to complete any necessary preparation; or that the trial do if practicable begin within a specified short period.

9.4.6 Where directions are given as in 9.4.5 above the onus is on the claimant to obtain a listing appointment with the Listing Officer in accordance with the direction.

9.4.7 If the claimant fails to do so any other party may seek such appointment; or the Listing Officer himself may make the appointment and give notice of the appointment to all parties.

9.4.8 At the listing hearing the Listing Officer will take account, in so far as it is practicable to do so, of any difficulties the parties may have as to availability of counsel, experts and witnesses. He will, nevertheless, try to ensure the speedy disposal of the trial by arranging a firm trial date or period as soon as possible within the trial window or, as the case may be, after the "not before" date directed by the court under Paragraph 9.4.5 above. If exceptionally it appears to the Listing Officer at the listing hearing that a trial date cannot be provided within a trial window, he may fix the trial date outside the trial period at the first available date. If a case summary has been prepared (see the Part 29 Practice Direction paragraphs 5.6 and 5.7) the claimant must produce a copy at the listing hearing together with a copy of particulars of claim and any orders relevant to the fixing of the trial date.

9.4.9 The Listing Officer will notify the Masters' Support Unit of any trial date or trial period given. In accordance with rule 29.2(3) notice will also be given to all the parties.

9.4.10 A party who wishes to appeal a date or period allocated by the Listing Officer must, within 7 days of the notification, make an application to the Judge nominated to hear such applications. The application notice should be filed in the Listing Office and served, giving one day's notice, on the other parties.

9.5 The Interim Hearings List:

1B–66 9.5.1 This List consists of interim applications whether in jury or non–jury actions, and appeals to Judges.

9.5.2 All matters in this List likely to take an hour or less will be listed before the

Interim Applications Judge in Court 37 in the West Green Building. All matters likely to last longer will be put into the Interim Hearings List to be heard by another Judge on a date to be fixed and notified by the Listing Officer to the parties.

9.5.3 Appeals from the Masters' decisions will appear in the Interim Hearings List. The appeal notice (stamped with the appropriate fee) must be filed in Room WG08. On filing the appeal notice the solicitors should uniform the Listing Officer whether they intend to instruct counsel and, if so, the names of counsel.

9.6 Listing before the Interim Applications Judge:

9.6.1 The work of the Interim Applications Judge is taken week by week by a High **1B–67** Curt Judge on a rota basis.

9.6.2 All applications must have a time estimate inserted by the parties. If an hour or less, the matter will be heard on a requested or ordered date notified by the Listing Office to the parties. If more than one hour, the matter will go into the Interim hearings Warned List (see Paragraph 9.5.2 above). The parties are required to give convenient dates before the date when the Warned List is due to commence and will if required attend on the Listing Officer to fix a date within the Warned List.

9.6.3 In order that a complete set of papers in proper order is available for the Judge to read before the hearing, the parties should not less than 3 days before the hearing lodge in Room WG08 a bundle, properly paginated in date order, and indexed, containing copies of the following documents:
1. the application notice or notice of appeal
2. any statements of case
3. copies of all written evidence (together with copy exhibits) on which any party intends to rely, and
4. any relevant order made in the proceedings

9.6.4 The bundle should be agreed if possible. In all but simple cases a skeleton argument and, where that would be helpful, a chronology should also be lodged. See paragraph 7.10.13 above and paragraphs 9.8.1 and 9.8.2 below in respect of skeleton arguments.

9.6.5 Except with the permission of the Judge no document may be used in evidence or relied on unless a copy of it has been included in the bundle referred to in paragraph 9.6.3 above. If any party seeks to rely on written evidence which has not been included in the bundle, that party should lodge the original (with copy exhibits) in Room WG08 in advance of the hearing, or otherwise with the Court Associate before the hearing commences.

9.6.6 In appeals from Masters and Circuit Judges to a High Court Judge, and from the decisions of District Judges sitting in the District Registries to a High Court Judge, the requirements as to a hearing bundle set out in paragraphs 9.6.3 and 9.6.4 above should be complied with. In addition, a copy of the judgment, or relevant parts thereof, given by the Master, Circuit Judge or District Judge should be made available.

9.6.7 Subject to the discretion of the Judge, any application or appeal normally made to the Interim Applications Judge may be made in the month of September. In the month of August, save with the permission of the Judge, appeals will be limited to those matters where, under Practice Direction 39B paragraph 2.5, an application might be made to a Master returnable in August without the Master's permission namely:–
1. to set aside a claim form or particulars of claim, or service of a claim form or particulars of claim
2. to set aside judgment
3. for a stay of execution
4. for any order by consent
5. for judgment or permission to enter judgment
6. for approval of settlements or for interim payment
7. for relief from forfeiture

8. for a charging order
9. for a third party debt order
10. for appointment or discharge of a receiver
11. for relief by way of interpleader by a sheriff or High Court enforcement officer
12. for transfer to a county court or for trial by a Master
13. for time where time is running in the month of August

9.6.8 As to applications in August, only those of real urgency will be dealt with, for example urgent applications in respect of injunctions or for possession under what remains of RSC Order 113 contained in Schedule 1 to the CPR.

9.6.9 It is desirable, where this is practical, that application notices or appeal notices are submitted to the Practice Master or a Judge prior to the hearing of the application or appeal so that they can be marked "fit for August" or "fit for vacation". If they are so marked, then normally the Judge will be prepared to hear the application or appeal in August, if marked "fit for August" or in September if marked "fit for vacation". The application to a Judge to have the papers so marked should normally be made in writing with the application shortly setting out the nature of the application or appeal and the reasons why it should be dealt with in August or in September, as the case may be: see PD 39B para.2.3(3).

9.7 The lists generally:

1B–68 9.7.1 Where a fixed date has been given it is the duty of the parties, notwithstanding that pre–trial checklists have been filed, to keep the Listing Officer fully informed as to the current position of the matter with regard to negotiations for settlement, whether all aspects of the claim are being proceeded with, an up to date estimate of the length of the hearing, and so on.

9.7.2 Applications for adjournment will not be granted except for the most cogent reasons. If an application is made because solicitors were unaware of the state of the List they may be ordered personally to pay the costs of the application.

9.7.3 A party who seeks to have a hearing before a Judge adjourned must inform the Listing Officer of his application as soon as possible. Applications for an adjournment immediately before a hearing begins should be avoided as they take up valuable time which could be used for dealing with effective matters and, if successful, may result in court time being wasted.

9.7.4 If the application is made by agreement, the parties should, by application notice in Form N244, apply to the Listing Officer who will consult either the Judge in Charge of the relevant list or, if necessary, the Interim Applications Judge. The Judge may grant the application on conditions that may include giving directions for a new hearing date.

9.7.5 If the application is opposed the application will be directed if practicable to the Judge assigned to hear the trial. A hearing will then be arranged through the Listing officer. A short summary of the reasons for the adjournment applied for should accompany the application notice. The parties must decide what if any evidence they seek to rely on.

9.7.6 The applicant will be expected to show that he has conducted his own case diligently. Any party should take all reasonable steps;
1. to ensure that his case is adequately prepared in sufficient time to enable the hearing to proceed, and
2. to prepare and serve any document (including any evidence) required to be served on any other party in sufficient time to enable that party also to be prepared.

9.7.7 If a party or his solicitor's failure to take reasonable steps necessitates an adjournment, the court will make such order as it sees fit including an order penalising the defaulting party in costs.

9.8 Listing Office—general matters:

1B–69 9.8.1 To facilitate the efficient listing of proceedings, parties are reminded that skeleton arguments concisely summarising each party's submissions must be prepared and filed with the Listing Office;

1. for trials, not less than 2 days before the trial, and
2. for substantial applications or appeals, not later than 1 day before the hearing.

9.8.2 If it is anticipated that a skeleton argument will be filed late, a letter of explanation should accompany it which will be shown to the Judge before whom the trial or hearing is to take place.

9.8.3 For parties' information, the following targets for the disposal of matters in the Lists have been agreed as set out below:

(1) Interim Hearings Warned List within 4 weeks from date of fixing
(2) Trials of 1 to 3 days, within 4–6 months after trial directions
(3) Trials of 3 to 5 days, within 6–8 months after trial directions
(4) Trials over 5 days but under 10 days, 8–12 months after trial directions
(5) Trials of 10 days or over but under 20 days, within 12–15 months after trial directions
(6) Trials of 20 days or over are likely to be fixed for a date exceeding 12 months.

SECTION 10

TRIAL, JUDGMENTS AND ORDERS

10.1 General:

10.1.1 The trial of a claim in the Royal Courts of Justice normally takes place before **1B–70** a High Court Judge (or a Deputy High Court Judge or a Circuit Judge sitting as a Judge of the High Court). A Master may assess the damages or sum due to a party under a judgment and, subject to any Practice Direction, he may try a claim which is proceeding under Part 8. A Master may also, with the consent of the parties, hear the trial of a claim. The Masters may, in such case, subject to their commitments, be able to do so.

10.1.2 Claims for malicious prosecution or false imprisonment are at present tried by a Judge sitting with a jury unless the court orders otherwise: see paragraph 9.3.1w above.

10.2 The Trial:

10.2.1 See paragraph 2.4. above about representation at the trial, and paragraphs **1B–71** 7.10.15 and 7.10.16 above about recording of proceedings.

10.2.2 Rule 39.3 sets out the consequences of a party's failure to attend the trial: and see also paragraph 2 of the Part 39 Practice Direction.

10.2.3 The Judge may fix a timetable for evidence and submissions if it has not already been fixed. The claimant's advocate will normally begin the trial with a short opening speech, and the Judge may then allow the other party to make a short speech. Each party should provide written summaries of their opening speeches if the points are not covered in their skeleton arguments

10.2.4 It is normally convenient for any outstanding procedural matters or applications to be dealt with in the course of, or immediately after, the opening speech. In a jury trial such matters would normally be dealt with before the jury is sworn in.

10.2.5 Unless the court orders otherwise, a witness statement will stand as the evidence in chief of the witness, provided he is called to give oral evidence: see rule 22.5(2). With the court's permission, a witness may amplify his witness statement or give evidence in relation to new matters which have arisen since the witness statement was served on the other parties.

10.2.6 The Court Associate will be responsible for any exhibits produced as evidence during the trial. After the trial, the exhibits are the responsibility of the party who produced them. Where a number of physical exhibits are involved, it is desirable, if possible, for the parties to agree a system of labelling and the manner of display beforehand.

10.2.7 The Associate will normally draw the formal judgment or order made at the trial. The reserved judgment of the Judge will be made available to the parties either by being handed down in writing or, where delivered orally, by request for a transcript of the same: see para.7.10.15 above.

10.2.8 At a jury trial, it is the parties' responsibility to provide sufficient bundles of documents for the use of the jury.

10.2.9 Facilities are available to assist parties or witnesses with special needs. The Queen's Bench Listing Office should be notified of any needs or requirements prior to the trial, in writing.

10.3 Judgments and orders:

1B–72 10.3.1 Part 40 deals with judgments and orders. Rule 40.2 contains the standard requirements, i.e. the matters to be included in any judgment or order. Note particularly what is to be included where application for permission to appeal was made at the hearing at which the judgment or order was given.

10.3.2 Drawing the order. Rule 40.3 contains extensive provision about the drawing up and filing of judgments and orders, including by whom they are to be drawn up and filed and the time for doing so. See also PD 40B para.1 for more information.

10.3.3 Of particular importance in relation to drawing Masters' orders in the Royal Courts of Justice is rule 40.3(4). This reads "Except for orders made by the court of its own initiative and unless the court otherwise orders, every judgment or order made in claims proceeding in the Queen's Bench Division at the Royal Courts of Justice..... will be drawn up by the parties, and rule 40.3 is modified accordingly." The procedure for drawing orders is as follows:–

1. The Master will either endorse the Order in full on the original Application Notice (or on the original order which fixed the date for the hearing) or will endorse on it a reference to the draft order which has been presented, and possibly amended, such as "O. as on (amended) initialled draft"
2. The party (usually the applicant or, at a case management conference, the claimant) having responsibility for drawing the Order (having "carriage") will type the Order, following exactly the wording of the Master's initialled draft, and make sufficient copies for the court file and for service on all other parties.
3. Within 7 days (see rule 40.3(3)(a)), or such other time as the Master may have directed, the party having carriage of the Order must present the original Application Notice bearing the Master's endorsed Order, or the draft Order initialled by the Master, together with the typed copies in Room E07 (The Masters Support Unit in the Action Department) where the court will compare the typed copies with the Master's endorsement or initialled draft.
4. If the typed copies faithfully reproduce the Master's endorsement or draft, then the court officer will seal the Orders, retaining one copy and the original documents initialled by the Masters for filing, and return the sealed copies for service.
5. Alternatively to having endorsed the order as in 1. above, the Master may, particularly where counsel are retained, tell counsel what his order is, direct them to draw it and sign it as an agreed minute and submit it to him (occasionally by e–mail) for his approval. The party having carriage will then submit typed copies of the approved Order to the court office for sealing.
6. In any case of doubt the court officer will refer the matter of sealing to the Master who made the order, or to the Practice Master, for him to decide whether or not the Order should be permitted to be sealed in the form presented.

10.3.4 Provisions concerning consent orders are contained in Rule 40.6 which sets out in paragraph (3) the types of consent judgments and orders that may be sealed and entered by a court officer, provided;

1. that none of the parties is a litigant in person, and
2. the approval of the court is not required by a rule, practice direction or an enactment.

Other types of consent order require an application to be made to a Master or Judge for the granting of the order. It is common for a respondent to a consent order not to attend the hearing but to provide a written consent. The consent may either be written on the document or contained in a letter, and must be signed by the respondent, or where there are solicitors on the record as acting for him, by his solicitors. The Master will be concerned to know, for example where a draft consent order is signed on behalf of a company, the status and authority of the signatory in question. All signatures should be accompanied by a legible statement in capital letters of the person's name. Paragraph 3 of the Part 40B Practice Direction contains further information about consent orders.

10.3.5 Under rule 40.7(1) a judgment or order takes effect from the day on which it is given or made, or such later date as the court may specify.

10.3.6 Rule 40.8 specifies the time from which interest is to run on a judgment, where interest is payable. Such interest runs from the date that the judgment is given, subject to the specific terms of rule 40.8.

10.3.7 Rule 40.11 sets out the time for complying with a judgment or order for the payment of money, which is 14 days unless the judgment or order specifies otherwise (for example by instalments), or any of the Rules specifies a different time, or the judgment or proceedings have been stayed.

10.3.8 The Part 40B Practice Direction also sets out useful provisions for:
  (a) expressly adjusting a final judgment figure where compensation recovery payments are concerned: see para.5,
  (b) expressly adjusting a final judgment figure where interim payments have been made: see para.6,
  (c) setting out in a judgment the consequences of failing to comply with an order that an act must be done by a certain time: see para.8, and
  (d) including in a money judgment provisions for payment by instalments: see para.12.

10.3.9 Where judgment is reserved, the Judge may deliver judgment by handing down the written text without reading it out in open court. Where this is the case, the advocates will be supplied with the full text of the judgment in advance of delivery. The advocates should then familiarise themselves with the contents and be ready to deal with any points which may arise when the judgment is delivered. Any direction or requirement as to confidentiality must be complied with.

10.3.10 Such judgment does not take effect until formally delivered in court. If the judgment is to be handed down in writing copies will then be made available to the parties and, if requested and so far as practicable, to the law reporters and the press.

10.3.11 The Judge will usually direct that the written judgment may be used for all purposes as the text of the judgment, and that no transcript need be made. Where such a direction is made, a copy will be provided to the Courts Recording and Transcription Unit, Room WB14, from where further copies may be obtained (and see Paragraph 7.10.15 above).

Judgment or order for payment of money on behalf of a child or protected beneficiary

10.3.12 The usual order made at trial will make provision for any immediate payment (e.g. for expenses) to the litigation friend or his/her legal representative and for the balance of the award to be placed to a special investment account (or other investment account as may be directed) pending application for investment directions. Such application is directed to made to a Master or District Judge in the case of a child's fund or to the Court of Protection in the case of a protected beneficiary's fund. The Judge's order will specify the time within which the application is to be made. Care should be taken to comply with this. The order will also deal with interest accrued to the date of judgment, and with any interest which accrues on the fund in the future. The order will also refer to majority directions in the case of a child (i.e. a specific direction as to what is to occur in relation to the fund when the child achieves the age of 18); and to any specific directions on investment which the Judge may see fit to give as part of his order. And see Paragraphs 6.8.11 to 6.8.15 above.

10.3.13 The litigation friend or legal representative will then apply:

1. in the case of a child, to the Master or District Judge in accordance with paragraphs 6.8.10 to 6.8.15 above and para.9.4 of the Part 21 Practice Direction. In the Royal Courts of Justice the application is sent to the Masters' Support Unit in Room E07; and
2. in the case of a protected beneficiary, to the Court of Protection in accordance with para.10 of the Practice Direction.

10.3.14 Where at trial the Judge has given judgment for an award of damages to a child or protected beneficiary by way of periodical payments his order will specify those matters that are required to be specified by rule 41.8.

Provisional damages

10.3.15 Rule 41.1 defines an award of provisional damages; and rule 41.2 lays down the circumstances in which (including at trial) the court may make such an award in a claim for personal injuries. Where there is a chance that a claimant may in the future develop a particular disease or suffer a particular deterioration in his physical or mental condition as a result of the event giving rise to the claim he may seek an award of damages on the assumption that he will not develop the disease or suffer the deterioration, with provision for him to make a further application within a specified time if he does develop the disease or suffer the deterioration. Rule 41.2(2) stipulates in precise terms what any order for provisional damages (if made) must contain.

10.3.16 The Part 41 Practice Direction gives further information about provisional damages awards and, in particular, about the preservation of the case file for the time specified in the order for making a further application, and the documents to be included in the case file. A precedent for a provisional damages judgment is annexed to the Practice Direction.

SECTION 11

APPEALS

11.1 General

1B–73 11.1.1 Appeals are governed by Part 52 and by the clear terms of the five new Practice Direction supplementing that Part.

11.1.2 The five Practice Direction are:

PD52A – Appeals; general provisions
PD52B – Appeals in the county courts and the High Court
PD52C – Appeals to the Court of Appeal
PD52D – Statutory appeals and appeals subject to special provision
PD52E – Appeals by way of case stated

11.1.3 Part 52 complements the provisions of sections 54 to 57 of the Access to Justice Act 1999 and provides a uniform procedure for appeals in the county courts and the High Court and a modified procedure for the Civil Division of the Court of Appeal.

11.1.4 In the case of any appeal the relevant Practice Direction or Directions must be read together with the rules in Part 52 and must be consulted in detail for their terms. Indeed, each of the Practice Direction is specifically described as supplementing Part 52; and by rule 52.2 all parties to an appeal must comply with the Practice Direction.

11.1.5 Under rule 52.1, the rules in Part 52 are to apply to appeals to
(a) the civil division of the Court of Appeal;
(b) the High Court; and
(c) a county court

11.1.6 Appeals only in (a) and (b) above arise for consideration in this Guide.

11.2 Permission to appeal:

11.2.1 Rule 52.3 contains the cardinal requirement that, save in certain specified **1B–74** cases, permission to appeal is required.

11.2.2 An application for permission to appeal may be made
   (a) to the lower court at the hearing at which the decision to be appealed was made; or
   (b) to the appeal court (i.e. the court to which the appeal is made) in an appeal notice.

See rule 52.3(2). By PD 52A para.4.1, in order to facilitate the making of an application to the lower court for permission to appeal in an appropriate case, the lower court may adjourn the hearing to give a party an opportunity so to apply. If an application to the lower court is refused, or if no application is made to the lower court, a party may nonetheless apply to the appeal court in accordance with rule 52.4: See rule 52.3(3) and PD52A para.4.1(b).

11.2.3 Permission to appeal may be given only where
   (a) the court considers that the appeal would have a real prospect of success; or
   (b) there is some other compelling reason why the appeal should be heard.

See rule 52.3(6).

11.2.4 An appeal court may consider an application for permission at a hearing or without a hearing. If it refuses permission without a hearing the person seeking permission may, within 7 days of notification of the refusal, request the decision to be reconsidered at a hearing: rule 52.3(4). This is however subject to provision that an order may be made refusing the right to request a hearing where the application is considered to be totally without merit: see rule 52.3(4A).

11.2.5 Permission may be given
   (a) limiting the issues to be heard, and
   (b) subject to conditions

See rule 52.3(7). Such conditions may, and not infrequently do, provide for security for the costs of the appeal.

11.2.6 Refusal of permission at a hearing by the appeal court is effectively the end of the road (see section.54(4) of the Access to Justice Act 1999), save in the extremely rare cases where the Court of Appeal or the High Court may re–open a final determination of an appeal, which expression includes an application for permission to appeal; see rule 52.17, and PD52A para.7 which governs the procedure in any such case.

11.2.7 Stay of proceedings. It should be noted that (except in certain immigration appeals), unless the appeal court or the lower court orders otherwise, an appeal does not operate as a stay of any order or decision of the lower court. Appellants seeking a stay should specifically include an application in the appeal notice, or make separate application in accordance with Part 23.

11.2.8 Second appeals. Where an application is made for permission to appeal a decision of the High Court or a county court which was itself made on appeal, the application for permission must be made to the Court of Appeal: rule 52.13(1) and PD52A para.4.7. The Court of Appeal will not give such permission unless it considers that the appeal would raise an important point of principle or practice, or there is some other compelling reason. If permission is given, the appeal will be heard in the Court of Appeal.

11.2.9 A court from which or to which an appeal is being made may, if it considers that an appeal which is to be heard in the county court or the High Court would raise an important point of principle or there is some other compelling reason for the Court of Appeal to hear it, transfer the appeal to the Court of Appeal: rule 52.14.

11.3 Routes of appeal and powers on appeal

11.3.1 Paragraphs 3.1 to 3.9 of Practice Direction 52A conveniently set out the **1B–75** destinations of appeal, i.e. the appropriate court to which an appeal must be made.

These provisions implement the Access to Justice 1999 (Destination of Appeals) Order 2000 (S.1 2000 No.1071).

11.3.2 The destinations set out in Table 1 in para.3.5 apply according to whether the decision appealed from is interim or final, as to which see para.11.3.3 below. Thus, by way of example, in relation to an appeal from a Circuit Judge in the county court, an appeal against an interim decision in a Part 7 claim will go to a High Court Judge. An appeal against a final decision in a Part 7 claim will, if the case is not in the multi–track, go to a High Court Judge; whereas if the case is in the multi–track the appeal will go to the Court of Appeal. In relation to a decision by a Master, or by a District Judge sitting in a District Registry of the High Court, the position is the same as above. Thus, the large majority of appeals from a Master, being appeals against an interim decision, will go to a High Court Judge. In relation to a decision by a High Court Judge, whether interim or final, the appeal will go to the Court of Appeal.

11.3.3 The distinction between interim and final decisions is set forth in paragraphs 3.6, 3.7 and 3.8 of the Practice Direction. A final decision is a decision that would finally determine (subject to any possible appeal or detailed assessment of costs) the entire proceedings whichever way the court decided the issues before it: para.3.6. A decision is to be treated as final where it is made at the conclusion of a hearing or trial which has been split into parts and would, if it had been made at the conclusion of the hearing or trial, have been a final decision: para.3.7. Para.3.8(1) sets out examples of final decisions, namely judgment on liability at the end of a split trial, and judgment at the conclusion of an assessment of damages following a judgment on liability. Para.3.8(2) sets out examples of decisions that are not final, amongst which are summary judgment and striking out a claim or statement of case.

11.3.4 Rule 52.10 sets out the appeal court's powers on an appeal, which include power to affirm, set aside or vary an order or judgment of the lower court, refer any claim or issue for determination by the lower court, or order a new trial or hearing. There is express power to vary an award of damages made by a jury.

11.3.5 It should be noted that an appeal will normally be limited to a review of the decision of the lower court: rule 52.11(1). Unless otherwise ordered, the appeal court will not receive oral evidence, or evidence which was not before the lower court: rule 52.11(2).

11.3.6 rule 52.11(3) contains the important guiding principle that the appeal court will allow an appeal where the decision of the lower court was
    (a) wrong; or
    (b) unjust because of a serious procedural or other irregularity in the proceedings in the lower court.

11.4 Appellant's Notice

1B–76 11.4.1 In all cases an appellant is required to file an appellant's notice. The notice is in Form N161. The venue for filing the appellant's notice is dealt with below.

11.4.2 If the appellant has not already obtained permission to appeal, and seeks that permission from the appeal court, he must include an application for such permission in the appellant's notice: see rule 52.4.

11.4.3 The time for filing the appellant's notice is:
    (a) such period as may be directed by the lower court, which may be longer or shorter than the period in (b) below; or
    (b) if the lower court makes no such direction, 21 days after the date of the decision of the lower court that it is sought to appeal.

11.4.4 Provisions for seeking a variation of time are contained in rule 52.6, whereby an application to vary the time limit must be made to the appeal court. A party may however, in an appeal in the county court or High Court, seek an extension of time from the lower court and, if he does so, he must seek it at the same time as applying to the lower court for permission to appeal: see PD 52B para.3.1. If applying after the time for filing has expired an appellant must include such application in his appeal notice stating the reason for the delay and the steps taken prior to making the application.

11.4.5 Service. Unless the appeal court orders otherwise, an appellant's notice must be served on each respondent as soon as practicable and in any event not later than 7 days after it is filed: rule 52.4 (3).

11.5 Respondent's Notice

11.5.1 A respondent to an appeal may himself seek to appeal the whole or part of the decision of the lower court; or he may wish to ask the appeal court to uphold the order of the lower court for reasons different from or additional to those given by the lower court. rule 52.5 sets out a respondent's obligations in such case, including his obligations as to filing and serving a respondent's notice. Such notice is to be in Form N162. Where, as will be required if the respondent is seeking to vary the order of the lower court, permission to appeal is required, such permission should be sought in the respondent's notice.   **1B–77**

11.6 Disposal of applications and appeals by consent

11.6.1 Section 6 of Practice Direction 52A deals with the position.   **1B–78**

11.6.2 An appellant who does not wish to proceed with an application or appeal may request the appeal court to dismiss such application or appeal. If such request is granted it will usually be subject to an order for costs against the appellant. A respondent may however state by letter that he consents to an order without costs. Where settlement has been reached, the parties may consent to dismissal of the application or appeal: paras.6.1 to 6.3.

11.6.3 Notwithstanding the above, where one of the parties is a child or protected party any disposal of an application or appeal requires the approval of the court. A draft order signed by the parties' solicitors should be sent to the appeal court, together with an opinion from the advocate acting for the child or protected party: para.6.5.

11.7 Procedure on appeals in the county court and the High Court

11.7.1 Practice Direction 52B sets out the procedure on   **1B–79**
   (a) appeals within a county court
   (b) appeals from a county court to the High Court, and
   (c) appeals within the High Court, including appeals from a Master or a District Judge sitting in a District Registry to a Judge of the High Court.

11.7.2 The venue for making the appeal, including filing all notices and making all applications, is the subject of section 2 of the PD. The tables at the end of the PD set out appeal centres which relate to the circuit on which the case has been heard and which will constitute the venue for the appeal. In appeals in the Royal Courts of Justice, appeal notices and applications should be filed in the High Court Appeals Listing Office in Room WG07. The office has a useful leaflet available to litigants entitled "I want to appeal" which provides information about High Court appeals.

11.7.3 Section 4 of the PD sets out the documents which must be filed with the appellant's notice. These include grounds of appeal which must be set out in a separate sheet and which must set out in simple language, clearly and concisely, why the order of the lower court was wrong or unjust because of a serious procedural or other irregularity.

11.7.4 Any application made in the appeal should be made in the appeal notice. Thus, for example, where an appellant qualifies for fee remission he may seek in his appellant's notice a transcript of the judgment of the lower court at public expense: para.4.3.

11.7.5 Para.6.2 of the PD deals specifically with the obtaining of a transcript of the judgment or other record of the reasons of the lower court and must be carefully followed in all cases.

11.7.6 Para.6.3 requires filing by the appellant, as soon as practicable but in any event within 35 days of filing the appellant's notice, of an appeal bundle which is to be paginated and indexed. The documents which (subject to any order) must be included in the bundle are set out in para.6.4(1). Those which should be considered for inclusion, but which should be included only where relevant, are set out in para.6.4(2).

11.7.7 Service of the appeal bundle, depending on the question whether and at what stage permission to appeal has been granted, is dealt with in para.6.5.

11.7.8 Skeleton arguments are the subject of para.8.3. They should be produced (subject to any order of the court) only where the complexity of the issues of fact or law justify them; or they would assist the court in respects not readily apparent from the papers in the appeal. In any event, it should be noted that skeleton arguments are subject to the specific requirements of section 5 of Practice Direction 52A which, if a skeleton argument is filed, should be carefully followed.

11.7.9 In appeals in the High Court to be heard in the Royal Courts of Justice, the High Court Appeals Office (Room WG07) will notify the parties of either the hearing date or the "listing window" during which the appeal is likely to be heard.

11.8 Procedure on appeals in the Court of Appeal

1B–80   11.8.1 Practice Direction 52C sets out the procedure in detail.

11.8.2 An appellant's notice in Form N161 must be filed and served in all cases, and must be accompanied by the appropriate fee or fee remission certificate.

11.8.3 The notice and accompanying documents (see para.11.8.4 below) must be filed in the Civil Appeals Office Registry, Room E307, Royal Courts of Justice, Strand, London WC2A 2LL.

11.8.4 The accompanying documents are described in para.3 of the Practice Direction. These include the appellant's skeleton argument in support of the appeal. Grounds of appeal are required by para.5 of the Practice Direction. These must, as in appeals within the High Court, identify as concisely as possible the respects in which the judgment of the court below is

(a) wrong; or

(b) unjust because of a serious procedural or other irregularity

It should be noted however that the reasons why the decision is wrong or unjust must not be included in the grounds of appeal but must be confined to the skeleton argument.

11.8.5 Paragraph 4 of the Practice Direction lays down procedural requirements for applying for an extension of time for filing an appellant's notice; and for the right of a respondent to an appeal to oppose an application for extension of time.

11.8.6 The Civil Appeals Office does not serve documents in an appeal. This is left to be effected by the parties: para.7.

11.8.7 Paragraphs 8 to 13 of the Practice Direction deal with respondent's notices and skeleton arguments including filing and service thereof. Thus a respondent who seeks to appeal against any part of the order below must file an appeal notice; and if he seeks a variation of the order he must obtain permission to appeal. A respondent's notice is in Form N162.

11.8.8 The procedure where permission to appeal is sought from the Court of Appeal is set out in section 4 (paragraphs 14 to 20). An application for permission will generally be considered without a hearing in the first instance subject (if permission is refused) to a request for an oral hearing. Whilst a respondent to an appeal must be served with any appeal notice, including an application therein for permission to appeal, a respondent need not take any action when served unless the court directs otherwise: para.19. Such directions may be called for (for example) where an appellant seeks permission to appeal at a permission hearing: see para.16 (2).

11.8.9 The "listing window notification" means the letter sent by the Civil Appeals Office notifying the parties of the window within which the appeal is likely to be heard. The "hear–by date" is the last day of the listing window. The Timetable Part 1 in section 5 of the Practice Direction sets out the precise timetable to be followed by each of the parties from the listing window notification to lodging of the appeal bundle. Cross–references to the various provisions of the Practice Direction regarding steps to be taken are set out in the Timetable. Thus, for example, within 7 days after the date of the listing window notification, the appellant must serve on every respondent the proposed bundle index as referred to in para.27 of the PD. That paragraph itself contains in detail those documents relevant to the appeal which must be included in the bundle; and those documents which should also be considered for inclusion in the bundle but should be included only where relevant to the appeal. Again by way of example, within 21 days after the listing window notification the appellant must serve on every respondent his appeal skeleton as referred to in para.31 of the PD.

11.8.10 The Timetable Part 2 sets out the steps to be taken by each of the parties once the hearing date has been fixed, again with cross–references. Thus, for example, not less than 42 days before the appeal hearing the appropriate number of appeal bundles must be lodged as directed by the court and copies must be served on all the other parties.

11.8.11 Bundles of authorities, as referred to in para.29 of the PD, must be lodged no later than 7 days before the date of the appeal hearing.

11.9 Statutory appeals and appeals subject to special provision

11.9.1 Practice Direction 52D deals with the procedure in those many cases where **1B–81** appeal from a court or tribunal is prescribed by statute. There is a Table set out in the PD which refers to the appropriate court for such appeals, including the many cases where the High Court is the appropriate court. In some cases the Chancery Division, rather than the Queen's Bench Division, will hear such appeals: see para.5.1. The Table has cross–references to the relevant paragraphs in PD 52D which govern the relevant procedure in the particular cases.

11.9.2 Where any statute prescribes a period of time within which an appeal must be filed then, unless the statute otherwise provides, the appeal court may not extend that period: see para.3.5 of the PD. Thus, in such cases, the appeal court may not exercise the powers generally available to it under rule 52.6.

11.9.3 Contempt of court. Appeals in cases of contempt of court fall under PD 52D. See the Table to the PD which prescribes the Court of Appeal as the appropriate court. Such appeals are brought under section 13 of the Administration of Justice Act 1960. By para.9 of the PD the appellant's notice must be served "on the court from whose order or decision the appeal is brought". This will require, in the case of appeals from the Queen's Bench Division in cases of contempt, service on the court by leaving a copy of the appellant's notice with the High Court Appeals Office in Room WG07, Royal Courts of Justice, Strand, London WC2A 2LL.

11.10 Appeals by way of case stated

11.10.1 Practice Direction 52E governs, firstly, the procedure to be followed, **1B–82** including filing and serving an appellant's notice, where a case has been stated by the Crown Court or a Magistrates' Court for the opinion of the High Court: see paras.2.1 to 2.4 of the PD. It governs, secondly, the procedure including the filing and serving of appellant's notices, where a Minister, Government Department, tribunal or other person has, whether on request or otherwise, stated a case for the opinion of the court or referred a question of law to the court by way of case stated: paras.3.1 to 3.10. An application for an order for a Minister or tribunal etc to state a case is made to the court which would be the appeal court if the case was stated: para.3.11. this may require consideration of the Table in Practice Direction 52D (see Paragraph 11.9.1 above) in order to determine which is the appropriate appeal court. Such application is made under Part 23 of the CPR and must contain the information set forth in para.3.13.

SECTION 12

ENFORCEMENT

12.1 General:

12.1.1 Enforcement in the High Court of judgments or orders is governed by CPR **1B–83**

Parts 70 to 74, CPR Part 81, and now, following an overhaul of the procedure governing writs of execution and what are now called writs of control taking effect from 6 April 2014, Parts 83 to 86. The former RSC Orders 45 to 47 and (with respect to interpleader proceedings) RSC Order 17, are now replaced by these new provisions. There is also power to appoint a receiver on or after judgment: see Part 69, and in particular rule 69.2(1)(c).

12.1.2 The new procedure with respect to writs of execution and writs of control is brought into force under the enabling Act, namely the Tribunal, Courts and Enforcement Act 2007, and under the Taking Control of Goods Regulations 2013 (SI 2013/1894). The provisions of the Act and Regulations must be read together with CPR Parts 83 to 86. Particular attention should be paid to section 62 of and schedule 12 to the Act in relation to the issue and execution of writs conferring a power to use the TCG procedure.

12.1.3 Issue of the writ of execution or control. The procedure is governed by rule 83.9. This provides that issue takes place on the writ being sealed by a court officer of the appropriate office. In all cases save those stipulated in rule 83.9 (1)(a)(b) and (c) this will be the Central Office of the Senior Courts at the Royal Courts of Justice. A request for the issue of the writ must be filed. Such request must be signed by the person entitled to execution, if acting in person, or by or on behalf of the solicitor of the person so entitled. Rule 83.9(5) lays down the documents which must be produced by the person presenting the writ in order to enable the writ to be sealed. It also requires the court officer to be satisfied that any period specified in the judgment or order for the payment of any money or the doing of any other act under the judgment or order has expired. Every writ of execution or control will bear the date on which it is issued: rule 83.9(6).

12.2 Judgments for land

1B–84 12.2.1 A judgment or order for the possession of land may be enforced in the High Court
    (a) by a writ of possession
    (b) in a case to which CPR rule 81.4 applies, by an order of committal, and
    (c) in a case to which CPR rule 81.20 applies, by an order of sequestration. See rule 83.13.

12.2.2 The court's permission is required to issue a writ of possession save (a) in mortgage claims, and (b) in claims against trespassers under Part 56 unless (in that case) the writ is to be issued after the expiry of three months from the date of the order: see rule 83.13.

12.2.3 Where such permission is required it will not, by virtue of rule 83.13(8), be granted unless it is shown that every person in actual possession of the whole or any part of the land has received such notice of the proceedings as appears to the court to be sufficient to enable him to apply to the court for any relief to which he may be entitled. Where the defendant or any other persons are in actual possession of the premises an affidavit applying for leave to issue a writ must, in addition to dealing with the matters required by rule 83.13(8), contain the following information:–
    (a) whether the premises or any part thereof is a dwelling house;
    (b) if so (i)
        (i) what is the rateable value of the dwelling house;
        (ii) whether it is let furnished or unfurnished and, if furnished, what is the amount of furniture therein;
    (c) any other matters which will assist the Master in determining whether the occupier is protected by the Rent Acts.

See the Practice Direction at [[1955] 1 W.L.R 1314 and [1955] 3 All E.R 646.

12.2.4 The duration, extension and priority of writs of possession are governed by rule 83.3. A writ will be valid for the period of 12 months beginning with the date of its issue. The court may, on application, extend the writ from time to time for a period of 12 months at any one time. If the application is made before the expiry of

12 months the extension will begin on the day after the expiry. If the application is made after the expiry any period of extension will begin on any day after the expiry that the court may allow. As to priority, irrespective of whether it has been extended, the priority of a writ of possession will be determined by reference to the time it was originally received by the person who is under a duty to endorse it: rule 83.3(9). Application should be made in Form N244 supported by witness statement.

12.2.5 Stay of execution of writ of possession. It should be noted that the court has no power to grant a stay of execution against trespassers. The extent to which the court will exercise a power of stay in other circumstances has been considered in *McPhail v Persons Names Unknown* [1973] Ch.447, C.A, and *Bain & Co v Church Commissioners for England* [1989] 1 W.L.R. 24.

12.2.6 In addition to the requirement under rule 83.13 to obtain permission for the issue of a writ of possession, rule 83.2 imposes further requirements to obtain permission in specified cases, e.g where 6 years or more have elapsed since the date of the judgment or order or any change has taken place in the parties entitled, or liable, under the judgment: see rule 83.2(3) (a) and (b).

12.3 Judgments for goods

12.3.1 Enforcement of a judgment or order for the delivery of goods, whether with **1B–85** or without the option for the judgment debtor to pay the assessed value of the goods, is the subject of rule 83.14.

12.3.2 In the case of a judgment or order that does not give the judgment debtor any such alternative the same may be enforced
- (a) by writ of delivery to recover the goods in Form N64, referred to as a "writ of specific delivery". No permission is required for the issue of such a writ in these circumstances;
- (b) in a case in which rule 81.4 applies, by an order of committal, and
- (c) in a case in which rule 81.20 applies, by a writ of sequestration.

12.3.3 In all such cases where a question of committal or sequestration arises the full terms of CPR Part 81 must be considered.

12.3.4 On the other hand, where the judgment or order gives the debtor the option of paying the assessed value, it may be enforced:
- (a) by writ of delivery to recover the goods or their assessed value. No permission to issue such a writ is required.
- (b) by order of the court, by writ of specific delivery. Permission is required. The judgment creditor should apply under Part 23 providing evidence to support his case why such an order should be made in the court's discretion. The application notice must be served on the judgment debtor.
- (c) in a case to which rule 81.20 applies, by writ of sequestration.

In the event that a judgment creditor relies on a judgment assessing the value of the goods such judgment may be enforced by the same means as any other judgment or order for the payment of money: rule 83.14(5).

12.4 Judgments for money

12.4.1 The usual means of execution in the High Court of a judgment or order for **1B–86** the payment of money is by the issue of what is now called a writ of control. The statutory framework for the whole process of such execution is found in Part 3 of the Tribunals, Courts and Enforcement Act 2007, including section 62(4), in schedule 12 to the Act, in the Taking Control of Goods Regulations 2013, and in Parts 83 and 84 of the CPR. PD84 contains a useful direction that the Act and the Regulations can both be found at **www.justice.gov.uk.courts/procedure–rules**; and also that a flow chart providing guidance and setting out the interrelationship of the Rules, the Act and the Regulations can be found at the same source. Such flow chart will, particularly, provide information as to the occasions on which, and how, an application to the court will need to be made in the process.

12.4.2 A writ of control confers powers on an enforcement agent to take control of goods for the purpose of sale thereof for a sum sufficient to satisfy the judgment debt and costs of the execution. The enforcement agent's fees, including fixed fees and additional fees in certain circumstances, are laid down by the Taking Control of Goods (Fees) Regulation 2014. Both the judgment creditor and the judgment debtor may require reasonable information from the enforcement agent or enforcement officer as to the execution of a writ: the enforcement agent or enforcement officer must provide that information within 7 days of the notice and the court may make an order against him if he fails to do so: rule 83.8.

12.4.3 Enforcement agent. The power to take control of goods is vested in an individual certificated to act as an enforcement agent. Section 63(2) of the Act defines who may act as an enforcement agent. The process of certification takes place under the Certification of Enforcement Agents Regulations 2014 (S1 2014/421). A judgment creditor may choose to address the sealed writ to a particular High Court Enforcement Officer for the relevant postcode of the judgment debtor; or he may simply address the writ with the postcode of the judgment debtor's residence or place of business in which case the writ will be allocated to a particular HCEO by rotation. Allocation will be carried by the Registry Trust Limited of 153–157 Cleveland Street, London W1T 6PQ (telephone 0207 391 7299) Further information can be found on the High Court Enforcement Officers Association website at **http://www.hceoa.org.uk**; or by telephone enquiry to the Association's office at 0844 824 4575.

12.4.4 The process of taking control of goods by the enforcement agent is the subject of the legislation under schedule 12 to the Act, the Regulations and Part 84 of the CPR. These provisions include, particularly, the steps that the enforcement agent may take, the hours of the day on which he may enter premises, and his ability to enter into a controlled goods agreement with the debtor under which terms are agreed in writing for the repayment by the debtor of the sum due under the judgment or order. The reader is advised to consult the legislation for its terms in any particular case but it may be helpful to point out that paragraphs 4 to 69 of schedule 12 delineate the general powers of the enforcement agent, including, at para.13, the four ways in which he may take control of the goods, whereas Part 84 of the CPR regulates specific matters that may, and often will, arise on applications in the process of taking control. Thus, to take examples, rule 84.3 provides that, in pre–existing proceedings, any application to the court must be made to the High Court or the County Court in accordance with rule 23.2. Further, whilst notice must be given to the judgment debtor not less than 7 days before the enforcement agent takes control, application may be made without notice to shorten that period: rule 84.4. An application to <u>extend</u> the period under which control may be taken is the subject of rule 84.5. An application to take control during prohibited hours, again without notice, may be made under rule 84.6. This will require evidence that unless the order is made it is likely that the judgment debtor will dispose of the goods in order to defeat the process. The enforcement agent will usually sell the goods at public auction. If however he seeks an order for sale by private treaty in a particular case he must apply under paragraph 41(2) of schedule 12 for that purpose. Rule 84.11 contains special provisions relating to any such application. An application by the enforcement agent to recover exceptional disbursements is the subject of rule 84.15. Disputes about the amount of fees recoverable are governed by application under rule 84.16. And, where a co–owner of the goods may be entitled to a share of the proceeds of sale, disputes in that respect are the subject of application under Rule 84.15.

12.4.5 Issue of a writ of control. This is the subject of rules 83.2 and 83.9. Permission to issue is required in the cases set forth in 83.2(3). As to the matters to be complied with to enable issue to take place see para.12.1.3 above.

12.4.6 Validity of the writ. The validity of a writ of control is governed by rule 83.4(3) whereby it will be valid for the period in which an enforcement agent may take control of the goods as specified in regulation 9(1) of the TCG Regulations. This period is defined as 12 months commencing with the date of notice of enforcement. Application for extension, limited to one application only, may be made in accordance with rule 84.5 and, if granted, will be for a period of 12 months: see regulation 9(3).

12.4.7 Goods which may be taken – exempt goods. Paragraph 9 of schedule 12 to the Act provides that an enforcement agent may take control of goods only if they are:

(a) on premises that he has power to enter under the schedule; or

(b) on a highway

Under paragraph 10 he may take control of goods only if they are goods of the debtor.

Under paragraph 11(1) "subject to paragraphs 9 and 10 and to any other enactment under which goods are protected, an enforcement agent:

(a) may take control of goods anywhere in England and Wales;

(b) may take control of any goods that are not exempt"

The definition of exempt goods for this purpose is set out in regulations 4 and 5 of the Taking Control of Goods Regulations 2013. The list in regulation 4 includes particularly, but not exhaustively:

"(a). items of equipment (for example tools, books, telephones, computer equipment and vehicles) which are necessary for use personally by the debtor in the debtor's employment, business, trade, profession, study or education, except that in any case the aggregate value of the items or equipment to which this exemption is applied shall not exceed £1,350;

(b) such clothing, bedding, furniture, household equipment, items and provisions as are reasonably required to satisfy the basic domestic needs of the debtor and every member of the debtor's household....."

The list should be read for its full terms.

12.4.8 Stay of writ of control. Under rule 83.7 at the time that a judgment or order for the payment of money is made or granted, or at any time thereafter, the debtor or other party liable to execution of a writ of control may apply to the court for a stay of execution. The power to grant a stay of any writ of control is vested in a Master or District Judge. The grounds on which application may be made include the debtor's inability to pay, in which case the witness statement in support must disclose the debtor's means: rule 83.7(4). It is specifically provided, in line with the position under the former RSC Order 47 rule 1(1), that if the court is satisfied that (a) there are special circumstances which render it inexpedient to enforce the judgment or order, or (b) that the applicant is unable for any reason to pay the money, then, notwithstanding anything in paragraph (5) or (6), the court may by order stay the execution of the judgment or order, either absolutely or for such period and subject to such conditions as the court thinks fit: see rule 83.7 (4). Paragraphs (5) and (6) set out what any application under rule 83.7 shall contain. Any application under this rule should always set out the applicant's case as fully as possible so that the Master may consider, if a stay is to be granted, what condition should be imposed.

12.4.9 Transfer of county court judgments for enforcement in the High Court. County court judgments or orders for the payment of money which are sought to be enforced wholly or partially by execution against goods must be enforced only in the High Court where the sum sought to be enforced is £5,000 or more; and may be enforced in the High Court where the sum is £600 or more: see art. 8(1) of the High Court and County Courts Jurisdiction Order 1991 (SI 1991/724) as amended. Transfers to the High Court in such cases very commonly arise, enabling the judgment creditor to issue a writ of control in the Central Office (or in the District Registry). The procedure does not apply to judgments arising on a regulated agreement under the Consumer Credit Act.

12.4.10 The procedure for transfer under para.12.4.9 above is now governed by rule 40.14A of the CPR. A request for a certificate of judgment is made in writing to the County Court. Such request must state that the certificate is required for the purpose of enforcing the judgment or order in the High Court and must also state that it is intended to enforce the judgment or order by execution against goods.

12.4.11 The certificate will set out details of the judgment or order to be enforced. It will be sealed with the seal of the County Court and will be signed and dated by an officer of that court. It will state on its face that it is granted for the purpose of enforcing the judgment or order by execution against goods in the High Court. Form N293A, adapted to refer to a writ of control in the High Court, should be used.

12.4.12 The judgment creditor should then comply with the Senior Master's Practice Direction published at [1998] 4 All E.R 63; and [1998] 1 WLR 1557, by filing the completed Form 293A, with a copy, in the Enforcement Section in the Central Office (Room E15). A court officer will check that it is correctly completed and will:–

1. allocate a reference number
2. date seal the certificate and copy, returning the original to the party and retaining a copy, and
3. enter the proceedings in a register kept for that purpose.

No fee is payable on registration. The certificate will be treated for enforcement purposes as a High Court judgment and interest at the appropriate rate will run from the date of the certificate.

12.4.13 the title of all subsequent documents will be set out as follows:–

In the High Court of Justice

Queen's Bench Division

High Court claim number:

County Court claim number:

(Sent from the [] County Court by certificate dated....)

Claimant ....

Defendant ....

12.4.14 When the writ of control is issued, the certificate of judgment to be retained by the party will be date – sealed by the court officer in the bottom left–hand corner and endorsed with either the name of the high Court Enforcement Officer or the postcode of the district to which the writ is directed.

12.4.15 it is important to remember in these cases involving transfer that, whilst an application for a stay of execution may be made to a Master in the High Court, any application to set aside or vary the judgment must be made to the County Court. Thus a Master may, and often does, order a stay of execution on terms that the judgment debtor (a) issues and serves within a limited time an application in the County Court to set aside or vary the judgment and (b) proceeds with such application with all due expedition.

12.4.16 Foreign currency. Where a party wishes to enforce a judgment or order expressed in a foreign currency by the issue of a writ of control the request for the writ must be endorsed by the applicant's solicitor or by the applicant if in person with the following certificate, in line with Practice Direction (QBD: Judgment: Foreign Currency) (No.1) [1976] 1 WLR 83:

"I/we certify that the rate current in London for the purchase of (state the unit of foreign currency in which the judgment is expressed) at the close of business on (state the nearest preceding date to the date of issue of the writ) was ( ) to the £ sterling and at this rate the sum of (state the amount of the judgment debt in the foreign currency) amounts to £....."

The schedule to the writ should be amended:

1. showing the amount of the judgment or order in the foreign currency at paragraph 1
2. inserting a new paragraph 2 as follows: "Amount of the sterling equivalent as appears from the certificate endorsed on the request for issue of the writ £......
3. re–numbering the remaining paragraphs accordingly.

The writ of control will then be issued for the sterling equivalent of the judgment in foreign currency as appears from the certificate.

12.5 Claims on controlled goods and executed goods

1B–87 12.5.1 Part 85 of the CPR introduces new rules, replacing in substance the

250

interpleader procedure provided by RSC Order 17 (revoked), for determining disputes arising on controlled goods and executed goods. It should be noted however that the stakeholder's interpleader procedure, which arose under the former RSC Ord.17, rule 1(1)(a) and which had no necessary relationship to execution, is now the subject of the separate new Part 86.

12.5.2 Any person making a claim to controlled goods must, under rule 85.4, as soon as practicable but in any event within 7 days of the goods being removed give notice in writing of his claim to the enforcement agent. Such notice must (inter alia) give his full name and address, a list of all goods in respect of which he claims and the grounds of claim in respect of each item. The subsequent provisions of rule 85.4 require an enforcement agent to give notice of the claim to the judgment creditor and any other claimants to the goods, and require the relevant parties to give notice as to whether the claims are admitted or disputed. Where the creditor or any other claimant to whom notice has been given fails to give the necessary notice the enforcement agent may seek directions and an order preventing the bringing of any claim against him in respect of having taken control of the goods.

12.5.3 Rule 85.5 regulates the procedure where a claim to controlled goods is disputed. Application is to be made by the <u>claimant to the goods</u>, supported by the documents set out in rule 85.5(2), which must be served on the creditor, any other claimant, and the enforcement agent. The application will be referred to a Master or District Judge who may then make a variety of directions as set out in rule 85.5(8), including listing a hearing of the application and giving directions for determination of any issue raised by the claim.

12.5.4 Rules 85.6 and 85.7 make similar provision in the case of claims to executed goods, i.e goods subject to a writ of execution. The term "writ of execution" is defined in rule 85.2(5) and does not include a writ of control.

12.5.5 Exempt goods. See Paragraph 12.4.7 above. A judgment debtor may make a claim to exempt goods, as defined in rule 85.2(R) both in relation to controlled goods and in relation to executed goods. In such case the procedure for determination of the claim is that laid down in rules 85.8 and 85.9, and is closely modelled on the foregoing provisions of rule 85. It should be noted that if an enforcement agent or relevant enforcement officer receives notice from the judgment creditor and any other claimant admitting the claim to exempt goods the enforcement power (in the case of controlled goods) ceases to be exercisable, and the right to execute (in the case of executed goods), ceases to have effect in respect of the exempt goods, and the enforcement agent and enforcement officer must as soon as reasonably practicable make the goods available for collection by the debtor.

12.2.6 Rules 85.10 and 85.11 make comprehensive provision for the final determination of any disputed claim under Part 85. Reference should be made to their terms. It should be noted that the court by which an issue is tried may give such judgment or make such order as finally to dispose of all questions arising in the application (rule 85.11(2)): and that Practice Direction 2B applies to the trial of an issue in such an application. Thus a Master or District Judge has, subject to PD 2B, jurisdiction to dispose of any issue arising in the application.

12.6 Stakeholder claims

12.6.1 These are the subject of Part 86, which replaces the jurisdiction previously **1B–88** available under RSC Order 17, rule 1(1)(a).

12.6.2 The jurisdiction will, as before, be invoked by persons, particularly deposit holders, who hold money subject to competing claims. The full ambit of the rule, and the definition of stakeholder, are set out in rule 86.1. A stakeholder may make an application to the court for a direction as to the person to whom he should pay a debt or money, or give any goods or chattels. His application is to be made to the court in which an existing claim against him is pending, or, if no claim is pending, to the court in which he might be sued: rule 86.2(2). The claim is to be made by Part 8 claim form (see Paragraph 4.3 above) unless made in an existing claim, in which case it should be made by application under Part 23. The claim must be supported by a witness statement stating that the stakeholder:

(a) claims no interest in the subject–matter in dispute other than for charges or costs

(b) does not collude with any other claimant to the subject–matter, and

(c) is willing to pay or transfer the subject–matter into court or dispose of it as the court may direct.

12.6.3 The rule provides for service of the claim form or application notice on the appropriate parties as detailed, for response by such parties, and provides that the matter will be referred to a Master or District Judge.

12.6.4 Under rules 86.3 and 86.4 the court has wide powers upon hearing any such application, including ordering that an issue between all parties be stated and tried. Furthermore, the court by which an issue is tried may give such judgment or make such order as finally to dispose of all questions arising in the stakeholder application: rule 86.4(2).

12.7 Injunctions and undertakings

1B–89 12.7.1 A judgment or order, or an undertaking, to do or abstain from doing an act may, upon breach, be enforced by an order of committal under the terms of CPR rule 81.4; or by an order of sequestration under rule 81.20 (see Paragraph 12.12 below). Applications for such orders in the Queen's Bench Division will, invariably, be listed before and heard by a Judge.

12.8 Examination of judgment debtor (Part 71):

1B–90 12.8.1 Part 71 of the CPR and the Practice Direction to that Part enable a judgment creditor to apply for a court order for oral examination on oath of a judgment debtor as to his means or to provide other information needed to enforce a judgment or order.

12.8.2 The application may be made without notice and must be issued in the court which made the judgment or order unless the proceedings have since been transferred to another court. Thus proceedings in the Queen's Bench Division in which judgment has been given there, or proceedings which have been transferred for enforcement to the Queen's Bench Division, may be the subject of an application to that Division for examination.

12.8.3 The application must (a) be in the form and (b) contain the information required by the PD71. Thus, under PD71 para.1.2 the application must, among other requirements, state the amount presently owed under the judgment or order, the name and address of the judgment debtor, and, if the judgment debtor is a company or other corporation, the name and address of the officer of the corporation whom the judgment creditor wishes to be ordered to attend court, and his position in the corporation.

12.8.4 An application for an order may be dealt with by a court officer without a hearing. But the court officer may in a case of any complexity refer it to a judge (which will include a Master or a District Judge); and he will refer it to a judge where the application requests that the questioning take place before a judge: see PD 71 para.1.3.

12.8.5 The order if made will be that the judgment debtor or other person to be questioned attend the county court for the district in which he resides or carries on business, unless a judge decides otherwise. The order will normally direct an examination before an officer of the court. It will provide for questioning to take place before a judge only if the judge considering the request decides that there are compelling reasons to make such an order: PD71 para.2.

12.8.6 A person served with an order must under rule 71.2 (b)

(a) attend court at the time and place specified in the order;

(b) when he does so, produce documents in his control which are described in the order. (Note that any specific document sought to be produced must be identified by the judgment creditor in his application); and

(c) answer on oath such questions as the court may require.

12.8.7 The order will contain a penal notice warning the person served of his position if he does not comply with the order: rule 71.2(7).

12.8.8 The order must, unless otherwise stated, be served personally not less than 14 days before the hearing. Thus the order will need to allow sufficient time for the judgment creditor to serve it.

12.8.9 The person ordered to attend may, within 7 days, ask the judgment creditor to pay him a sum reasonably sufficient to cover travelling expenses, which the judgment creditor must then pay.

12.8.10 Rule 71.6 makes provision for the judgment creditor to attend the hearing and ask questions; and indeed to conduct the questioning if the hearing is to be before a judge rather than a court officer.

12.8.11 Failure to comply. Rule 71.8 contains provisions for referring the matter to a High Court Judge where the person to be questioned fails to comply; and for a committal order to be made, subject to the terms of the rule. Such committal order will be suspended provided that the person attends court at a time and place specified in that order and complies with all the terms of that order and the original order. A warrant of committal will be issued only on proof to the criminal standard of proof that the judgment debtor has failed to comply with such orders: see PD71 paras.7 and 8. The Court of Appeal has, in *Broomleigh Housing Association Ltd v Okonkwo* [2010] EWCA Civ 113, given guidance to judges asked to make a suspended committal order under rule 71.8.

12.9 Third Party Debt Order proceedings (CPR Part 72):

12.9.1 Where a judgment creditor has obtained in the High Court (or in proceedings **1B–91** which have been transferred to the High Court for enforcement) a judgment or order for payment of a sum of money against a judgment debtor, and another person ("the third party") is indebted to the judgment debtor, the judgment creditor may apply to the Master for an order that the third party pays to the judgment creditor the amount of the debt due to the judgment debtor, or sufficient of it to satisfy the judgment debt. The third party must be within the jurisdiction.

12.9.2 The application should be made by filing an application notice in Practice Form N349, verified by a statement of truth, but the application notice need not be served on the judgment debtor. The application will normally be dealt with without a hearing and must be supported by evidence as set out in CPR 72 Practice Direction, para.1.2. If the Master is satisfied that such an order is appropriate, an interim order will be made in form N84 specifying the debt attached and appointing a time for the third party and the judgment debtor to attend and show cause why the order should not be made final. The order will direct that until the hearing the third party must not make any payment which reduces the amount he owes the judgment debtor to less than the amount specified in the order.

12.9.3 The third party debt order to show cause must be served on the third party, and on the judgment debtor, in accordance with CPR 72.5.

12.9.4 Special provisions are made for banks and building societies to disclose to the court the state of accounts held by a judgment debtor with them: see rule 72.6 and PD72 para.3; and for third parties other than banks or building societies to notify the court if they claim not to owe money to the judgment debtor.

12.9.5 A judgment debtor who is prevented from withdrawing money from his bank or building society may, in a case of hardship, apply to the court: see rule 72.7.

12.9.6 Written evidence must be filed by the parties under rule 72.8 in the event that a third party or judgment debtor objects to the making of a final order.

12.9.7 Where the third party or judgment debtor fails to attend the hearing or attends court but does not dispute the debt, the Master may make a final third party debt order under rule 72.8 in Form N85. The final order may be enforced in the same manner as any other order for the payment of money. Where the third party or judgment debtor disputes the debt, or takes other objection rule 72.8(6) provides for the various ways in which the Master may dispose of the matter at the hearing.

12.9.8 Where the judgment creditor seeks to enforce a judgment expressed in a foreign currency by third party debt order proceedings, the evidence in support of the application must contain words to the following effect:

"The rate current in London for the purchase of (state the unit of foreign currency in which the judgment is expressed) at the close of business on (state the nearest preceding date to the date of verifying the evidence) was ( ) to the £ sterling, and at this rate the sum of (state the amount of the judgment debt in the foreign currency) amounts to £...... I have obtained this information from (state source) and believe it to be true."

12.10 Charging Orders (CPR Part 73):

1B–92 12.10.1 A judgment creditor may apply for a charging order on the property or assets of the judgment debtor, which will have the effect of providing him with security. The High Court has jurisdiction to impose a charging order in the following cases:

1. where the property is a fund lodged in the High Court,
2. where the order to be enforced is a maintenance order of the High Court, and
3. where the judgment or order is made in the High Court (or has been transferred to the High Court) and exceeds £5,000.

12.10.2 The court to which application should be made is the court which gave the judgment or to which the proceedings have been transferred: rule 73.3(2). Note however that the High Court does not have jurisdiction to make a charging order under section 1(2)(c) of the Charging Orders Act 1979 unless the judgment or order to be enforced is for a sum exceeding £5,000. Thus, as quite frequently happens, if an application is made to the Master which does not meet this requirement, the application will be dismissed or transferred to the appropriate county court.

12.10.3 The property and assets of the judgment debtor on which a charge may be imposed by a charging order are specified by section.2 of the Charging Orders Act 1979. These include, particularly,

(a) any interest held by the judgment debtor beneficially
  (i) in land or specified securities, or
  (ii) under any trust, or
(b) any interest held by a person as trustee of a trust if the interest is in such land or securities and
  (i) the judgment or order was made against him as trustee of the trust, or
  (ii) the whole beneficial interest under the trust is held by the debtor unencumbered and for his own benefit, or
  (iii) in a case where there are two or more debtors all of whom are liable to the creditor for the same debt, they together hold the whole beneficial interest under the trust unencumbered and for their own benefit.

12.10.4 Whilst a charging order when made may be expressed to be over the judgment debtors' "interests" in accordance with Forms N86 (interim charging order) and N87 (final charging order) it may be clear that the effect of the order is to charge the land itself and not merely the interests in the proceeds of sale of the land: *Clark v Chief Land Registrar* [1994] ChD 370, C.A. The application for the order should make plain what interests are sought to be charged.

12.10.5 If an interim charging order is made on stocks or shares in more than one company, a separate order must be drawn in respect of each company. A judgment creditor may apply in a single application notice for charging orders over more than one asset, but if the court makes charging orders over more than one asset, there will be separate orders relating to each asset. If the judgment debt is expressed in a foreign currency, the evidence in support of any application for a charging order should contain a similar provision to that set out in Paragraph 12.6.8 above.

12.10.6 The application for a charging order is made to a Master and should be made in Practice Form N379 if the application relates to land, or N380 if the application relates to securities. Paragraph 1.2 of PD 73 sets out the information which the application must contain. The application is made without being served and will normally be dealt with without a hearing. If the Master is satisfied that such an order is appropriate, he will make an order in form N86 appointing a time for the judgment debtor to attend and show cause why the order should not be made absolute.

12.10.7 The interim order and the application notice and any documents in support must be served in accordance with rule 73.5. It should be noted particularly that they must be served not less than 21 days before the hearing: and must be served on the judgment debtor, on such other creditors as the court directs, and, if the interest relates to an interest under a trust, on such of the trustees as the court directs. As to other creditors, the Master will usually order service on other creditors (the identities of whom must be disclosed by the application) whose interests are likely to be unprotected. As to service on trustees, the Master will usually order service on a joint owner of the legal estate (such as the spouse of the judgment debtor).

12.10.8 After further consideration at the hearing the Master will either make the order final (with or without modifications) as in Form N87, or discharge it. He may order any necessary issue to be tried, such as an issue as to the existence and extent of the judgment debtor's interest in the property. The interim order will continue pending determination of such issue. Any order made must be served on all persons on whom the interim order was required to be served: rule 73.8(4).

12.10.9 Rule 73.7 deals with the effects of a charging order on funds in court, which includes securities held in court.

12.10.10 Although the court may make a charging order in a foreign currency, to facilitate enforcement it is usually preferable for it to be expressed in sterling. Thus if the judgment debt is in a foreign currency the evidence in support of the application should contain the sterling equivalent and request the charging order to be made in sterling. (See Paragraph 12.7.5 above).

Enforcement of Charging Order

12.10.11 Proceedings for the enforcement of a charging order by sale of the property charged must be begun by Part 8 claim form: rule 73.10. The claim should be made to the court which made the order unless that court does not have jurisdiction. In the High Court the claim is made to Chancery Chambers at the Royal Courts of Justice or to one of the Chancery district registries (see para.4.2 of PD73). The limit of the county court jurisdiction is £30,000 but the High Court may nonetheless transfer a claim before it above that limit to the county court, which will have the effect of conferring jurisdiction on the county court. The written evidence in support of the claim must set out all those matters contained in para.4.3 of PD73.

12.11 Receivers; equitable execution (CPR Part 69):

12.11.1 Equitable execution is a process which enables a judgment creditor to obtain **1B–93** payment of a judgment debt where the interest of the judgment debtor in property cannot be seized or reached by ordinary execution. Whilst in many cases sale pursuant to a charging order (see paragraph 12.7 above) may be appropriate, in some cases (such as where the debtor has a life interest in a trust fund) appointment of a receiver may be just and convenient. Likewise, a third party debt order cannot reach future debts which may become due to the judgment debtor. Part 69 of the CPR and the Practice Direction to that Part govern the position. Paragraph 4 of the PD sets out generally the evidence which must be filed in support of any application for a receiver. Its provisions should be followed in detail. It is particularly important, in the case of an application for appointment of a receiver by way of equitable execution, that the applicant should state why the judgment cannot be enforced by any other method: para.4.1(3)(d)

12.11.2 The application should be made to a Master or District Judge, who also have jurisdiction, under PD2B para.2.3(c), to make an injunction in connection with or ancillary to making an order appointing a receiver by way of equitable execution.

12.11.3 Whilst, under Rule 69.3, the application may be made without notice (and in cases of urgency this may well be appropriate), the more usual course is to apply on notice. The application should be in Form N244. It must be supported by written evidence. An order made without notice, which will be served as in paragraph 12.8.7 below, will include provision for persons affected to apply to set aside or vary the order.

12.11.4 Where a judgment creditor applies for the appointment of a receiver, in considering whether to make the appointment the court will have regard to
(1) the amount claimed
(2) the amount likely to be obtained by the receiver; and
(3) the probable costs of his appointment

See para 5 of the PD.

12.11.5 Rule 69.5 and para.7 of the PD deal with the giving of security by the receiver which will normally be required. The means of security are the subject of paras 7.2 and 7.3.

12.11.6 Rules 69.6, 69.7 and 69.8 deal respectively with the court's power to give directions (in particular on application by the receiver), the remuneration of the receiver, and the question of accounts. Under rule 69.7(5) the court may refer the determination of the receiver's remuneration to a costs judge.

12.11.7 An order appointing a receiver which may be in Form No.84 must be served by the party applying on
(a) the person appointed as receiver
(b) unless the court orders otherwise, on every other party to the proceedings; and
(c) such other persons as the court may direct

12.11.8 The court may at any time terminate the appointment of a receiver, and appoint another receiver in his place: see rule 69.2(3); and it may, on application by the receiver, discharge him on completion of his duties, on conditions including dealing with any money which he has received: see rules 69.10 and 69.11.

12.12 Committals, etc.,

1B–94 12.12.1 The court has power to punish contempt of court by an order of committal to prison or by other means. Such other means include an order for payment of a fine, an order for the sequestration of assets, or a hospital or guardianship order under certain provisions of the Mental Health Act 1983. Under section 14 of the Contempt of Court Act 1981, where no other limitation applies to the period of committal, the committal shall be for a fixed term and that term shall not on any occasion exceed two years. Under section.16, payment of a fine for contempt of court may be enforced upon the order of the court as a judgment of the High Court for the payment of money.

12.12.2 The substantive law of liability for contempt rests upon both common law and statutory principles (in part, as to the latter, under the Contempt of Court Act 1981).

12.12.3 The procedure under which the court exercises jurisdiction in contempt proceedings is governed by new legislation which came into effect on 1st October 2012 in the form of Part 81 of the CPR and the Practice Direction to that Part. Unless otherwise stated Part 81 applies to procedure in the Court of Appeal, the High Court and county courts: rule 81.1(3).

12.12.4 It should be noted that Part 81 is concerned only with procedure and does not itself confer any power on the court to make any of the above orders; nor does it affect any statutory or inherent power of the court to make a committal order of its own initiative: rule 81.2.

12.12.5 The structure of Part 81 is divided into sections. Section 2 (and in particular 81.4) is concerned with committal of a person who disobeys a judgment or order of the court to do an act within a fixed time, or disobeys a judgment or order not to do an act. Note that PD 40B para.8 requires that an order which requires an act to be done (other than a judgment or order for the payment of money) must specify the time within which the act should be done. Under rule 81.9, no order may be made under rule 81.4 unless the judgment or order in question has prominently displayed on the front of the copy served on the respondent a penal notice in terms of the rule.

12.12.6 Imprisonment for default in payment of a sum of money has long been abolished by Section 4 of the Debtors Act 1869, subject to the specific exceptions contained in that section. The further power, under s.5 of that Act, to commit to prison for non–payment of a debt due under a judgment or order of the court is now restricted, so far as relates to the jurisdiction of the High Court, to non–payment of a High Court maintenance order.

12.12.7 An order of committal may be made under rule 81.4 against any director or other officer of a company or corporation required to do or abstain from doing an act: see 81.4(3).

12.12.8 Rules 81.5 to 81.8 make provision for service, and the method of service, of judgments or orders, and undertakings, on persons required to do or abstain from doing an act, and rule 81.9 lays down the requirement for such judgments and orders to be endorsed with a penal notice.

12.12.9 Applications for an order of committal under rule 81.4 are made by application notice in the existing proceedings. The application must set out the grounds on which the application is made and must identify, separately and numerically, each act of contempt relied on. The application must be supported by evidence by affidavit: see rule 81.10. The application notice and evidence must be served personally on the respondent, subject to qualifications contained in the rule.

12.12.10 Such applications are made to the appropriate court as defined in PD81 para.10. If the application is one which must be made in the High Court then (save for the unusual cases where, under an enactment, a Master or District Judge has power to make a committal order) the application must be made to a High Court Judge or a person authorized to act as such. The application notice should be lodged in Room WG08, where a date for hearing will be set, and endorsed on or served with the application notice.

12.12.11 Section 3 of Part 81 regulates committal applications relating to interference with the due administration of justice in connection with proceedings. The full terms of rule 81.12 should be consulted. Applications for committal in such cases may be made only with the permission of the court: rule 81.12(3).

12.12.12 Rule 81.13 defines the court to which the application for permission under section 3 must be made. Again the rule should be consulted in detail. Thus, in connection with proceedings in the High Court (other than proceedings in a Divisional Court) the application for permission may be made only to a single judge of the Division in which the proceedings were commenced or to which they have subsequently been transferred. Where contempt is committed otherwise than in connection with proceedings, the application must be made to the Administrative Court (a part of the Queen's Bench Division).

12.12.13 An application for permission under section 3 must be made by Part 8 claim form. rule 81.14 makes provision as to the contents of the claim form; service (which is to be personal service unless the court otherwise directs); and response by the respondent. Where permission to proceed is given the court may give such directions as it thinks fit including listing before a single judge or a Divisional Court.

12.12.14 Section 4. This section provides the procedural code applicable in cases where the High Court has power under any enactment to punish any person charged with conduct in relation to proceedings before a court, tribunal or person. The section is supplemented by PD81 para.3.

12.12.15 Section 5. Contempt in the face of the court. This section, which is supplemented by PD81 para.4, provides that where contempt has occurred in the face of the court, and that court has power to commit for contempt, the court may deal with the matter of its own initiative and give directions for the disposal of the matter. In the Queen's Bench Division, if contempt occurs in the face of the court in proceedings before a Master, the Master is likely to direct under PD81 para.10.2 that the matter be referred to a single judge for disposal.

12.12.16 No application notice is necessary in cases falling under section 5, but the closely–written terms of para.4 of the Practice Direction, which envisage an opportunity for the respondent to reflect on his behaviour, should be given particular attention.

12.12.17 Section 6. Committal for making a false statement of truth or disclosure statement. Rule 81.17 contains detailed provisions as to the procedure to be followed in such cases, including provisions as to the interaction with other sections where the contempt involves not only the making of a false statement but other forms of contempt. A committal application in relation to a false statement in proceedings in the High Court may be made only with the permission of the court: rule 81.18(1). In such case the application for permission is made by application notice. PD81 para.5.2 governs the contents of the affidavit evidence required to support a permission application. In any such case the court may refer the matter to the Attorney General with a request to him to consider whether to bring proceedings for contempt.

12.12.18 Section 7. Writ of sequestration to enforce a judgment, order or undertaking. Rules 81.19 to 81.27 govern the position. The court may punish breach of an order to do or abstain from doing an act, or breach of an undertaking, by a writ of sequestration against the property of the person in breach. Permission is required to make the application. If the person in breach is a company or corporation the writ may in addition be issued against the property of any director or other officer. Rules 81.21 to 81.26 should be consulted as to service of the judgment or order in question; the requirement for endorsement thereof with a penal notice; and how to make the application for permission. The application is by application notice and is made to a single judge of the Division of the High Court in which the proceedings were commenced or to which they have been transferred; or in any other case to a single judge of the Queen's Bench Division.

12.12.19 Section 8. This section contains general rules, applicable to cases arising under all the above sections for:
- (a) the conduct of hearings, including restrictions on the evidence on which an applicant may rely at the hearing: rule 81.28;
- (b) stating the name of the respondent, and in general terms the nature of the contempt, where the hearing has been held in private under CPR 39.2: rule 81.28(5);
- (c) the power to suspend execution of a committal order: rule 81.29;
- (d) the issue of a warrant of committal where a committal order is made, and service of the committal order on the respondent: rule 81.30;
- (e) applications by a contemnor for his discharge from custody: rule 81.31; and
- (f) discharge of a person in custody where a writ of sequestration has been issued, and giving directions for dealing with the property taken in sequestration: rule 81.32.

12.12.20 Section 8 is further supplemented by the Practice Direction at paras.8 to 16. These paragraphs provide in particular
- (a) for observance of Convention rights. It is emphasized that the allegation of contempt be proved beyond reasonable doubt: para.9;
- (b) for the court to which a particular committal application, or permission application, should be made: paras.10 and 11;
- (c) for the form and contents of a claim form or application notice as appropriate: paras.12 and 13. It should be observed that the claim form or application notice must contain a prominent notice stating the possible consequences of the court making a committal order and of the respondent not attending the hearing. A form of notice which may be used is annexed to the Practice Direction at Annex 3;
- (d) for the form and filing of written evidence in a committal application: Para 14; and
- (e) for the hearing of a committal application. In particular the applicant must obtain from the court a date for hearing; and unless the court otherwise directs the hearing must not be less than 14 days after service of the claim form or application notice on the respondent. Such date must be specified on the claim form or application notice or in a notice of hearing served therewith.

258

12.13 Execution against property of Foreign or Commonwealth States

12.13.1 In cases where judgment has been obtained against a foreign or **1B–95** Commonwealth State and it is sought to execute the judgment by a writ, a charging order or a third party debt order, the following provisions introduced by the Queen's Bench Practice Direction No.37 on 28 July 1994 apply:

1. Before the writ is issued, the Master must be informed in writing and his direction sought. In cases where an application is to be made for an interim charging order or third party debt order, the evidence in support of the application must include a statement that the execution sought is against a foreign or Commonwealth State.
2. The Master, having been so informed will, as soon as practicable, inform the Foreign and Commonwealth Office ("FCO") of the application and will not permit the issue of a writ nor grant an interim order to show cause until the FCO has been so informed. The Protocol Division of the Head of Diplomatic Missions and International Organisations Unit of the FCO may be contacted by telephone on 0207 008 0991 or by Fax on 0207 008 0978.
3. Having regard to all the circumstances of the case, the Master may postpone the decision whether to issue the writ or grant the interim order to show cause for so long as he considers reasonable for the purpose of enabling the FCO to furnish further information relevant to his decision, but not for longer than 3 days from the time of his contacting the FCO. In the event that no further information is received from the FCO within 24 hours of its being informed, then the writ may be issued or the interim order to show cause may be sealed without further delay.

12.4 Recovery of enforcement costs:

12.14.1 Section 15(3) of the Courts and Legal Services Act 1990 enables a person **1B–96** taking steps to enforce a money judgment in the High Court to recover by execution the costs of any previous attempt to enforce that judgment. Subsection (4) excludes costs that the court considers to have been unreasonably incurred, whether because the earlier attempt was unreasonable in all the circumstances or for any other reason.

12.14.2 The application for an enforcement costs order is made to a Master and should be made in accordance with Part 23 but the application notice need not be served on the judgment debtor. The application will normally be dealt with without a hearing and must be supported by evidence substantially as set out in form PF 205. The witness should exhibit sufficient vouchers, receipts or other documents as are reasonably necessary to verify the amount of the costs of previous attempts to enforce the judgment.

12.14.3 If the Master is satisfied that such an order is appropriate, he will make an order for payment of the amount of such costs as he considers may be recoverable under subsection (3). If the amount of such costs is less than that claimed by the judgment creditor, the Master may either disallow the balance or give directions for a detailed assessment or other determination of the balance. If after assessment or other determination it appears that the judgment creditor is entitled to further costs beyond those originally allowed, he may issue a further writ or take other lawful steps to enforce those costs. Interest on the costs runs either from the date the Master made the enforcement costs order or from the date of the costs certificate.

12.5 Enforcement of Magistrates' Courts' orders:

12.15.1 The Magistrates' Courts Act 1980, s.87 provides that payment of a sum **1B–97** ordered to be paid on a conviction of a magistrates' court may be enforced by the High Court or a county court (otherwise than by the issue of a writ or other process against goods or by imprisonment or attachment of earnings) as if the sum were due to the clerk of the magistrates' court under a judgment or order of the High Court or county court, as the case may be.

12.15.2 In the Central Office, the application is made to a Master and should be made in accordance with Part 23. Where enforcement is sought by a third party debt order or charging order, the application for an interim order will normally be dealt with without a hearing. Otherwise the application notice and evidence in support should be served on the defendant.

12.15.3 The application must be supported by a witness statement in a form appropriate to the type of execution sought and must have exhibited to it the authority of the magistrates' court to take the proceedings which will recite the conviction, the amount outstanding and the nature of the proceedings authorised to be taken (Magistrates Courts Forms Rules 1981, Form 63).

12.15.4 The application notice and evidence in support together with an additional copy of the exhibit should be filed in Rooms E15–17 where it will be assigned a reference number from the register kept for that purpose. The Master, according to the type of enforcement sought, will then deal with the matter.

12.15.5 This practice will also be followed in the District Registries with such variations as circumstances may render necessary.

12.6 Enforcement in England and Wales of Foreign Judgments, and Enforcement of High Court Judgments abroad

1B–98   12.16.1 CPR 74 provides the procedure for enforcement of judgments in different jurisdictions as above.

12.16.2 Section I of Part 74 applies to enforcement in England and Wales of judgments of foreign courts. Section II applies to the enforcement in foreign countries of judgments of the High Court and county courts. Section III applies to the enforcement of United Kingdom judgments in other parts of the United Kingdom. Section IV applies to the enforcement in England and Wales of European Community judgments. Section V applies to (a) the certification of judgments in England and Wales as European Enforcement orders; and (b) the enforcement in England and Wales of judgments certified as European Enforcement Orders by other Member States.

12.16.3 If a foreign country is not a party to an agreement with this country on mutual recognition and enforcement of judgments, a fresh action will need to be brought here by claim form based on the judgment of the court of the foreign country.

Section I. Incoming judgments

1B–99   12.16.4 This section enables application to be made for registration of foreign judgments for enforcement in England and Wales in the following cases:
   (a) under section 9 of the Administration of Justice Act 1920;
   (b) under section 2 of the Foreign Judgments (Reciprocal Enforcement) Act 1933
   (c) under section 4 of the Civil Jurisdiction and Judgments Act 1982;
   (d) under the Judgments Regulation (i.e. Commercial Regulation (EC) No.44/2001 of December 22, 2000) as defined; and
   (e) under the Lugano Convention as defined
   The criteria for registration which the legislation in each of these cases lays down must of course be satisfied to enable a successful application to be made.

12.16.5 A list of the countries that are covered by each of the various cases set out above is contained in Her Majesty's Court Service "Notes for Guidance" on the above, which can be obtained from the Enforcement Section of the Central Office in Room E15. This also contains the standard forms used and sets out the procedure for registration (see paras.12.13.6 to 12.13.8 below).

12.16.6 The application for registration must be made to the High Court. Such applications are assigned to the Queen's Bench Division and may be heard by a Master. They may be made without notice: see rule 74.3(2). The Master may however direct that a Part 8 claim form should be issued and served.

12.16.7 The written evidence (including exhibits) required to be filed in each of the cases set out above is set out in detail in rule 74.4. Note that the evidence required differs in certain respects as between each of the cases. The requirements should be strictly followed. Assistance is obtained from PD74A paras.5, 6 and 6A in respect of the evidence required in support of such applications.

12.16.8 The order for registration, if made, will be for registration of the judgment in

260

the foreign currency in which it is expressed. It should not be converted into sterling in the evidence in support. When it comes to enforcement of the judgment, the amount should then be converted into sterling in accordance with the instructions set out in para 12.4.16 above.

12.16.9 The order for registration must be drawn up by or on behalf of the judgment creditor and served on the judgment debtor. Permission is not required to serve out of jurisdiction: rule 74.6. The order will be entered in the register of judgments kept in the Enforcement Section at the Central Office. The order will usually contain, at the Master's discretion, a direction that the costs of and caused by the application and the registration be assessed and added to the judgment debt.

12.16.10 The order must state the matters set out in rule 74.6(3). These include, in the case of registration under the 1920 Act and the 1933 Act, the right of the judgment debtor to apply to have the registration set aside; and, in the case of registration under the 1982 Act, the Judgments Regulation or the Lugano Convention, the right of the judgment debtor to appeal against the order.

12.16.11 Rule 74.7 governs the procedure on applications to set aside (including the time for doing so).

12.16.12 Rule 74.8 governs the procedure on appeal both against the grant or refusal of registration under the 1982 Act, the Lugano Convention, or the Judgments Regulation (including matters of extension of time for appealing). Permission is not required to appeal or to put in evidence.

12.16.13 In order to enforce the judgment following registration there must be filed evidence of service on the judgment debtor of the registration order and any other relevant order: rule 74.9.

Section II. Outgoing Judgments

12.16.14 This section covers enforcement in foreign countries of judgments of the **1B–100** High Court or county courts in England and Wales. The procedure is by way of application under rule 74.12 to the court where the judgment was given for a certified copy of the judgment. The application may be made without notice by application notice under Part 23. The application must, under PD 74A para.4.2, be made, in the case of a judgment given in the Chancery Division or Queen's Bench Division of the High Court, to a Master, Registrar or district judge; and, in the case of a county court judgment, to a district judge.

12.16.15 There is some question whether a judgment given in the county court and transferred to the High Court for enforcement may be regarded as a judgment which will be enforced in a foreign country under the Act of 1920 or the Act of 1933. In those cases the better course may be to commence the proceedings in the High Court, or to seek transfer of the proceedings from the county court at the outset so that judgment is obtained in the High Court.

12.16.16 The written evidence in support, including exhibits, is the subject of rule 74.13 and its requirements must be closely followed. These include, particularly, the requirements (i) to show that the judgment has been served; (ii) to state whether it provides for payment of a sum of money and, if so, the amount in respect of which it remains unsatisfied; and (iii) to state the required particulars of any interest on the judgment which is recoverable. This last requirement is not a requirement to state particulars of any interest incorporated in and forming part of the judgment sum itself.

12.16.17 The certified copy of the judgment when issued will be an office copy and will be accompanied by a certificate signed by a judge: see PD 74A para.7.1. If a Master has dealt with the application he will sign the certificate. The judgment and certificate will be sealed with the seal of the Senior Courts. In applications under the 1920, 1933 and 1982 Acts the certificate will be in Form 110 and will have annexed to it a copy of the claim form by which the proceedings were begun. In applications under the Judgments Regulation the certificate will be in the form of Annex V to the Regulation; and, in applications under the Lugano Convention, in the form of Annex V to the Convention. The forms of certificate are included in the "Notes for Guidance" referred to in para.12.16.5 above.

Section III. Judgments within the United Kingdom

1B–101 12.16.18 This section enables registration in the High Court of judgments (both money judgments and non–money judgments the enforcement of which is governed by s.18 of the 1982 Act) given by a court in another part of the United Kingdom; and likewise for the provision of certificates of judgments of the High Court and a county court for enforcement in another part of the United Kingdom. Rules 74.15 to 74.18 govern the procedure on application and the documents which must accompany the application. A certificate of a money judgment of a court in Scotland or Northern Ireland must be filed for enforcement in Room E17 within 6 months of its issue and be accompanied by a certified copy. Under Para 9 of Schedule 6 to the 1982 Act an application may be made to stay enforcement of the certificate. The application may be made without notice supported by a witness statement stating that the applicant is entitled and intends to apply to the judgment court to set aside or stay the judgment. As to outgoing judgments, the certificate will be in Form 111 for a money judgment. In the case of a non–money judgment, the certified copy of the judgment will be sealed and have annexed to it a certificate in Form 112: see PD 74A paras.8.1 to 8.3.

12.16.19 The certificates will be entered in the register of certificates kept for that purpose in the Central Office under PD 74A para.3.

Section IV. European Community Judgments

1B–102 12.16.20 This section deals with enforcement in England and Wales of European Community judgments, i.e. judgments not of the national courts of Member States but rather the judgments of the courts and institutions of the Community itself.

12.16.21 An application to the High Court for registration of such a judgment may be made without notice and must be supported by written evidence containing the material set out in rule 74.21.

12.16.22 The order for registration must contain the material set out in rule 74.22 and must be served on every person against whom the judgment was given: rule 74.22. The order will be entered in the register in Room E17.

12.16.23 Provision is made for application to vary or cancel a registration order under this section on the ground that it has been partly or wholly satisfied. Further, in any case where the European Court has made an order that the enforcement of a registered Community judgment should be suspended, provision is made for application to the High Court for registration of the European Court's order: rules 74.23 to 74.25.

12.16.24 The Merchant Shipping (Liner Conferences) Act 1982. Applications for registration of a recommendation, determination or award under this Act are made to a Commercial Judge by application notice under Part 23. The procedure is the subject of PD 74A Section II which should be consulted for its detail. The order giving permission must be drawn up by the applicant and will be entered in the register kept in the Admiralty and Commercial Registry under the direction of the Senior Master.

Section V. European Enforcement Orders

1B–103 12.16.25 The European Enforcement Order (EEO) creates a simplified method of enforcement for <u>uncontested</u> claims throughout the EU member states (except Denmark). Details of the procedure are contained in Section V of Part 74, as supplemented by Practice Direction 74B. The procedure is governed by Council Regulation (EC) No. 805/2004. A pack containing guidance for obtaining such orders is available in the Enforcement Section. A claim that does not meet the requirements of the Regulation, or which the judgment creditor does not wish to enforce using the Regulation may be enforceable using another method of enforcement.

12.16.26 An application for an EEO certificate of a judgment given in England and Wales must be made by Form N219 or N219A depending upon whether the judgment was by agreement/admission/settlement or in default of defence or objection. The application may be made without notice and will be dealt with without a hearing, unless the Master orders a hearing: see rule 74.28 and PD 74B para.2.

12.16.27 An application under Article 6(2) of the EEO Regulation for a certificate indicating the lack or limitation of enforceability of an EEO certificate must be made to the court of origin by application in accordance with Part 23: see rule 74.29 and PD 74B para.3.

12.16.28 An application under Article 10 of the EEO Regulation for rectification or withdrawal of an EEO certificate must be made to the court of origin and may be made by application in accordance with Part 23. It must be supported by written evidence: See rule 74.30 and para 4 of the PD.

12.16.29 A person seeking to enforce an EEO in England and Wales must lodge at the court in which enforcement proceedings are to be brought the documents required by Article 20 of the EEO Regulation: see rule 74.31 and para.5 of the PD.

12.16.30 Where an EEO certificate has been lodged and the judgment debtor applies to stay or limit the enforcement proceedings under Article 23 of the EEO Regulation, such application must be made by application in accordance with Part 23 to the court in which the EEO is being enforced: see rule 74.33 and PD 74B para.7. The written evidence must state that an application has been brought in the Member State of origin.

12.16.31 An application under Article 21 of the EEO Regulation that the court should refuse to enforce an EEO must be made by application in accordance with Part 23 to the court in which the EEO is being enforced: see rule 74.32 and PD 74 para.6.

Section 13

Miscellaneous

13.1 Service of incoming foreign process under:
(a) CPR 6.48 to 6.51 (section V of Part 6 of the CPR)   **1B–104**
(b) **The Hague Convention**
(c) **The Service Regulation**

Section V.

13.1.1 This section of Part 6 (rules 6.48 to 6.51) applies to service in England and Wales of any document in connection with civil or commercial proceedings in a foreign court or tribunal. It does not however, by reason of 6.48(b), apply where the Service Regulation applies, as to which see para.13.1.7 below.

13.1.2 Where the provisions of Section V are resorted to, a request for service is made to the Senior Master. The request is in writing and will be made:
(i) where the foreign court or tribunal is in a convention country (as defined in rule 6.49), from a consular or other authority of that country; or
(ii) from the Secretary of State for Foreign and Commonwealth Affairs, with a recommendation that service should be effected.

13.1.3 The request will be accompanied by a translation of the request into English, two copies of the document to be served, and, unless the foreign court or tribunal certifies that the person to be served understands English, two copies of a translation of it into English.

13.1.4 The method of service is for the Senior Master to determine. The usual practice is to require service by a county court bailiff and to provide him with a certificate to complete and return. The Senior Master may make an order for alternative service based on the certificate if appropriate.

13.1.5 Where the bailiff has served the document he will send the Senior Master a copy of the document with the certificate of service; or alternatively state why service could not be effected. The Senior Master may, but rarely does, request the process server to specify his costs. The Senior Master will then send to the country requesting service a sealed certificate stating when and how the document was served or the reason why it has not been served, together with a copy of the document. Where appropriate, the Senior Master will also state the amount of costs, certified by a costs judge: rule 6.52 (2).

The Hague Convention

13.1.6 Quite apart from and in addition to the availability of service under Section V, parties to proceedings in a foreign country subscribing to the Hague Convention (i.e. the Convention on the service abroad of judicial and extrajudicial documents in civil or commercial matters signed at the Hague on 15 November 1965) may and frequently do avail themselves of its provisions. Thus any person in another contracting State who is interested in a judicial proceeding (including his lawyer) may effect service in the United Kingdom "directly" or through a competent person other than a judicial officer or official, e.g through a solicitor. The full terms of Article 10 of the Convention, which relates to service, should be consulted. The UK has confirmed its position indicating its preference for the use of direct service through English solicitors on residents in England and Wales.

The Service Regulation

13.1.7 The Service Regulation (i.e. Council Regulation (EC) No.1393/2007) applies to service on a person in England and Wales of judicial and extrajudicial documents in civil and commercial matters arising in other European Union Member States and provides a complete code for such service. It should be noted that, under Article 20 para.1, the Regulation shall, in relation to matters to which it applies, prevail over other provisions contained in agreements or arrangements concluded by Member States, and in particular the Hague Convention. Under Article 20, para.2, however the Regulation shall not preclude individual Member States from maintaining or concluding agreements or arrangements to expedite further or simplify the transmission of documents, provided that they are compatible with the regulation. The Senior Master is the "transmitting agency" for England and Wales designated under Art.2, and is the "central body" for England and Wales designated under Art.3. Requests to him for assistance should be addressed for the attention of the Foreign Process Section at Room E16 of the Royal Courts of Justice. Standard forms of (a) request for service, (b) acknowledgment of receipt, (c) notice of return of request and document, (d) notice of retransmission of request and document to the appropriate receiving agency, (e) certificate of service or non-service of documents, and (f) information to the addressee about the right to refuse to accept a document are contained in Annexes I and II to the Regulation and may be obtained from the Foreign Process Section. The full terms of the Service Regulation are annexed to Practice Direction 6B to Part 6 of the CPR. Questions may arise under Art.15 of the Regulation as to "direct" service of any particular document which may need to be resolved on a case by case basis by enquiries to the Foreign Process Section.

13.2 Election Petitions

1B–105 13.2.1 Under Part III of the Representation of the People Act 1983, the result of a parliamentary or local government election may be questioned on the ground of some irregularity either before or during the election. The provisions of Part III have also been applied to European parliamentary elections.

13.2.2 The procedure for challenge is governed by the Act and by Election Petition Rules (as amended) made under the Act.

13.2.3 The Senior Master is the prescribed officer of the High Court for the purpose of receiving election petitions, in relation to both parliamentary and local government elections.

13.2.4 The challenge is made by the issue of an election petition:–
    (a) in the case of a parliamentary election, by one or more electors or by an unsuccessful candidate or an alleged candidate, and
    (b) in the case of a local government election, by four or more electors or by an alleged candidate

13.2.5 The member/councillor whose conduct is complained of is a respondent to the petition, as is the returning officer. The petition is issued in the Election Petitions

Office, Room E13, normally within 21 days after the return on the election has been made to the Clerk of the Crown (in the case of parliamentary elections), or after the day of the election (in the case of local elections). Petitioners are usually requested by the court to effect service themselves.

13.2.6 The petition is tried by an election court consisting of two High Court judges of the Queen's Bench Division in respect of parliamentary elections; or by a commissioner appointed by the court, being a lawyer of not less than 7 years standing, in the case of local elections. The trial usually takes place in the relevant constituency/local government area, although a direction may be given in special circumstances for it to be held elsewhere.

13.2.7 The election court shall determine whether the member whose election is complained of, or any and what other person, was duly elected or whether the election was void, and shall certify its determination. The procedure following such certification is laid down in sections 144 and 145 of the Act.

13.2.8 Outside the court offices' opening times, but while the building is still open to the public, election petitions and applications may be left in the letterbox located opposite Room E08. When the building is closed, petitions or applications may be left with Security at the main entrance (via a buzzer system available) up until midnight on the last day for lodging.

13.2.9 Applications for remedies or relief under various sections of the Act are also issued in Room E13 and are usually dealt with by a single judge or by the Senior Master.

13.2.10 Further information can be obtained from the leaflet entitled "I want to challenge the outcome of an election and how do I apply for relief", which can be found on the Justice website by inserting the reference LOC002 into the formfinder.

13.3 Bills of Sale Acts 1878 and 1882, and Section 344 of the Insolvency Act 1986

13.3.1 Every bill of sale to which the Bills of Sale Act 1878 or the Bills of Sale (1878) **1B–106** Amendment Act 1882 apply must be registered within 7 clear days of its making: see sections 8 and 10 of the 1878 Act and section 8 of the 1882 Act. And, under Section 11 of the 1878 Act, the registration of a bill of sale must be renewed at least once every five years.

13.3.2 The Queen's Bench Masters are the registrars for the purposes of the Acts and their duties may be performed by any one of them. The register is kept in the Enforcement Section of the Action Department in Room E15 and contains the particulars required under the Acts and a list of the names of the grantors of every registered bill of sale.

13.3.3 An application to register a bill of sale is made under section 10(2) of the 1878 Act by presenting at Room E15 the original bill together with every schedule or inventory annexed to it or referred to in it, and a true copy of the bill and of every such schedule or inventory and of every attestation of the execution of the bill, together with an affidavit containing the required particulars. Such affidavit must, in accordance with Section 10(2), prove
    (1) the time when the bill was made or given,
    (2) the due execution and attestation of the bill, and
    (3) the residence and occupation of the grantor of the bill and of every attesting witness.

13.3.4 The copy of the bill and the original affidavit are then filed at Room E15.

13.3.5 The evidence required may in the case of a security bill be in Form PF179 and in the case of an absolute bill in Form PF 180 save that in both cases
    (a) the time of day as well as the date of the granting of the bill must be stated so as to accord with section 10(2), and
    (b) the evidence must be in the form of an affidavit and sworn as such: see CPR 32.15(1).

13.3.6 An application to re–register a bill of sale under section 11 of the 1878 Act may be made as provided for in that section. Whilst Form PF 181 may be used, the evidence should again be in affidavit form so as to accord with section 11.

13.3.7 An application, which may be made under section 14 of the Act of 1878, to rectify an omission or misstatement in relation to registration, or renewal of registration (including particularly an application to extend time) must be made to a Queen's Bench Master and be accompanied by the prescribed fee. The procedure is now governed by PD8A paras 10A.1 to 5. The evidence in support, which may be by witness statement, must set out the particulars of the omission and the grounds on which the application is made. The Master will usually deal with the application without a hearing and without requiring service on any other person.

13.3.8 If satisfied than an omission to register or to file an affidavit of renewal within the time prescribed was accidental or due to inadvertence the Master may in his discretion extend time for that purpose. Likewise, if so satisfied in the case of omission or misstatement of the name, residence or occupation of any person, he may order the register to be rectified by insertion of the true particulars. Terms may be imposed as to security, or notice by advertisement, or otherwise as the Master may direct. In order to protect any creditors who have acquired rights of property in the assets which are the subject of the bill between the date of the bill and its actual registration any order to extend time will normally be made "without prejudice" to those rights. The order will be drawn up in Form PF182.

13.3.9 Memorandum of satisfaction. An application may be made under Section 15 of the 1878 Act for an order that a memorandum of satisfaction be written on a registered copy of a bill of sale. The procedure for so applying will depend on whether the person entitled to the benefit of the bill has or has not consented to the satisfaction. The procedure is governed by PD8A paras.11.1 to 11.5 which should be consulted in detail. Form PF183 contains the necessary contents of a witness statement or affidavit to support an application. Form PF184 contains the contents of a claim form where a claim form is required. And Form PF185 contains an order for the entry of satisfaction. In practice, where consent has been obtained, the Master will usually endorse "leave to enter memorandum of satisfaction" on the witness statement or affidavit without the need to draw an order. The endorsement is then sent to Room E15 for the entry to be made on the copy bill in the registry.

13.3.10 Search of the register. Under section 16 of the 1878 Act application may be made to search the register and obtain an office copy or extract of a registered bill of sale. The application is made to a Master. The procedure, and the necessary information to support the application, are the subject of PD8A paras.11A.1 to 4.

13.3.11 Assignment of book debts. Under section 344 of the Insolvency Act 1986 an assignment of book debts is void against the trustee of a bankrupt's estate as regards book debts which were not paid before the presentation of the bankruptcy petition unless the assignment has been registered under the Bills of Sale Act 1878. The register is kept as a separate register in Room E15 in the Central Office. The procedure on application to register is now the subject of PD8A paras.15B.1 to 6 which should be consulted in detail. Parties may use Form PF186 for their evidence in support. It is helpful if the original assignment is also produced.

13.4 Enrolment of deeds and other documents

1B–107   13.4.1 Any deed or document which by virtue of any enactment is required or authorised to be enrolled in the Senior Courts may be enrolled in the Central Office. The matter most commonly arises in cases of change of name by deed poll, in which case the procedure is governed by the Enrolment of Deeds (Change of Name) Regulations 1994. Such regulations are reproduced as an appendix to Practice Direction 5A paragraph 6. The Practice Direction itself contains further directions in the case of change of name of a child, which should be read together with the procedure set out in the Regulations and the Practice Direction. In cases of doubt the Senior Master or, in his absence, the Practice Master will refer the matter to the Master of the Rolls.

13.5 Bail

1B–108   13.5.1 With the coming into force on 5th April 2004 of Section 17 of the Criminal

Justice Act 2003 the powers of the High Court to entertain applications relating to bail have become restricted to specific circumstances. In those cases where such power exists the procedure is governed by RSC Order 79. rule 9(1) to (14); or, in the case of certain appeals by a prosecutor to the High Court against the grant of bail, by rule 9(15) and a Practice Direction supplementing the same.

13.6 References to the Court of Justice of the European Union

13.6.1 A party wishing to apply for an order under CPR 68 may do so by application **1B–109** before or at the trial or hearing. An application made before the trial or hearing should be made in accordance with Part 23.

13.6.2 "Order" means an order referring a question to the European Court for a preliminary ruling under Article 267 of the Treaty on the Functioning of the European Union or as provided for under any agreement to which the European Union or the Member States are parties: see rule 68.1(c).

13.6.3 The procedure for making a reference has been recently updated by the new Part 68 which came into force on 1st October 2013 and by its accompanying Practice Direction. The court and the parties will pay close attention to these, and also to the European Court Procedural Rules, and to the updated guidance by the European Court to national courts, namely "Recommendations to national courts and tribunals in relation to the initiation of preliminary ruling proceedings", published by the Official Journal on November 6, 2012. Both these latter two documents are available on the European Court's website at: **http://curia.europa.eu**.

13.6.4 An order may be made by the court of its own initiative or on application by a party, but will not normally be made by a Master or District Judge.

13.6.5 The reference must contain the matters specified in the European Court Procedure Rules (see particularly Articles 93–118 of the Rules) and must comply with any guidance given by the European Court (see above).

13.6.6 The reference itself must be set out in a schedule to the order. Under para.1.1 of the Practice Direction the court may direct the parties to produce a draft but responsibility for the terms of the reference lies with the court and not the parties.

13.6.7 The reference should identify as clearly and succinctly as possible the question on which the court seeks the ruling of the European Court.

13.6.8 Further directions as to the contents of the reference are set out in the Practice Direction. Particular attention is drawn to Article 94 of the European Court Procedure Rules and to Paragraphs 20 to 28 of the European Court's "Recommendations"

13.6.9 Transmission. It is the responsibility of the parties to provide a sealed copy of the order containing the reference to the Queen's Bench Division Associates' Department at Room WG03, Royal Courts of Justice. Strand, London WC2A 2LL. The parties should also provide the contact details of their legal representatives. The Senior Master will then send a copy of the order (and of any request to the European Court made under rule 68.3) to the Registrar of the European Court: see rule 68.4(2). It should be noted that under rule 68.4(3), unless the court orders otherwise, the Senior Master will send the documents to the Registrar without waiting for the time for appealing against the order to expire. Thus, parties should inform the Associates' Department in any case where the order provides that time for appealing should be awaited and should inform the Department of the determination of any appeal or application for permission to appeal.

13.6.10 Under para.2.2 of the Practice Direction the parties should prepare a bundle of key documents to be sent direct to the Registrar of the European Court.

13.6.11 Where an order for reference is made the proceedings will, unless the court orders otherwise, be stayed until the European Court has given its ruling: see rule 68.5.

13.7 Group Litigation Orders "GLOs"

1B–110 13.7.1 Parties considering applying for a GLO should consult Section III of Part 19 of the CPR and Practice Direction 19B which supplements that section. They should also consult the practitioners' textbooks as to the circumstances in which and the terms on which a GLO may be made.

13.7.2 CPR 19.10 defines a GLO as an order made under rule 19.11 to provide for the case management of claims which give rise to common or related issues of fact or law. The court may in its discretion under rule 19.11 make a GLO where there are or are likely to be a number of claims giving rise to such issues.

13.7.3 Applications are most commonly made in cases where the multiple parties are claimants, though an application may also be made where the multiple parties are defendants. PD19B deals only with applications in the former case.

13.7.4 The solicitors acting for the proposed applicant should consult the Law Society's Multi Party Action Information Service to obtain information about cases giving rise to the proposed GLO issues. They should, importantly, consider whether any other order would be more appropriate, in particular an order to consolidate the claims or for a representative action to be brought: see PD19B, para.2.3.

13.7.5 Any application must be made under Part 23; and may be made at any time before or after any relevant claims have been issued.

13.7.6 In the Queen's Bench Division, a GLO may not be made without the consent of the President of the Queen's Bench Division: para.3.3 (as amended). In London the application is made to the Senior Master at the Royal Courts of Justice, save where the claims are proceeding or are likely to proceed in a specialist list, in which case the application is made to the senior judge of that list. Outside London, the application is made to the Presiding Judge of the circuit in which the District Registry which has issued the application is situated: paras.3.5 and 3.6. If the Senior Master is minded to make a GLO he will send a copy of the application notice to the President.

13.7.7 A GLO, if made, must:
    (a) contain directions about the establishment of a register
    (b) specify the GLO issues, and
    (c) specify the management court which will manage the claims. See para.13.7.11 below.

Such order may give directions as to the management of claims which raise one or more of the GLO issues: CPR 19.11(2) and (3).

13.7.8 A form of order for the GLO is contained in Form PF19 which may be adapted according to the circumstances. Parties should submit to the Senior Master when applying a draft order of their own so that it may be checked before an order is made.

13.7.9 Once a GLO has been made a Group Register will be established on which will be entered such details as the court may direct of the cases which are the subject of the GLO: see PD 19B para.6.1. Paragraph 6.1A now makes it plain that a claim must be issued before it can be entered on the Register.

13.7.10 Questions as to whether a case should be admitted to the Register or should remain on the register may be dealt with on application or of the court's own motion under Paragraphs 6.2 to 6.4 of the Practice Direction.

13.7.11 The management of cases under a GLO is the subject of directions which are given by the management court under rule 19.13 and paras.8 to 15 of the Practice Direction. A managing judge is appointed as soon as possible. He will assume overall responsibility for the management of the claim and will generally hear the GLO issues. A Master or District Judge is usually appointed to deal with procedural matters. Directions that are likely to be given may include:
    1. that one or more of the claims proceed as test claims
    2. the appointment of lead solicitors for the claimants or defendants
    3. a cut–off date after which no claim will be admitted to the Register without permission.

4. that "Group Particulars of Claim" are served including general allegations relating to all the claims, and a schedule containing entries relating to each individual claim: see PD 19B para.14.1.

13.7.12 Publicising the GLO. A copy of the GLO should be sent:
   (1) to the Law Society, 113 Chancery Lane, London WC2A 1PL, and
   (a) to the Senior Master, Queen's Bench Division, Royal Courts of Justice, Strand, London WC2A 2LL.

Information, which may affect legal representatives of parties who have claims which raise one or more of the GLO issues, is thus available from those sources. Enquiries may be made of the office of the Senior Master in Room E103, from the Law Society's Multi Party Action Information Service, and from the Courts and Tribunals Service website at **http://www.justice.gov.uk/about/hmcts**.

13.7.13 A judgment given in a claim on the group register in relation to GLO issues is binding on the parties to all other claims on the register unless the court orders otherwise: rule 19.12.

13.7.14 Costs. CPR 46.6 contains rules as to costs where the court has made a GLO.

Annex 1

Plans of the Royal Courts of Justice

Keys to these plans are as follows: **1B–111**

Plan A The Royal Courts of Justice
   1. The Interim Applications Judge sits in Court 37 in the West Green Building
   2. The Queen's Bench Listing Office is in Room WG08 in the West Green Building
   3. The Masters' rooms, and the Bear garden and Ante–Room, are on the first floor of the East Block (at the south end)
   4. The rooms of the Action Department, including the Master's Support Unit, the Foreign Process Section, the Enforcement Section, and the Children's Funds Section (as described in paragraph 1.6.5 above) are on the ground floor of the East Block (at the south end)
   5. The Fees office is in Room E01, also on the ground floor of the East Block (at the south end)
   6. The Citizens' Advice Bureau is as marked by the main entrance. The Personal Support Unit is as marked on the first floor of the Central Block.

Plan B. East Block and Queen's Bench Masters' Rooms. The Queen's Bench Masters' rooms are as shown. Chambers applications (as described in paragraph 6.3.1 above) are heard in Room E102.

Plan A. The Royal Courts of Justice

1B–112

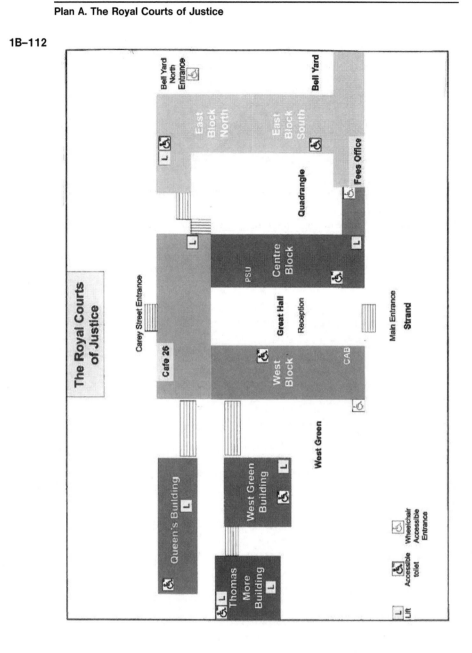

Plan B. East Block and Queen's Bench Masters' Rooms

1B–113

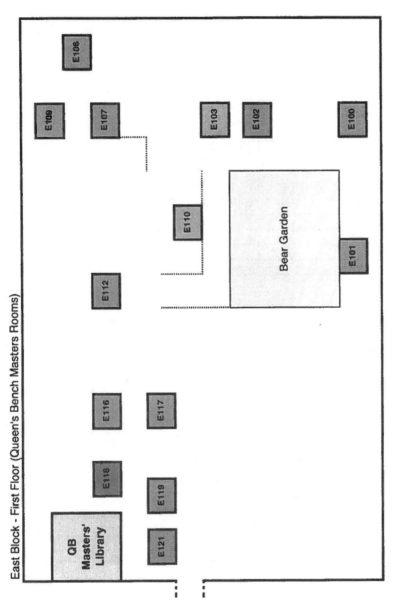

East Block - First Floor (Queen's Bench Masters Rooms)

Annex 2

Masters' abbreviations

The following is a list of abbreviations commonly used by Masters in the endorse- **1B–114** ments of their orders though there may be some variations as between individual Masters. They invariably endorse their orders with their own initials (as opposed to a full signature) and with the actual date when the order is made. Parties should familiarize themselves with the initials so that the identity of the Master (or Deputy Master) making the order is readily recognized.

Adj	Adjourn
A/D	Amended defence
ADR	Alternative dispute resolution
Affid	Affidavit
AMT	Allocate to multi–track
A/N	Application notice
A/P/C	Amended particulars of claim
Appn	Application
Appt	Appointment
AQ	Allocation questionnaire
Ack/service	Acknowledgment of service
BNLT	By no later than
CC	County Court
Cert	Certificate
CIA	Costs in the application
C in C	Costs in the case
CF	Claim form
Cl's costs iae	Claimant's costs in any event
Cl	Claimant
CMC	Case Management Conference
COS	Certificate of service
CPR	Civil procedure rule (s)
C/R	Costs reserved
C/sched	Counter schedule
DA	Detailed assessment
Def	Defendant/Defence
D/C	Defence and counterclaim
Dir	Directions
Disc	Disclosure
DQ	Directions questionnaire
DTBF	Date to be fixed
ET	Extension
Exch	Exchange
FC	Fixed costs
FCO	Final charging order
FD	Further directions
Final 3pDO	Final Third Party Debt Order
FI	Further information
FO	Further order
FOD	First open date
GLO	Group litigation order
IAE	In any event
IB	Indemnity basis
ICO	Interim charging order
Insp	Inspection
Interim 3pDO	Interim Third Party Debt Order
I/P	Interim payment
J	Judgment
JC	Judgment creditor

JD	Judgment debtor
JS	Joint statement
LA	Legal aid
O	Order
O exn	Order examination of judgment debtor
On COS	On producing certificate of service
Orse	Otherwise
P	Permission
P/C	Particulars of claim
PD	Practice Direction
PP	Periodical payments
PR	Permission to restore
PRA	Private Room Appointment
PRFD	Permission to restore for further directions
PTCL	Pre–trial check list
PTR	Pre–trial review
R/D/C	Reply and defence to counterclaim
Resp	Respondent
SA	Summary assessment
SAJ	Set aside judgment
SAO	Set aside order
SB	Standard basis
S/C	Statement of case
Sched	Schedule
S/D	Standard disclosure
S/O	Strike out
SOC	Strike out claim
SOE	Stay of execution
Solors	Solicitors
SOT	Statement of truth
Spec disc	Specific disclosure
TBA	To be assessed
TBD	To be determined
W/in	Within
W/out	Without
WS	Witness Statement

SECTION 2

SPECIALIST PROCEEDINGS

2A COMMERCIAL COURT

Part 58—Commercial Court

Related sources

In the second entry, for "March 2013" substitute:
April 2014

2A–3

Add new entry at end:

- CPR r.3.12 and PD3E: the Costs Management section of CPR Part 3 and PD3E will apply to all Admiralty and Commercial Court claims commenced on after April 22, 2014

ADMIRALTY AND COMMERCIAL COURTS GUIDE

B4 Part 7 claims

The form

Delete paragraph B4.1 and substitute:

2A–46 B4.1

(a) A claimant starting proceedings in the Commercial Court must use practice form **N1(CC)** for Part 7 claims.

(b) Within 7 days of issuing a Claim Form or when a case has been transferred into the Commercial Court, the receiving of the new claim number, the claimant(s) should complete an electronic Claim Information Form ("CIF") and file the same electronically to the following email address: comct.infosheet@hmcts.gsi.gov.uk. The form may be found at *http://hmctsformfinder.justice.gov.uk/HMCTS/GetForm.do?court_forms_id=4425* [Accessed May 21, 2014].

B7 Service of the claim form

Certificate of service

In paragraph B7.6, for rule 6.14(2) substitute:
2A–49 rule 6.17(2)

C.

PARTICULARS OF CLAIM, DEFENCE AND REPLY

C1 Form, content, serving and filing

Delete paragraph C1.1(b) and substitute:

2A–56 (b) Statements of case should be limited to 25 pages in length. The court will only exceptionally give permission for a longer statement of case to be served; and will do so only where a party shows good reasons for doing so. Where permission is given the court will require that a summary of the statement of case is also served. Any application to serve a statement of case longer than 25 pages should be made on paper to the court briefly stating the reasons for exceeding the 25 page limit.

In paragraph C1.2, add new entry (h):

(h) Where proceedings involve issues of construction of a document in relation to which a party wishes to contend that there is a relevant factual matrix that party should specifically set out in his pleading each feature of the matrix which is alleged to be of relevance. The "factual matrix" means the background knowledge which would reasonably have been available to the parties in the situation in which they found themselves at the time of the contract/document.

D2 Key features of case management in the Commercial Court

Delete paragraph number "D2" and substitute "D2.1".

2A–62 *In paragraph D2, add new entry D2.2:*

D2.2 The Costs Management section of CPR Part 3 and PD3E applies to all Admiralty and Commercial Court claims commenced on or after April 22, 2014 except where the claim is stated or valued at £10 million or more or where the court otherwise orders. Save in such cases the parties will be required to file and exchange costs budgets in accordance with rr.3.12 and 3.13. Unless an earlier costs management conference has been convened the issue of costs budgeting and whether a costs management order should be made will be considered at the first case management conference.

D6 List of issues

Add at end of paragraph D6.1: 2A–66

The common ground section should include features of the factual matrix which are agreed to be relevant. Any disagreements as to the relevant features of the factual matrix should be addressed in the List of Issues.

D19 Orders

Add new paragraph D19.4:

D19.4 Where the court makes an order under CPR 5.4C(4) that fact should be **2A–79** displayed prominently on the front of the order and the parties must inform the Clerk to the Commercial Court of the fact and terms of the order forthwith. Thereafter whenever a party files with the court a document which is subject to such order this should be stated on the front of the document and brought to the attention of the Clerk to the Commercial Court at the time of filing.

H.

EVIDENCE FOR TRIAL

H1 Witnesses of fact

Preparation and form of witness statements

Add at end of paragraph H1.1: 2A–103

Unless the court directs otherwise, witness statements should be no more than 30 pages in length.

2C PROCEEDINGS IN THE TECHNOLOGY AND CONSTRUCTION COURT

Delete the Technology and Construction Court Guide and substitute:

The Technology and Construction Court Guide

Contents 2C–35

2C–36   **Second Edition**

Issued 3rd October 2005, third revision with effect from 3 March 2014

Section 1

Introduction

1.1 Purpose of Guide

1.1.1 The Technology and Construction Court ("TCC") Guide is intended to provide straightforward, practical guidance on the conduct of litigation in the TCC. Whilst it is intended to be comprehensive, it naturally concentrates on the most important aspects of such litigation. It therefore cannot cover all the procedural points that may arise. It does, however, describe the main elements of the practice that is likely to be followed in most TCC cases. This Guide does not and cannot add to or amend the CPR or the relevant practice directions. The purpose and function of this Guide is to explain how the substantive law, rules and practice directions are applied in the TCC and cannot affect their proper interpretation and effect: see *Secretary of State for Communities and Local Government v Bovale* [2009] 1 WLR 2274 at [36].

1.1.2 The Guide reflects the flexible framework within which litigation in the TCC is habitually conducted. The guidance set out in the Guide is designed to ensure effective management of proceedings in the TCC. It must always be remembered that, if parties fail to comply with these requirements, the court may impose sanctions including orders for costs and, following the implementation of the Jackson reforms, will be more ready to do so.

1.1.3 In respect of those procedural areas for which specific provision is not made in this Guide, the parties, together with their advisors, will be expected to act reasonably and in accordance with both the spirit of the Guide and the overriding objective at CPR 1.1

1.1.4 It is not the function of the Guide to summarise the Civil Procedure Rules ("the CPR"), and it should not be regarded as a substitute for the CPR. The parties and their advisors are expected to familiarise themselves with the CPR and, in particular, to understand the importance of the "overriding objective" of the CPR. The TCC endeavours to ensure that all its cases are dealt with justly and at proportionate cost. This includes ensuring that the parties are on an equal footing; taking all practicable steps to save expenditure; dealing with the dispute in ways which are proportionate to the size of the claim and cross–claim and the importance of the case to the parties; and managing the case throughout in a way that takes proper account of its complexity and the different financial positions of the parties. The court will also endeavour to ensure expedition, and to allot to each case an appropriate share of the court's resources.

1.1.5 The TCC Guide has been prepared in consultation with the judges of the TCC in London, Cardiff, Birmingham, Manchester and Leeds, and with the advice and support of TECBAR, TeCSA, the Society for Construction Law, the Society for Computers and Law and the TCC Users' Committees in London, Cardiff,

Birmingham, Manchester, Liverpool and Leeds. The TCC Guide is published with the approval of the Head of Civil Justice and the deputy Head of Civil Justice.

1.2 The CPR

1.2.1 Proceedings in the TCC are governed by the CPR and the supplementary Practice Directions. CPR Part 60 and its associated **Practice Direction** deal specifically with the practice and procedure of the TCC.

1.2.2 Other parts of the CPR that frequently arise in TCC cases include Part 3 (Case Management Powers); Part 8 (Alternative Procedure for Claims); Parts 12 and 13 (Default Judgment and Setting Aside); Part 17 (Amendments); Part 20 (Counterclaims and Other Additional Claims); Part 24 (Summary Judgment); Part 25 (Interim Remedies and Security for Costs); Part 26 (Case Management); Part 32 (Evidence); Part 35 (Experts and Assessors); Part 44 (Costs); and Part 62 (Arbitration Claims).

1.3 The TCC

1.3.1 <u>What are TCC Claims?</u> CPR 60.1 (2) and (3) provide that a TCC claim is a claim which (i) involves technically complex issues or questions (or for which trial by a TCC judge is desirable) and (ii) has been issued in or transferred into the TCC specialist list. Paragraph 2.1 of the TCC Practice Direction identifies the following as examples of the types of claim which it may be appropriate to bring as TCC claims –

  (a) building or other construction disputes, including claims for the enforcement of the decisions of adjudicators under the Housing Grants, Construction and Regeneration Act 1996;
  (b) engineering disputes;
  (c) claims by and against engineers, architects, surveyors, accountants and other specialised advisors relating to the services they provide;
  (d) claims by and against local authorities relating to their statutory duties concerning the development of land or the construction of buildings;
  (e) claims relating to the design, supply and installation of computers, computer software and related network systems;
  (f) claims relating to the quality of goods sold or hired, and work done, materials supplied or services rendered;
  (g) claims between landlord and tenant for breach of a repairing covenant;
  (h) claims between neighbours, owners and occupiers of land in trespass, nuisance, etc.
  (i) claims relating to the environment (for example, pollution cases);
  (j) claims arising out of fires;
  (k) claims involving taking of accounts where these are complicated; and
  (l) challenges to decisions of arbitrators in construction and engineering disputes including applications for permission to appeal and appeals.

It should be noted that this list is not exhaustive and many other types of claim might well be appropriate for resolution in the TCC. In recent years the range of work in the TCC has become increasingly diverse, and many civil claims which are factually or technically complex are now heard in the TCC. This has included group actions for personal injury and public nuisance, and a number of procurement disputes arising in connection with the Public Contracts Regulations 2006. In addition, the TCC regularly deals with allegations of lawyers' negligence arising in connection with planning, property, construction and other technical disputes and with applications under the Arbitration Act 1996. However, with the exception of claims to enforce adjudicators' decisions or other claims with special features that justify a hearing before a High Court Judge, the TCC will not usually accept cases with a value of less than £250,000 (see Paragraph 1.3.6 below) unless there is good reason for it to do so. A non–exhaustive list of special features which will usually justify listing the case in the High Court is:

  (a) Adjudication and arbitration cases of any value;
  (b) International cases whatever their value (international cases will generally involve one or more parties resident outside the UK and/or involve an overseas project or development);

    (c) Cases involving new or difficult points of law in TCC cases;

    (d) Any test case or case which will be joined with others which will be treated as test cases;

    (e) Public procurement cases;

    (f) Part 8 claims and other claims for declarations;

    (g) Complex nuisance claims brought by a number of parties, even where the sums claimed are small;

    (h) Claims which cannot readily be dealt with effectively in a County Court or Civil Justice centre by a designated TCC judge;

    (i) Claims for injunctions.

For further guidance, see *West Country Renovations v McDowell* [2013] 1 WLR 416.

1.3.2 The Court. Both the High Court and the County Courts deal with TCC business. TCC business is conducted by TCC judges unless a TCC judge directs otherwise: see CPR 60.1(5)(b)(ii).

TCC business in the High Court is conducted by TCC judges who are High Court judges (who sit principally in the Rolls Building), and by designated circuit judges and recorders. Circuit judges and recorders only have jurisdiction to manage and try TCC cases if they have been nominated by the Lord Chancellor pursuant to Section 68(1)(a) of the Senior Courts Act 1981 or are authorised to sit in the TCC as High Court judges under Section 9 of that Act.

TCC business in the County Court is conducted by TCC judges who include circuit judges and recorders. TCC business may also be conducted by certain district judges ("TCC liaison district judges") provided that: (1) a TCC judge has so directed under CPR 60.1(5)(b)(ii); (2) the designated civil judge for the court has so directed in accordance with the Practice Direction at CPR 2BPD11.1(d).

It should be noted that those circuit judges who have been nominated pursuant to Section 68(1)(a) of the Senior Courts Act 1981 fall into two categories: "full time" TCC judges and "part time" TCC judges. "Full time" TCC judges spend most of their time dealing with TCC business, although they will do other work when there is no TCC business requiring their immediate attention. "Part time" TCC judges are circuit judges who are only available to sit in the TCC for part of their time. They have substantial responsibilities outside the TCC.

In respect of a court centre where there is no full time TCC judge, the term "principal TCC judge" is used in this Guide to denote the circuit judge who has principal responsibility for TCC work.

The phrase "Technology and Construction Court" or "TCC" or "the court" is used in this Guide to denote any court which deals with TCC claims. All of the courts which deal with TCC claims form a composite group of courts. When those courts are dealing with TCC business, CPR Part 60, its accompanying **Practice Direction and this Guide** govern the procedures of those courts. The High Court judge in charge of the TCC ("the Judge in Charge"), although based principally in London, has overall responsibility for the judicial supervision of TCC business in those courts.

1.3.3 The TCC in London. The principal centre for TCC work is the High Court in London at the Rolls Building, Fetter Lane, London, EC4. 1NL. The Rolls Building is a new specialist court building off Fetter Lane. The Judge in Charge of the TCC sits principally at the Rolls Building together with other High Court judges who are TCC judges. Subject to Paragraph 3.7.1 below, any communication or enquiry concerning a TCC case, which is proceeding at the Rolls Building, should be directed to the clerk of the judge who is assigned to that case and, if by email, copied to the TCC Registry. The various contact details for the judges' clerks are set out in **Appendix D**.

The TCC judges who are based at the Rolls Building will, when appropriate, sit at court centres outside London.

TCC County Court cases in London are brought in (or transferred to) the Central London Civil Justice Centre, 13–14 Park Crescent, London W1N 4HT. This court is shortly to move into new accommodation in the Royal Courts of Justice.

1.3.4 <u>District Registries.</u> TCC claims can be brought in the High Court outside London in any District Registry, although the Practice Direction states that it is preferable that, wherever possible, such claims should be issued in one of the following District Registries: Birmingham, Bristol, Cardiff, Chester, Exeter, Leeds, Liverpool, Newcastle, Nottingham and Manchester. There are currently full–time TCC Judges in Birmingham, Manchester and Leeds. Contact details are again set out in **Appendix D**. There are part time TCC judges and/or recorders nominated to deal with TCC business available at most court centres throughout England and Wales.

In a number of regions a "TCC liaison district judge" has been appointed. It is the function of the TCC liaison district judge:

(a) To keep other district judges in that region well informed about the role and remit of the TCC (in order that appropriate cases may be transferred to the TCC at an early, rather than late, stage).

(b) To deal with any queries from colleagues concerning the TCC or cases which might merit transfer to the TCC.

(c) To deal with any subsidiary matter which a TCC judge directs should be determined by a district judge pursuant to Rule 60.1 (5) (b) (ii).

(d) To deal with urgent applications in TCC cases pursuant to Paragraph 7.2 of the Practice Direction (i.e. no TCC judge is available and the matter is of a kind that falls within the district judge's jurisdiction).

(e) to hear TCC cases when a TCC judge has so directed under CPR 60.1(5)(b)(ii) and when the designated civil judge for the court has so directed in accordance with the Practice Direction at CPR 2BPD11.1(d).

1.3.5 <u>County Courts outside London.</u> TCC claims may also be brought in those county courts which are specified in the Part 60 **Practice Direction**. The specified county courts are: Birmingham, Bristol, Cardiff, Chester, Exeter, Leeds, Liverpool, Newcastle, Nottingham and Manchester. Contact details are again set out in **Appendix D**.

Where TCC proceedings are brought in a county court, statements of case and applications should be headed:

"In the ... County Court
Technology and Construction Court"

1.3.6 <u>The division between High Court and County Court TCC cases.</u> As a general rule TCC claims for more than £250,000 are brought in the High Court, whilst claims for lower sums are brought in the County Court. However, this is not a rigid dividing line (see Paragraph 1.3.1 above). The monetary threshold for High Court TCC claims tends to be higher in London than in the regions. Regard must also be had to the complexity of the case and all other circumstances. Arbitration claims and claims to enforce or challenge adjudicators' decisions are generally (but not invariably) brought in the High Court. The scale of fees differs in the High Court and the county court. This is a factor which should be borne in mind in borderline cases.

1.4 The TCC Users' Committees

1.4.1 The continuing ability of the TCC to meet the changing needs of all those involved in TCC litigation depends in large part upon a close working relationship between the TCC and its users.

1.4.2 <u>London.</u> The Judge in Charge chairs meetings of the London TCC Users' Committee (usually two meetings a year). The judge's clerk acts as secretary to the Committee and takes the minutes of meetings. That Committee is made up of representatives of the London TCC judges, the barristers and solicitors who regularly use the Court, the professional bodies, such as architects, engineers and arbitrators, whose members are affected by the decisions of the Court, and representatives of both employers and contractors' groups.

1.4.3 <u>Outside London.</u> There are similar meetings of TCC Users' Committees in Birmingham, Manchester, Liverpool, Cardiff and Leeds. Each Users' Committee is chaired by the full time TCC judge or the principal TCC judge in that location.

1.4.4 The TCC regards these channels of communication as extremely important and all those who are concerned with the work of the Court are encouraged to make full use of these meetings. Any suggestions or other correspondence raising matters for consideration by the Users' Committee should, in the first instance, be addressed to the clerk to the Judge in Charge at the Rolls Building or to the clerk to the appropriate TCC judge outside London.

1.5 Specialist Associations

1.5.1 There are a number of associations of legal representatives which are represented on the Users' Committees and which also liaise closely with the Court. These contacts ensure that the Court remains responsive to the opinions and requirements of the professional users of the Court.

1.5.2 The relevant professional organisations are the TCC Bar Association ("TECBAR") and the TCC Solicitors Association ("TeCSA"). Details of the relevant contacts at these organisations are set out on their respective websites, namely www.tecbar.org and www.tecsa.org.uk.

SECTION 2

PRE–ACTION PROTOCOL AND CONDUCT

2.1 Introduction

2C–37 2.1.1 There is a Pre–Action Protocol for Construction and Engineering Disputes. Where the dispute involves a claim against architects, engineers or quantity surveyors, this Protocol prevails over the Professional Negligence Pre–Action Protocol: see Paragraph 1.1 of the Protocol for Construction and Engineering Disputes and Paragraph A.1 of the Professional Negligence Pre–Action Protocol. The current version of the Construction and Engineering Pre–Action Protocol ("the Protocol") is set out in volume 1 of the White Book at Section C5.

2.1.2 The purpose of the Protocol is to encourage the frank and early exchange of information about the prospective claim and any defence to it; to enable parties to avoid litigation by agreeing a settlement of the claim before the commencement of proceedings; and to support the efficient management of proceedings where litigation cannot be avoided.

2.1.3 Proportionality. The overriding objective (CPR rule 1.1) applies to the pre–action period. The Protocol must not be used as a tactical device to secure advantage for one party or to generate unnecessary costs. In lower value TCC claims (such as those likely to proceed in the county court), the letter of claim and the response should be simple and the costs of both sides should be kept to a modest level. In all cases the costs incurred at the Protocol stage should be proportionate to the complexity of the case and the amount of money which is at stake. The Protocol does not impose a requirement on the parties to produce a detailed pleading as a letter of claim or response or to marshal and disclose all the supporting details and evidence or to provide witness statements or expert reports that may ultimately be required if the case proceeds to litigation. Where a party has serious concerns that the approach of the other party to the Pre–Action Protocol is not proportionate, then it is open for that party to issue a claim form and/or make an application (see Paragraph 4.1.5 below) to seek the assistance of the court.

2.2 To Which Claims Does The Protocol Apply?

2.2.1 The court will expect all parties to have complied in substance with the provisions of the Protocol in all construction and engineering disputes. The only exceptions to this are identified in Paragraph 2.3 below.

2.2.2 The court regards the Protocol as setting out normal and reasonable pre–action conduct. Accordingly, whilst the Protocol is not mandatory for a number of the claims noted by way of example in **Paragraph 1.3.1** above, such as computer cases or dilapidations claims, the court would, in the absence of a specific reason to the contrary, expect the Protocol generally to be followed in such cases prior to the commencement of proceedings in the TCC.

2.3 What Are The Exceptions?

2.3.1 A claimant does not have to comply with the Protocol if his claim:

(a) is to enforce the decision of an adjudicator;

(b) is to seek an urgent declaration or injunction in relation to adjudication (whether ongoing or concluded);

(c) includes a claim for interim injunctive relief;

(d) will be the subject of a claim for summary judgment pursuant to Part 24 of the CPR; or

(e) relates to the same or substantially the same issues as have been the subject of a recent adjudication or some other formal alternative dispute resolution procedure; or

(f) relates to a public procurement dispute.

The protocol does not contemplate an extended process and it should not be drawn out. Thus, the letter of claim should be concise and it is usually sufficient to explain the proposed claim(s), identifying key dates, so as to enable the potential defendant to understand and to investigate the allegations. Only essential documents need be supplied, and the period specified for a response should not be longer than one month without good reason. In particular, where a claim is brought by an litigant based outside the UK it will generally be appropriate to confine the steps to the time limits provided by the Protocol and, in many cases, to dispense with the meeting referred to in Paragraph 5.1 of the Protocol. In any event, such a meeting is not mandatory and may be dispensed with if it would involve disproportionate time and cost or it is clear that it would be unlikely to serve any useful purpose.

2.3.2 In addition, a claimant need not comply with any part of the Protocol if, by so doing, his claim may become time–barred under the Limitation Act 1980. In those circumstances, a claimant should commence proceedings without complying with the Protocol and must, at the same time, apply for directions as to the timetable and form of procedure to be adopted. The court may order a stay of those proceedings pending completion of the steps set out in the Protocol.

2.4 What Are The Essential Ingredients Of The Protocol?

2.4.1 The Letter of Claim. The letter of claim must comply with Section 3 of the Protocol. Amongst other things, it must contain a clear and concise summary of the facts on which each claim is based; the basis on which each claim is made; and details of the relief claimed, including a breakdown showing how any damages have been quantified. The claimant must also provide the names of experts already instructed and on whom he intends to rely.

2.4.2 The Defendant's Response. The defendant has 14 days to acknowledge the letter of claim and 28 days (from receipt of the letter of claim) either to take any jurisdiction objection or to respond in substance to the letter of claim. Paragraph 4.3.1 of the Protocol enables the parties to agree an extension of the 28 day period up to a maximum of 3 months. In any case of substance it is quite usual for an extension of time to be agreed for the defendant's response. The letter of response must comply with Section 4 of the Protocol. Amongst other things, it must state which claims are accepted, which claims are rejected and on what basis. It must set out any counterclaim to be advanced by the defendant. The defendant should also provide the names of experts who have been instructed and on whom he intends to rely. If the defendant fails either to acknowledge or to respond to the letter of claim in time, the claimant is entitled to commence proceedings.

2.4.3 Pre–action Meeting. The Construction and Engineering Protocol is the only Protocol under the CPR that generally requires the parties to meet, without prejudice, at least once, in order to identify the main issues and the root causes of their disagreement on those issues. The purpose of the meeting is to see whether, and if so how, those issues might be resolved without recourse to litigation or, if litigation is unavoidable, what steps should be taken to ensure that it is conducted in accordance with the overriding objective. At or as a result of the meeting, the parties should consider whether some form of alternative dispute resolution ("ADR") would be more suitable than litigation and if so, they should endeavour to agree which form of ADR to adopt. Although the meeting is "without prejudice", any party who attended the meeting is at liberty to disclose to the Court at a later stage that the meeting took place; who attended and who refused to attend, together with the grounds for their refusal; and any agreements concluded between the parties. (See also Paragraph 2.3.1 above in relation to claims brought by claimants based ouside the UK).

2.5 What Happens To The Material Generated By The Protocol?

2.5.1 The letter of claim, the defendant's response, and the information relating to attendance (or otherwise) at the meeting are not confidential or 'without prejudice' and can therefore be referred to by the parties in any subsequent litigation. The detail of any discussion at the meeting(s) and/or any note of the meeting cannot be referred to the court unless all parties agree.

2.5.2 Normally the parties should include in the bundle for the first case management conference: (a) the letter of claim, (b) the response, and (c) if the parties agree, any agreed note of the pre–action meeting: see Section 5 below. The documents attached to or enclosed with the letter and the response should not be included in the bundle.

2.6 What If One Party Has Not Complied With The Protocol?

2.6.1 There can often be a complaint that one or other party has not complied with the Protocol. The court will consider any such complaints once proceedings have been commenced. If the court finds that the claimant has not complied with one part of the Protocol, then the court may stay the proceedings until the steps set out in the Protocol have been taken or impose such other conditions as the court thinks appropriate pursuant to CPR 3.1(3).

2.6.2 **The Practice Direction in respect of Protocols** (Section C of volume 1 of the White Book) makes plain that the court may make adverse costs orders against a party who has failed to comply with the Protocol. The court will exercise any sanctions available with the object of placing the innocent party in no worse a position than he would have been if the Protocol had been complied with.

2.6.3 The court is unlikely to be concerned with minor infringements of the Protocol or to engage in lengthy debates as to the precise quality of the information provided by one party to the other during the Protocol stages. The court will principally be concerned to ensure that, as a result of the Protocol stage, each party to any subsequent litigation has a clear understanding of the nature of the case that it has to meet at the commencement of those proceedings.

2.7 Costs of compliance with the Protocol

2.7.1 If compliance with the Protocol results in settlement, the costs incurred will not be recoverable from the paying party, unless this is specifically agreed.

2.7.2 If compliance with the Protocol does not result in settlement, then the costs of the exercise cannot be recovered as costs, unless:

- those costs fall within the principles stated by Sir Robert Megarry V–C in *Re Gibson's Settlement Trusts* [1981] Ch 179; or
- the steps taken in compliance with the Protocol can properly be attributable to the conduct of the action: see the judgment of Coulson J in *Roundstone Nurseries v Stephenson* [2009] EWHC 1431 (TCC) where he held at [48]: ". . . as a matter of principle, it seems to me that costs incurred during the Pre–Action Protocol process may, in principle, be recoverable as costs incidental to the litigation: see *McGlinn v. Waltham (No. 1)* [2005] 3 All ER1126.

SECTION 3

COMMENCEMENT AND TRANSFER

3.1 Claim Forms

2C–38 3.1.1 All proceedings must be started using a claim form under CPR Part 7 or CPR

Part 8 or an arbitration claim form under CPR Part 62: see Paragraph 10.1 below. All claims allocated to the TCC are assigned to the Multi–Track: see CPR 60.6(1).

3.2 Part 7 Claims

3.2.1 The Part 7 claim form must be marked "Technology and Construction Court" in the appropriate place on the form.

3.2.2 Particulars of Claim may be served with the claim form, but this is not a mandatory requirement. If the Particulars of Claim are not contained in or served with the claim form, they must be served within **14 days** after service of the claim form.

3.2.3 A claim form must be verified by a statement of truth, and this includes any amendment to a claim form, unless the court otherwise orders.

3.3 Part 8 Claims

3.3.1 The Part 8 claim form must be marked "Technology and Construction Court" in the appropriate place on the form.

3.3.2 A Part 8 claim form will normally be used where there is no substantial dispute of fact, such as the situation where the dispute turns on the construction of the contract or the interpretation of statute. For example, claims challenging the jurisdiction of an adjudicator or the validity of his decision are sometimes brought under Part 8. In those cases the relevant primary facts are often not in dispute. Part 8 claims will generally be disposed of on written evidence and oral submissions.

3.3.3 It is important that, where a claimant uses the Part 8 procedure, his claim form states that Part 8 applies and that the claimant wishes the claim to proceed under Part 8.

3.3.4 A statement of truth is again required on a Part 8 claim form.

3.4 Service

3.4.1 Claim forms issued in the TCC at the Rolls Building in London are to be served by the claimant, not by the Registry. In some other court centres claim forms are served by the court, unless the claimant specifically requests otherwise.

3.4.2 The different methods of service are set out in CPR Part 6 and the accompanying Practice Direction.

3.4.3 Applications for an extension of time in which to serve a claim form are governed by CPR 7.6 and there are only limited grounds on which such extensions of time are granted. The evidence required on an application for an extension of time is set out in Paragraph 8.2 of Practice Direction A supplementing CPR Part 7.

3.4.4 When the claimant has served the claim form, he must file a certificate of service: CPR 6.17 (2). This is necessary if, for instance, the claimant wishes to obtain judgment in default (CPR Part 12).

3.4.5 Applications for permission to serve a claim form out of the jurisdiction are subject to CPR 6.30–6.47 inclusive.

3.5 Acknowledgment of Service

3.5.1 A defendant must file an acknowledgment of service in response to both Part 7 and Part 8 claims. Save in the special circumstances that arise when the claim form has been served out of the jurisdiction, the period for filing an acknowledgment of service is **14 days** after service of the claim form.

3.6 Transfer

3.6.1 Proceedings may be transferred from any Division of the High Court or from any specialist list to the TCC pursuant to CPR 30.5. The order made by the transferring court should be expressed as being subject to the approval of a TCC judge. The decision whether to accept such a transfer must be made by a TCC judge:

see CPR 30.5 (3). Many of these applications are uncontested, and may conveniently be dealt with on paper. Transfers from the TCC to other Divisions of the High Court or other specialist lists are also governed by CPR 30.5. In London there are sometimes transfers between the Chancery Division, the Commercial Court and the TCC, in order to ensure that cases are dealt with by the most appropriate judge. Outside London there are quite often transfers between the TCC and the mercantile and chancery lists. It should be noted that transfers from the Chancery Division may become subject to a requirement for permission from the Chancellor.

3.6.2 A TCC claim may be transferred from the High Court to a County Court or a County Court hearing centre, and from any County Court or County Court hearing centre to the High Court, if the criteria stated in CPR 30.3 are satisfied. In ordinary circumstances, proceedings will be transferred from the TCC in the High Court to the TCC in an appropriate County Court if the amount of the claim does not exceed £250,000.

3.6.3 Where no TCC judge is available to deal with a TCC claim which has been issued in a district registry or one of the county courts noted above, the claim may be transferred to another district registry or county court or to the High Court TCC in London (depending upon which court is appropriate).

3.6.4 On an application to transfer the case to the TCC from another court or Division of the High Court, there are a number of relevant considerations:

(a) Is the claim broadly one of the types of claim identified in Paragraph 2.1 of the Part 60 Practice Direction?

(b) Is the financial value of the claim and/or its complexity such that, in accordance with the overriding objective, the case should be transferred into the TCC?

(c) What effect would transfer have on the likely costs, the speed with which the matter can be resolved, and any other broader questions of convenience for the parties?

3.6.5 On an application to transfer into the TCC, when considering the relative appropriateness of different courts or divisions, the judge will ascertain where and in what areas of judicial expertise and experience the bulk or preponderance of the issues may lie. If there was little significant difference between the appropriateness of the two venues, and the claimant, having started in one court or division, was anxious to remain there, then the application to transfer in by another party is likely to be unsuccessful.

3.6.6 Where a TCC Claim is proceeding in a District Registry and it becomes apparent that the case would merit case management or trial before a High Court judge, the matter should be raised with the TCC judge at the District Registry who will consult the Judge in Charge: see Paragraph 3.7.3 below. If the case does merit the involvement of a High Court judge it is not necessary for the case to be transferred to London but rather a High Court judge can in appropriate cases sit outside London to deal with the case in the District Registry.

3.7 Assignment

3.7.1 Where a claim has been issued at or transferred to the TCC in London, the Judge in Charge of the TCC ("the Judge in Charge") shall assign it to a particular TCC judge.

3.7.2 In general the assigned TCC judge who case manages a case will also try that case. Although this continuity of judge is regarded as important, it is sometimes necessary for there to be a change of assigned judge to case manage or try a case because all High Court Judges in the Queen's Bench Division have other judicial duties.

3.7.3

(a) When a TCC case has been assigned to a named High Court judge, all communications about case management should be made to the assigned High Court judge's clerk with email communications copied to the TCC Registry at tcc@hmcourts–service.gsi.gov.uk.

(b) All communications in respect of the issue of claims or applications and all communications about fees, however, should be sent to the TCC Registry.

(c) All statements of case and applications should be marked with the name of the assigned judge.

3.7.4 There are currently full time TCC judges at Birmingham, Manchester and Leeds. There are principal TCC judges at other court centres outside London. TCC cases at these court centres are assigned to judges either (a) by direction of the full time or principal TCC judge or (b) by operation of a rota. It will not generally be appropriate for the Judge in Charge (who is based in London) to consider TCC cases which are commenced in, or transferred to, court centres outside London. Nevertheless, if any TCC case brought in a court centre outside London appears to require management and trial by a High Court judge, then the full time or principal TCC judge at that court centre should refer the case to the Judge in Charge for a decision as to its future management and trial.

3.7.5 When a TCC case has been assigned to a named circuit judge at a court centre other than in London, all communications to the court about the case (save for communications in respect of fees) shall be made to that judge's clerk. All communications in respect of fees should be sent to the relevant registry. All statements of case and applications should be marked with the name of the assigned judge.

3.8 Electronic Working in London

3.8.1 At the time of writing this guide claims in the TCC and Commercial Court Registry in London cannot be issued electronically.

3.8.2 It is planned that eworking in the TCC will be resumed in the near future when suitable software becomes available and that it will then be extended to courts outside London.

SECTION 4

ACCESS TO THE COURT

4.1 General Approach

4.1.1 There may be a number of stages during the case management phase when the parties will make applications to the court for particular orders: see Section 6 below. There will also be the need for the court to give or vary directions, so as to enable the case to progress to trial. **2C–39**

4.1.2 The court is acutely aware of the costs that may be incurred when both parties prepare for an oral hearing in respect of such interlocutory matters and is always prepared to consider alternative, and less expensive, ways in which the parties may seek the court's assistance.

4.1.3 There are certain stages in the case management phase when it will generally be better for the parties to appear before the assigned judge. Those are identified at Section 4.2 below. But there are other stages, and/or particular applications which a party may wish to make, which could conveniently be dealt with by way of a telephone hearing (Section 4.3 below) or by way of a paper application (Section 4.4 below).

4.1.4 Access prior to the issue of proceedings. Under Paragraph 4.1 of the Practice Direction supplementing CPR Part 60 it is provided that a party who intends to issue a TCC claim must make any application before the claim form is issued to a TCC judge. This provision allows a party, for instance, to issue an application for pre–action disclosure.

4.1.5 As a party will have issued a TCC claim in circumstances where Paragraph 6 of the Pre–Action Protocol for Construction and Engineering Disputes applies (limitation or time bar by complying with the pre–action protocol), this provision does not apply to that situation. The court might however be persuaded to deal with an application concerned with the pre–action protocol process under this provision although it may be necessary to insist on a claim form being issued.

4.1.6 Sometimes parties wish to use the TCC procedures for **Early Neutral Evaluation** (see Section 7.5) or the **Court Settlement Process** (see Section 7.6) prior to issuing a TCC claim, often as part of the pre–action protocol. The court will seek to accommodate the parties' wishes but again may have to insist on a claim form being issued.

4.2 Hearings in Court

4.2.1 First Case Management Conference. The court will normally require the parties to attend an oral hearing for the purposes of the first Case Management Conference. This is because there may be matters which the judge would wish to raise with the parties arising out of the answers to the case management information sheets and the parties' proposed directions: see Section 5.4 below. Even in circumstances where the directions and the case management timetable may be capable of being agreed by the parties and the court, the assigned judge may still wish to consider a range of case management matters face–to–face with the parties, including cost budgeting and ADR. See Paragraphs 7.2.3, 7.3.2, 8.1.3, 11.1–11.2.4, 13.3, 13.4, 15.4.2 and 16.3.2 below. For these reasons CPR 29.4 may be applied more sparingly in the TCC.

4.2.2 Whilst the previous paragraph sets out the ideal position, it is recognised that in low value cases the benefits of personal attendance might be outweighed by the costs involved. This is particularly so at court centres outside London, where the parties may have to travel substantial distances to court. Ultimately, the question whether personal attendance should be dispensed with at any particular case management conference must be decided by the judge, after considering any representations made and the circumstances of that particular case.

4.2.3 Pre–trial Review. It will normally be helpful for the parties to attend before the judge on a Pre–trial Review ("PTR"). It is always preferable for Counsel or other advocates who will be appearing at the trial to attend the PTR. Again, even if the parties can agree beforehand any outstanding directions and the detailed requirements for the management of the trial, it is still of assistance for the judge to raise matters of detailed trial management with the parties at an oral hearing. In appropriate cases, e.g. where the amount in issue is disproportionate to the costs of a full trial, the judge may wish to consider with the parties whether there are other ways in which the dispute might be resolved. See Paragraphs 14.1 to 14.5 below for detailed provisions relating to the PTR.

4.2.4 Interim Applications. Whether or not other interim applications require an oral hearing will depend on the nature and effect of the application being made. Disputed applications for interim payments, summary judgment and security for costs will almost always require an oral hearing. Likewise, the resolution of a contested application to enforce an adjudicator's decision will normally be heard orally. At the other end of the scale, applications for extensions of time for the service of pleadings or to comply with other orders of the court can almost always be dealt with by way of a telephone hearing or in writing and, indeed, orders sometimes expressly provide for this.

4.3 Telephone Hearings

4.3.1 Depending on the nature of the application and the extent of any dispute between the parties, the Court is content to deal with many case management matters and other interlocutory applications by way of a telephone conference.

4.3.2 Whilst it is not possible to lay down mandatory rules as to what applications should be dealt with in this way (rather than by way of an oral hearing in court), it may be helpful to identify certain situations which commonly arise and which can conveniently be dealt with by way of a telephone conference.

    (a) If the location of the court is inconvenient for one or more of the parties then the CMC and the PTR could, in the alternative to the procedure set out in Section 4.2 above, take place by way of a telephone conference. The judge's permission for such a procedure must be sought in advance.

    (b) If the parties are broadly agreed on the orders to be made by the court, but they are in dispute in respect of one or two particular matters, then a telephone hearing is a convenient way in which those outstanding matters can be dealt with by the parties and the assigned judge.

(c) Similarly, specific arguments about costs, once a substantive application has been disposed of, or arguments consequential on a particular judgment or order having been handed down, may also conveniently be dealt with by way of telephone hearing.

(d) Other applications which, depending on their size and importance, may conveniently be dealt with by way of a telephone hearing include limited applications in respect of disclosure and specific applications as to the scope and content of factual or expert evidence exchanged by the parties.

4.3.3 Telephone hearings are not generally suitable for matters which are likely to last for more than an hour (although the judge may be prepared, in an appropriate case, to list a longer application for a telephone hearing) or which require extensive reference to documents.

4.3.4 <u>Practical matters.</u> Telephone hearings can be listed at any time between 8.30 a.m. and 5.30 pm, subject to the convenience of the parties and the availability of the judge. It is not essential that all parties are on the telephone when those that are not find it more convenient to come to court. Any party, who wishes to have an application dealt with by telephone, should make such request by letter or e–mail to the judge's clerk, sending copies to all other parties. Except in cases of urgency, the judge will allow a period of two working days for the other parties to comment upon that request before deciding whether to deal with the application by telephone.

4.3.5 If permission is given for a telephone hearing, the court will normally indicate which party is to make all the necessary arrangements. In most cases, it will be the applicant. The procedure to be followed in setting up and holding a telephone hearing is generally that set out in Section 6 of the Practice Direction 23A supplementing CPR Part 23 and the TCC in London and at Regional Centres are "telephone conference enabled courts" for the purposes of that section. The party making arrangements for the telephone hearing must ensure that all parties and the judge have a bundle for that hearing with identical pagination.

It is vital that the judge has all the necessary papers, in good time before the telephone conference, in order that it can be conducted efficiently and effectively. Save in very simple cases involving no or only minimal amounts of documentation, it is usually essential that any bundle provided be paginated for a telephone hearing, failing which the judge may cancel it.

4.4 Paper Applications

4.4.1 CPR 23.8 and paragraphs 11.1–11.2 of Practice Direction 23A enable certain applications to be dealt with in writing. Parties in a TCC case are encouraged to deal with applications in writing, whenever practicable. Applications for abridgments of time, extensions of time and to reduce the trial time estimate can generally be dealt with in writing, as well as all other variations to existing directions which are wholly or largely agreed. Disputes over particular aspects of disclosure and evidence may also be capable of being resolved in this way.

4.4.2 If a party wishes to make an application to the court, it should ask itself the question: "Can this application be conveniently dealt with in writing?" If it can, then the party should issue the application and make its (short) written submissions both in support of its application and why it should be dealt with on paper. The application, any supporting evidence and the written submissions should be provided to all parties, as well as the court. These must include a draft of the precise order sought. There are some paper applications which can be made without notice to the other party or parties: see CPR 23.4(2), 23.9 and 23.10.

4.4.3 The party against whom the application is made, and any other interested party, should respond within **3 days** dealing both with the substantive application and the request for it to be dealt with in writing.

4.4.4 The court can then decide whether or not to deal with the application in writing. If the parties are agreed that the court should deal with it in writing, it will be rare for the court to take a different view. If the parties disagree as to whether or not the application should be dealt with in writing, the court can decide that issue and, if it decides to deal with it in writing can go on to resolve the substantive point on the basis of the parties' written submissions.

4.4.5 Further guidance in respect of paper applications is set out in Section 6.7 below.

4.4.6 It is important for the parties to ensure that all documents provided to the court are also provided to all the other parties, so as to ensure that both the court and the parties are working on the basis of the same documentation. The pagination of any bundle which is provided to the court and the parties must be identical.

4.5 E–mail Communications

4.5.1 Electronic Working under the provisions of CPR Part 5, Practice Direction 5C is not currently available.

4.5.2 The judges' clerks all have e–mail addresses identified in **Appendix D**. They welcome communication from the parties electronically. In addition, by agreement with the judge's clerk, it is also possible to provide documents to the Court electronically. However, it should be noted that HM Court Service imposes a restriction on the size of any e–mail, including its attachments. Larger attachments can be submitted by CD/DVD. Further, the provision of substantial documents electronically is to be used only with the permission of the judge and when time is short. The Court Service is not to be used as an outsource for printing.

4.5.3 Depending on the particular circumstances of an individual trial, the assigned judge may ask for an e–mail contact address for each of the parties and may send e–mail communications to that address. In addition, the judge may provide a direct contact e–mail address so that the parties can communicate directly with him out of court hours. In such circumstances, the judge and the parties should agree the times at which the respective e–mail addresses can be used.

4.5.4 Every e–mail communication to and from the court or a judge must be copied simultaneously to all the other parties. The subject line of every e–mail should include the name of the case (abbreviated if necessary) and the claim number.

4.6 Video Conferencing

4.6.1 In appropriate cases, particularly where there are important matters in dispute and the parties' representatives are a long distance from one another and/or the court, the hearing may be conducted by way of a Video Conference ("VC"). Prior arrangements will be necessary for any such hearing.

4.6.2 In London, a VC can be arranged through the VC facilities in the Rolls Building, but there is significant demand for these, so parties must notify the court well ahead In some cases, it may be possible to use Skype or other commercially viable software as a suitable alternative to VC facilities (but the parties must bear in mind that such software usually only provides an insecure link, and it will be essential in any event to ensure that all of the parties and the judge in question have access to the software and a relevant account).

4.6.3 Outside London, a VC can be arranged at the following TCC courts with the requisite facilities: Birmingham, Bristol, Cardiff, Central London, Chester, Exeter, Leeds, Liverpool, Newcastle–upon–Tyne, Nottingham, Manchester and Winchester.

4.7 Contacting the court out of hours

4.7.1 Occasionally it is necessary to contact a TCC judge out of hours. For example, it may be necessary to apply for an injunction to prevent the commencement of building works which will damage adjoining property; or for an order to preserve evidence. A case may have settled and it may be necessary to inform the judge, before he/she spends an evening or a weekend reading the papers.

4.7.2 <u>At the Rolls Building</u>. RCJ Security has been provided with the telephone numbers and other contact information of all the clerks to the TCC judges based at the Rolls Building and and their clerks and of the court manager. If contact is required with a judge out of hours, the initial approach should be to RCJ Security on

020–7947–6000. Security will then contact the judge's clerk and/or the court manager and pass on the message or other information. If direct contact with the judge or court manager is sought, RCJ Security must be provided with an appropriate contact number. This number will then be passed to the judge's clerk and/or the court manager, who will seek directions from the judge whether it is appropriate for the judge to speak directly with the contacting party.

4.7.3 <u>At other court centres</u>. At the Central London Civil Justice Centre and at all court centres outside London there is a court officer who deals with out of hours applications.

4.8 Lodging documents

4.8.1 In general documents should be lodged in hard copy only and not sent by email or fax. This causes unnecessary duplication as well as additional work for hard–pressed court staff. Fax communication with the court, in particular, is discouraged. If the court or judge's clerk agrees, some documents may be sent by email but otherwise only if matters are urgent may documents be sent by either email or fax, with a hard copy sent by way of confirmation and marked as such. In certain cases, the court may ask for documents to be submitted in electronic form by email or otherwise, where that is appropriate. The judge may ask for certain documents to be lodged in a particular form, such as pdf or Microsoft Word or Excel.

SECTION 5

COSTS AND CASE MANAGEMENT AND THE FIRST CMC

5.1 General

5.1.1 The general approach of the TCC to costs and case management is to give **2C–40** directions at the outset for the conduct of the case, up to trial, and then throughout the proceedings to serve the overriding objective of dealing with cases justly and at proportionate cost. Since the introduction of costs management the control of costs will be an important factor in how cases are managed from the outset: the parties must read this section in conjunction with Section 16, which concerns costs management and cost capping. The judge to whom the case has been assigned has wide case management powers, which will be exercised to ensure that:

- the real issues are identified early on and remain the focus of the ongoing proceedings;
- a realistic timetable is ordered which will allow for the fair and prompt resolution of the action;
- appropriate steps are taken to ensure that there is in place a suitable protocol for conducting e–disclosure (this should have been discussed by the parties at an early stage in the litigation and the parties may wish to use the TeCSA e–disclosure protocol (which can be found on its website).
- in document heavy cases the parties will be invited to consider the use of an electronic document management system; it is important that this is considered at an early stage because it will be closely linked to e–disclosure;
- costs are properly controlled and reflect the value of the issues to the parties and their respective financial positions. In cases commenced before 22 April 2014 and below the value set by the relevant Practice Direction (£2 million), this will be done by way of Costs Management Orders. For cases commenced after 22 April 2014, this limit is increased to £10 million by CPR 3.12 (as amended). The attention of the parties is drawn to the amended rule.

5.1.2 In order to assist the judge in the exercise of his costs and case management functions, the parties will be expected to co–operate with one another at all times. See CPR 1.3. Costs sanctions may be applied, if the judge concludes that one party is not reasonably co–operating with the other parties.

5.1.3 A hearing at which the judge gives general procedural directions is a case management conference ("CMC"). CMCs are relatively informal and business–like occasions. Representatives may sit when addressing the judge.

5.1.4 The following procedures apply in order to facilitate effective case management:

- Upon commencement of a case in the TCC, it is allocated automatically to the multi–track. The provisions of CPR Part 29 apply to all TCC cases (but see Paragraph 4.2.1 above).
- The TCC encourages a structured exchange of proposals and submissions for CMCs in advance of the hearing, including costs budgets, so as to enable the parties to respond on an informed basis to proposals made.
- The judges of the TCC operate pro–active case management. In order to avoid the parties being taken by surprise by any judicial initiative, the judge will consider giving prior notification of specific or unusual case management proposals to be raised at a case management conference.

5.1.5 The TCC's aim is to ensure that where possible the trial of each case takes place before the judge who has managed the case since the first CMC. Whilst continuity of judge is not always possible, because of the need to double– or triple–book judges and the need for High Court Judges to be deployed on other duties, or because cases can sometimes overrun their estimated length through no fault of the parties, this remains an aspiration of case management within the TCC.

5.1.6 To ensure that costs are properly controlled the judge will consider at all stages of case management whether there are ways in which costs can be reduced. If the judge considers that any particular aspect has unnecessarily increased costs, such as prolix pleadings or witness statements, the judge may make a costs order disallowing costs or ordering costs to be paid, either on the basis of a summary assessment, or by giving a direction to the costs judge as to what costs should be disallowed or paid on a detailed assessment: see also Paragraph 5.5.5 below.

5.2 The Fixing of the First CMC

5.2.1 Where a claim has been started in the TCC, or where it has been transferred into the TCC, Paragraph 8.1 of the Part 60 Practice Direction requires the court within **14 days** of the earliest of

- the filing by the defendant of an acknowledgement of service, or
- the filing by the defendant of the defence, or
- the date of the order transferring the case to the TCC

to fix the first CMC.

If some defendants but not others are served with proceedings, the claimant's solicitors should so inform the court and liaise about the fixing of the first CMC. See also Paragraph 4.2.1 above.

5.2.2 The first CMC will usually be fixed sufficiently far ahead to allow the parties time to discuss both e–disclosure and costs budgets. If any of the parties wishes to delay the first CMC for any reason, it can write to the judge's clerk explaining why a delayed CMC is appropriate (for example, in cases where the CMC would not otherwise take place until after service of the defence or the defences, it may be appropriate to postpone the first CMC until these are available). If such a request is agreed by the other party or parties, it is likely that the judge will grant the request.

5.3 The Case Management Information Sheet and Other Documents

It should be noted that for proceedings in the TCC, being a specialist court, the standard directions that can be found on line are not always appropriate.

5.3.1 All parties are expected to complete a detailed response to the case management information sheet sent out by the Registry when the case is commenced/transferred. A copy of a blank case management information sheet is attached as **Appendix A**. It is important that all parts of the form are completed, particularly those sections (eg. concerned with estimated costs) that enable the judge to give directions in accordance with the overriding objective.

5.3.2 The Registry will also send out a blank standard directions form to each party. A copy is attached at **Appendix B**. This provides an example of the usual directions made on the first CMC. The parties may either fill it in, indicating the directions and timetable sought, or, preferably, provide draft directions in a similar format. The parties should return both the questionnaire and the proposed directions to the court, so that the areas (if any) of potential debate at the CMC can be identified. The parties are encouraged to exchange proposals for directions and the timetable sought, with a view to agreeing the same before the CMC for consideration by the court. The parties should note that CPR 31.5 requires the parties no less than 14 days before the first CMC to file and serve a disclosure report and no less than 7 days before to discuss and seek to agree proposals for disclosure and file costs budgets. Failure to do the last may result in a party's recoverable costs being limited to the court fee.

5.3.3 If the case is large or complex, it is helpful for the advocates to prepare a Note to be provided to the judge the day before the CMC which can address the issues in the case, the suggested directions, and the principal areas of dispute between the parties. If such a Note is provided, it is unnecessary for the claimant also to prepare a Case Summary as well.

5.3.4 In smaller cases, a Case Summary for the CMC, explaining briefly the likely issues, can be helpful. Such Case Summaries should be non–contentious and should (if this is possible without incurring disproportionate cost) be agreed /between the parties in advance of the hearing.

5.4 Checklist of Matters likely to be considered at the first CMC

5.4.1 The following checklist identifies the matters which the judge is likely to want to consider at the first CMC, although it is not exhaustive:

- The need for, and content of, any further statements of case to be served. This is dealt with in Section 5.5 below.
- The outcome of the Protocol process, and the possible further need for ADR. ADR is dealt with in Section 7 below.
- The desirability of dealing with particular disputes by way of a Preliminary Issue hearing. This is dealt with in Section 8 below.
- The court may require a list of issues to be provided and updated during the course of the procedural steps, but this is often left to the pre–trial review.
- Whether the trial should be in stages (eg. stage 1 liability and causation, stage 2 quantum). In very heavy cases this may be necessary in order to make the trial manageable. In more modest cases, where the quantum evidence will be extensive, a staged trial may be in the interest of all parties.
- The appropriate orders in respect of the disclosure of documents and for a protocol to manage e–disclosure. This is dealt with in Section 11 below.
- The appropriate orders as to the exchange of written witness statements. This is dealt with in Section 12 below. It should be noted that, although it is normal for evidence–in–chief to be given by way of the written statements in the TCC, the judge may direct that evidence about particular disputes (such as what was said at an important meeting) should be given orally without reference to such statements.
- Whether it is appropriate for the parties to rely on expert evidence and, if so, what disciplines of experts should give evidence, on what issues, and whether any issues can be conveniently dealt with by single joint experts. This may be coupled with an order relating to the carrying out of inspections, the obtaining of samples, the conducting of experiments, or the performance of calculations. Considerations relating to expert evidence are dealt with in Section 13 below. The parties must be aware that, in accordance with the overriding objective, the judge will only give the parties permission to rely on expert evidence if it is both necessary and appropriate, and, even then, will wish to ensure that the scope of any such evidence is limited as far as possible.
- Review of the parties' costs budgets and the making of a Costs Management Order (subject to any financial threshold relevant to the case). In certain cases there is the possibility of making a costs capping order. See Section 16.3 below.
- Whether there will be any additional claims under Part 20. See Section 5.5.4 below.
- The appropriate timetable for the taking of the various interim steps noted above, and the fixing of dates for both the PTR and the trial itself (subject to Paragraph 5.4.2 below). The parties will therefore need to provide the

judge with an estimate for the length of the trial, assuming all issues remain in dispute. Unless there is good reason not to, the trial date will generally be fixed at the first CMC (although this may be more difficult at court centres with only one TCC judge). Therefore, to the extent that there are any relevant concerns as to availability of either witnesses or legal representatives, they need to be brought to the attention of the court on that occasion. The length of time fixed for the trial will depend on the parties' estimates, and also the judge's own view. If the parties' estimate of trial length subsequently changes, they should inform the clerk of the assigned judge immediately.

5.4.2 The fixing of the trial date at the CMC is usually as a provisional fixture. Therefore no trial fee is payable at this stage. The court should at the same time specify a date upon which the fixture will cease to be "provisional" and, therefore, the trial fee will become payable. This should ordinarily be two months before the trial date. It should be noted that:
- if the trial fee is not paid within 14 days of the due date, then the whole claim will be struck out: see CPR 3.7 (1) (a) and (4);
- if the court is notified at least 14 days before the trial date that the case is settled or discontinued, then the trial fee, which has been paid, shall be refunded: see **fee 2.2 in** Schedule 1 to the Civil Proceedings Fees Order 2004.

For all purposes other than payment of the trial fee, the provisional date fixed at the CMC shall be regarded as a firm date.

5.4.3 Essentially, the judge's aim at the first CMC is to set down a detailed timetable which, in the majority of cases, will ensure that the parties need not return to court until the PTR.

5.5 Further statements of case

5.5.1 Defence. If no defence has been served prior to the first CMC, then (except in cases where judgment in default is appropriate) the court will usually make an order for service of the defence within a specified period. The defendant must plead its positive case. Bare denials and non–admissions are, save in exceptional circumstances, unacceptable.

5.5.2 Further Information. If the defendant wants to request further information of the Particulars of Claim, the request should, if possible, be formulated prior to the first CMC, so that it can be considered on that occasion. All requests for further information should be kept within reasonable limits, and concentrate on the important parts of the case.

5.5.3 Reply. A reply to the defence is not always necessary. However, where the defendant has raised a positive defence on a particular issue, it may be appropriate for the claimant to set out in a reply how it answers such a defence. If the defendant makes a counterclaim, the claimant's defence to counterclaim and its reply (if any) should be in the same document.

5.5.4 Additional or Part 20 Claims. The defendant should, at the first CMC, indicate (so far as possible) any additional (Part 20) claims that it is proposing to make, whether against the claimant or any other party. Additional (Part 20) claims are required to be pleaded in the same detail as the original claim. They are a very common feature of TCC cases, because the widespread use of sub–contractors in the UK construction industry often makes it necessary to pass claims down a contractual chain. Defendants are encouraged to start any necessary Part 20 proceedings to join additional parties as soon as possible. It is undesirable for applications to join additional defendants to be made late in the proceedings.

5.5.5 Costs. If at any stage the judge considers that the way in which the case has been pleaded, particularly through the inclusion of extensive irrelevant material or obscurity, is likely to lead or has led to inefficiency in the conduct of the proceedings or to unnecessary time or costs being spent, the judge may order that the party should re–plead the whole or part of the case and may make a costs order disallowing costs or ordering costs to be paid, either on the basis of a summary assessment or by giving a direction to the costs judge as to what costs should be disallowed or paid on a detailed assessment: see also Paragraph 5.1.6 above and Paragraph 12.1.4 below.

5.6 Scott Schedules

5.6.1 It can sometimes be appropriate for elements of the claim, or any additional (Part 20) claim, to be set out by way of a Scott Schedule (ie. by a table, often in landscape format, in which the Claimant's case on liability and quantum is set out item by item in the first few columns and the Defendant's response is set out in the adjacent columns). For example, claims involving a final account or numerous alleged defects or items of disrepair, may be best formulated in this way, which then allows for a detailed response from the defendant. Sometimes, even where all the damage has been caused by one event, such as a fire, it can be helpful for the individual items of loss and damage to be set out in a Scott Schedule. The secret of an effective Scott Schedule lies in the information that is to be provided and its brevity: excessive repetition is to be avoided. This is defined by the column headings. The judge may give directions for the relevant column headings for any Schedule ordered by the court. It is important that the defendant's responses to any such Schedule are as detailed as possible. Each party's entries on a Scott Schedule should be supported by a statement of truth.

5.6.2 Nevertheless, before any order is made or agreement is reached for the preparation of a Scott Schedule, both the parties and the court should consider whether this course (a) will genuinely lead to a saving of cost and time or (b) will lead to a wastage of costs and effort (because the Scott Schedule will simply be duplicating earlier schedules, pleadings or expert reports). A Scott Schedule should only be ordered by the court, or agreed by the parties, in those cases where it is appropriate and proportionate.

5.6.3 When a Scott Schedule is ordered by the court or agreed by the parties, the format must always be specified. The parties must co–operate in the physical task of preparation. Electronic transfer between the parties of their respective entries in the columns will enable a clear and user–friendly Scott Schedule to be prepared, for the benefit of all involved in the trial.

5.7 Agreement Between the Parties

5.7.1 Many, perhaps most, of the required directions at the first CMC may be agreed by the parties. If so, the judge will endeavour to make orders in the terms which have been agreed pursuant to CPR 29.4, unless he considers that the agreed terms fail to take into account important features of the case as a whole, or the principles of the CPR. The agreed terms will always, at the very least, form the starting–point of the judge's consideration of the orders to be made at the CMC. If the agreed terms are submitted to the judge 3 days in advance of the hearing date, it may be possible to avoid the need for a hearing altogether, although it is normally necessary for the Court to consider the case with the parties (either at an oral hearing or by way of a telephone conference) in any event.

5.7.2 The approach outlined in Paragraph 5.7.1 above is equally applicable to all other occasions when the parties come before the court with a draft order that is wholly or partly agreed.

5.8 Drawing Up of Orders

5.8.1 Unless the court itself draws up the order, it may direct one party (usually the claimant or applicant) to do so within a specified time. If no such direction is given, then the advocate appearing for the Claimant (or applicant) must prepare and seek to agree a draft order and submit it for the judge's approval within 7 days of the conclusion of the hearing. This is to ensure that the draft is presented to the court whilst the case is still fresh in the judge's mind and he can satisfy himself that the draft is accurate to carry his order into effect. The party charged with drawing up the order must draw up the order and lodge it with the court for approval. Once approved, the order will be stamped by the court and returned to that party for service upon all other parties. The order should refer to the date on which the order was made by stating "Date order made: [date]". Orders should be referred to by this date, rather than later dates which reflect the process of submission of the draft order, approval by the judge and sealing by the court.

5.8.2 In exceptional cases where the parties cannot agree a minute of order (whether within the specified time or at all), then the party with carriage of the order should submit the order, so far as it has been agreed, to the judge together with a summary of those elements of those parts of the order which are not agreed, and setting out any rival wording proposed by the other side, within the specified time. That communication must be in an agreed form as far as possible stating neutrally the other parties' objections, and it must be copied to the other parties when it is submitted to the court. The court heavily discourages extended satellite correspondence over the precise form of order. If, exceptionally, the judge wishes to hear further submissions on the draft form of order before he approves it he will ask for those submissions. Unilateral further submissions to the court as to the minute of order are only to be made in exceptional circumstances (eg. where a party considers that there is a real risk that the court is being misled or its position is being seriously misrepresented). Parties who unreasonably refuse to agree a minute of order, or who take up court time arguing over the precise form of minute can expect to have costs orders made against them.

5.8.3 It is often the case that the parties, after the hearing, decide that it is sensible to include other directions in the draft order by consent, or to vary the timetable to accommodate such matters. Any such agreement must be clearly indicated in both the draft order (eg. by adding in the matters under a separate heading stating that such matters are being made "By Consent") and in an explanatory note for the judge submitted with the proposed order.

5.9 Further CMC

5.9.1 In an appropriate case, the judge will fix a review CMC, to take place part way through the timetable that has been set down, in order to allow the court to review progress, and to allow the parties to raise any matters arising out of the steps that have been taken up to that point. However, this will not be ordered automatically and will be confined to cases of significant complexity.

5.9.2 Each party will be required to give notice in writing to the other parties and the court of any directions which it will be seeking at the review CMC, two days in advance of the hearing.

5.10 The Permanent Case Management Bundle

5.10.1 In conjunction with the judge's clerk, the claimant's solicitor is responsible for ensuring that, for the first CMC and at all times thereafter, there is a permanent bundle of copy documents available to the judge, which contains:

- any relevant documents resulting from the Pre–Action Protocol;
- the claim form and all statements of case;
- all orders;
- all completed case management information sheets;
- all costs budgets;
- any proposed protocol for e–disclosure (if agreed);
- Disclosure Reports/Statements as required by CPR 31.5.3;
- Any case summaries (see Sections 5.3.3 and 5.3.4 above).

5.10.2 The permanent case management bundle can then be supplemented by the specific documents relevant to any particular application that may be made. Whether these supplementary documents should (a) become a permanent addition to the case management bundle or (b) be set on one side, will depend upon their nature. The permanent case management bundle may remain at court and be marked up by the judge; alternatively, the judge may direct that the permanent case management bundle be maintained at the offices of the claimant's solicitors and provided to the court when required.

SECTION 6

APPLICATIONS AFTER THE FIRST CMC

6.1 Relevant parts of the CPR

2C–41 6.1.1 The basic rules relating to all applications that any party may wish to make are set out inCPR Part 23 and its accompanying Practice Directions.

6.1.2 Part 7 of the Practice Direction accompanying CPR Part 60 is also of particular relevance.

6.2 Application Notice

6.2.1 As a general rule, any party to proceedings in the TCC wishing to make an application of any sort must file an application notice (CPR 23.3) and serve that application notice on all relevant parties as soon as practicable after it has been filed (CPR 23.4). Application notices should be served by the parties, unless (as happens in some court centres outside London) service is undertaken by the court. Where the circumstances may justify an application being made without notice, see Section 6.10 below.

6.2.2 The application notice must set out in clear terms what order is sought and, more briefly, the reasons for seeking that order: seeCPR 23.6.

6.2.3 The application notice must be served at least **3 days** before the hearing at which the Court deals with the application: CPR 23.7 (1). Such a short notice period is only appropriate for the most straight–forward type of application.

6.2.4 Most applications, in particular applications for summary judgment under CPR Part 24 or to strike out a statement of case underCPR 3.4, will necessitate a much longer notice period than **3 days**. In such cases, it is imperative that the applicant obtain a suitable date and time for the hearing of the application from the assigned judge's clerk before the application notice is issued. The applicant must then serve his application notice and evidence in support sufficiently far ahead of the date fixed for the hearing of the application for there to be time to enable the respondent to serve evidence in response. Save in exceptional circumstances, there should be a minimum period of **10 working days** between the service of the notice (and supporting evidence) and the hearing date. If any party considers that there is insufficient time before the hearing of the application or if the time estimate for the application itself is too short, that party must notify the Judge's clerk and the hearing may then be refixed by agreement.

6.2.5 When considering the application notice, the judge may give directions in writing as to the dates for the provision or exchange of evidence and any written submissions or skeleton arguments for the hearing.

6.2.6 In cases of great urgency applications may be made without formal notice to the other party, but that party should (save in exceptional cases) be informed of the hearing sufficiently in advance to enable him to instruct a representative to attend.

6.3 Evidence in Support

6.3.1 The application notice when it is served must be accompanied by all evidence in support: CPR 23.7 (2).

6.3.2 Unless the CPR expressly requires otherwise, evidence will be given by way of witness statements. Such statements must be verified by a statement of truth signed by the maker of the statement: CPR 22.1.

6.4 Evidence in opposition and Evidence in reply

6.4.1 Likewise, any evidence in opposition to the application should, unless the rules expressly provide otherwise, be given by way of witness statement verified by a statement of truth.

6.4.2 It is important to ensure that the evidence in opposition to the application is served in good time before the hearing so as to enable:
- the court to read and note up the evidence;
- the applicant to put in any further evidence in reply that may be considered necessary.

Such evidence should be served at least **5 working days** before the hearing.

6.4.3 Any evidence in reply should be served not less than **3 working days** before the hearing. Again, if there are disputes as to the time taken or to be taken for the preparation of evidence prior to a hearing, or any other matters in respect of a suitable timetable for that hearing, the court will consider the written positions of both parties and decide such disputes on paper. It will not normally be necessary for either a separate application to be issued or a hearing to be held for such a purpose.

6.4.4 If the hearing of an application has to be adjourned because of delays by one or other of the parties in serving evidence, the court is likely to order that party to pay the costs straight away, and to make a summary assessment of those costs.

6.5 Application Bundle

6.5.1 The bundle for the hearing of anything other than the most simple and straightforward application should consist of:
- the permanent case management bundle (see Section 5.8 above);
- the witness statements provided in support of the application, together with any exhibits;
- the witness statements provided in opposition to the application together with exhibits;
- any witness statements in reply, together with exhibits.

6.5.2 The permanent case management bundle will either be with the court or with the claimant's solicitors, depending on the order made at the first CMC: see Paragraph 5.9 above. If it is with the claimant's solicitors, it should be provided to the court not less than **2 working days** before the hearing. In any event, a paginated bundle (see Paragraph 6.5.4 below) containing any material specific to the application should also be provided to the court not less than **2 working days** before the hearing, unless otherwise directed by the judge. A failure to comply with this deadline may result in the adjournment of the hearing, and the costs thrown away being paid by the defaulting party.

6.5.3 In all but the simplest applications, the court will expect the parties to provide skeleton arguments and copies of any authorities to be relied on. The form and content of the skeleton argument is principally a matter for the author, although the judge will expect it to identify the issues that arise on the application, the important parts of the evidence relied on, and the applicable legal principles. For detailed guidance as to the form, content and length of skeleton arguments, please see Paragraph 7.11.12 of the Queen's Bench Guide; Appendix 3 of the Chancery Guide; and Appendix 9 of the Commercial Court Guide.

6.5.4 For an application that is estimated to last 1/2 day or less, the skeleton should be provided no later than **1 pm on the last working day before the hearing**. It should be accompanied by photocopies of the authorities relied on (preferably in the form of a common agreed bundle). An electronic copy of each skeleton argument (in Microsoft Word compatible format) should be sent to the clerk of the judge hearing the application: if a party is reluctant for other parties to be provided with its skeleton argument in Word, it may serve it in pdf (or other readable) form provided that it certifies that the version sent to the judge is identical in content to that served on the other party(ies).

6.5.5 For an application that is estimated to last more than 1/2 day, the skeleton should be provided no later than **4 pm one clear working day before the hearing**. It should be accompanied by photocopies of the authorities relied on (again, preferably in the form of a common agreed bundle).

6.5.6 The time limits at **Paragraphs 6.5.4** and **6.5.5** above will be regarded as the latest times by which such skeletons should be provided to the court. Save in exceptional circumstances, no extension to these periods will be permitted.

6.5.7 <u>Pagination.</u> It is generally necessary for there to be a paginated bundle for the hearing. Where the parties have produced skeleton arguments, these should be cross–referred to the bundle page numbers. Where possible bundles should be paginated right through, but this may be dispensed with where a document within a discrete section of the bundle has its own internal pagination.

6.6 Hearings

6.6.1 Arbitration applications may be heard in private: see CPR 62.10. All other applications will be heard in public in accordance with CPR 39.2, save where otherwise ordered.

6.6.2 Provided that the application bundle and the skeletons have been lodged in accordance with the time limits set out above, the parties can assume that the court will have a good understanding of the points in issue. However, the court will expect to be taken to particular documents relied on by the parties and will also expect to be addressed on any important legal principles that arise.

6.6.3 It is important that the parties ensure that every application is dealt with in the estimated time period. Since many applications are dealt with on Fridays, it causes major disruption if application hearings are not disposed of within the estimated period. If the parties take too long in making their submissions, the application may be adjourned, part heard, and the Court may impose appropriate costs sanctions.

6.6.4 At the conclusion of the hearing, unless the court itself draws up the order, it will direct the applicant to do so within a specified period.

6.7 Paper Applications

6.7.1 As noted in Section 4 above some applications may be suitable for determination on paper under the procedure set out in Paragraph 4.4 above.

6.7.2 In addition, certain simple applications (particularly in lower value cases) arising out of the management of the proceedings may be capable of being dealt with by correspondence without the need for any formal application or order of the court. This is particularly true of applications to vary procedural orders, which variations are wholly or largely agreed, or proposals to vary the estimated length of the trial. In such cases, the applicant should write to the other parties indicating the nature of its application and to seek their agreement to it. If, however, it emerges that there is an issue to be resolved by the court, then a formal application must be issued and dealt with as a paper application or, possibly, at an oral hearing.

6.7.3 It is essential that any communication by a party to the judge or the court is copied to all other parties, subject to Section 6.10 below (applications without notice).

6.8 Consent Orders

6.8.1 Consent Orders may be submitted to the Court in draft for approval without the need for attendance.

6.8.2 Two copies of the draft order should be lodged, at least one of which should be signed. The copies should be undated as the Court will set out the date the order is made: see **Paragraph 5.8.1** above.

6.8.3 As noted elsewhere, whilst the parties can agree between themselves the orders to be made either at the Case Management Conference or the Pre–Trial Review, it is normally necessary for the Court to consider the case with the parties (either at an oral hearing or by way of a telephone conference) on those occasions in any event.

6.8.4 Generally, when giving directions, the court will endeavour to identify the date by which the relevant step must be taken, and will not simply provide a period during which that task should be performed. The parties should therefore ensure that any proposed consent order also identifies particular dates, rather than periods, by which the relevant steps must be taken.

6.9 Costs

6.9.1 Costs are dealt with generally at Section 16 below.

6.9.2 The costs of any application which took a day or less to be heard and disposed of will be dealt with summarily, unless there is a good reason for the court not to exercise its powers as to the summary assessment of costs.

6.9.3 Accordingly, it is necessary for parties to provide to the court and to one another their draft statements of costs no later than **24 hours** before the start of the application hearing. Any costs which are incurred after these draft statements have been prepared, but which have not been allowed for (e.g. because the hearing has exceeded its anticipated length), can be mentioned at the hearing.

6.10 Applications without notice

6.10.1 All applications should be made on notice, even if that notice has to be short, unless:
- any rule or Practice Direction provides that the application may be made without notice; or
- there are good reasons for making the application without notice, for example, because notice would might defeat the object of the application.

6.10.2 Where an application without notice does not involve giving undertakings to the court, it will normally be made and dealt with on paper, as, for example, applications for permission to serve the claim form out of the jurisdiction, and applications for an extension of time in which to serve a claim form.

6.10.3 Any application for an interim injunction or similar remedy will require an oral hearing.

6.10.4 A party wishing to make an application without notice which requires an oral hearing before a judge should contact the TCC Registry at the earliest opportunity.

6.10.5 If a party wishes to make an application without notice at a time when no TCC judge is available, he should apply to the Queen's Bench Judge Chambers.

6.10.6 On all applications without notice it is the duty of the applicant and those representing him:
- to make full and frank disclosure of all matters relevant to the application;
- to ensure that a note of the hearing of the without notice application, the evidence and skeleton argument in support and any order made all be served with the order or as soon as possible thereafter.

6.10.7 The papers lodged the application should include two copies of a draft of the order sought. Save in exceptional circumstances where time is not met, all the evidence relied upon in support of the application and any other relevant documents must be lodged in advance with the TCC Registry. If the application is urgent, the Registry should be informed of the fact and of the reasons for the urgency. Counsel's estimate of reading time likely to be required by the court should also be provided.

SECTION 7

ADR

7.1 General

2C-42 7.1.1 The court will provide encouragement to the parties to use alternative dispute resolution ("ADR") and will, whenever appropriate, facilitate the use of such a procedure. In this Guide, ADR is taken to mean any process through which the parties attempt to resolve their dispute, which is voluntary. In most cases, ADR takes the form of inter–party negotiations or a mediation conducted by a neutral mediator. Alternative forms of ADR include early neutral evaluation either by a judge or some other neutral person who receives a concise presentation from each party and then provides his or her own evaluation of the case. The parties are advised to refer to the ADR Handbook.

7.1.2 Although the TCC is an appropriate forum for the resolution of all IT and construction/engineering disputes, the use of ADR can lead to a significant saving of costs and may result in a settlement which is satisfactory to all parties.d

7.1.3 Legal representatives in all TCC cases should ensure that their clients are fully aware of the benefits of ADR and that the use of ADR has been carefully considered prior to the first CMC.

7.2 Timing

7.2.1 ADR may be appropriate before the proceedings have begun or at any subsequent stage. However the later ADR takes place, the more the costs which will have been incurred, often unnecessarily. The timing of ADR needs careful consideration.

7.2.2 The TCC Pre–Action Protocol (Section 2 above) itself provides for a type of ADR, because it requires there to be at least one face–to–face meeting between the parties before the commencement of proceedings. At this meeting, there should be sufficient time to discuss and resolve the dispute. As a result of this procedure having taken place, the court will not necessarily grant a stay of proceedings upon demand and it will always need to be satisfied that an adjournment is actually necessary to enable ADR to take place.

7.2.3 However, at the first CMC, the court will want to be addressed on the parties' views as to the likely efficacy of ADR, the appropriate timing of ADR, and the advantages and disadvantages of a short stay of proceedings to allow ADR to take place. Having considered the representations of the parties, the court may order a short stay to facilitate ADR at that stage. Alternatively, the court may simply encourage the parties to seek ADR and allow for it to occur within the timetable for the resolution of the proceedings set down by the court.

7.2.4 At any stage after the first CMC and prior to the commencement of the trial, the court, will, either on its own initiative or if requested to do so by one or both of the parties, consider afresh the likely efficacy of ADR and whether or not a short stay of the proceedings should be granted, in order to facilitate ADR.

7.3 Procedure

7.3.1 In an appropriate case, the court may indicate the type of ADR that it considers suitable, but the decision in this regard must be made by the parties. In most cases, the appropriate ADR procedure will be mediation.

7.3.2 If at any stage in the proceedings the court considers it appropriate, an ADR order in the terms of **Appendix E** may be made. If such an order is made at the first CMC, the court may go on to give directions for the conduct of the action up to trial (in the event that the ADR fails). Such directions may include provision for a review CMC.

7.3.3 The court will not ordinarily recommend any individual or body to act as mediator or to perform any other ADR procedure. In the event that the parties fail to agree the identity of a mediator or other neutral person pursuant to an order in the terms of **Appendix E**, the court may select such a person from the lists provided by the parties. To facilitate this process, the court would also need to be furnished with the CVs of each of the individuals on the lists.

7.3.4 Information as to the types of ADR procedures available and the individuals able to undertake such procedures is available from TeCSA, TECBAR, the Civil Mediation Council, and from some TCC court centres outside London.

7.4 Non–Cooperation

7.4.1 Generally. At the end of the trial, there may be costs arguments on the basis that one or more parties unreasonably refused to take part in ADR. The court will determine such issues having regard to all the circumstances of the particular case. In *Halsey v Milton Keynes General NHS Trust* [2004] EWCA Civ 576; [2004] 1 WLR 3002, the Court of Appeal identified six factors that may be relevant to any such consideration:

    (a) the nature of the dispute;

    (b) the merits of the case;

    (c) the extent to which other settlement methods have been attempted;

    (d) whether the costs of the ADR would be disproportionately high;

    (e) whether any delay in setting up and attending the ADR would have been prejudicial;

    (f) whether the ADR had a reasonable prospect of success.

This case is the subject of extensive discussion in Civil Procedure, Volume 2, at Section 14. See also *PGF II SA v OMFS Company 1 Ltd* [2013] EWCA Civ 1288, [2014] BLR 1, particularly in relation to silence in the face of a request to mediate.

7.4.2 If an ADR Order Has Been Made. The court will expect each party to co–operate fully with any ADR procedure which takes place following an order of the court. If any other party considers that there has not been proper co–operation in relation to arrangements for mediation or any other ADR Procedure, the complaint will be considered by the court and cost orders and/or other sanctions may be ordered against the defaulting party in consequence. However, nothing in this paragraph should be understood as modifying the rights of all parties to a mediation or any other ADR Procedure to keep confidential all that is said or done in the course of that ADR Procedure.

7.5 Early Neutral Evaluation

7.5.1 An early neutral evaluation ("ENE") may be carried out by any appropriately qualified person, whose opinion is likely to be respected by the parties. In an appropriate case, and with the consent of all parties, a TCC judge may provide an early neutral evaluation either in respect of the full case or of particular issues arising within it. Unless the parties otherwise agree the ENE will be produced in writing and will set out conclusions and brief reasons. Such an ENE will not, save with the agreement of the parties, be binding on the parties.

7.5.2 If the parties would like an ENE to be carried out by the court, then they can seek an appropriate order from the assigned judge either at the first CMC or at any time prior to the commencement of the trial.

7.5.3 The assigned judge may choose to do the ENE himself. In such instance, the judge will take no further part in the proceedings once he has produced the ENE, unless the parties expressly agree otherwise. Alternatively, the assigned judge will select another available TCC judge to undertake the ENE.

7.5.4 The judge undertaking the ENE will give appropriate directions for the preparation and conduct of the ENE. These directions will generally be agreed by the parties and may include:

- a stay of the substantive proceedings whilst the ENE is carried out.
- a direction that the ENE is to be carried out entirely on paper with dates for the exchange of submissions.
- a direction that particular documents or information should be provided by a party.
- a direction that there will be an oral hearing (either with or without evidence), with dates for all the necessary steps for submissions, witness statements and expert evidence leading to that hearing. If there is an oral hearing the ENE will generally not last more than one day.
- a statement that the parties agree or do not agree that the ENE procedure and the documents, submissions or evidence produced in relation to the ENE are to be without prejudice, or, alternatively, that the whole or part of those items are not without prejudice and can be referred to at any subsequent trial or hearing.
- a statement whether the parties agree that the judge's evaluation after the ENE process will be binding on the parties or binding in certain circumstances (e.g. if not disputed within a period) or temporarily binding subject to a final decision in arbitration, litigation or final agreement.

7.6 Court Settlement Process

7.6.1 The Court Settlement Process is a form of mediation carried out by TCC judges. Whilst mediation may be carried out by any appropriately qualified person, in an appropriate case, and with the consent of all parties, a TCC judge may act as a Settlement Judge pursuant to a Court Settlement Order in the terms set out in **Appendix G**. This has proved to be successful in many cases.

7.6.2 If the parties would like to consider the use of the Court Settlement Process or would like further information, they should contact the TCC Registry in London or the TCC Liaison District Judges in the court centres outside London.

7.6.3 Where, following a request from the parties, the assigned TCC judge considers that the parties might be able to achieve an amicable settlement and that a TCC judge is particularly able to assist in achieving that settlement, that judge or another TCC judge, with the agreement of the parties, will make a Court Settlement Order (**Appendix G**) embodying the parties' agreement and fixing a date for the Court Settlement Conference to take place with an estimated duration proportionate to the issues in the case.

7.6.4 The TCC judge appointed as the Settlement Judge will then conduct the Court Settlement Process in accordance with that Court Settlement Order in a similar manner to that of a mediator. If no settlement is achieved then the case would proceed but, if the assigned judge carried out the Court Settlement Process, then the case would be assigned to another TCC judge. In any event, the Settlement Judge would take no further part in the court proceedings.

SECTION 8

PRELIMINARY ISSUES

8.1 General

8.1.1 The hearing of Preliminary Issues ("PI"), at which the court considers and **2C–43** delivers a binding judgment on particular issues in advance of the main trial, can be an extremely cost–effective and efficient way of narrowing the issues between the parties and, in certain cases, of resolving disputes altogether.

8.1.2 Some cases listed in the TCC lend themselves particularly well to this procedure. A PI hearing can address particular points which may be decisive of the whole proceedings; even if that is not the position, it is often possible for a PI hearing to cut down significantly on the scope (and therefore the costs) of the main trial.

8.1.3 At the first CMC the court will expect to be addressed on whether or not there are matters which should be taken by way of Preliminary Issues in advance of the main trial. Subject to **Paragraph 8.5** below, it is not generally appropriate for the court to make an order for the trial of preliminary issues until after the defence has been served. After the first CMC, and at any time during the litigation, any party is at liberty to raise with any other party the possibility of a PI hearing and the court will consider any application for the hearing of such Preliminary Issues. In many cases, although not invariably, a PI order will be made with the support of all parties.

8.1.4 Whilst, for obvious reasons, it is not possible to set out hard and fast rules for what is and what is not suitable for a PI hearing, the criteria set out in Section 8.2 below should assist the parties in deciding whether or not some or all of the disputes between them will be suitable for a PI hearing.

8.1.5 Drawbacks of preliminary issues in inappropriate cases. If preliminary issues are ordered inappropriately, they can have adverse effect. Evidence may be duplicated. The same witnesses may give evidence before different judges, in the event that there is a switch of assigned judge. Findings may be made at the PI hearing, which are affected by evidence called at the main hearing. The prospect of a PI hearing may delay the commencement of ADR or settlement negotiations. Also two trials are more expensive than one. For all these reasons, any proposal for preliminary issues needs to be examined carefully, so that the benefits and drawbacks can be evaluated. Also the court should give due weight to the views of the parties when deciding whether a PI hearing would be beneficial.

8.1.6 Staged trials. The breaking down of a long trial into stages should be differentiated from the trial of preliminary issues. Sometimes it is sensible for liability (including causation) to be tried before quantum of damages. Occasionally the subject matter of the litigation is so extensive that for reasons of case management the trial needs to be broken down into separate stages.

8.2 Guidelines

8.2.1 The Significance of the Preliminary Issues. The court would expect that any issue proposed as a suitable PI would, if decided in a particular way, be capable of:

- resolving the whole proceedings or a significant element of the proceedings; or
- significantly reducing the scope, and therefore the costs, of the main trial; or
- significantly improving the possibility of a settlement of the whole proceedings.

8.2.2 <u>Oral Evidence</u>. The court would ordinarily expect that, if issues are to be dealt with by way of a PI hearing, there would be either no or relatively limited oral evidence. If extensive oral evidence was required on any proposed PI, then it may not be suitable for a PI hearing. Although it is difficult to give specific guidance on this point, it is generally considered that a PI hearing in a smaller case should not take more than about 2 days, and in a larger and more complex case, should not take more than about 4 days.

8.3 Common Types of Preliminary Issue

The following are commonly resolved by way of a PI hearing:

(a) Disputes as to whether or not there was a binding contract between the parties.

(b) Disputes as to what documents make up or are incorporated within the contract between the parties and disputes as to the contents or relevance of any conversations relied on as having contractual status or effect.

(c) Disputes as to the proper construction of the contract documents or the effect of an exclusion or similar clause.

(d) Disputes as to the correct application of a statute or binding authority to a situation where there is little or no factual dispute.

(e) Disputes as to the existence and/or scope of a statutory duty.

(f) Disputes as to the existence and/or scope of a duty of care at common law in circumstances where there is no or little dispute about the relevant facts.

8.4 Other Possible Preliminary Issues

The following can sometimes be resolved by way of a preliminary issue hearing, although a decision as to whether or not to have such a hearing will always depend on the facts of the individual case:

8.4.1 <u>A Limitation Defence</u>. It is often tempting to have limitation issues resolved in advance of the main trial. This can be a good idea because, if a complex claim is statute–barred, a decision to that effect will lead to a significant saving of costs. However, there is also a risk that extensive evidence relevant to the limitation defence (relating to matters such as when the damage occurred or whether or not there has been deliberate concealment) may also be relevant to the liability issues within the main trial. In such a case, a preliminary issue hearing may lead to a) extensive duplication of evidence and therefore costs and b) give rise to difficulty if the main trial is heard by a different judge.

8.4.2 <u>Causation and 'No Loss' Points</u>. Causation and 'No Loss' points may be suitable for a PI hearing, but again their suitability will diminish if it is necessary for the court to resolve numerous factual disputes as part of the proposed PI hearing. The most appropriate disputes of this type for a PI hearing are those where the defendant contends that, even accepting all the facts alleged by the claimant, the claim must fail by reason of causation or the absence of recoverable loss.

8.4.3 <u>'One–Off' Issues</u>. Issues which do not fall into any obvious category, like economic duress, or misrepresentation, may be suitable for resolution by way of a PI hearing, particularly if the whole case can be shown to turn on them.

8.5 Use of PI as an adjunct to ADR

8.5.1 Sometimes parties wish to resolve their dispute by ADR, but there is one major issue which is a sticking point in any negotiation or mediation. The parties may wish to obtain the court's final decision on that single issue, in the expectation that after that they can resolve their differences without further litigation.

8.5.2 In such a situation the parties may wish to bring proceedings under CPR Part 8, in order to obtain the court's decision on that issue. Such proceedings can be rapidly progressed. Alternatively, if the issue is not suitable for Part 8 proceedings, the parties may bring proceedings under Part 7 and then seek determination of the critical question as a preliminary issue. At the first CMC the position can be explained and the judge can be asked to order early trial of the proposed preliminary issue, possibly without the need for a defence or any further pleadings.

8.6 Precise Wording of PI

8.6.1 If a party wishes to seek a PI hearing, either at the first CMC or thereafter, that party must circulate a precise draft of the proposed preliminary issues to the other parties and to the court well in advance of the relevant hearing.

8.6.2 If the court orders a PI hearing, it is likely to make such an order only by reference to specific and formulated issues, in order to avoid later debate as to the precise scope of the issues that have been ordered. Of course, the parties are at liberty to propose amendments to the issues before the PI hearing itself, but if such later amendments are not agreed by all parties, they are unlikely to be ordered.

8.7 Appeals

8.7.1 When considering whether or not to order a PI hearing, the court will take into account the effect of any possible appeal against the PI judgment, and the concomitant delay caused.

8.7.2 At the time of ordering preliminary issues, both the parties and the court should specifically consider whether, in the event of an appeal against the PI judgment, it is desirable that the trial of the main action should (a) precede or (b) follow such appeal. It should be noted, however, that the first instance court has no power to control the timetable for an appeal. The question whether an appeal should be (a) expedited or (b) stayed is entirely a matter for the Court of Appeal. Nevertheless, the Court of Appeal will take notice of any "indication" given by the lower court in this regard.

SECTION 9

ADJUDICATION BUSINESS

9.1 Introduction

9.1.1 The TCC is ordinarily the court in which the enforcement of an adjudicator's **2C–44** decision and any other business connected with adjudication is undertaken. Adjudicators' decisions predominantly arise out of adjudications which are governed by the mandatory provisions of the Housing Grants, Construction and Regeneration Act 1996 (as amended by the Local Democracy, Economic Development and Construction Act 2009 for contracts entered into on or after 1 October 2011) relating to the carrying out of construction operations in England and Wales ("HGCRA"). These provisions apply automatically to any construction contract as defined in the legislation. Some Adjudicators' decisions arise out of standard form contracts which contain adjudication provisions, and others arise from *ad hoc* agreements to adjudicate. The TCC enforcement procedure is the same for all kinds of adjudication.

9.1.2 In addition to enforcement applications, declaratory relief is sometimes sought in the TCC at the outset of or during an adjudication in respect of matters such as the jurisdiction of the adjudicator or the validity of the adjudication. This kind of application is dealt with in Paragraph 9.4 below.

9.1.3 The HGCRA provides for a mandatory 28–day period within which the entire adjudication process must be completed, unless a) the referring party agrees to an additional 14 days, or b) both parties agree to a longer period. In consequence, the TCC has moulded a rapid procedure for enforcing an adjudication decision that has not been honoured. Other adjudication proceedings are ordinarily subject to similar rapidity.

9.2 Procedure in Enforcement Proceedings

9.2.1 Unlike arbitration business, there is neither a practice direction nor a claim form concerned with adjudication business. The enforcement proceedings normally seek a monetary judgment so that CPR Part 7 proceedings are usually appropriate. However, if the enforcement proceedings are known to raise a question which is unlikely to involve a substantial dispute of fact and no monetary judgment is sought, CPR Part 8 proceedings may be used instead.

9.2.2 The TCC has fashioned a procedure whereby enforcement applications are dealt with promptly. The details of this procedure are set out below.

9.2.3 The claim form should identify the construction contract, the jurisdiction of the adjudicator, the procedural rules under which the adjudication was conducted, the adjudicator's decision, the relief sought and the grounds for seeking that relief.

9.2.4 The claim form should be accompanied by an application notice that sets out the procedural directions that are sought. Commonly, the claimant's application will seek an abridgement of time for the various procedural steps, and summary judgment under CPR Part 24. The claim form and the application should be accompanied by a witness statement or statements setting out the evidence relied on in support of both the adjudication enforcement claim and the associated procedural application. This evidence should ordinarily include a copy of the Notice of Intention to Refer and the adjudicator's decision. Further pleadings in the adjudication may be required where questions of the adjudicator's jurisdiction are being raised.

9.2.5 The claim form, application notice and accompanying documents should be lodged in the appropriate registry or court centre clearly marked as being a "paper without notice adjudication enforcement claim and application for the urgent attention of a TCC judge". A TCC judge will ordinarily provide directions in connection with the procedural application within **3 working days** of the receipt of the application notice at the courts.

9.2.6 The procedural application is dealt with by a TCC judge on paper, without notice. The paper application and the consequent directions should deal with:

(a) the abridged period of time in which the defendant is to file an acknowledgement of service;

(b) the time for service by the defendant of any witness statement in opposition to the relief being sought;

(c) an early return date for the hearing of the summary judgment application and a note of the time required or allowed for that hearing; and

(d) identification of the judgment, order or other relief being sought at the hearing of the adjudication claim.

The order made at this stage will always give the defendant liberty to apply.

9.2.7 A direction providing that the claim form, supporting evidence and court order providing for the hearing are to be served on the defendant as soon as practicable, or sometimes by a particular date, will ordinarily also be given when the judge deals with the paper procedural application.

9.2.8 The directions will ordinarily provide for an enforcement hearing within about **28 days** of the directions being made and for the defendant to be given at least **14 days** from the date of service for the serving of any evidence in opposition to the adjudication application. In more straightforward cases, the abridged periods may be less.

9.2.9 Draft standard directions of the kind commonly made by the court on a procedural application by the claimant in an action to enforce the decision of an adjudicator are attached as **Appendix F**.

9.2.10 The claimant should, with the application, provide an estimate of the time needed for the hearing of the application. This estimate will be taken into account by the judge when fixing the date and length of the hearing. The parties should, if possible jointly, communicate any revised time estimate to the court promptly and the judge to whom the case has been allocated will consider whether to refix the hearing date or alter the time period that has been allocated for the hearing.

9.2.11 If the parties cannot agree on the date or time fixed for the hearing, a paper application must be made to the judge to whom the hearing has been allocated for directions.

9.2.12 Parties seeking to enforce adjudication decisions are reminded that they might be able to obtain judgment in default of service of an acknowledgment of service or, if the other party does not file any evidence in response, they might be able to obtain an expedited hearing of the Part 24 application. Generally, it is preferable for a party to enter default judgment rather than seek an expedited hearing, because that reduces the costs involved (the terms of the order usually mention this explicitly).

9.3 The Enforcement Hearing

9.3.1 Where there is any dispute to be resolved at the hearing, the judge should be provided with copies of the relevant sections of the HGCRA, the adjudication procedural rules under which the adjudication was conducted, the adjudicator's decision and copies of any adjudication provisions in the contract underlying the adjudication.

9.3.2 Subject to any more specific directions given by the court, the parties should lodge, **by 4.00 pm one clear working day before the hearing**, a bundle containing the documents that will be required at the hearing. The parties should also file and serve short skeleton arguments and copies of any authorities which are to be relied on (preferably as an agreed joint bundle), summarising their respective contentions as to why the adjudicator's decision is or is not enforceable or as to any other relief being sought. For a hearing that is expected to last half a day or less, the skeletons should be provided **no later than 1 pm on the last working day before the hearing.** For a hearing that is estimated to last more than half a day, the skeletons should be provided **no later than 4 pm one clear working day before the hearing**.

9.3.3 The parties should be ready to address the court on the limited grounds on which a defendant may resist an application seeking to enforce an adjudicator's decision or on which a court may provide any other relief to any party in relation to an adjudication or an adjudicator's decision.

9.4 Other Proceedings Arising Out Of Adjudication

9.4.1 As noted above, the TCC will also hear any applications for declaratory relief arising out of the commencement of a disputed adjudication. Commonly, these will concern:
- Disputes over the jurisdiction of an adjudicator. It can sometimes be appropriate to seek a declaration as to jurisdiction at the outset of an adjudication, rather than both parties incurring considerable costs in the adjudication itself, only for the jurisdiction point to emerge again at the enforcement hearing.
- Disputes over whether there is a construction contract within the meaning of the Act (and, in older contracts, whether there was a written contract between the parties).
- Disputes over the permissible scope of the adjudication, and, in particular, whether the matters which the claimant seeks to raise in the adjudication are the subject of a pre–existing dispute between the parties.

9.4.2 Any such application will be immediately assigned to a named judge. In such circumstances, given the probable urgency of the application, the judge will usually require the parties to attend a CMC **within 2 working days** of the assignment of the case to him, and he will then give the necessary directions to ensure the speedy resolution of the dispute.

9.4.3 It sometimes happens that one party to an adjudication commences enforcement proceedings, whilst the other commences proceedings under Part 8, in order to challenge the validity of the adjudicator's award. This duplication of effort is unnecessary and it involves the parties in extra costs, especially if the two actions are commenced at different court centres. Accordingly there should be sensible discussions between the parties or their lawyers, in order to agree the appropriate venue and also to agree who shall be claimant and who defendant. All the issues raised by each party can and should be raised in a single action. However, in cases where an adjudicator has made a clear error (but has acted within his jurisdiction), it may on occasions be appropriate to bring proceedings under Part 8 for a declaration as a pre–emptive response to an anticipated application to enforce the decision.

Section 10

Arbitration

10.1 Arbitration Claims in the TCC

2C–45 10.1.1 "Arbitration claims" are any application to the court under the Arbitration Act 1996 and any other claim concerned with an arbitration that is referred to in CPR 62.2(1). Common examples of arbitration claims are challenges to an award on grounds of jurisdiction under Section 67, challenges to an award for serious irregularity under Section 68 or appeals on points of law under Section 69 of the Arbitration Act 1996. Arbitration claims may be started in the TCC, as is provided for in **Paragraph 2.3 of the Practice Direction – Arbitration** which supplements CPR Part 62.

10.1.2 In practice, arbitration claims arising out of or connected with a construction or engineering arbitration (or any other arbitration where the subject matter involved one or more of the categories of work set out in **Paragraph 1.3.1 above**) should be started in the TCC. The only arbitration claims that must be started in the Commercial Court are those (increasingly rare) claims to which the old law (i.e. the pre–1996 Act provisions) apply: see CPR 62.12.

10.1.3 The TCC follows the practice and procedure for arbitration claims established by CPR Part 62 and (broadly) the practice of the Commercial Court as summarised bySection O of the **Admiralty and Commercial Court Guide**. In the absence of any specific directions given by the court, the automatic directions set out in Section 6 of the **Practice Direction supplementing** CPR Part 62 govern the procedures to be followed in any arbitration claim from the date of service up to the substantive hearing.

10.2 Leave to appeal

10.2.1 Where a party is seeking to appeal a question of law arising out of an award pursuant to Section 69 of the Arbitration Act 1996 and the parties have not in their underlying contract agreed that such an appeal may be brought, the party seeking to appeal must apply for leave to appeal pursuant to Sections 69(2), 69(3) and 69(4) of that Act. That application must be included in the arbitration claim form as explained in **Paragraph 12 of the Practice Direction**.

10.2.2 In conformity with the practice of the Commercial Court, the TCC will normally consider any application for permission to appeal on paper after the defendant has had an appropriate opportunity to answer in writing the application being raised.

10.2.3 The claimant must include within the claim form an application for permission to appeal. No separate application notice is required.

10.2.4 The claim form and supporting documents must be served on the defendant. The judge will not consider the merits of the application for permission to appeal until (a) a certificate of service has been filed at the appropriate TCC registry or court centre and (b), subject to any order for specific directions, a further **28 days** have elapsed, so as to enable the defendant to file written evidence in opposition. Save in exceptional circumstances, the only material admissible on an application for permission to appeal is (a) the award itself and any documents annexed to or necessary to understand the award and (b) evidence relevant to the issue whether any identified question of law is of general public importance: see the requirements of **Paragraph 12 of the Practice Direction**.

10.2.5 If necessary, the judge dealing with the application will direct an oral hearing with a date for the hearing. That hearing will, ordinarily, consist of brief submissions by each party. The judge dealing with the application will announce his decision in writing or, if a hearing has been directed, at the conclusion of the hearing with brief reasons if the application is refused.

10.2.6 Where the permission has been allowed in part and refused in part:

(a) Only those questions for which permission has been granted may be raised at the hearing of the appeal.

(b) Brief reasons will be given for refusing permission in respect of the other questions.

10.2.7 If the application is granted, the judge will fix the date for the appeal, and direct whether the same judge or a different judge shall hear the appeal.

10.3 Appeals where leave to appeal is not required

10.3.1 Parties to a construction contract should check whether they have agreed in the underlying contract that an appeal may be brought without leave, since some construction and engineering standard forms of contract so provide. If that is the case, the appeal may be set down for a substantive hearing without leave being sought. The arbitration claim form should set out the clause or provision which it is contended provides for such agreement and the claim form should be marked "Arbitration Appeal – Leave not required"

10.3.2 Where leave is not required, the claimant should identify each question of law that it is contended arises out of the award and which it seeks to raise in an appeal under Section 69. If the defendant does not accept that the questions thus identified are questions of law or maintains that they do not arise out of the award or that the appeal on those questions may not be brought for any other reason, then the defendant should notify the claimant and the court of its contentions and apply for a directions hearing before the judge nominated to hear the appeal on a date prior to the date fixed for the hearing of the appeal. Unless the judge hearing the appeal otherwise directs, the appeal will be confined to the questions of law identified in the arbitration claim form.

10.3.3 In an appropriate case, the judge may direct that the question of law to be raised and decided on the appeal should be reworded, so as to identify more accurately the real legal issue between the parties.

10.4 The hearing of the appeal

10.4.1 Parties should ensure that the court is provided only with material that is relevant and admissible to the point of law. This will usually be limited to the award and any documents annexed to the award: see *Hok Sport Ltd v Aintree Racecourse Ltd* [2003] BLR 155 at 160. However, the court should also receive any document referred to in the award, which the court needs to read in order to determine a question of law arising out of the award: see *Kershaw Mechanical Services Ltd v Kendrick Construction Ltd* [2006] EWHC (TCC).

10.4.2 On receiving notice of permission being granted, or on issuing an arbitration claim form in a case where leave to appeal is not required, the parties should notify the court of their joint estimate or differing estimates of the time needed for the hearing of the appeal.

10.4.3 The hearing of the appeal is to be in open court unless an application (with notice) has previously been made that the hearing should be wholly or in part held in private and the court has directed that this course should be followed.

10.5 Section 68 applications—Serious Irregularity

10.5.1 In some arbitration claims arising out of construction and engineering arbitrations, a party will seek to appeal a question of law and, at the same time, seek to challenge the award under Section 68 of the Arbitration Act 1996 on the grounds of serious irregularity. This raises questions of procedure, since material may be admissible in a Section 68 application which is inadmissible on an application or appeal under Section 69. Similarly, it may not be appropriate for all applications to be heard together. A decision is needed as to the order in which the applications should be heard, whether there should be one or more separate hearings to deal with them and whether or not the same judge should deal with all applications. Where a party intends to raise applications under both sections of the Arbitration Act 1996, they should be issued in the same arbitration claim form or in separate claim forms issued together. The court should be informed that separate applications are intended and asked for directions as to how to proceed.

10.5.2 The court will give directions as to how the Section 68 and Section 69 applications will be dealt with before hearing or determining any application. These directions will normally be given in writing but, where necessary or if such is applied for by a party, the court will hold a directions hearing at which directions will be given. The directions will be given following the service of any documentation by the defendant in answer to all applications raised by the claimant.

10.6 Successive awards and successive applications

10.6.1 Some construction and engineering arbitrations give rise to two or more separate awards issued at different times. Where arbitration applications arise under more than one of these awards, any second or subsequent application, whether arising from the same or a different award, should be referred to the same judge who has heard previous applications. Where more than one judge has heard previous applications, the court should be asked to direct to which judge any subsequent application is to be referred.

10.7 Other applications and Enforcement

10.7.1 All other arbitration claims, and any other matter arising in an appeal or an application concerning alleged serious irregularity, will be dealt with by the TCC in the same manner as is provided for in CPR Part 62, **Practice Direction – Arbitration** and Section O **of The Admiralty and Commercial Courts Guide**.

10.7.2 All applications for permission to enforce arbitration awards are governed by Section III of Part 62 (Rules 62.17– 62.19).

10.7.3 An application for permission to enforce an award in the same manner as a judgment or order of the court may be made in an arbitration claim form without notice and must be supported by written evidence in accordance withCPR 62.18(6). Two copies of the draft order must accompany the application, and the form of the order sought must correspond to the terms of the award.

10.7.4 An order made without notice giving permission to enforce the award:
- must give the defendant 14 days after service of the order (or longer, if the order is to be served outside the jurisdiction) to apply to set it aside;
- must state that it may not be enforced until after the expiry of the 14 days (or any longer period specified) or until any application to set aside the order has been finally disposed of: CPR 62.18(9) and (10).

10.7.5 On considering an application to enforce without notice, the judge may direct that, instead, the arbitration claim form must be served on specified parties, with the result that the application will then continue as an arbitration claim in accordance with the procedure set out in Section I of Part 62: seeCPR 62.18(1)–(3).

SECTION 11

DISCLOSURE

11.1 General

2C–46   11.1.1 CPR 31.5 now provides a menu of different disclosure options, of which standard disclosure is but one.

11.1.2 What order is for disclosure is appropriate will normally be considered and made at the first case management conference. This is governed by CPR Part 31 and the Practice Direction supplementing it. This provides for various alternatives: (a) no disclosure (b) an order that a party discloses the documents on which it relies and at the same time requests any specific disclosure that it requires from the other parties (c) disclosure on an issue by issue basis (d) an order that each party discloses documents that it is reasonable to suppose will support its own case or damage that of another party (e) standard disclosure or any other form of disclosure..

In relation to electronic disclosure, see the provisions requiring the exchange of Electronic Documents Questionnaires (CPR 31.22 and PD13B).

11.2 Limiting disclosure and the cost of disclosure

11.2.1 In many cases being conducted in the TCC, standard disclosure will not be appropriate. This may for any one or more of the following reasons:

- The amount of documentation may be considerable, given the complexity of the dispute and the underlying contract or contracts, and the process of giving standard disclosure may consequently be disproportionate to the issues and sums in dispute.
- The parties may have many of the documents in common from their previous dealings so that disclosure is not necessary or desirable.
- The parties may have provided informal disclosure and inspection of the majority of these documents, for example when complying with the pre–action Protocol.
- The cost of providing standard disclosure may be disproportionate.
- In such cases, the parties should seek to agree upon a more limited form of disclosure, whether in one of the forms set out in CPR 31.5 or otherwise, or to dispense with formal disclosure altogether.

11.2.2 Where disclosure is to be provided, the parties should consider whether it is necessary for lists of documents to be prepared or whether special arrangements should be agreed as to the form of listing and identifying disclosable documents, the method, timing and location of inspection and the manner of copying or providing copies of documents. Where documents are scattered over several locations, or are located overseas or are in a foreign language, special arrangements will also need to be considered. Thought should also be given to providing disclosure in stages or to reducing the scope of disclosure by providing the relevant material in other forms.

11.2.3 Electronic data and documents give rise to particular problems as to searching, preserving, listing, inspecting and other aspects of discovery and inspection. These problems should be considered and, if necessary made the subject of special directions. Furthermore, in many cases disclosure, inspection and the provision of documents in electronic form or electronic copies of hard copies may be undertaken using information technology. Attention is drawn to the relevant provisions in CPR Part 31 and Practice Direction 31B: **Disclosure of Electronic Documents** A protocol for e–disclosure prepared by TeCSA, TECBAR and the Society for Computers and Law was launched on 1 November 2013 which provides a procedure and guidance in relation to these matters. The protocol was developed in consultation with the judges of the TCC, and is likely to be ordered by the court if the parties have not agreed on any alternative by the time of the first CMC. It is available on the TeCSA website.

11.2.4 All these matters should be agreed between the parties. If it is necessary to raise any of these matters with the court they should be raised, if possible, at the first CMC. If points arise on disclosure after the first CMC, they may well be capable of being dealt with by the court on paper.

SECTION 12

WITNESS STATEMENTS AND FACTUAL EVIDENCE FOR USE AT TRIAL

12.1 Witness statements

12.1.1 Witness statements should be prepared generally in accordance withCPR Part **2C–47** 22.1 (documents verified by a statement of truth) and CPR Part 32 (provisions governing the evidence of witnesses) and their practice directions, particularly Paragraphs 17 to 22 of the Practice Direction supplementing CPR Part 32.

12.1.2 Unless otherwise directed by the court, witness statements should <u>not</u> have annexed to them copies of other documents and should <u>not</u> reproduce or paraphrase at length passages from other documents. The only exception arises where a specific document needs to be annexed to the statement in order to make that statement reasonably intelligible.

12.1.3 When preparing witness statements, attention should be paid to the following matters:

- Even when prepared by a legal representative or other professional, the witness statement should be, so far as practicable, in the witness's own words.
- The witness statement should indicate which matters are within the witness's own knowledge and which are matters of information and belief. Where the witness is stating matters of hearsay or of either information or belief, the source of that evidence should also be stated.
- A witness statement should be no longer than necessary and should not be argumentative.
- A witness statement should not contain extensive reference to contemporaneous documents by way of narrative.
- The witness statement must include a statement by the witness that he believes the facts stated to be true.

12.1.4 Costs. If at any stage the judge considers that the way in which witness statements have been prepared, particularly by the inclusion of extensive irrelevant or peripheral material, is likely to lead or has led to inefficiency in the conduct of the proceedings or to unnecessary time or costs being spent, the judge may order that the witness should re–submit the witness statement in whole or part and may make a costs order disallowing costs or ordering costs to be paid, either on the basis of a summary assessment or by giving a direction to the costs judge as to what costs should be disallowed or paid on a detailed assessment: see Paragraph 5.5.5 above.

12.2 Other matters concerned with witness statements

12.2.1 Foreign language. If a witness is not sufficiently fluent in English to give his evidence in English, the witness statement should be in his or her own language and an authenticated translation provided. Where the witness has a broken command of English, the statement may be drafted by others so as to express the witness's evidence as accurately as possible. In that situation, however, the witness statement should indicate that this process of interpolation has occurred and also should explain the extent of the witness's command of English and how and to what parts of the witness statement the process of interpolation has occurred.

12.2.2 Reluctant witness. Sometimes a witness is unwilling or not permitted or is unavailable to provide a witness statement before the trial. The party seeking to adduce this evidence should comply with the provisions of CPR 32.9 concerned with the provision of witness summaries.

12.2.3 Hearsay. Parties should keep in mind the need to give appropriate notice of their intention to rely on hearsay evidence or the contents of documents without serving a witness statement from their maker or from the originator of the evidence contained in those documents. The appropriate procedure is contained in CPR 33.1 – 33.5.

12.2.4 Supplementary Witness Statements. The general principle is that a witness should set out in their witness statement their complete evidence relevant to the issues in the case. The witness statement should not include evidence on the basis that it might be needed depending on what the other party's witnesses might say. The correct procedure in such cases is for the witness to provide a supplementary witness statement or, as necessary, for a new witness to provide a witness statement limited to responding to particular matters contained in the other party's witness statement and to seek permission accordingly. In some cases it might be appropriate for the court to provide for the service of supplementary witness statements as part of the order at the first case management conference.

12.2.5 Supplementary Evidence in Chief. The relevant witness evidence should be contained in the witness statements, or if appropriate witness summaries, served in advance of the hearing. Where, for whatever reason, this has not happened and the witness has relevant important evidence to give, particularly where the need for such evidence has only become apparent during the trial, the judge has a discretion to permit supplementary evidence in chief.

12.3 Cross–referencing

12.3.1 Where a substantial number of documents will be adduced in evidence or contained in the trial bundles, it is of considerable assistance to the court and to all concerned if the relevant page references are annotated in the margins of the copy witness statements. It is accepted that this is a time–consuming exercise, the need for which will be considered at the PTR, and it will only be ordered where it is both appropriate and proportionate to do so. See further **Paragraphs 14.5.1** and **15.2.3** below.

12.4 Video link

12.4.1 If any witness (whose witness statement has been served and who is required to give oral evidence) is located outside England and Wales or would find a journey to court inconvenient or impracticable, his evidence might be given via a video link. Thought should be given before the PTR to the question whether this course would be appropriate and proportionate. Such evidence is regularly received by the TCC and facilities for its reception, whether in appropriate court premises or at a convenient venue outside the court building, are now readily available.

12.4.2 Any application for a video link direction and any question relating to the manner in which such evidence is to be given should be dealt with at the PTR. Attention is drawn to the Video–conferencing Protocol set out at Annex 3 to the Practice Direction supplementing CPR Part 32 – **Evidence**. The procedure described in Annex 3 is followed by the TCC.

Section 13

Expert evidence

13.1 Nature of expert evidence

13.1.1 Expert evidence is evidence as to matters of a technical or scientific nature and **2C–48** will generally include the opinions of the expert. The quality and reliability of expert evidence will depend upon (a) the experience and the technical or scientific qualifications of the expert and (b) the accuracy of the factual material that is used by the expert for his assessment. Expert evidence is dealt with in detail in CPR Part 35 ("Experts and Assessors") and in the **Practice Direction supplementing** Part 35. Particular attention should be paid to all these provisions, given the detailed reliance on expert evidence in most TCC actions. Particular attention should also be paid to the "Protocol for the instruction of experts to give evidence in civil claims" annexed to Practice Direction 35 – Experts and Assessors (it should be noted that this Protocol is expected to be replaced at some point with the "Guidance for the instruction of experts to give evidence in Civil claims").

13.1.2 The attention of the parties is drawn to the specific requirements in relation to the terms of the expert's declaration at the conclusion of the report.

13.1.3 The provisions in CPR Part 35 are concerned with the terms upon which the court may receive expert evidence. These provisions are principally applicable to independently instructed expert witnesses. In cases where a party is a professional or a professional has played a significant part in the subject matter of the action, opinion evidence will almost inevitably be included in the witness statements. Any points arising from such evidence (if they cannot be resolved by agreement) can be dealt with by the judge on an application or at the PTR.

13.2 Control of expert evidence

13.2.1 Expert evidence is frequently needed and used in TCC cases. Experts are often appointed at an early stage. Most types of case heard in the TCC involve more than one expertise and some, even when the dispute is concerned with relatively small sums, involve several different experts. Such disputes include those concerned with building failures and defects, delay and disruption, dilapidations, subsidence caused by tree roots and the supply of software systems. However, given the cost of preparing such evidence, the parties and the court must, from the earliest pre–action phase of a dispute until the conclusion of the trial, seek to make effective and proportionate use of experts. The scope of any expert evidence must be limited to what is necessary for the requirements of the particular case.

13.2.2 At the first CMC, or thereafter, the court may be asked to determine whether the cost of instructing experts is proportionate to the amount at issue in the proceedings, and the importance of the case to the parties. When considering an application for permission to call an expert, the court is to be provided with estimates of the experts' costs: see CPR 35.4(2). The permission may limit the issues to be considered by the experts: see CPR 35.4(3). This should ordinarily be linked to the party's costs budget.

13.2.3 The parties should also be aware that the court has the power to limit the amount of the expert's fees that a party may recover pursuant to CPR 35.4 (4).

13.3 Prior to and at the first CMC

13.3.1 There is an unresolved tension arising from the need for parties to instruct and rely on expert opinions from an early pre–action stage and the need for the court to seek, wherever possible, to reduce the cost of expert evidence by dispensing with it altogether or by encouraging the appointment of jointly instructed experts. This tension arises because the court can only consider directing joint appointments or limiting expert evidence long after a party may have incurred the cost of obtaining expert evidence and have already relied on it. Parties should be aware of this tension. So far as possible, the parties should avoid incurring the costs of expert evidence on uncontroversial matters or matters of the kind referred to in Paragraph 13.4.3 below, before the first CMC has been held.

13.3.2 In cases where it is not appropriate for the court to order a single joint expert, it is imperative that, wherever possible, the parties' experts co–operate fully with one another. This is particularly important where tests, surveys, investigations, sample gathering or other technical methods of obtaining primary factual evidence are needed. It is often critical to ensure that any laboratory testing or experiments are carried out by the experts together, pursuant to an agreed procedure. Alternatively, the respective experts may agree that a particular firm or laboratory shall carry out specified tests or analyses on behalf of all parties.

13.3.3 Parties should, where possible, disclose initial or preliminary reports to opposing parties prior to any pre–action protocol meeting, if only on a without prejudice basis. Such early disclosure will assist in early settlement or mediation discussions and in helping the parties to define and confine the issues in dispute with a corresponding saving in costs.

13.3.4 Before and at the first CMC and at each subsequent pre–trial stage of the action, the parties should give careful thought to the following matters:
- The number, disciplines and identity of the expert witnesses they are considering instructing as their own experts or as single joint experts.
- The precise issues which each expert is to address in his/her reports, to discuss without prejudice with opposing parties' experts and give evidence about at the trial.
- The timing of any meeting, agreed statement or report.
- Any appropriate or necessary tests, inspections, sampling or investigations that could be undertaken jointly or in collaboration with other experts. Any such measures should be preceded by a meeting of relevant experts at which an appropriate testing or other protocol is devised. This would cover (i) all matters connected with the process in question and its recording and (ii) the sharing and agreement of any resulting data or evidence.
- Any common method of analysis, investigation or reporting where it is appropriate or proportionate that such should be adopted by all relevant experts. An example of this would be an agreement as to the method to be used to analyse the cause and extent of any relevant period of delay in a construction project, where such is in issue in the case.
- The availability and length of time that experts will realistically require to complete the tasks assigned to them.

(Note that the amendment toCPR 35.4(3) permits the order granting permission to specify the issues which the expert evidence should address.)

13.3.5 In so far as the matters set out in the previous paragraph cannot be agreed, the court will give appropriate directions. In giving permission for the reception of any expert evidence, the court will ordinarily order the exchange of such evidence, with a definition of the expert's area of expertise and a clear description of the issues about which that expert is permitted to give evidence. It is preferable that, at the first CMC or as soon as possible thereafter, the parties should provide the court with the name(s) of their expert(s).

13.4 Single joint experts

13.4.1 An order may be made, at the first CMC or thereafter, that a single joint expert should address particular issues between the parties. Such an order would be made pursuant to CPR Parts 35.7 and 35.8.

13.4.2 Single joint experts are not usually appropriate for the principal liability disputes in a large case, or in a case where considerable sums have been spent on an expert in the pre–action stage. They are generally inappropriate where the issue involves questions of risk assessment or professional competence.

13.4.3 On the other hand, single joint experts can often be appropriate:
- in low value cases, where technical evidence is required but the cost of adversarial expert evidence may be prohibitive;
- where the topic with which the single joint expert's report deals is a separate and self–contained part of the case, such as the valuation of particular heads of claim;
- where there is a subsidiary issue, which requires particular expertise of a relatively uncontroversial nature to resolve;
- where testing or analysis is required, and this can conveniently be done by one laboratory or firm on behalf of all parties.

13.4.4 Where a single joint expert is to be appointed or is to be directed by the court, the parties should attempt to devise a protocol covering all relevant aspects of the appointment (save for those matters specifically provided for by CPR 35.6, 35.7 and 35.8).

13.4.5 The matters to be considered should include: any ceiling on fees and disbursements that are to be charged and payable by the parties; how, when and by whom fees will be paid to the expert on an interim basis pending any costs order in the proceedings; how the expert's fees will be secured; how the terms of reference are to be agreed; what is to happen if terms of reference cannot be agreed; how and to whom the jointly appointed expert may address further enquiries and from whom he should seek further information and documents; the timetable for preparing any report or for undertaking any other preparatory step; the possible effect on such timetable of any supplementary or further instructions. Where these matters cannot be agreed, an application to the court, which may often be capable of being dealt with as a paper application, will be necessary.

13.4.6 The usual procedure for a single joint expert will involve:
- The preparation of the expert's instructions. These instructions should clearly identify those issues or matters where the parties are in conflict, whether on the facts or on matters of opinion. If the parties can agree joint instructions, then a single set of instructions should be delivered to the expert. However, Rule 35.8 expressly permits separate instructions and these are necessary where joint instructions cannot be agreed
- The preparation of the agreed bundle, which is to be provided to the expert. This bundle must include CPR Part 35, the Practice Direction supplementing Part 35 and the Section 13 of the TCC Guide.
- The preparation and production of the expert's report.
- The provision to the expert of any written questions from the parties, which the expert must answer in writing.

13.4.7 In most cases the single joint expert's report, supplemented by any written answers to questions from the parties, will be sufficient for the purposes of the trial. Sometimes, however, it is necessary for a single joint expert to be called to give oral evidence. In those circumstances, the usual practice is for the judge to call the expert and then allow each party the opportunity to cross–examine. Such cross–examination should be conducted with appropriate restraint, since the witness has been instructed by the parties. Where the expert's report is strongly in favour of one party's position, it may be appropriate to allow only the other party to cross–examine.

13.5 Meetings of experts

13.5.1 The desirability of holding without prejudice meetings between experts at all stages of the pre–trial preparation should be kept in mind. The desired outcome of such meetings is to produce a document whose contents are agreed and which defines common positions or each expert's differing position. The purpose of such meetings includes the following:

- The provision to the expert of any written questions from the parties, which the expert must answer in writing.
- to define a party's technical case and to inform opposing parties of the details of that case;
- to clear up confusion and to remedy any lack of information or understanding of a party's technical case in the minds of opposing experts;
- to identify the issues about which any expert is to give evidence;
- to narrow differences and to reach agreement on as many "expert" issues as possible; and
- to assist in providing an agenda for the trial and for cross examination of expert witnesses, and to limit the scope and length of the trial as much as possible.

13.5.2 In many cases it will be helpful for the parties' respective legal advisors to provide assistance as to the agenda and topics to be discussed at an experts' meeting. However, (save in exceptional circumstances and with the permission of the judge) the legal advisors must not attend the meeting. They must not attempt to dictate what the experts say at the meeting.

13.5.3 Experts' meetings can sometimes usefully take place at the site of the dispute. Thought is needed as to who is to make the necessary arrangements for access, particularly where the site is occupied or in the control of a non–party. Expert meetings are often more productive, if (a) the expert of one party (usually the claimant) is appointed as chairman and (b) the experts exchange in advance agendas listing the topics each wishes to raise and identifying any relevant material which they intend to introduce or rely on during the meeting.

13.5.4 It is generally sensible for the experts to meet at least once before they exchange their reports.

13.6 Experts' Joint Statements

13.6.1 Following the experts' meetings, and pursuant to CPR 35.12 (3), the judge will almost always require the experts to produce a signed statement setting out the issues which have been agreed, and those issues which have not been agreed, together with a short summary of the reasons for their disagreement. In any TCC case in which expert evidence has an important role to play, this statement is a critical document and it must be as clear as possible.

13.6.2 It should be noted that, even where experts have been unable to agree very much, it is of considerable importance that the statement sets out their disagreements and the reasons for them. Such disagreements as formulated in the joint statement are likely to form an important element of the agenda for the trial of the action.

13.6.3 Whilst the parties' legal advisors may assist in identifying issues which the statement should address, those legal advisors must not be involved in either negotiating or drafting the experts' joint statement. Legal advisors should only invite the experts to consider amending any draft joint statement in exceptional circumstances where there are serious concerns that the court may misunderstand or be misled by the terms of that joint statement. Any such concerns should be raised with all experts involved in the joint statement.

13.7 Experts' Reports

13.7.1 It is the duty of an expert to help the court on matters within his expertise. This duty overrides any duty to his client: CPR 35.3. Each expert's report must be independent and unbiased. Paragraphs 3(vii), 3.3.1(vi) and 5.5(i) of the Pre–Action Protocol for Construction and Engineering Disputes contain provisions as to experts in TCC cases and accordingly Annex C to the Practice Direction—Pre–Action Conduct does not apply: see **The Practice Direction—Pre–Action Conduct.**

13.7.2 The parties must identify the issues with which each expert should deal in his or her report. Thereafter, it is for the expert to draft and decide upon the detailed contents and format of the report, so as to conform to **the Practice Direction supplementing** CPR Part 35 and **the Protocol for the Instruction of Experts to give Evidence in Civil Claims**. It is appropriate, however, for the party instructing an expert to indicate that the report (a) should be as short as is reasonably possible; (b) should not set out copious extracts from other documents; (c) should identify the source of any opinion or data relied upon; and (d) should not annex or exhibit more than is reasonably necessary to support the opinions expressed in the report. In addition, as set out in Paragraph 15.2 of the Protocol for the Instruction of Experts to give Evidence in Civil Claims, legal advisors may also invite experts to consider amendments to their reports to ensure accuracy, internal consistency, completeness, relevance to the issues or clarity of reports.

13.8 Presentation of Expert Evidence

13.8.1 The purpose of expert evidence is to assist the court on matters of a technical or scientific nature. Particularly in large and complex cases where the evidence has developed through a number of experts' joint statements and reports, it is often helpful for the expert at the commencement of his or her evidence to provide the court with a summary of their views on the main issues. This can be done orally or by way of a PowerPoint or similar presentation. The purpose is not to introduce new evidence but to explain the existing evidence.

13.8.2 The way in which expert evidence is given is a matter to be considered at the PTR. However where there are a number of experts of different disciplines the court will consider the best way for the expert evidence to be given. It is now quite usual for all expert evidence to follow the completion of the witness evidence from all parties. At that stage there are a number of possible ways of presenting evidence including:

- For one party to call all its expert evidence, followed by each party calling all of its expert evidence.
- For one party to call its expert in a particular discipline, followed by the other parties calling their experts in that discipline. This process would then be repeated for the experts of all disciplines.
- For one party to call its expert or experts to deal with a particular issue, followed by the other parties calling their expert or experts to deal with that issues. This process would then be repeated for all the expert issues.
- For the experts for all parties to be called to give concurrent evidence, colloquially referred to as "hot–tubbing". When this method is adopted there is generally a need for experts to be cross–examined on general matters and key issues before they are invited to give evidence concurrently on particular issues. Procedures vary but, for instance, a party may ask its expert to explain his or her view on an issue, then ask the other party's expert for his or her view on that issue and then return to that party's expert for a comment on that view. Alternatively, or in addition, questions may be asked by the judge or the experts themselves may each ask the other questions. The process is often most useful where there are a large number of items to be dealt with and the procedure allows the court to have the evidence on each item dealt with on the same occasion rather than having the evidence divided with the inability to have each expert's views expressed clearly. Frequently, it allows the extent of agreement and reason for disagreement to be seen more clearly. The giving of concurrent evidence may be consented to by the parties and the judge will consider whether, in the absence of consent, any modification is required to the procedure for giving concurrent evidence set out in the CPR (at PD35, Paragraph 11).

SECTION 14

THE PRE–TRIAL REVIEW

14.1 Timing and Attendance

14.1.1 The Pre–Trial Review ("PTR") will usually be fixed for a date that is 4–6 weeks **2C–49** in advance of the commencement of the trial itself. It is vital that the advocates, who are going to conduct the trial, should attend the PTR and every effort should be made to achieve this. It is usually appropriate for the PTR to be conducted by way of an oral hearing or, at the very least, a telephone conference, so that the judge may raise matters of trial management even if the parties can agree beforehand any outstanding directions and the detailed requirements for the management of the trial. In appropriate cases, e.g. where the amount in issue is disproportionate to the costs of a full trial, the judge may wish to consider with the parties whether there are other ways in which the dispute might be resolved.

14.2 Documents

14.2.1 The parties must complete the PTR Questionnaire (a copy of which is at **Appendix C** attached) and return it in good time to the court. In addition, the judge may order the parties to provide other documents for the particular purposes of the PTR.

14.2.2 In an appropriate case, the advocates for each party should prepare a Note for the PTR, which addresses:
- any outstanding directions or interlocutory steps still to be taken;
- the issues for determination at the trial;
- the most efficient way in which those issues might be dealt with at the trial, including all questions of timetabling of witnesses.

These Notes should be provided to the court **by 4 pm one clear working day before the PTR**.

14.2.3 The parties should also ensure that, for the PTR, the court has an up–to–date permanent case management bundle, together with a bundle of the evidence (factual and expert) that has been exchanged. This Bundle should also be made available to the court **by 4 pm one clear day before the PTR**.

14.3 Outstanding Directions

14.3.1 It can sometimes be the case that there are still outstanding interlocutory steps to be taken at the time of the PTR. That will usually mean that one, or more, of the parties has not complied with an earlier direction of the court. In that event, the court is likely to require prompt compliance, and may make costs orders to reflect the delays.

14.3.2 Sometimes a party will wish to make an application to be heard at the same time as the PTR. Such a practice is unsatisfactory, because it uses up time allocated for the PTR, and it gives rise to potential uncertainty close to the trial date. It is always better for a party, if it possibly can, to make all necessary applications well in advance of the PTR. If that is not practicable, the court should be asked to allocate additional time for the PTR, in order to accommodate specific applications. If additional time is not available, such applications will not generally be entertained.

14.4 Issues

14.4.1 The parties should, if possible, provide the judge at the PTR with an agreed list of the main issues for the forthcoming trial (including, where appropriate, a separate list of technical issues to be covered by the experts). The list of issues should not be extensive and should focus on the key issues. It is provided as a working document to assist in the management of the trial and not as a substitute for the pleadings.

14.4.2 If the parties are unable to agree the precise formulation of the issues, they should provide to the court their respective formulations. Because the list of issues should focus on the key issues the opportunity for disagreement should be minimised. The judge will note the parties' formulations, but, because the issues are those which arise on the pleadings, is unlikely to give a ruling on this matter at the PTR unless the different formulations show that there is a dispute as to the pleaded case.

14.5 Timetabling and Trial Logistics

14.5.1 Much of the PTR will be devoted to a consideration of the appropriate timetable for the trial, and other logistical matters. These will commonly include:

- Directions in respect of oral and written openings and any necessary reading time for the judge.
- Sequence of oral evidence; for example, whether all the factual evidence should be called before the expert evidence.
- Timetabling of oral evidence. To facilitate this exercise, the advocates should, after discussing the matter and whether some evidence can be agreed, provide a draft timetable indicating which witnesses need to be cross–examined and the periods during it is proposed that they should attend. Such timetables are working documents.
- The manner in which expert evidence is to be presented: see **Paragraph 13.8** above.
- Whether any form of time limits should be imposed. (Since the purpose of time limits is to ensure that that the costs incurred and the resources devoted to the trial are proportionate, this is for the benefit of the parties. The judge will endeavour to secure agreement to any time limits imposed.)
- Directions in respect of the trial bundle: when it should be agreed and lodged; the contents and structure of the bundle; avoidance of duplication; whether witness statements and/or expert reports should be annotated with cross references to page numbers in the main bundle (see **Paragraph 12.3** above); and similar matters.
- Whether there should be a core bundle; if so how it should be prepared and what it should contain. (The court will order a core bundle in any case where (a) there is substantial documentation and (b) having regard to the issues it is appropriate and proportionate to put the parties to cost of preparing a core bundle).
- Rules governing any email communication during trial between the parties and the court.
- Any directions relating to the use of electronic document management systems at trial (this subject to agreement between the parties).
- Any directions relating to the use of simultaneous transcription at trial (this subject to agreement between the parties).
- Whether there should be a view by the judge.
- The form and timing of closing submissions.
- Whether there is a need for a special court (because of the number of parties or any particular facilities required).
- Whether there is need for evidence by video link.
- Any applications for review or variation of costs budgets.

14.5.2 The topics identified in Paragraph 14.5.1 are discussed in greater detail in Section 15 below.

SECTION 15

THE TRIAL

15.1 Arrangements prior to the trial—witnesses

15.1.1 Prior to the trial the parties' legal representatives should seek to agree on the **2C–50** following matters, in so far as they have not been resolved at the PTR: the order in which witnesses are to be called to give evidence; which witnesses are not required for cross examination and whose evidence in consequence may be adduced entirely from their witness statements; the timetable for the trial and the length of time each advocate is to be allowed for a brief opening speech. When planning the timetable, it should be noted that trials normally take place on Mondays to Thursdays, since Fridays are reserved for applications.

15.1.2 The witnesses should be notified in advance of the trial as to: (a) when each is required to attend court and (b) the approximate period of time for which he or she will be required to attend.

15.1.3 It is the parties' responsibility to ensure that their respective witnesses are ready to attend court at the appropriate time. It is never satisfactory for witnesses to be interposed, out of their proper place. It would require exceptional circumstances for the trial to be adjourned for any period of time because of the unavailability of a witness.

15.2 Opening notes, trial bundle and oral openings

15.2.1 Opening notes. Unless the court has ordered otherwise, each party's advocate should provide an opening note, which outlines that party's case in relation to each of the issues identified at the PTR. Each opening note should indicate which documents (giving their page numbers in the trial bundle) that party considers that the judge should pre–read. The claimant's opening note should include a neutral summary of the background facts, as well as a chronology and cast list. The other parties' opening notes should be shorter and should assume familiarity with the factual background. In general terms, all opening notes should be of modest length and proportionate to the size and complexity of the case. Subject to any specific directions at the PTR, the claimant's opening note should be served two clear working days before the start of the trial; the other parties opening notes should be served by 1 pm on the last working day before the trial.

15.2.2 Trial bundles. Subject to any specific directions at the PTR, the trial bundles should be delivered to court at least three working days before the hearing. It is helpful for the party delivering the trial bundles to liaise in advance with the judge's clerk, in order to discuss practical arrangements, particularly when a large number of bundles are to be delivered. The parties should provide for the court an agreed index of all trial bundles. There should also be an index at the front of each bundle. This should be a helpful guide to the contents of that bundle. (An interminable list, itemising every letter or sheet of paper is not a helpful guide. Nor are bland descriptions, such as "exhibit "JT3", of much help to the bundle user.) The spines and inside covers of bundles should be clearly labelled with the bundle number and brief description.

15.2.3 As a general rule the trial bundles should be clearly divided between statements of case, orders, contracts, witness statements, expert reports and correspondence/minutes of meetings. The correspondence/minutes of meetings should be in a separate bundle or bundles and in chronological order. Documents should only be included if they are relevant to the issues in the case or helpful as background material. Documents should not be duplicated, and unnecessary duplication of e–mail threads should be avoided where possible. Exhibits to witness statements should generally be omitted, since the documents to which the witnesses are referring will be found elsewhere in the bundles. The bundles of contract documents and correspondence/minutes of meetings should be paginated, so that every page has a discrete number. The other bundles could be dealt with in one of two ways:

- The statements of case, witness statements and expert reports could be placed in bundles and continuously paginated.
- Alternatively, the statements of case, witness statements and expert reports could be placed behind tabbed divider cards, and then the internal numbering of each such document can be used at trial. If the latter course is adopted, it is vital that the internal page numbering of each expert report continues sequentially through the appendices to that report.

The court encourages the parties to provide original copies of expert reports in this way so that any photographs, plans or charts are legible in their original size and, where appropriate, in colour. In such cases sequential numbering of every page including appendices is essential.

The ultimate objective is to create trial bundles, which are user friendly and in which any page can be identified with clarity and brevity (e.g. "bundle G page 273" or "defence page 3" or "Dr Smith page 12"). The core bundle, if there is one (as to which see **Paragraph 14.5.1** above), will be a separate bundle with its own pagination or contain documents from other bundles retaining the original bundle number behind a divider marked with the bundle number.

15.2.4 In document heavy cases the parties should consider the use of an electronic document management system that can be used at the trial. In order for the most effective use to be made of such a system, it is a matter that may require consideration at an early stage in the litigation.

15.2.5 Opening speeches. Subject to any directions made at the PTR, each party will be permitted to make an opening speech. These speeches should be prepared and presented on the basis that the judge will have pre–read the opening notes and the documents identified by the parties for pre–reading. The claimant's advocate may wish to highlight the main features of the claimant's case and/or to deal with matters raised in the other parties' opening notes. The other parties' advocates will then make shorter opening speeches, emphasising the main features of their own cases and/or responding to matters raised in the claimant's opening speech.

15.2.6 It is not usually necessary or desirable to embark upon legal argument during opening speeches. It is, however, helpful to foreshadow those legal arguments which (a) explain the relevance of particular parts of the evidence or (b) will assist the judge in following a party's case that is to be presented during the trial.

15.2.7 Narrowing of issues. Experience shows that often the issues between the parties progressively narrow as the trial advances. Sometimes this process begins during the course of opening speeches. Weaker contentions may be abandoned and responses to those contentions may become irrelevant. The advocates will co–operate in focussing their submissions and the evidence on the true issues between the parties, as those issues are thrown into sharper relief by the adversarial process.

15.3 Simultaneous transcription

15.3.1 Many trials in the TCC, including the great majority of the longer trials, are conducted with simultaneous transcripts of the evidence being provided. There are a number of transcribing systems available. It is now common for a system to be used involving simultaneous transcription onto screens situated in court. However, systems involving the production of the transcript in hard or electronic form at the end of the day or even after a longer period of time are also used. The parties must make the necessary arrangements with one of the companies who provide this service. The court can provide a list, on request, of all companies who offer such a service.

15.3.2 In long trials or those which involve any significant amount of detailed or technical evidence, simultaneous transcripts are helpful. Furthermore, they enable all but the shortest trials to be conducted so as to reduce the overall length of the trial appreciably, since the judge does not have to note the evidence or submissions in longhand as the trial proceeds. Finally, a simultaneous transcript makes the task of summarising a case in closing submissions and preparing the judgment somewhat easier. It reduces both the risk of error or omission and the amount of time needed to prepare a reserved judgment.

15.3.3 If possible, the parties should have agreed at or before the PTR whether a simultaneous transcript is to be employed. It is usual for parties to agree to share the cost of a simultaneous transcript as an interim measure pending the assessment or agreement of costs, when this cost is assessable and payable as part of the costs in the case. Sometimes, a party cannot or will not agree to an interim cost sharing arrangement. If so, it is permissible for one party to bear the cost, but the court cannot be provided with a transcript unless all parties have equal access to the transcript. Unlike transcripts for use during an appeal, there is no available means of obtaining from public funds the cost of a transcript for use at the trial.

15.4 Time limits

15.4.1 Generally trials in the TCC are conducted under some form of time limit arrangement. Several variants of time limit arrangements are available, but the TCC has developed the practice of imposing flexible guidelines in the form of directions as to the sharing of the time allotted for the trial. These are not mandatory but an advocate should ordinarily be expected to comply with them.

15.4.2 The practice is, in the usual case, for the court to fix, or for the parties to agree, at the PTR or before trial an overall length of time for the trial and overall lengths of time within that period for the evidence and submissions. The part of those overall lengths of time that will be allocated to each party must then be agreed or directed.

15.4.3 The amount of time to be allotted to each party will not usually be the same. The guide is that each party should have as much time as is reasonably needed for it to present its case and to test and cross examine any opposing case, but no longer.

15.4.4 Before the trial, the parties should agree a running order of the witnesses and the approximate length of time required for each witness. A trial timetable should be provided to the court when the trial starts and, in long trials, regularly updated.

15.4.5 The practice of imposing a strict guillotine on the examination or cross examination of witnesses, is not normally appropriate. Flexibility is encouraged, but the agreed or directed time limits should not ordinarily be exceeded without good reason. It is unfair on a party, if that party's advocate has confined cross–examination to the agreed time limits, but an opposing party then greatly exceeds the corresponding time limits that it has been allocated.

15.4.6 An alternative form of time limit, which is sometimes agreed between the parties and approved by the court, is the "chess clock arrangement". The available time is divided equally between the parties, to be used by the parties as they see fit. Thus each side has X hours. One representative on each side operates the chess clock. The judge has discretion "to stop the clock" in exceptional circumstances. A chess clock arrangement is only practicable in a two–party case.

15.5 Oral evidence

15.5.1 Evidence in chief is ordinarily adduced by the witness confirming on oath the truth and accuracy of the previously served witness statement or statements. A limited number of supplementary oral questions will usually be allowed (a) to give the witness an opportunity to become familiar with the procedure and (b) to cover points omitted by mistake from the witness statement or which have arisen subsequent to its preparation.

15.5.2 In some cases, particularly those involving allegations of dishonest, disreputable or culpable conduct or where significant disputes of fact are not documented or evidenced in writing, it is desirable that the core elements of a witness's evidence–in–chief are given orally. The giving of such evidence orally will often assist the court in assessing the credibility or reliability of a witness.

15.5.3 If any party wishes such evidence to be given orally, a direction should be sought either at the PTR or during the openings to that effect. Where evidence in chief is given orally, the rules relating to the use of witness statements in cross–examination and to the adducing of the statement in evidence at any subsequent stage of the trial remain in force and may be relied on by any party.

15.5.4 It is usual for all evidence of fact from all parties to be adduced before expert evidence and for the experts to give evidence in groups with all experts in a particular discipline giving their evidence in sequence: see **Paragraph 13.8.2** above for ways for expert evidence to be given. Usually, but not invariably, the order of witnesses will be such that the claimant's witnesses give their evidence first, followed by all the witnesses for each of the other parties in turn. If a party wishes a different order of witnesses to that normally followed, the agreement of the parties or a direction from the judge must be obtained in advance.

15.5.5 In a multi–party case, attention should be given (when the timetable is being discussed) to the order of cross–examination and to the extent to which particular topics will be covered by particular cross–examiners. Where these matters cannot be agreed, the order of cross–examination will (subject to any direction of the judge) follow the order in which the parties are set out in the pleadings. The judge will seek to limit cross examination on a topic which has been covered in detail by a preceding cross examination.

15.5.6 In preparing witness statements and in ascertaining what evidence a witness might give in an original or supplementary witness statement or as supplementary evidence–in–chief, lawyers may discuss the evidence to be given by a witness with that witness. The coaching of witnesses or the suggestion of answers that may be given, either in the preparation of witness statements or before a witness starts to give evidence, is not permitted. In relation to the process of giving evidence, witness familiarisation is permissible, but witness coaching is not. The boundary between witness familiarisation and witness coaching is discussed in the context of criminal proceedings by the Court of Appeal in *R v Momodou* [2005] EWCA Crim 177 at [61] – [62]. Once a witness has started giving evidence, that witness cannot discuss the case or their evidence either with the lawyers or with anyone else until they have finally left the witness box. Occasionally a dispensation is needed (for example, an expert may need to participate in an experts' meeting about some new development). In those circumstances the necessary dispensation will either be agreed between the advocates or ordered by the judge.

15.6 Submissions during the trial

15.6.1 Submissions and legal argument should be kept to a minimum during the course of the trial. Where these are necessary, (a) they should, where possible, take place when a witness is not giving evidence and (b) the judge should be given forewarning of the need for submissions or legal argument. Where possible, the judge will fix a time for these submissions outside the agreed timetable for the evidence.

15.7 Closing submissions

15.7.1 The appropriate form of closing submissions can be determined during the course of the trial. Those submissions may take the form of (a) oral closing speeches or (b) written submission alone or (c) written submissions supplemented by oral closing speeches. In shorter or lower value cases, oral closing speeches immediately after the evidence may be the most cost effective way to proceed. Alternatively, if the evidence finishes in the late afternoon, a direction for written closing submissions to be delivered by specified (early) dates may avoid the cost of a further day's court hearing. In longer and heavier cases the judge may (in consultation with the advocates) set a timetable for the delivery of sequential written submissions (alternatively, an exchange of written submissions) followed by an oral hearing. In giving directions for oral and/or written closing submissions, the judge will have regard to the circumstances of the case and the overriding objective.

15.7.2 It is helpful if, in advance of preparing closing submissions, the parties can agree on the principal topics or issues that are to be covered. It is also helpful for the written and oral submissions of each party to be structured so as to cover those topics in the same order.

15.7.3 It is both customary and helpful for the judge to be provided with a photocopy of each authority and statutory provision that is to be cited in closing submissions.

15.8 Views

15.8.1 It is sometimes necessary or desirable for the judge to be taken to view the subject–matter of the case. In normal circumstances, such a view is best arranged to take place immediately after the openings and before the evidence is called. However, if the subject matter of the case is going to be covered up or altered prior to the trial, the view must be arranged earlier. In that event, it becomes particularly important to avoid a change of judge. Accordingly, the court staff will note on the trial diary the fact that the assigned judge has attended a view. In all subsequent communications between the parties and court concerning trial date, the need to avoid a change of judge must be borne firmly in mind.

15.8.2 The matters viewed by the judge form part of the evidence that is received and may be relied on in deciding the case. However, nothing said during the view to (or in the earshot of) the judge, has any evidential status, unless there has been an agreement or order to that effect.

15.8.3 The parties should agree the arrangements for the view and then make those arrangements themselves. The judge will ordinarily travel to the view unaccompanied and, save in exceptional circumstances when the cost will be shared by all parties, will not require any travelling costs to be met by the parties.

15.9 Judgments

15.9.1 Depending on the length and complexity of the trial, the judge may (a) give judgment orally immediately after closing speeches; (b) give judgment orally on the following day or soon afterwards; or (c) deliver a reserved judgment in writing at a later date.

15.9.2 If a party wishes to obtain a transcript of an oral judgment, it should notify the judge's clerk so that any notes made by the judge can be retained in order to assist the judge when correcting the transcript.

15.9.3 Where judgment is reserved. The judge will normally indicate at the conclusion of the trial what arrangements will be followed in relation to (a) the making available of any draft reserved judgment and (b) the handing down of the reserved judgment in open court. If a judgment is reserved, it will be handed down as soon as possible. Save in exceptional circumstances, any reserved judgment will be handed down within 3 months of the conclusion of the trial. Any enquiries as to the progress of a reserved judgment should be addressed in the first instance to the judge's clerk, with notice of that enquiry being given to other parties. If concerns remain following the judge's response to the parties, further enquiries or communication should be addressed to the judge in charge of the TCC.

15.9.4 If the judge decides to release a draft judgment in advance of the formal hand down, this draft judgment will be confidential to the parties and their legal advisers. Solicitors and counsel on each side should send to the judge a note (if possible, agreed) of any clerical errors or slips which they note in the judgment. However, this is not to be taken as an opportunity to re–argue the issues in the case.

15.10 Disposal of judge's bundle after conclusion of the case

15.10.1 The judge will have made notes and annotations on the bundle during the course of the trial. Accordingly, the normal practice is that the entire contents of the judge's bundle are disposed of as confidential waste. The empty ring files can be recovered by arrangement with the judge's clerk.

15.10.2 If any party wishes to retrieve from the judge's bundle any particular items of value which it has supplied (e.g. plans or photographs), a request for these items should be made to the judge's clerk promptly at the conclusion of the case. If the judge has not made annotations on those particular items, they will be released to the requesting party.

SECTION 16

COSTS AND COSTS MANAGEMENT

16.1 General

2C–51   16.1.1 All disputes as to costs will be resolved in accordance with CPR Part 44, and in particular CPR 44.2.

16.1.2 The judge's usual approach will be to determine which party can be properly described as 'the successful party', and then to investigate whether there are any good reasons why that party should be deprived of some or all of their costs.

16.1.3 It should be noted that, in view of the complex nature of TCC cases, a consideration of the outcome on particular issues or areas of dispute can sometimes be an appropriate starting point for any decision on costs.

16.1.4 As set out in **Paragraphs 5.1.6, 5.5.5 and 12.1.4** above, if the judge considers that any particular aspect is likely to or has led to unnecessarily increased costs, the judge may make a costs order disallowing costs or ordering costs to be paid, either on the basis of a summary assessment, or by giving a direction to the costs judge as to what costs should be disallowed or paid on a detailed assessment.

16.2 Summary Assessment of Costs

16.2.1 Interlocutory hearings that last one day or less will usually be the subject of a summary assessment of costs in accordance with CPR 44.6 and Section 9 of PD44. The parties must ensure that their statements of costs, on which the summary assessment will be based, are provided to each other party, and the Court, no later than **24 hours** before the hearing in question: see **Paragraph 6.9.3** above.

16.2.2 The Senior Courts Costs Office Guide to the Summary Assessment of Costs sets out clear advice and guidance as to the principles to be followed in any summary assessment. Generally summary assessment proceeds on the standard basis. In making an assessment on the standard basis, the court will only allow a reasonable amount in respect of costs reasonably incurred and any doubts must be resolved in favour of the paying party.

16.2.3 In arguments about the hourly rates claimed, the judge will have regard to the principles set out by the Court of Appeal in *Wraith v Sheffield Forgemasters Ltd* [1998] 1 WLR 132: ie. the judge will consider whether the successful party acted reasonably in employing the solicitors who had been instructed and whether the costs they charged were reasonable compared with the broad average of charges made by similar firms practising in the same area.

16.2.4 When considering hourly rates, the judge in the TCC may have regard to any relevant guideline rates.

16.2.5 The court will also consider whether unnecessary work was done or an unnecessary amount of time was spent on the work.

16.2.6 It may be that, because of pressures of time, and/or the nature and extent of the disputes about the level of costs incurred, the court is unable to carry out a satisfactory summary assessment of the costs. In those circumstances, the court will direct that costs be assessed on the standard (or indemnity) basis and will order an amount to be paid on account of costs under CPR 44.3 (8).

16.3 Costs Management

16.3.1 Following a pilot scheme in the TCC and elsewhere, Section II of CPR 3 introduces the new regime of Costs Management. This implements the recommendations of the Jackson Report.

16.3.2 The rules now require each party to file a costs budget in the prescribed form at the outset of the litigation (before the first CMC). Although not expressly stated in Practice Direction 3E, the budgets should be discussed between the parties prior to the budgets being filed with the court. The court will fix the first CMC sufficiently far ahead to enable this to be done.

16.3.3 At the first CMC the court will consider the costs budgets. If they are agreed, the court will make an order recording the extent to which the budgets have been agreed: see CPR 3.15(2)(a). In such cases the parties' costs will be subject to detailed assessment as in the pre costs management regime. The penalty for failure to serve a budget is draconian: the party will be limited to recovering the court fees only (see CPR 3.14), as applied by the Court of Appeal in *Mitchell v News Group Newspapers* [2013] EWCA Civ 1537.

16.3.4 Where a budget or parts of a budget are not agreed, the court will consider the budget and make such revisions as it thinks fit. These will then be recorded in a Costs Management Order: see CPR 3.15(2)(b).

16.3.5 Precedent H is the form for a costs budget. This divides the litigation into different phases, and the court will consider the amount of the fees and disbursements for each phase separately. Costs budgets are to be supported by a statement of truth (see CPR 3EPD.1).

16.3.6 Once approved, the costs shown in each phase of the costs budget will usually be recoverable on a detailed assessment if they have been incurred. Recovery will not usually be permitted where a party has overspent its budget for a particular phase, even though it may have underspent on another phase. The court will not depart from the approved figure in the budget unless satisfied that there is good reason to do so: see CPR 3.18.

16.3.7 Precedent H allows a party to provide an allowance for certain contingencies, but these must be set out in the budget and the reason for them given. It is open to a party to apply to the court to amend its costs budget if there is good reason to do so.

16.3.8 In cases where items in the costs budgets are in issue, it of great help to the court if counsel can prepare a brief summary of the differences (if necessary, there is available on the market an Excel programme that can do this).

16.3.9 The parties should note that a different regime applied to cases commenced before 1 April 2013: see PD51G (Costs Management in Mercantile Courts and Technology and Construction Courts – Pilot Scheme). For cases commenced on or after 1 April 2013: see CPR 3.11–3.18 and PD3E, including the current £2 million cap (a revised Precedent H has been in force since 1 October 2013). For cases commencing after 22 April 2014 the costs management regime will apply where the value of the case is below £10 million: see CPR 3.12 (as amended).

16.4 Costs Capping Orders

16.4.1 In exercising case management powers, the judge may make costs cap orders which, in normal circumstances, will be prospective only. New rules are set out in CPR 3, Section III. The judge should only do so, however, where:
- it is in the interests of justice to do so;
- there is a substantial risk that without such an order costs will be disproportionately incurred; and
- the court is not satisfied that the risk can be adequately controlled by case management and detailed assessment of costs after a trial.

See CPR 3 Section III "Costs Capping"

16.4.2 The possibility of a costs cap order should be considered at the first CMC. The later such an order is sought, the more difficult it may be to impose an effective costs cap.

16.4.3 The procedure for making an application for a costs capping order are set out in CPR 3.20 and PD3F **Costs Capping** (these include a new requirement that parties must file a costs budget rather than an estimate of costs with any application for a costs capping order).

16.5 Costs: Miscellaneous

16.5.1 Pursuant to CPR 44.8 and Section 10 PD44, solicitors have a duty to tell their clients within 7 days if an order for costs was made against the clients and they were not present at the hearing, explaining how the order came to be made. They must also give the same information to anyone else who has instructed them to act on the case or who is liable to pay their fees.

SECTION 17

ENFORCEMENT

17.1 General

2C–52 17.1.1 The TCC is concerned with the enforcement of judgments and orders given by the TCC and with the enforcement of adjudicators' decisions and arbitrators' awards. Adjudication and arbitration enforcement have been dealt with in, respectively, Sections 9 and 10 above.

17.2 High Court

17.2.1 <u>London.</u> A party wishing to make use of any provision of the CPR concerned with the enforcement of judgments and orders made in the TCC in London can use the TCC Registry in London or any other convenient TCC District Registry listed in **Appendix A**.

17.2.2 <u>Outside London.</u> Where the judgment or order in respect of which enforcement is sought was made by a judge of the TCC out of London, the party seeking enforcement should use the Registry of the court in which the judgment or order was made.

17.2.3 Where orders are required or sought to support enforcement of a TCC judgment or order, a judge of the TCC is the appropriate judge for that purpose. If available, the judge who gave the relevant judgment or made the relevant order is the appropriate judge to whom all applications should be addressed.

17.3 County Court

17.3.1 A TCC County Court judgment (like any other County Court judgment):
- if for less than £600, must be enforced in the County Court;
- if for between £600 and £4999, can be enforced in either the County Court or the High Court, at the option of the judgment creditor;
- if for £5,000 or more, must be enforced in the High Court.

17.3.2 If a judgment creditor in a TCC County Court wishes to transfer any enforcement proceedings to any other County Court hearing centre (whether a TCC County Court or not), he must make a written request to do so pursuant to Section 2 of the Practice Direction **supplementing** Part 70. Alternatively, at the end of the trial the successful party may make an oral application to the trial judge to transfer the proceedings to some other specified County Court or County Court hearing centre for the purposes of enforcement.

17.4 Enforcement on paper

17.4.1 Where the application or order is unopposed or does not involve any substantial dispute, the necessary order should be sought by way of a paper application.

17.5 Charging Orders and Orders For Sale

17.5.1 One of the most common methods of enforcement involves the making of a charging order over the judgment debtor's property. There are three stages in the process.

17.5.2 The judgment creditor can apply to the TCC for a charging order pursuant to CPR 73.3 and 73.4. The application is in Form N379 in which the judgment creditor must identify the relevant judgment and the property in question. The application is initially dealt with by the judge without a hearing, and he may make an interim charging order imposing a charge over the judgment debtor's interest in the property and fixing a hearing to consider whether or not to make the charging order final.

17.5.3 The interim charging order must be served in accordance with CPR 73.5. If the judgment debtor or any other person objects to the making of a final charging order, then he must set out his objection in accordance with CPR 73.8. There will then be a hearing at which the court will decide whether or not to make the charging order final.

17.5.4 Ultimately, if the judgment remains unsatisfied, the party who has obtained the final charging order may seek an order for the sale of the property in accordance with CPR 73.10. Although Paragraph 4.2 of PD 73 might suggest that a claim for an order for sale to enforce a charging order must be started in the Chancery Division, there is no such restriction in the rule itself and practical difficulties have arisen for parties who have obtained a judgment, an interim charging order and a final charging order in the TCC and who do not want to have to transfer or commence fresh proceedings in another division in order to obtain an order for sale. The TCC will, in appropriate circumstances, in accordance with the overriding objective, make orders for sale in such circumstances, particularly if the parties are agreed that is the most convenient cost–effective course: see *Packman Lucas Limited v Mentmore Towers Ltd* [2010] EWHC 1037 (TCC).

17.5.5 In deciding whether or not to make an order for sale, the court will consider, amongst other things, the size of the debt, and the value of the property relative to that debt, the conduct of the parties and the absence of any other enforcement option on the part of the judgment creditor.

SECTION 18

THE TCC JUDGE AS ARBITRATOR

18.1 General

2C–53 18.1.1 Section 93(1) of the Arbitration Act 1996 ("the 1996 Act") provides that a judge of the TCC (previously an Official Referee) may "if in all the circumstances he thinks fit, accept appointment as a sole arbitrator or as an umpire by or by virtue of an arbitration agreement." Judges of the TCC may accept appointments as sole arbitrators or umpires pursuant to these statutory provisions. The 1996 Act does not limit the appointments to arbitrations with the seat in England and Wales.

18.1.2 However, a TCC judge cannot accept such an appointment unless the Lord Chief Justice "has informed him that, having regard to the state of (TCC) business, he can be made available": see Section 93(3) of the 1996 Act. In exceptional cases a judge of the TCC may also accept an appointment as a member of a three–member panel of arbitrators if the Lord Chief Justice consents but such arbitrations cannot be under Section 93 of the 1996 Act because Section 93(6) of the 1996 Act modifies the provisions of the 1996 Act where there is a judge–arbitrator and this could not apply to arbitral tribunals with three arbitrators, one of whom was a judge–arbitrator.

18.1.3 Application should be made in the first instance to the judge whose acceptance of the appointment is sought. If the judge is willing to accept the appointment, he will make application on behalf of the appointing party or parties, through the judge in charge of the TCC, to the Lord Chief Justice for his necessary approval. He will inform the party or parties applying for his appointment once the consent or refusal of consent has been obtained.

18.1.4 Subject to the workload of the court and the consent of the Lord Chief Justice, the TCC judges will generally be willing to accept such requests, particularly in short cases or where an important principle or point of law is concerned. Particular advantages have been noted by both TECBAR and TeCSA in the appointment of a TCC judge to act as arbitrator where the dispute centres on the proper interpretation of a clause or clauses within one of the standard forms of building and engineering contracts.

18.2 Arbitration Management and Fees

18.2.1 Following the appointment of the judge–arbitrator, the rules governing the arbitration will be decided upon, or directed, at the First Preliminary Meeting, when other appropriate directions will be given. The judge–arbitrator will manage the reference to arbitration in a similar way to a TCC case.

18.2.2 The judge sitting as an arbitrator will sit in a TCC court room (suitably rearranged) unless the parties and the judge–arbitrator agree to some other arrangement.

18.2.3 Fees are payable to the Court Service for the judge–arbitrator's services and for any accommodation provided. The appropriate fee for the judge–arbitrator, being a daily rate, is published in the Fees Order and should be paid through the TCC Registry.

18.3 Modifications to the Arbitration Act 1996 for judge–arbitrators

18.3.1 As Section 93 envisages that appointments of judge–arbitrators will be in arbitrations where the seat of the arbitration is in England and Wales, Schedule 2 of the 1996 Act modifies the provisions of the Act which apply to arbitrations where the seat is in England and Wales.

18.3.2 In relation to arbitrations before judge–arbitrators, Paragraph 2 of Schedule 2 to the Arbitration Act 1996 provides that references in Part I of the 1996 Act to "the court" shall be construed in relation to a judge–arbitrator, or in relation to the appointment of a judge–arbitrator, as references to "the Court of Appeal". This means that, for instance, any appeal from a judge–arbitrator under Section 69 of the 1996 Act is therefore heard, in the first instance, by the Court of Appeal.

APPENDIX A

CASE MANAGEMENT INFORMATION SHEET

This Appendix is the same as Appendix A to the Part 60 Practice Direction.   **2C–55**

APPENDIX B

CASE MANAGEMENT DIRECTIONS FORM

Action no HT—............. [*Insert name of judge in title of order*]   **2C–56**

[*Delete or amend the following directions, as appropriate to the circumstances of the case*]

1. Trial date ... ... For the purposes of payment of the trial fee, but for no other purposes, this date is provisional. This date will cease to be provisional and the trial fee will become payable on ... [*usually 2 months before the trial date*].

2. Estimated length of trial ....

3. Directions, if appropriate, (a) for the trial of any preliminary issues or (b) for the trial to be divided into stages ...

4. This action is to be [consolidated] [managed and tried with] action no ... The lead action shall be ... All directions given in the lead action shall apply to both actions, unless otherwise stated.

5. Further statements of case shall be filed and served as follows:
   - Defence and any counterclaim by 4 pm on ...
   - Reply (if any) and defence to counterclaim (if any) by 4 pm on ...

6. Permission to make the following amendments ...

7. Disclosure
   - By 5 pm on ...
   - To be standard disclosure/on the basis set out in CPR 31(5) (7) ...
   - On the basis set out in CPR 31(5) (7) ...
   - Specific directions in respect of electronic disclosure ... [where appropriate the TeCSA/TECBAR/SCL e–disclosure protocol is to be followed]

8. There shall be a Scott Schedule in respect of defects/ items of damage/ other ...
   - The column headings shall be as follows ...
   - Claimant/defendant to serve Scott Schedule by 5 pm on ...
   - Defendant/claimant to respond to Scott Schedule by 5 pm on ...

9. Signed statements of witnesses of fact to be served by 5 pm on ... [Supplementary statements of witnesses of fact to be served by 5 pm on ...]

10. The parties have permission to call the following expert witnesses in respect of the following issues:
    - ...
    - ...
    - ...

11. In respect of any expert evidence permitted under Paragraph 10:
    - Directions for carrying out inspections/taking samples/conducting experiments/ performance of calculations shall be ...
    - Experts in like fields to hold discussions in accordance with Rule 35.12 by ...

- Experts' statements Rule 35.12 (3) to be prepared and filed by 5 pm on …
- Experts' reports to be served by 5 pm on …

12. A single joint expert shall be appointed by the parties to report on the following issue(s) …. The following directions shall govern the appointment of the single joint expert:
    - ….
    - ….

13. The following documents shall be provided to the court electronically or in computer readable form, as well as in hard copy …

14. Costs Management
    - The costs budgets filed by the parties are approved.
    - The costs budget filed by the Claimant/Defendant is approved.
    - The following parties' costs budgets are approved subject to the following revisions:
        - …
        - …

15. A review case management conference shall be held on … at …am/pm. Time allowed …

16. The pre–trial review shall be held on … at … am/pm. Time allowed …

17. The above dates and time limits may be extended by agreement between the parties. Nevertheless:
    - The dates and time limits specified in paragraphs … may not be extended by more than [14] days without the permission of the court.
    - The dates specified in Paragraph 1 (trial) and paragraph 15 (pre–trial review) cannot be varied without the permission of the court.

18. Costs in the case.
DATED this day of 201

APPENDIX C

PRE–TRIAL REVIEW QUESTIONNAIRE

2C–57 This Appendix is the same as Appendix C to the Part 60 Practice Direction.

APPENDIX D

CONTACT DETAILS FOR TECHNOLOGY AND CONSTRUCTION COURT

2C–58 **The High Court of Justice, Queen's Bench Division, Technology and Construction Court**
The Rolls Building
7 Rolls Buildings
Fetter Lane
London EC4A 1NL
Management
Court Manager: Mr Wilf Lusty (wilf.lusty@hmcts.gsi.gov.uk)
List Officer: Mr Steven Gibbon (steven.gibbon@hmcts.gsi.gov.uk)
Court Manager: Tel: 020 7947 7427
Listing: Tel: 020 7947 7156
Registry Tel: 020 7947 7591
Fax: 0870 761 7724 (Goldfax)
TCC Judges
Mr Justice Edwards–Stuart (Judge in Charge of the TCC from 1 September 2013)
Clerk: Philip Morris (philip.morris@hmcts.gsi.gov.uk)
Tel: 020 7947 7205
Fax: 0870 761 7694 (Goldfax)
Mr Justice Ramsey
Clerk: Mr David Hamilton (david.hamilton5@hmcts.gsi.gov.uk)
Tel: 020 7947 6331
Fax: 0870 761 7694 (Goldfax)

Mr Justice Akenhead
Clerk: Mr Sam Taylor (sam.taylor1@hmcts.gsi.gov.uk)
Tel: 020 7947 7445
Fax: 0870 761 7694 (Goldfax)
Mr Justice Coulson
Clerk: Mr Simon Smith (simon.smith@hmcts.gsi.gov.uk)
Tel: 020 7947 6547
Fax: 0870 761 7694 (Goldfax)
Mr Justice Stuart–Smith
Clerk: Maxine Barfoot (maxine.barfoot@hmcts.gsi.gov.uk)
Tel: 020 7073 4837

The following High Court Judges may be available, when necessary and by arrangement with the President of the Queen's Bench Division, to sit in the TCC:

Mr Justice Burton
Mrs Justice Carr
Mr Justice Field
Mr Justice Foskett
Mr Justice Ouseley
Mr Justice Simon
Mr Justice Teare

The following judges are also TCC judges who may be available when necessary and by arrangement with the President of the Queen's Bench Division, to sit in the TCC:

His Honour Judge Anthony Thornton QC
His Honour Judge David Mackie QC

Birmingham District Registry: Birmingham County Court
33 Bull Street
Birmingham
West Midlands B4 6DS

TCC listing and clerk to His Honour Judge David Grant: Peter Duke (Peter.Duke@hmcts.gsi.gov.uk) birmingham.tcc@hmcts.gsi.gov.uk

Tel: 0121 681 4441
Fax: 0121 250 6437

TCC Judges
His Honour Judge David Grant (principal TCC Judge)
His Honour Judge Simon Brown QC (Mercantile Judge)
His Honour Judge Charles Purle QC (Chancery Judge)
His Honour Judge David Cooke
His Honour Martin McKenna
His Honour Judge Simon Barker QC

Bristol District Registry: Bristol County Court
TCC Listing Office
Bristol Civil Justice Centre
2 Redcliff Street
Bristol BS1 6GR

TCC Listing Officer: Victoria Haddock
Tel: 0117 366 4866
Email: bristoltcclisting@hmcts.gsi.gov.uk
Switchboard Tel: 0117 366 4800

TCC Judges
His Honour Judge Mark Havelock–Allan QC (principal TCC judge)
His Honour Judge Patrick McCahill QC
District Judge Brian Watson (TCC Liaison Judge)

Cardiff District Registry: Cardiff County Court
Cardiff Civil Justice Centre
2 Park Street
Cardiff CF10 1ET
Main switchboard: 029 2037 6400

Fax: 029 2037 6475
Listing office: 029 2037 6412
Circuit Judges Listing Manager: Tracey Davies
Tel: 029 2037 6483, tracey.davies2@hmcts.gsi.gov.uk
Specialist Listing Officer: Amanda Thomas
Tel: 029 2037 6412, amanda.thomas6@hmcts.gsi.gov.uk
TCC Judges
His Honour Judge Andrew Keyser QC (principal TCC judge)
His Honour Judge Milwyn Jarman QC
His Honour Judge Anthony Seys Llewellyn QC
Central London Civil Justice Centre
26 Park Crescent, London W1B 1HT
(but as from 20 May 2014 Thomas More Building, Royal Courts of Justice, Strand, London WC2 2LL)
TCC/Chancery Section: Geanette Rodney
Tel: 0207 917 7821
(from 20 May 2014: 020 7947 7800; and for counter appointments 020 7947 7502)
Fax: 020 7917 7935
Goldfax: 0970 330 571
Email for e-applications: CLCCTCC@hmcts.gsi.gov.uk
Circuit Judge Listing: 020 7917 7932
Email: hearingsatcentrallondon.countycourt@hmcts.gsi.gov.uk
Email for skeleton arguments: CentralLondonCJSKEL@hmcts.gsi.gov.uk
TCC Judges
His Honour Judge Edward Bailey (principal TCC Judge)
His Honour Judge John Hand QC
His Honour Judge Timothy Lamb
Her Honour Judge Deborah Taylor
His Honour Judge Marc Dight
Chester District Registry: Chester County Court
The Chester Civil Justice Centre
Trident House
Little St John Street
Chester CH1 1SN
Tel: 01244 404200
Fax: 0870 324 0311
email: hearings@chester.countycourt.gsi.gov.uk
TCC Judge
His Honour Judge Derek Halbert
Exeter District Registry: Exeter County Court
Southernhay Gardens
Exeter
Devon EX1 1UH
Tel: 01392 415 350
Fax: 01392 415645
email: hearings@exeter.countycourt.gsi.gov.uk
TCC Judge
His Honour Judge Barry Cotter QC
Leeds Combined Court Centre
The Courthouse
1 Oxford Row
Leeds LS1 3BG
TCC Chancery and Mercantile Listing Officer: Richard Sutherland
Tel: 0113 306 2440 / 2441
Fax: 08707617740
e-mail: richard.sutherland@hmcts.gsi.gov.uk
TCC Judges
His Honour Judge Mark Raeside QC (Judge in Charge of TCC in North East Region)

His Honour Judge John Behrens
His Honour Judge Roger Kaye QC
His Honour Judge Andrew Saffman
Liverpool District Registry: Liverpool Combined Court Centre
Liverpool Civil & Family Courts
35 Vernon Street
Liverpool L2 2BX
TCC listing officer: Jackie Jones
Tel: 0151 296 2444
Fax: 0151 295 2201
TCC Judges
His Honour Judge Wood QC
Manchester District Registry
Manchester Civil Justice Centre
1 Bridge Street West
Manchester M60 9DJ
TCC clerk: Isobel Rich
Tel: 0161 240 5305
Fax: 0161 240 5399
e–mail: manchester.tcc@hmcts.gsi.gov.uk
TCC Judges
His Honour Judge Philip Raynor QC (full time TCC judge)
His Honour Judge Stephen Davies (full time TCC judge)
The following judges at Manchester are nominated to deal with TCC business:
HHJ David Waksman QC
HHJ Mark Pelling QC
HHJ David Hodge QC
HHJ Nigel Bird
HHJ Graham Platts
HHJ Allan Gore QC
Mold County Court
Law Courts
Civic Centre
Mold
Flintshire
Wales CH7 1AE TCC
Listing officer: Selina Wilkes
Tel: 01352 707405
Fax: 01352 753874
TCC Judges
Will attend from Cardiff when required
Newcastle upon Tyne Combined Court Centre
The Law Courts
The Quayside
Newcastle upon Tyne NE1 3LA
Tel: 0191 201 2029
Listing Officer: Mrs Carol Gallagher
Email: carol.gallagher@hmcts.gsi.gov.uk
Tel: 0191 201 2047
Fax: 0191 201 2001
TCC Judges
His Honour Judge Christopher Walton
District Judge Atherton
Nottingham District Registry: Nottingham County Court
60 Canal Street
Nottingham NG1 7EJ
Tel 0115 910 3500

Fax: 0115 910 3510
TCC Judges
His Honour Judge Richard Inglis
His Honour Judge Nigel Godsmark QC
Sheffield Combined Court Centre
The Law Courts
50 West Bar
Sheffield S3 8PH
Tel: 0114 281 2419
Fax: 0114 281 2585
TCC Judge
His Honour Judge John Bullimore
Winchester Combined Court Centre
The Law Courts
Winchester
Hampshire SO23 9EL
Switchboard: 01962 814 100
Fax: 01962 814 260
Diary Manager: Mr Wayne Hacking
Email: wayne.hacking@hmcts.gsi.gov.uk
Tel: 023 8021 3254
Civil Listing Officer: Mrs Karen Hart
Email: karen.hart@hmcts.gsi.gov.uk
Tel: 01962 814 113
TCC Judge
His Honour Judge Iain Hughes QC

APPENDIX E

DRAFT ADR ORDER

2C–59 1. By [date/time] the parties shall exchange lists of three neutral individuals who have indicated their availability to conduct a mediation or ENE or other form of ADR in this case prior to [date].

2. By [date/time] the parties shall agree an individual from the exchanged lists to conduct the mediation or ENE or other form of ADR by [date]. If the parties are unable to agree on the neutral individual, they will apply to the Court in writing by [date/time] and the Court will choose one of the listed individuals to conduct the mediation or ENE or other form of ADR.

3. There will be a stay of the proceedings until [date/time] to allow the mediation or ENE or other form of ADR to take place. On or before that date, the Court shall be informed as to whether or not the case has been finally settled. If it has not been finally settled, the parties will:

    a) comply with all outstanding directions made by the Court;

    b) attend for a review CMC on [date/time].

DATED this day of 201

APPENDIX F

DRAFT DIRECTIONS ORDER IN ADJUDICATION ENFORCEMENT PROCEEDINGS

2C–60   **BEFORE** the Hon Mr Justice [] sitting in the High Court of Justice, Queen's Bench Division, Technology and Construction Court

    UPON reading the application notice dated [], and the witness statement of [] dated [],

    IT IS HEREBY ORDERED THAT:

    1) The Claimant shall as soon as practicable after receipt of this Order serve this application upon the Defendant together with:

        a) The Claim Form, Response Pack and any statement relied upon

b) This Order.

2) The time for the Defendant to file its Acknowledgement of Service is abridged to [four] working days. The Defendant is advised that failure to comply with the requirement to file this Acknowledgment can lead to judgment in default being entered against it. The Claimant is reminded that if there is such failure, serious consideration should be given to entering judgment in default as a cheaper option than taking the matter through to a hearing.

3) Any further evidence shall be served and filed:

  a) By the Defendant, on or by [about 14 days after order]

  b) By the Claimant, in response to that of the Defendant, on or by [7 days later];

  and in either case no later than 4.00 pm that day.

4) The Claimant has permission to issue an application for summary judgment prior to service by the Defendant of either Acknowledgement of Service or a Defence, pursuant to CPR Rule 24.4. The period of notice to be given to the Defendant is abridged to [four] working days.

5) There shall be an oral hearing on [] at [] with a time estimate of [] for the hearing of the Claimant's summary judgment application (this time may be varied at short notice to accommodate the listing requirements of the court).

6) The Claimant shall serve and file a paginated bundle comprising all relevant documents, statements, pleadings and otherwise by 1.00 pm on [].

7) Any skeleton arguments and any authorities to be relied upon (an agreed bundle, if possible) shall be served and filed by 1.00 pm on [].

8) The costs of and incidental to these directions are reserved.

9) The parties have permission to apply to set aside or vary these directions on [two] working days' written notice to the other.

Dated this day of 201

APPENDIX G

DRAFT COURT SETTLEMENT ORDER

Court Settlement

1. The Court Settlement Process under this Order is a confidential, voluntary and **2C–61** non–binding dispute resolution process in which the Settlement Judge assists the Parties in reaching an amicable settlement at a Court Settlement Conference.

2. This Order provides for the process by which the Court assists in the resolution of the disputes in the Proceedings. This Order is made by consent of the Parties with a view to achieving the amicable settlement of such disputes. It is agreed that the Settlement Judge may vary this Order at any time as he thinks appropriate or in accordance with the agreement of the Parties.

3. The following definitions shall apply:

  (1) The Parties shall be [names]

  (2) The Proceedings are [identify]

  (3) The Settlement Judge is [name]

The Court Settlement Process

4. The Settlement Judge may conduct the Court Settlement Process in such manner, as the Judge considers appropriate, taking into account the circumstances of the case, the wishes of the Parties and the overriding objective in Part 1 of the Civil Procedure Rules. A Preliminary Court Settlement Conference shall be held, either in person or in some other convenient manner, at which the Parties and the Settlement Judge shall determine, in general terms, the procedure to be adopted for the Court Settlement Process, the venue of the Court Settlement Conference, the estimated duration of the Court Settlement Conference and the material which will be read by the Settlement Judge in advance of the Court Settlement Conference.

5. Unless the Parties otherwise agree, during the Court Settlement Conference the

Settlement Judge may communicate with the Parties together or with any Party separately, including private meetings at which the Settlement Judge may express views on the disputes. Each Party shall cooperate with the Settlement Judge. A Party may request a private meeting with the Settlement Judge at any time during the Court Settlement Conference. The Parties shall give full assistance to enable the Court Settlement Conference to proceed and be concluded within the time stipulated by the Settlement Judge.

6. In advance of the Court Settlement Conference, each Party shall notify the Settlement Judge and the other Party or Parties of the names and the role of all persons involved in the Court Settlement Conference. Each Party shall nominate a person having full authority to settle the disputes.

7. No offers or promises or agreements shall have any legal effect unless and until they are included in a written agreement signed by representatives of all Parties (the "Settlement Agreement").

8. If the Court Settlement Conference does not lead to a Settlement Agreement, the Settlement Judge may, if requested by the Parties, send the Parties such assessment setting out his views on such matters as the Parties shall request, which may include, for instance, his views on the disputes, his views on prospects of success on individual issues, the likely outcome of the case and what would be an appropriate settlement. Such assessment shall be confidential to the parties and may not be used or referred to in any subsequent proceedings.

Termination of the Settlement Process

9. The Court Settlement Process shall come to end upon the signing of a Settlement Agreement by the Parties in respect of the disputes or when the Settlement Judge so directs or upon written notification by any Party at any time to the Settlement Judge and the other Party or Parties that the Court Settlement Process is terminated.

Confidentiality

10. The Court Settlement Process is private and confidential. Every document, communication or other form of information disclosed, made or produced by any Party specifically for the purpose of the Court Settlement Process shall be treated as being disclosed on a privileged and without prejudice basis and no privilege or confidentiality shall be waived by such disclosure.

11. Nothing said or done during the course of the Court Settlement Process is intended to or shall in any way affect the rights or prejudice the position of the Parties to the dispute in the Proceedings or any subsequent arbitration, adjudication or litigation. If the Settlement Judge is told by a Party that information is being provided to the Settlement Judge in confidence, the Settlement Judge will not disclose that information to any other Party in the course of the Court Settlement Process or to any other person at any time.

Costs

12. Unless otherwise agreed, each Party shall bear its own costs and shall share equally the Court costs of the Court Settlement Process.

Settlement Judge's Role in Subsequent Proceedings

13. The Settlement Judge shall from the date of this Order not take any further part in the Proceedings nor in any subsequent proceedings arising out of the Court Settlement Process and no party shall be entitled to call the Settlement Judge as a witness in any subsequent adjudication, arbitration or judicial proceedings arising out of or connected with the Court Settlement Process.

Exclusion of Liability

14. For the avoidance of doubt, the Parties agree that the Settlement Judge shall have the same immunity from suit in relation to a Court Settlement Process as the Settlement Judge would have if acting otherwise as a Judge in the Proceedings.

Particular Directions

15. A Court Settlement Conference shall take place on [date] at [place] commencing at [time].

16. If by [date] the Parties have not concluded a settlement agreement, the matter shall be listed on the first available date before an appropriate judge who shall be allocated for the future management and trial of the Proceedings.

17. The Court Settlement Process shall proceed on the basis of such documents as might be determined at the Preliminary Court Settlement Conference and which may include the documents filed in the court proceedings and further documents critical to the understanding of the issues in the dispute and the positions of the Parties.

Dated this day of 201

2D ADMIRALTY JURISDICTION AND PROCEEDINGS

PART 61 — ADMIRALTY CLAIMS

Constituting a limitation fund

Delete the last sentence (beginning "However a contrary view") and substitute:
The Court of Appeal has decided that on its proper construction art.11.2 of the **2D–76.1**
Limitation of Liability for Maritime Claims 1976 as enacted by s.185(1) of the Merchant Shipping Act 1995 provides that a limitation fund may be constituted by producing a guarantee which is considered by the court to be adequate security for the fund, see *Kairos Shipping v Enka & Co. (The "Atlantic Confidence")* [2014] EWCA Civ 217; [2014] 1 Lloyds Rep. 586.

2E ARBITRATION PROCEEDINGS

Arbitration Act 1996

THE ARBITRATION AGREEMENT

Agreement to submit to arbitration

Add at end:
In *Christian Kruppa v Alessandro Benedetti and Bertrand de Pallieres* [2014] EWHC 1887 **2E–99**
(Comm) Cooke J. held that a clause providing that in the event of any dispute the parties would endeavour first to resolve the matter through Swiss arbitration, failing which the English courts would have non–exclusive jurisdiction, was not an arbitration agreement within the meaning of the section.

STAY OF LEGAL PROCEEDINGS

A Party to an arbitration agreement

In the second paragraph, for "Fortress Value Recovery Fund I LLC v Blue Skye Special Opportunities Fund LP [2013] EWCA Civ 367; [2013] 2 All E.R. (Comm) 315; [2013] 1 Lloyd's Rep. 606; [2013] 1 C.L.C. 752" substitute:
Fortress Value Recovery Fund I LLC v Blue Skye Special Opportunities Fund LP [2013] **2E–107**
EWCA Civ 367; [2013] 1 W.L.R. 3466; [2013] 2 All E.R. (Comm) 315; [2013] 1 Lloyd's Rep. 606; [2013] 1 C.L.C. 752

Inoperative

Add at end:
An arbitration is not inoperative under this section by reason of one party's failure **2E–113**
to pay an advance on costs, which breach was not a repudiatory breach: *BDMS v Rafael Advanced Defence Systems* [2014] EWHC 451 (Comm); [2014] 1 Lloyd's Rep 576 Hamblen J.

Note

Add new paragraph at end:

2E–187   As to the approach under this section, see *Emmott v Michael Wilson & Partners Ltd* [2009] EWHC 1 (Comm); [2009] 2 All E.R. (Comm) 856 (Teare J) and *Patley Wood Farm LLP v Nihal Mohammed Kamal Brake and others* [2013] EWHC 4035 (Ch) Peter Smith J establishing that there is a discretion, and that the exercise is not a rubber stamping exercise, and considering factors which will be relevant in the exercise of the discretion.

Interim Injunctions

At the end of the second paragraph (ending "for the purposes of s.44(3)") add:

2E–197   In *Zim Integrated Shipping Services v European Container AS and others* Males J held that s.44(3) might possibly extend to an order preventing a party from terminating a charterparty but held it would be inappropriate to exercise the discretion to secure the claim where the claimant had knowingly chosen to deal with respondents who had very few assets.

POWERS OF THE COURT IN RELATION TO AWARD

"On the ground of serious irregularity"

In the first paragraph, for "Primera Maritime Hellas v Jiangsum Eastern Heavy Industry [2013] EWHC 3066 (Comm)", substitute:

2E–262   *Primera Maritime Hellas v Jiangsum Eastern Heavy Industry* [2013] EWHC 3066 (Comm); [2014] 1 Lloyd's Rep. 255

In the seventh paragraph, for "Primera Maritime Hellas v Jiangsum Eastern Heavy Industry [2013] EWHC 3066 (Comm)", substitute:

   Primera Maritime Hellas v Jiangsum Eastern Heavy Industry [2013] EWHC 3066 (Comm); [2014] 1 Lloyd's Rep. 255 Flaux J, *Transition Feeds LLP v Itochu Europe PLC* [2013] EWHC 3629 (Comm) Field J.

Appeals to the Court of Appeal

In the sixth paragraph, for "Bunge SA v Kyla Shipping Co Ltd [2013] EWCA Civ 734; [2013] 3 All E.R. 1006; [2013] 2 All E.R. (Comm) 577", substitute:

2E–268   *Bunge SA v Kyla Shipping Co Ltd* [2013] EWCA Civ 734; [2013] 3 All E.R. 1006; [2013] 2 All E.R. (Comm) 577; [2013] 2 Lloyd's Rep. 463

Time for appeal/Exhaustion of Specified Remedies s.70(2)

At the end of the first paragraph, add:

2E–271   See also the judgment of Andrew Smith J. in *A Ltd v B Ltd* [2014] EWHC 1870 (Comm) as to whether an applicant who had had its appeal dismissed for delay had exhausted the available remedies.

Terms

Add at end:

2E–273   When considering an application for security under s.70(6) the principles are stated by the Court of Appeal in *Republic of Kazakhstan v Istil Group Inc* [2006] 1 WLR 596 at [31]–[32]. The Court has to act in accordance with the overriding objective and the correct approach is the same as that under CPR 25.12 and 25.13. See also the judgment of Teare J. in *X v Y* [2013] EWHC 1104 (Comm); [2013] 2 Lloyd's Rep. 230 applying a test of "real risk" that assets are not available to satisfy any order for costs.

Section 70(7)

After "C.L.C. 944 (FlauxJ.))" add:

2E–274   See also Teare J. in *X v Y* [2013] EWHC 1104 (Comm); [2013] 2 Lloyd's Rep. 230 and Eder J. in *Konkola Copper Mines v U&M Mining Zambia* [2014] EWHC 2146 (Comm) considering this approach.

Note

In the last paragraph, for "London Steamship Owners Mutual Insurance Association v Kingdom of Spain [2013] EWHC 2840 (Comm)", substitute:

London Steamship Owners Mutual Insurance Association v Kingdom of Spain [2013] **2E–278**
EWHC 2840 (Comm); [2014] 1 All E.R. (Comm) 300; [2014] 1 Lloyd's Rep. 137; 150
Con. L.R. 181 Walker J.

SUPPLEMENTARY

In s.82(1), delete the definition for "legal proceedings" and substitute:

Minor definitions
"legal proceedings" means civil proceedings in England and Wales in the High **2E–294**
Court or the county court or in Northern Ireland in the High Court or a
county court;

Note

Delete Note and substitute:

In subsection (1) definition "legal proceedings" amended by the Crime and Courts **2E–294.1**
Act 2013 Sch.9 para.60(1), (2), with effect from April 22, 2014 (see SI 2014/954).

Grounds of refusal

At the end of the last paragraph, add:

In (1) *Anthony Lombard–Knight* (2) *Jakob Kinde v Rainstorm Pictures Inc* [2014] EWCA **2E–360**
Civ 356 the Court of Appeal held that the failure to have copies of the arbitration
agreement certified was not a good ground for setting aside an order for enforcement
under the section. The Convention was intended to promote enforcement, not put
purposeless hurdles in its way.

Subsection (5)

Add at end:

IPCO (Nigeria) v Nigerian National Petroleum [2014] EWHC 576 (Comm); [2014] 1 **2E–361**
Lloyd's Rep. 625 Field J considering the circumstances in which a decision to adjourn
an enforcement decision in the face of allegations of fraud will be made.

2F INTELLECTUAL PROPERTY PROCEEDINGS

PART 63—INTELLECTUAL PROPERTY CLAIMS

Commercial Success

In the second paragraph, for "toother" substitute:
to other **2F–7.5**

In the fourth paragraph, for "para.2F–104" substitute:
para. 2F–10.4

Expert evidence in design right cases and copyright cases

In the second paragraph, after "EWCA Civ 886", delete the sentence beginning: "Whilst **2F–14.7**
sometimes it is" to the end.

Delete the Patents County Court Guide at paragraphs 2F–149 to 2F–181 and substitute:

Intellectual Property Enterprise Court Guide
Issued April 2014 **2F–149**
By authority of the Chancellor of the High Court

1. General

1.1 Introduction
This is the general Guide to the Intellectual Property Enterprise Court (the IPEC).

It is written for all users of the IPEC, whether a litigant in person or a specialist IP litigator.

The Guide aims to help users and potential users of the IPEC by explaininghow the procedures will operate, providing guidelines where appropriate and dealing with various practical aspects of proceedings before the IPEC.

The IPEC has a multi–track and a small claims track. This means that there are two alternative procedures for making a claim in the IPEC. The IPEC multi–track has a limit on damages of up to £500,000. Costs orders will be made which are proportionate to the nature of the dispute and subject to a cap of no more than £50,000. The small claims track is for suitable claims in the IPEC with a value of up to £10,000. Costs orders on the small claims track are highly restricted.

The focus of this Guide is the IPEC's multi–track. There is a separate Guide for the IPEC's small claims track.

The Guide cannot be wholly comprehensive of all issues which may arise on the multi–track in the IPEC. In circumstances which are not covered by this guide, reference may be made to the Patents Court Guide and the Chancery Guide. See paragraph 3.12 below for where to find these and also the IPEC Small Claims Guide.

Civil Procedure Rules

Throughout this Guide there will be reference to the Civil Procedure Rules and also to Practice Directions which set out how the Rules are to be applied. These are generally abbreviated to 'CPR' and 'PD' respectively. The Civil Procedure Rules are divided into 'Parts', each of which is concerned with an aspect of the rules.

A rule is identified by the Part in which it is found and the number of the rule. Thus, for instance, 'CPR r.63.2' is rule 2 in Part 63 and 'CPR r.63.27(1)(a)' refers to sub–rule (1)(a) of rule 27 in Part 63. The Parts are also often divided into 'Sections' and where it is appropriate the relevant Section of the Part will be identified. In most instances in this Guide 'CPR' will be taken as read, so the rule and sub–rule just mentioned, for example, will be referred to as 'r.63.2' and 'r.63.27(1)(a)'.

Practice Directions are also identified by the Part in which they fall, by paragraph number and sometimes by the relevant Section of the Practice Direction, e.g. 'PD 30 para. 9.1' or 'PD 45 Section IV'.

The Civil Procedure Rules, including the Practice Directions, are contained in a publication usually referred to as 'The White Book' and are also available on the court service website, see paragraph 3.12 below.

History of the IPEC

Following the report of the Committee chaired by Sir Derek Oulton in 1987, the Patents County Court (PCC) was set up in 1990. The PCC was intended to provide a less costly and less complex alternative to the High Court, Patents Court. The Patents Court is intended for larger and more complex claims.

Based initially in Wood Green in North London, the PCC moved to Park Crescent near Regent's Park in the West End of London in the mid 1990s. In 2002 the court moved to Field House, Breams Buildings, and to St Dunstan's House, Fetter Lane in 2008.

In June 2009, the Intellectual Property Court Users' Committee (IPCUC) published a consultation paper setting out proposals for reform of the PCC and in July 2009 the working party's final report was published. The proposals were adopted in the final report of the Review of Civil Litigation Costs by Lord Justice Jackson and on1st October 2010 a new set of procedures was implemented in the PCC.

In 2011 the PCC moved to the Rolls Building along with the Chancery Division of the High Court (including the Patents Court), the Commercial Court and the Technology and Construction Court.

Following on from the proposals set out in the Jackson Review and in response to a further recommendation made in the Hargreaves Review, a small claims track within the PCC was set up and came into effect on 1 October 2012.

On 1st October 2013 the PCC was reconstituted as a specialist list in the Chancery Division of the High Court to form the Intellectual Property Enterprise Court (IPEC). The reference to "intellectual property" in the name of the court is intended to recognise its broad intellectual property jurisdiction.

The practices and procedures in the IPEC after reconstitution are and are intended to be the same as the practices and procedures in the PCC before reconstitution. Save for a few minor adjustments to the rules which would have been desirable even if the court had not been reconstituted, the provisions of the Rules and Practice Directions applicable in the IPEC are identical to the Rules and Practice Directions which were applicable in the PCC.

Transitional provisions

The transitional provisions governing the reconstitution of the PCC as the IPEC are set out in The Civil Procedure (Amendment No. 7) Rules 2013, SI 2013 No. 1974 (L.19) paragraph 30. Generally it will be sufficient to know the following. Proceedings which were already in the PCC as at 1st October 2013 will continue in the IPEC afterwards as if they had been started in that court (paragraph 30(a)). Anything done in accordance with the rules which applied in the PCC before reconstitution will be treated as being done in accordance with the corresponding rules of the IPEC (paragraph 30(b)) and any judgment or order of the PCC has the same effect as if it had been a judgment or order of the IPEC (paragraph 30(c)).

1.2 Jurisdiction

The IPEC is set up to handle intellectual property cases of all kinds including patents, designs (registered and unregistered, Community and UK national), trade marks (UK and Community), passing off, copyright, database right, other rights conferred by the Copyright Designs and Patents Act 1988 and actions for breach of confidence.

For example, the IPEC may hear and determine actions and counterclaims for:

- Infringement of patents, designs, trade marks, copyright and other intellectual property rights
- Revocation or invalidity of patents, registered designs and trade marks
- Amendment of patents
- Declarations of non–infringement
- Determination of entitlement to a patent, design or any other intellectual property
- Employee's compensation in respect of a patented invention
- Unjustified threats of proceedings for infringement of patents, designs or trade marks
- Misuse of trade secrets and other breaches of confidence.

As part of the Chancery Division the IPEC has jurisdiction over any case which can be heard before that Division. Consequently the IPEC may hear proceedings primarily concerned with intellectual property but covering other subject matter, such as breach of fiduciary duty, defamation or malicious falsehood.

(a)

Legal basis for jurisdiction of the IPEC

The IPEC is as specialist list within the Chancery Division of the High Court and is administered at the Rolls Building. Whereas the basis for the jurisdiction of its predecessor court, the PCC, was a complex matter derived in part from the Copyright Designs and Patents Act 1988 and from other sources, the nature of the IPEC as a specialist list in the Chancery Division, means it has the same jurisdiction as the High Court and the former complexities relating to the jurisdiction of the PCC, no longer arise.

The small claims track

The jurisdiction of the IPEC small claims track is a subset of the normal jurisdiction of the IPEC available on the IPEC multi–track. CPR r.63.27(1)(a) limits the kinds of intellectual property claim which may be allocated to the IPEC small claims track. The IPEC small claims track may deal with any IP claim within the jurisdiction of the IPEC save for those referred to in r.63.2. In practice this means the small claims track may hear claims relating to copyright, trade marks and passing off, and unregistered designs (UK or Community) and breach of confidence. Claims relating to patents, registered designs (UK or Community) and plant varieties may only be heard on the IPEC multi–track.

(b)

Applicable rules of procedure

The rules applicable to proceedings started in or transferred to the IPEC are as follows:

- The general Civil Procedure Rules (CPR) provide the framework for proceedings in the IPEC as they apply to all civil courts in England and Wales.
- CPR Part 63—Intellectual Property Claims applies to all intellectual property claims. Part 63 includes rules specific to intellectual property cases and in some areas modifies the general parts of the CPR.
- Practice Direction 63 (PD 63) supplements CPR Part 63.
- Part 63 and PD 63 are arranged in sections as follows:
  - Section I relates to proceedings which concern patents and registered designs (Community or national). It is applicable to proceedings in the IPEC which relate to those rights.
  - Section II allocates all other IP cases to particular courts including the Chancery Division, the IPEC and certain county courts where there is a Chancery District Registry.
  - Section III deals with service of documents and participation by the Comptroller.
  - Section IV does not relate to proceedings in the IPEC.
  - Section V relates to all proceedings started in or transferred to the IPEC. This section contains the new procedural rules applicable after 1st October 2010 with minor modifications introduced since then.
- Attention is drawn to two other parts of the general CPR which contain provisions specific to the IPEC:
  - Part 30 and in particular PD 30 paras. 9.1 and 9.2 which relate to the transfer of proceedings to the IPEC from other courts and vice versa. Part 30 includes r.30.5 which, when it applies to transfers to the IPEC from the County Court or from the Chancery Division, is modified by Part 63 r.63.18.
  - Part 45 Section IV and Section IV of PD 45 which relate to costs.

Transition between the PCC and the IPEC

Parts 63 and 45 of the CPR, and the relevant PDs have been amended to reflect the reconstitution of the IPEC as a specialist list of the Chancery Division and the renaming of the court from the PCC to the IPEC, with effect from 1st October 2013. Since the procedures in the IPEC are the same as the procedures in the PCC before reconstitution, the cases decided in the PCC before 1st October 2013 will generally remain applicable as precedents in the IPEC after 1st October 2013.

(c)

Legal remedies

All the remedies available in the High Court are available in the IPEC including preliminary and final injunctions, damages, accounts of profits, delivery up and disclosure. In particular search and seizure (Anton Piller) and asset freezing (Mareva) orders are available in the IPEC.

There is one exception. The IPEC small claims track has the power to order final injunctions (and award damages and other final remedies) but not preliminary injunctions, search and seizure (Anton Piller) and asset freezing (Mareva) orders (r63.27(4)). All these remedies are however available on the IPEC multi–track.

(d)

Enforcement

Orders of the IPEC are generally enforced in the same way as any other orders of the High Court in England and Wales. Orders for the payment of money can be enforced by obtaining information from judgment debtors (CPR rule 71), making charging orders (CPR rule 73) and in the other ways available under the CPR. All proceedings for the enforcement of any financial element of an IPEC judgment are dealt with by a district judge (r.63.18(2)(c)). The IPEC has the power to commit for contempt of court and has the power to issue a bench warrant to secure attendance at court (see e.g. *Westwood v Knight* [2012] EWPCC 14).

(e)

The cap on damages in the IPEC

There is a cap on the damages recoverable in the IPEC of £500,000. The same cap also applies to the sum recoverable on an account of profits. The £500,000 figure does not include interest (save for interest due under an agreement) or costs (CPR r63.17A). The cap is a limit on the amount or value of the claim for damages (or an account). It is not an automatic cap on the value of the proceedings as a whole (such as the value of any injunction which may be sought).

The cap itself may be waived by agreement of the parties (CPR r63.17A(3)).

1.3 Allocation

The limit on damages available in the IPEC provides a clear distinction between that court and the other parts of the High Court such as the Patents Court and general Chancery Division. Otherwise there is no sharp dividing line between cases which should be brought in the IPEC and actions which should be brought in other courts.

In deciding which is the appropriate court in which to commence a claim, users should bear in mind that the IPEC has been established to handle the smaller, shorter, less complex, less important, lower value actions and the procedures applicable in the court are designed particularly for cases of that kind. The court aims to provide cheaper, speedier and more informal procedures to ensure that small and medium sized enterprises and private individuals are not deterred from innovation by the potential cost of litigation to safeguard their rights. Longer, heavier, more complex, more important and more valuable actions belong in the Patents Court or the general Chancery list of the High Court.

Parties may agree with each other to maintain a case in the IPEC if they wish to make use of the procedures available in it. The court will endeavour to accommodate parties in that respect. The court will, however, maintain its list in such a way as to ensure that it maintains access to justice for small and medium sized enterprises and individuals.

If a party to litigation in either the IPEC or a different court believes that the other court is a more appropriate forum for the case, they should apply to transfer it. In the IPEC an application to transfer to a different court must be made at or before the case management conference (CPR rule 63.25(4)). There are a number of cases in which the transfer provisions now applicable were considered in the PCC. They include *ALK Abello v Meridian* [2010] EW PCC 014, *Caljan Rite–Hite v Solvex* [2011] EW HC 669 (Ch), *A.S. Watson v The Boots Company* [2011] EWPCC 26, *Comic Enterprises v Twentieth Century Fox* [2012] EW PCC 13, *Environmental Recycling v Stillwell* [2012] EWHC 2097 (Pat), *Destra v Comada* [2012] EW PCC 39.

The following guidelines are provided to assist users in determining which court is suitable:

- Size of the parties. If both sides are small or medium sized enterprises then the case may well be suitable for the IPEC. If one party is a small or medium sized enterprise but the other is a larger undertaking then again the case may be suitable for the IPEC but other factors ought to be considered such as the value of the claim and its likely complexity.
- The complexity of the claim. The procedure in the IPEC is streamlined and trials will seldom last more than 2 days. A trial which would appear to require more time than that even with the streamlined procedure of the IPEC is likely to be unsuitable.
- The nature of the evidence. Experiments in a patent case may be admitted in the IPEC but a case which will involve substantial complex experimental evidence will be unsuitable for the IPEC.
- Conflicting factual evidence. Cross–examination of witnesses will be strictly controlled in the IPEC. The court is well able to handle cases involving disputed factual matters such as allegations of prior use in patents and independent design as a defence to copying; but if a large number of witnesses are required the case may be unsuitable for the IPEC.
- Value of the claim. Subject to the agreement of the parties, there is a limit on the damages available in the IPEC of £500,000. However, assessing the value of a claim is not only concerned with damages. Putting a value on a claim is a notoriously difficult exercise, taking into account factors such as possible damages, the value of an injunction and the possible effect on competition in a market if a patent was revoked. As a general rule of thumb, disputes where the value of sales, in the UK, of products protected by the intellectual property in issue (by the owner, licensees and alleged infringer) exceeds £1 million per year are unlikely to be suitable for the IPEC in the absence of agreement.

Allocation between the IPEC multi–track and small claims track (r.63.27)

If the claim has a value of £10,000 or less and if it is concerned with the intellectual property rights applicable in the IPEC small claims track (essentially copyright, trade marks and passing off or unregistered design rights (UK or Community)) then that track is likely to be the appropriate track in the IPEC. Otherwise the case should proceed on the normal IPEC multi–track.

If the claimant in its Particulars of Claim states that it wishes the claim to be allocated to the small claims track and the defendant does not object, the claim will go to the small claims track provided it has the necessary features just referred to (value not more than £10,000 and it concerns appropriate intellectual property rights) (r.63.27(1)). If the claim has those necessary features but the parties disagree about whether the claim should be heard in the small claims track, the court will allocate the claim to the appropriate track in accordance with Part 26 and in particular the criteria listed in r.26.8 (r.63.27(3)).

The separate Guide to the IPEC small claims track deals with cases proceeding on that track.

1.4 The judges of the Intellectual Property Enterprise Court

The Enterprise Judge of the IPEC is a Specialist Circuit Judge. The judges of the High Court, Patents Court are able to sit as judges of the IPEC as necessary. Certain senior members of the Intellectual Property Bar are qualified and able to sit in the IPEC when the need arises.

Cases on the IPEC small claims track are handled by district judges (r63.18(2)(b)).

1.5 Judges able and willing to sit out of London

If the parties so desire, for the purpose of saving time or costs, the IPEC will sit out of London. Before any approach is made to the Judge's Clerk, the parties should discuss between themselves the desirability of such a course. If there is a dispute as to venue, the court will resolve the matter on an application. Where there is no dispute, the Judge's Clerk should be contacted as soon as possible so that arrangements can be put in place well before the date of the proposed hearing.

1.6 Intellectual Property Enterprise Court Users' Committee

The IPEC has a Users' Committee which considers the problems and concerns of intellectual property litigators in the IPEC. Anyone having views concerning the improvement of intellectual property litigation in the IPEC is invited to make his or her views known to the committee, preferably through the relevant professional representative on the committee or its secretary (contact details are in Annex A).

If matters relate to intellectual property litigation more widely, then this may be a matter for the Intellectual Property Court Users' Committee. Views can be expressed to the IPEC Users' Committee, who will refer on matters outside its remit, or direct to representatives of the Intellectual Property Court Users' Committee or its secretary.

1.7 Representation

A person may represent themselves in litigation in the IPEC as a litigant in person. However, intellectual property matters are often quite complex and cases will often benefit from the assistance of a knowledgeable legal representative.

Patent and trade mark attorneys[1] and solicitors all have rights to represent clients in the IPEC. These professionals may additionally instruct barristers to help prepare the case and/or argue the case in court. In some instances, a barrister may accept instructions directly from the public.

Each of these professions has a different qualification and skill set. So, in some cases, it may be appropriate to instruct more than one legal representative to act as a team.

---

[1] The rights of patent attorneys and trade mark attorneys to conduct litigation and appear in the IPEC are determined by the Intellectual Property Regulation Board (IPREG) (www.ipreg.org.uk). Attorneys with an Intellectual Property Litigation Certificate may conduct litigation and appear in the IPEC. The equivalent rights of solicitors are governed by the Solicitors Regulation Authority (SRA). Discussions between the judiciary and the SRA have made clear that notwithstanding the constitution of the IPEC as a part of the High Court all solicitors have right of audience in the IPEC.

More information about these different professions can be found at the following websites:

- Chartered Institute of Patent Attorneys—www.cipa.org.uk regarding patent attorneys and patent attorney litigators
- Law Society—www.lawsociety.org.uk regarding solicitors; and for IP specialist solicitors the IPLA—www.ipla.org.uk
- Institute of Trade Mark Attorneys—www.itma.org.uk regarding trade mark and design litigators
- Bar Council—www.barcouncil.org.uk regarding barristers, and for IP specialist barristers—www.ipba.co.uk

Where a person bringing or defending a case in the IPEC cannot afford to pay for their own legal representative, then they may be eligible to seek free or pro bono advice. The National Pro Bono Centre houses national clearing houses for legal pro bono work delivered in England and Wales: i.e. the Bar Pro Bono Unit, LawWorks (the Solicitors' Pro Bono Group) and ILEX Pro Bono Forum. The website is at: www.nationalprobonocentre.org.uk.

A litigant wishing to seek pro bono legal assistance should approach the Citizens Advice Bureau or a Law Centre first. There is a CAB office in the Royal Courts of Justice, Strand, London.

The IPEC Users Committee is working with CIPA to look at setting up a CIPA pro bono scheme and also actively considering other ways to widen the availability of pro bono legal assistance in the IPEC.

1.8 Appeals (rule 52)

If a party wishes to appeal, permission is generally required. Permission may be sought from the judge making the order or from the court to which the appeal is addressed.

Appeals from the multi–track in the Intellectual Property Enterprise Court

Depending on the nature of the order being appealed, the destination of an appeal from the multi–track in the IPEC is either the Court of Appeal or the High Court. Final orders are appealed to the Court of Appeal whereas interim orders are appealed to the High Court (Chancery Division). See r.63.19(1A) which provides that for the purposes of Practice Direction 52A, a decision of the enterprise judge shall be treated as a decision by a circuit judge hearing a specialist claim in the County Court. Paragraphs 3.6 to 3.8 of PD 52A explain the difference between a final order and an interim order.

When permission is sought from the judge making the order, the order must identify the route of appeal (r.40.2(4)).

Appeals from the IPEC small claims track

The destination of an appeal from a decision on the IPEC small claims track is to the Enterprise Judge in the IPEC. Although r.63.19(3) provides that for the purposes of Practice Direction 52A a decision of district judge shall be treated as a decision by a district judge hearing a specialist claim in the County Court, it also expressly provides than an appeal from such a decision (by implication whether interim or final) shall be heard by an Enterprise Judge.

2. Procedure in the Intellectual Property Enterprise Court

2.1 Before issuing proceedings

Attention is drawn to the Practice Direction—Pre–Action Conduct. This is to be **2F–150** found at the start of Section C of Volume 1 of the White Book and is also available on the internet—see paragraph 3.12 below.

Compliance with this Practice Direction will affect the timetable, once proceedings are issued (see further below). However, as unjustified threats to bring legal proceedings in respect of many IP rights can themselves be subject to litigation, each claimant will have to make their own decision as to whether it is appropriate to write to a prospective defendant to see if matters can be settled before any proceedings are issued.

2.2 Issuing proceedings

'Issuing proceedings' is the term used for starting proceedings. The IPEC is situated in the Rolls Building in London at the address in Annex A and this is where proceedings in the IPEC must be started.

Most proceedings are issued using claim form N1 which can be obtained from the public counter at the Rolls Building or downloaded from the court website (see paragraph 3.12 below). A claimant should ensure that there is a copy of the claim form for the court, one for each defendant, as well as a copy for itself. The claim form must be completed and then filed at the Rolls Building. This may be done by post.

2.3 Service of the claim form

'Service' of a document means delivering it to another party in the proceedings. A copy of the claim form should be served by the claimant on each defendant together with a response pack. A response pack consists of the documents that a defendant will need to read and complete in order to make its initial response to the claim, namely (a) a form for defending the claim, (b) a form for admitting the claim and (c) a form for acknowledging service. The response pack may also be downloaded from the court website (see paragraph 3.12 below). The claimant should make sure the defendant's copy of the claim form is obtained from the court at issue.

CPR Part 6 and the associated Practice Direction deal with how to make sure that documents are correctly served. A typical means of service on a company is by first class post to the company's principal or last known place of business, although CPR Part 6 sets out a number of alternative methods. Attention is also drawn to r.63.14 where a party is being served at an address for service for a registered right and with regard to when a copy of a document should also be sent to the UK Intellectual Property Office.

Generally a claimant should serve its Particulars of Claim with the claim form (see below).

2.4 Response by a defendant

A defendant served with Particulars of Claim has a choice as to how to respond. It may serve its Defence within 14 days of service of the Particulars of Claim. But if the defendant either needs more time to serve its Defence or wishes to challenge the jurisdiction of the Court, it should file an Acknowledgment of Service with the Court. CPR r.10.3 sets out the period for filing an Acknowledgment of Service. Generally it must be done within 14 days of service of the claim form or, if the claim form states that the Particulars of Claim are to follow, within 14 days of service of the Particulars of Claim. The CPR only requires the Acknowledgement of Service to be filed with the Court, although subsequent documents, such as the Defence, must both be filed with the Court and served on the other parties (see r.15.6). In any event it may often be helpful to send a copy of any document filed with the court to the other party, to ensure that those documents are received in a timely manner.

2.5 Statements of Case

(a)

Introduction

The statements of case are the documents where each party sets out its case. For the claimant this will primarily be the Particulars of Claim. The defendant responds with the Defence or the Defence and Counterclaim. The claimant may then serve a Reply or a Reply and Defence to Counterclaim, as appropriate.

These statements of case need to be full, but not unnecessarily lengthy. Statements of case can stand as evidence at trial in the IPEC, where relevant individuals have verified them with a statement of truth, as discussed further below.

(b)

Time limits for filing and serving statements of case

The relevant time limits are necessarily but unfortunately dispersed across different Parts of the CPR. The following is a summary guide.

The better practice is for a claimant to file the Particulars of Claim with the court along with the claim form and to serve the Particulars of Claim on the other parties at the same time as serving the claim form. However the Particulars of Claim can be served up to 14 days later (r.7.4(1)). If served later, the Particulars of Claim must be filed with the court no later than 7 days after service on the defendant (r.7.4(3)).

If no Acknowledgement of Service has been filed, the period for filing the Defence with the court is 14 days after service of the Particulars of Claim (r.15.4(1)(a)). If an Acknowledgement of Service has been filed, then the time limit for filing the Defence depends on whether the Particulars of Claim confirms that the Pre–Action Conduct Practice Direction has been complied with (r.63.22(2) and (3)). The time limit is 42 days if it does and 70 days if it does not. In the event that the defendant also wishes to make a counterclaim against the claimant, this should follow on from the Defence in the same document and should be headed 'Counterclaim' (PD 20, para. 6.1).

The Defence (or Defence and Counterclaim) must be served on every other party (r.15.6). This should be done at the same time as filing the Defence. The CPR does not specify a time limit for serving the Defence but undue delay may cause adverse consequences in costs later.

The time limit for the claimant filing a Reply with court is 28 days from the service of the Defence. The same time limit applies to service of the Reply on other parties (r.63.22(4)).

If the claimant has been served with a Defence and Counterclaim it must respond with a Reply and Defence to Counterclaim. This should follow on from the Reply in the same document and should be headed 'Defence to Counterclaim' (PD 20, para. 6.2). The time limits for a Reply and Defence to Counterclaim are the same as for a Reply.

An optional final statement of case from the defendant is a Reply to the Defence to Counterclaim. This must be both filed and served 14 days from the service of the Defence to Counterclaim (r.63.22(5)).

Some time limits are stricter than others in the IPEC. The parties are not at liberty to extend the time limits set out in r.63.22 without the prior consent of the judge. Applications for any extension of time must be made in good time and set out good reasons as to why they are required. They are almost always dealt with without a hearing.

(c)

Content of statements of case

Statements of case must comply with the requirements of CPR Part 16, with an important modification: a particular feature of statements of case in the IPEC is that they must comply with r.63.20 (1). They must set out concisely all facts and arguments relied on. A key purpose of this requirement is to facilitate the conduct of the case management conference which will be conducted on an issue by issue basis. The court and the parties need to know what the issues are going to be in sufficient detail for that process to take place. Therefore the facts and arguments that all parties intend to present at trial should have been finalised by the time of the CMC and set out in the statements of case.

However, attention is drawn to the requirement for the matters to be set out concisely. Unnecessarily lengthy statements of case will not be permitted. It is unlikely that legal arguments will need to be set out in any detail; all that is likely to be required is a brief statement of the nature of the argument to be relied on.

In proceedings relating to a patent or registered design the statements of case should also comply with PD 63 paras. 4.1 to 4.6 (r.63.6).

In all proceedings copies of important documents referred to in a statement of case (e.g. an advertisement relied on or documents cited in Grounds of Invalidity) should be served with the statement of case. Where any such document requires translation, a translation should be served at the same time.

Guidance on the preparation of a statement of case for particular proceedings is as follows:

Patent proceedings

- Statements of case should comply with PD 63 paras. 4.1 to 4.6 (r.63.6).
- Lengthy expositions of construction of patent claims are unlikely to be necessary or desirable. However the parties will be expected to identify the claims in issue (for infringement and validity) and identify the relevant features of those claims.
- It is likely to be necessary to break down a patent claim into suitable integers (i.e. separate parts) in order to explain a case on infringement with reference to specific elements of the alleged infringing product or process. This may be

most conveniently done in the form of a table or chart annexed to the statement of case. Points on construction should emerge from this exercise and may need to be identified but lengthy argument on them is not required.

- A submission of lack of novelty of a patent is likely to require a similar approach to infringement (i.e. a claim break down, perhaps in the form of a table, with the claim integers compared with the relevant parts of the prior art disclosure(s) relied upon).
- A case of obviousness of a patent is likely to require a statement addressing the allegedly obvious step(s).
- Where a party raises the issue of validity of a patent, the patentee (or other relevant party) should identify which of the claims of the patent are alleged to have independent validity in his reply (or defence) to the allegation of invalidity.
- A specific statement of what facts are said to be relevant and common general knowledge is likely to be necessary. A short summary of the relevant technical background may be helpful.

Registered design proceedings
- Statements of case should comply with PD 63 paras. 4.1 to 4.6 (r.63.6).
- The nature and characteristics of the informed user should be identified.

Trade Mark proceedings
- Similarities relied on between a mark and a sign will not generally require elaboration. But in an appropriate case some detail may be necessary in relation to allegations that goods or services are similar. Parties to trade mark cases should identify the nature and characteristics of the relevant consumer (if relevant).

Copyright proceedings
- A defence of independent design in a copyright case (or similar) will need to be addressed in appropriate detail.

(d)

Statements of truth
Attention is drawn to r63.21, which modifies Part 22 in its application to the IPEC. The statement of truth must be made by a person with knowledge of the facts alleged (or by persons who between them have such knowledge). If more than one person signs the statement of truth, the individuals should indicate in some suitable manner which parts of the statement of case they are verifying.

Statements of case (or parts of them) suitably verified may be permitted to stand as evidence at trial. The court's permission to do so is required (r.32.6) but will generally be given. This is a matter to raise at the case management conference (see e.g. *Westwood v Knight* [2010] EW PCC 16).

Attention is drawn to r.32.14 which sets out the consequences of verifying a statement of case containing a false statement without an honest belief in its truth, and to the procedures set out in PD 32 para. 28.

2.6 Case management (r.63.23)
The case management conference ("CMC") in the IPEC is conducted by a judge. The purpose of the CMC is to manage the conduct of the case in order to bring the proceedings to a trial in a manner proportionate to the nature of the dispute, the financial position of the parties, the degree of complexity of the case, the importance of the case and the amount of money at stake. At the first CMC, the court will identify the issues and decide whether to make orders under paragraph 29.1 of PD 63. These include orders permitting the filing of further material in the case such as witness statements, experts' reports, disclosure and orders permitting cross–examination at trial and skeleton arguments. The trial date will be fixed at the CMC.

(a)

Directions questionnaire
All cases are allocated to the multi–track automatically by operation of r.63.1(3) unless the case is to be allocated to the small claims track in which case r.63.27 applies (see the Guide to the IPEC small claims track).

346

The effect of these provisions means that for cases on the multi–track the IPEC generally dispenses with the need for a directions questionnaire.

(b)

The date for the case management conference

The date for the CMC will normally be arranged as follows. The claimant should apply for a CMC within 14 days after all defendants who intend to file and serve a Defence have done so. Where a case has been transferred from another court, the claimant should apply for a CMC within 14 days of the transfer. Any party may apply for a CMC at an earlier date than these dates. If the claimant has not applied for a CMC within 14 days then the defendant should do so. In any event the Court can and will aim to fix a date for a CMC if the parties have not done so within a reasonable period. These requirements are mandatory for cases within Section I of Part 63 (essentially patents and registered designs; see PD 63 paras. 5.3 to 5.7) but should be followed in all cases in the IPEC as a matter of efficient case management.

(c)

The case management conference

The CMC will be conducted as a hearing in open court. However where all parties consent the court may determine the CMC on paper (r.63.23(3)).

A bundle of documents (see Annex C) should be filed with the court at the Rolls Building (full address in Annex A) in advance. Two days before the CMC is usually sufficient.

In general, parties should endeavour to agree directions prior to the date fixed for the CMC. Although the court has the right to amend directions which have been agreed, this will only happen where there is manifest reason for doing so.

The CMC is an important part of the procedure because no material may be filed in the case by way of evidence, disclosure or written submissions unless permission is given for it by the judge and the proper time for that permission to be given is the CMC (see e.g. *Westwood v Knight* [2010] EWPCC 16). Save in exceptional circumstances the court will not permit a party to submit material in a case in addition to that ordered at the CMC (r.63.23(2), see e.g. *Liversidge v Owen Mumford* [2012] EW PCC 33 and *Redd v Red Legal* [2012] EW PCC 50).

The basis on which the court will decide whether to permit material to be filed in a case is by applying the cost–benefit test (PD 63 para. 29.2(2)) and by giving permission in relation to specific and identified issues only ((PD 63 para. 29.2(1)). PD 63 para. 29.1 lists the material which the court may order: disclosure of documents, a product or process description, experiments, witness statements, experts' reports, cross–examination at trial, and written submissions or skeleton arguments. The parties need to attend the CMC in a position to assist the court in making appropriate orders on this basis. In particular, the parties should consider:

(a) The need for and scope of any evidence from factual or expert witnesses. Note the court will consider whether there is sufficient evidence in the statements of case or whether further evidence is required.

(b) The need for and scope of any oral testimony and cross–examination. Note that the court will confine any permitted cross–examination to particular issues and to time limits.

(c) The need for, and scope of, any disclosure of documents. No disclosure reports are required in the IPEC. Only specific disclosure will be ordered, i.e. disclosure of particular documents or particular classes of document, in relation to one or more of the issues in the proceedings identified in the CMC. In some cases a class of documents can be identified solely by reference to an issue or issues to which the documents relate.

(d) The need for any experiments, process or product descriptions or supply of any samples.

(e) The need for written submissions or skeleton arguments.

(f) The likely timetable up to trial. This may include dates on which disclosure of documents, product and process description and experiments is to take place as well as a schedule for witness statements and experts reports including provisions for any evidence in reply (if required).

(g) The need for an oral hearing or whether a decision can be made on the papers.

If an oral hearing is considered to be appropriate, the court will order that the hearing be of a fixed duration of no more than 2 days.

A specimen CMC order is attached to this Guide at Annex B.

(d)

A review of the issues

At the case management conference the court will identify the issues in the proceedings (r.63.23(1)). This is an important part of the CMC. The parties should exchange their proposed list of the issues. These need not be lengthy documents. They should be agreed if possible in advance but rather than incurring the cost debating lists of issues before the CMC, the most cost effective approach is generally to leave the argument over to the CMC itself.

(e)

Matters arising in particular cases before the IPEC

The following specific matters come up regularly and experience has shown that the approaches described below may be reasonable and proportionate.

In patent cases:

- to require the patentee to rely on no more than three independently valid claims; and
- to require a party challenging validity to rely on no more than three items of prior art.

These limits are intended to be flexible and in an appropriate case they can and have been relaxed. The reference to prior art includes all starting points for the obviousness analysis. In other words it does not encompass a party's general reliance on common general knowledge as part of its case on obviousness but it does include an argument of obviousness over common general knowledge alone.

Also in patent cases, evidence over and above the material in the statement of case may well only be required in relation to common general knowledge and obviousness.

In copyright and unregistered design right cases, if the issues include a defence of independent design, cross–examination and a measure of disclosure is likely to be required.

In registered design cases, there may be no need for cross–examination at all.

In Community design cases there is likely to be a limit on the extent to which the design corpus may be explored.

In general, if expert evidence is required, it may be possible for that evidence to be given by "in house" experts.

(f)

Amendments to the statement of case

On occasions a party may wish to amend its statement of case. If the other parties agree then generally no difficulties arise. If not then the court's permission is needed. This is best sought at the CMC but if the need for amendment arises after the CMC then it can be done by a separate application. In considering whether to permit the amendment the court will consider all the circumstances including proportionality and the cost–benefit test (see *Temple Island v New English Teas* [2011] EWPCC 19).

(g)

Expression of a preliminary, non–binding opinion on the merits

If both parties wish the court to do so, if it is likely to assist the parties in reaching a settlement, the IPEC is willing to express a preliminary and non–binding opinion on the merits of the case (see *Weight Watchers v Love Bites* [2012] EWPCC 12 and *Fayus v Flying Trade* [2012] EW PCC 43).

(h)

Costs in a multi–party case

If the case includes more than one defendant or group of defendants who are separately represented, the parties should consider the question of the likely effect of the costs capping provisions (see *Gimex v Chillbag* [2012] EW PCC 34 and *Liversidge v Owen Mumford (costs)* [2012] EWPCC 40). If in doubt the parties should raise the matter at the CMC.

(i)

Security for costs

In certain circumstances it is open to a defendant to seek security for costs. This means requiring the claimant to safeguard a sum of money to ensure that, in the event that the defendant were to win the action, the defendant's entitlement to its costs is secured. The rules relating to security for costs are set out at r.25.12–14.

(j)

Alternative dispute resolution

At the CMC the parties may apply for time in which to seek alternative dispute resolution (see paragraph 2.12 below) before the proceedings progress further. Occasionally the court may invite the parties to explore alternative means of resolving the case.

2.7 Transfers to and from the IPEC (r.63.18 and r.63.25(4) and (5))

Applications to transfer a case to another court should be made at the case management conference. The court will have regard to the provisions of PD 30 (Transfer) and in particular paragraph 9.1 which relates to transfers to and from the IPEC. The considerations set out above in the section on Allocation will be taken into account. In addition, in considering an application to transfer to another part of the High Court the following further matters will be taken into account:

- The holder of an intellectual property right who does not wish to incur costs on the normal High Court scale but apprehends that an alleged infringer may seek to have the matter transferred to another part of the High Court, may consider an undertaking to limit the enforcement of their rights; e.g. by foregoing an injunction or by reference to a certain value of sales (cf. *Liversidge v Owen Mumford* [2011] EWPCC 34).
- A defendant seeking transfer to another part of the High Court when the claimant cannot afford the cost of normal High Court litigation may offer to allow the claimant to withdraw their claim without prejudice to a right to restart litigation and/or without an adverse costs award.

An application to transfer a case after the CMC will only be considered in exceptional circumstances.

A judge sitting in the County Court or the general Chancery Division has the power to transfer a case to the IPEC (r.63.18(1) modifying r.30.5).

2.8 Re-allocation of cases within the IPEC between the multi–track and the small claims track (r.63.27 and r.26.10)

A case proceeding on one track in the IPEC may subsequently be re–allocated to the other track if it is appropriate to do so. A case will be re–allocated from the small claims track to the multi–track if it emerges that the nature of the claim makes it inappropriate for the small claims track. Circumstances in which it may be appropriate to re–allocate a case between the multi–track and the small claims track could arise if it emerges that the current track is inappropriate having regard to the value of the case or to its complexity or the relief sought.

A claim will not be re–allocated (unless it has to be) if that would cause substantial disruption to the progress of litigation.

2.9 Applications (r.63.25)

Any application to the court except for the CMC will be dealt with without a hearing unless the court considers it necessary to hold a hearing (r.63.25(3)). Provisions relating to telephone hearings of applications are set out at paragraph 3.5 below.

Once the application is received by a respondent, by r.63.25(2) the respondent to the application must file and serve on all relevant parties a response within 5 days of service of the application notice. When an application is to be resolved on paper, it is imperative that the applicant tells the court the date on which the application notice was served. This is necessary so that the court can know when the 5 day period provided for by r.63.25(2) has expired. Unless the matter is urgent or for some other good reason, the court will generally not deal with a paper application until it can be seen that the 5 day period provided for by r.63.25(2) has expired.

Applications for judgment in default

If a defendant fails to file either an Acknowledgment of Service or a Defence within two weeks of service on it of the Particulars of Claim the claimant may make an application for judgment in default. A claimant may also make an application for a default judgment if the defendant files an Acknowledgment of Service but fails to file a Defence within the relevant time limit (see above). These can generally be dealt with as paper applications, provided the application notice has been served on the relevant defendant and the court is informed of the date on which this took place in order to give effect to the 5 day period provided for by r.63.25(2).

2.10 Fast track and expedition

The IPEC does not operate a separate Part 28 "fast track", a procedure confined to the County Court. All cases in the IPEC are either on the multi–track or the small claims track.

The normal operation of the procedure on the IPEC multi–track is intended to ensure that trials and applications are heard and dealt with in a timely fashion. Nevertheless the court can accommodate urgent applications (such as applications for interim remedies) and, when necessary, trials can be dealt with on an expedited (speedy) basis. Applications for expedited trials may be made at any time but should be made as soon as possible and notice given to all parties.

2.11 The trial

At trial the Court will take an active part in controlling the proceedings and setting limits on the time allocated during a trial. To facilitate this process the court will consider the timetable for the trial at the CMC, subject to revision at the beginning of trial. The timetable will be set taking into account the parties' time estimates but the time estimates will not be determinative of the trial timetable. So far as appropriate the court will allocate equal time to the parties. Cross–examination will be strictly controlled.

Because costs are capped there is no requirement for costs budgets in the IPEC.

The court will endeavour to ensure that the trial lasts no more than 2 days. Many cases in the IPEC are heard in a single day.

Trial on paper

In an appropriate case and if the parties consent, the IPEC is able and willing to conduct a trial entirely on paper (for an example see *Hoffmann v DARE* [2012] EW PCC 2).

2.12 Costs

Costs in the IPEC are subject to a cap provided by Part 45 rules 45.30 to 45.32 and see also PD 45 Section IV. Subject to certain limited exceptions the court will not order a party to pay total costs of more than £50,000 on the final determination of a claim in relation to liability and no more than £25,000 on an inquiry as to damages or account of profits.

Tables A and B of PD 45 Section IV set out the maximum amount of scale costs which the court will award for each stage of a claim in the IPEC. However these tables only apply to proceedings started on or after 1 October 2013. Proceedings begun earlier than that date are subject to the lower scale costs set out in Tables A and B of PD 45 Section 25C, even in relation to matters occurring after 1 October 2013 (*PPL v Hamilton (No.2)* [2013] EWHC 3801 (IPEC)).

In proceedings started on or after 1 October 2013 court fees, costs relating to enforcement of an order and wasted costs are excluded from the costs cap (r.45.31(4A)).

The Costs Management procedures in CPR Part 3 Section II r.3.12 – r.3.18 including the provisions for costs budgets and the like, do not apply in the IPEC (CPR r.3.12(1), because proceedings in the IPEC are subject to scale costs).

In the IPEC all costs are assessed summarily (r.45.41(3)). In preparing their statement of costs, parties should bear in mind that they will need to explain which stage of the claim the costs were incurred in relation to. The general approach to the summary assessment process is explained in *Westwood v Knight* [2011] EW PCC 11.

The application of an issue based approach to costs in the context of the IPEC scales and the cap is addressed in *BOS v Cobra* [2012] EW PCC 44.

For cases which have been transferred to the IPEC from elsewhere, either the County Court or another part of the High Court, the IPEC will deal with costs incurred in proceedings before transfer on a case by case basis. Costs incurred in the High Court before transfer are usually dealt with by being summarily assessed as High Court costs (e.g. *Westwood v Knight* [2011] EWPCC 11).

Costs at the interim stage

At the interim stage costs of an application in the IPEC will be reserved to the conclusion of the trial (r.63.26(1)). When a party has behaved unreasonably in relation to an application the court may make an order for costs at the conclusion of the hearing and such costs will not be part of the costs covered by the cap (r.63.26(2)).

2.13 Alternative Dispute Resolution

The primary role of the IPEC is as a forum for deciding intellectual property rights cases. However, the IPEC encourages parties to consider the use of ADR (such as, but not confined to, mediation and conciliation) as an alternative means of resolving disputes or particular issues within disputes.

Settlement of a dispute by ADR has many advantages. It can result in significant saving of costs. It also has the potential to provide the parties with a wider range of solutions than can be offered by litigation. For example, while the solution to litigation is usually limited to "win/lose" on the issues put in front of the court, ADR may provide a creative "win/win" solution, as some forms of ADR can explore other ways for the parties to co–operate. ADR can also explore settlement in several countries at the same time.

Legal representatives should consider and advise their clients as to the possibility of seeking to resolve the dispute via ADR. However not all cases are suitable for settlement this way. In an appropriate case, the IPEC has the power to adjourn a case for a specified period of time to encourage and enable the parties to use ADR. At the Case Management Conference, the IPEC Judge will sometimes ask whether the parties have been advised about ADR and whether an adjournment in the proceedings is being sought. However, this will not usually be a reason to delay the CMC itself.

There are many forms of ADR. Most of these are not free. They include:

(a) Conciliation—This can involve the use of a third party to see if agreement may be reached or to offer a non–binding opinion on the dispute. Some trade bodies offer conciliation services.

(b) Mediation—This involves the appointment of a trained mediator to see whether a legally binding agreement can be negotiated. The parties will usually sign a framework agreement for the procedure of the mediation. Mediation can involve the mediator meeting with both parties together and/ or meeting the parties in separate rooms and shuttling between them. The UKIPO offers a specialist IP mediation service (details on the IPO website). Other mediation services are also available.

(c) Arbitration—This involves the appointment of an arbitrator or private decision maker, under a set of procedural rules. The arbitrator will then make a binding decision on the case. Arbitration replaces the court action, but the decision of the arbitrator is private to the parties. NB since arbitration is a private matter between the parties, arbitrators cannot revoke intellectual property rights.

(d) Early Neutral Evaluation—This involves the appointment of an expert to give an opinion about one or more issues in a dispute. Such opinions are not binding but assist the parties in reaching a settlement of the case.

(e) Binding expert determination—This involves the appointment of an expert to make a decision about one or more issues in a dispute. Such decisions can be legally binding, by agreement between the parties.

(f) IPO Opinions—The UK IPO runs a scheme to give non–binding opinions on patent infringement and patent validity. The opinion is given on the basis of written papers provided by the party applying for the opinion. The other party has the right to file observations, but does not become a party to proceedings before the IPO. The parties can agree to be bound by the outcome of any such opinion.

3. General arrangements

3.1 Issuing proceedings and applications

(a)

Issuing proceedings

Claim forms are issued at the public counter of the Rolls Building (address in Annex A). A claim form may also be issued by post. **2F–151**

The fee for issuing proceedings depends on the nature of the claim, including its value. Guidance may be sought from the Court. Information on the latest court fees can be found at www.justice.gov.uk.

(b)

Transferring proceedings to the Intellectual Property Enterprise Court

Cases transferred to the IPEC will be taken to the Rolls Building (address in Annex A).

(c)

Issuing interim applications

The issue of all interim process is dealt with at the public counter of the Rolls Building (address in Annex A). Users are reminded that:

- The first case management conference (r.63.23) will be conducted at a hearing unless all parties consent to determination on paper.
- The court will deal with all other applications without a hearing unless it considers one necessary (r.63.25(3)). A party may nonetheless request a hearing.

The fee will be determined on the face of the application notice when it is issued and prior to consideration (if any) by the court of whether a hearing is necessary. Accordingly applications marked for determination at a hearing will be charged the appropriate fee for a hearing. Applications marked for determination otherwise than at a hearing will be charged the appropriate fee for a paper application.

Personal attendance to issue process

The Fee and the application notice should be taken to the public counter at the Rolls Building. The Application will be issued and returned.

Postal application to issue process

Applications should be sent to the address in Annex A. The Clerk will issue and return the application.

3.2 Arrangements for listing

(a)

First case management conference (r.63.23)

If the application is for the first case management conference (r63.23), the date for the hearing will be fixed by liaison with the Chancery Listing Office at the Rolls Building (address in Annex A).

(b)

Interim Applications when a hearing has been ordered

For applications marked for determination at a hearing, the court will promptly consider whether a hearing is necessary. If the court considers it necessary to hold a hearing, the date will be fixed by the Chancery Listing Office at the Rolls Building (address in Annex A).

(c)

Trials

Trial dates will be fixed at the Case Management Conference (CMC) and parties attending the Case Management Conference should have the necessary information in order to fix a trial date. This may include dates relating to the availability of witnesses and parties as well as the availability of legal representatives.

The trial fee must be paid within 14 days of the trial date being set.

3.3 Time Estimates for applications

The parties must provide time estimates for all applications in respect of which a hearing is sought. Parties must appreciate the need to give a realistic and accurate time estimate and ensure that it includes a discrete reading time for the court to read the papers prior to the hearing of the application.

Where parties and their legal advisors consider that a time estimate that has been provided is unrealistic, they have a duty to notify the new time estimate to the Judge's Clerk as soon as possible.

3.4 Documents and trial timetable

The preparation of papers for the hearing of applications and trials is of considerable importance and should be approached intelligently. Annex C hereto provides guidance to the preparation of the bundle of documents for use at trial or an application, which should be followed. Legal representatives and litigants in person who fail to do so may be required to explain why and may be penalised personally in costs.

Papers for the hearing should be lodged directly at the Rolls Building. If there is insufficient time to lodge hard copies before the deadline, documents of significance (and particularly skeleton arguments) should be supplied by email to the Judge's Clerk. As an alternative documents may also be faxed to the Judge's Clerk followed up by hard copies.

It is the responsibility of both parties to ensure that all relevant documents are lodged by noon two days before the date fixed for hearing unless some longer or shorter period has been ordered by the judge or is prescribed by this guide.

The judge requests that all important documents also be supplied on a USB stick or via e-mail in a format convenient for the judge's use (normally the current or a recent version of Microsoft Word or as a text searchable pdf). For trial, these will usually include skeleton arguments, important patents and drawings, the witness statements and expert reports.

Prior to trial the parties should ensure that they comply with the requirements of PD 63 para. 9, namely that a trial bundle, reading guide and detailed trial timetable are provided for the judge. These will generally have been specifically dealt with in the Order following the CMC but if not, the directions on timing in PD 63 para. 9 should be followed.

If they are used, skeleton arguments should be lodged in time for the judge to read them before an application or trial. Any skeleton argument must also be served on the other parties in the case:

(a) In the case of applications, if a skeleton argument is used, it should normally be filed by 10:30am the previous working day (or, in the case of short applications, 3pm).

(b) In the case of trials, skeletons may only be used where they have been ordered at the CMC and they should normally be lodged at least three working days before commencement of the trial.

3.5 Telephone applications

The IPEC will hear applications by telephone conference in accordance with the Practice Direction under Part 23 and PD 63 para. 30.1. The party making the application is responsible for setting up the telephone application and informing the parties, Counsels' clerks (where barristers are instructed) and the Judge's Clerk or the Chancery Listing Office of the time of the conference call.

It is possible for the application to be recorded, and if recording by the court rather than by British Telecom (or other service provider) is requested, arrangements should be made with the Judge's Clerk. The recording will not be transcribed. The tape will be kept by the Judge's Clerk for a period of six months. Arrangements for transcription, if needed, must be made by the parties.

This procedure should be used where it will save costs.

3.6 Consent Orders

The court is normally willing to make consent orders without the need for the attendance of any parties. A draft of the agreed order and the written consent of all the parties or their respective legal representatives should be supplied to the Judge's Clerk. Unless the judge assigned to hear the application considers a hearing is needed, he or she will make the order in the agreed terms by signing it. It will be drawn up accordingly and sent to the parties.

3.7 The trial

The Court will normally hear trials from 10.30am to 4.15pm with a break from 1pm to 2pm for lunch. CMCs and other hearings will normally be heard at 10.30am but may be heard at a different time if appropriate.

If appropriate, arrangements can be made for witnesses to give their oral evidence by video link. This needs to be arranged well in advance with the parties and the court.

Where a transcript of evidence is being made and supplied to the judge, the transcript should be supplied by e–mail and in hard copy.

3.8 Draft judgments

Many judgments, particularly after a full trial, will be reserved and handed down at a later date, as advised by the Judge's Clerk or the Chancery Listing Office. Where possible the date for handing down the judgment will be set at the CMC. Usually the parties' legal representatives (or litigants in person) will be provided with a copy of the draft judgment in order for advocates to notify the court of typographical and obvious errors (if any). The text may be shown, in confidence, to the parties, but only for the purpose of obtaining instructions and on the strict understanding that the judgment, or its effect, is not to be disclosed to any other person, or used in the public domain, and that no action is taken (other than internally) in response to the judgment. If the parties would prefer not to be shown the draft judgment on this basis they should inform the court at the time the judgment is reserved.

3.9 Orders following judgment

Where a judgment is made available in draft before being given in open court the parties should, in advance of that occasion, exchange drafts of the desired consequential order. It is highly undesirable that one party should spring a proposal on the other for the first time when judgment is handed down. Where the parties are agreed as to the consequential order and have supplied to the judge a copy of the same signed by all parties or their representatives, attendance at the handing down of the judgment is not necessary.

3.10 Enforcement

Enforcement of orders is undertaken at the IPEC in the Rolls Building. Enforcement of any financial element of an IPEC judgment will be dealt with by a district judge. W here appropriate, cases may be transferred elsewhere for enforcement.

3.11 Contacting the Intellectual Property Enterprise Court

Contact details for the IPEC are in Annex A.

3.12 Information available on the Internet

Copies of this Guide, the Guide to the Intellectual Property Enterprise Court Small Claims Track, the Guide to the Patents Court, the Chancery Guide and all other IPEC guidance and forms are available at http://hmctsformfinder.justice.gov.uk/HMCTS/FormFinder.do

The Civil Procedure Rules (CPR) and Practice Directions are at: www.justice.gov.uk/courts/procedure–rules/civil/rules

Statutes and other legislation are at: www.legislation.gov.uk

The IPEC daily list of court hearings appears at the end of the Chancery List on the Daily Court Lists page at www.justice.gov.uk. The full address is: http://www.justice.gov.uk/courts/court–lists/list–chancery–judges

A link to a diary setting out a list of the forthcoming trials in the IPEC as well as a list of recent trials and applications is available at: http://www.justice.gov.uk/courts/rcj–rolls–building/intellectual–property–enterprise–court

Judgments of the IPEC are usually available at the bailli website at: http://www.bailii.org/ew/cases

Annex A – Contact details

The Intellectual Property Enterprise Court

2F–152   The home of the IPEC is in the Rolls Building at this address:

> The Rolls Building
> 7 Rolls Building Fetter Lane
> London

EC4A 1NL

DX160040 Strand 4

The IPEC is presided over by a specialist circuit judge, at present His Honour Judge Hacon.

The contact details for the Clerk to the Intellectual Property Enterprise Court, Christy Irvine, are:

Christy.Irvine@hmcts.gsi.gov.uk

Tel: 020 7947 6265

Chancery Listing Office

The Chancery Listing Office may be contacted at:

Michael Mcilroy

Chancery Listing Officer

7 Rolls Buildings

EC4A 1NL

DX 160040 Strand 4

Tel: 020 7947 7717/6690

Team email chanceryjudgeslisting@hmcts.gsi.gov.uk

Whether you contact listing by fax, e–mail or by post please avoid duplication of work by only sending documents once.

Postal application to issue process

Applications should be addressed to the Issue Section at the Rolls Building (address above) and clearly marked Intellectual Property Enterprise Court.

The public counter

The public counters are on the ground floor of the Rolls Building (address above). The counters are open Monday to Friday (except public holidays) from 10am–4.30pm.

General Enquiries

A general email address for the IPEC is: ipec@hmcts.gsi.gov.uk

Apart from the issuing of proceedings, all communications with the Court should be addressed to the Clerk to the Intellectual Property Enterprise Court.

Enquiries relating to a case which has been allocated to the IPEC small claims track may be made to the clerks in the IPEC small claims track (see the Guide to the IPEC small claims track).

Please note the court staff cannot give legal advice.

Intellectual Property Enterprise Court Users Committee

The secretary to the IPECUC is:

Alan Johnson,

Bristows,

100 Victoria Embankment,

London

EC4Y 0DH

Tel: 020 7400 8000

Fax: 020 7400 8050

Email: Alan.Johnson@bristows.com

IP Court Users Committee

The secretary to the IP Court users committee is:

Philip Westmacott,

Bristows,

100 Victoria Embankment,

London

EC4Y 0DH

Tel: 020 7400 8000

Fax: 020 7400 8050

Email: Philip.Westmacott@bristows.com

Annex B – Specimen CMC Order

UPON HEARING the Case Management Conference on [date]

UPON the issues being identified in the Schedule to this order

IT IS ORDERED THAT:

Disclosure

1. The parties will make and serve on the other of them by 4pm on [date] a list in accordance with form N265 of [the following categories of] documents in their control which relate to issues X:

    (a)

    (b)

    (c)

2. If any party wishes to inspect or have copies of such documents as are in another party's control it shall give notice in writing that it wishes to do so and such inspection shall be allowed at all reasonable times upon reasonable notice and any copies shall be provided within 14 days of the request, upon the undertaking of the party requesting the copies to pay the reasonable copying charges.

Evidence

3. The statements of case shall stand as evidence in chief.

4. The parties may serve witness statements dealing with [issues X] on or before 4pm on [date].

5. The parties may serve witness statements in reply on or before 4pm on [date].

6. The parties may each serve an expert's report dealing with [issues Y] on or before 4pm on [date].

7. The parties may serve an expert's report in reply on or before 4pm on [date].

8. The witnesses dealing with [issues X and Y] may be cross–examined at trial. No other witness will be cross–examined.

Trial

9. The time allocated for the trial is [1] day.

10. Time estimates for the cross–examination and speeches of the parties and a reading guide for the judge will be filed by 4pm on [date]. The court will consider the time estimates and allocate time taking them into account.

11. The parties shall file skeleton arguments, on or before 4pm on [date].

12. The claimant shall no less than 3 weeks before the date of the trial serve on the other parties a list of all documents that it proposes to include in the trial bundle.

13. The other parties shall each no less than 2 days thereafter serve on the claimant a list of any additional documents that it proposes should be included in the trial bundle.

14. The claimant shall no less than 2 weeks before the date of the trial serve on the other parties an agreed bundle of documents for use at the trial and no less than 1 week before the date of the trial file the agreed bundle with the court. The bundle shall be prepared in accordance with Annex C to the IPEC Guide.

15. The trial of the Claim shall take place on [date].

16. Judgment in the action shall be handed down on [date].

Costs

17. Costs are reserved to the trial.

Schedule

List of issues:

1. Infringement of claim 5

2. Novelty of claim 1 over [citation 1]

3. Inventive step of claim 1 over [citation 1]

4. Inventive step of claim 1 over [citation 2]

5. Inventive step of claim 5 over [citation 2]

Annex C – Guidelines on bundles

Guidelines on bundles

1. The 'bundle' is the name given to the one or more files containing the docu-

ments to be used at a trial or other hearing. Preparation of the bundle is primarily the responsibility of the claimant unless the court has directed otherwise. This must be done in consultation with the other parties. It is the duty of all parties to co–operate in order to agree the content of the bundle in good time before the trial or other hearing.

2. In no circumstances should rival bundles be presented to the court.

Typical content of a bundle

3. Below is set out a typical list of the documents that should go into the bundle for the trial, for the case management conference (CMC) or for any other hearing. Some hearings will not require all the indicated documents. For example at the CMC there will not normally yet exist any experts' reports, disclosure documents or earlier orders of the court and there may be no witness statements.

The parties are also free to agree that types of document other than those listed below should go into the bundle if it is important for the judge to see them.

Statements of Case

Claim Form and Particulars of Claim

Defence and Counterclaim

Reply and Defence to Counterclaim

Part 18 Requests for further information and Responses

Orders

All earlier orders of the court made in the proceedings

Evidence

Witness statements

Experts' reports

Exhibits

Documents exhibited to the statements of case, witness statements and experts' reports

Disclosure

Documents produced in disclosure on which any party seeks to rely

Correspondence

Correspondence between parties or their legal advisors may be included, but strictly only to the extent that will be relevant at the trial or other hearing.

Avoidance of duplication

4. No more than one copy of any one document should be included, unless there is good reason for doing otherwise.

Chronological order

5. In general the documents in each of the categories (statements of case, witness statements, orders, etc) should be arranged in date order starting with the earliest document.

6. The sequence of exhibits in an exhibits file (see paragraph 18 below) should reflect the order in which they are referred to in the relevant statement of case, witness statement or expert's report.

Pagination of a bundle for a trial

7. The bundle prepared for a trial should be paginated continuously from start to finish, i.e. beginning with 1 for the first page of the first file and continuing the numbering up to the last page of the last file. (This is not necessary for other hearings).

8. These page numbers should be inserted in bold figures, at the bottom of the page and in a form that can clearly be distinguished from any other pagination on the document.

Format and presentation

9. Where possible, the documents should be in A4 format.

10. Where the colour of any image or writing in a document is important, the document must be copied in colour.
11. Documents in a foreign language should be translated; the translation should immediately follow the document translated. The translation should be agreed or, if it cannot be agreed, each party's proposed translation should be included.
12. Subject to paragraph 18 below, the bundle should contain the minimum convenient number of files with appropriate use of dividers for each file. The size of each file should be tailored to its contents. It is not useful to have a large lever–arch file with just a few pages inside; on the other hand bundles should not be overloaded as they tend to break. **No bundle should contain more than 300 pages.**
13. Large documents, such as plans, should be placed in a file in a way such that the document is easily accessible.

Contents lists and labels
14. Each file in the bundle should have a list of contents at the front. It is not necessary to put the full heading of the action on the contents list. Documents should be identified briefly but enough to know what each document is, e.g. "AGS3 – Defendant's Accounts"
15. The contents list of a correspondence file need not identify each letter, email etc. if these are presented in chronological order.
16. Labels on the outside of files should use large and clearly visible lettering, e.g. "File A. Statements of Case." A label should be used on the front as well as on the spine.
17. A label should also be stuck on to the front inside cover of a file, in such a way that it can be clearly seen even when the file is open.

Exhibits in a separate bundle
18. Exhibits to statements of case, witness statements or experts' reports should generally be put in a separate bundle so that the reader can see both the text of the statement and the document referred to at the same time. This need not be done if there are very few exhibits; in such cases exhibits should immediately follow the document to which they are exhibited.

SECTION 3

OTHER PROCEEDINGS

3A   HOUSING

Rent Act 1977

Part XI—General

Jurisdiction and Procedure

County court jurisdiction

Delete s.141(1)–(3) and substitute:

3A–220   (1) The county court shall have jurisdiction, either in the course of any proceedings relating to a dwelling or on an application made for the purpose by the landlord or the tenant, to determine any question—

    (a) as to whether a tenancy is a protected tenancy or whether any person is a statutory tenant of a dwelling–house; or

    (b) as to the rent limit; or

    (c) [...]

(d) as to the application of Part V and sections 103 to 106 of this Act to a contract; or

(e) as to whether a protected, statutory or regulated tenancy is a protected, statutory or regulated furnished tenancy; or as to any matter which is or may become material for determining any such question.

(2) [...]

(3) The county court shall have jurisdiction to deal with any claim or other proceedings arising out of any of the provisions of this Act specified in subsection (5) below, notwithstanding that by reason of the amount of the claim or otherwise the case would not, apart from this subsection, be within the jurisdiction of the county court.

Note

Add at end:

Subsections (1), (3) amended, subject to savings and transitional provisions, by the **3A–221** Crime and Courts Act 2013 Sch.9 para.52, with effect from April 22, 2014 (see SI 2014/954); for savings and transitional provisions see Sch.8 to the Act.

SCHEDULES

SCHEDULE 1—STATUTORY TENANCIES

PART II—RELINQUISHING TENANCIES AND CHANGING TENANTS

No pecuniary consideration to be required on change of tenant under paragraph 13

Add new paragraph 3A–241.1:

Spouse

For there to be a surviving spouse of a deceased tenant, there has to have been a **3A–241.1** marriage which was valid under English law, although it may be that some or all foreign ceremonies of marriage would allow a person to qualify. (*Northumberland & Durham Property Trust Ltd v Ouaha* [2014] EWCA Civ 571; 7 April 2014).

Housing Act 1985

FORFEITURE FOR NON–PAYMENT OF RENT

Service of summons and re–entry

Delete s.139(1)(c) and substitute:

(c) the power under section 72(1) of the Tribunals, Courts **3A–310** and Enforcement Act 2007 (commercial rent arrears recovery) is exercisable to recover the arrears; and

Note

At the end of the first paragraph, add:

Subsection (1)(c) amended, subject to savings, by the Tribunals, Courts and Enforce- **3A–311** ment Act 2007, Sch.14, para.40, with effect from April 6, 2014 (SI 2014/768; for savings see art.2(2) to (6)).

Security of tenure

In the first paragraph, for "and Notting Hill Housing Trust v Brackley [2001] EWCA Civ 601; [2001] 35 E.G. 106; [2002] H.L.R. 212; [2001] L. & T.R. 467)." substitute:

; *Notting Hill Housing Trust v Brackley* [2001] EWCA Civ 601; [2002] H.L.R. 212; **3A–348** *Newlon Housing Trust v Al–Sulaimen* [1999] 1 A.C. 313, HL and *Muema v Muema* [2013] EWHC 3864 (Fam), 10 June 2013).

In the first paragraph, for "corepublic" substitute
core public

Demotion because of anti–social behaviour

Delete s.82A(2) and substitute:

3A–349   (2) The landlord may apply to the county court for a demotion order.

For s.82A(4)(a)(i) & (ii), substitute:

(4) (a) that the tenant or a person residing in or visiting the dwelling–house has engaged or has threatened to engage in—

> (i) conduct that is capable of causing nuisance or annoyance to some person (who need not be a particular identified person) and that directly or indirectly relates to or affects the landlord's housing management functions, or
>
> (ii) conduct that consists of or involves using housing accommodation owned or managed by the landlord for an unlawful purpose, and.

For s.82A(7A), substitute:

(7A) In subsection (4)(a)(ii) "housing accommodation" includes—

> (a) flats, lodging–houses and hostels;
>
> (b) any yard, garden, outhouses and appurtenances belonging to the accommodation or usually enjoyed with it;
>
> (c) any common areas used in connection with the accommodation.

Note

Add at end:

3A–350   Subsection (2) amended, subject to savings and transitional provisions, by the Crime and Courts Act 2013 Sch.9 para.52, with effect from April 22, 2014 (see SI 2014/954); for savings and transitional provisions see Sch.8 to the Act. Further amended by Anti–social Behaviour, Crime and Policing Act 2014 Sch.11 para.6. That amendment is not yet in force.

For the heading to s.83, substitute:

Proceedings for possession or termination: general notice requirements

Add new s.83(A1):

3A–358   (A1) This section applies in relation to proceedings for an order mentioned in s.82(1A) other than—

> (a) proceedings for possession of a dwelling–house under s.84A (absolute ground for possession for anti–social behaviour), including proceedings where possession is also sought on one or more of the grounds set out in Sch.2, or
>
> (b) proceedings for possession of a dwelling–house under s.107D (recovery of possession on expiry of flexible tenancy).

For s.83(1), substitute:

(1) The court shall not entertain proceedings to which this section applies unless—

    (a) the landlord has served a notice on the tenant complying with the provisions of this section, or

    (b) the court considers it just and equitable to dispense with the requirement of such a notice.

Note

Add at end:

Further amended by Anti–social Behaviour, Crime and Policing Act 2014, Sch.11, **3A–359** para.7. That amendment is not yet in force.

Add new paragraphs 3A–362.1 to 3A–362.4:

Notice requirements in relation to proceedings for possession on absolute ground for anti–social behaviour

83ZA.—(1) This section applies in relation to proceedings for pos- **3A–362.1** session of a dwelling–house under section 84A (absolute ground for possession for anti–social behaviour), including proceedings where possession is also sought on one or more of the grounds set out in Schedule 2.

(2) The court must not entertain the proceedings unless the landlord has served on the tenant a notice under this section.

(3) The notice must—

    (a) state that the court will be asked to make an order under section 84A for the possession of the dwelling–house,

    (b) set out the reasons for the landlord's decision to apply for the order (including the condition or conditions in section 84A on which the landlord proposes to rely), and

    (c) inform the tenant of any right that the tenant may have under section 85ZA to request a review of the landlord's decision and of the time within which the request must be made.

(4) In a case where possession is also sought on one or more of the grounds set out in Schedule 2, the notice must also—

    (a) specify the ground on which the court will be asked to make the order, and

    (b) give particulars of that ground.

(5) A notice which states that the landlord proposes to rely upon condition 1, 3 or 5 in section 84A—

    (a) must also state the conviction on which the landlord proposes to rely, and

    (b) must be served on the tenant within—

        (i) the period of 12 months beginning with the day of the conviction, or

        (ii) if there is an appeal against the conviction, the period of 12 months beginning with the day on which the appeal is finally determined or abandoned.

(6) A notice which states that the landlord proposes to rely upon condition 2 in section 84A—

    (a) must also state the finding on which the landlord proposes to rely, and

(b) must be served on the tenant within—
  (i) the period of 12 months beginning with the day on which the court has made the finding, or
  (ii) if there is an appeal against the finding, the period of 12 months beginning with the day on which the appeal is finally determined, abandoned or withdrawn.

(7) A notice which states that the landlord proposes to rely upon condition 4 in section 84A—
  (a) must also state the closure order concerned, and
  (b) must be served on the tenant within—
    (i) the period of 3 months beginning with the day on which the closure order was made, or
    (ii) if there is an appeal against the making of the order, the period of 3 months beginning with the day on which the appeal is finally determined, abandoned or withdrawn.

(8) A notice under this section must also inform the tenant that, if the tenant needs help or advice about the notice and what to do about it, the tenant should take it immediately to a Citizens' Advice Bureau, a housing aid centre, a law centre or a solicitor.

(9) The notice—
  (a) must also specify the date after which proceedings for the possession of the dwelling–house may be begun, and
  (b) ceases to be in force 12 months after the date so specified.

(10) The date specified in accordance with subsection (9)(a) must not be earlier than—
  (a) in the case of a periodic tenancy, the date on which the tenancy could, apart from this Part, be brought to an end by notice to quit given by the landlord on the same day as the notice under this section;
  (b) in the case of a secure tenancy for a term certain, one month after the date of the service of the notice.

(11) Where a notice under this section is served with respect to a secure tenancy for a term certain, it has effect also with respect to any periodic tenancy arising on the termination of that tenancy by virtue of section 86; and subsection (10)(a) does not apply to the notice.

Note

3A–362.2   Inserted by Anti–social Behaviour, Crime and Policing Act 2014 s.95. This new provision is not yet in force. It will be brought into force by a commencement order.

Secure tenancy
3A–362.3   See Housing Act 1985 s.79.

Editorial introduction
3A–362.4   A landlord wishing to obtain possession order under the absolute ground for possession for anti–social behaviour in s.84A must first serve a statutory notice in accordance with this section. There is no power to dispense with that notice. There is no statutory form of notice, but the notice must:
  (a) state that the court will be asked to make an order under section;
  (b) set out the reasons for the landlord's decision to apply for the order;
  (c) inform the tenant of any right that the tenant may have under s.85ZA to request a review;
  (d) give details of any conviction, finding or closure order on which the landlord relies;

(e) comply with various time limits; and

(f) state that if the tenant needs help or advice about the notice, the tenant should take it immediately to a Citizens' Advice Bureau, a housing aid centre, a law centre or a solicitor.

Additional requirements in relation to certain proceedings for possession

In s.83A(2)(a), after "section 83" add:

or 83ZA   **3A–363**

In s.83A(2)(b), for "subsection (4)(a) of that section", substitute:

subsection 83(4)(a) or section 83ZA(9)(a)

In s.83A(3)(a), after "section 83" add:

or 83ZA

In s.83A(4)(a), after "section 83" add:

or 83ZA

In s.83A(5), for "the notice", substitute:

a notice

In s.83A(5), after "section 83" add:

or a notice is served under section 83ZA

Note

Add at end:

Amended by the Anti–social Behaviour, Crime and Policing Act 2014, Sch.11, **3A–364** para.8. That amendment is not yet in force.

Grounds for orders for possession

In s.84(1), after "in accordance with" add:

> section 84A (absolute ground for possession for anti–social **3A–366** behaviour) or

In s.84(2)(a), for "that schedule", substitute:

> Schedule 2

For s.83(3), substitute:

(3) Where a notice under section 83 or 83ZA has been served on the tenant, the court shall not make an order on any of the grounds mentioned in subsection (2) unless the ground is specified in the notice; but the grounds so specified may be altered or added to with the leave of the court.

Note

Add at end:

Further amended by the Anti–social Behaviour, Crime and Policing Act 2014 Sch.11 **3A–367** para.9. That amendment is not yet in force.

Add new paragraphs 3A–379.1 to 3A–379.9:

Absolute ground for possession for anti–social behaviour

84A.—(1) If the court is satisfied that any of the following condi- **3A–379.1** tions is met, it must make an order for the possession of a dwelling–

house let under a secure tenancy. This is subject to subsection (2) (and to any available defence based on the tenant's Convention rights, within the meaning of the Human Rights Act 1998).

(2) Subsection (1) applies only where the landlord has complied with any obligations it has under section 85ZA (review of decision to seek possession).

(3) Condition 1 is that—

> (a) the tenant, or a person residing in or visiting the dwelling–house, has been convicted of a serious offence, and
>
> (b) the serious offence—
>
>> (i) was committed (wholly or partly) in, or in the locality of, the dwelling–house,
>>
>> (ii) was committed elsewhere against a person with a right (of whatever description) to reside in, or occupy housing accommodation in the locality of, the dwelling–house, or
>>
>> (iii) was committed elsewhere against the landlord of the dwelling–house, or a person employed (whether or not by the landlord) in connection with the exercise of the landlord's housing management functions, and directly or indirectly related to or affected those functions.

(4) Condition 2 is that a court has found in relevant proceedings that the tenant, or a person residing in or visiting the dwelling–house, has breached a provision of an injunction under section 1 of the Anti–social Behaviour, Crime and Policing Act 2014, other than a provision requiring a person to participate in a particular activity, and—

> (a) the breach occurred in, or in the locality of, the dwelling–house, or
>
> (b) the breach occurred elsewhere and the provision breached was a provision intended to prevent—
>
>> (i) conduct that is capable of causing nuisance or annoyance to a person with a right (of whatever description) to reside in, or occupy housing accommodation in the locality of, the dwelling–house, or
>>
>> (ii) conduct that is capable of causing nuisance or annoyance to the landlord of the dwelling–house, or a person employed (whether or not by the landlord) in connection with the exercise of the landlord's housing management functions, and that is directly or indirectly related to or affects those functions.

(5) Condition 3 is that the tenant, or a person residing in or visiting the dwelling–house, has been convicted of an offence under section 30 of the Anti–social Behaviour, Crime and Policing Act 2014 consisting of a breach of a provision of a criminal behaviour order prohibiting a person from doing anything described in the order, and the offence involved—

> (a) a breach that occurred in, or in the locality of, the dwelling–house, or
>
> (b) a breach that occurred elsewhere of a provision intended to prevent—

      (i) behaviour that causes or is likely to cause harassment, alarm or distress to a person with a right (of whatever description) to reside in, or occupy housing accommodation in the locality of, the dwelling–house, or

      (ii) behaviour that causes or is likely to cause harassment, . alarm or distress to the landlord of the dwelling–house, or a person employed (whether or not by the landlord) in connection with the exercise of the landlord's housing management functions, and that is directly or indirectly related to or affects those functions.

(6) Condition 4 is that—

  (a) the dwelling–house is or has been subject to a closure order under section 80 of the Anti–social Behaviour, Crime and Policing Act 2014, and

  (b) access to the dwelling–house has been prohibited (under the closure order or under a closure notice issued under section 76 of that Act) for a continuous period of more than 48 hours.

(7) Condition 5 is that—

  (a) the tenant, or a person residing in or visiting the dwelling–house, has been convicted of an offence under—

    (i) section 80(4) of the Environmental Protection Act 1990 (breach of abatement notice in relation to statutory nuisance), or

    (ii) section 82(8) of that Act (breach of court order to abate statutory nuisance etc.), and

  (b) the nuisance concerned was noise emitted from the dwelling–house which was a statutory nuisance for the purposes of Part 3 of that Act by virtue of section 79(1)(g) of that Act (noise emitted from premises so as to be prejudicial to health or a nuisance).

(8) Condition 1, 2, 3, 4 or 5 is not met if—

  (a) there is an appeal against the conviction, finding or order concerned which has not been finally determined, abandoned or withdrawn, or

  (b) the final determination of the appeal results in the conviction, finding or order being overturned.

(9) In this section—

- "relevant proceedings" means proceedings for contempt of court or proceedings under Schedule 2 to the Anti–social Behaviour, Crime and Policing Act 2014;

- "serious offence" means an offence which—

    was committed on or after the day on which subsection (3) comes into force,

    is specified, or falls within a description specified, in Schedule 2A at the time the offence was committed and at the time the court is considering the matter, and

    is not an offence that is triable only summarily by virtue of section 22 of the Magistrates' Courts Act 1980 (either–way offences where value involved is small).

(10) The Secretary of State may by order amend Schedule 2A as it applies in relation to dwelling–houses in England by—

(a) adding an indictable offence;

(b) removing an offence.

(11) The Welsh Ministers may by order amend Schedule 2A as it applies in relation to dwelling–houses in Wales by—

(a) adding an indictable offence;

(b) removing an offence.

(12) An order under subsection (10) or (11)—

(a) is to be made by statutory instrument;

(b) may make different provision for different purposes;

(c) may include incidental, supplementary, consequential, transitional or saving provision.

(13) A statutory instrument containing an order under subsection (10) or (11) may not be made unless a draft of the instrument has been laid before and approved by a resolution of—

(a) each House of Parliament (in the case of an order of the Secretary of State), or

(b) the National Assembly for Wales (in the case of an order of the Welsh Ministers).

(c) may include incidental, supplementary, consequential, transitional or saving provision.

Note

3A–379.2   Inserted by Anti–social Behaviour, Crime and Policing Act 2014 s.94. This new provision is not yet in force. It will be brought into force by a commencement order.

"secure tenancy"

3A–379.3   See Housing Act 1985 s.79.

"defence based on the tenant's Convention rights"

3A–379.4   See e.g. *Manchester CC v Pinnock* [2010] UKSC 45; [2010] 3 W.L.R. 1441, November 3, 2010, and *Hounslow London Borough Council v Powell* [2011] UKSC 8; [2011] 2 W.L.R. 287, SC.

"review of decision to seek possession"

3A–379.5   See section 85ZA.

"a serious offence"

3A–379.6   See Schedule 2A.

"locality"

3A–379.7   As to the meaning of locality in the context of Housing Act 1996 s.152, see *Manchester CC v Lawler* (1999) 31 H.L.R. 119, CA where it was said that it is a matter of fact for the judge in each case to determine whether the conduct complained of has occurred in the locality (held that an incident in a shopping centre three streets away from the property was "in the locality").

"an injunction under section 1 of the Anti–social Behaviour, Crime and Policing Act 2014"

3A–379.8   See 3A–1777.

Editorial introduction

3A–379.9   This section introduces a new mandatory or "absolute" ground for possession. Unlike discretionary grounds for possession, the court has to make an order for possession and cannot consider reasonableness. Courts do though have to consider whether eviction is necessary and proportionate, having regards to the Human Rights Act, and, in particular, Article 8.

A landlord can only rely on this ground for possession if a statutory notice has been served in accordance with s.83ZA (see above). The new ground for possession applies if any of five conditions is proved:

Condition 1

The tenant, or a person residing in or visiting the dwelling–house, has been convicted of a serious offence, which was committed in, or in the locality of, the dwelling–house, or was committed against a person with a right to reside in, or occupy housing accommodation in the locality of, the dwelling–house, or was committed against the landlord, or a person employed in connection with the exercise of the landlord's housing management functions.

Condition 2

The tenant, or a person residing in or visiting the dwelling–house, has breached a provision of an injunction granted under s.1 of the Anti–social Behaviour, Crime and Policing Act 2014. There are various requirements as to the nature of the breach.

Condition 3

The tenant, or a person residing in or visiting the dwelling–house, has been convicted of breaching a provision of a criminal behaviour order (Anti–social Behaviour, Crime and Policing Act 2014 s.30). There are various requirements as to the nature of the breach.

Condition 4

The dwelling–house is or has been subject to a closure order under Anti–social Behaviour, Crime and Policing Act 2014 s.80 and access has been prohibited for a continuous period of more than 48 hours.

Condition 5

The tenant, or a person residing in or visiting the dwelling–house, has been convicted of an offence under Environmental Protection Act 1990 s.80(4) (breach of abatement notice in relation to statutory nuisance), or s.82(8) (breach of court order to abate statutory nuisance etc.), and the nuisance concerned was noise emitted from the dwelling–house which was a statutory nuisance.

Add new paragraphs 3A–389.1 to 3A–389.6:

Review of decision to seek possession on absolute ground for anti–social behaviour

85ZA.—(1) A tenant may request a review of a landlord's decision **3A–389.1** to seek an order for possession of a dwelling–house under section 84A if the interest of the landlord belongs to—

    (a) a local housing authority, or

    (b) a housing action trust.

(2) Such a request must be made in writing before the end of the period of 7 days beginning with the day on which the notice under section 83ZA is served.

(3) On a request being duly made to it, the landlord must review its decision.

(4) The landlord must notify the tenant in writing of the decision on the review.

(5) If the decision is to confirm the original decision, the landlord must also notify the tenant of the reasons for the decision.

(6) The review must be carried out, and the tenant notified, before the day specified in the notice under section 83ZA as the day after which proceedings for the possession of the dwelling–house may be begun.

(7) The Secretary of State may by regulations make provision about the procedure to be followed in connection with a review under this section that relates to an order for possession of a dwelling–house in England.

(8) The Welsh Ministers may by regulations make provision about the procedure to be followed in connection with a review under this section that relates to an order for possession of a dwelling–house in Wales.

(9) Regulations under subsections (7) and (8) may, in particular, make provision—

(a) requiring the decision on review to be made by a person of appropriate seniority who was not involved in the original decision, and

(b) as to the circumstances in which the person concerned is entitled to an oral hearing, and whether and by whom the person may be represented at such a hearing.

(10) Regulations under this section—

(a) may contain transitional or saving provision;

(b) are to be made by statutory instrument which—

(i) in the case of regulations made by the Secretary of State, is subject to annulment in pursuance of a resolution of either House of Parliament;

(ii) in the case of regulations made by the Welsh Ministers, is subject to annulment in pursuance of a resolution of the National Assembly for Wales.

Note

3A–389.2   Inserted by Anti–social Behaviour, Crime and Policing Act 2014 s.96. This new provision is not yet in force. It will be brought into force by a commencement order.

"a local housing authority"

3A–389.3   See Section 1—a district council, a London borough council, the Common Council of the City of London, a Welsh county council or county borough council, or the Council of the Isles of Scilly.

"housing action trust"

3A–389.4   See Housing Act 1988 s.62.

Regulations

3A–389.5   At present there are no regulations.

Editorial introduction

3A–389.6   A tenant who wishes to dispute the landlord's claim for possession under the absolute ground contained in s.84A must request a review of a landlord's decision to seek an order for possession within seven days beginning with the day on which the s.83ZA notice was served. In those circumstances, the landlord must review its decision. The procedure to be followed on any such review is to be contained in regulations. The regulations may state the seniority of the person who is to carry out the review and whether the tenant is entitled to an oral hearing. After the review, the landlord must notify the tenant of its decision in writing, and, if it confirms its original decision, it must also give its reasons.

In s.85A, delete title and substitute:

Proceedings for possession on non–absolute grounds: anti–social behaviour

Editorial note

Add at end:

3A–391   It was amended by the Anti–social Behaviour, Crime and Policing Act 2014 , Sch.11, para.10. That amendment is not yet in force.

Add new paragraph 3A–395.4.1:

spouse

For there to be a surviving spouse of a deceased tenant, there has to have been a marriage which was valid under English law, although it may be that some or all foreign ceremonies of marriage would allow a person to qualify. (*Northumberland & Durham Property Trust Ltd v Ouaha* [2014] EWCA Civ 571; 7 April 2014, a case decided under Rent Act 1977.) **3A–395.4.1**

SUPPLEMENTARY PROVISIONS

Jurisdiction of county court

Delete s.110(1) and substitute:

(1) The county court has jurisdiction to determine questions aris- **3A–443** ing under this Part and to entertain proceedings brought under this Part and claims, for whatever amount, in connection with a secure tenancy.

Add new paragraph 3A–443.1:

Note

Subsection (1) amended, subject to savings and transitional provisions, by the Crime **3A–443.1** and Courts Act 2013 Sch.9 para.52, with effect from April 22, 2014 (see SI 2014/954); for savings and transitional provisions see Sch.8 to the Act.

SCHEDULES

SECTION 79   SCHEDULE 1

TENANCIES WHICH ARE NOT SECURE TENANCIES

Family intervention tenancies

In paragraph 4ZA(3)(a) for "possession order under section 84", substitute:

relevant possession order **3A–487.1**

In paragraph 4ZA(3)(a)(i), delete: "on ground 2 or 2A of Part 1 of Schedule 2".

In paragraph 4ZA(12), after the entry for "the new tenant", add:

- "relevant possession order" means—

  a possession order under section 84 that is made on ground 2, 2ZA or 2A of Part 1 of Schedule 2, or

  a possession order under section 84A;

Sch.1, para.4ZA—family intervention tenancies

Add at end:

It was amended by the Anti–social Behaviour, Crime and Policing Act 2014 , **3A–502.1** Sch.11, para.12. That amendment was implemented on May 13, 2014 by the Anti–social Behaviour, Crime and Policing Act 2014 (Commencement No. 2, Transitional and Transitory Provisions) Order 2014 SI 949 and the Anti–social Behaviour, Crime and Policing Act 2014 (Commencement No. 1 and Transitory Provisions) (Wales) Order 2014 SI 1241 (W.129) (C.50).

SECTION 84   SCHEDULE 2

GROUNDS FOR POSSESSION OF DWELLING-HOUSES LET UNDER SECURE TENANCIES

Ground 2

Delete paragraph (a) and substitute: **3A–505**

(a) has been guilty of conduct causing or likely to cause a nuisance or annoyance to a person residing, visiting or otherwise engaging in a lawful activity in the locality, (aa) has been guilty of conduct causing or likely to cause a nuisance or annoyance to the landlord of the dwelling–house, or a person employed (whether or not by the landlord) in connection with the exercise of the landlord's housing management functions, and that is directly or indirectly related to or affects those functions, or

Add new paragraph 3A–505.1:

Ground 2ZA

3A–505.1 The tenant or an adult residing in the dwelling–house has been convicted of an indictable offence which took place during, and at the scene of, a riot in the United Kingdom.

In this Ground—

(a) "adult" means a person aged 18 or over;

(b) "indictable offence" does not include an offence that is triable only summarily by virtue of section 22 of the Magistrates' Courts Act 1980 (either way offences where value involved is small);

(c) "riot" is to be construed in accordance with section 1 of the Public Order Act 1986.

Ground 2A

3A–506 *Add at end:*

This Ground applies only in relation to dwelling–houses in England.

PART V

APPROVAL OF REDEVELOPMENT SCHEMES FOR PURPOSES OF GROUND 10A

In Part V, paragraph 5(3), after "section 83" add:

3A–523 or 83ZA

Note

Add at end:

3A–524 Ground 2 was amended by the Anti–social Behaviour, Crime and Policing Act 2014 s.98. The amendment was brought into force on May 13, 2014 by the Anti–social Behaviour, Crime and Policing Act 2014 (Commencement No.2, Transitional and Transitory Provisions) Order 2014 SI 949 Art.2 and the Anti–social Behaviour, Crime and Policing Act 2014 (Commencement No.1 and Transitory Provisions) (Wales) Order 2014 (SI 2014/1241 (W.129) (C.50)).

Add new paragraph 3A–526.1:

Sch.2 Ground 2ZA—Riot

3A–526.1 Ground 2ZA was inserted by the Anti–social Behaviour, Crime and Policing Act 2014 s.99. The ground was brought into force by the Anti–social Behaviour, Crime and Policing Act 2014 (Commencement No. 2, Transitional and Transitory Provisions) Order 2014 SI No. 949. It is only available where the relevant office was committed on or after May 13, 2014.

For the definition of "indictable offences" in Ground 2ZA, see the Interpretation Act 1978 Sch.1, which provides that "indictable offence" means an offence which, if committed by an adult, is triable on indictment, whether it is exclusively so triable or triable either way. For the purposes of this ground, it does not include an offence that is triable only summarily by virtue of s.22 of the Magistrates' Courts Act 1980 (either way offences where value involved is small).

"Riot" is to be construed in accordance with section 1 of the Public Order Act 1986 which provides:

(1) Where 12 or more persons who are present together use or threaten unlawful violence for a common purpose and the conduct of them (taken together) is such as would cause a person of reasonable firmness present at the scene to fear for his personal safety, each of the persons using unlawful violence for the common purpose is guilty of riot.

(2) It is immaterial whether or not the 12 or more use or threaten unlawful violence simultaneously.

(3) The common purpose may be inferred from conduct.

(4) No person of reasonable firmness need actually be, or be likely to be, present at the scene.

(5) Riot may be committed in private as well as in public places.

SECTION 84A(9) SCHEDULE 2A

ABSOLUTE GROUND FOR POSSESSION FOR ANTI–SOCIAL BEHAVIOUR: SERIOUS OF-
FENCES

Add new paragraph 3A–532:

Violent offences
1. Murder. **3A–532**
2. Manslaughter.
3. Kidnapping.
4. False imprisonment.
5. An offence under any of the following sections of the Offences against the Person Act 1861—

(a) section 4 (soliciting murder),
(b) section 16 (threats to kill),
(c) section 18 (wounding with intent to cause grievous bodily harm),
(d) section 20 (malicious wounding),
(e) section 21 (attempting to choke, suffocate or strangle in order to commit or assist in committing an indictable offence),
(f) section 22 (using chloroform etc. to commit or assist in the committing of any indictable offence),
(g) section 23 (maliciously administering poison etc. so as to endanger life or inflict grievous bodily harm),
(h) section 24 (maliciously administering poison etc. with intent to injure, aggrieve or annoy any other person),
(i) section 27 (abandoning or exposing children whereby life is endangered or health permanently injured),
(j) section 28 (causing bodily injury by explosives),
(k) section 29 (using explosives etc. with intent to do grievous bodily harm),
(l) section 30 (placing explosives with intent to do bodily injury),
(m) section 31 (setting spring guns etc. with intent to do grievous bodily harm),
(n) section 38 (assault with intent to resist arrest),
(o) section 47 (assault occasioning actual bodily harm).

6. An offence under any of the following sections of the Explosive Substances Act 1883—

(a) section 2 (causing explosion likely to endanger life or property),
(b) section 3 (attempt to cause explosion, or making or keeping explosive with intent to endanger life or property),
(c) section 4 (making or possession of explosive under suspicious circumstances).

7. An offence under section 1 of the Infant Life (Preservation) Act 1929 (child destruction).

8. An offence under section 1 of the Children and Young Persons Act 1933 (cruelty to children).

9. An offence under section 1 of the Infanticide Act 1938 (infanticide).

10. An offence under any of the following sections of the Public Order Act 1986—

(a) section 1 (riot),
(b) section 2 (violent disorder),
(c) section 3 (affray).

11. An offence under either of the following sections of the Protection from Harassment Act 1997—

(a) section 4 (putting people in fear of violence),
(b) section 4A (stalking involving fear of violence or serious alarm or distress).

12. An offence under any of the following provisions of the Crime and Disorder Act 1998—

(a) section 29 (racially or religiously aggravated assaults),
(b) section 31(1)(a) or (b) (racially or religiously aggravated offences under section 4 or 4A of the Public Order Act 1986),
(c) section 32 (racially or religiously aggravated harassment etc.).

13. An offence under either of the following sections of the Female Genital Mutilation Act 2003—

(a) section 1 (female genital mutilation),

(b) section 2 (assisting a girl to mutilate her own genitalia).

14. An offence under section 5 of the Domestic Violence, Crime and Victims Act 2004 (causing or allowing the death of a child or vulnerable adult).

Sexual offences

15. An offence under section 33A of the Sexual Offences Act 1956 (keeping a brothel used for prostitution).

16. An offence under section 1 of the Protection of Children Act 1978 (indecent photographs of children).

17. An offence under section 160 of the Criminal Justice Act 1988 (possession of indecent photograph of a child).

18. An indictable offence under Part 1 of the Sexual Offences Act 2003 (sexual offences).

Offensive weapons

19. An offence under either of the following sections of the Prevention of Crime Act 1953—

(a) section 1 (prohibition of the carrying of offensive weapons without lawful authority or reasonable excuse),

(b) section 1A (threatening with offensive weapon in public).

20. An offence under any of the following provisions of the Firearms Act 1968—

(a) section 16 (possession of firearm with intent to endanger life),

(b) section 16A (possession of firearm with intent to cause fear of violence),

(c) section 17(1) (use of firearm to resist arrest),

(d) section 17(2) (possession of firearm at time of committing or being arrested for offence specified in Schedule 1 to the Act of 1968),

(e) section 18 (carrying a firearm with criminal intent),

(f) section 19 (carrying a firearm in a public place),

(g) section 20 (trespassing with firearm),

(h) section 21 (possession of firearms by persons previously convicted of crime).

21. An offence under either of the following sections of the Criminal Justice Act 1988—

(a) section 139 (having article with blade or point in public place),

(b) section 139AA (threatening with article with blade or point or offensive weapon).

Offences against property

22. An offence under any of the following sections of the Theft Act 1968—

(a) section 8 (robbery or assault with intent to rob),

(b) section 9 (burglary),

(c) section 10 (aggravated burglary).

23. An offence under section 1 of the Criminal Damage Act 1971 (destroying or damaging property).

24. An offence under section 30 of the Crime and Disorder Act 1998 (racially or religiously aggravated criminal damage).

Road traffic offences

25. An offence under section 35 of the Offences against the Person Act 1861 (injuring persons by furious driving).

26. An offence under section 12A of the Theft Act 1968 (aggravated vehicle–taking involving an accident which caused the death of any person).

27. An offence under any of the following sections of the Road Traffic Act 1988—

(a) section 1 (causing death by dangerous driving),

(b) section 1A (causing serious injury by dangerous driving),

(c) section 3A (causing death by careless driving when under influence of drink or drugs).

Drug–related offences
28. An offence under any of the following provisions of the Misuse of Drugs Act 1971—
- (a) section 4 (restriction of production and supply of controlled drugs),
- (b) section 5(3) (possession of controlled drugs with intent to supply),
- (c) section 8(a) or (b) (occupiers etc. of premises to be punishable for permitting unlawful production or supply etc. of controlled drugs there).

29. An offence under section 6 of that Act (restrictions of cultivation of cannabis plant) where the cultivation is for profit and the whole or a substantial part of the dwelling–house concerned is used for the cultivation.

Inchoate offences
30.(1) An offence of attempting or conspiring the commission of an offence specified or described in this Schedule.
- (2) An offence under Part 2 of the Serious Crime Act 2007 (encouraging or assisting) where the offence (or one of the offences) which the person in question intends or believes would be committed is an offence specified or described in this Schedule.
- (3) An offence of aiding, abetting, counselling or procuring the commission of an offence specified or described in this Schedule.

Scope of offences
31. Where this Schedule refers to offences which are offences under the law of England and Wales and another country or territory, the reference is to be read as limited to the offences so far as they are offences under the law of England and Wales.

Housing Act 1988

Demotion because of anti–social behaviour

Delete s.6A(2) and substitute:

(2) The landlord may apply to the county court for a demotion order. **3A–765**

Delete s.6A(4)(a) and substitute:

- (a) that the tenant or a person residing in or visiting the dwelling–house has engaged or has threatened to engage in—
  - (i) conduct that is capable of causing nuisance or annoyance to some person (who need not be a particular identified person) and that directly or indirectly relates to or affects the landlord's housing management functions, or
  - (ii) conduct that consists of or involves using housing accommodation owned or managed by the landlord for an unlawful purpose, and

Delete s.6A(10A) and substitute:

(10A) In subsection (4)(a)(ii) "housing accommodation" includes—
- (a) flats, lodging–houses and hostels;
- (b) any yard, garden, outhouses and appurtenances belonging to the accommodation or usually enjoyed with it;
- (c) any common areas used in connection with the accommodation.

Note

Add at end:

Subsection (2) amended, subject to savings and transitional provisions, by the Crime **3A–765.1** and Courts Act 2013 Sch.9 para.52, with effect from April 22, 2014 (see SI 2014/954); for savings and transitional provisions see Sch.8 to the Act. It was amended by Anti–social Behaviour, Crime and Policing Act 2014 Sch.11 para.17. That amendment is not yet in force.

Orders for possession

In s.7(3), after "below" add:

3A–769 (and to any available defence based on the tenant's Convention rights, within the meaning of the Human Rights Act 1998)

In s.7(5A)(a), for "and 5" substitute:

5 and 7A

In s.7(6)(a), after "Ground 2" add:

, Ground 7A

Note

Add at end:

3A–770 It was further amended by the Anti–social Behaviour, Crime and Policing Act 2014 Sch.11 para.18. That amendment is not yet in force.

Notice of proceedings for possession

In s.8(3)(b), for "subsections (4)" substitute:

3A–784 subsections (3A)

Add new s.8(3A):

(3A) If a notice under this section specifies in accordance with subsection (3)(a) Ground 7A in Schedule 2 to this Act (whether with or without other grounds), the date specified in the notice as mentioned in subsection (3)(b) is not to be earlier than—

    (a) in the case of a periodic tenancy, the earliest date on which, apart from section 5(1), the tenancy could be brought to an end by a notice to quit given by the landlord on the same date as the date of service of the notice under this section;

    (b) in the case of a fixed term tenancy, one month after the date on which the notice was served.

In s.8(4), for "(whether with or without other grounds)" substitute:

(whether without other grounds or with any ground other than Ground 7A)

In s.8(4A), after "other than Ground", add:

7A or

Add new ss.8(4C) to 8(4F):

(4C) A notice under this section that specifies in accordance with subsection (3)(a) Ground 7A in Schedule 2 to this Act (whether with or without other grounds) must be served on the tenant within the time period specified in subsection (4D), (4E) or (4F).

(4D) Where the landlord proposes to rely on condition 1, 3 or 5 in Ground 7A, the notice must be served on the tenant within—

    (a) the period of 12 months beginning with the day of the conviction, or

    (b) if there is an appeal against the conviction, the period of 12 months beginning with the day on which the appeal is finally determined or abandoned.

(4E) Where the landlord proposes to rely on condition 2 in Ground 7A, the notice must be served on the tenant within—

(a) the period of 12 months beginning with the day on which the court has made the finding, or

(b) if there is an appeal against the finding, the period of 12 months beginning with the day on which the appeal is finally determined, abandoned or withdrawn.

(4F) Where the landlord proposes to rely on condition 4 in Ground 7A, the notice must be served on the tenant within—

(a) the period of 3 months beginning with the day on which the closure order was made, or

(b) if there is an appeal against the making of the order, the period of 3 months beginning with the day on which the appeal is finally determined, abandoned or withdrawn.

In s.8(5), after "Ground" insert:

7A or

Note

Add at end:

and by the Anti–social Behaviour, Crime and Policing Act 2014 s.97. This latter **3A–785** amendment is not yet in force. It will be brought into force by a commencement order.

Notice of proceedings for possession

Add at end:

Subsections (4D), (4E) and (4F) specify time limits in relation to notices which apply **3A–791** if the landlord seeks possession under mandatory Ground 7A (anti–social behaviour).

In s.9A, delete the title and substitute:

Proceedings for possession on non–absolute grounds: anti–social behaviour

Editorial note

Add at end:

It was amended by the Anti–social Behaviour, Crime and Policing Act 2014 , Sch.11, **3A–810** para.19. That amendment is not yet in force.

Determination of rent by rent assessment committee

Delete the fourth paragraph beginning "Note that ss.14A". **3A–841**

Add at end:

, but see *Preston v Area Estates Ltd* [2014] EWHC 1206 (Admin); 26 March 2014.

Add new paragraph 3A–860.2:

spouse

For there to be a surviving spouse of a deceased tenant, there has to have been a **3A–860.2** marriage which was valid under English law, although it may be that some or all foreign ceremonies of marriage would allow a person to qualify. (*Northumberland & Durham Property Trust Ltd v Ouaha* [2014] EWCA Civ 571; 7 April 2014, a case decided under Rent Act 1977.)

Restriction on levy of distress for rent

Delete s.19 and substitute:

[s.19 repealed, subject to savings, by the Tribunals, Courts and Enforcement Act **3A–867** 2007, Sch.14, para.45, Sch.23, Pt 4, with effect from April 6, 2014 (SI 2014/768); for savings see art.2(2) to (6).]

Recovery of possession on expiry or termination of assured shorthold tenancy

In the third paragraph (beginning "Although s.21(4)(a)") after "2 E.G.L.R. 67)." add:

3A–896   See too *Spencer v Taylor* [2013] EWCA Civ 1600

In the fifth paragraph, after "possession of the dwelling house"." add:

It does not require the notice to expire on any particular date nor does it require a date to be specified in the notice. (*Spencer v Taylor* [2013] EWCA Civ 1600, 20 November 2013).

In the sixth paragraph, after "the end of the tenancy"."add:

; but see *Spencer v Taylor* [2013] EWCA Civ 1600, 20 November 2013.

CHAPTER VI

GENERAL PROVISIONS

Jurisdiction of county courts

Delete s.40 and substitute:

3A–938   **40.**—(1) The county court shall have jurisdiction to hear and determine any question arising under any provision of—

    (a) Chapters I to III and V above, or

    (b) sections 27 and 28 above,

         other than a question falling within the jurisdiction of the appropriate tribunal by virtue of any such provision.

(2) [...]

(3) Where any proceedings under any provision mentioned in subsection (1) above are being taken in the county court, the court shall have jurisdiction to hear and determine any other proceedings joined with those proceedings, notwithstanding that, apart from this subsection, those other proceedings would be outside the court's jurisdiction.

(4) If any person takes any proceedings under any provision mentioned in subsection (1) above in the High Court, he shall not be entitled to recover any more costs of those proceedings than those to which he would have been entitled if the proceedings had been taken in the county court: and in such a case the taxing master shall have the same power of directing on what county court scale costs are to be allowed, and of allowing any item of costs, as the judge would have had if the proceedings had been taken in the county court.

(5) Subsection (4) above shall not apply where the purpose of taking the proceedings in the High Court was to enable them to be joined with any proceedings already pending before that court (not being proceedings taken under any provision mentioned in subsection (1) above).

Note

Add at end:

3A–939   Subsections (1), (3), (4) amended, subject to savings and transitional provisions, by the Crime and Courts Act 2013 Sch.9 para.52, with effect from April 22, 2014 (see SI 2014/954); for savings and transitional provisions see Sch.8 to the Act.

SECTION 1   SCHEDULE 1

TENANCIES WHICH CANNOT BE ASSURED TENANCIES

Family intervention tenancies

3A–953.1   *In paragraph 12ZA(3)(i), for "ground 14" substitute:*

ground 7A of Part 1 of Schedule 2 or ground 14, 14ZA

Note

Add at end:

It was further amended by the Anti–social Behaviour, Crime and Policing Act 2014, **3A–958**
Sch.11, para.20. That amendment was implemented on May 13, 2014 by the Anti–
social Behaviour, Crime and Policing Act 2014 (Commencement No.2, Transitional
and Transitory Provisions) Order 2014 (SI 2014/949) and the Anti–social Behaviour,
Crime and Policing Act 2014 (Commencement No.1 and Transitory Provisions) (Wales)
Order 2014 (SI 2014/1241 (W.129) (C.50)).

SECTION 7   ## SCHEDULE 2

GROUNDS FOR POSSESSION OF DWELLING-HOUSES LET ON ASSURED TENANCIES

Add new paragraph 3A–977.1:

Ground 7A

Any of the following conditions is met.   **3A–977.1**

Condition 1 is that—

> the tenant, or a person residing in or visiting the dwelling–house, has been
> convicted of a serious offence, and
> the serious offence—
>
>> (i) was committed (wholly or partly) in, or in the locality of, the dwelling–
>> house,
>>
>> (ii) was committed elsewhere against a person with a right (of whatever de-
>> scription) to reside in, or occupy housing accommodation in the locality
>> of, the dwelling–house, or
>>
>> (iii) was committed elsewhere against the landlord of the dwelling–house, or
>> a person employed (whether or not by the landlord) in connection with
>> the exercise of the landlord's housing management functions, and
>> directly or indirectly related to or affected those functions.

Condition 2 is that a court has found in relevant proceedings that the tenant, or a
person residing in or visiting the dwelling–house, has breached a provision of an
injunction under section 1 of the Anti–social Behaviour, Crime and Policing Act 2014,
other than a provision requiring a person to participate in a particular activity, and—

> (a) the breach occurred in, or in the locality of, the dwelling–house, or
> (b) the breach occurred elsewhere and the provision breached was a provision
> intended to prevent—
>
>> (i) conduct that is capable of causing nuisance or annoyance to a person
>> with a right (of whatever description) to reside in, or occupy housing ac-
>> commodation in the locality of, the dwelling–house, or
>>
>> (ii) conduct that is capable of causing nuisance or annoyance to the landlord
>> of the dwelling–house, or a person employed (whether or not by the
>> landlord) in connection with the exercise of the landlord's housing
>> management functions, and that is directly or indirectly related to or af-
>> fects those functions.

Condition 3 is that the tenant, or a person residing in or visiting the dwelling–
house, has been convicted of an offence under section 30 of the Anti–social Behaviour,
Crime and Policing Act 2014 consisting of a breach of a provision of a criminal behaviour order prohibiting a person from doing anything described in the order, and the
offence involved—

> (a) a breach that occurred in, or in the locality of, the dwelling–house, or
> (b) a breach that occurred elsewhere of a provision intended to prevent—
>
>> (i) behaviour that causes or is likely to cause harassment, alarm or distress
>> to a person with a right (of whatever description) to reside in, or occupy
>> housing accommodation in the locality of, the dwelling–house, or
>>
>> (ii) behaviour that causes or is likely to cause harassment, alarm or distress
>> to the landlord of the dwelling–house, or a person employed (whether
>> or not by the landlord) in connection with the exercise of the landlord's
>> housing management functions, and that is directly or indirectly related
>> to or affects those functions.

Condition 4 is that—

(a) the dwelling–house is or has been subject to a closure order under section 80 of the Anti–social Behaviour, Crime and Policing Act 2014, and

(b) access to the dwelling–house has been prohibited (under the closure order or under a closure notice issued under section 76 of that Act) for a continuous period of more than 48 hours.

Condition 5 is that—

(a) the tenant, or a person residing in or visiting the dwelling–house, has been convicted of an offence under—

(i) section 80(4) of the Environmental Protection Act 1990 (breach of abatement notice in relation to statutory nuisance), or

(ii) section 82(8) of that Act (breach of court order to abate statutory nuisance etc.), and

(b) the nuisance concerned was noise emitted from the dwelling–house which was a statutory nuisance for the purposes of Part 3 of that Act by virtue of section 79(1)(g) of that Act (noise emitted from premises so as to be prejudicial to health or a nuisance).

Condition 1, 2, 3, 4 or 5 is not met if—

(a) there is an appeal against the conviction, finding or order concerned which has not been finally determined, abandoned or withdrawn, or

(b) the final determination of the appeal results in the conviction, finding or order being overturned.

In this ground—

- "relevant proceedings" means proceedings for contempt of court or proceedings under Schedule 2 to the Anti–social Behaviour, Crime and Policing Act 2014;

- "serious offence" means an offence which—

(a) was committed on or after the day on which this ground comes into force,

(b) is specified, or falls within a description specified, in Schedule 2A to the Housing Act 1985 at the time the offence was committed and at the time the court is considering the matter, and

(c) is not an offence that is triable only summarily by virtue of section 22 of the Magistrates' Courts Act 1980 (either–way offences where value involved is small).

Ground 14

3A–984 *At the end of entry (a) before ", or" add:*

has been guilty of conduct causing or likely to cause a nuisance or annoyance to the landlord of the dwelling–house, or a person employed (whether or not by the landlord) in connection with the exercise of the landlord's housing management functions, and that is directly or indirectly related to or affects those functions, or

Add new paragraph 3A–984.1:

Ground 14ZA

3A–984.1 The tenant or an adult residing in the dwelling–house has been convicted of an indictable offence which took place during, and at the scene of, a riot in the United Kingdom.

In this Ground—

- "adult" means a person aged 18 or over;

- "indictable offence" does not include an offence that is triable only summarily by virtue of section 22 of the Magistrates' Courts Act 1980 (either way offences where value involved is small);

- "riot" is to be construed in accordance with section 1 of the Public Order Act 1986.

This Ground applies only in relation to dwelling–houses in England.

Add new paragraph 3A–991.1:

Note

Ground 7A was inserted by the Anti–social Behaviour, Crime and Policing Act 2014 **3A–991.1**
s.97. This new provision is not yet in force. It will be brought into force by a commencement order.

Ground 14ZA was inserted by the Anti–social Behaviour, Crime and Policing Act
2014 s.99. The ground was brought into force by the Anti–social Behaviour, Crime
and Policing Act 2014 (Commencement No. 2, Transitional and Transitory Provisions)
Order 2014 SI No. 949. It is only available where the relevant offence was committed
on or after May 13, 2014

Add new paragraph 3A–999.1:

Ground 7A

Anti–social behaviour

This new ground for possession applies if any of five conditions is proved: **3A–999.1**

Condition 1

The tenant, or a person residing in or visiting the dwelling–house, has been
convicted of a serious offence, which was committed in, or in the locality of, the dwelling–house, or was committed against a person with a right to reside in, or occupy
housing accommodation in the locality of, the dwelling–house, or was committed
against the landlord, or a person employed in connection with the exercise of the
landlord's housing management functions.

Condition 2

The tenant, or a person residing in or visiting the dwelling–house, has breached a
provision of an injunction granted under section 1 of the Anti–social Behaviour,
Crime and Policing Act 2014. There are various requirements as to the nature of the
breach.

Condition 3

The tenant, or a person residing in or visiting the dwelling–house, has been
convicted of breaching a provision of a criminal behaviour order (Anti–social Behaviour, Crime and Policing Act 2014 s.30). There are various requirements as to the
nature of the breach.

Condition 4

The dwelling–house is or has been subject to a closure order under the Anti–social
Behaviour, Crime and Policing Act 2014 s.80 and access has been prohibited for a
continuous period of more than 48 hours.

Condition 5

The tenant, or a person residing in or visiting the dwelling–house, has been
convicted of an offence under Environmental Protection Act 1990 s.80(4) (breach of
abatement notice in relation to statutory nuisance), or s.82(8) (breach of court order to
abate statutory nuisance etc.), and the nuisance concerned was noise emitted from the
dwelling–house which was a statutory nuisance.

Discretionary Grounds

Ground 14

In the first paragraph, (after the former "nuisance or annoyance" ground.) add:
It was amended by the Anti–social Behaviour, Crime and Policing Act 2014 s.98. **3A–1006**
The amendment was brought into force on May 13 2014 by the Anti–social Behaviour,
Crime and Policing Act 2014 (Commencement No. 2, Transitional and Transitory Pro-
visions) Order 2014 SI 949 Art 2 and the Anti–social Behaviour, Crime and Policing
Act 2014 (Commencement No. 1 and Transitory Provisions) (Wales) Order 2014 SI
1241 (W.129) (C.50).

Add new paragraph 3A–1006.1:

Ground 14ZA Riot

For the definition of "indictable offences" in Ground 14ZA, see the Interpretation **3A–1006.1**
Act 1978 Sch.1, which provides that "indictable offence" means an offence which, if

committed by an adult, is triable on indictment, whether it is exclusively so triable or triable either way. For the purposes of this ground, it does not include an offence that is triable only summarily by virtue of s.22 of the Magistrates' Courts Act 1980 (either way offences where value involved is small).

"Riot" is to be construed in accordance with s.1 of the Public Order Act 1986 which provides:

(1) Where 12 or more persons who are present together use or threaten unlawful violence for a common purpose and the conduct of them (taken together) is such as would cause a person of reasonable firmness present at the scene to fear for his personal safety, each of the persons using unlawful violence for the common purpose is guilty of riot.

(2) It is immaterial whether or not the 12 or more use or threaten unlawful violence simultaneously.

(3) The common purpose may be inferred from conduct.

(4) No person of reasonable firmness need actually be, or be likely to be, present at the scene.

(5) Riot may be committed in private as well as in public places.

Housing Act 1996

Part III

Landlord and tenant

Supplementary

Jurisdiction of county courts

Delete s.95(1)–(4) and substitute:

3A–1062 (1) Any jurisdiction expressed by a provision to which this section applies to be conferred on the court shall be exercised by the county court.

(2) There shall also be brought in the county court any proceedings for determining any question arising under or by virtue of any provision to which this section applies.

(3) Where, however, other proceedings are properly brought in the High Court, that court has jurisdiction to hear and determine proceedings to which subsection (1) or (2) applies which are joined with those proceedings.

(4) Where proceedings are brought in the county court by virtue of subsection (1) or (2), that court has jurisdiction to hear and determine other proceedings joined with those proceedings despite the fact that they would otherwise be outside its jurisdiction.

Add new paragraph 3A–1062.1:

Note

3A–1062.1 Subsections (1), (2), (4) amended, subject to savings and transitional provisions, by the Crime and Courts Act 2013 Sch.9 para.52, with effect from April 22, 2014 (see SI 2014/954); for savings and transitional provisions see Sch.8 to the Act.

Part V

Conduct of tenants

Supplementary

Jurisdiction of county court

Delete s.138(1) and substitute:

(1) The county court has jurisdiction to determine questions aris- **3A–1112** ing under this Chapter and to entertain proceedings brought under this Chapter and claims, for whatever amount, in connection with an introductory tenancy.

Note

Add at end:

Subsection (1) amended, subject to savings and transitional provisions, by the Crime **3A–1113** and Courts Act 2013 Sch.9 para.52, with effect from April 22, 2014 (see SI 2014/954); for savings and transitional provisions see Sch.8 to the Act.

SUPPLEMENTARY

Jurisdiction of county court

Delete s.143N(1) and substitute:

(1) The county court has jurisdiction— **3A–1185**
    (a) to determine questions arising under this Chapter;
    (b) to determine questions arising under this Chapter;
    (c) to determine claims (for whatever amount) in connection with a demoted tenancy.

Note

Delete the second paragraph and substitute:

Subsection (1) amended by the Crime and Courts Act 2013 Sch.9 para.37, with ef- **3A–1186** fect from April 22, 2014 (see SI 2014/954).

Note

Add at end:

This section was repealed by the Anti–social Behaviour, Crime and Policing Act **3A–1199** 2014 Sch.11, para.22. The repeal has not yet been implemented.

Relevant landlord

Add at end:

This section was repealed by the Anti–social Behaviour, Crime and Policing Act **3A–1210** 2014 Sch.11, para.22. The repeal has not yet been implemented.

Note

Add at end:

This section was repealed by the Anti–social Behaviour, Crime and Policing Act **3A–1215** 2014 Sch.11, para.22. The repeal has not yet been implemented.

Note

Add at end:

This section was repealed by the Anti–social Behaviour, Crime and Policing Act **3A–1222** 2014 Sch.11, para.22. The repeal has not yet been implemented.

Injunctions: supplementary

Delete s.153E(6) and substitute:

(6) The court is the High Court or the county court. **3A–1227**

Note

Delete Note and substitute:

Subsection (6) amended, subject to savings and transitional provisions, by the Crime **3A–1228** and Courts Act 2013 Sch.9 para.52, with effect from April 22, 2014 (see SI 2014/954); for savings and transitional provisions see Sch.8 to the Act. This section was repealed by the Anti–social Behaviour, Crime and Policing Act 2014 Sch.11, para.22. The repeal has not yet been implemented.

381

Powers of arrest: ex–parte applications for injunctions

Delete s.154(1) and substitute:

3A–1230   (1) In determining whether to exercise its power under section 153C(3) or 153D(4) to attach a power of arrest to an injunction which it intends to grant on an ex–parte application, the High Court or the county court shall have regard to all the circumstances including—

(a) whether it is likely that the applicant will be deterred or prevented from seeking the exercise of the power if the power is not exercised immediately, and

(b) whether there is reason to believe that the respondent is aware of the proceedings for the injunction but is deliberately evading service and that the applicant or any person of a description mentioned in any of paragraphs (a) to (d) of section 153A(3) (as the case may be) will be seriously prejudiced if the decision as to whether to exercise the power were delayed until substituted service is effected.

Note

Delete Note and substitute:

3A–1231   Subsection (1) amended, subject to savings and transitional provisions, by the Crime and Courts Act 2013 Sch.9 para.52, with effect from April 22, 2014 (see SI 2014/954); for savings and transitional provisions see Sch.8 to the Act. This section was repealed by the Anti–social Behaviour, Crime and Policing Act 2014 Sch.11 para.22. The repeal has not yet been implemented.

Arrest and remand

Delete s.155(6) and substitute:

3A–1233   (6) Schedule 15 (which makes provision corresponding to that applying in magistrates' courts in civil cases under sections 128 and 129 of the Magistrates' Courts Act 1980) applies in relation to the powers of the High Court and the county court to remand a person under this section.

Note

Delete Note and substitute:

3A–1234   Subsection (6) amended, subject to savings and transitional provisions, by the Crime and Courts Act 2013 Sch.9 para.52, with effect from April 22, 2014 (see SI 2014/954); for savings and transitional provisions see Sch.8 to the Act. This section was repealed by the Anti–social Behaviour, Crime and Policing Act 2014 Sch.11 para.22. The repeal has not yet been implemented.

Note

Add at end:

3A–1237.1   This section was repealed by the Anti–social Behaviour, Crime and Policing Act 2014 Sch.11, para.22. The repeal has not yet been implemented.

Powers of arrest: supplementary provisions

Delete s.157(1) and substitute:

3A–1240   (1) If in exercise of its power under section 153C(3) or 153D(4) the High Court or the county court attaches a power of arrest to any provisions of an injunction, it may provide that the power of arrest is to have effect for a shorter period than the other provisions of the injunction.

Note

Delete Note and substitute:

Subsection (1) amended, subject to savings and transitional provisions, by the Crime **3A–1241** and Courts Act 2013 Sch.9 para.52, with effect from April 22, 2014 (see SI 2014/954); for savings and transitional provisions see Sch.8 to the Act. This section was repealed by the Anti–social Behaviour, Crime and Policing Act 2014 Sch.11 para.22. The repeal has not yet been implemented.

Interpretation: Chapter III

In s.158(1), delete the definition for "relevant judge" and substitute:

"relevant judge", in relation to an injunction, means— **3A–1243**
>   (a) where the injunction was granted by the High Court, a judge of that court,
>   (b) where the injunction was granted by the county court, a judge of that court;

Note

Delete Note and substitute:

In subs.(1), in definition "relevant judge", para.(b) substituted by the Crime and **3A–1244** Courts Act 2013 Sch.9 para.37, with effect from April 22, 2014 (see SI 2014/954). This section was repealed by the Anti–social Behaviour, Crime and Policing Act 2014 Sch.11, para.22. The repeal has not yet been implemented.

PART VII

HOMELESSNESS AND THREATENED HOMELESSNESS

Reviews

At the end of the last paragraph in the third bullet point in the third paragraph, (after "the reviewing officer to comply with the "minded–to" provisions of reg.8(2).") add:

See too *Wandsworth LBC v NJ* [2013] EWCA Civ 1373, November 7, 2013. **3A–1425**

Accommodation pending reviews and appeals

In the final paragraph, for "Johnson v City of Westminster [2013] EWCA Civ 773, June 26, 2013,", substitute:

Johnson v City of Westminster [2013] EWCA Civ 773; [2013] H.L.R 45, June 26, 2013, **3A–1426**

Procedure on a review

Delete s.203(5) and substitute:

(5) In any case they shall inform the applicant of his right to ap- **3A–1433** peal to the county court on a point of law, and of the period within which such an appeal must be made (see section 204).

Add new paragraph 3A–1433.1:

Note

Subsection (5) amended, subject to savings and transitional provisions, by the Crime **3A–1433.1** and Courts Act 2013 Sch.9 para.52, with effect from April 22, 2014 (see SI 2014/954); for savings and transitional provisions see Sch.8 to the Act.

"extension of time for bringing appeal"

Add at end:

There is no rule of law that instructing seemingly competent solicitors is, of itself, **3A–1441** sufficient to amount to "good reason" or "good cause" for any subsequent delay. Absent any direct evidence as to why the application to extend time had been made late, a judge was entitled to hold that the second condition was not made out. (*Poorsalehy v Wandsworth LBC* [2013] EWHC 3687 (QB); November 7, 2013).

Part VIII

Miscellaneous and general provisions

Miscellaneous

Anti–social behaviour: landlords' policies and procedures

Delete s.218A(8)–(8A) and substitute:

3A–1488 (8) Anti–social behaviour is—

(a) conduct that is capable of causing nuisance or annoyance to some person (who need not be a particular identified person) and that directly or indirectly relates to or affects the landlord's housing management functions, or

(b) conduct that consists of or involves using or threatening to use housing accommodation owned or managed by the landlord for an unlawful purpose.

Note

Add at end:

3A–1489 It was further amended by Anti–social Behaviour, Crime and Policing Act 2014 Sch.11 para.23. That amendment is not yet in force.

SCHEDULE 15

ARREST FOR ANTI–SOCIAL BEHAVIOUR: POWERS OF HIGH COURT AND COUNTY COURT TO REMAND

Introductory

Delete para.1(2) and substitute:

3A–1497 (2) In this Schedule "the court" means the High Court or the county court and includes—

(a) in relation to the High Court, a judge of that court, and

(b) in relation to the county court, a judge of that court.

Note

Delete Note and substitute:

3A–1497.1 Paragraph 1 amended by the Crime and Courts Act 2013 Sch.9 para.37, with effect from April 22, 2014 (see SI 2014/954).

Schedule 15

Add at end:

3A–1501 This Schedule was repealed by the Anti–social Behaviour, Crime and Policing Act 2014 Sch.11 para.22. The repeal has not yet been implemented.

Crime and Disorder Act 1998

Add new paragraph 3A–1502.1:

Note

3A–1502.1 These provisions were repealed by the Anti–social Behaviour, Crime and Policing Act 2014 Sch.11 para.24. The repeal has not yet been implemented.

Note

Add at end:

3A–1504 This section was repealed by the Anti–social Behaviour, Crime and Policing Act 2014 Sch.11 para.24. The repeal has not yet been implemented.

Add at end:

This section was repealed by the Anti–social Behaviour, Crime and Policing Act **3A–1510**
2014 Sch.11 para.24. The repeal has not yet been implemented.

Orders in county court proceedings

Delete s.1B(1) and substitute:

(1) This section applies to any proceedings in the county court **3A–1512**
('the principal proceedings').

Note

Add at end:

Subsection (1) amended, subject to savings and transitional provisions, by the Crime **3A–1513**
and Courts Act 2013 Sch.9 para.52, with effect from April 22, 2014 (see SI 2014/954);
for savings and transitional provisions see Sch.8 to the Act. This section was repealed
by the Anti–social Behaviour, Crime and Policing Act 2014 Sch.11 para.24. The repeal
has not yet been implemented.

Note

Add at end:

This section was repealed by the Anti–social Behaviour, Crime and Policing Act **3A–1520**
2014 Sch.11 para.24. The repeal has not yet been implemented.

Note

Add at end:

This section was repealed by the Anti–social Behaviour, Crime and Policing Act **3A–1523**
2014 Sch.11 para.24. The repeal has not yet been implemented.

Housing Act 2004

Proceedings relating to tenancy deposits

Delete s.214(1) and substitute:

(1) Where a tenancy deposit has been paid in connection with a **3A–1622**
shorthold tenancy, the tenant or any relevant person (as defined by
section 213(10)) may make an application to the county court on the
grounds—
  (a) that section 213(3) or (6) has not been complied with in
      relation to the deposit, or
  (b) that he has been notified by the landlord that a particular
      authorised scheme applies to the deposit but has been
      unable to obtain confirmation from the scheme
      administrator that the deposit is being held in accordance
      with the scheme.

Note

Add at end:

Subsection (1) amended, subject to savings and transitional provisions, by the Crime **3A–1623**
and Courts Act 2013 Sch.9 para.52, with effect from April 22, 2014 (see SI 2014/954);
for savings and transitional provisions see Sch.8 to the Act.

Sanctions for non–compliance

Delete s.215(2A)(b) and substitute:

  (b) an application to the county court has been made under **3A–1628** section 214(1) and has been determined by the court, withdrawn or settled by agreement between the parties.

Note

Add at end:

3A–1629   Subsection (2A) amended, subject to savings and transitional provisions, by the Crime and Courts Act 2013 Sch.9 para.52, with effect from April 22, 2014 (see SI 2014/954); for savings and transitional provisions see Sch.8 to the Act.

Prevention of Social Housing Fraud Act 2013

Note

Add at end:

3A–1766   In Wales, the section was brought into force on November 5, 2013 by the Prevention of Social Housing Fraud Act 2013 (Commencement) (Wales) Order 2013 (SI 2013/2861 (C.115)).

Add new paragraphs 3A–1776 to 3A–1845:

Anti–social Behaviour, Crime and Policing Act 2014

3A–1776   (2014, c.12)

ARRANGEMENT OF SECTIONS

PART 1

INJUNCTIONS

Injunctions

PART 1

INJUNCTIONS

INJUNCTIONS

Power to grant injunctions

1.—(1) A court may grant an injunction under this section against   **3A–1777**
a person aged 10 or over ("the respondent") if two conditions are
met.

(2) The first condition is that the court is satisfied, on the balance
of probabilities, that the respondent has engaged or threatens to
engage in anti–social behaviour.

(3) The second condition is that the court considers it just and
convenient to grant the injunction for the purpose of preventing the
respondent from engaging in anti–social behaviour.

(4) An injunction under this section may for the purpose of
preventing the respondent from engaging in anti–social behaviour—

> (a) prohibit the respondent from doing anything described in
> the injunction;

> (b) require the respondent to do anything described in the
> injunction.

(5) Prohibitions and requirements in an injunction under this section must, so far as practicable, be such as to avoid—

> (a) any interference with the times, if any, at which the re-
> spondent normally works or attends school or any other
> educational establishment;

> (b) any conflict with the requirements of any other court or-
> der or injunction to which the respondent may be subject.

(6) An injunction under this section must—

> (a) specify the period for which it has effect, or

> (b) state that it has effect until further order.
> In the case of an injunction granted before the respon-
> dent has reached the age of 18, a period must be speci-
> fied and it must be no more than 12 months.

(7) An injunction under this section may specify periods for which
particular prohibitions or requirements have effect.

(8) An application for an injunction under this section must be
made to—

> (a) a youth court, in the case of a respondent aged under 18;

> (b) the High Court or the county court, in any other case.
> Paragraph (b) is subject to any rules of court made under
> section 18(2).

Note

This section is not yet in force. It will be brought into force by a commencement   **3A–1778**
order.

"anti–social behaviour"

3A–1779 See section 2.

rules

3A–1780 At present there are no Rules.

Editorial introduction

3A–1781 This Part of this Act replaces the power to grant anti–social behaviour injunctions contained in Housing Act 1996 s.153A to 156. Those earlier provisions are repealed.

These provisions enable the High Court, the county court or (in certain circumstances) the youth court to grant an injunction if the court is satisfied, on the balance of probabilities, that the respondent has engaged or threatens to engage in anti–social behaviour and it is just and convenient to grant the injunction for the purpose of preventing the respondent from engaging in anti–social behaviour. Such an injunction can only be granted on the application of a local authority, a housing provider, the chief officer of police for a police area, the chief constable of the British Transport Police Force, Transport for London, the Environment Agency, the Natural Resources Body for Wales, the Secretary of State exercising security management functions, or a Special Health Authority exercising security management functions on the direction of the Secretary of State, or the Welsh Ministers exercising security management functions, or a person or body exercising security management functions on the direction of the Welsh Ministers or under arrangements made between the Welsh Ministers and that person or body (see section 5). There is power to grant an injunction on an application made without notice being given to the respondent (see section 6). The injunction must either specify the period for which it has effect, or state that it has effect until further order. If the respondent has not reached the age of 18, a period of no more than 12 months must be specified. A court granting an injunction under section 1 may attach a power of arrest to a prohibition or requirement of the injunction if the anti–social behaviour in which the respondent has engaged or threatens to engage consists of or includes the use or threatened use of violence against other persons, or there is a significant risk of harm to other persons from the respondent. Section 8 gives the court power to vary or discharge an injunction.

If an injunction is breached, the applicant may apply to a judge for a warrant of arrest (section 10) or, if a power of arrest was attached to a provision of the injunction, a constable may arrest the respondent without warrant if he or she has reasonable cause to suspect that the respondent is in breach of the provision (section 9). A person arrested under a power of arrest must be brought before a judge within the period of 24 hours beginning with the time of the arrest. Section 11 and Schedule 1 contain provisions enabling courts to remand respondents who have been arrested in custody.

Sentences for breach of injunctions

3A–1782 Any sentence imposed for breach of an injunction depends on the culpability of the offender and the harm caused by the particular breach. Guidance as to the appropriate range of sentence can however be gleaned from cases decided under Housing Act 1996 s.153A which this Act replaced.

In *Tower Hamlets LBC v Long* (2000) 32 H.L.R. 219, CA, the Court of Appeal held that an immediate sentence of imprisonment was appropriate where a tenant had waged a personal vendetta against another tenant in breach of an injunction. However a prison sentence of three months was reduced to three weeks. In *Nottingham City Council v Cutts* (2001) 33 H.L.R. 7, CA, the Court of Appeal dismissed an appeal against an immediate sentence of twelve months imprisonment where there had been previous breaches and where the actual breaches consisted of attempts to punch, racist and other foul language, threats to kill and kicking and banging of doors. The judge "was undoubtedly right in the case to impose a substantial term of imprisonment". Although the sentence was "a stiff one" it was not "manifestly excessive". See too *Leicester City Council v Lewis* (2001) 33 H.L.R. 37, CA and *Leeds CC v MacDonald*, November20, 2007, unrep.

In *Barnet LBC v Hurst* [2002] EWCA Civ 1009; [2003] 1 W.L.R. 722, the Court of Appeal held that a sentence of nine months imprisonment for a defendant who had breached an undertaking not to assault, threaten, harass or cause nuisance to anyone residing in or visiting a block of flats where his father lived by being loud and noisy and disturbing the neighbours' sleep was manifestly too long. The sentence was reduced to three months. The maximum sentence of two years imprisonment should be reserved for the worst cases (*Turnbull v Middlesbrough BC* [2003] EWCA Civ 1327).

In *Longhurst Homes Ltd v Killen* [2008] EWCA Civ 402; March 11, 2008, a case of repeated, unpleasant and intimidating behaviour, but where no actual violence had been used, the Court of Appeal dismissed an appeal against nine months' imprisonment, stating that the judge was entitled to reach the conclusion that an immediate sentence of imprisonment was called for in the face of breaches of the injunction which had been deliberate and repeated. Although the overall sentence was stiff, and one which would not necessarily have been imposed by every judge, the judge had not stepped outside the bracket legitimately available to her.

In *Birmingham City Council v Flatt* [2008] EWCA Civ 739, June 12, 2008, the Court of Appeal stated that it does not follow that imprisonment is to be regarded as the automatic consequence of breach of an order and it is common practice to take some other course on the first occasion when someone breaches an injunction. However, in this case, the defendant had a history of violent and threatening conduct towards others. He had denied the breaches and shown no remorse. A sentence of imprisonment was not wrong in principle. Although the length of the sentence (four months' imprisonment for driving a vehicle at a neighbour, causing him injury and making false accusations about other neighbours) was at the top end of the range of sentences available for such a breach, it was not manifestly excessive and the judge had been entitled to take the view that this was not a case for a suspended sentence order.

Time spent in custody on remand is not deducted from the sentence imposed on a committal for contempt of court (*Delaney v Delaney* [1996] Q.B. 387, CA; *Sevketoglu v Sevketoglu* [2003] EWCA Civ 1570)—but it is important to note that pursuant to Criminal Justice Act 2003 s.258, a defendant can expect to serve half of the period of imprisonment imposed (see *Wear Valley DC v Robson* [2008] EWCA Civ 1470; [2009] H.L.R. 27—six months' imprisonment for breaching an ASBI on five separate occasions by playing loud music, banging on residents' doors, using foul language, behaving in a drunken and abusive manner, allowing other alcoholics to visit his flat and threatening to smash up the flat evicted, described as a severe sentence, but wholly appropriate.).

Meaning of "anti–social behaviour"

2.—(1) In this Part "anti–social behaviour" means—   3A–1783

(a) conduct that has caused, or is likely to cause, harassment, alarm or distress to any person,

(b) conduct capable of causing nuisance or annoyance to a person in relation to that person's occupation of residential premises, or

(c) conduct capable of causing housing–related nuisance or annoyance to any person.

(2) Subsection (1)(b) applies only where the injunction under section 1 is applied for by—

(a) a housing provider,

(b) a local authority, or

(c) a chief officer of police.

(3) In subsection (1)(c) "housing–related" means directly or indirectly relating to the housing management functions of—

(a) a housing provider, or

(b) a local authority.

(4) For the purposes of subsection (3) the housing management functions of a housing provider or a local authority include—

(a) functions conferred by or under an enactment;

(b) the powers and duties of the housing provider or local authority as the holder of an estate or interest in housing accommodation.

Note

3A–1784   This section is not yet in force. It will be brought into force by a commencement order.

"housing–related"

3A–1785   See section 2(3)(b). This is intended "to have a broad sweep". In *Swindon BC v Redpath* [2009] EWCA Civ 943, September 11, 2009; [2010] 1 All E.R. 1003, Lord Neuberger said that the phrase "housing related" conduct in Housing Act 1996 s.153A(3) (one of the provisions which this Act replaced) "can clearly be engaged in by someone who is not a tenant or an occupier of property owned by the relevant landlord; equally, it can be engaged in by someone who neither resides nor works within the area in which the conduct occurs" (para.64).

"housing provider"

3A–1786   See section 20.

"local authority"

3A–1787   See section 20.

CONTENTS OF INJUNCTIONS

Requirements included in injunctions

3A–1788   **3.**—(1) An injunction under section 1 that includes a requirement must specify the person who is to be responsible for supervising compliance with the requirement. The person may be an individual or an organisation.

(2) Before including a requirement, the court must receive evidence about its suitability and enforceability from—

    (a) the individual to be specified under subsection (1), if an individual is to be specified;

    (b) an individual representing the organisation to be specified under subsection (1), if an organisation is to be specified.

(3) Before including two or more requirements, the court must consider their compatibility with each other.

(4) It is the duty of a person specified under subsection (1)—

    (a) to make any necessary arrangements in connection with the requirements for which the person has responsibility (the "relevant requirements");

    (b) to promote the respondent's compliance with the relevant requirements;

    (c) if the person considers that the respondent—

      (i) has complied with all the relevant requirements, or

      (ii) has failed to comply with a relevant requirement,
        to inform the person who applied for the injunction and the appropriate chief officer of police.

(5) In subsection (4)(c) "the appropriate chief officer of police" means—

    (a) the chief officer of police for the police area in which it appears to the person specified under subsection (1) that the respondent lives, or

    (b) if it appears to that person that the respondent lives in more than one police area, whichever of the relevant chief officers of police that person thinks it most appropriate to inform.

(6) A respondent subject to a requirement included in an injunction under section 1 must—

390

   (a) keep in touch with the person specified under subsection
      (1) in relation to that requirement, in accordance with
      any instructions given by that person from time to time;
   (b) notify the person of any change of address.
      These obligations have effect as requirements of the
      injunction.

Note

This section is not yet in force. It will be brought into force by a commencement **3A–1789**
order.

Power of arrest

4.—(1) A court granting an injunction under section 1 may attach   **3A–1790**
a power of arrest to a prohibition or requirement of the injunction
if the court thinks that—

   (a) the anti–social behaviour in which the respondent has
      engaged or threatens to engage consists of or includes the
      use or threatened use of violence against other persons,
      or
   (b) there is a significant risk of harm to other persons from
      the respondent.
      "Requirement" here does not include one that has the
      effect of requiring the respondent to participate in partic-
      ular activities.

  (2) If the court attaches a power of arrest, the injunction may
specify a period for which the power is to have effect which is
shorter than that of the prohibition or requirement to which it
relates.

Note

This section is not yet in force. It will be brought into force by a commencement **3A–1791**
order.

APPLICATIONS FOR INJUNCTIONS

Applications for injunctions

5.—(1) An injunction under section 1 may be granted only on the   **3A–1792**
application of—

   (a) a local authority,
   (b) a housing provider,
   (c) the chief officer of police for a police area,
   (d) the chief constable of the British Transport Police Force,
   (e) Transport for London,
   (f) the Environment Agency,
   (g) the Natural Resources Body for Wales,
   (h) the Secretary of State exercising security management
      functions, or a Special Health Authority exercising secu-
      rity management functions on the direction of the Secre-
      tary of State, or
   (i) the Welsh Ministers exercising security management func-
      tions, or a person or body exercising security manage-
      ment functions on the direction of the Welsh Ministers or

under arrangements made between the Welsh Ministers and that person or body.

(2) In subsection (1) "security management functions" means—

(a) the Secretary of State's security management functions within the meaning given by section 195(3) of the National Health Service Act 2006;

(b) the functions of the Welsh Ministers corresponding to those functions.

(3) A housing provider may make an application only if the application concerns anti–social behaviour that directly or indirectly relates to or affects its housing management functions.

(4) For the purposes of subsection (3) the housing management functions of a housing provider include—

(a) functions conferred by or under an enactment;

(b) the powers and duties of the housing provider as the holder of an estate or interest in housing accommodation.

(5) The Secretary of State may by order—

(a) amend this section;

(b) amend section 20 in relation to expressions used in this section.

Note

3A–1793   This section is not yet in force. It will be brought into force by a commencement order.

"a local authority"

3A–1794   See section 20.

"a housing provider"

3A–1795   See section 20.

Applications without notice

3A–1796   **6.**—(1) An application for an injunction under section 1 may be made without notice being given to the respondent.

(2) If an application is made without notice the court must either—

(a) adjourn the proceedings and grant an interim injunction (see section 7), or

(b) adjourn the proceedings without granting an interim injunction, or

(c) dismiss the application.

Note

3A–1797   This section is not yet in force. It will be brought into force by a commencement order.

INTERIM INJUNCTIONS

Interim injunctions

3A–1798   **7.**—(1) This section applies where the court adjourns the hearing of an application (whether made with notice or without) for an injunction under section 1.

(2) The court may grant an injunction under that section lasting

until the final hearing of the application or until further order (an "interim injunction") if the court thinks it just to do so.

(3) An interim injunction made at a hearing of which the respondent was not given notice may not have the effect of requiring the respondent to participate in particular activities.

(4) Subject to that, the court has the same powers (including powers under section 4) whether or not the injunction is an interim injunction.

Note

This section is not yet in force. It will be brought into force by a commencement order. **3A–1799**

VARIATION AND DISCHARGE

Variation or discharge of injunctions

8.—(1) The court may vary or discharge an injunction under section 1 on the application of— **3A–1800**

    (a) the person who applied for the injunction, or

    (b) the respondent.

(2) In subsection (1) "the court" means—

  (a) the court that granted the injunction, except where paragraph (b) applies;

  (b) the county court, where the injunction was granted by a youth court but the respondent is aged 18 or over.

(3) The power to vary an injunction includes power—

    (a) to include an additional prohibition or requirement in the injunction, or to extend the period for which a prohibition or requirement has effect;

    (b) to attach a power of arrest, or to extend the period for which a power of arrest has effect.

(4) If an application under this section is dismissed, the party by which the dismissed application was made may make no further application under this section without—

    (a) the consent of the court, or

    (b) the agreement of the other party.

(5) Section 3 applies to additional requirements included under subsection (3)(a) above as it applies to requirements included in a new injunction.

Note

This section is not yet in force. It will be brought into force by a commencement order. **3A–1801**

BREACH OF INJUNCTIONS

Arrest without warrant

9.—(1) Where a power of arrest is attached to a provision of an injunction under section 1, a constable may arrest the respondent without warrant if he or she has reasonable cause to suspect that the respondent is in breach of the provision. **3A–1802**

(2) A constable who arrests a person under subsection (1) must inform the person who applied for the injunction.

(3) A person arrested under subsection (1) must, within the period of 24 hours beginning with the time of the arrest, be brought before—

> (a) a judge of the High Court or a judge of the county court, if the injunction was granted by the High Court;
> (b) a judge of the county court, if—
>> (i) the injunction was granted by the county court, or
>> (ii) the injunction was granted by a youth court but the respondent is aged 18 or over;
> (c) a justice of the peace, if neither paragraph (a) nor paragraph (b) applies.

(4) In calculating when the period of 24 hours ends, Christmas Day, Good Friday and any Sunday are to be disregarded.

(5) The judge before whom a person is brought under subsection (3)(a) or (b) may remand the person if the matter is not disposed of straight away.

(6) The justice of the peace before whom a person is brought under subsection (3)(c) must remand the person to appear before the youth court that granted the injunction.

Note

3A–1803 This section is not yet in force. It will be brought into force by a commencement order.

Issue of arrest warrant

3A–1804 **10.**—(1) If the person who applied for an injunction under section 1 thinks that the respondent is in breach of any of its provisions, the person may apply for the issue of a warrant for the respondent's arrest.

(2) The application must be made to—

> (a) a judge of the High Court, if the injunction was granted by the High Court;
> (b) a judge of the county court, if—
>> (i) the injunction was granted by the county court, or
>> (ii) the injunction was granted by a youth court but the respondent is aged 18 or over;
> (c) a justice of the peace, if neither paragraph (a) nor paragraph (b) applies.

(3) A judge or justice may issue a warrant under this section only if the judge or justice has reasonable grounds for believing that the respondent is in breach of a provision of the injunction.

(4) A warrant issued by a judge of the High Court must require the respondent to be brought before that court.

(5) A warrant issued by a judge of the county court must require the respondent to be brought before that court.

(6) A warrant issued by a justice of the peace must require the respondent to be brought before—

> (a) the youth court that granted the injunction, if the person is aged under 18;
> (b) the county court, if the person is aged 18 or over.

(7) A constable who arrests a person under a warrant issued under this section must inform the person who applied for the injunction.

(8) If the respondent is brought before a court by virtue of a warrant under this section but the matter is not disposed of straight away, the court may remand the respondent.

Note

This section is not yet in force. It will be brought into force by a commencement **3A–1805** order.

Remands

11. Schedule 1 (remands under sections 9 and 10) has effect.　　**3A–1806**

Note

This section is not yet in force. It will be brought into force by a commencement **3A–1807** order.

Remands and Bail

The Schedule includes provisions relating to remands in custody and the grant of **3A–1808** bail and the taking of recognizances. There is power to remand for medical reports.

It was held that the county court had power to review a decision to grant bail or to remand in custody under the provisions of Housing Act 1996 Chapter III (which this Act replaced), especially when there has been a change in circumstance. Accordingly, the Court of Appeal's task on any appeal against a refusal to grant bail is one of review rather than rehearing. (*Newham LBC v Jones* [2002] EWCA Civ 1779 a case where an appeal was dismissed. Although the circuit judge did not specifically refer to the Bail Act 1976 when refusing bail, he did express concerns over the seriousness of the allegations and further breaches of the injunction).

Powers in respect of under–18s

12. Schedule 2 (breach of injunctions: powers of court in respect　**3A–1809** of under–18s) has effect.

Note

This section is not yet in force. It will be brought into force by a commencement **3A–1810** order.

EXCLUSION FROM HOME

Power to exclude person from home in cases of violence or risk of harm

13.—(1) An injunction under section 1 may have the effect of　　**3A–1811** excluding the respondent from the place where he or she normally lives ("the premises") only if—

　　(a) the respondent is aged 18 or over,
　　(b) the injunction is granted on the application of—
　　　　(i) a local authority,
　　　　(ii) the chief officer of police for the police area that the premises are in, or
　　　　(iii) if the premises are owned or managed by a housing provider, that housing provider, and
　　(c) the court thinks that—
　　　　(i) the anti–social behaviour in which the respondent has engaged or threatens to engage consists of or includes

the use or threatened use of violence against other persons, or

(ii) there is a significant risk of harm to other persons from the respondent.

(2) For the purposes of this section a housing provider owns a place if—

(a) the housing provider is a person (other than a mortgagee not in possession) entitled to dispose of the fee simple of the place, whether in possession or in reversion, or

(b) the housing provider is a person who holds or is entitled to the rents and profits of the place under a lease that (when granted) was for a term of not less then 3 years.

Note

3A–1812   This section is not yet in force. It will be brought into force by a commencement order.

"a local authority"

3A–1813   See section 20.

"a housing provider"

3A–1814   See section 20.

Exclusion orders

3A–1815   An application for an injunction under section 1 may have the effect of excluding the respondent from the place where he or she normally lives, but only if the court thinks that the anti–social behaviour in which the respondent has engaged or threatens to engage consists of or includes the use or threatened use of violence against other persons, or there is a significant risk of harm to other persons from the respondent. This power applies only if the respondent is aged 18 or over.

Although courts have power to make ouster orders and/or exclusion orders without notice if the facts are sufficiently serious to warrant such a draconian order, very great care is needed. Further, judges making such orders should generally be scrupulous to prescribe that the order may only be served at a reasonable time of the day (for example, between 9 am and 4.30 pm on a weekday) (*Moat Housing Group–South Ltd v Harris* [2005] EWCA Civ 287; [2006] Q.B. 606; [2005] 3 W.L.R. 691; [2005] 4 All E.R. 1051).

SUPPLEMENTAL

Requirements to consult etc

3A–1816   **14.**—(1) A person applying for an injunction under section 1 must before doing so—

(a) consult the local youth offending team about the application, if the respondent will be aged under 18 when the application is made;

(b) inform any other body or individual the applicant thinks appropriate of the application.
This subsection does not apply to a without–notice application.

(2) Where the court adjourns a without–notice application, before the date of the first on–notice hearing the applicant must—

(a) consult the local youth offending team about the application, if the respondent will be aged under 18 on that date;

(b) inform any other body or individual the applicant thinks appropriate of the application.

(3) A person applying for variation or discharge of an injunction under section 1 granted on that person's application must before doing so—

>   (a) consult the local youth offending team about the application for variation or discharge, if the respondent will be aged under 18 when that application is made;
>   (b) inform any other body or individual the applicant thinks appropriate of that application.

(4) In this section—

>   "local youth offending team" means —
>
>>   (a) the youth offending team in whose area it appears to the applicant that the respondent lives, or
>>   (b) if it appears to the applicant that the respondent lives in more than one such area, whichever one or more of the relevant youth offending teams the applicant thinks it appropriate to consult;
>
>   "on–notice hearing" means a hearing of which notice has been given to the applicant and the respondent in accordance with rules of court;
>   "without–notice application" means an application made without notice under section 6.

Note

This section is not yet in force. It will be brought into force by a commencement order. **3A–1817**

Consultation

A person applying on notice for an injunction against a respondent aged under 18 must consult the local youth offending team about the application. This subsection does not apply to a without–notice application. **3A–1818**

Appeals against decisions of youth courts

15.—(1) ...   **3A–1819**

Special measures for witnesses

16.—(1) Chapter 1 of Part 2 of the Youth Justice and Criminal Evidence Act 1999 (special measures directions in the case of vulnerable and intimidated witnesses) applies to proceedings under this Part as it applies to criminal proceedings, but with—   **3A–1820**

>   (a) the omission of the provisions of that Act mentioned in subsection (2) (which make provision appropriate only in the context of criminal proceedings), and
>   (b) any other necessary modifications.

(2) The provisions are—

>   (a) section 17(4) to (7);
>   (b) section 21(4C)(e);
>   (c) section 22A;
>   (d) section 27(10);
>   (e) section 32.

(3) Rules of court made under or for the purposes of Chapter 1 of Part 2 of that Act apply to proceedings under this Part—

>   (a) to the extent provided by rules of court, and
>   (b) subject to any modifications provided by rules of court.

(4) Section 47 of that Act (restrictions on reporting special measures directions etc) applies with any necessary modifications—

    (a) to a direction under section 19 of that Act as applied by this section;

    (b) to a direction discharging or varying such a direction. Sections 49 and 51 of that Act (offences) apply accordingly.

Note

3A–1821   This section is not yet in force. It will be brought into force by a commencement order.

"rules of court"

3A–1822   At present, there are no relevant rules of court.

Special measures

3A–1823   Youth Justice and Criminal Evidence Act 1999 provides that witnesses, especially children and vulnerable witnesses, may be granted special measures so that they are more at ease when giving evidence. Such special measures may include giving evidence from behind a screen or curtain, by live link, in private or by means of video–recorded evidence in chief.

Children and young persons: disapplication of reporting restrictions

3A–1824   **17.** Section 49 of the Children and Young Persons Act 1933 (restrictions on reports of proceedings in which children and young persons are concerned) does not apply to proceedings under this Part.

Note

3A–1825   This section is not yet in force. It will be brought into force by a commencement order.

Rules of court

3A–1826   **18.**—(1) Rules of court may provide that an appeal from a decision of the High Court, the county court or a youth court—

    (a) to dismiss an application for an injunction under section 1 made without notice being given to the respondent, or

    (b) to refuse to grant an interim injunction when adjourning proceedings following such an application,
    may be made without notice being given to the respondent.

(2) Rules of court may provide for a youth court to give permission for an application for an injunction under section 1 against a person aged 18 or over to be made to the youth court if—

    (a) an application to the youth court has been made, or is to be made, for an injunction under that section against a person aged under 18, and

    (b) the youth court thinks that it would be in the interests of justice for the applications to be heard together.

(3) In relation to a respondent attaining the age of 18 after proceedings under this Part have begun, rules of court may—

    (a) provide for the transfer of the proceedings from the youth court to the High Court or the county court;

(b) prescribe circumstances in which the proceedings may or must remain in the youth court.

Note

This section is not yet in force. It will be brought into force by a commencement order. **3A–1827**

"rules of court"

At present, there are no relevant rules of court. **3A–1828**

Guidance

19.—(1) The Secretary of State may issue guidance to persons entitled to apply for injunctions under section 1 (see section 5) about the exercise of their functions under this Part. **3A–1829**

(2) The Secretary of State may revise any guidance issued under this section.

(3) The Secretary of State must arrange for any guidance issued or revised under this section to be published.

Note

This section is not yet in force. It will be brought into force by a commencement order. **3A–1830**

Guidance

At present, the Secretary of State has not issued any guidance. **3A–1831**

Interpretation etc

20.—(1) In this Part— **3A–1832**

"anti–social behaviour" has the meaning given by section 2;

"harm" includes serious ill–treatment or abuse, whether physical or not;

"housing accommodation" includes—

(a) flats, lodging–houses and hostels;

(b) any yard, garden, outhouses and appurtenances belonging to the accommodation or usually enjoyed with it;

(c) any common areas used in connection with the accommodation;

"housing provider" means —

(a) a housing trust, within the meaning given by section 2 of the Housing Associations Act 1985, that is a charity;

(b) a housing action trust established under section 62 of the Housing Act 1988;

(c) in relation to England, a non–profit private registered provider of social housing;

(d) in relation to Wales, a Welsh body registered as a social landlord under section 3 of the Housing Act 1996;

(e) any body (other than a local authority or a body within paragraphs (a) to (d)) that is a landlord under a secure tenancy within the meaning given by section 79 of the Housing Act 1985;

"local authority" means —

> (a) in relation to England, a district council, a county council, a London borough council, the Common Council of the City of London or the Council of the Isles of Scilly;
>
> (b) in relation to Wales, a county council or a county borough council;

"respondent" has the meaning given by section 1(1).

(2) A person's age is treated for the purposes of this Part as being that which it appears to the court to be after considering any available evidence.

Note

3A–1833 This section is not yet in force. It will be brought into force by a commencement order.

Saving and transitional provision

3A–1834 **21.**—(1) In this section "existing order" means any of the following injunctions and orders—

> (a) an anti–social behaviour injunction under section 153A of the Housing Act 1996;
>
> (b) an injunction under section 153B of that Act (injunction against unlawful use of premises);
>
> (c) an injunction in which anything is included by virtue of section 153D(3) or (4) of that Act (power to include provision banning person from premises or area, or to include power of arrest, in injunction against breach of tenancy agreement);
>
> (d) an order under section 1 or 1B of the Crime and Disorder Act 1998 (anti–social behaviour orders etc);
>
> (e) an individual support order under section 1AA of that Act made in connection with an order under section 1 or 1B of that Act;
>
> (f) an intervention order under section 1G of that Act;
>
> (g) a drinking banning order under section 3 or 4 of the Violent Crime Reduction Act 2006.

(2) The repeal or amendment by this Act of provisions about any of the existing orders specified in subsection (1)(a) to (d), (f) and (g) does not apply in relation to—

> (a) an application made before the commencement day for an existing order;
>
> (b) an existing order (whether made before or after that day) applied for before that day;
>
> (c) anything done in connection with such an application or order.

(3) The repeal or amendment by this Act of provisions about an order specified in subsection (1)(e) does not apply in relation to—

> (a) an individual support order made before the commencement day;
>
> (b) anything done in connection with such an order.

(4) As from the commencement day there may be no variation of an existing order that extends the period of the order or of any of its provisions.

(5) At the end of the period of 5 years beginning with the commencement day—

    (a) in relation to any of the existing orders specified in subsection (1) (a), (b) and (d) to (g) that is still in force, this Part has effect, with any necessary modifications (and with any modifications specified in an order under section 185(7)), as if the provisions of the order were provisions of an injunction under section 1;

    (b) the provisions of this Part set out in subsection (6) apply to any injunction specified in subsection (1)(c) that is still in force as they apply to an injunction under section 1;

    (c) subsections (2) to (4) cease to have effect.

(6) The provisions referred to in subsection (5)(b) are—

    (a) section 1(7);

    (b) sections 4(2) and 9 (if a power of arrest is attached);

    (c) sections 6 to 8;

    (d) section 10;

    (e) section 11 and Schedule 1;

    (f) section 12 and Schedule 2;

    (g) section 18(1).

(7) In deciding whether to grant an injunction under section 1 a court may take account of conduct occurring up to 6 months before the commencement day.

(8) In this section "commencement day" means the day on which this Part comes into force.

Note

This section is not yet in force. It will be brought into force by a commencement order.   **3A–1835**

SECTION 11   **SCHEDULE 1**

REMANDS UNDER SECTIONS 9 AND 10

Introductory

1—(1) This Schedule applies where—   **3A–1836**

    (a) a judge has power to remand a person under section 9(5),

    (b) a justice of the peace is required to remand a person under section 9(6), or

    (c) a court has power to remand a person under section 10(8).

(2) A reference in the following paragraphs of this Schedule to a judge is to be read as including a justice of the peace.

Remand in custody or on bail

2—(1) The judge or the court may remand the person—   **3A–1837**

    (a) in custody, or

    (b) on bail.

    But a person aged under 18 may not be remanded in custody unless paragraph 6 applies.

(2) A reference in this Schedule to remanding a person in custody is a reference to committing the person to custody to be brought before the court at the end of the period of remand or at whatever earlier time the court may require.

(3) The judge or the court may remand the person on bail—

    (a) by taking from the person a recognizance, with or without sureties, conditioned as provided in paragraph 3, or

    (b) by fixing the amount of the recognizances with a view to their being taken subsequently and, in the meantime, committing the person to custody as mentioned in sub–paragraph (2).

(4) Where a person is brought before the court after remand, the court may further remand the person.

3A–1838 3—(1) Where a person is remanded on bail, the judge or the court may direct that the person's recognizance be conditioned for his or her appearance—

(a) before the court at the end of the period of remand, or

(b) at every time and place to which during the course of the proceedings the hearing may from time to time be adjourned.

(2) Where a recognizance is conditioned for a person's appearance as mentioned in sub–paragraph (1)(b), the fixing of a time for the person next to appear is to be treated as a remand.

(3) Nothing in this paragraph affects the power of the court at any subsequent hearing to remand the person afresh.

3A–1839 4—(1) The judge or the court may not remand a person for a period exceeding 8 clear days unless—

(a) paragraph 5 or 6 applies, or

(b) the person is remanded on bail and both that person and the person who applied for the injunction consent to a longer period.

(2) Where the judge or the court has power to remand a person in custody, the person may be committed to the custody of a constable if the remand is for a period not exceeding 3 clear days.

Remand for medical examination and report

3A–1840 5—(1) This paragraph applies where—

(a) the judge or the court has reason to think that a medical report will be needed, and

(b) the judge or the court remands the person in order to enable a medical examination to take place and a report to be made.

(2) If (in the case of a person aged 18 or over) the person is remanded in custody, the adjournment may not be for more than 3 weeks at a time.

(3) If the person is remanded on bail, the adjournment may not be for more than 4 weeks at a time.

3A–1841 6—(1) If the judge or the court—

(a) is satisfied, on the written or oral evidence of a registered medical practitioner, that there is reason to suspect that the person is suffering from mental disorder, and

(b) is of the opinion that it would be impracticable for a report on the person's mental condition to be made if he or she were remanded on bail,

the judge or the court may remand the person to a hospital or registered establishment specified by the judge or the court for such a report to be made.

(2) In sub–paragraph (1)—

"hospital" has the meaning given by section 145(1) of the Mental Health Act 1983;

"mental disorder" has the meaning given by section 1 of that Act (reading subsection (2B) of that section as if it included a reference to sub–paragraph (1) above);

"registered establishment" has the meaning given by 34(1) of that Act.

(3) Subsections (4) to (10) of section 35 of the Mental Health Act 1983 apply for the purposes of sub–paragraph (1) with any necessary modifications (in particular, with references to the accused person being read as references to the person mentioned in that sub–paragraph, and references to the court being read as references to the judge or the court).

Further remand

3A–1842 7—(1) If the court is satisfied that a person who has been remanded is unable by reason of illness or accident to appear or be brought before the court at the end of the period of remand, the court may further remand the person in his or her absence.

(2) The power in sub–paragraph (1) may, in the case of a person who was

remanded on bail, be exercised by enlarging the person's recognizance and those of any sureties for the person to a later time.

(3) Where a person remanded on bail is bound to appear before the court at any time and the court has no power to remand the person under sub–paragraph (1), the court may (in the person's absence) enlarge the person's recognizance and those of any sureties for the person to a later time.

(4) The enlargement of the person's recognizance is to be treated as a further remand.

(5) Paragraph 4(1) (limit of remand) does not apply to the exercise of the powers conferred by this paragraph.

Postponement of taking recognizance

8 Where under paragraph 2(3)(b) the court fixes the amount in which the **3A–1843** principal and the sureties, if any, are to be bound, the recognizance may afterwards be taken by a person prescribed by rules of court, with the same consequences as if it had been entered into before the court.

Requirements imposed on remand on bail

9 The court may when remanding a person on bail under this Schedule require **3A–1844** the person to comply, before release on bail or later, with any requirements that appear to the court to be necessary to secure that the person does not interfere with witnesses or otherwise obstruct the course of justice.

Note

This Schedule is not yet in force. It will be brought into force by a commencement **3A–1845** order.

3B BUSINESS TENANCIES

Landlord and Tenant Act 1954

s.30(1)(c) other substantial breaches of obligations, or any other reason connected with the tenant's use or management of the holding

Add at end:

The two limbs of s.30(1)(c) are separate and it is not necessary to establish a breach **3B–179** of obligation under the first limb in order to rely on the second limb. Further, the reasons relied on under the second limb need not be directly concerned with the relationship of the parties as landlord and tenant (*Horne and Meredith Properties Ltd v Cox* [2014] EWCA Civ 423—a long history of litigation in which "tenant's conduct had grossly exceeded any reasonable balance" was sufficient.)

3C CONTEMPT OF COURT

A. An Outline of the Law of Contempt of Court

2. Principal forms of contempt liability

(e) Contempt of court and enforcement of judgments etc by order of committal

Add new paragraph at end:

Standing to make an application for committal for breach of a court order in accor- **3C–17** dance with the procedure set out in Section 2 of Part 81 lies with the party for whose assistance the order was made. In *Clarke v Chadbourn* [1985] 1 W.L.R. 78, Sir Robert Megarry V–C explained that where that party chooses not to make an application, and there is a "public element involved", it would be for the Attorney–General to judge whether the public interest required him to intervene in order to enforce the order. His lordship added that, if neither the party nor the Attorney–General sought to enforce the order the court will act of its own initiative to punish the contempt "only in exceptional cases of clear contempts which cannot wait to be dealt with". See also *Bedfordshire Police v U* [2013] EWHC 2350 (Fam), [2014] 2 W.L.R. 780 (Holman J.).

At the end of the third paragraph, add:

3C–18 Section 5 states that the court's power is limited to committing to prison for a term not exceeding six weeks; the burden of proving that the debtor has the means to pay and has refused or neglected or refuses or neglects to pay the same lies on the applicant.

In the second paragraph, for "RSC Ord 45, r.8", substitute:

3C–19 CPR r.70.2A (formerly RSC Ord.45 r.8)

In the third paragraph, before "Applications to commit", add:

3C–22 The Family Court also deals with applications to commit for breach of forced marriage protection orders made under Pt 4A of the Family Law Act 1996, which may be made with a power of arrest attached, as for example in the case of *Bedfordshire Police v U* [2013] EWHC 2350 (Fam), [2014] 2 W.L.R. 780 (Holman J.), where it was held that the police, having arrested the respondent for breach of the order, did not have standing to make an application to commit the respondent for contempt.

After the first paragraph, add as a new paragraph:

3C–24 In *Coll v Floreat Merchant Banking Ltd* [2014] EWHC 1741 (QB), June 3, 2014, unrep. (Hickinbottom J), where the claimant (C) (1) alleged that solicitors (Y) for the defendants (D) had acted in breach of an undertaking given to her before the commencement of the proceedings and (2) applied under r.81.11 for permission to make an application for the committal to prison of Y (whom C sought to join as additional defendants for that purpose) and of D whom C alleged were involved in the breach, the judge stated that the question of whether the court has jurisdiction to commit for breach of a solicitor's undertaking, other than one made to the court, has never been authoritatively determined. In dismissing the application the judge held (1) that where a solicitor has failed to perform a negative undertaking, the appropriate course for the party disadvantaged to take is to seek an injunction (or undertaking to the court in lieu) preventing further non–compliance which, if breached, will found an application to commit, (2) given the other procedures nowadays available for regulating the conduct of solicitors, there will generally be no compelling reason for seeking to commit a solicitor for breach of an undertaking not to the court (assuming such power to commit exists), and (3) because of the "potential for tactical mischief", on public policy grounds such proceedings should generally be discouraged, particularly where the undertaking is given by a solicitor acting for a party in civil proceedings.

(f) Corporations and contempt liability

In the first paragraph, after "Biba Ltd v Stratford Investments Ltd [1973] Ch. 281)." add:

3C–24.1 Put shortly, for a director or officer to be liable, it is necessary to show that he or she knew of and was responsible for the company's breach of the court order, undertaking to the court, or other contempt (see *Dar Al Arkan Real Estate Development Co v Al Refai* [2014] EWCA Civ 715, May 23, 2014, CA, unrep., at para.33 per Beatson L.J., and authorities referred to there).

4. Procedure

In the second paragraph, for "81.8.6", substitute:

3C–35 81.18.6

6. Appeal in cases of contempt of court

(b) Route of appeal and permission to appeal

At the end of the eighth paragraph, add:

3C–39 The Court of Appeal has suggested that consideration should be given to imposing a permission requirement where the appellant had not submitted to the court's jurisdiction and had deliberately absented himself from the committal proceedings (*Thursfield v Thursfield* [2013] EWCA Civ 840, [2013] C.P. Rep. 44, CA).

B. Debtors Acts 1869 & 1878

Debtors Act 1869

General Note

After the fourth paragraph, add as a new paragraph:

The ordinary and natural meaning of "means" in s.5(2) is income or assets of some **3C–41** kind; a mere finding to the effect that a person had earning potential which he was choosing not to exercise or maximise would not amount to a finding that it had been proved to the satisfaction of the court that he "either has or has had...the means to pay" (*Constantinides v Constantinides* [2013] EWHC 3688 (Fam); [2014] 1 W.L.R. 1934 (Holman J.), where difference noted in wording between s.5(2) and the Magistrates' Courts Act 1980 s.93(6), which provides for imprisonment by a magistrates' court for default in paying a maintenance order, and held that the latter provision should be construed and applied so that it has the same practical effect as the former).

In the sixth paragraph, before "The result is", add:

(As to meaning of "maintenance order" in this context, see *ZUK v ZUK* [2012] EWCA Civ 1871, [2013] 2 F.L.R. 1466, CA.)

C. Contempt of Court Act 1981

Contempt of Court Act 1981

Directions prohibiting publication

After the first paragraph, add as a new paragraph:

In *A v British Broadcasting Corporation* [2014] UKSC 25; [2014] 2 W.L.R. 1243, SC, **3C–75** the Supreme Court examined the scope and effect of s.11 in a Scottish appeal. The Court (1) stated that (a) when an application is made to the court under s.11 to allow a name or matter to be withheld, that is not an application for relief made against any person as no remedy or order is sought against any respondent, (b) if ancillary directions under s.11 are also sought, prohibiting any publication of the name or matter in question, that equally is not an application for relief made against any respondent, and (c) in such circumstances there is no respondent who should be notified, or who might be present or represented at the hearing, and (2) held that there is therefore no obligation under s.12(2) of the Human Rights Act 1998 (see para.3D–47 below) to allow the media an opportunity to be heard before such an order can be granted. The Court explained that where a s.11 order is made ex parte the media's right under art.13 to an effective remedy for any violation of their art.10 rights is secured (as the instant case indicated) by procedures enabling them to challenge such orders at a hearing where they are able to make representations. The Court further stated that the power given to the court by s.11 is not restricted to making orders to protect the public interest in the administration of justice and enables orders to be made for the purpose of protecting an individual's Convention rights, and the court's power to give directions under the section is not restricted to those circumstances where members of the public are present in the court room and the court allows a name or matter to be withheld.

PENALTIES FOR CONTEMPT AND KINDRED OFFENCES

Proceedings in England and Wales

Delete s.14(4A) and substitute:

(4A) For the purposes of the preceding provisions of this section **3C–84** the county court shall be treated as a superior court and not as an inferior court.

Add new s.14(4B):

(4B) The preceding provisions of this section do not apply to the family court, but—

> (a) this is without prejudice to the operation of section 31E(1)(a) of the Matrimonial and Family Proceedings Act 1984 (family court has High Court's powers) in relation to

> the powers of the High Court that are limited or conferred
> by those provisions of this section, and
>
> (b) section 31E(1)(b) of that Act (family court has county
> court's powers) does not apply in relation to the powers of
> the county court that are limited or conferred by those
> provisions of this section.

Note

Add at end:

3C–85   Paragraph (4B) was inserted by the Crime and Courts Act 2013 s.17(6), Sch.10 Pt 2 para.53, with effect from the establishment of the Family Court on April 22, 2014. Subsection (4A) amended, subject to savings and transitional provisions, by the Crime and Courts Act 2013 Sch.9 para.52, with effect from April 22, 2014 (see SI 2014/954); for savings and transitional provisions see Sch.8 to the Act.

Term of imprisonment or fine for contempt

At the end of the fifth paragraph (beginning "The section has been"), add:

3C–87   A judge is entitled to treat the respondent's failure to attend the committal hearing in the face of an order requiring him to do so as an aggravating factor (*Thursfield v Thursfield* [2013] EWCA Civ 840, [2013] C.P. Rep. 44, CA).

It is conceivable that conduct justifying the committal of a person for contempt or for a kindred offence may also constitute a criminal offence. In *Chelmsford County Council v Ramet* [2014] EWHC 6 (Fam), January 2, 2014, unrep., the President explained that where proceedings are brought against a person for contempt or a for kindred offence (in that case, proceedings under the County Courts Act 1984 s.14(1)(b)), and that person has already been convicted in a criminal court and sentenced for conduct inclusive of conduct alleged in the proceedings, the court may sentence "only for such conduct as was not the subject of the criminal proceedings", as a person may not be punished twice for the same offence.

After the sixteenth paragraph (beginning "In JSC BTA Bank") add as a new paragraph:

In *Smith v Doncaster Metropolitan Borough Council* [2014] EWCA Civ 16, January 16, 2014, CA, unrep., a committal order was made for breach of a planning injunction, a 12 months' custodial sentence with both a punitive element and a coercive element was imposed, but the order was suspended on conditions. After the occurrence of developments rendering the coercive element ineffectual, a High Court judge granted the applicant's application for activation of the order, made on the grounds that the contemnor (C) had failed to comply fully with the conditions, and sent C to prison for nine months. In dismissing C's appeal against a judge's dismissal of his application for release, the Court of Appeal stated that where (as in this case) persistent failure to comply with an injunction after the imposition of a sentence of committal aggravates the gravity of the contemnor's conduct, the weight to be given to the punitive element will be increased; consequently, the fact that the coercive element of the sentence no longer had any purpose did not require that the sentence be discharged.

Penalties for breach of orders made in family proceedings

Add new paragraph at beginning:

3C–88   Provisions in Pt 4A of the Matrimonial and Family Proceedings Act 1984 (ss.31A to 31P) taking effect on April 22, 2014, inserted therein by the Crime and Courts Act 2013, established the Family Court. Section 31E(1) states that, in any proceedings in the Family Court, the court may make any order (a) which could be made by the High Court if the proceedings were in the High Court, or (b) which could be made by the county court if the proceedings were in the county court. At the same time, the Family Procedure (Amendment No. 2) Rules 2014 (SI 2014/667) inserted in the FPR a new Part, Part 37 (Applications and Proceedings in Relation to Contempt of Court) containing free–standing rules for family proceedings on contempt and committal, modelled on the provisions contained in CPR Part 81. In effect, the Family Court inherited, as it were, the powers of the High Court and the former county courts in relation to contempt. However, s.31H(1) of the 1984 Act states that the Lord Chancellor may by regulations make provision limiting or removing, in circumstances specified in the regulations, any of the powers exercisable by the Family Court when dealing with a person for contempt of court. The regulations made under s.31H are the Family Law (Contempt of Court) (Powers) Regulations 2014 (SI 2014/833). They contain detailed provisions specifying the scope of the contempt powers that may be exercised by judges of different levels sitting in the Family Court.

3E   INSOLVENCY PROCEEDINGS

PRACTICE DIRECTION—INSOLVENCY PROCEEDINGS

Delete "Practice Direction—Insolvency Proceedings" and substitute:

Contents

3E–0.1

PART ONE: GENERAL PROVISIONS

Editorial note

3E–0.2   The Insolvency Practice Direction which came into force on February 23, 2012 has undergone some amendment. The version that now applies came into force on July 29, 2014.

The principal changes are as follows:

- The revised Practice Direction includes a table of contents (which follows the lead given by Professor Scott who first prepared one to give an overview of the 2012 Practice Direction when it was published in this volume that year) which makes it easier to use.
- Account has been taken of the move of the registrars' courts in London to the Rolls Building in Fetter Lane and of the creation of the single county court.
- The provisions relating to winding up petitions and their content (see in particular para.11.2) have been revised to take account of (a) petitions presented in respect of foreign companies and (b) changes made by the Companies Act 2006.
- Further clarification has been given in relation to the complex provisions governing service.
- A new Part Four contains a reminder about the need to comply with certain requirements of the Financial Markets and Insolvency (Final Settlement) Regulations 1999.
- In response to user pressure, the requirements relating to the searches to be carried out before presenting a bankruptcy petition have been changed so as to allow a search to be conducted through the Land Registry rather than requiring searches to be made at a number of courts which could have jurisdiction in respect of a debtor. Increased court fees had made the old search requirements disproportionately expensive.

Part One

General Provisions

1.   Definitions

3E–1   **1.1** In this Practice Direction:

(1) "The Act" means the Insolvency Act 1986 and includes the Act as applied to limited liability partnerships by the Limited Liability Partnerships Regulations 2001 or to any other person or body by virtue of the Act or any other legislation;

(2) "The Insolvency Rules" means the rules for the time being in force and made under s.411 and s.412 of the Act in relation to insolvency proceedings, and, save where otherwise provided, any reference to a rule is to a rule in the Insolvency Rules;

(3) "CPR" means the Civil Procedure Rules and "CPR" followed by a Part or rule identified by number means the Part or rule with that number in those Rules;

(4) "EC Regulation on Insolvency Proceedings" means Council Regulation (EC) No 1346/2000 of 29 May 2000 on Insolvency Proceedings;

(5) "Service Regulation" means Council Regulation (EC) No. 1393/2007 of 13 November 2007 on the service in the Member States of judicial and extrajudicial documents in civil and commercial matters (service of documents);

(6) "Insolvency proceedings" means:

  (a) any proceedings under the Act, the Insolvency Rules, the Administration of Insolvent Estates of Deceased Persons Order 1986 (S.I. 1986 No.1999), the Insolvent Partnerships Order 1994 (S.I. 1994 No. 2421) or the Limited Liability Partnerships Regulations 2001;

  (b) any proceedings under the EC Regulation on Insolvency Proceedings or the Cross–Border Insolvency Regulations 2006 (S.I. 2006/1030);

(7) References to a "company" include a limited liability partnership and references to a "contributory" include a member of a limited liability partnership;

(8) References to a "Registrar" are to a Registrar in Bankruptcy of the High Court and (save in cases where it is clear from the context that a particular provision applies only to the Royal Courts of Justice) include a District Judge in a District Registry of the High Court and in any county court hearing centre having relevant insolvency jurisdiction;

(9) "Court" means the High Court or any county court hearing centre having relevant insolvency jurisdiction;

(10) "Royal Courts of Justice" means the Royal Courts of Justice, 7 Rolls Buildings, Fetter Lane, London EC4A 1NL or such other place in London where the Registrars sit;

(11) In Part Six of this Practice Direction:

  (a) "appointee" means:

    (i) a provisional liquidator appointed under section 135 of the Act;

    (ii) a special manager appointed under section 177 or section 370 of the Act;

    (iii) a liquidator appointed by the members of a company or partnership or by the creditors of a company or partnership or by the Secretary of State pursuant to section 137 of the Act, or by the court pursuant to section 140 of the Act;

    (iv) an administrator of a company appointed to manage the property, business and affairs of that company under the Act or other enactment and to which the provisions of the Act are applicable;

    (v) a trustee in bankruptcy (other than the Official Receiver) appointed under the Act;

    (vi) a nominee or supervisor of a voluntary arrangement under Part I or Part VIII of the Act;

    (vii) a licensed insolvency practitioner appointed by the court pursuant to section 273 of the Act;

    (viii) an interim receiver appointed by the court pursuant to section 286 of the Act;

  (b) "assessor" means a person appointed in accordance with CPR 35.15;

  (c) "remuneration application" means any application to fix, approve or challenge the remuneration or expenses of an appointee or the basis of remuneration;

(d) "remuneration" includes expenses (where the Act or the Insolvency Rules give the court jurisdiction in relation thereto) and, in the case of an administrator, any pre–appointment administration costs or remuneration.

2.   Coming into force

3E–2   **2.1** This Practice Direction shall come into force on 29 July 2014 and shall replace all previous Practice Directions, Practice Statements and Practice Notes relating to insolvency proceedings. For the avoidance of doubt, this Practice Direction does not affect the Practice Direction relating to contributories' winding up petitions (Practice Direction 49B—Order under section 127 Insolvency Act 1986).

3.   Distribution of business

3E–3   **3.1** As a general rule all petitions and applications (except those listed in paragraphs 3.2 and 3.3 below) should be listed for initial hearing before a Registrar in accordance with rule 7.6A(2) and (3).

3.2 The following applications relating to insolvent companies should always be listed before a Judge:

(1) applications for committal for contempt;

(2) applications for an administration order;

(3) applications for an injunction pursuant to the Court's inherent jurisdiction (e.g. to restrain the presentation or advertisement of a winding up petition) or pursuant to section 37 of the Senior Courts Act 1981 or section 38 of the County Courts Act 1984 but not applications for any order to be made pursuant to the Act or the Rules;

(4) applications for the appointment of a provisional liquidator;

(5) interim applications and applications for directions or case management after any proceedings have been referred or adjourned to the Judge (except where liberty to apply to the Registrar has been given).

3.3 The following applications relating to insolvent individuals should always be listed before a Judge:

(1) applications for committal for contempt;

(2) applications for an injunction pursuant to the Court's inherent jurisdiction (e.g. to restrain the presentation of a bankruptcy petition) or pursuant to section 37 of the Senior Courts Act 1981 or section 38 of the County Courts Act 1984 but not applications for any order to be made pursuant to the Act or the Rules;

(3) interim applications and applications for directions or case management after any proceedings have been referred or adjourned to the Judge (except where liberty to apply to the Registrar has been given).

3.4 When deciding whether to hear proceedings or to refer or adjourn them to the Judge, the Registrar should have regard to the following factors:

(1) the complexity of the proceedings;

(2) whether the proceedings raise new or controversial points of law;

(3) the likely date and length of the hearing;

(4) public interest in the proceedings.

4.   Court documents

4.1 All insolvency proceedings should be commenced and applica-   **3E–4** tions in proceedings should be made using the forms prescribed by the Act, the Insolvency Rules or other legislation under which the same is or are brought or made and/or should contain the information prescribed by the Act, the Insolvency Rules or other legislation.

4.2 Every court document in insolvency proceedings under Parts I to VII of the Act shall be headed:

IN THE HIGH COURT OF JUSTICE......

CHANCERY DIVISION

[..............DISTRICT REGISTRY] or in the Royal Courts of Justice

[COMPANIES COURT]

or

IN THE COUNTY COURT AT [...............]

followed by

IN THE MATTER OF [name of company]

AND IN THE MATTER OF THE INSOLVENCY ACT 1986

4.3 Every court document in insolvency proceedings under Parts IX to XI of the Act shall be headed:

IN THE [HIGH COURT OF JUSTICE] or [COUNTY COURT AT [...............]]

IN BANKRUPTCY

IN THE MATTER OF [name of bankrupt]

or

RE: [name of bankrupt].

Every application should also be headed:

AND IN THE MATTER OF THE INSOLVENCY ACT 1986

4.4 Every court document in proceedings to which the Act applies by virtue of other legislation should also be headed:

IN THE MATTER OF [THE FINANCIAL SERVICES AND MARKETS ACT 2000 or as the case may be]

AND IN THE MATTER OF THE INSOLVENCY ACT 1986

5.   Evidence

3E–5   **5.1** Subject to the provisions of rule 7.9 or any other provisions or directions as to the form in which evidence should be given, written evidence in insolvency proceedings must be given by witness statement.

6.   Service of court documents in insolvency proceedings

3E–6   **6.1** Except where the Insolvency Rules otherwise provide (and, in this regard, the attention of practitioners is particularly drawn to rule 12A.16(2)), CPR Part 6 applies to the service of court documents both within and out of the jurisdiction as modified by this Practice Direction or as the court may otherwise direct.

6.2 Except where the Insolvency Rules otherwise provide, or as may be required under the Service Regulation, service of documents in insolvency proceedings will be the responsibility of the parties and will not be undertaken by the court.

6.3 A document which, pursuant to rule 12A.16(3)(b), is treated as a claim form, is deemed to have been served on the date specified in CPR Part 6.14, and any other document (including any document which is treated as a claim form pursuant to rule 12A.16(3)(a) but which is not a document of a type specified in rule 12A.16(2)) is deemed to have been served on the date specified in CPR Part 6.26, unless the court otherwise directs. (Pursuant to rule 12A.16(2), the provisions of CPR Part 6 do not apply to the service of any of the following documents within the jurisdiction: (a) a winding–up petition; (b) a bankruptcy petition; (c) any document relating to such a petition; or (d) any administration, winding–up or bankruptcy order.)

6.4 Except as provided below, service out of the jurisdiction of an application which is to be treated as a claim form under rule 12A.16(3) requires the permission of the court.

6.5 An application which is to be treated as a claim form under rule 12A.16(3) may be served out of the jurisdiction without the permission of the court if:

(1) the application is by an office–holder appointed in insolvency proceedings in respect of an individual or company with its centre of main interests within the jurisdiction exercising a statutory power under the Act, and the person to be served is to be served within the EU; or

(2) it is a copy of an application, being served on a Member State liquidator (as defined by Article 2 of the EC Regulation on Insolvency Proceedings).

6.6 An application for permission to serve out of the jurisdiction must be supported by a witness statement setting out:

(1) the nature of the claim or application and the relief sought;

(2) that the applicant believes that the claim has a reasonable prospect of success; and

(3) the address of the person to be served or, if not known, in what place or country that person is, or is likely, to be found.

6.7 CPR 6.36 and 6.37(1) and (2) do not apply in insolvency proceedings.

7. Jurisdiction

7.1 Where CPR 2.4 provides for the court to perform any act, that act may be performed by a Registrar. **3E–7**

8. Drawing up of orders

8.1 The court will draw up all orders except orders on the application of the Official Receiver or for which the Treasury Solicitor is responsible or where the court otherwise directs. **3E–8**

9. Urgent applications

9.1 In the Royal Courts of Justice the Registrars (and in other courts exercising insolvency jurisdiction the District Judges) operate urgent applications lists for urgent and time–critical applications and may be available to hear urgent applications at other times. Parties asking for an application to be dealt with in the urgent applications lists or urgently at any other time must complete the certificate below: **3E–9**

No:

Heading of action

I estimate that this matter is likely to occupy the court for
.... mins/hours.

I certify that it is urgent for the following reasons:

....
[name of representative]

....
[telephone number]

Counsel/Solicitor for the ....

WARNING. If, in the opinion of the Registrar/District Judge, the application is not urgent then such sanction will be applied as is thought appropriate in all the circumstances.

Part Two

Company Insolvency

10. Administrations

10.1 In the absence of special circumstances, an application for the extension of an administration should be made not less than one month before the end of the administration. The evidence in support of any later application must explain why the application is being made late. The court will consider whether any part of the costs should be disallowed where an application is made less than one month before the end of the administration. **3E–10**

11. Winding–up petitions

11.1 Before presenting a winding–up petition the creditor must conduct a search to ensure that no petition is already pending. Save in exceptional circumstances a second winding up petition should not be presented whilst a prior petition is pending. A petitioner who presents his own petition while another petition is pending does so at risk as to costs.

11.2 Save where by reason of the nature of the company or its place of incorporation the information cannot be stated (in which case as much similar information as is available should be given), every creditor's winding–up petition must (in the case of a company) contain the following:

(1) the full name and address of the petitioner;

(2) the name and any registered number/s of the company in respect of which a winding up order is sought;

(3) the date of incorporation of the company and the legislation under which it was incorporated;

(4) the address of the company's registered office and, in the case of any overseas company, the address of any establishment registered under the Companies Act or Acts;

(5) (a) In the case of companies incorporated under any of the Companies Acts prior to the Companies Act 2006, a statement of the nominal capital of the company, the manner in which its shares are divided up and the amount of the capital paid up or credited as paid up; or

(b) In the case of any other companies, a statement of the known issued share capital of the company, the manner in which its shares are divided up and the amount of the capital paid up or credited as paid up.

(6) (a) In the case of companies incorporated under any of the Companies Acts prior to the Companies Act 2006, brief details of the principal objects for which the company was established followed, where appropriate, by the words "and other objects stated in the memorandum of association of the company"; or

(b) In the case of companies incorporated under the Companies Act 2006, either:

(i) a statement confirming that its objects are unrestricted pursuant to section 31(1) of the Companies Act 2006, or alternatively

(ii) a statement confirming that its objects are restricted by its Articles of Association and brief details of such restrictions;

(7) details of the basis on which it is contended that the company is insolvent including, where a debt is relied on, sufficient particulars of the debt (the amount, nature and approximate date(s) on which it was incurred) to enable the company and the court to identify the debt;

(8) a statement that the company is insolvent and unable to pay its debts;

(9) a statement that for the reasons set out in the evidence verifying the petition the EC Regulation on Insolvency Proceedings either applies or does not and if the former whether the

proceedings will be main, territorial or secondary proceedings;

(10) the statement that, "In the circumstances it is just and equitable that the company be wound up under the provisions of the Insolvency Act 1986";

(11) a prayer that the company be wound up, for such other order as the court thinks fit and any other specific relief sought.

Similar information (so far as is appropriate) should be given where the petition is presented against a partnership.

11.3 The statement of truth verifying the petition in accordance with rule 4.12 should be made no more than ten business days before the date of issue of the petition.

11.4 Where the company to be wound up has been struck off the register, the petition should state that fact and include as part of the relief sought an order that it be restored to the register. Save where the petition has been presented by a Minister of the Crown or a government department, evidence of service on the Treasury Solicitor or the Solicitor for the affairs of the Duchy of Lancaster or the Solicitor to the Duchy of Cornwall (as appropriate) should be filed exhibiting the bona vacantia waiver letter.

11.5 Gazetting of the petition

11.5.1 Rule 4.11 must be complied with (unless waived by the court): it is designed to ensure that the class remedy of winding up by the court is made available to all creditors, and is not used as a means of putting improper pressure on the company to pay the petitioner's debt or costs. Failure to comply with the rule, without good reason accepted by the court, may lead to the summary dismissal of the petition on the return date (rule 4.11(6)) or to the court depriving the petitioner of the costs of the hearing. If the court, in its discretion, grants an adjournment, this will usually be on terms that notice of the petition is gazetted or otherwise given in accordance with the rule in due time for the adjourned hearing. No further adjournment for the purpose of gazetting will normally be granted.

11.5.2 Copies of every notice gazetted in connection with a winding up petition, or where this is not practicable a description of the form and content of the notice, must be lodged with the court as soon as possible after publication and in any event not later than five business days before the hearing of the petition. This direction applies even if the notice is defective in any way (e.g. is published on a date not in accordance with the Insolvency Rules , or omits or misprints some important words) or if the petitioner decides not to pursue the petition (e.g. on receiving payment).

11.6 Errors in petitions

11.6.1 Applications for permission to amend errors in petitions which are discovered after a winding up order has been made should be made to the member of court staff in charge of the winding up list in the Royal Courts of Justice or to a District Judge in any other court.

11.6.2 Where the error is an error in the name of the company, the member of court staff in charge of the winding up list in the Royal Courts of Justice or a District Judge in any other court may make any necessary amendments to ensure that the winding up order is drawn up with the correct name of the company inserted. If there is any doubt, e.g. where there might be another company in existence which could be confused with the company to be wound up, the member of court staff in charge of the winding up list will refer the application to a Registrar at the Royal Courts of Justice and a District Judge may refer it to a Judge.

11.6.3 Where it is discovered that the company has been struck off the Register of Companies prior to the winding up order being made, the matter must be restored to the list as soon as possible to enable an order for the restoration of the name to be made as well as the order to wind up and, save where the petition has been presented by a Minister of the Crown or a government department, evidence of service on the Treasury Solicitor or the Solicitor for the Affairs of the Duchy of Lancaster or the Solicitor to the Duchy of Cornwall (as appropriate) should be filed exhibiting the bona vacantia waiver letter.

11.7 Rescission of a winding up order

11.7.1 An application to rescind a winding up order must be made by application.

11.7.2 The application should normally be made within five business days after the date on which the order was made (rule 7.47(4)) failing which it should include an application to extend time. Notice of any such application must be given to the petitioning creditor, any supporting or opposing creditor and the Official Receiver.

11.7.3 Applications will only be entertained if made (a) by a creditor, or (b) by a contributory, or (c) by the company jointly with a creditor or with a contributory. The application must be supported by a witness statement which should include details of assets and liabilities and (where appropriate) reasons for any failure to apply within five business days.

11.7.4 In the case of an unsuccessful application the costs of the petitioning creditor, any supporting creditors and of the Official Receiver will normally be ordered to be paid by the creditor or the contributory making or joining in the application. The reason for this is that if the costs of an unsuccessful application are made payable by the company, they fall unfairly on the general body of creditors.

11.8 Validation orders

11.8.1 A company against which a winding up petition has been presented may apply to the court after presentation of the petition for relief from the effects of section 127(1) of the Act by seeking an order that a disposition or dispositions of its property, including payments out of its bank account (whether such account is in credit or overdrawn), shall not be void in the event of a winding up order being made on the hearing of the petition (a validation order).

11.8.2 An application for a validation order should generally be made to the Registrar. An application should be made to the Judge only if: (a) it is urgent and no Registrar is available to hear it; or (b) it is complex or raises new or controversial points of law; or (c) it is estimated to last longer than 30 minutes.

11.8.3 Save in exceptional circumstances, notice of the making of the application should be given to: (a) the petitioning creditor; (b) any person entitled to receive a copy of the petition pursuant to rule 4.10; (c) any creditor who has given notice to the petitioner of his intention to appear on the hearing of the petition pursuant to rule 4.16; and (d) any creditor who has been substituted as petitioner pursuant to rule 4.19.

11.8.4 The application should be supported by a witness statement which, save in exceptional circumstances, should be made by a director or officer of the company who is intimately acquainted with the company's affairs and financial circumstances. If appropriate, supporting evidence in the form of a witness statement from the company's accountant should also be produced.

11.8.5 The extent and contents of the evidence will vary according to the circumstances and the nature of the relief sought, but in the majority of cases it should include, as a minimum, the following information:

(1) when and to whom notice has been given in accordance with paragraph 11.8.3 above;

(2) the company's registered office;

(3) the company's nominal and paid up capital;

(4) brief details of the circumstances leading to presentation of the petition;

(5) how the company became aware of presentation of the petition;

(6) whether the petition debt is admitted or disputed and, if the latter, brief details of the basis on which the debt is disputed;

(7) full details of the company's financial position including details of its assets (including details of any security and the amount(s) secured) and liabilities, which should be supported, as far as possible, by documentary evidence, e.g. the latest filed accounts, any draft audited accounts, management accounts or estimated statement of affairs;

(8) a cash flow forecast and profit and loss projection for the period for which the order is sought;

(9) details of the dispositions or payments in respect of which an order is sought;

(10) the reasons relied on in support of the need for such dispositions or payments to be made;

(11) any other information relevant to the exercise of the court's discretion;

(12) details of any consents obtained from the persons mentioned in paragraph 11.8.3 above (supported by documentary evidence where appropriate);

(13) details of any relevant bank account, including its number and the address and sort code of the bank at which such account is held and the amount of the credit or debit balance on such account at the time of making the application.

11.8.6 Where an application is made urgently to enable payments to be made which are essential to continued trading (e.g. wages) and it is not possible to assemble all the evidence listed above, the court may consider granting limited relief for a short period, but there should be sufficient evidence to satisfy the court that the interests of creditors are unlikely to be prejudiced.

11.8.7 Where the application involves a disposition of property the court will need details of the property (including its title number if the property is land) and to be satisfied that any proposed disposal will be at a proper value. Accordingly, an independent valuation should be obtained and exhibited to the evidence.

11.8.8 The court will need to be satisfied by credible evidence either that the company is solvent and able to pay its debts as they fall due or that a particular transaction or series of transactions in respect of which the order is sought will be beneficial to or will not prejudice the interests of all the unsecured creditors as a class (*Denney v John Hudson & Co Ltd* [1992] BCLC 901; *Re Fairway Graphics Ltd* [1991] BCLC 468).

11.8.9 A draft of the order sought should be attached to the application.

11.8.10 Similar considerations to those set out above are likely to apply to applications seeking ratification of a transaction or payment after the making of a winding–up order.

12. Applications

3E–12   **12.1** In accordance with rule 13.2(2) , in the Royal Courts of Justice the member of court staff in charge of the winding up list has been authorised to deal with applications:

(1) to extend or abridge time prescribed by the Insolvency Rules in connection with winding up (rule 4.3);

(2) for permission to withdraw a winding up petition (rule 4.15);

(3) for the substitution of a petitioner (rule 4.19);

(4) by the Official Receiver for limited disclosure of a statement of affairs (rule 4.35);

(5) by the Official Receiver for relief from duties imposed upon him by the Insolvency Rules (rule 4.47);

(6) by the Official Receiver for permission to give notice of a meeting by advertisement only (rule 4.59);

(7) to transfer proceedings from the High Court (Royal Courts of Justice) to the county court hearing centre (in which proceedings to wind up companies may be commenced under the Act) after the making of a winding–up order (rule 7.11).

12.2 In District Registries or the County Court such applications must be made to a District Judge.

Part Three

Personal Insolvency

13. Statutory demands

13.1 Service abroad of statutory demands

3E–13   **13.1.1** A statutory demand is not a document issued by the court. Permission to serve out of the jurisdiction is not, therefore, required.

13.1.2 Rule 6.3(2) ('Requirements as to service') applies to service of the statutory demand whether within or out of the jurisdiction.

13.1.3 A creditor wishing to serve a statutory demand out of the jurisdiction in a foreign country with which a civil procedure convention has been made (including the Hague Convention) may and, if the assistance of a British Consul is desired, must adopt the procedure prescribed by CPR Part 6.42 and 6.43 . In the case of any doubt whether the country is a 'convention country', enquiries should be made of the Queen's Bench Masters' Secretary Department, Royal Courts of Justice, Strand, London WC2A 2LL.

13.1.4 In all other cases, service of the demand must be effected by private arrangement in accordance with rule 6.3(2) and local foreign law.

13.1.5 When a statutory demand is to be served out of the jurisdiction, the time limits of 21 days and 18 days respectively referred to in the demand must be amended as provided in the next paragraph. For this purpose reference should be made to the table set out in the practice direction supplementing Section IV of CPR Part 6.

13.1.6 A creditor should amend the statutory demand as follows:

(1) for any reference to 18 days there must be substituted the appropriate number of days set out in the table plus 4 days;

(2) for any reference to 21 days there must be substituted the appropriate number of days in the table plus 7 days.

13.1.7 Attention is drawn to the fact that in all forms of the statutory demand the figure 18 and the figure 21 occur in more than one place.

13.2 Substituted service of statutory demands

13.2.1 The creditor is under an obligation to do all that is reasonable to bring the statutory demand to the debtor's attention and, if practicable, to cause personal service to be effected (rule 6.3(2)).

13.2.2 In the circumstances set out in rule 6.3(3) the demand may instead be advertised. As there is no statutory form of advertisement, the court will accept an advertisement in the following form:

STATUTORY DEMAND

(Debt for liquidated sum payable immediately following a judgment or order of the court)

To (Block letters)

of

TAKE NOTICE that a statutory demand has been issued by:

Name of Creditor:

Address:

The creditor demands payment of £ the amount now due on a judgment or order of the (High Court of Justice Division (County Court at........) dated the [day] of [month] 20[].

The statutory demand is an important document and it is deemed to have been served on you on the date of the first appearance of this advertisement. You must deal with this demand within 21 days of the service upon you or you could be made bankrupt and your property and goods taken away from you. If you are in any doubt as to your position, you should seek advice immediately from a solicitor or your nearest Citizens' Advice Bureau. The statutory demand can be obtained or is available for inspection and collection from:

Name:

Address:

(Solicitor for) the creditor

Tel. No. Reference:

You have only 21 days from the date of the first appearance of this advertisement before the creditor may present a bankruptcy petition. You have only 18 days from the date of the first appearance of this advertisement within which to apply to the court to set aside the demand.

13.2.3 Where personal service is not effected or the demand is not advertised in the limited circumstances permitted by rule 6.3(3), substituted service is permitted, but the creditor must have taken all those steps which would justify the court making an order for substituted service of a petition. The steps to be taken to obtain an order for substituted service of a petition are set out below. Failure to comply with these requirements may result in the court declining to issue the petition (rule 6.11(9)) or dismissing it.

13.2.4 In most cases, evidence of the following steps will suffice to justify acceptance for presentation of a petition where the statutory demand has been served by substituted service (or to justify making an order for substituted service of a petition):

(1) One personal call at the residence and place of business of the debtor where both are known or at either of such places as is known. Where it is known that the debtor has more than one residential or business address, personal calls should be made at all the addresses.

(2) Should the creditor fail to effect personal service, a letter should be written to the debtor referring to the call(s), the purpose of the same and the failure to meet the debtor, adding that a further call will be made for the same purpose on the [day] of [month] 20[] at [] hours at [place]. Such letter may be sent by first class prepaid post or left at or delivered to

the debtor's address in such a way as it is reasonably likely to come to the debtor's attention. At least two business days' notice should be given of the appointment and copies of the letter sent to or left at all known addresses of the debtor. The appointment letter should also state that:

(a) in the event of the time and place not being convenient, the debtor should propose some other time and place reasonably convenient for the purpose;

(b) (In the case of a statutory demand) if the debtor fails to keep the appointment the creditor proposes to serve the debtor by [advertisement] [post] [insertion through a letter box] or as the case may be, and that, in the event of a bankruptcy petition being presented, the court will be asked to treat such service as service of the demand on the debtor;

(c) (In the case of a petition) if the debtor fails to keep the appointment, application will be made to the Court for an order for substituted service either by advertisement, or in such other manner as the court may think fit.

(3) When attending any appointment made by letter, inquiry should be made as to whether the debtor has received all letters left for him. If the debtor is away, inquiry should also be made as to whether or not letters are being forwarded to an address within the jurisdiction (England and Wales) or elsewhere.

(4) If the debtor is represented by a solicitor, an attempt should be made to arrange an appointment for personal service through such solicitor. The Insolvency Rules enable a solicitor to accept service of a statutory demand on behalf of his client but there is no similar provision in respect of service of a bankruptcy petition.

(5) The certificate of service of a statutory demand filed pursuant to rule 6.11 should deal with all the above matters including all relevant facts as to the debtor's whereabouts and whether the appointment letter(s) have been returned. It should also set out the reasons for the belief that the debtor resides at the relevant address or works at the relevant place of business and whether, so far as is known, the debtor is represented by a solicitor.

13.3 Setting aside a statutory demand

13.3.1 The application (Form 6.4) and witness statement in support (Form 6.5) exhibiting a copy of the statutory demand must be filed in court within 18 days of service of the statutory demand on the debtor. Where service is effected by advertisement the period of 18 days is calculated from the date of the first appearance of the advertisement. Three copies of each document must be lodged with the application to enable the court to serve notice of the hearing date on the applicant, the creditor and the person named in Part B of the statutory demand.

13.3.2 Where copies of the documents are not lodged with the application, any order of the Registrar fixing a venue is conditional upon copies of the documents being lodged on the next business day after the Registrar's order otherwise the application will be deemed to have been dismissed.

13.3.3 Where the debt claimed in the statutory demand is based on a judgment, order, liability order, costs certificate, tax assessment or decision of a tribunal, the court will not at this stage inquire into the validity of the debt nor, as a general rule, will it adjourn the application to await the result of an application to set aside the judgment, order decision, costs certificate or any appeal.

13.3.4 Where the debtor (a) claims to have a counterclaim, set–off or cross demand (whether or not he could have raised it in the action in which the judgment or order was obtained) which equals or exceeds the amount of the debt or debts specified in the statutory demand or (b) disputes the debt (not being a debt subject to a judgment, order, liability order, costs certificate or tax assessment) the court will normally set aside the statutory demand if, in its opinion, on the evidence there is a genuine triable issue.

13.3.5 A debtor who wishes to apply to set aside a statutory demand after the expiration of 18 days from the date of service of the statutory demand must apply for an extension of time within which to apply. If the applicant wishes to apply for an injunction to restrain presentation of a petition the application must be made to the Judge. Paragraphs 1 and 2 of Form 6.5 (witness statement in support of application to set aside statutory demand) should be used in support of the application for an extension of time with the following additional paragraphs:

> "(3) To the best of my knowledge and belief the creditor(s) named in the demand has/have not presented a petition against me.
>
> (4) The reasons for my failure to apply to set aside the demand within 18 days after service are as follows: ..."

If application is made to restrain presentation of a bankruptcy petition the following additional paragraph should be added:

> "(5) Unless restrained by injunction the creditor(s) may present a bankruptcy petition against me"

14.   Bankruptcy petitions

14.1 Listing of petitions

3E–14   **14.1.1** All petitions presented will be listed under the name of the debtor unless the court directs otherwise.

14.2 Content of petitions

14.2.1 The attention of practitioners is drawn to the following points:

> (1) A creditor's petition does not require dating, signing or witnessing but must be verified in accordance with rule 6.12.
>
> (2) In the heading it is only necessary to recite the debtor's name e.g. Re John William Smith or Re J W Smith (Male). Any alias or trading name will appear in the body of the petition.

14.2.2 Where the petition is based solely on a statutory demand, only the debt claimed in the demand may be included in the petition.

14.2.3 The attention of practitioners is also drawn to rules 6.7 and 6.8, and in particular to rule 6.8(1) where the 'aggregate sum' is made up of a number of debts.

14.2.4 The date of service of the statutory demand should be recited as follows:

(1) In the case of personal service, the date of service as set out in the certificate of service should be recited and whether service is effected before/after 16.00 hours on Monday to Friday or before/after 12.00 hours on a Saturday.

(2) In the case of substituted service (other than by advertisement), the date alleged in the certificate of service should be recited.

(3) In the strictly limited case of service by advertisement under rule 6.3, the date to be alleged is the date of the advertisement's appearance or, as the case may be, its first appearance (see rules 6.3(3) and 6.11(8)).

14.3 Searches

14.3.1 The petitioning creditor shall, before presenting a petition, conduct an Official Search with the Chief Land Registrar in the register of pending actions for pending petitions presented against the debtor and shall include the following certificate at the end of the petition:

> "I/we certify that within 7 days ending today I/we have conducted a search for pending petitions presented against the debtor and that to the best of my/our knowledge information and belief [no prior petitions have been presented which are still pending] [a prior petition (No [])' has been presented and is/may be pending in the [Court] and I/we am/are issuing this petition at risk as to costs].

Signed..... Dated...."

14.4 Deposit

14.4.1 The deposit will be taken by the court and forwarded to the Official Receiver. In the Royal Courts of Justice the petition fee and deposit should be paid in the Fee Room, which will record the receipt and will impress two entries on the original petition, one in respect of the court fee and the other in respect of the deposit. In a District Registry or the county court hearing centre, the petition fee and deposit should be handed to the duly authorised officer of the court's staff who will record its receipt.

14.4.2 In all cases cheque(s) for the whole amount should be made payable to 'HM Courts and Tribunals Service' or 'HMCTS'.

14.5 Certificates of continuing debt and of notice of adjournment

14.5.1 On the hearing of a petition where a bankruptcy order is sought, in order to satisfy the court that the debt on which the petition is founded has not been paid or secured or compounded for the court will normally accept as sufficient a certificate signed by the person representing the petitioning creditor in the following form:

> "I certify that I have/my firm has made enquiries of the petitioning creditor(s) within the last business day prior to

the hearing/adjourned hearing and to the best of my knowledge and belief the debt on which the petition is founded is still due and owing and has not been paid or secured or compounded for save as to ...

Signed ....Dated ......"

14.5.2 For convenience, in the Royal Courts of Justice this certificate is incorporated in the attendance sheet for the parties to complete when they come to court and which is filed after the hearing. A fresh certificate will be required on each adjourned hearing.

14.5.3 On any adjourned hearing of a petition where a bankruptcy order is sought, in order to satisfy the court that the petitioner has complied with rule 6.29, the petitioner will be required to file evidence of the date on which, manner in which and address to which notice of the making of the order of adjournment and of the venue for the adjourned hearing has been sent to:

(1) the debtor, and

(2) any creditor who has given notice under rule 6.23 but was not present at the hearing when the order for adjournment was made or was present at the hearing but the date of the adjourned hearing was not fixed at that hearing. For convenience, in the Royal Courts of Justice this certificate is incorporated in the attendance sheet for the parties to complete when they come to court and which is filed after the hearing and is as follows:

"I certify that the petitioner has complied with rule 6.29 by sending notice of adjournment to the debtor [supporting/opposing creditor(s)] on [date] at [address]".

A fresh certificate will be required on each adjourned hearing.

14.6 Extension of hearing date of petition

14.6.1 Late applications for extension of hearing dates under rule 6.28, and failure to attend on the listed hearing of a petition, will be dealt with as follows:

(1) If an application is submitted less than two clear working days before the hearing date (for example, later than Monday for Thursday, or Wednesday for Monday) the costs of the application will not be allowed under rule 6.28(3).

(2) If the petition has not been served and no extension has been granted by the time fixed for the hearing of the petition, and if no one attends for the hearing, the petition may be dismissed or re–listed for hearing about 21 days later. The court will notify the petitioning creditor's solicitors (or the petitioning creditor in person), and any known supporting or opposing creditors or their solicitors, of the new date and times. Written evidence should then be filed on behalf of the petitioning creditor explaining fully the reasons for the failure to apply for an extension or to appear at the hearing, and (if appropriate) giving reasons why the petition should not be dismissed.

(3) On the re–listed hearing the court may dismiss the petition if

not satisfied it should be adjourned or a further extension granted.

14.6.2 All applications for an extension should include a statement of the date fixed for the hearing of the petition.

14.6.3 The petitioning creditor should contact the court (by solicitors or in person) on or before the hearing date to ascertain whether the application has reached the file and been dealt with. It should not be assumed that an extension will be granted.

14.7 Substituted service of bankruptcy petitions

14.7.1 In most cases evidence that the steps set out in paragraph 13.3.4 [13.2.4] have been taken will suffice to justify an order for substituted service of a bankruptcy petition.

14.8 Validation orders

14.8.1 A person against whom a bankruptcy petition has been presented ('the debtor') may apply to the court after presentation of the petition for relief from the effects of section 284(1) – (3) of the Act by seeking an order that any disposition of his assets or payment made out of his funds, including any bank account (whether it is in credit or overdrawn) shall not be void in the event of a bankruptcy order being made on the petition (a 'validation order').

14.8.2 Save in exceptional circumstances, notice of the making of the application should be given to (a) the petitioning creditor(s) or other petitioner, (b) any creditor who has given notice to the petitioner of his intention to appear on the hearing of the petition pursuant to rule 6.23 1986, (c) any creditor who has been substituted as petitioner pursuant to rule 6.30 Insolvency Rules 1986 and (d) any creditor who has carriage of the petition pursuant to rule 6.31 Insolvency Rules 1986.

14.8.3 The application should be supported by a witness statement which, save in exceptional circumstances, should be made by the debtor. If appropriate, supporting evidence in the form of a witness statement from the debtor's accountant should also be produced.

14.8.4 The extent and contents of the evidence will vary according to the circumstances and the nature of the relief sought, but in a case where the debtor is trading or carrying on business it should include, as a minimum, the following information:

(1) when and to whom notice has been given in accordance with paragraph 14.8.2 above;

(2) brief details of the circumstances leading to presentation of the petition;

(3) how the debtor became aware of the presentation of the petition;

(4) whether the petition debt is admitted or disputed and, if the latter, brief details of the basis on which the debt is disputed;

(5) full details of the debtor's financial position including details of his assets (including details of any security and the amount(s) secured) and liabilities, which should be supported, as far as possible, by documentary evidence, e.g. accounts, draft accounts, management accounts or estimated statement of affairs;

(6) a cash flow forecast and profit and loss projection for the period for which the order is sought;

(7) details of the dispositions or payments in respect of which an order is sought;

(8) the reasons relied on in support of the need for such dispositions or payments to be made;

(9) any other information relevant to the exercise of the court's discretion;

(10) details of any consents obtained from the persons mentioned in paragraph 14.8.2 above (supported by documentary evidence where appropriate);

(11) details of any relevant bank account, including its number and the address and sort code of the bank at which such account is held and the amount of the credit or debit balance on such account at the time of making the application.

14.8.5 Where an application is made urgently to enable payments to be made which are essential to continued trading (e.g. wages) and it is not possible to assemble all the evidence listed above, the court may consider granting limited relief for a short period, but there must be sufficient evidence to satisfy the court that the interests of creditors are unlikely to be prejudiced.

14.8.6 Where the debtor is not trading or carrying on business and the application relates only to a proposed sale, mortgage or re–mortgage of the debtor's home evidence of the following will generally suffice:

(1) when and to whom notice has been given in accordance with 14.8.2 above;

(2) whether the petition debt is admitted or disputed and, if the latter, brief details of the basis on which the debt is disputed;

(3) details of the property to be sold, mortgaged or re–mortgaged (including its title number);

(4) the value of the property and the proposed sale price, or details of the mortgage or re–mortgage;

(5) details of any existing mortgages or charges on the property and redemption figures;

(6) the costs of sale (e.g. solicitors' or agents' costs);

(7) how and by whom any net proceeds of sale (or sums coming into the debtor's hands as a result of any mortgage or re–mortgage) are to be held pending the final hearing of the petition;

(8) any other information relevant to the exercise of the court's discretion;

(9) details of any consents obtained from the persons mentioned in 14.8.2 above (supported by documentary evidence where appropriate).

14.8.7 Whether or not the debtor is trading or carrying on business, where the application involves a disposition of property the court will need to be satisfied that any proposed disposal will be at a proper value. Accordingly an independent valuation should be obtained and exhibited to the evidence.

14.8.8 The court will need to be satisfied by credible evidence that the debtor is solvent and able to pay his debts as they fall due or that a particular transaction or series of transactions in respect of which the order is sought will be beneficial to or will not prejudice the interests of all the unsecured creditors as a class (*Denney v John Hudson & Co Ltd* [1992] BCLC 901, [1992] BCC 503, CA; *Re Fairway Graphics Ltd* [1991] BCLC 468).

14.8.9 A draft of the order sought should be attached to the application.

14.8.10 Similar considerations to those set out above are likely to apply to applications seeking ratification of a transaction or payment after the making of a bankruptcy order.

15. Applications

15.1 In accordance with rule 13.2(2) , in the Royal Courts of Justice **3E–15** the member of court staff in charge of the winding up list has been authorised to deal with applications:
  (1) by petitioning creditors to extend the time for hearing petitions (rule 6.28);
  (2) by the Official Receiver:
    (a) to transfer proceedings from the High Court to a county court hearing centre (rule 7.13);
    (b) to amend the title of the proceedings (rules 6.35 and 6.47).

15.2 In District Registries or the County Court such applications must be made to the District Judge.

16. Orders without attendance

16.1 In suitable cases the court will normally be prepared to make **3E–16** orders under Part VIII of the Act (Individual Voluntary Arrangements), without the attendance of the parties, provided there is no bankruptcy order in existence and (so far as is known) no pending petition. The orders are:
  (1) A 14 day interim order adjourning the application for 14 days for consideration of the nominee's report, where the papers are in order, and the nominee's signed consent to act includes a waiver of notice of the application or the consent by the nominee to the making of an interim order without attendance.
  (2) A standard order on consideration of the nominee's report, extending the interim order to a date seven weeks after the date of the proposed meeting, directing the meeting to be summoned and adjourning to a date about three weeks after the meeting. Such an order may be made without attendance if the nominee's report has been delivered to the court and complies with section 256(1) of the Act and rule 5.11(2) and (3) and proposes a date for the meeting not less than 14 days from that on which the nominee's report is filed in court under rule 5.11 nor more than 28 days from that on which that report is considered by the court under rule 5.13.
  (3) A "concertina" order, combining orders as under (1) and (2)

above. Such an order may be made without attendance if the initial application for an interim order is accompanied by a report of the nominee and the conditions set out in (1) and (2) above are satisfied.

(4) A final order on consideration of the chairman's report. Such an order may be made without attendance if the chairman's report has been filed and complies with rule 5.27(1). The order will record the effect of the chairman's report and may discharge the interim order.

16.2 Provided that the conditions under sub–paragraphs (2) and (4) above are satisfied and that the appropriate report has been lodged with the court in due time the parties need not attend or be represented on the adjourned hearing for consideration of the nominee's report or of the chairman's report (as the case may be) unless they are notified by the court that attendance is required. Sealed copies of the order made (in all four cases as above) will be posted by the court to the applicant or his solicitor and to the nominee.

16.3 In suitable cases the court may also make consent orders without attendance by the parties. The written consent of the parties will be required. Examples of such orders are as follows:

(1) on applications to set aside a statutory demand, orders:
   (a) dismissing the application, with or without an order for costs as may be agreed (permission will be given to present a petition on or after the seventh day after the date of the order, unless a different date is agreed);
   (b) setting aside the demand, with or without an order for costs as may be agreed; or

(2) On petitions where there is a negative list of supporting or opposing creditors in Form 6.21, or a statement signed by or on behalf of the petitioning creditor that no notices have been received from supporting or opposing creditors, orders:
   (a) dismissing the petition, with or without an order for costs as may be agreed; or
   (b) if the petition has not been served, giving permission to withdraw the petition (with no order for costs).

(3) On other applications, orders:
   (a) for sale of property, possession of property, disposal of proceeds of sale;
   (b) giving interim directions;
   (c) dismissing the application, with or without an order for costs as may be agreed;
   (d) giving permission to withdraw the application, with or without an order for costs as may be agreed.

16.4 If, as may often be the case with orders under subparagraphs 3(a) or (b) above, an adjournment is required, whether generally with liberty to restore or to a fixed date, the order by consent may include an order for the adjournment. If adjournment to a date is requested, a time estimate should be given and the court will fix the first available date and time on or after the date requested.

16.5 The above lists should not be regarded as exhaustive, nor should it be assumed that an order will be made without attendance as requested.

16.6 Applications for consent orders without attendance should be lodged at least two clear working days (and preferably longer) before any hearing date.

16.7 Whenever a document is lodged or a letter sent, the correct case number should be quoted. A note should also be given of the date and time of the next hearing (if any).

17.   Bankruptcy restrictions undertakings

17.1 Where a bankrupt has given a bankruptcy restrictions 3E–17 undertaking, the Secretary of State or official receiver must file a copy in court and send a copy to the bankrupt as soon as reasonably practicable (rule 6.250). In addition the Secretary of State must notify the court immediately that the bankrupt has given such an undertaking in order that any hearing date can be vacated.

18.   Persons at risk of violence

18.1 Where an application is made pursuant to rule 5.67, 5.68, 5A 3E–18 18, or 6.235B or otherwise to limit disclosure of information as to a person's current address by reason of the possibility of violence, the relevant application should be accompanied by a witness statement which includes the following:

(1) The grounds upon which it is contended that disclosure of the current address as defined by the Insolvency Rules might reasonably be expected to lead to violence against the debtor or a person who normally resides with him or her as a member of his or her family or where appropriate any other person.

(2) Where the application is made in respect of the address of the debtor, the debtor's proposals with regard to information which may safely be given to potential creditors in order that they can recognise that the debtor is a person who may be indebted to them, in particular the address at which the debtor previously resided or carried on business and the nature of such business.

(3) The terms of the order sought by the applicant by reference to the court's particular powers as set out in the rule under which the application is made and, unless impracticable, a draft of the order sought.

(4) Where the application is made by the debtor in respect of whom a nominee or supervisor has been appointed or against whom a bankruptcy order has been made, evidence of the consent of the nominee/supervisor, or, in the case of bankruptcy, the trustee in bankruptcy, if one has been appointed, and the official receiver if a trustee in bankruptcy has not been appointed. Where such consent is not available the statement must indicate whether such consent has been refused.

The application shall in any event make such person a respondent to the application.

18.2 The application shall be referred to the Registrar who will consider it without a hearing in the first instance but without prejudice to the right of the court to list it for hearing if:

(1) the court is minded to refuse the application;

(2) the consent of any respondent is not attached;

(3) the court is of the view that there is another reason why listing is appropriate.

Part Four

Financial Markets and Insolvency (Settlement Finality) Regulations 1999—Required Information

19.   Financial Markets and Insolvency (Settlement Finality) Regulations 1999—Required Information

3E–19   **19.1** In any case in which the court is asked to make an order to which regulation 22(1) of the Financial Markets and Insolvency (Settlement Finality) Regulations 1999 (SI 1999/2979) applies, the party applying for the order must include in the petition or application a statement to that effect, identifying the system operator of the relevant designated system, the relevant designating authority, and the email or other addresses to which the court will be required to send notice pursuant to regulation 22(1) if an order is made.

19.2 At the date of this Practice Direction, the Regulations apply where, in respect of "a participant in a designated system" (as those terms are defined in the Regulations), an order is made for administration, winding–up, bankruptcy, sequestration, bank insolvency, bank administration, building society insolvency, building society special administration or investment bank special administration. Applicants must before making the application check for any amendments to the Regulations.

Part Five

Appeals

20.   Appeals

3E–20   **20.1** An appeal from a decision of the County Court (whether made by a District Judge, a Recorder or a Circuit Judge) or of a Registrar in insolvency proceedings lies to a Judge of the High Court.

20.2 An appeal from a decision of a Judge of the High Court, whether at first instance or on appeal, lies to the Court of Appeal.

20.3 A first appeal, whether under 20.1 or 20.2 above, is subject to the permission requirements of CPR Part 52, rule 3.

20.4 An appeal from a decision of a Judge of the High Court which was made on a first appeal requires the permission of the Court of Appeal.

20.5 Filing Appeals

20.5.1 An appeal from a decision of a Registrar must be filed at the Royal Courts of Justice in London.

20.5.2 An appeal from a decision of a District Judge sitting in a district registry of the High Court may be filed:

(1) at the Royal Courts of Justice in London; or

(2) in that district registry.

20.6 The court centres at which appeals from decisions of the County Court at hearing centres on any particular Circuit must be filed, managed and heard (unless the appeal court otherwise orders) are as follows:

Midland Circuit: Birmingham

North Eastern Circuit: Leeds or Newcastle upon Tyne

Northern Circuit: Manchester or Liverpool

Wales Circuit: Cardiff, Caernarfon or Mold

Western Circuit: Bristol

South Eastern Circuit: Royal Courts of Justice.

20.7 Where the lower court is the County Court:

(1) an appeal or application for permission to appeal from a decision of a District Judge will be heard or considered by a High Court Judge or by any person authorised under section 9 of the Senior Courts Act 1981 to act as a judge of the High Court in the Chancery Division;

(2) an appeal or application for permission to appeal from a decision of a Recorder or a Circuit Judge will be heard or considered by a High Court Judge or by a person authorised under paragraphs (1), (2) or (4) of the table in section 9(1) of the Senior Courts Act 1981 to act as a judge of the High Court in the Chancery Division;

(3) other applications in any appeal or application for permission to appeal may be heard or considered and directions may be given by a High Court Judge or by any person authorised under section 9 of the Senior Courts Act 1981 to act as a judge of the High Court in the Chancery Division.

20.8 In the case of appeals from decisions of Registrars or District Judges in the High Court, appeals, applications for permission to appeal and other applications may be heard or considered and directions may be given by a High Court Judge or by any person authorised under section 9 of the Senior Courts Act 1981 to act as a judge of the High Court in the Chancery Division.

20.9.1 CPR Part 52 and Practice Directions 52A, 52B and 52C and its Forms shall, as appropriate, apply to appeals in insolvency proceedings, saved as provided in paragraph 20.9.4 below.

20.9.2 Paragraphs 4.3 to 4.5 of Practice Direction 52A and Section 2 and Tables A and B of Practice Direction 52B shall not apply.

20.10 For the avoidance of any doubt, references in this Part to the County Court include, in respect of decisions made before 22 April 2014, a county court.

Part Six

Applications Relating to the Remuneration of Appointees

21. Remuneration of Appointees

21.1 Introduction

21.1.1 This Part of the Practice Direction applies to any remuneration application made under the Act or the Insolvency Rules. **3E–21**

21.2 The objective and guiding principles

21.2.1 The objective of this Part of the Practice Direction is to ensure that the remuneration of an appointee which is fixed and approved by the court is fair, reasonable and commensurate with the nature and extent of the work properly undertaken by the appointee in any given case and is fixed and approved by a process which is consistent and predictable.

21.2.2 Set out below are the guiding principles by reference to which remuneration applications are to be considered both by applicants, in the preparation and presentation of their application, and by the court determining such applications.

21.2.3 The guiding principles are as follows:

(1) "Justification"

It is for the appointee who seeks to be remunerated at a particular level and / or in a particular manner to justify his claim and in order to do so the appointee should be prepared to provide full particulars of the basis for and the nature of his claim for remuneration.

(2) "The benefit of the doubt"

The corollary of guiding principle (1) is that on any remuneration application, if after considering the evidence before it and after having regard to the guiding principles (in particular guiding principle (3)), the matters contained in paragraph 21.4.2 (in particular paragraph 21.4.2 (10)) and the matters referred to in paragraph 21.4.3 (as appropriate) there remains any element of doubt as to the appropriateness, fairness or reasonableness of the remuneration sought or to be fixed (whether arising from a lack of particularity as to the basis for and the nature of the appointee's claim to remuneration or otherwise) such element of doubt should be resolved by the court against the appointee.

(3) "Professional integrity"

The court should (where this is the case) give weight to the fact that the appointee is a member of a regulated profession and as such is subject to rules and guidance as to professional conduct and the fact that (where this is the case) the appointee is an officer of the court.

(4) "The value of the service rendered"

The remuneration of an appointee should reflect the value of the service rendered by the appointee, not simply reimburse the appointee in respect of time expended and cost incurred.

(5) "Fair and reasonable"

The amount of the appointee's remuneration should represent fair and reasonable remuneration for the work properly undertaken or to be undertaken.

(6) "Proportionality"

(a) "Proportionality of information"

In considering the nature and extent of the information which should be provided by an appointee in respect of a remuneration application the court, the appointee and any other parties to the application shall have regard to what is proportionate by reference to the amount of remuneration to be fixed, the nature, complexity and extent of the work to be completed (where the application relates to future remuneration) or that has been completed by the appointee and the value and nature of the assets and liabilities with which the appointee will have to deal or has had to deal.

(b) "Proportionality of remuneration"

The amount of remuneration to be fixed by the court should be proportionate to the nature, complexity and extent of the work to be completed (where the application relates to future remuneration) or that has been completed by the appointee and the value and nature of the assets and/or potential assets and the liabilities and/or potential liabilities with which the appointee will have to deal or has had to deal, the nature and degree of the responsibility to which the appointee has been subject in any given case, the nature and extent of the risk (if any) assumed by the appointee and the efficiency (in respect of both time and cost) with which the appointee has completed the work undertaken.

(7) "Professional guidance"

In respect of an application for the fixing and approval of the remuneration of an appointee, the appointee may have regard to the relevant and current statements of practice promulgated by any relevant regulatory and professional bodies in relation to the fixing of the remuneration of an appointee. In considering a remuneration application, the court may also have regard to such statements of practice and the extent of compliance with such statements of practice by the appointee.

(8) "Timing of application"

The court will take into account whether any application should have been made earlier and if so the reasons for any delay in making it.

21.3 Hearing of remuneration applications

21.3.1 On the hearing of the application the court shall consider the evidence then available to it and may either summarily determine the application or adjourn it giving such directions as it thinks appropriate.

21.3.2 Whilst the application will normally be determined summarily by a Registrar sitting alone, where it is sufficiently complex, the court may direct that:

(1) an assessor or a Costs Judge prepare a report to the court in respect of the remuneration which is sought to be fixed and approved; and/or

(2) the application be heard by the Registrar sitting with or without an assessor or a Costs Judge or by a Judge sitting with or without an assessor or a Costs Judge.

21.4 Relevant criteria and procedure

21.4.1 When considering a remuneration application the court

433

shall have regard to the objective, the guiding principles and all relevant circumstances including the matters referred to in paragraph 21.4.2 and where appropriate paragraph 21.4.3, each of which should be addressed in the evidence placed before the court.

21.4.2 On any remuneration application, the appointee should:

(1) Provide a narrative description and explanation of:

    (a) the background to, the relevant circumstances of and the reasons for the appointment;

    (b) the work undertaken or to be undertaken in respect of the appointment; the description should be divided, insofar as possible, into individual tasks or categories of task (general descriptions of work, tasks, or categories of task should (insofar as possible) be avoided);

    (c) the reasons why it is or was considered reasonable and/or necessary and/or beneficial for such work to be done, giving details of why particular tasks or categories of task were undertaken and why such tasks or categories of task are to be undertaken or have been undertaken by particular individuals and in a particular manner;

    (d) the amount of time to be spent or that has been spent in respect of work to be completed or that has been completed and why it is considered to be fair, reasonable and proportionate;

    (e) what is likely to be and has been achieved, the benefits that are likely to and have accrued as a consequence of the work that is to be or has been completed, the manner in which the work required in respect of the appointment is progressing and what, in the opinion of the appointee, remains to be achieved.

(2) Provide details sufficient for the court to determine the application by reference to the criteria which are required to be taken into account by reference to the Insolvency Rules and any other applicable enactments or rules relevant to the fixing of the remuneration.

(3) Provide a statement of the total number of hours of work undertaken or to be undertaken in respect of which the remuneration is sought, together with a breakdown of such hours by individual member of staff and individual tasks or categories of tasks to be performed or that have been performed. Where appropriate, a proportionate level of detail should also be given of:

    (a) the tasks or categories of tasks to be undertaken as a proportion of the total amount of work to be undertaken in respect of which the remuneration is sought and the tasks or categories of tasks that have been undertaken as a proportion of the total amount of work that has been undertaken in respect of which the remuneration is sought; and

    (b) the tasks or categories of task to be completed by individual members of staff or grade of personnel including the appointee as a proportion of the total amount of work to be completed by all members of staff including the appointee in respect of which the remuneration is sought, or the tasks or categories of task that have been completed by individual members of staff or grade of personnel as a proportion of the total amount of work that has been completed by all members of staff including the appointee in respect of which the remuneration is sought.

(4) Provide a statement of the total amount to be charged for the work to be undertaken or that has been undertaken in respect of which the remuneration is sought which should include:

(a) a breakdown of such amounts by individual member of staff and individual task or categories of task performed or to be performed;

(b) details of the time expended or to be expended and the remuneration charged or to be charged in respect of each individual task or category of task as a proportion (respectively) of the total time expended or to be expended and the total remuneration charged or to be charged.

In respect of an application pursuant to which some or all of the amount of the appointee's remuneration is to be fixed on a basis other than time properly spent, the appointee shall provide (for the purposes of comparison) the same details as are required by this paragraph (4), but on the basis of what would have been charged had he been seeking remuneration on the basis of the time properly spent by him and his staff.

(5) Provide details of each individual to be engaged or who has been engaged in work in respect of the appointment and in respect of which the remuneration is sought, including details of their relevant experience, training, qualifications and the level of their seniority.

(6) Provide an explanation of:

(a) the steps, if any, to be taken or that have been taken by the appointee to avoid duplication of effort and cost in respect of the work to be completed or that has been completed in respect of which the remuneration is sought;

(b) the steps to be taken or that have been taken to ensure that the work to be completed or that has been completed is to be or was undertaken by individuals of appropriate experience and seniority relative to the nature of the work to be or that has been undertaken.

(7) Provide details of the individual rates charged by the appointee and members of his staff in respect of the work to be completed or that has been completed and in respect of which the remuneration is sought. Such details should include:

(a) a general explanation of the policy adopted in relation to the fixing or calculation of such rates and the recording of time spent;

(b) where, exceptionally, the appointee seeks remuneration in respect of time spent by secretaries, cashiers or other administrative staff whose work would otherwise be regarded as an overhead cost forming a component part of the rates charged by the appointee and members of his staff, a detailed explanation as to why such costs should be allowed should be provided.

(8) Where the remuneration application is in respect of a period of time during which the charge–out rates of the appointee and/or members of his staff engaged in work in respect of the appointment have increased, provide an explanation of the nature, extent and reason for such increase and the date when such increase took effect. This paragraph (8) does not apply to applications to which paragraph 21.4.3 applies.

(9) Provide details of any remuneration previously fixed or approved in relation to the appointment (whether by the court or otherwise) including in particular the amounts that were previously sought to be fixed or approved and the amounts that were in fact fixed or approved and the basis upon which such amounts were fixed or approved.

(10) In order that the court may be able to consider the views of any persons who the appointee considers have an interest in the assets that are under his control, provide details of:

    (a) what (if any) consultation has taken place between the appointee and those persons and if no such consultation has taken place an explanation as to the reason why;

    (b) the number and value of the interests of the persons consulted including details of the proportion (by number and by value) of the interests of such persons by reference to the entirety of those persons having an interest in the assets under the control of the appointee.

(11) Provide such other relevant information as the appointee considers, in the circumstances, ought to be provided to the court.

21.4.3 This paragraph applies to applications where some or all of the remuneration of the appointee is to be fixed and approved on a basis other than time properly spent. On such applications in addition to the matters referred to in paragraph 21.4.2 (as applicable) the appointee shall:

(1) Provide a full description of the reasons for remuneration being sought by reference to the basis contended for.

(2) Where the remuneration is sought to be fixed by reference to a percentage of the value of the assets which are realised or distributed, provide a full explanation of the basis upon which any percentage rates to be applied to the values of the assets realised and/or distributed have been chosen.

(3) Provide a statement that to the best of the appointee's belief the percentage rates or other bases by reference to which some or all of the remuneration is to be fixed are similar to the percentage rates or other bases that are applied or have been applied in respect of other appointments of a similar nature.

(4) Provide a comparison of the amount to be charged by reference to the basis contended for and the amount that would otherwise have been charged by reference to the other available bases of remuneration, including the scale of fees in Schedule 6 to the Insolvency Rules.

21.4.4 If and insofar as any of the matters referred to in paragraph 21.4.2 or 21.4.3 (as appropriate) are not addressed in the evidence, an explanation for why this is the case should be included in such evidence.

21.4.5 For the avoidance of doubt and where appropriate and proportionate, paragraphs 21.4.2 to 21.4.4 (inclusive) are applicable to applications for the apportionment of remuneration as between a new appointee and a former appointee in circumstances where some or all of the former appointee's remuneration was based upon a set amount under the Insolvency Rules and the former appointee has ceased (for whatever reason) to hold office before the time has elapsed or the work has been completed in respect of which the set amount of remuneration was fixed.

21.4.6 The evidence placed before the court by the appointee in respect of any remuneration application should include the following documents:

(1) a copy of the most recent receipts and payments account;

(2) copies of any reports by the appointee to the persons having an interest in the assets under his control relevant to the period for which the remuneration sought to be fixed and approved relates;

(3) any schedules or such other documents providing the information referred to in paragraphs 21.4.2 and 21.4.3 where these are likely to be of assistance to the court in considering the application;

(4) evidence of any consultation with those persons having an interest in the assets under the control of appointee in relation to the remuneration of the appointee.

21.4.7 On any remuneration application the court may make an order allowing payments of remuneration to be made on account subject to final approval whether by the court or otherwise.

21.4.8 Unless otherwise ordered by the court (or as may otherwise be provided for in any enactment or rules of procedure) the costs of and occasioned by an application for the fixing and/or approval of the remuneration of an appointee, including those of any assessor, shall be paid out of the assets under the control of the appointee.

Insolvency proceedings

Delete paragraph 3E–21 and substitute:

The substantive law relating to insolvency is found primarily in the Insolvency Act **3E–21.1** 1986 (as amended) and the Insolvency Rules 1986 (as amended) (SI 1986/1925). The law governing the insolvency of partnerships is to be found in the Insolvent Partnerships Order 1994 (SI 1994/2421) as amended and that governing the insolvency of limited liability partnerships in the Limited Liability Partnerships Act 2000 and related secondary legislation (in particular the Limited Liability Partnerships Regulations 2001 (SI 2001/1090)). The administration of the estates of deceased insolvent individuals is governed by the Administration of Insolvent Estates of Deceased Persons Order 1986 (SI 1986/1999).

The Bankruptcy Act 1914 and the Bankruptcy Rules 1952 continue to govern bankruptcies commenced under that Act. The Companies Act 1948 and the Companies (Winding–Up) Rules 1949 (SI 1949/330) continue to apply to corporate insolvencies commenced under the 1948 Act.

Insolvency proceedings are defined as proceedings under the Insolvency Act 1986 and the Insolvency Rules 1986 (r.13.7, Insolvency Rules 1986).

Applications in the liquidation of companies

Delete paragraph 3E–84 and substitute:

3E–84   The winding up of a company (whether voluntary or by the court) does not bring the life of the company to an end. The company, acting by its liquidator, may bring proceedings in its own name even after it has been wound up, for example to collect a debt or enforce some other right. Such proceedings should generally be issued in the court having the appropriate jurisdiction, for example the relevant county court in the case of an action for debt. Where the cause of action is the company's the proceedings should be brought in the name of the company. However, where the cause of action is the liquidator's (for example, a claim under ss.212, 213, 214, 238 or 239 of the Insolvency Act 1986) any application should be made in the name of the liquidator. The liquidator may not bring an action that should be brought in the name of the company in his own name in order to avoid having to give security for costs (*Kirkpatrick & Tan v Snoozebox Ltd* [2014] All ER (D) 177 (Jun)).

3F   PERSONAL INJURY

Access to Health Records Act 1990

Applications to the court

Delete s.8(5) and substitute:

3F–30   (5) The jurisdiction conferred by this section shall be exercisable by the High Court or the county court or, in Scotland, by the Court of Session or the sherrif.

Note

Delete Note and substitute:

3F–30.0   Subsection (5) amended, subject to savings and transitional provisions, by the Crime and Courts Act 2013 Sch.9 para.52; for savings and transitional provisions see Sch.8 to the Act and art.3 of SI 2014/954.

3G   DATA PROTECTION ACT 1998

Introduction

In the first paragraph, for "The courts have referred" substitute:

3G–1   The UK courts have referred

In the first paragraph, after "rights under art.8 in conjunction with the Act.", add:

The CJEU has increasingly referred to the European Union Charter of Fundamental Rights when considering data protection cases.

In the first paragraph, for "is mandated by Directive 2006/24" substitute:

was mandated by Directive 2006/24 EC. That directive was ruled to be invalid by the CJEU in April 2014 because it breaches Articles 7 and 8 of the EU Charter of Fundamental Rights, in joined cases C–293/12 and C–594/12

Add new entries at the end of the list:

C–543109 *Deutsche Telekom AG*
C–131/12 *Costeja*
C141/12 and C–372/12 *YS v Minister voor Immigratie Integratie en Asiel*

Data Protection Act 1998

At the end of the second paragraph, add:

3G–5   *Southern Pacific Personal Loans Ltd, Re* [2013] EWHC 2485 Ch held the liquidators of a company are not data controllers.

Add at end:

In *Costeja* CJEU Case 131/12 the Court held that a search engine is a data controller for the contents of personal data delivered as part of a search result.

In the first paragraph, after "before it is considered to relate to him", delete "It held that the term **3G–7**
has a narrow meaning:".

*At the end of the first paragraph, for "Thus the name, and information immediately associated
with the name, such as a statement in a report of a meeting that Mr X was present, will fall
within the definition but the remainder of the report will not be personal data about Mr X merely
by virtue of that one reference." substitute:*

In *Edem v Information Commissioner* [2014] EWCA Civ 92 the Court of Appeal made
it clear that the tests or "notions" applied in *Durant* should not be applicable in most
cases, citing the Technical Guidance produced by the Information Commissioner as an
accurate statement of the statutory position (per Lord Justice Moses para.21).

*At the end of the fourth paragraph, delete "Followed in ICO v FSA and Edem [2012] UKUT464
(AAC).".*

At the end of the fourth paragraph, add:

In the cases of *YS v Minister voor Immigratie en Asiel (MIIA)* C–141/2 and *MIIA v M, S*
C–372/12 the CJEU held that legal analysis of a case which does not itself include
identifiable data is not personal data even if the results of the analysis may have an
impact on the individual.

In the fifth paragraph, for "The EU Commission has reviewed", substitute:
The EU Commission reviewed

In the fifth paragraph, for "if the United Kingdom fails to change its law" substitute:
against the UK. No further action has been taken and it is assumed that the decision in *Edem* has now resolved the issue

Editorial note

At the end of the 23rd paragraph (beginning "'Personal data'"), add:
The CJEU described the purpose of subject access being to allow the individual to **3G–11**
check the accuracy of data and ensure they are processed in compliance with the
directive in *YS v Minister voor Immigratie Integratie en Asiel* case C–141/12.

At the beginning of the 24th paragraph (beginning "'Third party data'"), add:
In *AB v Ministry of Justice* [2014] EWHC 1847 (QB) the High Court held that a
covering letter which enclosed correspondence from a complainant did not qualify as
personal data of the complainant.

Editorial note

At the end of the second paragraph, add:
The provision of Directive 95/46/EC on which the right is based, art.14 was **3G–15**
considered by the CJEU in case C–131/ 12 *Google v AEPD & Cooteja*. The CJEU held
that the data subject had the right to require the removal of links to his name in
results displayed by a search engine. Any section 10 application should now be
considered in the light of the CJEU ruling.

Editorial note

*In the second paragraph, for "The level of damages in discrimination cases are not an appropri-
ate guide for awards under data protection." substitute:*
Also commented (Lady Justice Arden) that the level of damages in discrimination **3G–21**
cases are not a helpful guide. The Vento Guidelines were however applied in *WXY v
Gewanter* [2013] EWHC 589 in a case of harassment and misuse of personal
information. In *Vidal–Hall v Google Inc* [2014] EWHC 13 (QB) on an application for
leave to serve proceedings out of the jurisdiction the question of whether moral damages could be claimed for data protection breach was left open.

After the second paragraph, add as a new paragraph:
In *AB v Ministry of Justice* [2014] EWHC 1847 the High Court awarded nominal
damages (of £100) and an award of compensation for distress of £2,250 where a
subject access request had not been adequately handled.

At the end of the seventh paragraph, add:
In *WXY v Gewanter* [2013] EWHC 589 (QB) damages of £24,950.00 were awarded,
of which £5,000 were aggravated damages for harassment including the misuse of
personal information.

Editorial note

Add at end as new paragraph:

3G–24.0   In *R. v NE London NHS Foundation Trust* [2011] EWCA Civ 1529 the court considered the term "required under an enactment" and held it requires an express power.

Note

After "compulsory assessment or consensual audit." add:

3G–57.2   It may be served where the data controller repeats a breach voluntarily: *CLCH v ICO* [2013] UKUT 0551.

Add at end:

   In *Niebel v ICO* EA/2012/0260 the Tribunal held that the receipt of spam texts was not of a kind likely to cause substantial damage or distress. In *Scottish Borders Council v Information Commissioner* EA/2012/0212 the Tribunal similarly found that the breach of security in issue was not of a nature to cause substantial damage or distress.

Add new paragraph at end:

   In *Central London Community Healthcare NHS Trust v Information Commissioner* [2013] UKUT 551 (AAC) the Upper Tribunal held that a voluntary report of a breach of data protection is not an assessment for the purposes of S55A (3A).

Monetary penalty notices: enforcement

Delete s.55D(2)(a) and substitute:

3G–60   (2) (a) if the county court so orders, as if it were payable under an order of that court;

Add new paragraph 3G–60.1:

Note

3G–60.1   Subsection (2)(a) amended, subject to savings and transitional provisions, by the Crime and Courts Act 2013 Sch.9 para.52, with effect from April 22, 2014 (see SI 2014/954); for savings and transitional provisions see Sch.8 to the Act.

3H   CONSUMER CREDIT AND CONSUMER LAW

Consumer Credit Act 1974

PART II

CREDIT AGREEMENTS, HIRE AGREEMENTS AND LINKED TRANSACTIONS

Consumer credit agreements

After s.8(3) add:

3H–20   (4) Subsection (1) does not apply in relation to an agreement that is a green deal plan (see instead section 189B).

Note

Add at end:

3H–21   Subsection (4) inserted, subject to savings, by the Consumer Credit Act 1974 (Green Deal) (Amendment) Order 2014 (2014/436), art.3, with effect from February 28, 2014 (for savings see art.1(3)).

Exclusion of certain agreements from Part V

Delete s.74(2A) and substitute:

(2A) In the case of an agreement to which Part 2 or 3 of the **3H–122** Consumer Contracts (Information, Cancellation and Additional Charges) Regulations 2013 applies, the reference in subsection (2) to a small agreement is to read as if in section 17(1)(a) and (b) "£42" were substituted for "£50".

Note

In the second paragraph, delete the last sentence beginning "With effect from" and substitute:

Subs.(2A) replaced, with effect from June 13, 2014, by the Consumer Contracts (In- **3H–123** formation, Cancellation and Additional Charges) Regulations 2013 (SI 2013/3134).

Exclusion of certain agreements from Part V

Add at end:

A dealer in fine musical instruments granted to the owner of a valuable viola a loan **3H–124** of £50,000, interest free, to be repaid from the proceeds of a sale of the viola which the dealer was to seek to achieve. This being the only occasion on which the dealer had ever made such a loan agreement, it was not made "in the course of a business", was a non–commercial agreement and was thus excluded by s.74(1)(a) from the application of Part V: *Bassano v Toft* [2014] EWHC 377 (QB), [2014] C.C.L.R.8.

Liability of creditor for breaches by supplier

In the last paragraph, delete from "; where the debtor is entitled" to the end, and substitute:

Where the debtor is entitled to rescind his supply agreement, s.75(1) does not give **3H–129** the debtor the right to rescind the loan agreement which financed that supply agreement. Nevertheless, where a debtor–creditor–supplier agreement is within s.12(b) of the Consumer Credit Act 1974 and is also tied into a specific supply transaction, the law implies a term into that credit agreement that it is conditional upon the survival of the supply agreement. The debtor, upon rejecting the goods and thereby rescinding the supply agreement for breach of contract, may also rescind the credit agreement by invoking that implied term and without invoking s.75. The same reasoning applies to an agreement within s.12(c) where the credit agreement ties the loan to a particular transaction: *Durkin v DSG Retail Limited* [2014] UKSC 21, [2014] 1 W.L.R. 1148.

Notice of sums in arrears under fixed–sum credit agreements etc

In s.86B(12A)(b)(iii) delete: "(within the meaning of section 1 of the Energy Act 2011)". **3H–166**

Note

Add at end:

Subsection (12A)(b) amended, subject to savings, by the Consumer Credit Act 1974 **3H–167** (Green Deal) (Amendment) Order 2014 (2014/436), art.8, with effect from February 28, 2014 (for savings see art.1(3)).

Unfair relationships

Add at end:

For where a single (draconian) clause in a supply agreement led to a finding of an **3H–329** unfair creditor–debtor relationship, see *Link Financial v North Wilson* [2014] EWHC 252 (Ch); [2014] C.C.L.R. 6.

3I   DISCRIMINATION

Equality Act 2010

Part 9

ENFORCEMENT

Chapter 2

CIVIL COURTS

Jurisdiction

In s.114(1), for "A county court" substitute:

3I–78   The county court

Add new paragraph 3I–78.1:

Note

3I–78.1   Subsection (1) amended, subject to savings and transitional provisions, by the Crime and Courts Act 2013 Sch.9 para.52, with effect from April 22, 2014 (see SI 2014/954); for savings and transitional provisions see Sch.8 to the Act.

Remedies

In s.119(1), for "a county court" substitute:

3I–80   the county court

Add new paragraph 3I–80.1:

Note

3I–80.1   Subsection (1) amended, subject to savings and transitional provisions, by the Crime and Courts Act 2013 Sch.9 para.52, with effect from April 22, 2014 (see SI 2014/954); for savings and transitional provisions see Sch.8 to the Act.

Obtaining information, etc.

In s.183(8)(a), for "a county court" substitute:

3I–83   the county court

Note

Add at end:

3I–83.1   Subsection (8) amended, subject to savings and transitional provisions, by the Crime and Courts Act 2013 Sch.9 para.52, with effect from April 22, 2014 (see SI 2014/954); for savings and transitional provisions see Sch.8 to the Act.

Conduct giving rise to separate proceedings

In s.140(6)(a), for "a county court" substitute:

3I–84   the county court

Add new paragraph 3I–84.1:

Note

3I–84.1   Subsection (6) amended, subject to savings and transitional provisions, by the Crime and Courts Act 2013 Sch.9 para.52, with effect from April 22, 2014 (see SI 2014/954); for savings and transitional provisions see Sch.8 to the Act.

3K   CIVIL RECOVERY PROCEEDINGS

Editorial note

3K–2   *In the second paragraph delete "Consequently, all civil recovery proceedings in train as of April 1, 2008, were taken over by SOCA on that date and SOCA was empowered to bring proceedings."*

After the third paragraph, add as a new paragraph:

Then, on October 7, 2013, SOCA was abolished by the Crime and Courts Act 2013. Most of its functions, including in particular the civil recovery functions, were transferred to the National Crime Agency. Consequently, the current claimants who may conduct civil recovery proceedings are the National Crime Agency, the Crown Prosecution Service (into which the Revenue and Customs Prosecutions Office has since been subsumed) and the Serious Fraud Office.

Part 5 powers—power to make a recovery order

In the first paragraph, for "R. (Greater Manchester Police v Salford Magistrates' Court; and Serious Organised Crime Agency v Matthews [2009] EWHC 1544 (Admin)" substitute:

R. (Greater Manchester Police) v Salford Magistrates' Court [2008] EWHC 1651 (Admin); *Serious Organised Crime Agency v Matthews* [2009] EWHC 1544 (Admin); and *Serious Organised Crime Agency v Namli* [2014] EWCA Civ 411 **3K–3**

Part 5 powers—making a recovery order

Add new paragraph at end:

As the proceedings are civil, the trial judge has a wide discretion to hold a trial in the absence of the defendant. The normal civil rules apply. The court should apply the overriding objective in CPR Pt 3 and the general fair trial guarantees in art.6(1) of the ECHR (*Robb v National Crime Agency* [2014] EWCA Civ 171). **3K–5**

3L   EUROPEAN PROCEDURES (CPR PART 78)

Part 78—European Procedures

European Order for Payment (EOP) Procedure—Editorial introduction

Add new paragraph at end:

In *Goldbet Sportwetten GmbH v Sperinded LTLAG (C–144/12)* [2013] Bus. L.R. 1115; [2014] I.L.Pr. 1 on a question raised by an Austrian Court the Advocate General of the EU opinion was that in the meaning of Regulation 936/2012, lodging a statement of opposition to a European Order for Payment did not constitute the entry of an appearance in the meaning of Regulation 44/2001 art 24.EU Law Citator. **3L–5**

SECTION 6

ADMINISTRATION OF FUNDS, PROPERTY AND AFFAIRS

6A   COURT FUNDS

Administration of Justice Act 1982

Part VI

Funds in Court

Management and investment of funds in court

Delete s.38(1)(aa) and substitute:

(aa) the family court; **6A–5**

Note

Add at end:

Subsection (1)(aa) inserted by the Crime and Courts Act 2013 (Family Court: **6A–5.1**

Consequential Provision) Order 2014 (SI 2014/605), art.17, with effect from April 22, 2014 (being the date on which s.17(3)of the Crime and Courts Act 2013 is brought fully into force.

Court Funds Rules 2011

Application of the Rules

6A–20   *In r.2(b)(iii), delete "or".*

In r.2(b)(iv), for "." substitute:

; or

After r.2(b)(iv) add:

(v) the family court.

Add at end:

Note

Amended by the Crime and Courts Act 2013 (Family Court: Consequential Provision) (No.2) Order 2014 (SI 2014/879), art.133, with effect from April 22, 2014.

SECTION 7

LEGAL REPRESENTATIVES—COSTS AND LITIGATION FUNDING

7A1   LITIGATION FUNDING BEFORE APRIL 1, 2013

Access to Justice (Membership Organisation) Regulations 2005

FUNDING ARRANGEMENTS

CONDITIONAL FEES

Add new paragraph at end:

7A1–55   On a detailed assessment before a costs judge a preliminary point arose as to the construction of the CFA in respect of which the defendant contended that the condition upon which payment became due to the solicitors had not been fulfilled. Both the Costs Judge and the judge on appeal considered the wording of the CFA in detail and the Judge concluded that the provisions did not raise any ambiguity which needed to be resolved by the consideration of business common sense. The judge's conclusion was obvious from the words used. Following the iterative process set out in *Rainy Sky SA v Kookmin Bank* [2011] UKSC 50; [2011] 1 W.L.R. 2900 the Judge could see no reason, within the CFA or in general, why the construction which he had given should be thought to create any legal or commercial difficulty for either side. So far as the claimants were concerned they would be bound under the CFA to pay their solicitors their normal rates and success fee once they had achieved some positive result from the litigation even if not complete success on all aspects of the claim. So far as the defendants were concerned they were only bound to reimburse the claimants for those costs which were proportionate to the matters in issue reasonably and proportionately incurred and reasonable and proportionate in amount: *Ultimate Products Ltd v Woolley* [2014] EWHC 1919 (Ch) Mr Christopher Pymont QC.

Add new paragraph at end:

7A1–56   The court had to decide upon the position where a party loses mental capacity in the course of proceedings, in particular whether such loss of capacity has the automatic

444

and immediate effect of terminating the solicitor's retainer. The claimant (who subsequently lost capacity) had entered into a CFA with her solicitors. The court held that termination of a solicitor's authority by reason of mental incapacity did not in itself frustrate the underlying contract of retainer. A retainer such as a CFA entered into with a person known to have fluctuating capacity was not frustrated by the loss of such capacity (the court explained in some detail the reason for this conclusion at paragraphs 38 to 43 of the judgment): *Blankley v Central Manchester & Manchester Children's University Hospitals NHS Trust* [2014] EWHC 168 (QB) Phillips J.

Success fees

After the eighth paragraph, add as a new paragraph:

A client entered into a CFA which provided for a two–stage success fee 50 per cent **7A1–58** payable if the claim settled more than three months before the trial date or the opening of the trial window and 100 per cent if it settled or was determined in favour of the claimant thereafter. The case settled five days before a liability trial and the claimant served a notice of commencement and bill of costs which included a success fee of 75 per cent on the solicitor's charges. The defendant challenged this claim and offered 30 per cent. At the detailed assessment the Master took into account the increased risk of a well–placed Part 36 offer with the additional difficulty in assessing the adjustment for contributory negligence. He had regard to the decision in *C v W* [2008] EWCA Civ 1459 in which the Court of Appeal substituted a success fee of 20 per cent for the risk of failure to beat a rejected Part 36 offer where there was an issue of contributory negligence. The Master's decision on a reasonable success fee was reached independently of the decision of the Master as to staging. The material issue was whether the requested success fee of 75 per cent was reasonable whether the staged or not. The Master's award of 30 per cent was upheld: *Bright v Motor Insurers Bureau* [2014] EWHC 1557 QB Slade J.

Add new paragraph at end:

A conditional fee agreement defined the claim as "for trade mark infringement and passing off". The claimant succeeded at trial on the passing off claim but the trade mark infringement claim was stayed pending the outcome of other proceedings. The defendant's argument that the claimant had not won as the claim had not been finally decided in the claimant's favour was rejected. Success was defined by obtaining a remedy, not a remedy in respect of each cause of action included in the definition of "claim". Provided that some damages were derived from the claim, the claimant had achieved success: *Ultimate Products Limited v Woolley* [2014] EWHC 1919 (Ch) Christopher Pymont QC.

7A2 LITIGATION FUNDING AFTER APRIL 1, 2013

Delete Law Society Model Conditional Fee Agreement and substitute:

Law Society Model Conditional Fee Agreement (2014) (Personal Injury and Clinical Negligence cases)

CFA   **7A2–35**

[1]

For use in personal injury and clinical negligence cases only.

This agreement is a binding legal contract between you and your solicitor/s. Before you sign, please read everything carefully. This agreement must be read in conjunction with the Schedules and the Law Society Conditions attached.

I/We, [....] the solicitors/s
You   [...]   of,
[....], the client

---

[1] This model Conditional Fee Agreement for use in Personal Injury and Clinical Negligence cases is reproduced with the kind permission of the Law Society.

Section 7:   Legal Representatives

What is covered by this agreement

- Your claim for damages for personal injury suffered on or about the [....] of [....] as a result of [....]
- Any application for pre–action or non–party disclosure.
- Any appeal by your opponent.
- Any appeal you make against an interim order or an assessment of costs.
- Any proceedings you take to enforce a judgment, order or agreement.
- Negotiations about and/or a court assessment of the costs of this claim.

What is not covered by this agreement

- Any counterclaim against you.
- Any appeal you make against the final judgment order.

Paying us if you win

If you win your claim, you pay our basic charges, our expenses and disbursements and a success fee together with the premium for any insurance you take out. You are entitled to seek recovery from your opponent of part or all of our basic charges and our expenses and disbursements, but not the success fee or any insurance premium.

[**The overall amount we will charge you for our basic charges, success fees, expenses and disbursements is limited as set out in Schedule 2 below.**]

It may be that your opponent makes a formal offer to settle your claim which you reject on our advice, and your claim for damages goes ahead to trial where you recover damages that are less than that offer. If this happens, we will [**not add our success fee to the basic charges**] [**not claim any costs**] for the work done after we received notice of the offer or payment. In these circumstances, you may be ordered to pay your opponent's costs, but only up to the amount of damages and interest awarded to you.

Expenses and Disbursements

If you receive interim damages, we may require you to pay our expenses and disbursements at that point and a reasonable amount for our future expenses and disbursements.

If you receive provisional damages, we are entitled to payment of our basic charges, our expenses and disbursements and success fee at that point.

If you win overall but on the way lose an interim hearing, you may be required to pay your opponent's charges of that hearing, but usually only up to the amount of damages awarded to you.

If on the way to winning or losing you are awarded any costs, by agreement or court order, then we are entitled to payment of those costs, together with a success fee on those charges if you win overall.

What do I pay if I lose?

If you lose you will normally have the benefit of Qualified One–Way Cost Shifting so the court will not usually enforce an order for costs against you, unless:

- the proceedings have been struck out; or
- the claim is fundamentally dishonest; or
- the claim includes a claim for the financial benefit of someone else.

If you lose, you do not pay our charges [**but we may require you to pay our expenses and disbursements**].

The Success Fee

The success fee is set out in Schedule 1.

Basic Charges

Details of our basic charges are set out in Schedule 2.

Ending this agreement

If you have a right to cancel this agreement under Schedule 3 (see below) and do so within the 14 day time limit, you will pay nothing. Otherwise if you end this agreement before you win or lose, you pay our basic charges and expenses and disbursements. If you go on to win, you also pay a success fee.

We may end this agreement before you win or lose, with the consequences set out in the Law Society Conditions.

Other points

Definitions of words used in this CFA are explained in the Law Society Conditions.

You have the right to cancel this agreement in the circumstances set out in Schedule 3.

We add VAT, at the rate that applies when the work is done, to the total of the basic charges and success fee. Our VAT Registration Number is **[Insert]**.

[You may be able to take out an insurance policy against the risk of paying expenses and disbursements (but not our charges) if you lose, or some or all of your opponent's costs even if you win. You will be responsible for paying the insurance premium for this if you win. If you lose the premium [is still/is not] payable. Full details are contained in the insurance policy documents. We will give further information about insurance policies to you so that you can decide whether you wish to take one out].

The parties acknowledge and agree that this agreement is not a Contentious Business Agreement within the terms of the Solicitors Act 1974.

Signatures

Signed by the solicitor: ....

Signed by the client: ....

Dated: ....

Note: We are not bound to act on a conditional fee basis until both you and we have signed this agreement.

Schedule 1

Success fee

The success fee is set at [....................]% of our basic charges, where the claim concludes at trial; or [....................] % of our basic charges where the claim concludes before a trial has commenced.

The success fee percentage reflects the following:

(a) the fact that if you lose, we will not earn anything;

(b) our assessment of the risks of your case;

(c) any other appropriate matters;

(d) the fact that if you win we will not be paid our basic charges until the end of the claim;

(e) our arrangements with you about paying expenses and disbursements.

(f) the arrangements about payment of our costs if your opponent makes a Part 36 offer or payment which you reject on our advice, and your claim for damages goes ahead to trial where you recover damages that are less than that offer or payment.

The Success Fee cannot be more than 100% of the basic charges in total.

Cap on the amount of Success Fee which you will pay us in the event of Success in proceedings at first instance

There is a maximum limit on the amount of the success fee which we can recover from you.

That maximum limit is 25% of the total amount of any:

(i) general damages for pain suffering and loss of amenity; and

(ii) damages for pecuniary loss, other than future pecuniary loss;

which are awarded to you in the proceedings covered by this agreement. The maximum limit is applicable to these damages net of any sums recoverable by the Compensation Recovery Unit of the Department of Work and Pensions. The maximum limit is inclusive of any VAT which is chargeable.

[These maximum limits include any success fee payable to a barrister who has a CFA with us.]

However, this maximum limit applies only to a success fee for proceedings at first instance and not to a success fee on other proceedings (such as, for example, an appeal against a final judgment or order).

447

We will provide you with a copy of any relevant judgment or of our calculation of any settlement showing how much of your damages should be attributed to General Damages and Past Pecuniary Loss, net of any sums recoverable by the Compensation Recovery Unit. **[If you do not agree our calculation and this makes a difference to the amount of the Success Fee payable you, then we will put the matter for determination by an independent barrister of at least 10 years call, to be appointed by agreement between us or, in default of agreement, by the President of the Law Society of England and Wales, such barrister to act as expert and not as arbitrator and his decision shall be binding. The barrister's costs for assessing this issue are to be paid by you if the barrister agrees with us, but otherwise are to be paid by us.]**

You also have the right to apply to the court for assessment of our costs, including our success fee.

Schedule 2

Basic charges

These are for work done from now until this agreement ends. These are subject to review.

How we calculate our basic charges

These are calculated for each hour engaged on your matter. Routine letters and telephone calls will be charged as units of one tenth of an hour. Other letters and telephone calls will be charged on a time basis. The hourly rates are:

Grade of Fee Earner	Hourly Rate
1 Solicitors with over eight years post qualification experience including at least eight years litigation experience.	
2 Solicitors and legal executives with over four years post qualification experience including at least four years litigation experience.	
3 Other solicitors and legal executives and fee earners of equivalent experience	
4 Trainee solicitors, para legals and other fee earners.	

We review the hourly rate in **[month]** each year and we will notify you of any change in the rate in writing.

[Fixed Fees/Costs]

[The above hourly rates may not apply if your claim is subject to a specific fixed fee arrangement agreed between us. If a specific fixed fee arrangement has been agreed with you it is set out below and that fee plus expenses payable by you will be the amount of legal costs payable by you less any amount recovered from your opponent.]

[Overall cap on your liability for costs]

[We will limit the total amount of charges, success fees, expenses and disbursements (inclusive of VAT) payable by you (net of any contribution to your costs paid by your opponent) to a maximum of [25%] of the damages you receive].

Schedule 3

Schedule 3

Notice of the Right to Cancel

This only applies if you sign the Conditional Fee Agreement:

(i) At your home, workplace or at someone else's home; or
(ii) At our offices but following a visit by us (or by someone acting on our behalf) to your home, workplace or someone else's home; or
(iii) At our offices but following a meeting between us away from our offices.

You have the right to cancel this contract, without reason, if you wish and can do so by delivering, sending (including electronic mail) a cancellation notice to the person mentioned below at any time within 14 days starting with the day of receipt of this Notice.

The person to whom a cancellation notice may be given is [   ] of [Name of Firm] at [Address of Firm]   ] [Case Reference]

Notice of cancellation is deemed to be served as soon as it is posted or sent to us.

You can use the cancellation form provided below if you wish.

Signed on behalf of [Name of Firm]: ....

Dated: ....

If you wish to cancel the contract, you **must do so in writing** and deliver personally or send (which [may] [may not] be by electronic mail) this to the person named below. You may use this form if you want to but you do not have to.

....

(Complete, detach and return this form ONLY IF YOU WISH TO CANCEL THE CONTRACT)

To: [   ] of [Name of Firm]
at [Address of firm   ]
Case Reference No: [................]

I hereby give notice that I wish to cancel my Conditional Fee Agreement with your firm.

Signed: ....
Name (please print): ....

Address: ....

....

Date: ....

Law Society Conditions

The Law Society Conditions below are part of this agreement. Any amendments or additions to them will apply to you. You should read the conditions carefully and ask us about anything you find unclear.

Our responsibilities

We must:

- always act in your best interests, subject to our duty to the court;
- explain to you the risks and benefits of taking legal action;
- give you our best advice about whether to accept any offer of settlement;
- give you the best information possible about the likely costs of your claim for damages.

Your responsibilities

You must:

- give us instructions that allow us to do our work properly;
- not ask us to work in an improper or unreasonable way;
- not deliberately mislead us;
- co–operate with us;
- go to any medical or expert examination or court hearing.

Dealing with costs if you win

- **[Subject to any overall cap agreed with you]** you are liable to pay all our basic charges, our expenses and disbursements and the success fee (up to the maximum limit) **[together with the premium of any insurance policy you take out]**.
- Normally, you can claim part or all of our basic charges and our expenses and disbursements from your opponent. You provide us with your irrevocable agreement to pursue such a claim on your behalf. However, you cannot claim from your opponent the success fees **[or the premium of any insurance policy you take out]**.
- If we and your opponent cannot agree the amount, the court will decide how much you can recover. If the amount agreed or allowed by the court does not cover all our basic charges and our expenses and disbursements, then you pay the difference **[up to any maximum agreed with you]**.
- You, not your opponent, pay our success fee **[and any insurance premium]**.
- You agree that after winning, the reasons for setting the success fee at the amount stated may be disclosed to the court and any other person required by the court.
- If your opponent is receiving Community Legal Service funding, we are unlikely to get any money from him or her. So if this happens, you have to pay us our basic charges, expenses and disbursements and success fee.

We are allowed to keep any interest your opponent pays on the charges.

You agree to pay into a designated account any cheque received by you or by us from your opponent and made payable to you. Out of the money, you agree to let us take the balance of the basic charges; success fee; **[insurance premium]**; our remaining expenses and disbursements; and VAT.

You take the rest.

If your opponent fails to pay monies due to you

If your opponent does not pay any damages or charges owed to you, we have the right to take recovery action in your name to enforce a judgment, order or agreement. The charges of this action become part of the basic charges.

Payment for advocacy

The cost of advocacy and any other work by us, or by any solicitor agent on our behalf, forms part of our basic charges. We shall discuss with you the identity of any barrister instructed, and the arrangements made for payment.

Barristers who have a conditional fee agreement with us

If you win, you are normally entitled to recover their fee from your opponent, but not their success fee. The barrister's success fee is shown in the separate conditional fee agreement we make with the barrister. You must pay the barrister's success fee shown in the separate conditional fee agreement we make with the barrister. We will discuss the barrister's success fee with you before we instruct him or her. If you lose, you pay the barrister nothing.

[The barrister's success fee is included within the maximum limit to the recoverable success fee in proceedings at first instance as explained in Schedule 1].

Barristers who do not have a conditional fee agreement with us

If you win, then you will normally be entitled to recover all or part of their fee from your opponent. If you lose, then you must pay their fee.

What happens when this agreement ends before your claim for damages ends?

(a) Paying us if you end this agreement

You can end the agreement at any time. Unless you have a right to cancel this agreement under Schedule 3 and do so within the 14 day time limit we then have the right to decide whether you must:

- pay our basic charges and our expenses and disbursements including barristers' fees but not the success fee when we ask for them; or
- pay our basic charges, and our expenses and disbursements including barristers' fees and success fees if you go on to win your claim for damages.

(b) Paying us if we end this agreement

(i) We can end this agreement if you do not keep to your responsibilities. We then have the right to decide whether you must:

- pay our basic charges and our expenses and disbursements including barristers' fees but not the success fee when we ask for them; or
- pay our basic charges and our expenses and disbursements including barristers' fees and success fees if you go on to win your claim for damages.

(ii) We can end this agreement if we believe you are unlikely to win. If this happens, you will **[pay us nothing] [only have to pay our expenses and disbursements]. [These will include barristers' fees if the barrister does not have a conditional fee agreement with us.]**

(iii) We can end this agreement if you reject our opinion about making a settlement with your opponent. You must then:

- pay the basic charges and our expenses and disbursements, including barristers' fees;
- pay the success fee if you go on to win your claim for damages.

If you ask us to get a second opinion from a specialist solicitor outside our firm, we will do so. You pay the cost of a second opinion.

(iv) **[We can end this agreement if you do not pay your insurance premium when asked to do so.]**

(c) Death

This agreement automatically ends if you die before your claim for damages is concluded. We will be entitled to recover our basic charges up to the date of your death from your estate.

If your personal representatives wish to continue your claim for damages, we may offer them a new conditional fee agreement, as long as they agree to pay the success fee on our basic charges from the beginning of the agreement with you.

What happens after this agreement ends

After this agreement ends, we may apply to have our name removed from the record of any court proceedings in which we are acting unless you have another form of funding and ask us to work for you.

We have the right to preserve our lien unless another solicitor working for you undertakes to pay us what we are owed including a success fee if you win.

Explanation of words used

(a) Advocacy

Appearing for you at court hearings.

(b) Basic charges

Our charges for the legal work we do on your claim for damages as set out in Schedule 2.

(c) Claim

Your demand for damages for personal injury whether or not court proceedings are issued.

(d) Counterclaim

A claim that your opponent makes against you in response to your claim.

(e) Damages

Money that you win whether by a court decision or settlement.

(f) Our disbursements

Payment we make on your behalf such as:

- court fees;
- experts' fees;
- accident report fees;
- travelling expenses.

(g) Interim damages

Money that a court says your opponent must pay or your opponent agrees to pay while waiting for a settlement or the court's final decision.

(h) Interim hearing

A court hearing that is not final.

(i) Lien

Our right to keep all papers, documents, money or other property held on your behalf until all money due to us is paid. A lien may be applied after this agreement ends.

(j) Lose

The court has dismissed your claim or you have stopped it on our advice.

(k) Formal Offer to Settle

An offer to settle your claim made in accordance with Part 36 of the Civil Procedure Rules.

(l) Provisional damages

Money that a court says your opponent must pay or your opponent agrees to pay, on the basis that you will be able to go back to court at a future date for further damages if:

- you develop a serious disease; or
- your condition deteriorates;

in a way that has been proved or admitted to be linked to your personal injury claim.

(m) Qualified One–Way Cost Shifting

The rules in respect of costs payable if you lose a personal injury claim set out in [Part 44 Section II] of the Civil Procedure Rules.

(n) Success fee

The percentage of basic charges that we add to your bill if you win your claim for damages.

(o) Trial

The final contested hearing or the contested hearing of any issue to be tried separately and a reference to a claim concluding at trial includes a claim settled after the trial has commenced or a judgment.

(p) Win

Your claim for damages is finally decided in your favour, whether by a court decision or an agreement to pay you damages or in any way that you derive benefit from pursuing the claim.

'Finally' means that your opponent:

- is not allowed to appeal against the court decision; or
- has not appealed in time; or
- has lost any appeal.

7B   BARRISTERS

INTRODUCTION

After the third paragraph (ending "liable for them.") add as a new paragraph:

7B–1   A conditional fee agreement which provided that a barrister would be able to claim fees directly from the losing party had the effect of giving the barrister an equitable assignment of an entitlement to his fees. This did not entitle the barrister to revert to the client for any shortfall where he had already negotiated a form of final settlement in respect of his fees with the losing party. This was so even where the client later negotiated payment of costs from that other party: *French v Hartman & Anor* [2014] EWHC 15 April (QB) Green J.

7C SOLICITORS ACT 1974

Solicitors Act 1974

Enforcement of contentious business agreements

Delete s.61(6) and substitute:

(6) In this section and in sections 62 and 63 "the court" means— **7C–79**

(a) in relation to an agreement under which any business has been done in the county court having jurisdiction to enforce and set aside agreements, any such court in which any of that business has been done;

(b) in relation to an agreement under which no business has been done in any such court and under which not more than £50 is payable, the High Court;

(c) in relation to an agreement under which no business has been done in any such court and under which not more than £50 is payable, any county court which would, but for the provisions of subsection (1) prohibiting the bringing of an action on the agreement, have had jurisdiction in any action on it;

and for the avoidance of doubt it is hereby declared that in paragraph (a) "court having jurisdiction to enforce and set aside agreements" includes the county court.

Note

Delete the second paragraph and substitute:

Subsection (6) amended by the Crime and Courts Act 2013 Sch.9 paras 52, 130, with **7C–80** effect from April 22, 2014 (see SI 2014/954).

REMUNERATION—GENERAL

Power of court to order solicitor to deliver bill, etc.

Delete s.68(2) and substitute:

(2) The county court and the family court each have the same ju- **7C–97** risdiction as the High Court to make orders making such provision as is mentioned in subsection (1) in cases where the bill of costs or the documents relate wholly or partly to contentious business done by the solicitor in the county court or (as the case may be) the family court.

Note

Delete Note and substitute:

In subs.(2) words "the county" substituted, and word "The" substituted, by the **7C–97.1** Crime and Courts Act 2013 Sch.9 paras 52, 130, with effect from April 22, 2014 (see SI 2014/954); otherwise amended by the Crime and Courts Act 2013 (Family Court:

Consequential Provision) Order 2014 (SI 2014/605) art.12, with effect from April 22, 2014 (being the day on which s.17(3) of the Crime and Courts Act 2013 is brought fully into force).

Orders for the delivery of a bill of costs

Add new paragraph at end:

7C–98   In *Assaubayev v Michael Wilson & Partners Ltd* [2014] EWHC 821 (QB) a claim for an order for the delivery up of a bill and for an order for detailed assessment of that bill was struck out on the ground that the defendant, an international law firm, was not a solicitor within the meaning of the 1974 Act.

Action to recover solicitor's costs

Delete s.69(3) and substitute:

7C–101   (3) Where a bill of costs relates wholly or partly to contentious business done in the county court and the amount of the bill does not exceed £5,000, the powers and duties of the High Court under this section and sections 70 and 71 in relation to that bill may be exercised and performed by the county court.

Note

Delete the second paragraph and substitute:

7C–102   Subsection (3) amended by the Crime and Courts Act 2013 Sch.9 paras 52, 130, with effect from April 22, 2014 (see SI 2014/954).

Subsection (2)—The bill

Add new paragraph at end:

7C–106   Where one firm of solicitors acted as agent for another, and provided the principal with an invoice for the work done to enable negotiations to be carried out with the paying party, this was not a bill of costs for the purposes of s.69 of the Solicitors Act 1974: *Kingston Solicitors v Reiss Solicitors* [2014] EWCA Civ February 4.

Subsection (9)—"One–fifth of the amount of the bill"

In the first paragraph, before the sixth sentence beginning "The amount, on which one–fifth is taken", add:

7C–123   Where a number of bills were assessed together and the total of the bills was reduced by more than one–fifth, but individually most of the bills had not been reduced by more than one–fifth, the Master had erred in finding special circumstances to deprive the client of the costs of the assessment: *Stone Rowe Brewer LLP v Just Costs Ltd* (2014) 2 Costs LR 266.

Special provisions as to contentious business done in county courts

Delete s.74(1) and substitute:

7C–139   (1) The remuneration of a solicitor in respect of contentious business done by him in the county court shall be regulated in accordance with sections 59 to 73, and for that purpose those sections shall have effect subject to the following provisions of this section.

Delete s.74(2) and substitute:

(2) [. . .]

In s.74(3), for "a county court" substitute:

the county court

Note

Delete the second paragraph and substitute:

7C–139.1   Subsections (1), (3) amended and subs.(2) repealed by the Crime and Courts Act 2013 Sch.9 paras 26, 52 with effect from April 22, 2014 (see SI 2014/954).

Interpretation

In s.87(1), for the definition of "bank" substitute: **7C–143**

"bank" means the Bank of England, a person (other than a building society) who has permission under Part 4A of the Financial Services and Markets Act 2000 to accept deposits or an EEA firm of the
kind mentioned in paragraph 5(b) of Schedule 3 to that Act which
has permission under paragraph 15 of that Schedule (as a result of
qualifying for authorisation under paragraph 12 of that Schedule) to
accept deposits;

Delete s.87(1A)(a) and substitute:

(a) a person who has permission under Part 4A of the Financial
Services and Markets Act 2000 to effect or carry out contracts of
insurance of a relevant class;

Note

Add at end:

Amended by Financial Services Act 2012, s.114(1), Sch.18 Pt 2 para.38 with effect **7C–144**
from April 1, 2013 (SI 2013/423).

7D   LEGAL AID

Community Legal Service (Cost Protection) Regulations 2000

Costs order against Commission

In reg.5(3A)(b), after "High Court" add:

, family court **7D–70**

Note

Add at end:

Amended by the Crime and Courts Act 2013 (FamilyCourt: Consequential Provision) (No.2) Order 2014 (SI 2014/879), art.78, with effect from April 22, 2014.

SECTION 8

LIMITATION

Limitation Act 1980

Accrual of cause of action

After "gave rise to a cause of action.", add:

In *British Telecommunications Plc v Luck* [2014] EWHC 290 Teare J. held that a claim **8–5**
for fraudulent or negligent misrepresentation had not been issued outside the limitation period, given that the cause of action had accrued when the claimants ceased to
be members of their former employer's pension scheme, which was just less than six
years before they commenced proceedings.

Add new paragraph 8–12.1:

Accrual of cause of action

In *JJ Metcalfe v (1) James Dennison (2) Jane Dennison* [2013] QBD (TCC) a claim for **8–12.1** an unpaid sum under a building contract was statute barred as the cause of action accrued at the date of completion of the works, which had been more than six years before the claim was brought. That conclusion was not affected by the fact that the contract provided that recovery procedures would not be commenced until after expiry of an agreed credit term.

In *Russell v Cornwell* [2014] EWHC 1509 (QB) a client's claim against a solicitor for breach of contract and professional negligence was time barred where it had been issued over 11 years after the claimant had withdrawn its instructions. The cause of action had not accrued when a trustee in bankruptcy later applied to set aside a transfer of a house to the client from her husband, and had instead accrued whilst the solicitors had been instructed.

Claim to recover money

Add at end:

8–20   In *James Dawson v Thomson Airways Ltd* [2014] EWCA Civ 845 it was held that a claim for compensation for a delayed flight under Regulation 261/2004 art.7 lay outside the scope of the Montreal Convention on International Carriage by Air 1999. It was therefore subject to the six–year limitation period laid down by the Limitation Act 1980 s.9 rather than the two–year period specified by the Convention.

After the tenth paragraph, add as a new paragraph:

8–39   **Divisible injury.** In *Malone v Relyon Heating Engineering Ltd* [2014] EWCA Civ 904 the trial judge had found that the cause of action regarding the entire period of employment had accrued when the injury was "completed", namely when the claimant ceased working in 2004, although the claimant had knowledge by 2001. The Court of Appeal held that, given that apportionment was possible in hearing loss cases and was appropriate in the instant case, the judge should have considered, separately, whether to allow the case to proceed for the pre–2001 injury, bearing in mind the prejudice caused by the delay since 2004, and whether to allow it to proceed for the post–2001 injury.

Section 21—actions for breach of trust and actions for breach of fiduciary duty

Add new paragraph at beginning:

8–60   In *Williams v Central Bank of Nigeria* [2014] UKSC 10 constructive trustees who had exposed themselves to equitable remedies by dishonestly assisting in the misapplication of trust funds by the trustee, or by receiving trust funds knowing the transfer to be in breach of trust, were not true trustees. The Limitation Act 1980 s.21(1) did not disapply the statutory limitation period in respect of actions brought against them by beneficiaries.

Notes on s.32

After the fourth paragraph, add as a new paragraph:

8–85.1   In *Horner v Allison* [2014] EWCA Civ 117 it was held that the judge had not erred in applying the Limitation Act 1980 s.32(1) to extend the limitation period in a claim for deceit. He had been entitled to find that the claimant did not know, and could not have discovered, until the Revenue made a determination, that a tax relief scheme in which he had been induced to participate was fraudulent.

Discretion to disapply relevant limitation period

At the end of the third paragraph, add:

8–92   In *Blue Water Recoveries Ltd v Secretary of State for Transport* [2014] QBD (TCC) June 27, 2014 it was held that it was not appropriate to order a hearing of preliminary issues in relation to limitation because such a hearing would concern contentious issues of fact that could only be determined by calling witnesses from each side to be cross–examined, all the issues would have to be decided in the defendant's favour for the case to be brought to an end, and it was unlikely that costs would be reduced.

In the fourth paragraph, after "are in fact considered." add:

In *Collins v (1) Secretary of State for Business Innovation & Skills (2) Stena Line Irish Sea Ferries Ltd* [2014] EWCA Civ 717 it was held that the judge had not erred in declining to extend time for a personal injury claim under the Limitation Act 1980 s.33. Although pre–limitation period effluxion of time was to be treated as just one of the relevant factors to be taken into account under s.33(3), he had been entitled to consider the lengthy historic delay between the alleged breaches of duty and the date when the claimant had constructive knowledge of his injury as a factor in making it less equitable to extend time under s.33(1).

After the thirteenth paragraph, add as a new paragraph:

In *McArdle v Jason Marmion* [2013] NIQB 123 it was held that despite an inexcusable and unjustified 17–year delay in commencing a personal injury action arising out of a road traffic accident, the fact that a wealth of evidence had been gathered close to the accident meant that the passage of time had not significantly diminished the defendant's ability to defend himself and that it was fair and just to disapply the usual three–year limitation period.

After the eighteenth paragraph, add as a new paragraph:

In *Francisquini v Southwark LBC* [2014] EWHC 1278 (QB), the claimant was permitted to add a personal injury claim to other claims arising from a fire in which his daughter and grandchildren had died, notwithstanding that the new claim was outside the limitation period. The claimant's delay had caused only minor prejudice to the defendants, which was outweighed by the prejudice that would be caused by requiring him to sue his former solicitors for professional negligence for advising that he did not have a personal injury claim.

Scope and operation of this section

Add new paragraph at end:

In *Wm Morrison Supermarkets Plc v MasterCard Inc* [2013] EWHC 3271 (Comm), **8–104** permission was given for an amendment to plead a new claim after the end of the limitation period pursuant to the Limitation Act 1980 s.35. However, the new claim could only relate back six years from the date of the judgment and not to the beginning of the limitation period for the pre–existing claim.

SECTION 9

JURISDICTIONAL AND PROCEDURAL LEGISLATION

9A MAIN STATUTES

Senior Courts Act 1981

OTHER PROVISIONS

Assistance for transaction of judicial business [...]

Delete s.9 and substitute:

9.—(1) A person within any entry in column 1 of the following **9A–30** Table may subject to the proviso at the end of that Table at any time, at the request of the appropriate authority, act—

    (a) as a judge of a relevant court specified in the request; or

    (b) if the request relates to a particular division of a relevant court so specified, as a judge of that court in that division.

	1	2	**9A–31**
1.	A judge of the Court of Appeal.	The High Court, the family court, the county court and the Crown Court.	
2.	A person who has been a judge of the Court of Appeal.	The Court of Appeal, the High Court, the family court, the county court and the Crown Court.	

3.	A puisne judge of the High Court.	The Court of Appeal.
4.	A person who has been a puisne judge of the High Court.	The Court of Appeal, the High Court, the family court, the county court and the Crown Court.
4A.	The Senior President of Tribunals	The Court of Appeal and the High Court.
5.	A Circuit judge.	The High Court and the Court of Appeal.
6.	A Recorder or a person within subsection (1ZB).	The High Court.

The entry in column 2 specifying the Court of Appeal in relation to a Circuit judge only authorises such a judge to act as a judge of a court in the criminal division of the Court of Appeal.

(1ZA) The Senior President of Tribunals is to be treated as not being within any entry in column 1 of the Table other than entry 4A.

(1ZB) A person is within this subsection if the person—

    (a) is a Chamber President, or a Deputy Chamber President, of a chamber of the Upper Tribunal or of a chamber of the First–tier Tribunal,

    (b) is a judge of the Upper Tribunal by virtue of appointment under paragraph 1(1) of Schedule 3 to the Tribunals, Courts and Enforcement Act 2007,

    (c) is a transferred–in judge of the Upper Tribunal (see section 31(2) of that Act),

    (d) is a deputy judge of the Upper Tribunal (whether under paragraph 7 of Schedule 3 to, or section 31(2) of, that Act), or

    (e) is the President of Employment Tribunals (England and Wales) or the President of Employment Tribunals (Scotland).

(1A) A person shall not act as a judge by virtue of subsection (1) after the day on which he attains the age of 75.

(2) In subsection (1)

"the appropriate authority"—

    (a) the Lord Chief Justice or a judicial office holder (as defined in section 109(4) of the Constitutional Reform Act 2005) nominated by him to exercise his functions under this section, or

    (b) at any time when the Lord Chief Justice or the nominated judicial office holder is unable to make such a request himself, or there is a vacancy in the office of Lord Chief Justice, the Master of the Rolls;

"relevant court", in the case of a person within any entry in column 1 of the Table, means a court specified in relation to that entry in column 2 of the Table.

(2A) The power of the appropriate authority to make a request under subsection (1) is subject to subsections (2B) to (2D).

(2B) In the case of a request to a person within entry 1, 3, 4A, 5 or 6 in column 1 of the Table, the appropriate authority may make the request only after consulting the Lord Chancellor.

(2C) In any other case the appropriate authority may make a request only with the concurrence of the Lord Chancellor.

(2CA) In the case of a request to a person within entry 5 or 6 in column 1 of the Table to act as a judge of the Court of Appeal, the appropriate authority may make the request only if the person is a member of the pool for requests under subsection (1) to persons within that entry.

(2D) In the case of a request to a Circuit judge to act as a judge of the Court of Appeal, the appropriate authority may make the request only with the concurrence of the Judicial Appointments Commission.

(3) The person to whom a request is made under subsection (1) must comply with the request, but this does not apply to—

    (a) a request made to a person who has been a judge of the Court of Appeal,

    (b) a request made to a person who has been a puisne judge of the High Court and is not a judge of the Court of Appeal, or

    (c) a request made to the Senior President of Tribunals if the holder of that office is a judge of the Court of Session or of the High Court, or Court of Appeal, in Northern Ireland.

(4) Without prejudice to section 24 of the Courts Act 1971 (temporary appointment of deputy Circuit judges [...]), if it appears to the Lord Chief Justice, after consulting the Lord Chancellor, that it is expedient as a temporary measure to make an appointment under this subsection in order to facilitate the disposal of business in the High Court or the Crown Court or any other court or tribunal to which persons appointed under this subsection may be deployed, he may appoint a person qualified for appointment as a puisne judge of the High Court to be a deputy of the High Court during such period or on such occasions as the Lord Chief Justice, after consulting the Lord Chancellor, thinks fit; and during the period or on the occasions for which a person is appointed as a deputy judge under this subsection, he may act as a puisne judge of the High Court.

(4A) No appointment of a person as a deputy judge of the High Court shall be such as to extend beyond the day on which he attains the age of 70, but this subsection is subject to section 26(4) to (6) of the Judicial Pensions and Retirement Act 1993 (Lord Chancellor's power to authorise continuance in office up to the age of 75).

(5) Every person while acting under this section shall, subject to subsections (6) and (6A), be treated for all purposes as, and accordingly may perform any of the functions of, a judge of the court in which he is acting.

(6) A person shall not by virtue of subsection (5)—

    (a) be treated as a judge of the court in which he is acting for the purposes of section 98(2) or of any statutory provision relating to—

        (i) the appointment, retirement, removal or disqualification of judges of that court;

        (ii) the tenure of office and oaths to be taken by such judges; or

(iii) the remuneration, allowances or pensions of such judges; or

(b) subject to section 27 of the Judicial Pensions and Retirement Act 1993, be treated as having been a judge of a court in which he has acted only under this section.

(6A) A Circuit judge, Recorder or person within subsection (1ZB) shall not by virtue of subsection (5) exercise any of the powers conferred on a single judge by sections 31, 31B, 31C and 44 of the Criminal Appeal Act 1968 (powers of single judge in connection with appeals to the Court of Appeal and appeals from the Court of Appeal to the Supreme Court).

(7) [...]

(8) Such remuneration and allowances as the Lord Chancellor may, with the concurrence of the Minister for the Civil Service, determine may be paid out of money provided by Parliament—

(a) to any person who has been—

(i) a judge of the Supreme Court; or

(ii) a judge of the Court of Appeal; or

(iii) a judge of the High Court,

and is by virtue of subsection (1) acting as mentioned in that subsection;

(b) to any deputy judge of the High Court appointed under subsection (4).

(8A) A person may be removed from office as a deputy judge of the High Court—

(a) only by the Lord Chancellor with the agreement of the Lord Chief Justice, and

(b) only on—

(i) the ground of inability or misbehaviour, or

(ii) a ground specified in the person's terms of appointment.

(8B) Subject to the preceding provisions of this section, a person appointed under subsection (4) is to hold and vacate office as a deputy judge of the High Court in accordance with the terms of the person's appointment, which are to be such as the Lord Chancellor may determine.

(9) The Lord Chief Justice may nominate a senior judge (as defined in section 109(5) of the Constitutional Reform Act 2005) to exercise functions of the Lord Chief Justice under this section.

Note

9A–32 *Delete the second paragraph.*

Judicial bias—"incapable" and "apparent"

In the sixth paragraph (beginning "On application or on"), after "a Norwich Pharmacal application in related proceedings.", add:

9A–48 In *Dar Al Arkan Real Estate Development Co v Al Refai* [2014] EWHC 1055 (Comm), April 1, 2014, unrep. (Andrew Smith J.), before trial of a Commercial Court claim, the defendants (D) brought committal proceedings against the claimants (C) for breach of an interim court order. A judgment by the judge granting D's earlier application to discharge an interim injunction obtained by C contained detailed and specific views about the credibility of the witnesses and conclusions adverse to C, not only on some questions that might arise on the hearing of the committal application, but on issues that were likely to be crucial and possibly on all the real issues that would arise. In the circumstances the judge concluded that he should accede to C's request and should recuse himself on the ground of apparent bias.

C. CONTEMPT OF COURT ACT 1981

Mandatory, prohibiting and quashing orders

In s.29(4), for "a county court" substitute:

the county court

9A–96

Note

Add at end:

Subsection (4) amended, subject to savings and transitional provisions, by the Crime **9A–97**
and Courts Act 2013 Sch.9 para.52, with effect from April 22, 2014 (see SI 2014/954);
for savings and transitional provisions see Sch.8 to the Act.

Powers of High Court exercisable before commencement of action

Delete s.33(3) and substitute:

(3) This section applies in relation to the family court as it applies **9A–110**
in relation to the High Court.

Note

Delete the second paragraph and substitute:

Subsection (3) inserted by the Crime and Courts Act 2013 Sch.10 para.55, with effect **9A–111**
from April 22, 2014 (see SI 2014/954).

Power of High Court to order disclosure of documents, inspection of property etc. in proceedings for personal injuries or death

Delete s.34(5) and substitute:

(5) Subsections (2) and (3) apply in relation to the family court as **9A–115**
they apply in relation to the High Court.

Note

Delete the second paragraph and substitute:

Subsection (5) inserted by the Crime and Courts Act 2013 Sch.10 para.56, with effect **9A–116**
from April 22, 2014 (see SI 2014/954).

Provisions supplementary to ss.33 and 34

Delete s.35(1) and substitute:

(1) A court shall not make an order under section 33 or 34 if it **9A–118**
considers that compliance with the order, if made, would be likely to
be injurious to the public interest.

Note

Delete the second paragraph and substitute:

Subsection (1) amended by the Crime and Courts Act 2013 Sch.10 para.57, with ef- **9A–119**
fect from April 22, 2014 (see SI 2014/954).

Powers of High Court with respect to injunctions and receivers

Delete s.37(6) and substitute:

(6) This section applies in relation to the family court as it applies **9A–128**
in relation to the High Court.

461

Note

Delete the second paragraph and substitute:

9A–129   Subsection (6) inserted by the Crime and Courts Act 2013 Sch.10 para.58, with effect from April 22, 2014 (see SI 2014/954).

Execution of instrument by person nominated by High Court

Delete s.39(1) and substitute:

9A–136   (1) Where the High Court or family court has given or made a judgment or order directing a person to execute any conveyance, contract or other document, or to indorse any negotiable instrument, then, if that person—

> (a) neglects or refuses to comply with the judgment or order; or
>
> (b) cannot after reasonable inquiry be found,
>> that court may, on such terms and conditions, if any, as may be just, order that the conveyance, contract or other document shall be executed, or that the negotiable instrument shall be indorsed, by such person as the court may nominate for that purpose.

Note

Delete the second paragraph and substitute:

9A–137   Subsection (1) amended by the Crime and Courts Act 2013 Sch.10 para.59, with effect from April 22, 2014 (see SI 2014/954).

Restriction of vexatious legal proceedings

Delete s.42(1) and substitute:

9A–148   (1) If, on an application made by the Attorney General under this section, the High Court or the family court is satisfied that any person has habitually and persistently and without any reasonable ground—

Note

Delete the second paragraph and substitute:

9A–149   Subsection (1) amended by the Crime and Courts Act 2013 Sch.10 para.60, with effect from April 22, 2014 (see SI 2014/954).

Power of High Court to vary committal in default

In s.43ZA(1) for "distress", in both places, substitute:

9A–156   goods

Add new s.43ZA(3):

(3) In subsection (1) references to want of sufficient goods to satisfy a sum are references to circumstances where—

> (a) there is power to use the procedure in Schedule 12 to the Tribunals, Courts and Enforcement Act 2007 to recover the sum from a person, but
>
> (b) it appears, after an attempt has been made to exercise the power, that the person's goods are insufficient to pay the amount outstanding (as defined by paragraph 50(3) of that Schedule).

Note

Add at end:

Subsection (1) amended and subs.(3) inserted, subject to savings, by the Tribunals, **9A–157** Courts and Enforcement Act 2007, Sch.13, para.66, with effect from April 6, 2014 (SI 2014/768); for savings see art.2(2) to (6).

C. Section 49(3)

(v) Related actions

Add at end:

In determining whether discretion should be exercised in favour of a stay the court **9A–191** should consider (1) the extent of the relatedness of the proceeding and the risk of mutually irreconcilable decisions, (2) the stage reached in each set of proceedings, and (3) the proximity of the courts to the subject matter of the case, but those factors are not exhaustive (see *Nomura International plc v Banca Monte Dei Paschi Di Siena SpA* [2013] EWHC 3187 (Comm), [2014] 1 W.L.R. 1584 (Eder J.) at para.72 et seq, and authorities referred to there).

COSTS

Costs in civil division of Court of Appeal, High Court and county courts

Delete s.51(1) and substitute:

(1) Subject to the provisions of this or any other enactment and to **9A–199** rules of court, the costs of and incidental to all proceedings in—

    (a) the civil division of the Court of Appeal;
    (b) the High Court,
    (ba) the family court;
        and
    (c) the county court,
        shall be in the discretion of the court.

Delete s.51(8) and substitute:

(8) Where—

    (a) a person has commenced proceedings in the High Court; but
    (b) those proceedings should, in the opinion of the court, have been commenced in the county court or family court in accordance with any provision made under section 1 of the Courts and Legal Services Act 1990 or by or under any other enactment,
        the person responsible for determining the amount which is to be awarded to that person by way of costs shall have regard to those circumstances.

Note

Delete the second and third paragraphs and substitute:

Subsections (1), (8) amended by the Crime and Courts Act 2013 Sch.9 para.29, **9A–200** Sch.10 para.61, with effect from April 22, 2014 (see SI 2014/954).

Assessors and scientific advisers

Delete s.70(5) and substitute:

(5) Subsections (1) and (2) apply in relation to the family court as **9A–261** they apply in relation to the High Court.

Note

Delete the second paragraph and substitute:

9A–262   Subsection (5) inserted by the Crime and Courts Act 2013 Sch.10 para.62, with effect from April 22, 2014 (see SI 2014/954).

SCHEDULE 1

Distribution of Business in High Court

Family Division

Delete para.3(d) and substitute:

9A–400   (d) [. . .]

Note

Delete the second paragraph and substitute:

9A–401   Paragraph 3(d) revoked by the Crime and Courts Act 2013 Sch.10 para.63, with effect from April 22, 2014 (see SI 2014/954).

County Courts Act 1984

Jurisdiction of county courts

At the end of the first paragraph, add:

9A–410   With effect from April 22, 2014, the County Court Jurisdiction Order 2014 (SI 2014/503) increased, from £30,000 to £350,000, the equity jurisdiction of the County Court under s.23 of the 1984 Act (see para.9A–448 below). For other effects of that Order on the jurisdiction of the County Court, see para.9A–710 below.

Penalty for assaulting officers

Delete s.14(1) and substitute:

9A–435   (1) If any person assaults an officer of the county court while in the execution of his duty, he shall be liable—

    (a) on summary conviction, to imprisonment for a term not exceeding 3 months or to a fine of an amount not exceeding level 5 on the standard scale, or both; or

    (b) on an order made by the court in that behalf, to be committed for a specified period not exceeding 3 months to prison or to such a fine as aforesaid, or to be so committed and to such a fine,

and an officer of the court may take the offender into custody, with or without warrant, and bring him before the court.

Delete s.14(3) and substitute:

    (3) [. . .]

Note

Delete Note and substitute:

9A–435.1   Subsection (1) amended and subs.(3) repealed by the Crime and Courts Act 2013 Sch.9 para.9, with effect from April 22, 2014 (see SI 2014/954).

"committed to prison"

At the end of the paragraph, for "and 3C–38" substitute:

9A–436   and 3C–36. In *Chelmsford County Council v Ramet* [2014] EWHC 6 (Fam), January 2, 2014, unrep., the President explained that, where a person against whom proceedings under s.14(1)(b) (or s.118) are brought has already been convicted in a criminal court for the assault and sentenced for conduct inclusive of conduct alleged in the s.14(1)(b) (or s.118) proceedings, the County Court may sentence "only for such conduct as was not the subject of the criminal proceedings", as a person may not be punished twice for the same offence.

Part II

Jurisdiction and Transfer of Proceedings

Actions of contract and tort

General jurisdiction in actions of contract and tort

Delete s.15 and substitute:

15.—(1) Subject to subsection (2), the county court shall have juris- **9A–437**
diction to hear and determine any action founded on contract or
tort.

(2) The county court shall not, except as in this Act provided, have
jurisdiction to hear and determine—
- (a) [...]
- (b) any action in which the title to any toll, fair, market or
  franchise is in question; or
- (c) any action for libel or slander.

Note

Delete the second paragraph and substitute:

Subsections (1), (2) amended by the Crime and Courts Act 2013 Sch.9 para.10(1), **9A–438**
with effect from April 22, 2014 (see SI 2014/954).

Money recoverable by statute

Delete s.16 and substitute:

16. The county court shall have jurisdiction to hear and determine **9A–440**
an action for the recovery of a sum recoverable by virtue of any
enactment for the time being in force, if—

(a) it is not provided by that or any other enactment that such
sums shall only be recoverable in the High Court or shall only be recoverable summarily;

(b) [...]

Note

Delete the second paragraph and substitute:

Amended by the Crime and Courts Act 2013 Sch.9 para.10(1), with effect from April **9A–441**
22, 2014 (see SI 2014/954).

Abandonment of part of claim to give court jurisdiction

Delete s.17(1) and substitute:

(1) Where a plaintiff has a cause of action for more than a county **9A–442**
court limit in which, if it were not for more than the county court
limit, the county court would have jurisdiction, the plaintiff may
abandon the excess, and thereupon the county court shall have jurisdiction to hear and determine the action, but the plaintiff shall not
recover in the action an amount exceeding the county court limit.

Note

Delete Note and substitute:

Subsection (1) amended by the Crime and Courts Act 2013 Sch.9 para.10(1), with **9A–442.1**
effect from April 22, 2014 (see SI 2014/954).

Jurisdiction by agreement in certain actions

Delete s.18 and substitute:

9A–443   **18.** If the parties to any action, other than an action which, if commenced in the High Court, would have been assigned to the Chancery Division or to the Family Division or have involved the exercise of the High Court's Admiralty jurisdiction, agree, by a memorandum signed by them or by their respective legal representatives, that a county court shall have jurisdiction in the action, that court shall have jurisdiction to hear and determine the action accordingly.

Note

Delete the third paragraph and substitute:

9A–444   Amended by the Crime and Courts Act 2013 Sch.9 para.10(1), (2), with effect from April 22, 2014 (see SI 2014/954).

Recovery of land and cases where title in question

Actions for recovery of land and actions where title is in question

Delete s.21(1)–(3) and substitute:

9A–445   (1) The county court shall have jurisdiction to hear and determine any action for the recovery of land.

(2) The county court shall have jurisdiction to hear and determine any action in which the title to any hereditament comes into question.

(3) Where a mortgage of land consists of or includes a dwelling–house and no part of the land is situated in Greater London then, subject to subsection (4), if the county court has jurisdiction by virtue of this section to hear and determine an action in which the mortgagee under that mortgage claims possession of the mortgaged property, no court other than the county court shall have jurisdiction to hear and determine that action.

Note

Delete the second paragraph and substitute:

9A–446   Subsections (1)–(3) amended by the Crime and Courts Act 2013 Sch.9 para.10(1), with effect from April 22, 2014 (see SI 2014/954).

Equity proceedings

Equity jurisdiction

In s.23, for "A county court [The county court]" substitute:

9A–448   The county court

Delete s.23(b)(iii) and the word "or" preceding it.

Note

Delete Note and substitute:

9A–448.1   Amended by the Crime and Courts Act 2013 Sch.9 para.10, with effect from April 22, 2014; and the County Court Jurisdiction Order 2014 (SI 2014/503), art.3, with effect from April 22, 2014 (see SI 2014/954); and the High Court and County Court Jurisdiction (Amendment) Order 2014 (SI 2014/821), with effect from April 22, 2014.

Note

Delete Note and substitute:

The text of this section has been amended so as to indicate that, for the purposes of **9A–449** the equity jurisdiction, the county court limit is £350,000 (see the County Court Jurisdiction Order 2014 (SI 2014/503), art.3. See further para.9A–710 below.

Jurisdiction by agreement in certain equity proceedings

Delete s.24(1)–(2) and substitute:

(1) If, as respects any proceedings to which this section applies, the **9A–450** parties agree, by a memorandum signed by them or by their respective legal representatives or agents, that the county court shall have jurisdiction in the proceedings, that court shall, notwithstanding anything in any enactment, have jurisdiction to hear and determine the proceedings accordingly.

(2) Subject to subsection (3), this section applies to any proceedings in which the county court would have jurisdiction by virtue of—

(a) section 113(3) of the Settled Land Act 1925,
(b) section 63A of the Trustee Act 1925,
(c) sections 3(7), 49(4), 66(4), 89(7), 90(3), 91(8), 92(2), 136(3), 181(2), 188(2) of, and paragraph 3A of Part III and paragraph 1(3A) and (4A) of Part IV of Schedule 1 to, the Law of Property Act 1925,
(d) sections 17(2), 38(4), 41(1A) and 43(4) of the Administration of Estates Act 1925,
(e) section 6(1) of the Leasehold Property (Repairs) Act 1938,
(f) sections 1(6A) and 5(11) of the Land Charges Act 1972, and
(g) section 23 of this Act,
but for the limits of the jurisdiction of the court provided in those enactments.

Note

Delete the second paragraph and substitute:

Subsections (1), (2) amended by the Crime and Courts Act 2013 Sch.9 para.10(1), **9A–451** Sch.9 para.10(2), with effect from April 22, 2014 (see SI 2014/954).

FAMILY PROVISION PROCEEDINGS

Jurisdiction under Inheritance (Provisions for Family and Dependants) Act 1975

Delete s.25 and substitute:

25. The county court shall have jurisdiction to hear and determine **9A–452** any application for an order under section 2 of the Inheritance (Provision for Family and Dependants) Act 1975 (including any application for permission to apply for such an order and any application made, in the proceedings on an application for such an order under any other provision of that Act).

Note

Delete the second paragraph and substitute:

Amended by the Crime and Courts Act 2013 Sch.9 para.10(1), with effect from April **9A–453** 22, 2014 (see SI 2014/954).

Remedies available in county courts

Delete s.38(2)–(4) and substitute:

9A–468   (2) Any order made by the county court may be—

(a) absolute or conditional;

(b) final or interlocutory.

(3) Neither the county court nor the family court has power—

(a) to order mandamus, certiorari or prohibition; or

(b) to make any order of a prescribed kind.

(4) Regulations under subsection (3)—

(a) may provide for any of their provisions not to apply in such circumstances or descriptions of case as may be specified in the regulations;

(b) may provide for the transfer of the proceedings to the High Court for the purpose of enabling an order of a kind prescribed under subsection (3) to be made;

(c) [...]

(d) may make provision amending or repealing any provision made by or under any enactment, so far as may be necessary or expedient in consequence of the regulations; and

(e) may make different provision for different purposes.

Note

Delete the second paragraph and substitute:

9A–469   Subsections (2), (3), (4) amended by the Crime and Courts Act 2013 Sch.9 para.10(1), Sch.10 para.66, with effect from April 22, 2014 (see SI 2014/954).

"Regulations"

Add at end:

9A–470   The County Court Remedies Regulations 1991 were revoked and replaced by the County Court Remedies Regulations 2014 (SI 2014/982) with effect from April 9, 2014.

"any order which could be made by the High Court"

Add new paragraph at beginning:

9A–471   In the County Court Remedies Regulations 1991 the orders of a prescribed kind which the County Court did not have power to make included freezing injunctions and search orders. The County Court Remedies Regulations 2014 (SI 2014/982), which revoked and replaced the 1991 Regulations with effect from April 22, 2014, make no provision for freezing injunctions; consequently, that remedy is no longer prescribed and the County Court has unrestricted jurisdiction to make orders for that form of injunctive relief. An application in the County Court for a freezing order must be made to a Circuit Judge.

TRANSFER OF PROCEEDINGS

Transfer of proceedings to county court

Delete s.40(1)–(4) and substitute:

9A–472   (1) Where the High Court is satisfied that any proceedings before it are required by any provision of a kind mentioned in subsection (8) to be in the county court it shall—

(a) order the transfer of the proceedings to the county court; or

(b) if the court is satisfied that the person bringing the

proceedings knew, or ought to have known, of that requirement, order that they be struck out.

(2) Subject to any such provision, the High Court may order the transfer of any proceedings before it to the county court.

(3) An order under this section may be made either on the motion of the High Court itself or on the application of any party to the proceedings.

(4) [. . .]

Delete s.40(6)–(7) and substitute:

(6) Where proceedings for the enforcement of any judgment or order of the High Court are transferred under this section—

(a) the judgment or order may be enforced as if it were a judgment or order of the county court; and

(b) subject to subsection (7), it shall be treated as a judgment or order of that court for all purposes.

(7) Where proceedings for the enforcement of any judgment or order of the High Court are transferred under this section—

(a) the powers of any court to set aside, correct, vary or quash a judgment or order of the High Court, and the enactments relating to appeals from such a judgment or order, shall continue to apply; and

(b) the powers of any court to set aside, correct, vary or quash a judgment or order of the county court, and the enactments relating to appeals from such a judgment or order, shall not apply.

Delete s.40(9) and substitute:

(9) [. . .]

Note

Delete the second paragraph and substitute:

Subsections (1), (2), (6), (7) amended and subss.(4), (9) repealed by the Crime and **9A–473** Courts Act 2013 Sch.9 para.10(1), (10), Sch.10, para.67, with effect from April 22, 2014 (see SI 2014/954).

Transfer to High Court by order of High Court

Delete s.41(1)–(2) and substitute:

(1) If at any stage in proceedings commenced in the county court **9A–479** or transferred to a county court under section 40, the High Court thinks it desirable that the proceedings, or any part of them, should be heard and determined in the High Court, it may order the transfer to the High Court of the proceedings or, as the case may be, of that part of them.

(2) The power conferred by subsection (1) is without prejudice to section 29 of the Senior Courts Act 1981 (power of High Court to issue prerogative orders).

Note

Delete the second paragraph and substitute:

Subsections (1), (2) amended by the Crime and Courts Act 2013 Sch.9 para.10(1), **9A–480** Sch.10 para.67, with effect from April 22, 2014 (see SI 2014/954).

Transfer to High Court by order of a county court [the county court]

Delete s.42(1)–(2) and substitute:

(1) Where the county court is satisfied that any proceedings before **9A–482**

it are required by any provision of a kind mentioned in subsection (7) to be in the High Court, it shall—

(a) order the transfer of the proceedings to the High Court; or

(b) if the court is satisfied that the person bringing the proceedings knew, or ought to have known, of that requirement, order that they be struck out.

(2) Subject to any such provision, the county court may order the transfer of any proceedings before it to the High Court.

Delete s.42(5)-(6) and substitute:

(5) Where the proceedings for the enforcement of any judgment or order of a county court are transferred under this section—

(a) the judgment or order may be enforced as if it were a judgment or order of the High Court; and

(b) subject to subsection (6), it shall be treated as a judgment or order of that court for all purposes.

(6) Where proceedings for the enforcement of any judgment or order of the county court are transferred under this section—

(a) the powers of any court to set aside, correct, vary or quash a judgment or order of a county court, and the enactments relating to appeals from a judgment or order, shall continue to apply; and

(b) the powers of any court to set aside, correct, vary or quash a judgment or order of the High Court, and the enactments relating to appeals from such a judgment or order, shall not apply.

Delete s.42(8) and substitute:

(8) [. . .]

Note

Delete the second paragraph and substitute:

9A–483   Subsections (1), (2), (5), (6) amended and subs.(8) repealed by the Crime and Courts Act 2013 Sch.9 para.10(1), Sch.10 para.67, with effect from April 22, 2014 (see SI 2014/954).

Costs in transferred cases

Delete s.45(1) and substitute:

9A–486   (1) Where an action, counterclaim or matter is ordered to be transferred—

(a) from the High Court to the county court; or

(b) from the county court to the High Court; or

(c) [. . .]

Note

Delete the second paragraph and substitute:

9A–487   Subsection (1) amended by the Crime and Courts Act 2013 Sch.9 para.10(1), Sch.9 para.10(11), with effect from April 22, 2014 (see SI 2014/954).

PART III

PROCEDURE

PARTIES

Proceedings by the Crown

Delete s.46(1)–(2) and substitute:

(1) Subject to the provisions of any enactment limiting the jurisdic- **9A–488**
tion of the county court, whether by reference to the subject matter
of the proceedings to be brought or the amount sought to be
recovered in the proceedings or otherwise, proceedings by the Crown
may be instituted in the county court.

(2) Subject to section 40(5), all rules of law and enactments regulating the removal or transfer of proceedings from the county court to
the High Court and the transfer of proceedings in the High Court to
the county court shall apply respectively to the removal or transfer of
proceedings in the High Court to the county court shall apply
respectively to the removal or transfer of proceedings by the Crown
in a county court and to the transfer of proceedings by the Crown in
the High Court.

Note

Delete Note and substitute:

Subsections (1), (2) amended by the Crime and Courts Act 2013 Sch.9 para.10(1), **9A–488.1**
with effect from April 22, 2014 (see SI 2014/954).

DISCOVERY AND RELATED PROCEDURES

Powers of court exercisable before commencement of action

Delete s.52(1)–(2) and substitute:

(1) On the application of any person in accordance with rules of **9A–500**
court, the county court shall, in such circumstances as may be
prescribed, have power to make an order providing for any one or
more of the following matters, that is to say—

    (a) the inspection, photographing, preservation, custody and
        detention of property which appears to the court to be
        property which may become the subject–matter of subse-
        quent proceedings in the court, or as to which any ques-
        tion may arise in any such proceedings; and

    (b) the taking of samples of any such property as is mentioned
        in paragraph (a) and the carrying out of any experiment
        on or with any such property.

(2) On the application, in accordance with rules of court, of a
person who appears to the county court to be likely to be a party to
subsequent proceedings in that court, the county court shall in such
circumstances as may be prescribed, have power to order a person
who appears to the court to be likely to be a party to the proceedings
and to be likely to have or to have had in his possession, custody or
power any documents which are relevant to an issue arising or likely
to arise out of that claim—

(a) to disclose whether those documents are in his possession, custody or power; and

(b) to produce such of those documents as are in his possession, custody or power to the applicant or, on such conditions as may be specified in the order—

   (i) to the applicant's legal advisers; or

   (ii) to the applicant's legal advisers and any medical or other professional adviser of the applicant; or

   (iii) if the applicant has no legal adviser, to any medical or other professional adviser of the applicant.

Note

Delete the second paragraph and substitute:

9A–501   Subsections (1), (2) amended by the Crime and Courts Act 2013 Sch.9 para.10(1), with effect from April 22, 2014 (see SI 2014/954).

Power of court to order disclosure of documents, inspection of property, etc., in proceedings for personal injuries or death

Delete s.53(2)–(4) and substitute:

9A–506   (2) On the application, in accordance with county court rules, of a party to any proceedings, the county court shall, in such circumstances as may be prescribed, have power to order a person who is not a party to the proceedings and who appears to the court to be likely to have in his possession, custody or power any documents which are relevant to an issue arising out of the said claim—

(a) to disclose whether those documents are in his possession, custody or power; and

(b) to produce such of those documents as are in his possession, custody or power to the applicant or, on such conditions as may be specified in the order—

   (i) to the applicant's legal advisers; or

   (ii) to the applicant's legal advisers and any medical or other professional adviser of the applicant; or

   (iii) if the applicant has no legal adviser, to any medical or other professional adviser of the applicant.

(3) On the application, in accordance with county court rules, of a party to any proceedings, the county court shall, in such instances as may be prescribed, have power to make an order providing for any one or more of the following matters, that is to say—

(a) the inspection, photographing, preservation, custody and detention of property which is not the property of, or in the possession of, any party to the proceedings but which is the subject–matter of the proceedings or as to which any question arises in the proceedings;

(b) the taking of samples of any such property as is mentioned in paragraph (a) and the carrying out of any experiment on or with any such property.

(4) The preceding provisions of this section are without prejudice to the exercise by the county court of any power to make orders which is exercisable apart from those provisions.

Note

Add at end:

Subsections (2), (3), (4) amended by the Crime and Courts Act 2013 Sch.9 para.10(1), **9A–507** with effect from April 22, 2014 (see SI 2014/954).

Provisions supplementary to sections 52 and 53

Delete s.54(1) and substitute:

(1) The county court shall not make an order under section 52 or **9A–510** 53 if it considers that compliance with the order, if made, would be likely to be injurious to the public interest.

Note

Delete the second paragraph and substitute:

Subsection (1) amended by the Crime and Courts Act 2013 Sch.9 para.10(1), with **9A–511** effect from April 22, 2014 (see SI 2014/954).

WITNESSES AND EVIDENCE

Penalty for neglecting or refusing to give evidence

Delete s.55 and substitute:

55.—(1) Subject to subsections (2) and (3), any person who— **9A–513**
  (a) having been summoned in pursuance of rules of court as a witness in the county court refuses or neglects, without sufficient cause, to appear or to produce any documents required by the summons to be produced; or
  (b) having been so summoned or being present in court and being required to give evidence, refuses to be sworn or give evidence,
  shall forfeit such fine as the court may direct.
(2) The court shall not have power under subsection (1) to direct that a person shall forfeit a fine of an amount exceeding £1000.
(3) No person summoned in pursuance of rules of court as a witness in the county court shall forfeit a fine under this section unless there has been paid or tendered to him at the time of the service of the summons such sum in respect of his expenses (including, in such cases as may be prescribed, compensation for loss of time) as may be prescribed for the purposes of this section.
(4) The court may at its discretion direct that the whole or any part of any such fine, after deducting the costs, shall be applicable towards indemnifying the party injured by the refusal or neglect.
(4A) [. . .]
(5) [. . .]

Note

Delete the second paragraph and substitute:

Subsections (1)–(5) amended by the Crime and Courts Act 2013 Sch.9 para.10(1), **9A–514** (12), with effect from April 22, 2014 (see SI 2014/954).

Examination of witnesses abroad

Delete s.56 and substitute:

56. The High Court shall have the same power to issue a commis- **9A–516** sion, request or order to examine witnesses abroad for the purpose of proceedings in the county court as it has for the purpose of an action or matter in the High Court.

Note

Delete Note and substitute:

9A–516.1   Amended by the Crime and Courts Act 2013 Sch.9 para.10(1), with effect from April 22, 2014 (see SI 2014/954).

Evidence of prisoners

Delete s.57(1) and substitute:

9A–518   (1) Subject to subsection (2), in any proceedings pending before the county court, the court may, if it thinks fit, upon application on affidavit by any party, issue an order for bringing up before the court any person (in this section referred to as a "prisoner") confined in any place under any sentence or following the transfer of proceedings against him for trial or otherwise, to be examined as a witness in the proceedings.

Delete s.57(5) and substitute:

(5) This section applies in relation to the family court as it applies in relation to the county court.

Note

Delete the second paragraph and substitute:

9A–519   Subsection (1) amended and subs.(5) inserted by the Crime and Courts Act 2013 Sch.9 para.10(1), (13), Sch.10 para.68, with effect from April 22, 2014 (see SI 2014/954).

Persons who may take affidavits for use in county courts

Delete s.58 and substitute:

9A–521   58.—(1) An affidavit to be used in the county court may be sworn before—

  (a) a judge of the county court; or

  (b) any justice of the peace; or

  (c) an officer of the county court appointed by a judge of the county court for the purpose.

  as well as before a commissioner for oaths or any other person authorised to take affidavits under the Commissioners for Oaths Acts 1889 and 1891 [...].

(2) An affidavit sworn before any judge or officer may be sworn without the payment of any fee.

Note

Delete the second paragraph and substitute:

9A–522   Subsections (1), (2) amended by the Crime and Courts Act 2013 Sch.9 para.10(1), (14), (15), with effect from April 22, 2014 (see SI 2014/954).

RIGHT OF AUDIENCE

Right of audience

Delete s.60(2) and substitute:

9A–527   (2) Where an action is brought in the county court by a local authority for either or both of the following—

(a) the recovery of possession of a house belonging to the authority;

(b) the recovery of any rent, mesne profits, damages or other sum claimed by the authority in respect of the occupation by any person of such a house,

then, except where rules of court provide otherwise, any officer of the authority authorised by the authority for the purpose may address the court.

Note

Delete the second paragraph and substitute:

Subsection (2) amended by the Crime and Courts Act 2013 Sch.9 para.10(1), (16), **9A–528** with effect from April 22, 2014 (see SI 2014/954).

Rights of audience etc of employees of housing management bodies

Delete s.60A(2) and substitute:

(2) This section applies to relevant housing proceedings in a county **9A–530** court that are not excluded by rules of court and are brought—

(a) in the name of a local housing authority, and

(b) by the housing management body in the exercise of functions of that local housing authority delegated to that body under a housing management agreement.

Note

Delete the second paragraph and substitute:

Subsection (2) amended by the Crime and Courts Act 2013 Sch.9 para.10(17), with **9A–531** effect from April 22, 2014 (see SI 2014/954).

Right of audience by direction of Lord Chancellor

Delete s.61(1) and substitute:

(1) The Lord Chancellor may, with the concurrence of the Lord **9A–532** Chief Justice, at any time direct that such categories of persons in relevant legal employment as may be specified in the direction may address the court in any proceedings in the county court, or in proceedings in the county court of such description as may be so specified.

Delete s.61(3) and substitute:

(3) A direction under this section may be given subject to such conditions and restrictions as appear to the Lord Chancellor to be necessary or expedient, and may be expressed to have effect as respects every place where the county court sits or as respects one or more specified places where the county court sits.

Delete s.61(3A) and substitute:

(3A) Subsections (1) to (3) apply in relation to the family court as they apply in relation to the county court.

Note

Delete the second paragraph and substitute:

Amended by the Crime and Courts Act 2013 Sch.9 para.10(1), (18), Sch.10 para.69, **9A–533** with effect from April 22, 2014 (see SI 2014/954).

Mode of trial

General power of judge to determine questions of law and fact

Delete s.62 and substitute:

9A–535   **62.** Subject to the provisions of this Act and of county court rules, a judge of the county court shall be the sole judge in all proceedings brought in the court, and shall determine all questions of fact as well as of law.

Note

Delete Note and substitute:

9A–535.1   Amended by the Crime and Courts Act 2013 Sch.9 para.10(1), (19), with effect from April 22, 2014 (see SI 2014/954).

Assessors

Delete s.63 and substitute:

9A–537   **63.**—(1) In any proceedings the judge may, if he thinks fit, summon to his assistance, in such manner as may be prescribed, one or more persons of skill and experience in the matter to which the proceedings relate who may be willing to sit with in the county court a judge of the court and act as assessors.

(2) [...]

(3) Subject to subsection (4), the remuneration of assessors for sitting under this section shall be determined by the court and shall be costs in the proceedings unless otherwise ordered by the court.

(4) Where one or more assessors are summoned for the purposes of assisting a judge in reviewing the taxation of the costs of any proceedings the remuneration of any such assessor—

> (a) shall be at such rate as may be determined by the Lord Chancellor with the approval of the Treasury; and
>
> (b) shall be payable out of moneys provided by Parliament.

(5) Where any person is proposed to be summoned as an assessor, objection to him, either personally or in respect of his qualification, may be taken by any party in the prescribed manner.

Note

Delete the second paragraph and substitute:

9A–538   Amended by the Crime and Courts Act 2013 Sch.9 para.10(20), with effect from April 22, 2014 (see SI 2014/954).

Assessors summoned to assist judge

In the second paragraph, after "the judge was not required by law to sit with assessors.", add:

9A–539   In delivering the lead judgment in *Cary v Commissioner of Police of the Metropolis* [2014] EWCA Civ 987, July 17, 2014, CA, unrep., Christopher Clarke LJ examined and explained the development and effects of the statutory provisions providing for the appointment of assessors in discrimination claims falling within the jurisdiction of the County Court according to the type of discrimination in issue, down to the all–embracing Equality Act 2010 (and starting with the Race Relations Act 1968). (The enactments preceding the 2010 Act are sometimes described as "the legacy discrimination enactments".) In that case, where the Court of Appeal was particularly concerned with the meaning within s.63(1) of the phrase "in the matter to which the proceedings relate", the Court gave guidance on the practice and procedure to be followed by court and parties for the selection and appointment of assessors in discrimination cases under the 2010 Act.

Reference to arbitration

Delete s.64(1)–(4) and substitute:

(1) Rules of court—   9A–540

    (a) may prescribe cases in which proceedings in the county court are (without any order of the court) to be referred to arbitration, and

    (b) may prescribe the manner in which and the terms on which cases are to be so referred, and

    (c) may, where cases are so referred, require other matters within the jurisdiction of the court in dispute between the parties also to be referred to arbitration.

(2) Rules of court—

    (a) may prescribe cases in which proceedings in the county court may be referred to arbitration by order of the court, and

    (b) may authorise the court also to order other matters in dispute between the parties and within the jurisdiction of the court to be so referred.

(2A) Rules of court may prescribe the procedures and rules of evidence to be followed on any reference under subsection (1) or (2).

(2B) Rules made under subsection (2A) may, in particular, make provision with respect to the manner of taking and questioning evidence.

(3) On a reference under subsection (1) or (2) the award of the arbitrator, arbitrators or umpire shall be entered as the judgment in the proceedings and shall be as binding and effectual to all intents, subject to subsection (4), as if it had been given by the court.

(4) The court may, if it thinks fit, on application made to it within such time as may be prescribed, set aside the award, or may, with the consent of the parties, revoke the reference or order another reference to be made in the manner specified in this section.

Note

Delete the second paragraph and substitute:

Amended by the Crime and Courts Act 2013 Sch.9 para.10(21)–(23), with effect **9A–541** from April 22, 2014 (see SI 2014/954).

Power of judge to refer to district judge or referee

Delete s.65 and substitute:

65.—(1) Subject to rules of court, a judge of the county court may **9A–543** refer to another judge of the county court for inquiry and report—

    (a) any proceedings which require any prolonged examination of documents or any scientific or local investigation which cannot, in the opinion of the judge, conveniently be made before him;

    (b) any proceedings where the question in dispute consists wholly or in part of matters of account;

    (c) with the consent of the parties, any other proceedings;

    (d) subject to any right to have particular cases tried with a jury, any question arising in any proceedings.

(2) [. . .]

(3) Where any proceedings or question are referred under subsection (1), a judge of the county court may direct how the reference shall be conducted, and may remit any report for further inquiry and report, and on consideration of any report or further report may give such judgment or make such order in the proceedings as may be just.

(4) A judge of the county court may, after deciding or reserving any question of liability, refer to another judge of the county court any mere matter of account which is in dispute between the parties and, after deciding the question of liability, may give judgment on the other judge's report.

Note

Delete the second paragraph and substitute:

9A–544   Amended by the Crime and Courts Act 2013 Sch.9 para.10(24), with effect from April 22, 2014 (see SI 2014/954).

JURIES

Trial by jury

Delete s.66(1)–(2) and substitute:

9A–546   (1) In the following proceedings in the county court the trial shall be without a jury—

(a) Admiralty proceedings;

(b) proceedings arising—

(i) under Part I of the Rent (Agriculture) Act 1976, or

(ii) under any provision of the Rent Act 1977 other than a provision contained in Part V, sections 103 to 106 or Part IX, or

(iii) under Part I of the Protection from Eviction Act 1977; or

(iv) under Part I of the Housing Act 1988.

(c) any appeal to the county court under the Housing Act 1985;

(2) In all other proceedings in the county court the trial shall be without a jury unless the court otherwise orders on an application made in that behalf by any party to the proceedings in such manner and within such time before the trial as may be prescribed.

Delete s.66(4) and substitute:

(4) There shall be payable, in respect of the trial with a jury of proceedings in the county court, such fees as may be prescribed by an order under section 92 of the Courts Act 2003 (fees).

Note

Delete the second paragraph and substitute:

9A–547   Amended by the Crime and Courts Act 2013 Sch.9 para.10(1), with effect from April 22, 2014 (see SI 2014/954).

Impanelling and swearing of jury

Delete s.67 and substitute:

9A–550   **67.** Where any proceedings in the county court are to be tried with a jury, eight jurymen shall be impanelled and sworn as occasion requires to give their verdicts in the proceedings brought before them, and being once sworn need not be re–sworn in each trial.

Note

Delete Note and substitute:

Amended by the Crime and Courts Act 2013 Sch.9 para.10(25), with effect from April 22, 2014 (see SI 2014/954). **9A–550.1**

Duty of judge to determine foreign law in jury trials

Delete s.68 and substitute:

68. Where, for the purpose of disposing of any proceedings which are being tried in the county court by the judge with a jury, it is necessary to ascertain the law of any other country which is applicable to the facts of the case, any question as to the effect of the evidence given with respect to that law shall, instead of being submitted to the jury, be decided by a judge of the court alone. **9A–552**

Note

Delete Note and substitute:

Amended by the Crime and Courts Act 2013 Sch.9 para.10(1), (26), with effect from April 22, 2014 (see SI 2014/954). **9A–552.1**

INTEREST ON DEBTS AND DAMAGES

Power to award interest on debts and damages

Delete s.69(1) and substitute:

(1) Subject to rules of court, in proceedings (whenever instituted) before the county court for the recovery of a debt or damages there may be included in any sum for which judgment is given simple interest, at such rate as the court thinks fit or as may be prescribed, on all or any part of the debt or damages in respect of which judgment is given, or payment is made before judgment, for all or any part of the period between the date when the cause of action arose and— **9A–554**

    (a) in the case of any sum paid before judgment, the date of the payment; and

    (b) in the case of the sum for which judgment is given, the date of the judgment.

Note

Delete the second paragraph and substitute:

Amended by the Crime and Courts Act 2013 Sch.9 para.10(1), with effect from April 22, 2014 (see SI 2014/954). **9A–555**

JUDGMENTS AND ORDERS

Finality of judgments and orders

Delete s.70 and substitute:

70. Every judgment and order of the county court shall, except as **9A–557**

provided by this or any other Act or as may be prescribed, be final and conclusive between the parties.

Note

Delete Note and substitute:

9A–557.1   Amended by the Crime and Courts Act 2013 Sch.9 para.10(1), with effect from April 22, 2014 (see SI 2014/954).

Satisfaction of judgments and orders for payment of money

Delete s.71(2) and substitute:

9A–559   (2) If at any time it appears to the satisfaction of the county court that any party to any proceedings in the court is unable from any cause to pay any sum recovered against him (whether by way of satisfaction of the claim or counterclaim in the proceedings or by way of costs or otherwise) or any instalment of such a sum, the court may, in its discretion, suspend or stay any judgment or order given or made in the proceedings for such time and on such terms as the court thinks fit, and so from time to time until it appears that the cause of inability has ceased.

Note

Delete Note and substitute:

9A–559.1   Amended by the Crime and Courts Act 2013 Sch.9 para.10(27), Sch.10 para.70, with effect from April 22, 2014 (see SI 2014/954).

Set–off in cases of cross judgments in county courts and High Court

Delete s.72(1) and substitute:

9A–561   (1) Where one person has obtained a judgment or order in a county court against another person, and that other person has obtained a judgment or order against the first–mentioned person in the county court or in the High Court, either such person may, in accordance with rules of court, give notice in writing to the court or the several courts as the case may be, and may apply to the court or any of the said courts in accordance with rules of court for leave to set off any sums, including costs, payable under several judgments or orders.

Note

Delete Note and substitute:

9A–561.1   Amended by the Crime and Courts Act 2013 Sch.9 para.10(28), with effect from April 22, 2014 (see SI 2014/954).

Interest on judgment debts, etc.

Delete s.74(2) and substitute:

9A–563   (2) The sums to which subsection (1) applies are—
    (a) sums payable under judgments or orders given or made in the county court, including sums payable by instalments; and
    (b) sums which by virtue of any enactment are, if the county court so orders, recoverable as if payable under an order

of that court, and in respect of which the county court has so ordered.

Delete s.74(5A) and substitute:

(5A) The power conferred by subsection (1) includes power to make provision enabling the county court to order that the rate of interest applicable to a sum expressed in a currency other than sterling shall be such rate as the court thinks fit (instead of the rate otherwise applicable).

(5B) This section applies in relation to the family court as it applies in relation to the county court.

Note

Delete the second paragraph and substitute:

Amended by the Crime and Courts Act 2013 Sch.9 para.10(1), with effect from April **9A–564** 22, 2014 (see SI 2014/954). Subsection (5B) inserted by the Crime and Courts Act 2013 (County Court and Family Court: Consequential Provision) Order 2014 (SI 2014/1773), art.2, with effect from July 4, 2014.

Application of practice of High Court

Delete s.76 and substitute:

76. In any case not expressly provided for by or in pursuance of **9A–566** this Act, the general principles of practice in the High Court may be adopted and applied to proceedings in the county court.

Note

Delete Note and substitute:

Amended by the Crime and Courts Act 2013 Sch.9 para.10(1), with effect from April **9A–566.1** 22, 2014 (see SI 2014/954).

PART IV

APPEALS ETC.

APPEALS

Appeals: general provisions

Delete s.77(1)–(1A) and substitute:

(1) Subject to the provisions of this section and the following provi- **9A–568** sions of this Part of this Act, and to any order made by the Lord Chancellor under section 56(1) of the Access to Justice Act 1999, if any party to any proceedings in the county court is dissatisfied with the determination of a judge or jury, he may appeal from it to the Court of Appeal in such manner and subject to such conditions as may be provided by Civil Procedure Rules.

(1A) Without prejudice to the generality of the power to make rules of court , such rules may make provision for any appeal from the exercise by a judge of the county court of any power given to him by virtue of any enactment to be to another judge of the county court.

Note

Delete the second paragraph and substitute:

9A–569   Amended by the Crime and Courts Act 2013 Sch.9 para.10(1), (29), (30), with effect from April 22, 2014 (see SI 2014/954).

Agreement not to appeal

Delete s.79(1) and substitute:

9A–572   (1) No appeal shall lie from any judgment, direction, decision or order of a judge of the county court if, before the judgment, direction, decision or order is given or made, the parties agree, in writing signed by themselves or their legal representatives or agents, that it shall be final.

Note

Delete the second paragraph and substitute:

9A–573   Amended by the Crime and Courts Act 2013 Sch.9 para.10(1), (31), with effect from April 22, 2014 (see SI 2014/954).

Judge's note on appeal

Delete s.80(1) and substitute:

9A–574   (1) At the hearing of any proceedings in the county court in which there is a right of appeal or from which an appeal may be brought with leave, the judge shall, at the request of any party, make a note—

    (a) of any question of law raised at the hearing; and

    (b) of the facts in evidence in relation to any such question; and

    (c) of his decision on any such question and of his determination of the proceedings.

Note

Delete the second paragraph and substitute:

9A–575   Amended by the Crime and Courts Act 2013 Sch.9 para.10(1), with effect from April 22, 2014 (see SI 2014/954).

Decision of Court of Appeal on probate appeals to be final

Delete s.82 and substitute:

9A–579   **82.** No appeal shall lie from the decision of the Court of Appeal on any appeal from the county court in any proceedings in respect of any contentious matter arising with any grant, or revocation, of probate or administration that under section 105 of the Senior Courts Act 1981 has been applied for through the principal registry of the Family Division or a district probate registry.

Note

Delete Note and substitute:

9A–579.1   Amended by the Crime and Courts Act 2013 Sch.9 para.10(1), (32), with effect from April 22, 2014 (see SI 2014/954).

CERTIORARI AND PROHIBITION

Stay of proceedings in case of certiorari or prohibition

Delete s.83 and substitute:

9A–580   **83.**—(1) The grant by the High Court of leave to make an application for an order of certiorari or prohibition to the county court shall, if the High Court so directs, operate as a stay of the proceedings in question until the determination of the application, or until the High Court otherwise orders.

(2) Where any proceedings are so stayed, the county court shall from time to time adjourn the hearing of the proceedings to such day as the court thinks fit.

Note

Delete Note and substitute:

Amended by the Crime and Courts Act 2013 Sch.9 para.10(33), with effect from April 22, 2014 (see SI 2014/954). **9A–580.1**

Prohibition

Delete s.84 and substitute:

84.—(1) Where an application is made to the High Court for an order or prohibition addressed to the county court, the matter shall be finally disposed of by order. **9A–581**

(2) Upon any such application, no judge of the county court is to be served with notice of it or, except by the order of a judge of the High Court—

    (a) be required to appear or be heard; or

    (b) be liable to any order for the payment of the costs of the application;

        but the application shall be proceeded with and hear in the same manner in all respects as an appeal duly brought from a decision of a judge of the county court, and notice of the application shall be given to or served upon the same parties as in the case of an order made or refused by a judge of the county court in a matter within his jurisdiction.

Note

Delete Note and substitute:

Amended by the Crime and Courts Act 2013 Sch.9 para.10(34), with effect from April 22, 2014 (see SI 2014/954). **9A–581.1**

Part V

Enforcement of Judgments and Orders

Execution against goods

Execution of judgments or orders for payment of money

Delete s.85 and substitute:

85.—(1) Subject to Article 8 of the High Court and County Courts Jurisdiction Order 1991, any sum of money payable under a judgment or order of the county court may be recovered, in case of default or failure of payment, forthwith or at the time or times and in the manner thereby directed, under a warrant under subsection (2). **9A–582**

(2) A judge of the county court, on the application of the party prosecuting any such judgment or order, shall issue a warrant of control whereby any person authorised by or on behalf of the Lord Chancellor is empowered to use the procedure in Schedule 12 to the Tribunals, Courts and Enforcement Act 2007 (taking control of goods) to recover the money payable under the judgment or order.

2(A) The person to whom a warrant under subsection (2) must be directed is to be determined in accordance with arrangements made by a person authorised by or on behalf of the Lord Chancellor.

(3) [Omitted]

(4) It shall be the duty of every constable within his jurisdiction to assist in the execution of every such warrant.

Note

Delete Note and substitute:

9A–582.1   Amended by SI 1991/724. Amended by the Crime and Courts Act 2013 Sch.9 para.10(35), with effect from April 22, 2014 (see SI 2014/954). Subsections (1), (2) amended and subs.(2A) inserted, subject to savings, by the Tribunals, Courts and Enforcement Act 2007 Sch.13 para.69, Sch.23 Pt 3, with effect from April 6, 2014 (SI 2014/768); for savings see art.2(2) to (6).

Execution of orders for payment by instalments

In s.86(1), for "execution on the order", substitute:

9A–584   a warrant of control to recover any of that sum

In s.86(2), for "execution is to issue", substitute:

a warrant of control is to be issued

In s.86(2), for "execution may issue", substitute:

a warrant of control may be issued

In s.86(3), for "execution or successive executions may issue", substitute:

a warrant or successive warrants of control may be issued

In s.86(3), for "no execution shall issue unless at the time when it issues", substitute:

no warrant of control may be issued unless when it is issued

Note

Add at end:

9A–585   Subsections (1), (2) and (3) amended, subject to savings, by the Tribunals, Courts and Enforcement Act 2007, Sch.13, para.70, with effect from April 6, 2014 (SI 2014/768); for savings see art.2(2) to (6).

In s.87, for the title, substitute:

Endorsement of amount on warrant

Delete s.87 and substitute:

9A–587   **87.**—(1) In or upon every warrant of control issued from the county court against the goods of any person, the court shall cause to be inserted or indorsed the total amount to be recovered, inclusive of the fee for issuing the warrant but exclusive of the fees for its execution.

(2) [Omitted]

Note

Delete Note and substitute:

9A–587.1   Amended by the Crime and Courts Act 2013 Sch.9 para.10(1), (36), with effect from April 22, 2014 (see SI 2014/954). Heading and subs.(1) amended, subject to savings, by the Tribunals, Courts and Enforcement Act 2007 Sch.13 para.71, Sch.23 Pt 3, with effect from April 6, 2014 (SI 2014/768; for savings see art.2(2) to (6)).

Delete ss.89 to 91 and substitute:

[ss.89 to 91 repealed, subject to savings, by the Tribunals, Courts and Enforcement **9A–591** Act 2007, Sch.13, para.72, Sch.23, Pt 3, with effect from April 6, 2014 (SI 2014/768); for savings see art.2(2) to (6).]

Penalty for rescuing goods seized

Delete s.92 and substitute:

92.—(1) If any person rescues or attempts to rescue any goods **9A–598** seized in execution under process of the county court, he shall be liable—

    (a) on summary conviction, to imprisonment for a term not exceeding one month or to a fine of an amount not exceeding level 4 on the standard scale, or both; or

    (b) on an order made by the county court in that behalf, to be committed for a specified period not exceeding one month to prison or to a fine of an amount not exceeding level 4 on the standard scale or to be so committed and to such a fine,

and an officer of the court may take the offender into custody, with or without warrant, and bring him before the county court.

(2) A judge of the county court may at any time revoke an order committing a person to prison under this section and, if he is already in custody, order his discharge.

(3) This section does not apply in the case of goods seized under Schedule 12 to the Tribunals, Courts and Enforcement Act 2007.

Note

Delete the second paragraph and substitute:

Amended by the Crime and Courts Act 2013 Sch.9 para.10(1), (39), with effect from **9A–599** April 22, 2014 (see SI 2014/954). Subsection (3) inserted, subject to savings, by the Tribunals, Courts and Enforcement Act 2007 Sch.13 para.73, with effect from April 6, 2014 (SI 2014/768); for savings see art.2(2) to (6).

Delete ss.93 to 98 and substitute:

[ss.93 to 98 repealed, subject to savings, by the Tribunals, Courts and Enforcement **9A–601** Act 2007, Sch.13, para.73, Sch.23, Pt 3, with effect from April 6, 2014 (SI 2014/768); for savings see art.2(2) to (6).]

CLAIMS IN RESPECT OF GOODS SEIZED

In s.99, for title substitute:

Endorsement of warrants of control etc.

Delete s.99 and substitute:

99.—(1) This section applies to—   **9A–612**

    (a) a warrant of control issued under section 85(2);

    (b) a warrant of delivery or of possession, but only if it includes a power to take control of and sell goods to recover a sum of money and only for the purposes of exercising that power.

(2) The person to whom the warrant is directed must, as soon as possible after receiving it, endorse it by inserting on the back the date and time when he received it.

(3) No fee may be charged for endorsing a warrant under this section.

Note

Delete Note and substitute:

9A–612.1   Section 99 substituted, subject to savings, by the Tribunals, Courts and Enforcement Act 2007, s.69, with effect from April 6, 2014 (SI 2014/768; for savings see art.2(2) to (6)).

Delete s.100 and substitute:

9A–614   [s.100 repealed, subject to savings, by the Tribunals, Courts and Enforcement Act 2007, Sch.13, para.73, Sch.23, Pt 3, with effect from April 6, 2014 (SI 2014/768); for savings see art.2(2) to (6).]

Delete paragraph 9A–614.1

Interpleader by district judge

Add new s.101(4):

9A–616   (4) This section does not apply in the case of goods seized under Schedule 12 to the Tribunals, Courts and Enforcement Act 2007.

Interpleader by district judge

Add at end:

9A–617   Subsection (4) inserted, subject to savings, by the Tribunals, Courts and Enforcement Act 2007, Sch.13, para.75, with effect from April 6, 2014 (SI 2014/768); for savings see art.2(2) to (6).

Delete ss.102 and 103 and substitute:

9A–618   [ss.102, 103 repealed, subject to savings, by the Tribunals, Courts and Enforcement Act 2007, Sch.13, para.76, Sch.23, Pt 3, with effect from April 6, 2014 (SI 2014/768; for savings see art.2(2) to (6)).]

Information as to writs and warrants of execution

Delete s.104 and substitute:

9A–624   **104.**—(1) Where a writ against the goods of any person issued from the High Court is delivered to an enforcement officer who is under a duty to execute the writ or to a sheriff, then on demand from a judge of the county court that person shall—

> (a) in the case of an enforcement officer, by writing signed by that officer or a person acting under his authority, and
>
> (b) in the case of a sheriff, by writing signed by any clerk in the officer of the under–sheriff,
>
> inform the judge of the precise time the writ was delivered to him.

(2) The person to whom a warrant issued by a county court is directed the county court shall on demand show his warrant to any enforcement officer, any person acting under the authority of an enforcement officer and any sheriff's officer.

(3) Any writing purporting to be signed as mentioned in subsection (1) and the endorsement on any warrant issued from a county court shall respectively be sufficient justification to any judge, or enforcement officer or sheriff, acting on it.

(4) In this section "enforcement officer" means an individual who is authorised to act as an enforcement officer under the Courts Act 2003.

Note

Delete Note and substitute:
Amended by the Crime and Courts Act 2013 Sch.9 para.10(1), (49), with effect from April 22, 2014 (see SI 2014/954). Subsection (2) amended, subject to savings, by the Tribunals, Courts and Enforcement Act 2007 Sch.13 para.77, with effect from April 6, 2014 (SI 2014/768); for savings see art.2(2) to (6). **9A–624.1**

MISCELLANEOUS PROVISIONS AS TO ENFORCEMENT OF JUDGMENTS AND ORDERS

Penalty for non–attendance on judgment summons

Delete s.110 and substitute:

110.—(1) If a debtor summoned to attend the county court by a judgment summons fails to attend on the day and at the time fixed for any hearing of the summons, the court may adjourn or further adjourn the summons to a specified time on a specified day and order the debtor to attend at that time on that day. **9A–634**

(2) If—
  (a) a debtor, having been ordered under subsection (1) to attend at a specified time on a specified day, fails to do so;
  (b) [...]
  the court may make an order committing him to prison for a period not exceeding 14 days in respect of the failure or refusal.

(3) In any case where the court has power to make an order of committal under subsection (2) for failure to attend, he may in lieu of or in addition to making that order, order the debtor to be arrested and brought before the court either forthwith or at such time as the court may direct.

(4) A debtor shall not be committed to prison under subsection (2) for having failed to attend as required by an order under subsection (1) unless there was paid to him at the time of the service of the judgment summons, or paid or tendered to him at the time of the service of the order, such sum in respect of his expenses as may be prescribed for the purposes of this section.

(5) The court may at any time revoke an order committing a person to prison under this section and, if he is already in custody, order his discharge.

Note

Delete Note and substitute:
Amended by the Crime and Courts Act 2013 Sch.9 para.10(1), (50), with effect from April 22, 2014 (see SI 2014/954). **9A–634.1**

PART VI

ADMINISTRATION ORDERS

Power to make administration order

Delete s.112(1)–(4) and substitute:

(1) Where a debtor— **9A–639**

(a) is unable to pay forthwith the amount of a judgment obtained against him, and

(b) alleges that his whole indebtedness amounts to a sum not exceeding the county court limit, inclusive of the debt for which the judgment was obtained;
the county court may make an order providing for the administration of his estate.

(2) In this Part of this Act
"administration order" means an order under this section.

(3) Before an administration order is made, the county court shall, in accordance with rules of court, send to every person whose name the debtor has notified to the county court]as being a creditor of his, a notice that that person's name has been so notified.

(4) So long as an administration order is in force, a creditor whose name is included in the schedule to the order shall not, without the leave of the county court, be entitled to present, or join in, a bankruptcy petition against the debtor unless—

(a) his name was so notified; and

(b) the debt by virtue of which he presents, or joins in, the petition, exceeds £1,500; and

(c) the notice given under subsection (3) was received by the creditor within 28 days immediately preceding the day on which the petition is presented.

Note

Delete the second paragraph and substitute:

9A–640   Amended by the Crime and Courts Act 2013 Sch.9 para.10(1), (51), with effect from April 22, 2014 (see SI 2014/954).

Notice of order and proof of debts

Delete s.113 and substitute:

9A–642   **113.** Where an administration order has been made—

(a) notice of the order—
 (i) [...]
 (ii) shall be posted on an appropriate website, and
 (iii) shall be sent to every person whose name the debtor has notified to the appropriate court as being a creditor of his or who has proved;

(b) any creditor of the debtor, on proof of his debt before the county court, shall be entitled to be scheduled as a creditor of the debtor for the amount of his proof;

(c) any creditor may object in the prescribed manner to any debt scheduled, or to the manner in which payment is directed to be made by instalments;

(d) any person who, after the date of the order, becomes a creditor of the debtor shall, on proof of his debt before the county court, be scheduled as a creditor of the debtor for the amount of his proof, but shall not be entitled to any dividend under the order until the creditors who are scheduled as having been creditors before the date of the order have been paid to the extent provided by the order.

Note

Delete the second paragraph and substitute:

Amended by the Crime and Courts Act 2013 Sch.9 para.10(51), with effect from **9A–643** April 22, 2014 (see SI 2014/954).

Effect of administration order

Delete s.114(2)–(3) and substitute:

(2) Subject to subsection (3), when an administration order is made, **9A–645** the county court is to stay any proceedings in the county court which are pending against the debtor in respect of any debt so notified or scheduled, but may allow costs already incurred by the creditor, and such costs may, on application, be added to the debt.

(3) The requirement to stay proceedings shall not operate as a requirement to stay any proceedings in bankruptcy which are pending against the debtor.

Note

Delete the second paragraph and substitute:

Amended by the Crime and Courts Act 2013 Sch.9 para.10(1), (51), with effect from **9A–646** April 22, 2014 (see SI 2014/954).

Execution by district judge

Delete s.115(1) and substitute:

(1) Where it appears to the appropriate court at any time while an **9A–648** administration order is in force that property of the debtor exceeds in value the minimum amount, the court shall, at the request of any creditor, and without fee, issue execution against the debtor's goods.

Note

Delete Note and substitute:

Amended by the Crime and Courts Act 2013 Sch.9 para.10(51), with effect from **9A–648.1** April 22, 2014 (see SI 2014/954).

Delete s.116 and substitute:

[s.116 repealed, subject to savings, by the Tribunals, Courts and Enforcement Act **9A–651** 2007, Sch.14, para.39, Sch.23, Pt 4, with effect from April 6, 2014 (SI 2014/768; for savings see art.2(2) to (6)).]

PART VII

COMMITTALS

Power to commit for contempt

Delete s.118 and substitute:

118.—(1) If any person— **9A–654**
  (a) wilfully insults a judge of the county court, or any juror or witness, or any officer of the court during his sitting or attendance in court, or in going to or returning from the court; or
  (b) wilfully interrupts the proceedings of the county court or otherwise misbehaves in court;

any officer of the court, with or without the assistance of any other person, may, by order of the judge, take the offender into custody and detain him until the rising of the court, and the judge may, if he thinks fit,—

(i) make an order committing the offender for a specified period not exceeding one month to prison; or

(ii) impose upon the offender, for every offence, a fine of an amount not exceeding £2,500, or may both make such an order and impose such a fine.

(2) A judge of the county court may at any time revoke an order committing a person to prison under this section, and if he is already in custody, order his discharge.

(3) [. . .]

Note

Delete the second paragraph and substitute:

9A–655   Amended by the Crime and Courts Act 2013 Sch.9 para.10(1), (54), with effect from April 22, 2014 (see SI 2014/954).

Power to commit for contempt

In the third paragraph, for "Rule 3.8 of the family Procedure Rules 2010", substitute:

9A–656   Rule 37.38 of the Family Procedure Rules 2010 (as inserted by SI 2014/667)

Issue and execution of orders of committal

Delete s.119(1) and substitute:

9A–657   (1) Whenever any order or warrant for the committal of any person to prison is made or issued by the county court (whether in pursuance of this or any other Act or of rules of court), the order or warrant shall be directed to the officers of the court, who shall thereby be empowered to take the body of the person against whom the order is made or warrant issued.

Note

Delete the second paragraph and substitute:

9A–658   Amended by the Crime and Courts Act 2013 Sch.9 para.10(1), (55), with effect from April 22, 2014 (see SI 2014/954).

Prisons to which committals may be made

Delete s.120 and substitute:

9A–660   **120.** Any person committed to prison by the county court, in pursuance of this or any other Act or of rules of court, shall be committed to such prison as may from time to time be directed in the case of that court by order of the Secretary of State.

Note

Delete the second paragraph and substitute:

9A–661   Amended by the Crime and Courts Act 2013 Sch.9 para.10(56), with effect from April 22, 2014 (see SI 2014/954).

Power of judge to order discharge

Delete s.121 and substitute:

9A–662   **121.** If at any time it appears to the satisfaction of a county court that any debtor arrested or confined in prison by order of the court is unable from any cause to pay any sum recovered against him (whether by way of satisfaction of a claim or counterclaim or by way of costs or otherwise), or any instalments thereof, and ought to be discharged, the court may order his discharge upon such terms (including liability to re–arrest if the terms are not complied with) as the court thinks fit.

Note

Delete Note and substitute:

Amended by the Crime and Courts Act 2013 Sch.9 para.10(57), with effect from April 22, 2014 (see SI 2014/954). **9A–662.1**

Execution of committal orders out of jurisdiction of court

Delete s.122 and substitute:

122. [. . .] **9A–663**

Note

Delete Note and substitute:

Section 122 repealed by the Crime and Courts Act 2013 Sch.9 para.10(58), with effect from April 22, 2014 (see SI 2014/954). **9A–663.1**

Delete s.123 and substitute:

[s.123 repealed, subject to savings, by the Tribunals, Courts and Enforcement Act 2007, Sch.13, para.78, Sch.23, Pt 3, with effect from April 6, 2014 (SI 2014/768; for savings see art.2(2) to (6)).] **9A–665**

Liability of bailiff for neglect to levy execution

Delete s.124 and substitute:

124.—(1) Where a county court issues a warrant of execution, control, possession or delivery and the person to whom it is directed loses the opportunity of executing it by reason of neglect, connivance or omission, any party aggrieved thereby may complain to the district judge to the court. **9A–667**

(2) On any such complaint the court, if the neglect, connivance or omission is proved to his satisfaction, shall order that person to pay such damages as it appears that the complainant has sustained by reason of it, not exceeding in any case the sum for which the warrant was issued.

Note

Delete Note and substitute:

Amended by the Crime and Courts Act 2013 Sch.9 para.10(60), with effect from April 22, 2014 (see SI 2014/954). Subsections (1), (2) amended, subject to savings, by the Tribunals, Courts and Enforcement Act 2007 Sch.13 para.79, with effect from April 6, 2014 (SI 2014/768); for savings see art.2(2) to (6). **9A–667.1**

Irregularity in executing warrants

Delete s.125(1) and substitute:

(1) No officer of the county court in executing any warrant of the court, and no person at whose instance any such warrant is executed, shall be deemed a trespasser by reason of any irregularity or informality— **9A–669**

(a) in any proceeding on the validity of which the warrant depends; or

(b) in the form of the warrant or in the mode of executing it;

but, except in the case of a warrant of control (to which Schedule 12 to the Tribunals, Courts and Enforcement Act 2007 applies), any person aggrieved may bring an action for any special damage sustained by him by reason of the irregularity or informality against the person guilty of it.

Note

Delete Note and substitute:

9A–669.1 Amended by the Crime and Courts Act 2013 Sch.9 para.10(1), (61), with effect from April 22, 2014 (see SI 2014/954). Subsection (1) amended, subject to savings, by the Tribunals, Courts and Enforcement Act 2007, Sch.13, para.80, with effect from April 6, 2014 (SI 2014/768); for savings see art.2(2) to (6).

Actions against bailiffs acting under warrants

Delete s.126 and substitute:

9A–670 **126.**—(1) No action shall be commenced against any bailiff for anything done in obedience to a warrant issued by the county court, unless—

(a) a demand for inspection of the warrant and for a copy of it is made or left at the office of the bailiff by the party intending to bring the action, or his legal representative or agent; and

(b) the bailiff refuses or neglects to comply with the demand within six days after it is made.

(2) The demand must be in writing and signed by the person making it.

(3) If an action is commenced against a bailiff in a case where such a demand has been made and not complied with, judgment shall be given for the bailiff if the warrant is produced or proved at the trial, notwithstanding any defect of jurisdiction or other irregularity in the warrant.

(4) In this section "bailiff" in relation to a warrant means the person to whom the warrant is directed, and (except in paragraph (a) of subsection (1)) includes any person acting by the order and in aid of that person.

(5) This section does not apply to an action for anything done under a power to use the procedure in Schedule 12 to the Tribunals, Courts and Enforcement Act 2007.

Note

Delete the second paragraph and substitute:

9A–671 Amended by the Crime and Courts Act 2013 Sch.9 para.10(62), with effect from April 22, 2014 (see SI 2014/954). Subsections (3), (4) amended, subject to savings, by the Tribunals, Courts and Enforcement Act 2007 Sch.13 para.81, Sch.23 Pt 3, with effect from April 6, 2014 (SI 2014/768); for savings see art.2(2) to (6).

Enforcement of fines

Delete s.129 and substitute:

9A–674 **129.** Payment of any fine imposed by the county court under this Act may be enforced upon the order of the court in like manner—

    (a) as payment of a debt adjudged by the court to be paid may be enforced under this Act; or

    (b) as payment of a sum adjudged to be paid by a conviction of a magistrates' court may be enforced under the Magistrates' Courts Act 1980 (disregarding section 81(1) of that Act).

Note

Delete Note and substitute:

Amended by the Crime and Courts Act 2013 Sch.9 para.10(63), with effect from **9A–674.1** April 22, 2014 (see SI 2014/954).

Payment and application of fees, fines, etc.

Delete s.130(3) and substitute:

(3) The Lord Chancellor, with the concurrence of the Treasury, **9A–675** shall from time to time make such rules as he thinks fit for securing the balances and other sums of money in the hands of any officers of the county court, and for the due accounting for and application of those balances and sums.

Note

Delete Note and substitute:

Amended by the Crime and Courts Act 2013 Sch.9 para.10(1), with effect from April **9A–675.1** 22, 2014 (see SI 2014/954).

Appointment of auditors and other officers

Delete s.131 and substitute:

131. The Lord Chancellor may, subject to the consent of the Trea- **9A–676** sury as to numbers and salaries, appoint as officers in his department such auditors and other officers as he may consider necessary for the purpose of the family court or the county court.

Note

Delete Note and substitute:

Amended by the Crime and Courts Act 2013 Sch.9 para.10(1), Sch.10 para.71, with **9A–676.1** effect from April 22, 2014 (see SI 2014/954).

Payment of salaries and expenses

Delete s.132 and substitute:

132. There shall be paid out of money provided by Parliament— **9A–677**

    (a) all salaries, remuneration and other sums payable under Part I of this Act or under section 131;

    (b) the expenses of supplying the the county court and its offices, and the family court and its offices, with law and office books and stationery and postage stamps;

    (c) expenses incurred in conveying to prison persons the family court or the county court; and

    (d) all other expenses arising out of any jurisdiction for the time being conferred on the family court or any officer of the family court or on the county court of any officer of the county court.

Note

Delete Note and substitute:

9A–677.1   Amended by the Crime and Courts Act 2013 Sch.9 para.10(65), Sch.10 para.72, with effect from April 22, 2014 (see SI 2014/954).

SUMMONSES AND OTHER DOCUMENTS

Proof of service of summonses, etc.

Delete s.133 and substitute:

9A–678   **133.**—(1) Where any summons or other process issued from a county court is served by an officer of the court, the service may be proved by a certificate in a prescribed form showing the fact and mode of the service.

(2) Any officer of the court wilfully and corruptly giving a false certificate under subsection (1) in respect of the service of a summons or other process shall be guilty of an offence and on conviction thereof, shall be removed from office and shall be liable—

(a) on conviction on indictment, to imprisonment for any term not exceeding 2 years; or

(b) on summary conviction, to imprisonment for any term not exceeding 6 months or to a fine not exceeding the statutory maximum or to both such imprisonment and fine.

Note

Delete the second paragraph and substitute:

9A–679   Amended by the Crime and Courts Act 2013 Sch.9 para.10(66), with effect from April 22, 2014 (see SI 2014/954).

Penalty for falsely representing document to have been issued from county court

Delete s.136(1) and substitute:

9A–682   (1) It shall not be lawful to deliver or cause to be delivered to any person any document which was not issued under the authority of the county court but which, by reason of its form or contents or both, has the appearance of having been issued under such authority.

Note

Delete Note and substitute:

9A–682.1   Amended by the Crime and Courts Act 2013 Sch.9 para.10(1), with effect from April 22, 2014 (see SI 2014/954).

Lessee to give notice of summons for recovery of land

Delete s.137 and substitute:

9A–683   **137.**—(1) Every lessee to whom there is delivered any summons issued from the county court for the recovery of land demised to or held by him, or to whose knowledge any such summons comes, shall forthwith give notice of the summons to his lessor or his bailiff or receiver.

(2) If a lessee fails to give notice as required by subsection (1), he shall be liable to forfeit to the person of whom he holds the land an amount equal to the value of 3 years' improved or rack rent of the

land to be recovered by action in the county court or any other court having jurisdiction in respect of claims for such an amount.

Note

Delete Note and substitute:

Amended by the Crime and Courts Act 2013 Sch.9 para.10(1), (67), with effect from April 22, 2014 (see SI 2014/954). **9A–683.0**

Power to enforce undertakings of solicitors

Delete s.142 and substitute:

142. The county court shall have the same power to enforce an undertaking given by a solicitor in relation to any proceedings in that court as the High Court has to enforce an undertaking so given in relation to any proceedings in the High Court. **9A–704**

Note

Delete Note and substitute:

Amended by the Crime and Courts Act 2013 Sch.9 para.10(1), with effect from April 22, 2014 (see SI 2014/954). **9A–704.1**

Prohibition on persons other than solicitors receiving remuneration for business done in county courts

Delete s.143(1) and substitute:

(1) No person other than— **9A–706**
    (a) a legal representative; or
    (b) a person exercising a right of audience or a right to conduct litigation by virtue of an order made under section 11 of the Courts and Legal Services Act 1990 (representation in county courts),

shall be entitled to have or recover any fee or reward for acting on behalf of a party in proceedings in the county court.

Note

Delete the second paragraph and substitute:

Amended by the Crime and Courts Act 2013 Sch.9 para.10(1), with effect from April 22, 2014 (see SI 2014/954). **9A–707**

Note

Delete paragraph 9A–710 and substitute:

Section 145 was amended by the Constitutional Reform Act 2005 s.15(1) and Sch.4 para.170 (see para.9A–4 above). The County Court Jurisdiction Order 2014 (SI 2014/ 503) was made under this section and came into effect on April 22, 2014. That Order revoked the County Courts Jurisdiction Order 1981 (SI 1981/1122), as amended by article 2 of, and Part II of the Schedule to, the High Court and County Courts Jurisdiction Order 1991 (SI 1991/724). The 2014 Order increased, from £30,000 to £350,000, the equity jurisdiction of the County Court under s.23 of the 1984 Act. In relation to certain other statutory provisions referring to "the county court limit", the 2014 Order re–states that limit at £30,000; those provisions are: the Settled Land Act 1925 s.13, the Trustee Act 1925 s.63A(1), (2), and (3)(c) & (d), the Administration of Estates Act 1925 ss.38, 41 and 43. In addition to 2014 Order re–states the limit for the purposes of the Charging Orders Act s.1 at £5,000. See further paras. 9A–410 and 9A–449 above. **9A–710**

Interpretation

Delete s.147(1) and substitute:

(1) In this Act, unless the context otherwise requires— **9A–712**

"action" means any proceedings in the county court which may be commenced as prescribed by plaint;

"Admiralty proceedings" means proceedings which, if commenced in the High Court, would involve the exercise of the High Court's Admiralty jurisdiction;

"the county court limit" means—

> (a) in relation to any enactment contained in this Act for which a limit for the time being specified by an Order under section 145, that limit,
>
> (b) [...]
>
> (c) in relation to any enactment contained in this Act and not within paragraph (a), the county court limit for the time being specified by any other Order in Council or order defining the limit of county court jurisdiction for the purposes of that enactment;

"court" means the county court;

"deposit–taking institution" means a person who may, in the course of his business, lawfully accept deposits in the United Kingdom;

"hearing" includes trial, and "hear" and "heard" shall be construed accordingly;

"hereditament" includes both a corporeal and incorporeal hereditament;

"judgment summons" means a summons issued on the application of a person entitled to enforce a judgment or order under section 5 of the Debtors Act 1869 requiring a person, or where two or more persons are liable under the judgment or order, requiring any one or more of them, to attend court;

"landlord", in relation to any land, means the person entitled to the immediate reversion or, if the property therein is held in joint tenancy, any of the persons entitled to the immediate reversion;

"legal representative" means an authorised advocate or authorised litigator, as defined by section 119(1) of the Courts and Legal Services Act 1990;

"matter" means every proceeding in the county court which may be commenced as prescribed otherwise than by plaint;

"officer", in relation to the county court, means any clerk, bailiff, usher or messenger in the service of that court;

"party" includes every person served with notice of, or attending, any proceeding, whether named as a party to that proceeding or not;

"prescribed" means prescribed by rules of court;

"proceedings" includes both actions and matters;

"return day" means the day appointed in any summons or proceeding for the appearance of the defendant or any other day fixed for the hearing of any proceedings;

"ship" includes any description of vessel used in navigation;

"solicitor" means solicitor of the Senior Courts.

Note

Delete seventh and eighth paragraphs and substitute:
Amended by the Crime and Courts Act 2013 Sch.9 para.10(1), (68), with effect from **9A–713** April 22, 2014 (see SI 2014/954).

Subsection (1) amended, subject to savings, by the Tribunals, Courts and Enforcement Act 2007 Sch.13 para.82, Sch.23 Pt 3, with effect from April 6, 2014 (SI 2014/768); for savings see art.2(2) to (6).

"The county court limit"

Delete paragraph 9A–714 and substitute:
See para.9A–710 above. **9A–714**

SECTION 148(2) SCHEDULE 3

TRANSITORY AND TRANSITIONAL PROVISIONS AND SAVINGS

High bailiffs

Delete para.7 and substitute:
7. References to a high bailiff in any enactment, Order in Council, order, rule, **9A–729** regulation or any document whatsoever shall be construed as a reference to a judge of the county court.

Note

Delete the second paragraph and substitute:
Paragraph 5A inserted and para.7 amended by the Crime and Courts Act 2013 **9A–734** Sch.9 para.10(70), (71), with effect from April 22, 2014 (see SI 2014/954).

Civil Procedure Act 1997

RULES AND DIRECTIONS

Civil Procedure Rules

Delete s.1(1) and substitute:

(1) There are to be rules of court (to be called " Civil Procedure **9A–738** Rules") governing the practice and procedure to be followed in—
    (a) the civil division of the Court of Appeal,
    (b) the High Court, except in relation to its jurisdiction under the Extradition Act 2003, and
    (c) the county court.

Note

Delete Note and substitute:
Amended by the Crime and Courts Act 2013 Sch.9 para.67, with effect from April **9A–738.1** 22, 2014 (see SI 2014/954). Paragraph (1)(b) of s.1 was amended by the Anti–social Behaviour, Crime and Policing Act 2014 s.174(2) with effect from October 1, 2014, for the purpose of transferring responsibility for making rules concerning the High Court's jurisdiction under the Extradition Act 2003 from the Civil Procedure Rule Committee to the Criminal Procedure Rule Committee.

Rule Committee

Delete s.2(2) and substitute:

(2) The persons to be appointed in accordance with subsections **9A–740** (1A) and (1B) are
    (a) either two or three judges of the Senior Courts,
    (b) one Circuit judge,
    (c) either one or two district judges,

(d) one person who is a Master referred to in Part II of Schedule 2 to the Senior Courts Act 1981,

(e) three persons who have a Senior Courts qualification (within the meaning of section 71 of the Courts and Legal Services Act 1990), including at least one with particular experience of practice in the county court,

(f) three persons who have been authorised by a relevant approved regulator to conduct litigation in relation to all proceedings in the Senior Courts, including at least one with particular experience of practice in the county court,

(g) two persons with experience in and knowledge of the lay advice sector and consumer affairs.

Note

Delete the second paragraph and substitute:

9A–740.1   Subsection (2) amended by the Crime and Courts Act 2013 Sch.9 para.10(1), (67), with effect from April 22, 2014 (see SI 2014/954).

SECTION 1   SCHEDULE 1

CIVIL PROCEDURE RULES

Removal of proceedings

Delete para.3 and substitute:

9A–767   3.—(1) Civil Procedure Rules may provide for the removal of proceedings at any stage—

(a) within the High Court (for example, between different divisions or different district registries), or

(b) within the county court.

(2) In sub-paragraph (1)—

(a) "provide for the removal of proceedings" means—

(i) provide for transfer of proceedings, or

(ii) provide for any jurisdiction in any proceedings to be exercised (whether concurrently or not) elsewhere within the High Court or, as the case may be, elsewhere within the county court without the proceedings being transferred, and

(b) "proceedings" includes any part of proceedings.

Note

Delete Note and substitute:

9A–772   Amended by the Crime and Courts Act 2013 Sch.9 para.67, with effect from April 22, 2014 (see SI 2014/954).

Access to Justice Act 1999

PART IV

APPEALS, COURTS, JUDGES AND COURT PROCEEDINGS

APPEALS

Permission to appeal

Delete s.54(1) and substitute:

9A–841   (1) Rules of court may provide that any right of appeal to—

(a) the county court,

(aa) the family court,

(b) the High Court, or

(c) the Court of Appeal,
   may be exercised only with permission.

Add new paragraph 9A–841.1:

Note

Amended by the Crime and Courts Act 2013 Sch.9 para.52, Sch.10 para.79, with ef-   **9A–841.1**
fect from April 22, 2014 (see SI 2014/954).

Second appeals

Delete s.55(1) and substitute:

(1) Where an appeal is made to the county court, the family court   **9A–843**
or the High Court in relation to any matter, and on hearing the appeal the court makes a decision in relation to that matter, no appeal
may be made to the Court of Appeal from that decision unless the
Court of Appeal considers that—
   (a) the appeal would raise an important point of principle or
       practice, or
   (b) there is some other compelling reason for the Court of
       Appeal to hear it.

Note

Delete the second and third paragraphs and substitute:
Amended by the Crime and Courts Act 2013 Sch.9 para.52, Sch.10 para.80, with ef-   **9A–844**
fect from April 22, 2014 (see SI 2014/954).

Power to prescribe alternative destination of appeals

Delete s.56(1) and substitute:

(1) The Lord Chancellor may by order provide that appeals which   **9A–845**
would otherwise lie to—
   (a) the county court,
  (aa) the family court,
   (b) the High Court, or
   (c) the Court of Appeal,
       shall lie instead to another of those courts, as specified in
       the order.

Note

Delete the second and third paragraphs and substitute:
Amended by the Crime and Courts Act 2013 Sch.9 para.52, Sch.10 para.81, with ef-   **9A–847**
fect from April 22, 2014 (see SI 2014/954).

Assignment of appeals to Court of Appeal

Delete s.57(1) and substitute:

(1) Where in any proceedings in the county court, the family court   **9A–848**
or the High Court a person appeals, or seeks permission to appeal,
to a court other than the Court of Appeal or the Supreme Court
   (a) the Master of the Rolls, or
   (b) the court from which or to which the appeal is made, or
       from which permission to appeal is sought, or
   (c) the President of the Family Division where it is the family

court from which or to which the appeal is made, or from which permission to appeal is sought.

may direct that the appeal shall be heard instead by the Court of Appeal.

Note

Delete the second and third paragraphs and substitute:

9A–848.1   Amended by the Crime and Courts Act 2013 Sch.9 para.52, Sch.10 para.82, with effect from April 22, 2014 (see SI 2014/954).

Courts Act 2003

Schedule 7—Enforcement of Certain Writs and Warrants

Writs of execution against goods

Application of paragraphs 7 to 11

Delete Sch.7, para.6 and substitute:

9A–954   6.—(1) Paragraph 7 applies to any writ of execution against goods which is issued from the High Court.
(2) Paragraphs 8 to 11—
> (a) do not apply to any writ that confers power to use the procedure in Schedule 12 to the Tribunals, Courts and Enforcement Act 2007, but
> (b) apply to any other writ of execution against goods which is issued from the High Court.

Add new paragraph 9A–954.1:

Note

9A–954.1   Paragraph 6 substituted with savings by the Tribunals, Courts and Enforcement Act 2007, Sch.13, para.151, with effect from April 6, 2014 (SI 2014/768; for savings see art.2(2) to (6)).

Effect of writ

Delete para.8(4)–(5) and substitute:

9A–956   (4) Sub–paragraph (2) does not apply if the person acquiring goods of the execution debtor had notice, at the time of the acquisition, that—
> (a) an application for the issue of a warrant of execution against the goods of the execution debtor had been made to the county court, and
> (b) the warrant issued on the application remained unexecuted in the hands of a person charged with its execution.

(5) [...]

Note

Delete Note and substitute:

9A–956.1   Paragraph 8(5) repealed with savings by the Tribunals, Courts and Enforcement Act 2007 Sch.13 para.151, Sch.23 Pt 3, with effect from April 6, 2014 (SI 2014/768); for savings see art.2(2) to (6). Paragraph 8(4) amended, subject to savings and transitional provisions, by the Crime and Courts Act 2013 Sch.9 para.40(d), with effect from April 22, 2014 (see SI 2014/954); for savings and transitional provisions see Sch.8 to the Act and art.3 of SI 2014/954.

Tribunals, Courts and Enforcement Act 2007

Editorial note

Delete the first paragraph (beginning "This Act recieved") and substitute:

9A–1056.1   Part 3 (Enforcement by Taking Control of Goods) (ss.62 to 89) was brought into force with effect from April 6, 2014 by the Tribunals, Courts and Enforcement Act 2007 (Commencement No. 11) Order 2014 (SI 2014/768). Section 85 does not come into force in relation to licences to occupy land as commercial premises (see SI 2014/768. art.2(2)), so that parties may continue to negotiate for a commercial licence to include terms granting similar rights to distress for rent or CRAR, as such rights are not otherwise available in the licence context.

Certificates to act as an enforcement agent

Delete s.64(1) and substitute:

(1) A certificate may be issued under this section by a judge of the county court. **9A–1058**

Note

Delete Note and substitute:

Subsection (1) amended, subject to savings and transitional provisions, by the Crime and Courts Act 2013 Sch.9 para.46, with effect from April 6, 2014 (see SI 2014/830); for savings and transitional provisions see Sch.8 to the Act and art.3 of SI 2014/954. **9A–1058.1**

9B OTHER STATUTES AND REGULATIONS

Administration of Justice Act 1960

CONTEMPT OF COURT, HABEAS CORPUS AND CERTIORARI

Publication of information relating to proceedings in private

In s.12(1)(b), for "a county court" substitute:

the county court **9B–15**

Note

Add at end:

Subsection (1) amended, subject to savings and transitional provisions, by the Crime and Courts Act 2013 Sch.9 para.52, with effect from April 22, 2014 (see SI 2014/954); for savings and transitional provisions see Sch.8 to the Act. **9B–16**

Appeal in cases of contempt of court

Delete s.13(2)–(2A) and substitute:

(2) An appeal under this section shall lie in any case at the instance of the defendant and, in the case of an application for committal or attachment, at the instance of the applicant; and the appeal shall lie— **9B–18**

  (a) from an order or decision of any inferior court not referred to in the next following paragraph, to the High Court;
  (b) from an order or decision of the county court or any other inferior court from which appeals generally lie to the civil division of the Court of Appeal, and from an order or decision (other than a decision on an appeal under this section) of a single judge of the High Court, or of any court having the powers of the High Court or of a judge of that court, to the civil division of the Court of Appeal;
  (bb) from an order or decision of the Crown Court to the Court of Appeal;

    (c) from a decision of a single judge of the High Court on an appeal under this section, from an order or decision of a Divisional Court or the Court of Appeal (including a decision of either of those courts on an appeal under this section), and from an order or decision (except one made in Scotland or Northern Ireland) of the Court Martial Appeal Court, to the Supreme Court.

(2A) Paragraphs (a) to (c) of subsection (2) of this section do not apply in relation to appeals under this section from an order or decision of the family court, but (subject to any provision made under section 56 of the Access of Justice Act 1999 or by or under any other enactment) such an appeal shall lie to the Court of Appeal.

Delete s.13(5) and substitute:

(5) In this section "court" includes any tribunal or person having power to punish for contempt; and references in this section to an order or decision of a court in the exercise of jurisdiction to punish for contempt of court include references—

    (a) to an order or decision of the High Court, the family court, the Crown Court or the county court under any enactment enabling that court to deal with an offence as if it were contempt of court;

    (b) to an order or decision of the county court, under section 14, 92 or 118 of the County Courts Act 1984;

    (c) to an order or decision of a magistrates' court under subsection (3) of section 63 of the Magistrates' Courts Act 1980,

but do not include references to order under section five of the Debtors Act 1869, or under any provision of the Magistrates' Courts Act 1980, or the County Courts Act 1984, except those referred to in paragraphs (b) and (c) of this subsection and except sections 38 and 142 of the last mentioned Act so far as those sections confer jurisdiction in respect of contempt of court.

Note

Delete the second paragraph and substitute:

9B–19   Subsection (2A) inserted, and subss.(2), (5) amended, subject to savings and transitional provisions, by the Crime and Courts Act 2013 Sch.9 para.52, Sch.10 para.15, with effect from April 22, 2014 (see SI 2014/954); for savings and transitional provisions see Sch.8 to the Act and art.3 of SI 2014/954.

County Courts (Interest on Judgment Debts) Order 1991

In art.1(2), for the definition of "relevant judgement" substitute:

Citation, commencement, interpretation and savings

9B–70   "relevant judgment" means

        (a) a judgment or order of the county court for the payment of a sum of money—

            (i) of not less than £5,000; or

            (ii) in respect of a debt which is a qualifying debt for the purposes of the Late Payment of Commercial Debts (Interest) Act 1998; or

        (b) a judgment or order of, or registered in, the family court for the payment of a sum of money of not less than £5,000,and, in relation to a judgment debt, means the judgment or order which gives rise to the judgment debt;

Add new art.9B–70.1:

Note

In para.(2), definition of "relevant judgment" substituted by the Crime and Courts **9B–70.1** Act 2013 (County Court and Family Court: Consequential Provision) Order 2014 (SI 2014/1773), art.5, with effect from July 4, 2014.

The general rule

Add new art.2(5):

(5) A judgment debt under a relevant judgment of, or registered **9B–71** in, the family court does not carry interest under this Order if by virtue of any other enactment it does not carry interest.

Add new paragraph 9B–71.1:

Note

Paragraph 2(5) inserted by the Crime and Courts Act 2013 (County Court and Fam- **9B–71.1** ily Court: Consequential Provision) Order 2014 (SI 2014/1773), art.6, with effect from July 4, 2014.

Interest and enforcement or other proceedings

In art.4(1), for "a county court" substitute:

the county court or the family court **9B–73**

Add new paragraph 9B–73.1:

Note

Article 4(1) amended by the Crime and Courts Act 2013 (County Court and Family **9B–73.1** Court: Consequential Provision) Order 2014 (SI 2014/1773), art.7, with effect from July 4, 2014.

Rate of interest

In art.5(2), for "a county" substitute:

the appropriate **9B–74**

Add new art.5(3):

(3) In paragraph (2) "the appropriate court" means—
  (a) the county court if the judgment debt is under a relevant judgment of the county court;
  (b) the family court if the judgment debt is under a relevant judgment of, or registered in, the family court.

Add new paragraph 9B–74.1:

Note

Article 5(2) amended and art.5(3) inserted by the Crime and Courts Act 2013 **9B–74.1** (County Court and Family Court: Consequential Provision) Order 2014 (SI 2014/1773), art.8, with effect from July 4, 2014.

Delete title and substitute:

County Court Remedies Regulations 2014

(S.I. 2014 No. 982)

Introductory note

Delete paragraph 9B–77 and substitute:

These Regulations, made under powers conferred on the Lord Chancellor by the **9B–77**

County Courts Act 1984 s.38 (Remedies available in County Court), revoked and replaced the County Court Remedies Regulations 1991 (SI 1991/1222) with effect from April 22, 2014. Section 38(1) provides that the County Court may make any orders which the High Court could make if the proceedings were in the High Court. However, s.38(3) provides that the County Court does not have power to make an order of a prescribed kind. In this case "prescribed" means prescribed in these Regulations. In the County Court Remedies Regulations 1991 the orders of a prescribed kind which the County Court did not have power to make included freezing injunctions and search orders. The 2014 Regulations make no provision for freezing injunctions; consequently, that remedy is no longer prescribed and the County Court has unrestricted jurisdiction to make orders for that form of injunctive relief.

Delete paragraph 9B–78 and substitute:

9B–78 **1.**—(1) These Regulations may be cited as the County Court Remedies Regulations 2014 and come into force on 22nd April 2014 or, if made on or after that date, on the day after the day on which they are made.

(2) In these Regulations—

"judge of the County Court" is to be construed in accordance with section 5 of the County Courts Act 1984 Act; and

"search order" means an order under section 7 of the Civil Procedure Act 1997 (order requiring a party to admit another party to premises for the purpose of preserving evidence, etc.).

2. The County Court Remedies Regulations 1991 ("the 1991 Regulations") are revoked.

3.—(1) Subject to the following provisions of this regulation, the County Court shall not grant a search order or vary or revoke a search order made by the High Court.

(2) Paragraph (1) shall not apply to a judge of the Court of Appeal or a High Court Judge sitting as a judge of the County Court.

(3) Paragraph (1) shall not—

(a) affect or modify powers expressly conferred on the County Court by or under any enactment other than section 38 of the County Courts Act 1984; or

(b) prevent the County Court from varying a search order where all the parties are agreed on the terms of the variation.

4. An application to the High Court for a search order in County Court proceedings shall be deemed to include an application for transfer of the proceedings to the High Court.

5.—(1) After an application for a search order has been disposed of by the High Court, the proceedings shall, unless the High Court orders otherwise, be transferred to the County Court if—

(a) they were transferred to the High Court; or

(b) apart from these Regulations, they should have been commenced in the County Court.

(2) Where a search order is made on an application made without notice, the application shall not be treated as disposed of for the purposes of paragraph (1) until any application to set aside or vary the order has been heard, or until the expiry of 28 days (or such other period as the Court may specify) during which no such application has been made.

Add new paragraph 9B–78.1:

Note

Amended by the Crime and Courts Act 2013 (Family Court: Consequential Provision) (No.2) Order 2014 (SI 2014/879), art.23, with effect from April 22, 2014.　**9B–78.1**

Courts and Legal Services Act 1990

PART I

PROCEDURE ETC. IN CIVIL COURTS

ALLOCATION AND TRANSFER OF BUSINESS

Allocation of business between High Court and county courts

Delete s.1 and substitute:

1.—(1) The Lord Chancellor may by order make provision—　**9B–102**
   (a) conferring jurisdiction on the High Court in relation to proceedings in which the family court or the county court has jurisdiction;
   (b) conferring jurisdiction on the family court or the county court in relation to proceedings in which the High Court has jurisdiction;
   (c) allocating proceedings to the High Court or to the family court or to the county court;
   (d) specifying proceedings which may be commenced only in the High Court;
   (da) specifying proceedings which may be commenced only in the family court,
   (e) specifying proceedings which may be commenced only in the county court;
   (f) specifying proceedings which may be taken only in the High Court;
   (fa) specifying proceedings which may be taken only in the family court;
   (g) specifying proceedings which may be taken only in the county court.

(1A) An order under subsection (1)(a) or (b) may be made only with the concurrence of the Lord Chief Justice.

(2) Without prejudice to the generality of section 120(2), any such order may differentiate between categories of proceedings by reference to such criteria as the Lord Chancellor sees fit to specify in the order.

(3) The criteria so specified may, in particular, relate to—
   (a) the value of an action (as defined by the order);
   (b) the nature of the proceedings;
   (c) the parties to the proceedings;
   (ca) any relationship between the proceedings and any other proceedings;
   (d) the degree of complexity likely to be involved in any aspect of the proceedings; and
   (e) the importance of any question likely to be raised by, or in the course of, the proceedings.

(4) [. . .]
(5) [. . .]

(6) [. . .]

(7) Any such order may—

   (a) amend or repeal any provision falling within subsection (8) and relating to—

      (i) the jurisdiction, practice or procedure of the Senior Courts; or

      (ii) the jurisdiction, practice or procedure of the county court,

      or

      (iii) the jurisdiction, practice or procedure of the family court,

      so far as the Lord Chancellor considers it to be necessary, or expedient, in consequence of any provision made by the order; or

   (b) make such incidental or transitional provision as the Lord Chancellor considers necessary, or expedient, in consequence of any provision made by the order.

(8) A provision falls within this subsection if it is made by any enactment other than this Act or made under any enactment.

(9) Before making any such order the Lord Chancellor shall consult the Lord Chief Justice, the Master of the Rolls, the President of the Queen's Division, the President of the Family Division, the Chancellor of the High Court and the Senior Presiding Judge (appointed under section 72).

(10) No such order shall be made so as to confer jurisdiction on the family court or the county court to hear any application for judicial review.

(11) For the purposes of this section the commencement of proceedings may include the making of any application in anticipation of any proceedings or in the course of any proceedings.

(12) [. . .]

(13) The Lord Chief Justice may nominate a judicial office holder (as defined in section 109(4) of the Constitutional Reform Act 2005) to exercise his functions under this section.

Note

Delete the seventh paragraph and substitute:

9B–103   Amended by the Crime and Courts Act 2013, Sch.9 para.32, Sch.10 para.76, with effect from April 22, 2014 (see SI 2014/954).

Enforcement

Delete s.15(3) and substitute:

9B–115   (3) Where a person takes steps to enforce a judgment or order of the High Court, the family court or the county court for the payment of any sum due, the costs of any previous attempt to enforce that judgment shall be recoverable to the same extent as if they had been incurred in the taking of those steps.

Note

Delete Note and substitute:

9B–116   Subsection (1) repealed by the Courts Act 2003 s.109(3) Sch.10. Subsection (3) amended, subject to savings and transitional provisions, by the Crime and Courts Act

2013 Sch.9 para.34, with effect from April 22, 2014 (see SI 2014/954) (for savings and transitional provisions see Sch.8 to the Act and art.3 of SI 2014/954); and by the Crime and Courts Act 2013 (Family Court: Consequential Provision) Order 2014 (SI 2014/605) art.19, with effect from April 22, 2014 (being the day on which s.17(3) of the Crime and Courts Act 2013 comes into force).

Legal Services Act 2007

PRO BONO REPRESENTATION

Payments in respect of pro bono representation

Delete s.194(10) and substitute:

(10) In this section—   **9B–550**

"legal representative", in relation to a party to proceedings, means a person exercising a right of audience or conducting litigation on the party's behalf;

"civil court" means—

(a) the Supreme Court when it is dealing with a relevant civil appeal,

(b) the civil division of the Court of Appeal,

(c) the High Court, or

(ca) the family court,

(d) the county court;

"relevant civil appeal" means an appeal to the Supreme Court—

(a) from the High Court in England and Wales under Part 2 of the Administration of Justice Act 1969,

(b) from the Court of Appeal under section 40(2) of the Constitutional Reform Act 2005, or

(c) under section 13 of the Administration of Justice Act 1960 (appeal in cases of contempt of court) other than an appeal from an order or decision made in the exercise of jurisdiction to punish for criminal contempt of court;

"free of charge" means otherwise than for or in expectation of fee, gain or reward.

Note

Delete the second paragraph and substitute:

Amended by the Crime and Courts Act 2013 Sch.9 para.101, with effect from April **9B–550.1** 22, 2014 (see SI 2014/954) and by the Crime and Courts Act 2013 (Family Court: Consequential Provision) Order 2014 (SI 2014/605), art.25, with effect from April 22, 2014 (being the date on which section 17(3)of the Crime and Courts Act 2013 is brought fully into force).

SCHEDULE 3

EXEMPT PERSONS

Rights of audience

Delete para.1(7) and substitute:

(7) The person is exempt if—   **9B–594**

(a) the person is an individual whose work includes assisting in the conduct of litigation,

(b) the person is assisting in the conduct of litigation—

(i) under instructions given (either generally or in relation to the proceedings) by an individual to whom sub–paragraph (8) applies, and

(ii) under the supervision of that individual, and

(c) the proceedings are not reserved family proceedings and are being heard in chambers—

(i) in the High Court or county court, or

(ii) in the family court by a judge who is not, or by two or more judges at least one of whom is not, within section 31C(1)(y) of the Matrimonial and Family Proceedings Act 1984 (lay justices).

Delete para.1(10) and substitute:

(10) For the purposes of this paragraph—

"family proceedings" has the same meaning as in the Matrimonial and Family Proceedings Act 1984 (c. 42) and also includes any proceedings in the family court and any other proceedings which are family proceedings for the purposes of the Children Act 1989 (c. 41);

"reserved family proceedings" means such category of family proceedings as the Lord Chancellor may, after consulting the President of the Law Society and with the concurrence of the President of the Family Division, by order prescribe;

and any order made under section 27(9) of the Courts and Legal Services Act 1990 (c. 41) before the day appointed for the coming into force of this paragraph is to have effect on and after that day as if it were an order made under this sub–paragraph.

Note

Delete Note and substitute:

9B–594.1 Amended by the Crime and Courts Act 2013 Sch.10 para.98, with effect from April 22, 2014 (see SI 2014/954).

High Court and County Courts Jurisdiction Order 1991

Interpretation

Delete art.1A and substitute:

9B–929.1 **1A.** In this Order—

(a) "the EOP Regulation" means Regulation (EC) No 1896/2006 of the European Parliament and of the Council of 12 December 2006 creating a European order for payment procedure;

(b) "the ESCP Regulation" means Regulation (EC) No 861/2007 of the European Parliament and of the Council of 11 July 2007 establishing a European small claims procedure; and

(c) "the London insolvency district" means the insolvency district designated by the London Insolvency District (County Court at Central London) Order 2014.

Add new paragraph 9B–929.2:

Note

9B–929.2 Amended by the High Court and County Court Jurisdiction (Amendment) Order 2014 (SI 2014/821) with effect from April 22, 2014.

Jurisdiction

In art.2(1), for "A county court" substitute:

9B–930 The County Court

In art.2(1), in the words following subpara.(r), delete from "except as provided" to the end.

In art.2(2), for "A county court" substitute:

The County Court

In art.2(3), for "A county court" substitute:

The County Court

In art.2(4), for "A county court" substitute:

The County Court

In art.2(5), for "A county court" substitute:

The County Court

In art.2(6), for "A county court" substitute:

The County Court

In art.2(7), for "A county court" substitute:

The County Court

In art.2(7), for "a county court" substitute:

the County Court

In art.2(7A), for "A patents county court and the county courts listed in paragraph (7B)" substitute:

The County Court

Delete art.2(7B) and substitute:

(7B) The County Court has jurisdiction in respect of any contentious probate matter arising in connection with an application for the grant or revocation of probate or administration where—

    (a) the grant or application is made through the principal registry of the Family Division or a district probate registry under section 105 of the Senior Courts Act 1981; and

    (b) it is shown to the satisfaction of the County Court that the value of the deceased's net estate at the date of death does not exceed £30,000.

(7C) In paragraph (7B), "net estate", in relation to a deceased person, means the estate of that person exclusive of any property the deceased was possessed of or entitled to as a trustee and not beneficially, and after making allowances for funeral expenses and for debts and liabilities.

Omit art.2(8).

Note

Add at end (before the full stop):

; and the High Court and County Court Jurisdiction (Amendment) Order 2014 (SI **9B–931** 2014/821) with effect from April 22, 2014.

Injunctions

In art.3, for "a county court", both times it appears, substitute:

the County Court   **9B–933**

Add new paragraph 9B–933.1:

Note

Amended by the High Court and County Court Jurisdiction (Amendment) Order **9B–933.1** 2014 (SI 2014/821) with effect from April 22, 2014.

Allocation

Delete art.4 and substitute:

4. Subject to articles 5, 6, 6A to 6E, proceedings in which both the **9B–935** County Court and the High Court have jurisdiction may be commenced either in the County Court or in the High Court.

Delete art.4A and substitute:

4A. Except for proceedings to which article 5 applies, a claim for money in which the County Court has jurisdiction may only be commenced in the High Court if the value of the claim is more than £100,000.

In art.6A, for "a county court" substitute:

the County Court

In art.6B, for "a county court" substitute:

the County Court

Add new arts 6C to 6F:

6C. Proceedings for the exercise of the jurisdiction to wind up a company registered in England and Wales may be commenced only in the High Court if the place which has longest been the company's registered office during the 6 months immediately preceding the presentation of the petition for winding up is in the district that is the London insolvency district for the purposes of the second Group of Parts of the Insolvency Act 1986.

6D. Proceedings under section 1 of the Variation of Trusts Act 1958 may be commenced and taken only in the High Court.

6E. Proceedings under sections 98, 641(1)(b) and 645 to 651 of the Companies Act 2006 may be commenced and taken only in the High Court.

6F. The enactments listed in Part 1 of the Schedule to this Order are amended as specified therein, being amendments which are consequential on the amendments in articles 6C to 6E.

Note

Delete Note and substitute:

9B–936   Amended by the High Court and County Courts Jurisdiction (Amendment) Order 1993 (SI 1993/1407); the Access to Neighbouring Land Act 1992 s.7(2), and the High Court and County Court Jurisdiction (Amendment) Order 2014 with effect from April 22, 2014. Article 6B was inserted by SI 2008/2934. Article 4A was substituted and art.5(1) was amended in relation to proceedings issued on or after April 6, 2009 by the High Court and County Courts Jurisdiction (Amendment) Order 2009 (SI 2009/577). Articles 6C to 6F were inserted by the High Court and County Court Jurisdiction (Amendment) Order 2014 (SI 2014/821) with effect from April 22, 2014.

Enforcement

In art.8(1)(b), for "a county court" substitute:

9B–939   the County Court

In art.8(1A), for "a county court", both times it appears, substitute:

the County Court

In art.8(2)(a), for "a county court" substitute:

the County Court

Note

Add at end:

9B–940   Amended by the High Court and County Court Jurisdiction (Amendment) Order 2014 (SI 2014/821) with effect from April 22, 2014.

Enforcement of traffic penalties

In art.8A(1), for "Northampton" substitute:

9B–943   the

Note

Add at end (before the full stop):

; and the High Court and County Court Jurisdiction (Amendment) Order 2014 (SI **9B–944** 2014/821) with effect from April 22, 2014.

Enforcement of possession orders against trespassers

In art.8B, for "a county court", both times it appears, substitute:

the County Court   **9B–946**

Note

Add at end:

Amended by the High Court and County Court Jurisdiction (Amendment) Order **9B–947** 2014 (SI 2014/821) with effect from April 22, 2014.

Crown proceedings—transitional provisions

In art.11, for "a county court" substitute:

the County Court   **9B–952**

Add new paragraph 9B–952.1:

Note

Amended by the High Court and County Court Jurisdiction (Amendment) Order **9B–952.1** 2014 (SI 2014/821) with effect from April 22, 2014.

Attachment of Earnings Act 1971

CASES IN WHICH ATTACHMENT IS AVAILABLE

Courts with power to attach earnings

Delete s.1 and substitute:

1.—(1) The High Court may make an attachment of earnings or- **9B–955** der to secure payments under a High Court maintenance order.

(1A) The family court may make an attachment of earnings order to secure payments under a High Court or family court maintenance order.

(2) The county court may make an attachment of earnings order to secure—

    (a) [...]

    (b) the payment of a judgment debt, other than a debt of less than £5 or such other sum as may be prescribed by rules of court; or

    (c) payments under an administration order.

(3) A magistrates' court may make an attachment of earnings order to secure—

    (a) [...]

    (b) [...]

    (c) the payment of any sum required to be paid under regulations under section 23 or 24 of the Legal Aid, Sentencing and Punishment of Offenders Act 2012

(4) The following provisions of this Act apply, except where otherwise stated, to attachment of earnings orders made, or to be made, by any court.

(5) Any power conferred by this Act to make an attachment of

earnings order includes a power to make such an order to secure the discharge of liabilities arising before the coming into force of this Act.

Note

Delete the second paragraph and substitute:

9B–956   Amended by the Crime and Courts Act 2013 Sch.9 para.25, Sch.10 para.21, with effect from April 22, 2014 (see SI 2014/954).

Principal definitions

Delete s.2(b) and substitute:

9B–959   (b) "High Court maintenance order", "county court maintenance order" and "magistrates' court and "family court" maintenance order" mean respectively a maintenance order enforceable by the High Court, the county court and a magistrates court; and the family court;

Note.

Delete the second paragraph and substitute:

9B–959.1   Amended by the Crime and Courts Act 2013 Sch.9 para.25, Sch.10 para.22, with effect from April 22, 2014 (see SI 2014/954).

Application for order and conditions of court's power to make it

Delete s.3(1) and substitute:

9B–960   (1) The following persons may apply for an attachment of earnings order:—

   (a) the person to whom payment under the relevant adjudication is required to be made (whether directly or through any court or an officer of any court);

   (b) where the relevant adjudication is an administration order, any one of the creditors scheduled to the order;

   (c) without prejudice to paragraph (a) above, an officer of the family court if the application is to the family court for an order to secure maintenance payments and there is in force an order that those payments be made to the court or an officer of the court;

   (d) in the following cases the debtor—

      (i) where the application is to a magistrates' court; or

      (ii) where the application is to the High Court or the family court for an order to secure maintenance payments.

Delete s.3(4) and substitute:

   (4) Where proceedings are brought—

   (a) in the High Court or the family court for the enforcement of a maintenance order by committal under section 5 of the Debtors Act 1869;
   then, the court may make an attachment of earnings order to secure payments under the maintenance order, instead of dealing with the case under section 5 of the said Act of 1869.

Delete s.3(6)–(7) and substitute:

   (6) Where proceedings are brought in the county court for an or-

der of committal under section 5 of the Debtors Act 1869 in respect of a judgment debt for any of the taxes, contributions premiums or liabilities specified in Schedule 2 to this Act, the court may, in any circumstances in which it has power to make such an order, make instead an attachment of earnings order to secure the payment of the judgment debt.

(7) The county court shall not make an attachment of earnings order to secure the payment of a judgment debt if there is in force an order or warrant for the debtor's committal, under section 5 of the Debtors Act 1869, in respect of that debt; but in any such case the court may discharge the order or warrant with a view to making an attachment of earnings order instead.

Note

Delete the second paragraph and substitute:
Amended by the Crime and Courts Act 2013 Sch.9 para.25, Sch.10 para.23, with effect from April 22, 2014 (see SI 2014/954). Subsection (4)(b) amended, subject to savings, by the Tribunals, Courts and Enforcement Act 2007 Sch.13, para.36, with effect from April 6, 2014 (SI 2014/768; for savings see art.2(2) to (6)). **9B–961**

ADMINISTRATION ORDERS IN THE COUNTY COURT

Extension of power to make administration order

Delete s.4(1) and substitute:

(1) Where, on an application to the county court for an attachment of earnings order to secure the payment of a judgment debt, it appears to the court that the debtor also has other debts, the court— **9B–962**

    (a) shall consider whether the case may be one in which all the debtor's liabilities should be dealt with together and that for that purpose an administration order should be made; and

    (b) if of opinion that it may be such a case, shall have power (whether or not it makes the attachment of earnings order applied for), with a view to making an administration order, to order the debtor to furnish to the court a list of all his creditors and the amounts which he owes to them respectively.

Note

Delete second paragraph and substitute:
Amended by the Crime and Courts Act 2013 Sch.9 para.25, with effect from April 22, 2014 (see SI 2014/954). **9B–963**

Attachment of earnings to secure payments under administration order

Delete s.5 and substitute:

5.—(1) Where the county court makes an administration order in respect of a debtor's estate, it may also make an attachment of earnings order to secure the payments required by the administration order. **9B–964**

(2) At any time when an administration order is in force a county court may (with or without an application) make an attachment of earnings order to secure the payments required by the administration order, if it appears to the court that the debtor has failed to make any such payment.

(3) The power of the county court under this section to make an

attachment of earnings order to secure the payments required by an administration order shall, where the debtor is already subject to an attachment of earnings order to secure the payment of a judgment debt, include power to direct that the last–mentioned order shall take effect (with or without variation under section 9 of this Act) as an order to secure the payments required by the administration order.

Note

Delete Note and substitute:

9B–964.1 Amended by the Crime and Courts Act 2013 Sch.9 para.25, with effect from April 22, 2014 (see SI 2014/954).

CONSEQUENCES OF ATTACHMENT ORDER

Effect and contents of order

Delete s.6(7) and substitute:

9B–965 (7) For the purposes of an attachment of earnings order, the collecting officer of the court shall be (subject to later variation of the order under section 9 of this Act)—

> (a) in the case of an order made by the High Court, either—
>> (i) the proper officer of the High Court, or
>> (ii) the appropriate officer of the family court or the county court if the order so specifies;
> (aa) in the case of an order made by the family court, the appropriate officer of that court;
> (b) in the case of an order made by the county court, the appropriate officer of that court; and
> (c) in the case of an order made by a magistrates' court, the designated officer for that court or for another magistrates' court specified in the order.

Note

Delete the second paragraph and substitute:

9B–966 Amended by the Crime and Courts Act 2013 Sch.9 para.25, Sch.10 para.24, with effect from April 22, 2014 (see SI 2014/954).

Interrelation with alternative remedies open to creditors

Delete s.8(2)–(3) and substitute:

9B–969 (2) Where the county court has made an attachment of earnings order to secure the payment of a judgment debt—

> (a) no order or warrant of commitment shall be issued in consequence of any proceedings for the enforcement of the debt begun before the making of the attachment of earnings order; and
> (b) so long as the order is in force, no execution for the recovery of the debt shall issue against any property of the debtor without the leave of the county court.

(3) An attachment of earnings order made to secure maintenance payments shall cease to have effect upon the making of an order of commitment or the issue of a warrant of commitment for the enforcement of the related maintenance order.

Note

Delete the second paragraph and substitute:

Amended by the Crime and Courts Act 2013 Sch.9 para.25, Sch.10 para.25, with ef- **9B–970**
fect from April 22, 2014 (see SI 2014/954).

Normal deduction rate to be reduced in certain cases

Delete s.10(2)–(3) and substitute:

(2) In the case of an order made by the High Court or the family **9B–973**
court, the collecting officer shall give the prescribed notice to the
person to whom he is required to pay sums received under the attachment of earnings order, and to the debtor; and the court shall
make the appropriate variation order, unless the debtor requests it
to discharge the attachment of earnings order, or to vary it in some
other way, and the court thinks fit to comply with the request.

(3) [...]

Note

Delete Note and substitute:

Amended by the Crime and Courts Act 2013 Sch.10 para.26, with effect from April **9B–973.1**
22, 2014 (see SI 2014/954).

Attachment order in respect of maintenance payments to cease to have effect on the occurrence of certain events

Delete s.11(1) and substitute:

(1) An attachment of earnings order made to secure maintenance **9B–974**
payments shall cease to have effect—

(a) upon the grant of an application for registration of the related maintenance order under section 2 of the Maintenance Orders Act 1958 (which provides for the registration in the family court of a High Court maintenance
order);

(b) where the related maintenance order is registered under
Part I of the said Act of 1958, upon the giving of notice
with respect thereto under section 5 of that Act (notice
with view to cancellation of registration);

(c) subject to subsection (3) below, upon the discharge of the
related maintenance order while it is not registered under
Part I of the said Act of 1958;

(d) upon the related maintenance order ceasing to be registered in a court in England or Wales, or becoming
registered in a court in Scotland or Northern Ireland,
under Part II of the Maintenance Orders Act 1950.

Note

Delete Note and substitute:

Amended by the Crime and Courts Act 2013 Sch.10 para.27, with effect from April **9B–974.1**
22, 2014 (see SI 2014/954).

ADMINISTRATIVE PROVISIONS

Application of sums received by collecting officer

Delete s.13(3) and substitute:

(3) Where the county court makes an attachment of earnings order **9B–976**

to secure the payment of a judgment debt and also, under section 4(1) of this Act, orders the debtor to furnish to the court a list of all his creditors, sums paid to the collecting officer in compliance with the attachment of earnings order shall not be dealt with by him as mentioned in subsection (1) above, but shall be retained by him pending the decision of the court whether or not to make an administration order and shall then be dealt with by him as the court may direct.

Note

Delete Note and substitute:

9B–976.1   Amended by the Crime and Courts Act 2013 Sch.9 para.25, with effect from April 22, 2014 (see SI 2014/954).

Power of court to determine whether particular payments are earnings

Delete s.16(2) and substitute:

9B–981   (2) The persons referred to in subsection (1) above are—

  (a) the employer;

  (b) the debtor.

  (c) the person to whom payment under the relevant adjudication is required to be made (whether directly or through an officer of any court); and

  (d) without prejudice to paragraph (c) above, where the application is in respect of an attachment of earnings order made to secure payments under a family court maintenance order, the collecting officer.

Note

Delete Note and substitute:

9B–981.1   Amended by the Crime and Courts Act 2013 Sch.10 para.29, with effect from April 22, 2014 (see SI 2014/954).

Consolidated attachment orders

Delete s.17(1) and substitute:

9B–982   (1) The powers of the county court under sections 1 and 3 of this Act shall include power to make an attachment of earnings order to secure the payment of any number of judgment debts; and the powers of a magistrates' court under those sections or under Schedule 5 to the Courts Act 2003, and the powers of a fines officer under that Schedule, shall include power to make an attachment of earnings order to secure the discharge of any number of such liabilities as are specified in section 1(3)of this Act and paragraph 1 of Schedule 5 to the Courts Act 2003.

Note

Delete the second paragraph and substitute:

9B–983   Amended by the Crime and Courts Act 2013 Sch.9 para.25, with effect from April 22, 2014 (see SI 2014/954).

Certain action not to be taken by collecting officer except on request

Delete s.18 and substitute:

18.—(1) Where payments under a maintenance order are payable **9B–984** to the family court or an officer of the family court for transmission to a person, no officer of the family court is to—

    (a) apply for an attachment of earnings order to secure payments under the maintenance order; or

    (b) except as provided by section 10(3) of this Act, apply for an order discharging or varying such an attachment of earnings order; or

    (c) apply for a determination under section 16 of this Act, unless he is requested in writing to do so by a person entitled to receive the payments through the family court or an officer of that court.

  (2) Where an officer of the family court is so requested—

    (a) he shall comply with the request unless it appears to him unreasonable in the circumstances to do so; and

    (b) the person by whom the request was made shall have the same liabilities for all the costs properly incurred in or about any proceedings taken in pursuance of the request as if the proceedings has been taken by that person.

  (3) [...]

Note

Delete the second paragraph and substitute:
Amended by the Crime and Courts Act 2013 Sch.10 para.30, with effect from April 22, 2014 (see SI 2014/954).

Jurisdiction in respect of persons residing outside England and Wales

Delete s.20 and substitute:

20.—(1) It is hereby declared that the family court has jurisdiction **9B–987** to hear an application by or against a person residing outside England and Wales for the discharge or variation of an attachment of earnings order made by the family court to secure maintenance payments; and where such an application is made, the following provisions shall have effect.

  (2) If the person resides in Scotland or Northern Ireland, section 15 of the Maintenance Orders Act 1950 (which relates to the service of process on persons residing in those countries) shall have effect in relation to the application as it has effect in relation to the proceedings therein mentioned.

  (3) Subject to the following subsection, if the person resides outside the United Kingdom and does not appear at the time and place appointed for the hearing of the application, the court may, if it thinks it reasonable in all the circumstances to do so, proceed to hear and determine the application at the time and place appointed for the hearing, or for any adjourned hearing, in like manner as if the person had then appeared.

(4) Subsection (3) above shall apply only if it is proved to the satisfaction of the court, on oath or in such other manner as may be prescribed, that the applicant has taken such steps as may be prescribed to give to the said person notice of the application and of the time and place appointed for the hearing of it.

Note

Delete Note and substitute:

9B–987.1 Amended by the Crime and Courts Act 2013 Sch.10 para.31, with effect from April 22, 2014 (see SI 2014/954).

Costs on application under s.16

Delete s.21 and substitute:

9B–988 **21.**—(1) On making a determination under section 16 of this Act, a magistrates' court may in its discretion make such order as it thinks just and reasonable for payment by any of the persons mentioned in subsection (2) of that section of the whole or any part of the costs of the determination.

(2) Costs ordered to be paid under this section shall—

(a) in the case of costs to be paid by the debtor to the person in whose favour the attachment of earnings order in question was made, be deemed to be a sum due to the designated officer for the magistrates' court; and

(b) in any other case, be enforceable as a civil debt.

Note

Delete the second paragraph and substitute:

Amended by the Crime and Courts Act 2013 Sch.10 para.32, with effect from April 22, 2014 (see SI 2014/954).

Enforcement provisions

Delete s.23(1)–(1A) and substitute:

9B–991 (1) If, after being served with notice of an application to a county court for an attachment of earnings order or for the variation of such an order or with an order made under section 14(2)(b) above, the debtor fails to attend on the day and at the time specified for any hearing of the application or specified in the order, the court may adjourn the hearing and order him to attend at a specified time on another day; and if the debtor—

(a) fails to attend at that time on that day; or

(b) attends, but refuses to be sworn or give evidence,
he may be ordered by the court to be imprisoned for not more than fourteen days.

(1A) In any case where the court has power to make an order of imprisonment under subsection (1) for failure to attend, the court may, in lieu of or in addition to making that order, order the debtor to be arrested and brought before the court either forthwith or at such time as the court may direct.

Delete s.23(3)–(4) and substitute:

(3) Where a person commits an offence under subsection (2) above in relation to proceedings in, or to an attachment of earnings order

made by, the High Court or the county court, he shall be liable on summary conviction to a fine of not more than level 2 on the standard scale or he may be ordered by a judge of the High Court or by the county court (as the case may be) to pay a fine of not more than £250 or, in the case of an offence specified in subsection (4) below, to be imprisoned for not more than fourteen days; and where a person commits an offence under subsection (2) otherwise than as mentioned above in this subsection, he shall be liable on summary conviction to a fine of not more than level 2 on the standard scale.

(4) The offences referred to above in the case of which a judge or court may impose imprisonment are—

(a) an offence under subsection (2)(c) or (d), if committed by the debtor; and

(b) an offence under subsection (2)(e) or (f), whether committed by the debtor or any other person.

Delete s.23(7)–(8) and substitute:

(7) Where under this section a person is ordered by a judge of the High Court or by the county court to be imprisoned, or court may at any time revoke the order and, if the person is already in custody, order his discharge.

(8) Any fine imposed by a judge of the High Court under subsection (3) above and any sums ordered by the High Court to be paid under subsection (6) above shall be recoverable in the same way as a fine imposed by that court in the exercise of its jurisdiction to punish for contempt of court; section 129 of the County Courts Act 1984 (enforcement of fines) shall apply to payment of a fine imposed by the county court under subsection (3) and of any sums ordered by the county court to be paid under subsection (6); and any sum ordered by a magistrates' court to be paid under subsection (6) shall be recoverable as a sum adjudged to be paid on a conviction by that court.

Delete s.23(10A)–(11) and substitute:

(10A) This section applies in relation to the family court as it applies in relation to the county court, but as if the reference in subsection (8) to section 129 of the County Courts Act 1984 were a reference to section 31L(1) of the Matrimonial and Family Proceedings Act 1984.

(11) [...]

Note

Delete the second paragraph and substitute:
Amended by the Crime and Courts Act 2013 Sch.9 para.25, Sch.10 para.33, with ef- **9B–992** fect from April 22, 2014 (see SI 2014/954).

General interpretation

Delete s.25(1) and substitute:

(1) In this Act, except where the context otherwise requires— **9B–995**
"administration order" means an order made under, and so referred to in, Part VI of the County Courts Act 1984;
"the court", in relation to an attachment of earnings order, means the court which made the order, subject to rules of

court as to the venue for, and the transfer of, proceedings in the county court and magistrates' courts;

"debtor" and "relevant adjudication" have the meanings given by section 2 of this Act;

"the employer", in relation to an attachment of earnings order, means the person who is required by the order to make deductions from earnings paid by him to the debtor;

"the fines officer", in relation to a debtor who is subject to a collection order made under Schedule 5 to the Courts Act 2003, means any fines officer working at the fines office specified in that order;

"judgment debt" has the meaning given by section 2 of this Act;

"maintenance order" has the meaning given by section 2 of this Act;

"maintenance payments" means payments required under a maintenance order;

"prescribed" means prescribed by rules of court;

and, in relation to a magistrates' court, references to a single justice are to a justice of the peace acting for the same petty sessions area as the court.

Note

Delete the second paragraph and substitute:

9B–996 Amended by the Crime and Courts Act 2013 Sch.9 para.25(6), with effect from April 22, 2014 (see SI 2014/954).

SCHEDULE 1

MAINTENANCE ORDERS TO WHICH THIS ACT APPLIES

Delete paras 11, 12, 13, 14, 14A, 15 and 16 and substitute:

9B–1004 11. A maintenance order within the meaning of Part I of the Maintenance Orders (Reciprocal Enforcement) Act 1972 registered in the family court under the said Part I.

12. An order under section 34(1)(b) of the Children Act 1975 (payments of maintenance in respect of a child to his custodian).

13. A maintenance order within the meaning of Part I of the Civil Jurisdiction and Judgments Act 1982 which is registered in the family court under that Part.

14. A maintenance judgment within the meaning of Council Regulation (EC) No. 44/2001 of 22nd December 2000 on jurisdiction and the recognition and enforcement of judgments in civil and commercial matters, as amended from time to time and as applied by the Agreement made on 19th October 2005 between the European Community and the Kingdom of Denmark on jurisdiction and the recognition and enforcement of judgments in civil and commercial matters (OJ No. L 299 16.11.2005 at p62) which is registered in a court in England and Wales under that Regulation.

14A.—(1) A decision, court settlement or authentic instrument which falls to be enforced by the family court by virtue of the Maintenance Regulation and the Civil Jurisdiction and Judgments (Maintenance) Regulations 2011.

(2) In this paragraph—

"the Maintenance Regulation" means Council Regulation (EC) No 4/2009 including as applied in relation to Denmark by virtue of the Agreement made on 19th October 2005 between the European Community and the Kingdom of Denmark;

"decision", "court settlement" and "authentic instrument" have the meanings given by Article 2 of that Regulation.

15. An order made under Schedule 5 to the Civil Partnership Act 2004 (financial relief in the High Court or the county court etc financial relief: provision corresponding to provision made by Part 2 of the Matrimonial Causes Act 1973),for periodical or other payments.

16. An order made under Schedule 6 to the 2004 Act (financial relief: provision corresponding

to provision made by the Domestic Proceedings and Magistrates' Courts Act 1978), for maintenance or other payments to or in respect of a civil partner or child.

Note

Delete the second paragraph and substitute:

Amended by the Crime and Courts Act 2013 Sch.9 para.25(3), with effect from April **9B–1005** 22, 2014 (see SI 2014/954). Further amended by the Crime and Courts Act 2013 (Family Court: Consequential Provision) Order 2014 (SI 2014/605), art.5, with effect from April 22, 2014 (being the date on which s.17(3) of the Crime and Courts Act 2013 is brought fully into force).

Charging Orders Act 1979

CHARGING ORDERS

Charging orders

Delete s.1 and substitute:

1.—(1) Where, under a judgment or order of the High Court or **9B–1017** the family court or the county court, a person (the "debtor") is required to pay a sum of money to another person (the "creditor") then, for the purpose of enforcing that judgment or order, the appropriate court may make an order in accordance with the provisions of this Act imposing on any such property of the debtor as may be specified in the order a charge for securing the payment of any money due or to become due under the judgment or order.

(2) The appropriate court is—

    (a) in a case where the property to be charged is a fund in court, the court in which that fund is lodged;

    (b) in a case where paragraph (a) above does not apply and the order to be enforced is a maintenance order of the High Court or an order for costs made in family proceedings in the High Court, the High Court or the county court;

    (c) in a case where neither paragraph (a) nor paragraph (b) above applies and the judgment or order to be enforced is a judgment or order of the High Court for a sum exceeding the county court limit, the High Court or the county court; and

    (d) in any other case, the county court.

    In this section "county court limit" means the county court limit for the time being specified in an Order in Council under section 145 of the County Courts Act 1984, as the county court limit for the purposes of this section and "maintenance order" has the same meaning as in section 2(a) of the Attachment of Earnings Act 1971.

(3) An order under subsection (1) above is referred to in this Act as a "charging order".

(4) Where a person applies to the High Court for a charging order to enforce more than one judgment or order, that court shall be the appropriate court in relation to the application if it would be the appropriate court, apart from this subsection, on an application relating to one or more of the judgments or orders concerned.

(5) In deciding whether to make a charging order the court shall consider all the circumstance of the case and, in particular, any evidence before it as to—

    (a) the personal circumstances of the debtor, and

    (b) whether any other creditor of the debtor would be likely to be unduly prejudiced by the making of the order.

(6) Subsections (7) and (8) apply where, under a judgment or order of the High Court or the family court or the county court, a debtor is required to pay a sum of money by instalments.

(7) The fact that there has been no default in payment of the instalments does not prevent a charging order from being made in respect of that sum.

(8) But if there has been no default, the court must take that into account when considering the circumstances of the case under subsection (5).

(9) In this section "family proceedings" means proceedings in the Family Division of the High Court which are business assigned, by or under section 61 of (and Schedule 1 to) the Senior Courts Act 1981, to that Division of the High Court and no other.

Note

Delete the second paragraph and substitute:

9B–1018   Amended by the Crime and Courts Act 2013 Sch.9 para.52, Sch.10 para.38(2), with effect from April 22, 2014 (see SI 2014/954). Further amended by the Crime and Courts Act 2013 (Family Court: Consequential Provision) Order 2014 (SI 2014/605), art.15, with effect from April 22, 2014 (being the date on which s.17(3) of the Crime and Courts Act 2013 is brought fully into force).

"appropriate court may make an order"

For "County Court Jurisdiction Order 1981 (SI 1981/1123)", substitute:

9B–1020   County Court Jurisdiction Order 2014 (SI 2014/503), art.3,

Provisions supplementing sections 1 and 2

Delete s.3(4A) and substitute:

9B–1022   (4A) Subsections (4C) to (4E) apply where—

    (a) a debtor is required to pay a sum of money in instalments under a judgment or order of the High Court or the county court (an "instalments order"), and

    (b) a charge has been imposed by a charging order in respect of that sum.

Note

Delete the third paragraph and substitute:

9B–1023   Amended by the Crime and Courts Act 2013 Sch.9 para.52, with effect from April 22, 2014 (see SI 2014/954).

SUPPLEMENTAL

Interpretation

Delete s.6(2) and substitute:

9B–1026   (2) For the purposes of sections 1 and 3 of this Act references to a judgment or order of the High Court or the county court shall be taken to include references to a judgment, order, decree or award (however called) of any court or arbitrator (including any foreign court or arbitrator) which is or has become enforceable (whether wholly or to a limited extent) as if it were a judgment or order of the High Court or the county court.

Note

Delete the third paragraph and substitute:
Amended by the Crime and Courts Act 2013 Sch.9 para.52, with effect from April **9B–1027** 22, 2014 (see SI 2014/954).

Civil Evidence Act 1968

Findings of adultery and paternity as evidence in civil proceedings

Delete s.12(5) and substitute:
(5) In this section—   **9B–1036**
"matrimonial proceedings" means any matrimonial cause in the High Court or family court in England and Wales or in the High Court in Northern Ireland, any consistorial action in Scotland, or any appeal arising out of any such cause or action;
"relevant proceedings" means—
(a) proceedings on a complaint under section 42 of the National Assistance Act 1948 or section 26 of the Social Security Act 1986;
(b) proceedings under the Children Act 1989;
(c) proceedings which would have been relevant proceedings for the purposes of this section in the form in which it was in force before the passing of the Children Act 1989;
"affiliation proceedings" means, in relation to Scotland, any action of affiliation and aliment;
and in this subsection "consistorial action" does not include an action of aliment only between husband and wife raised in the Court of Session or an action of interim aliment raised in the sheriff court.

Note

Delete the second paragraph and substitute:
Amended by the Crime and Courts Act 2013 Sch.10 para.17, with effect from April **9B–1037** 22, 2014 (see SI 2014/954).

Litigants in Person (Costs and Expenses) Act 1975

Costs or expenses recoverable

Delete s.1(1)(a) and substitute:
(1) (a) in England and Wales in the county court or in Northern **9B–1210** Ireland in a county court, in the family court, in the Senior Courts, in the Court of Judicature or in the Supreme Court on appeal from the High Court or the Court of Appeal,

Note

Delete the second paragraph and substitute:
Amended by the Crime and Courts Act 2013 Sch.9 para.103, Sch.10 para.35, with **9B–1210.1** effect from April 22, 2014 (see SI 2014/954).

Late Payment of Commercial Debts (Interest) Act 1998

When does the statutory interest start to run?

At the end of the third paragraph (beginning "Interest runs on"), add:

9B–1338   See also *E–Nik Ltd v Secretary of State for Communities and Local Government* [2012] EWHC 3027 (Comm), [2013] 2 All E.R (Comm) 868 (Burton J.).

Distress for Rent Rules 1988

Editorial Introduction

Add at end:

9B–1365   The Distress for Rent Rules 1988 are revoked subject to transitional and saving provisions, by the Tribunals, Courts and Enforcement Act 2007 (Consequential, Transitional and Saving Provisions) Order 2014 (SI 2014/600), Sch, Pt.2, with effect from April 6, 2014 (for transitional and saving provisions see arts 3–6).

Crime and Courts Act 2013

Add new paragraph 9B–1425.1:

Note

9B–1425.1   This section was brought into force on January 7, 2014, by the Crime and Courts Act 2013 (Commencement No. 7 and Saving and Consequential Provisions) Order 2013 (SI 2013/3176).

Effect of section

Add at end:

9B–1430   This section was brought into force on June 25, 2013, by s.61(6) of the Act.

Add SI 2014/421:

Certification of Enforcement Agents Regulations 2014

9B–1432   (2014 /421)

Citation, commencement and extent

9B–1433   **1.**—(1) These Regulations may be cited as the Certification of Enforcement Agents Regulations 2014 and come into force on 6th April 2014.

(2) These Regulations extend to England and Wales only.

Interpretation

General interpretation

9B–1434   **2.** In these Regulations—

"the Act" means the Tribunals, Courts and Enforcement Act 2007;

"the 1888 Act" means the Law of Distress Amendment Act 1888(b);

"the 1895 Act" means the Law of Distress Amendment Act 1895(c);

"the 1988 Rules" means the Distress for Rent Rules 1988(a);

"applicant" means a person applying for a certificate to be issued under section 64 of the Act;

"certificate" means a certificate under section 64 of the Act to act as an enforcement agent and includes a certificate under section 7 of the 1888 Act which by virtue of section 64(4) of the Act has effect as a certificate under section 64 of the Act;

"certificated person" means a person to whom a certificate has been issued;

"commercial rent arrears recovery" has the meaning given by section 72 of the Act;

"complainant" means a person who makes a complaint to the court under regulation 9;

"court" means the County Court;

"enforcement agent" has the meaning given in paragraph 2(1) of Schedule 12 (enforcement agents);

"Schedule 12" means Schedule 12 to the Act;

"the security" means the security required by regulation 6(1) of these Regulations.

Issue of certificates

Issue of certificates

3. A certificate may be issued under section 64 of the Act only—   **9B–1435**

(a) on application by the person to whom the certificate is to be issued; and

(b) if the judge is satisfied that—

(i) the applicant is a fit and proper person to hold a certificate;

(ii) the applicant possesses sufficient knowledge of the law and procedure relating to powers of enforcement by taking control of goods and of commercial rent arrears recovery to be competent to exercise those powers;

(iii) the forms which the applicant intends to use when exercising powers of taking control of goods or commercial rent arrears recovery conform to the design and layout prescribed in the Schedule to these Regulations;

(iv) the applicant has lodged the security required by regulation 6(1), or such security is already subsisting; and

(v) the applicant does not carry on, and is not and will not be employed in, a business which includes buying debts.

Information about certificates and applications

4.—(1) The court must compile and maintain a list of all certificated **9B–1436** persons who hold a certificate which has not expired or been cancelled.

(2) The list required by paragraph (1) must contain, for each certificated person—

(a) the certificated person's name;

(b) the name of the certificated person's employer, if any; (c)

(c) the date of issue of the certificate; and

(d) the date on which the certificate ceases to have effect.

(3) The list required by paragraph (1) must be published on a website maintained by or on behalf of Her Majesty's Courts and Tribunals Service.

(4) The court must also publish, on the website referred to in paragraph (3), notice of every application made to the court for a certificate to be issued under section 64.

(5) The notice required by paragraph (4) must contain the following information—

(a) the applicant's name;

(b) the name of the applicant's employer, if any;

(c) the date on which the application will be heard, which must be at least eight days after the date in sub–paragraph (f);

(d) that any person who knows of any reason or reasons why the applicant may not be a fit and proper person to hold a certificate may give the reason or reasons to the court;

(e) that reasons given under sub–paragraph (d) must be given in writing;

(f) the date by which a person must give a reason or reasons to the court under sub–paragraph (d), which must be at least 30 days from the date on which the notice is published on the website.

When application may be heard

9B–1437   **5.** No application for a certificate to be issued will be heard before the date in regulation 4(5)(c).

Security

9B–1438   **6.**—(1) The applicant must, before a certificate is issued—

(a) lodge in court by way of bond security totalling £10,000; or

(b) satisfy the judge that security totalling that amount is already subsisting by way of bond.

(2) The security must be retained once the certificate has been issued for the purpose of securing the certificated person's duties as an enforcement agent and the payment of any reasonable costs, fees and expenses incurred in the investigation of any complaint made to the court against the certificated person in the capacity of an enforcement agent.

(3) The certificated person must maintain the security throughout the duration of the certificate.

(4) If at any time during the duration of the certificate the security no longer exists, or is reduced in value so it totals less than £10,000, the certificated person must, by such time as the court may direct, provide fresh security to the satisfaction of the court.

Duration of certificates

9B–1439   **7.**—(1) A certificate has effect, unless cancelled, for two years from the date on which it was issued, subject in the case of a replacement certificate to regulation 8(3).

(2) Every certificate must state the date on which it ceases to have effect.

Issue of replacement certificate following change of relevant details

8.—(1) If there is for any certificated person a change in any of the **9B–1440** matters referred to in regulation 4(2)(a) and (b) (name, business address and employer of a certificated person), the certificated person must as soon as possible notify the court in writing of the change or changes, and produce the certificate to the court.

(2) Where a certificated person notifies the court and produces the certificate in accordance with paragraph (1), the certificate must be cancelled, and a replacement certificate issued to the certificated person, as soon possible.

(3) The replacement certificate must reflect the change notified, but in all other respects, including the date on which it ceases to have effect, must be the same as the cancelled certificate.

(4) No fee is payable for cancellation of a certificate and issue of a replacement certificate under this regulation.

Complaints and cancellation of certificates

Complaints as to fitness to hold a certificate

9.—(1) Any person who considers that a certificated person is by **9B–1441** reason of the certificated person's conduct in acting as an enforcement agent, or for any other reason, not a fit person to hold a certificate, may submit a complaint in writing to the court.

(2) No fee is payable for submitting a complaint under paragraph (1).

(3) A complaint submitted under paragraph (1) must provide details of the matters complained of and explain the reason or reasons why the certificated person is not a fit person to hold a certificate.

(4) No complaint submitted under paragraph (1) may be considered by the judge until the certificated person has been provided with a copy of the complaint and given an opportunity to respond to it in writing.

(5) If on considering the complaint and the certificated person's response the judge is satisfied that the certificated person remains a fit and proper person to hold a certificate, the complaint must be dismissed.

(6) If—
    (a) the certificated person fails to respond; or
    (b) on considering the complaint and the certificated person's response the judge is not satisfied that the certificated person remains a fit and proper person to hold a certificate,
    the complaint must be considered at a hearing.

(7) If a complaint is to be considered at a hearing under paragraph (6)—
    (a) the certificated person must attend for examination and may make representations; and

(b) the complainant may attend and make representations, or may make representations in writing.

(8) If after a hearing the judge is satisfied that the certificated person remains a fit and proper person to hold a certificate, the complaint must be dismissed.

(9) No appeal lies against the dismissal of a complaint under paragraph (5) or paragraph (8).

Cancellation or suspension of certificates

9B–1442   10.—(1) If, following consideration of a complaint at a hearing, the judge is satisfied that the certificated person is not a fit and proper person to hold a certificate, the judge may—

(a) cancel the certificate; or

(b) suspend the certificate.

(2) If the certificate is cancelled, the judge may order that the certificated person must, before making any further application to be issued with a certificate, have fulfilled such conditions as to training or any other conditions the judge considers necessary for the certificated person to be a fit and proper person to hold a certificate.

(3) If the certificate is suspended the judge may order that the suspension is not to be lifted until the certificated person has fulfilled such conditions as to training or any other conditions the judge considers necessary for the certificated person to be a fit and proper person to hold a certificate.

(4) The court must, whether the certificate is suspended or cancelled, consider whether to make an order under regulation 13(2).

Application of security after consideration of complaint at a hearing

9B–1443   11.—(1) When a complaint has been considered at a hearing, the judge may, if satisfied that the complaint was well founded, order that the security be forfeited either wholly or in part, and that the forfeited amount be paid, in such proportions as the judge considers appropriate—

(a) to the complainant by way of compensation for failure in due performance of the certificated person's duties as an enforcement agent or for the complainant's costs or expenses in attending and making representations; and

(b) where costs or expenses have been incurred by the court in considering the complaint at a hearing, to Her Majesty's Paymaster General by way of reimbursement of those costs or expenses.

(2) The judge may make an order under paragraph (1) whether or not the certificate is cancelled or suspended.

(3) If an order is made under paragraph (1) but the certificate is not cancelled, regulation 6(4) applies.

(4) If the certificate is cancelled, the security must, subject to the making of an order under paragraph (1), be cancelled and the balance of any deposit, following payment of any amounts ordered to be forfeited, returned to the certificated person.

Surrender of certificate

9B–1444   12.—(1) When a certificate is cancelled or expires, it must be surrendered to the court, unless the judge directs otherwise.

(2) If a certificated person ceases to carry on business as an enforcement agent, the certificated person must unless the judge orders

528

otherwise surrender the certificate to the court, and the certificate will be treated as if it had expired on the date on which it was surrendered.

(3) The security must be cancelled and the balance of any deposit returned to the certificated person following surrender of a certificate.

Continuing effect of certificate in certain circumstances

13.—(1) This regulation applies in any case where— 9B–1445
    (a) a certificate is cancelled or has expired, or is suspended; and
    (b) before the cancellation, expiry or suspension, the certificated person took control of goods (within the meaning given by paragraph 13(1) of Schedule 12 (ways of taking control)).

(2) In such a case, unless the court orders otherwise, the goods continue to be controlled goods and the certificate continues to have effect, for the purpose of any action which may be taken in relation to the goods as controlled goods under Schedule 12, as if it had not been cancelled, or expired, or suspended as the case may be.

Transitional, saving and consequential provisions

Applications for grant of certificate made under the 1988 Rules

14.—(1) The 1988 Rules continue to apply in relation to— 9B–1446
    (a) an application for the grant of a certificate which was made before 6th April 2014 by a person who does not hold a certificate but was not determined before that date;
    (b) an application for the grant of a certificate to replace an existing certificate which ceases to have effect on or before 6th August 2014.

(2) A certificate granted on or after 6th April 2014 pursuant to an application referred to in paragraph (1)(a) or (b) has effect as a certificate under section 64 of the Act in the same way as a certificate under section 7 of the 1888 Act which is in force on that date.

Duration of certificates granted under section 7 of the 1888 Act

15. A certificate under section 7 of the 1888 Act which is in force 9B–1447
on 6th April 2014 shall have effect for the period provided for when it was granted.

Add new paragraph 9B–1448:

Note

The Schedule to the Certification of Enforcement Agents Regulations (SI 2014/421) 9B–1448
contains new enforcement regulation forms, which we publish in the Forms Volume under the heading "Enforcement Regulation Forms".

SECTION 10

COURT FEES

Civil Proceedings Fees Order 2008

Citation and commencement

In r.1(2)(a), for "Bulk" substitute:

Business 10–1

Note

Add at end:

10–1.1 Further amended by the Civil Proceedings Fees (Amendment) Order 2014 (SI 2014/ 874), with effect from April 22, 2014.

In r.2, for "county courts" substitute:

10–2 County Court

Add new paragraph 10–2.1:

Note

10–2.1 Amended by the Civil Proceedings Fees (Amendment) Order 2014 (SI 2014/874), with effect from April 22, 2014.

In r.3(e), for "county court" substitute:

10–3 County Court

Add new paragraph 10–3.1:

Note

10–3.1 Amended by the Civil Proceedings Fees (Amendment) Order 2014 (SI 2014/874), with effect from April 22, 2014.

Delete Sch.1 and substitute:

SCHEDULE 1

FEES TO BE TAKEN

10–7

Column 1 *Number and description of fee*	Column 2 *Amount of fee*
1 Starting proceedings (High Court and county court)	
1.1 On starting proceedings (including proceedings issued after permission to issue is granted but excluding CCBC cases brought by Centre users or cases brought by Money Claim OnLine users) to recover a sum of money where the sum claimed:	
(a) does not exceed £300;	£35
(b) exceeds £300 but does not exceed £500;	£50
(c) exceeds £500 but does not exceed £1,000;	£70
(d) exceeds £1,000 but does not exceed £1,500;	£80
(e) exceeds £1,500 but does not exceed £3,000;	£115
(f) exceeds £3,000 but does not exceed £5,000;	£205
(g) exceeds £5,000 but does not exceed £15,000;	£455
(h) exceeds £15,000 but does not exceed £50,000;	£610
(i) exceeds £50,000 but does not exceed £100,000;	£910
(j) exceeds £100,000 but does not exceed £150,000;	£1,115
(k) exceeds £150,000 but does not exceed £200,000;	£1,315
(l) exceeds £200,000 but does not exceed £250,000;	£1,515
(m) exceeds £250,000 but does not exceed £300,000;	£1,720
(n) exceeds £300,000 or is not limited.	£1,920

Column 1 *Number and description of fee*	Column 2 *Amount of fee*
1.2 On starting proceedings to recover a sum of money in CCBC cases brought by Centre users, where the sum claimed:	
(a) does not exceed £300;	£25
(b) exceeds £300 but does not exceed £500;	£35
(c) exceeds £500 but does not exceed £1,000;	£60
(d) exceeds £1,000 but does not exceed £1,500;	£70
(e) exceeds £1,500 but does not exceed £3,000;	£105
(f) exceeds £3,000 but does not exceed £5,000;	£185
(g) exceeds £5,000 but does not exceed £15,000;	£410
(h) exceeds £15,000 but does not exceed £50,000;	£550
(i) exceeds £50,000 but does not exceed £100,000.	£815
1.3 On starting proceedings to recover a sum of money brought by Money Claim OnLine users where the sum claimed:	
(a) does not exceed £300;	£25
(b) exceeds £300 but does not exceed £500;	£35
(c) exceeds £500 but does not exceed £1,000;	£60
(d) exceeds £1,000 but does not exceed £1,500;	£70
(e) exceeds £1,500 but does not exceed £3,000;	£105
(f) exceeds £3,000 but does not exceed £5,000;	£185
(g) exceeds £5,000 but does not exceed £15,000;	£410
(h) exceeds £15,000 but does not exceed £50,000;	£550
(i) exceeds £50,000 but does not exceed £100,000.	£815
Fees 1.1, 1.2 and 1.3. Where the claimant is making a claim for interest on a specified sum of money, the amount on which the fee is calculated is the total amount of the claim and the interest.	
1.4 On starting proceedings for the recovery of land:	
(a) in the High Court;	£480
(b) in the County Court, other than where fee 1.4(c) applies;	£280
(c) using the Possession Claims Online website.	£250
1.5 On starting proceedings for any other remedy (including proceedings issued after permission to issue is granted):	
in the High Court	£480
in the County Court	£280
Fees 1.1, 1.4 and 1.5. Recovery of land or goods. Where a claim for money is additional or alternative to a claim for recovery of land or goods, only fee 1.4 or 1.5 is payable.	
Fees 1.1 and 1.5. Claims other than recovery of land or goods. Where a claim for money is additional to a non money claim (other than a claim for recovery of land or goods), then fee 1.1 is payable in addition to fee 1.5.	

Column 1 *Number and description of fee*	Column 2 *Amount of fee*
Where a claim for money is alternative to a non money claim (other than a claim for recovery of land or goods), only fee 1.1 is payable in the High Court, and, in the County Court, whichever is greater of fee 1.1 or fee 1.5 is payable.	
Fees 1.1 and 1.5. Where more than one non money claim is made in the same proceedings, fee 1.5 is payable once only, in addition to any fee which may be payable under fee 1.1.	
Fees 1.1 and 1.5 are not payable where fee 1.8(b), fee 1.9(a), fee 3 or fee 10.1 applies.	
Fees 1.1 and fee 1.5. Amendment of claim or counterclaim. Where the claim or counterclaim is amended, and the fee paid before amendment is less than that which would have been payable if the document, as amended, had been so drawn in the first instance, the party amending the document must pay the difference.	
1.6 On the filing of proceedings against a party or parties not named in the proceedings.	£50
Fee 1.6 is payable by a defendant who adds or substitutes a party or parties to the proceedings or by a claimant who adds or substitutes a defendant or defendants.	
1.7 On the filing of a counterclaim.	The same fee as if the remedy sought were the subject of separate proceedings
No fee is payable on a counterclaim which a defendant is required to make under rule 57.8 of the CPR(a) (requirement to serve a counterclaim if a defendant makes a claim or seeks a remedy in relation to a grant of probate of a will, or letters of administration of an estate, of a deceased person).	
1.8(a) On an application for permission to issue proceedings.	£50
(b) On an application for an order under Part 3 of the Solicitors Act 1974(b) for the assessment of costs payable to a solicitor by a client or on starting costs–only proceedings.	£50
1.9(a) For permission to apply for judicial review.	£140
1.9(b) On a request to reconsider at a hearing a decision on permission.	£350
Where fee 1.9(b) has been paid and permission is granted at a hearing, the amount payable under fee 1.9(c) is £350.	
Where the court has made an order giving permission to proceed with a claim for judicial review, there is payable by the claimant within 7 days of service on the claimant of that order:	
1.9(c) if the judicial review procedure has been started.	£700
1.9(d) if the claim for judicial review was started otherwise than by using the judicial review procedure.	£140
2 General Fees (High Court and County Court)	

C. CONTEMPT OF COURT ACT 1981

Column 1 *Number and description of fee*	Column 2 *Amount of fee*
2.1 On the claimant filing a pre–trial check list (listing questionnaire); or where the court fixes the trial date or trial week without the need for a pre–trial check list; or where the claim is on the small claims track, within 14 days of the date of despatch of the notice (or the date when oral notice is given if no written notice is given) of the trial week or the trial date if no trial week is fixed a fee payable for the hearing of:	
(a) a case on the multi–track;	£1,090
(b) a case on the fast track.	£545
(c) a case on the small claims track where the sum claimed:	
(i) does not exceed £300;	£25
(ii) exceeds £300 but does not exceed £500;	£55
(iii) exceeds £500 but does not exceed £1,000;	£80
(iv) exceeds £1,000 but does not exceed £1,500;	£115
(v) exceeds £1,500 but does not exceed £3,000;	£170
(vi) exceeds £3,000.	£335
Fee 2.1 is payable by the claimant except where the action is proceeding on the counterclaim alone, when it is payable by the defendant: or	
within 14 days of the date of despatch of the notice (or the date when oral notice is given if no written notice is given) of the trial week or the trial date if no trial week is fixed.	
Where a case is on the multi–track or fast track and, after a hearing date has been fixed, the court receives notice in writing from the party who paid the hearing fee that the case has been settled or discontinued then the following percentages of the hearing fee will be refunded:	
(i) 100% if the court is notified more than 28 days before the hearing;	
(ii) 75% if the court is notified between 15 and 28 days before the hearing;	
(iii) 50% if the court is notified between 7 and 14 days before the hearing.	
Where a case is on the small claims track and, after a hearing date has been fixed, the court receives notice in writing from the party who paid the hearing fee, at least 7 days before the date set for the hearing, that the case has been settled or discontinued the hearing fee will be refunded in full.	
Fee 2.1 is not payable in respect of a case where the court fixed the hearing date on the issue of the claim.	
2.2 In the High Court on filing:	£240
an appellant's notice: or	
a respondent's notice where the respondent is appealing or wishes to ask the appeal court to uphold the order of the lower court for reasons different from or additional to those given by the lower court:	
2.3 In the County Court on filing:	
an appellant's notice, or	
a respondent's notice where the respondent is appealing or wishes to ask the appeal court to uphold the order of the lower court for reasons different from or additional to those given by the lower court:	

Column 1 Number and description of fee	Column 2 Amount of fee
(a) in a claim allocated to the small claims track;	£120
(b) in all other claims.	£140
Fees 2.2 and 2.3 do not apply on appeals against a decision made in detailed assessment proceedings.	
2.4 On an application on notice where no other fee is specified.	£155
2.5 On an application by consent or without notice where no other fee is specified.	£50
For the purpose of fee 2.5 a request for a judgment or order on admission or in default does not constitute an application and no fee is payable.	
Fee 2.5 is not payable in relation to an application by consent for an adjournment of a hearing where the application is received by the court at least 14 days before the date set for that hearing.	
Fees 2.4 and 2.5 are not payable when an application is made in an appeal notice or is filed at the same time as an appeal notice.	
2.6 On an application for a summons or order for a witness to attend court to be examined on oath or an order for evidence to be taken by deposition, other than an application for which fee 7.2 or 8.3 is payable.	£50
2.7 On an application to vary a judgment or suspend enforcement, including an application to suspend a warrant of possession.	£50
Where more than one remedy is sought in the same application only one fee is payable.	
2.8 Register of judgments, orders and fines kept under section 98 of the Courts Act 2003:	
On a request for the issue of a certificate of satisfaction.	£15
3 Companies Act 1985, Companies Act 2006 and Insolvency Act 1986 (High Court and County Court)	
3.1 On entering a bankruptcy petition:	
(a) if presented by a debtor or the personal representative of a deceased debtor;	£180
(b) if presented by a creditor or other person.	£280
3.2 On entering a petition for an administration order.	£280
3.3 On entering any other petition.	£280
One fee only is payable where more than one petition is presented in relation to a partnership.	
3.4 (a) On a request for a certificate of discharge from bankruptcy.	£70
(b) after the first certificate, for each copy.	£10
3.5 On an application under the Companies Act 1985(c), the Companies Act 2006(d) or the Insolvency Act 1986(e) other than one brought by petition and where no other fee is specified.	£280
Fee 3.5 is not payable where the application is made in existing proceedings.	
3.6 On an application for the conversion of a voluntary arrangement into a winding up or bankruptcy under Article 37 of Council Regulation (EC) No 1346/2000.	£160

Column 1 Number and description of fee	Column 2 Amount of fee
3.7 On an application, for the purposes of Council Regulation (EC) No 1346/2000, for an order confirming creditors' voluntary winding up (where the company has passed a resolution for voluntary winding up, and no declaration under section 89 of the Insolvency Act 1986 has been made).	£50
3.8 On filing:	£50
a notice of intention to appoint an administrator under paragraph 14 of Schedule B1 to the Insolvency Act 1986(f) or in accordance with paragraph 27 of that Schedule; or	
Where a person pays fee 3.8 on filing a notice of intention to appoint an administrator, no fee is payable on that same person filing a notice of appointment of that administrator.	
3.9 On submitting a nominee's report under section 2(2) of the Insolvency Act 1986.	£50
3.10 On filing documents in accordance with paragraph 7(1) of Schedule A1(g) to the Insolvency Act 1986.	£50
3.11 On an application by consent or without notice within existing proceedings where no other fee is specified.	£50
3.12 On an application with notice within existing proceedings where no other fee is specified.	£155
3.13 On a search in person of the bankruptcy and companies records, in a County Court.	£45
Requests and applications with no fee:	
No fee is payable on a request or on an application to the Court by the Official Receiver when applying only in the capacity of Official Receiver to the case (and not as trustee or liquidator), or on an application to set aside a statutory demand.	
4 Copy Documents (Court of Appeal, High Court and County Court)	
4.1 On a request for a copy of a document (other than where fee 4.2 applies):	
(a) for ten pages or less;	£10
(b) for each subsequent page.	50p
Note: The fee payable under fee 4.1 includes:	
where the court allows a party to fax to the court for the use of that party a document that has not been requested by the court and is not intended to be placed on the court file;	
where a party requests that the court fax a copy of a document from the court file; or	
where the court provides a subsequent copy of a document which it has previously provided.	
4.2 On a request for a copy of a document on a computer disk or in other electronic form, for each such copy.	£10
5 Determination of costs (Senior Court and County Court) Fee 5 does not apply to the determination in the Senior Courts of costs incurred in the Court of Protection.	

Column 1 *Number and description of fee*	Column 2 *Amount of fee*
5.1 On the filing of a request for detailed assessment where the party filing the request is legally aided, is funded by the Legal Aid Agency or is a person for whom civil legal services have been made available under arrangements made by the Lord Chancellor under Part 1 of the Legal Aid, Sentencing and Punishment of Offenders Act 2012(h) and no other party is ordered to pay the costs of the proceedings.	£200
5.2 On the filing of a request for detailed assessment in any case where fee 5.1 does not apply; or on filing a request for a hearing date for the assessment of costs payable to a solicitor by a client pursuant to an order under Part 3 of the Solicitors Act 1974 where the amount of the costs claimed:	
(a) does not exceed £15,000;	£335
(b) exceeds £15,000 but does not exceed £50,000;	£675
(c) exceeds £50,000 but does not exceed £100,000;	£1,005
(d) exceeds £100,000 but does not exceed £150,000;	£1,345
(e) exceeds £150,000 but does not exceed £200,000;	£1,680
(f) exceeds £200,000 but does not exceed £300,000;	£2,520
(g) exceeds £300,000 but does not exceed £500,000;	£4,200
(h) exceeds £500,000.	£5,600
Where there is a combined party and party and legal aid, or a combined party and party and Legal Aid Agency, or a combined party and party and Lord Chancellor, or a combined party and party and one or more of legal aid, Legal Aid Agency or Lord Chancellor determination of costs, fee 5.2 will be attributed proportionately to the party and party, legal aid, Legal Aid Agency or Lord Chancellor (as the case may be) portions of the bill on the basis of the amount allowed.	
5.3 On a request for the issue of a default costs certificate.	£60
5.4 On commencing an appeal against a decision made in detailed assessment proceedings.	£210
5.5 On a request or application to set aside a default costs certificate.	£110
6 Determination in the Senior Court of costs incurred in the Court of Protection	
6.1 On the filing of a request for detailed assessment:	
(a) where the amount of the costs to be assessed (excluding VAT and disbursements) does not exceed £3,000;	£115
(b) in all other cases.	£225
6.2 On an appeal against a decision made in detailed assessment proceedings.	£65
6.3 On a request or application to set aside a default costs certificate.	£65
7 Enforcement in the High Court	
7.1 On sealing a writ of control/possession/delivery	£60
Where the recovery of a sum of money is sought in addition to a writ of possession and delivery, no further fee is payable.	
7.2 On an application for an order requiring a judgment debtor or other person to attend court to provide information in connection with enforcement of a judgment or order.	£50

Column 1 *Number and description of fee*	Column 2 *Amount of fee*
7.3(a) On an application for a third party debt order or the appointment of a receiver by way of equitable execution.	£100
(b) On an application for a charging order.	£100
Fee 7.3(a) is payable in respect of each third party against whom the order is sought. Fee 7.3(b) is payable in respect of each charging order applied for.	
7.4 On an application for a judgment summons.	£100
7.5 On a request or application to register a judgment or order, or for permission to enforce an arbitration award, or for a certificate or a certified copy of a judgment or order for use abroad.	£60
8 Enforcement in the county court	
8.1 On an application for or in relation to enforcement of a judgment or order of the County Court or through the County Court, by the issue of a warrant of control against goods except a warrant to enforce payment of a fine:	
(a) in CCBC cases or cases in which a warrant of control is requested in accordance with paragraph 11.2 of Practice Direction 7E to the Civil Procedure Rules (Money Claim OnLine cases);	£70
(b) in any other case.	£100
8.2 On a request for a further attempt at execution of a warrant at a new address following a notice of the reason for non–execution (except a further attempt following suspension and CCBC cases brought by Centre users).	£30
8.3 On an application for an order requiring a judgment debtor or other person to attend court to provide information in connection with enforcement of a judgment or order.	£50
8.4(a) On an application for a third party debt order or the appointment of a receiver by way of equitable execution.	£100
(b) On an application for a charging order.	£100
Fee 8.4(a) is payable in respect of each third party against whom the order is sought. Fee 8.4(b) is payable in respect of each charging order applied for.	
8.5 On an application for a judgment summons.	£100
8.6 On the issue of a warrant of possession or a warrant of delivery.	£110
Where the recovery of a sum of money is sought in addition, no further fee is payable.	
8.7 On an application for an attachment of earnings order (other than a consolidated attachment of earnings order) to secure payment of a judgment debt.	£100
Fee 8.7 is payable for each defendant against whom an order is sought. Fee 8.7 is not payable where the attachment of earnings order is made on the hearing of a judgment summons.	
8.8 On a consolidated attachment of earnings order or on an administration order.	For every £1 or part of a £1 of the money paid into court in respect of debts due to creditors – 10p

Column 1 *Number and description of fee*	Column 2 *Amount of fee*
Fee 8.8 is calculated on any money paid into court under any order at the rate in force at the time when the order was made (or, where the order has been amended, at the time of the last amendment before the date of payment).	
8.9 On an application for the enforcement of an award for a sum of money or other decision made by any court, tribunal, body or person other than the High Court or a County Court.	£40
8.10 On a request for an order to recover a sum that is:	
a specified debt within the meaning of the Enforcement of Road Traffic Debts Order 1993(i) ; or pursuant to an enactment, treated as a specified debt for the purposes of that Order.	£7
No fee is payable on: an application for an extension of time to serve a statutory declaration or a witness statement in connection with any such order; or a request to issue a warrant of control to enforce any such order.	
8A Service in the county court	
8A.1 On a request for service by a bailiff of an order to attend court for questioning	£100
9 Sale (County Court only)	
9.1 For removing or taking steps to remove goods to a place of deposit.	The reasonable expenses incurred
Fee 9.1 is to include the reasonable expenses of feeding and caring for any animals.	
9.2 For the appraisement of goods.	5p in the £1 or part of a £1 of the appraised value
9.3 For the sale of goods (including advertisements, catalogues, sale and commission and delivery of goods).	15p in the £1 or part of a £1 on the amount realised by the sale or such other sum as the district judge may consider to be justified in the circumstances
9.4 Where no sale takes place by reason of an execution being withdrawn, satisfied or stopped.	(a) 10p in the £1 or part of a £1 on the value of the goods seized, the value to be the appraised value where the goods have been appraised or such other sum as the district judge may consider to be justified in the circumstances; and in addition (b) any sum payable under fee 9.1 and 9.2.
FEES PAYABLE IN HIGH COURT ONLY	
10 Miscellaneous proceedings or matters	
Bills of Sale	
10.1 On filing any document under the Bills of Sale Acts 1878(j) and the Bills of Sale Act (1878) Amendment Act 1882(k) or on an application under section 15 of the Bills of Sale Act 1878 for an order that a memorandum of satisfaction be written on a registered copy of the bill.	£25
Searches	

Column 1 *Number and description of fee*	Column 2 *Amount of fee*
10.2 For an official certificate of the result of a search for each name, in any register or index held by the court; or in the Court Funds Office, for an official certificate of the result of a search of unclaimed balances for a specified period of up to 50 years.	£45
10.3 On a search in person of the court's records, including inspection, for each 15 minutes or part of 15 minutes.	£10
Judge sitting as arbitrator	
10.4 On the appointment of:	
(a) a judge of the Commercial Court as an arbitrator or umpire under section 93 of the Arbitration Act 1996(l); or	£2,455
(b) a judge of the Technology and Construction Court as an arbitrator or umpire under section 93 of the Arbitration Act 1996.	£2,455
10.5 For every day or part of a day (after the first day) of the hearing before:	
(a) a judge of the Commercial Court; or	£2,455
(b) a judge of the Technology and Construction Court, so appointed as arbitrator or umpire.	£2,455
Where fee 10.4 has been paid on the appointment of a judge of the Commercial Court or a judge of the Technology and Construction Court as an arbitrator or umpire but the arbitration does not proceed to a hearing or an award, the fee will be refunded.	
11 Fees payable in Admiralty matters	
In the Admiralty Registrar and Marshal's Office:	
11.1 On the issue of a warrant for the arrest of a ship or goods.	£225
11.2 On the sale of a ship or goods	
Subject to a minimum fee of £205:	
(a) for every £100 or fraction of £100 of the price up to £100,000;	£1
(b) for every £100 or fraction of £100 of the price exceeding £100,000.	50p
Where there is sufficient proceeds of sale in court, fee 11.2 will be payable by transfer from the proceeds of sale in court.	
11.3 On entering a reference for hearing by the Registrar.	£70
FEES PAYABLE IN HIGH COURT AND COURT OF APPEAL ONLY	
12 Affidavits	
12.1 On taking an affidavit or an affirmation or attestation upon honour in lieu of an affidavit or a declaration except for the purpose of receipt of dividends from the Accountant General and for a declaration by a shorthand writer appointed in insolvency proceedings: for each person making any of the above.	 £11
12.2 For each exhibit referred to in an affidavit, affirmation, attestation or declaration for which fee 12.1 is payable.	£2
FEES PAYABLE IN COURT OF APPEAL ONLY	
13 Fees payable in appeals to the Court of Appeal	

Column 1 Number and description of fee	Column 2 Amount of fee
13.1(a) Where in an appeal notice, permission to appeal or an extension of time for appealing is applied for (or both are applied for): on filing an appellant's notice, or where the respondent is appealing, on filing a respondent's notice.	£235
13.1(b) Where permission to appeal is not required or has been granted by the lower court: on filing an appellant's notice, or on filing a respondent's notice where the respondent is appealing.	£465
13.1(c) On the appellant filing an appeal questionnaire (unless the appellant has paid fee 13.1(b), or the respondent filing an appeal questionnaire (unless the respondent has paid fee 13.1(b)).	£465
13.2 On filing a respondent's notice where the respondent wishes to ask the appeal court to uphold the order of the lower court for reasons different from or additional to those given by the lower court.	£235
13.3 On filing an application notice.	£235
Fee 13.3 is not payable for an application made in an appeal notice.	

Note

Add at end:

10–7.1   Entry 3.5 amended by the Civil Proceedings Fees (Amendment No.2) Order 2014 (SI 2014/1834) with effect from August 4, 2014.

Entry 8.1 amended by the Civil Proceedings Fees (Amendment No.3) Order 2014 (SI 2014/2059) with effect from August 4, 2014.

Entries 7.1, 8.1 and 8.10 amended by the Courts and Tribunals Fees (Miscellaneous Amendments) Order 2014 (SI 2014/590) art.3, with effect from April 6, 2014. New Schedule 1 substituted by the Civil Proceedings Fees (Amendment) Order 2014 (SI 2014/874), with effect from April 22, 2014.

SCHEDULE 2

REMISSIONS AND PART REMISSIONS

Interpretation

Delete para.1(1) and substitute:

10–8   (1) In this Schedule—

   "child" means a person—

   (a) whose main residence is with a party and who is aged—

   (i) under 16 years; or

   (ii) 16 to 19 years; and is—

   (aa) not married or in a civil partnership; and

   (bb) enrolled or accepted in full–time education that is not advanced education, or approved training; or

   (b) in respect of whom a party or their partner pays child support maintenance or periodic payments in accordance with a maintenance agreement, and "full–time education", "advanced education" and "approved training" have the meaning given by the Child Benefit (General) Regulations 2006;

   "child support maintenance" has the meaning given in section 3(6) of the Child Support Act 1991;

   "couple" has the meaning given in section 3(5A) of the Tax Credits Act 2002 ;

"disposable capital" has the meaning given in paragraph 5;

"excluded benefits" means any of the following—

(a) any of the following benefits payable under the Social Security Contributions and Benefits Act 1992 or the corresponding provisions of the Social Security Contributions and Benefits (Northern Ireland) Act 1992—

   (i) attendance allowance paid under section 64;

   (ii) severe disablement allowance;

   (iii) carer's allowance;

   (iv) disability living allowance;

   (v) constant attendance allowance under section 104 as an increase to a disablement pension;

   (vi) any payment made out of the social fund;

   (vii) housing benefit;

   (viii) widowed parents allowance;

(b) any of the following benefit payable under the Tax Credits Act 2002—

   (i) any disabled child element or severely disabled child element of the child tax credit;

   (ii) any childcare element of the child tax credit;

(c) any direct payment made under the Community Care, Services for Carers and Children's Services (Direct Payments) (England) Regulations 2009, the Community Care, Services for Carers and Children's Services (Direct Payments) (Wales) Regulations 2011, the Carers and Direct Payments Act (Northern Ireland) 2002, section 12B(1) of the Social Work (Scotland) Act 1968 or the Social Care (Self–directed Support) (Scotland) Act 2013;

(d) a back to work bonus payable under section 26 of the Jobseekers Act 1995, or article 28 of the Jobseekers (Northern Ireland) Order 1995;

(e) any exceptionally severe disablement allowance paid under the Personal Injuries (Civilians) Scheme 1983;

(f) any payments from the Industrial Injuries Disablement Benefit;

(g) any pension paid under the Naval, Military and Air Forces etc (Disablement and Death) Service Pension Order 2006;

(h) any payment made from the Independent Living Funds;

(i) any payment made from the Bereavement Allowance;

(j) any financial support paid under an agreement for the care of a foster child;

(k) any housing credit element of pension credit;

(l) any armed forces independence payment;

(m) any personal independence payment payable under the Welfare Reform Act 2012;

(n) any payment on account of benefit as defined in the Social Security (Payments on Account of Benefit) Regulations 2013;

(o) any of the following amounts, as defined by the Universal Credit Regulations 2013, that make up an award of universal credit—

   (i) an additional amount to the child element in respect of a disabled child;

   (ii) a housing costs element;

   (iii) a childcare costs element;

   (iv) a carer element;

   (v) a limited capability for work or limited capacity for work and work–related activity element.

"family help (higher)" has the meaning given in paragraph 15(3) of the Civil Legal Aid (Merits Criteria) Regulations 2013;

"family help (lower)" has the meaning given in paragraph 15(2) of the Civil Legal Aid (Merits Criteria) Regulations 2013;

"gross monthly income" has the meaning given in paragraph 13;

"Independent Living Funds" means the funds listed at regulation 20(2)(b) of the Criminal Legal Aid (Financial Resources) Regulations 2013;

"legal representation" has the meaning given in paragraph 18(2) of the Civil Legal Aid (Merits Criteria) Regulations 2013;

"maintenance agreement" has the meaning given in subsection 9(1) of the Child Support Act 1991;

"partner" means a person with whom the party lives as a couple and includes a person with whom the party is not currently living but from whom the party is not living separate and apart;

"party" means the individual who would, but for this Schedule, be liable to pay the fee under this Order;

"restraint order" means—

(a) an order under section 42(1A) of the Senior Courts Act 1981;

(b) an order under section 33 of the Employment Tribunals Act 1996;

(c) a civil restraint order under rule 3.11 of the Civil Procedure Rules 1998, or a practice direction made under that rule; or

(d) a civil restraint order under rule 4.8 of the Family Procedure Rules 2010, or the practice direction referred to in that rule.

Note

Add at end:

10–15.3.10   Sch.2 amended by the Courts and Tribunals Fees (Miscellaneous Amendments) Order 2014 (SI 2014/590) art.3, with effect from April 6, 2014.

In para.1 definition "excluded benefits" amended by the Civil Proceedings Fees (Amendment No.2) Order 2014 (SI 2014/1834), with effect from August 4, 2014.

SECTION 11

OVERRIDING OBJECTIVE OF CPR

E. DUTY OF THE PARTIES (R.1.3)

At the end of the eighth paragraph, add:

11–14   Presumably, where one party (A) is aware that court staff have made an error in discharging the court's responsibilities in relation to the handling of a claim, by which his opponent (B) is or may be prejudiced, and A has reason to believe that B is unaware of the error and the procedural consequences of it for him or is unsure whether he is and does, A is not by virtue of r.1.3 or on any other ground under a duty clearly to alert B to his predicament. However, A's reluctance in that respect may be a matter which the court will find difficult to ignore when determining applications made by B for relief from the consequences of the court's mistakes; see e.g. *Power v Meloy Whittle Robinson Solicitors* [2014] EWCA Civ 898, July 2, 2014, CA, unrep. (where claimant, prejudiced by court's mis–service of claim form, making application for service by an alternative method).

SECTION 12

CPR: APPLICATION, AMENDMENTS AND INTERPRETATION

B. EXTENT AND APPLICATION OF CPR

2. EXTENT OF POWER TO MAKE CPR

At the end of the fourth paragraph, add:

The question whether the presumption against the extra–territorial effect of legisla- **12–4** tion applies to particular provisions in the CPR is one that has to be determined in context; ibid (see also *Dar Al Arkan Real Estate Development Co v Al Refai* [2014] EWCA Civ 7125, May 23, 2014, CA, unrep., where submission that certain provisions in Pt 6 and Pt 81 did not have the effect of enabling a committal order to be made against a foreign director who was not within the jurisdiction was rejected).

Add at end:

In *Dunhill v Burgin* [2014] UKSC 18; [2014] 1 W.L.R. 933, SC, the Supreme Court rejected the submission that the provision in r.21.10 (Compromise etc. by or on behalf of a child or protected party) to the effect that a settlement is invalid unless approved by the court is ultra vires.

3. APPLICATION OF THE CPR

(b) Proceedings to which CPR do not apply (CPR r.2.1)

(v) *Family proceedings*

In the third paragraph, delete the sentence beginning "In relation to enforcement" and substitute:

The establishment (with effect from April 22, 2014) of the Family Court, required **12–11** substantial amendments to the FPR. Among them were the insertion of a new Part, Part 37, containing free–standing rules for family proceedings on contempt and committal, modelled on provisions contained in CPR Part 81.

C. STRUCTURE OF CPR

3. SCHEDULES (CPR PT 50)

(c) Schedule rules remaining in effect

(i) *Schedule 1—RSC provisions*

Delete the list and substitute:

Order 54 (Applications for writ of habeas corpus) **12–27**
Order 79 (Criminal proceedings)
Order 109 (The Administration of Justice Act 1960)
Order 110 (Environmental Control Proceedings)
Order 115 (Confiscation and forfeiture in connection with criminal proceedings)

(ii) *Schedule 2—CCR provisions*

Delete the list and substitute:

Order 1 (Application of RSC to county court proceedings) r.6 **12–28**
Order 27 (Attachment of earnings), excluding r.7A(3), r.8 and r.17
Order 28 (Judgment summonses), excluding r.12

Order 39 (Administration orders)
Order 44 (The Agricultural Holdings Act 1986) r.4
Order 46 (The Legitimacy Act 1976)
Order 49 (Miscellaneous Statutes) rr.7, 12, 18A and 19

By r.40 of the Civil Procedure (Amendment) Rules 2014 (SI 2014/407), r.A1 and r.1A were inserted in CCR Order 28 before r.1 of that Order.

D. STATUTORY INSTRUMENTS AMENDING CPR

3. COMMENCEMENT DATES FOR STATUTORY INSTRUMENTS AMENDING CPR

Add at end:

12-31

Civil Procedure (Amendment No.4) Rules 2013 (SI 2013/1412)—July 1, 2013

Civil Procedure (Amendment No.5) Rules 2013 (SI 2013/1571)—June 26, 2013

Civil Procedure (Amendment No.6) Rules 2013 (SI 2013/1695)—July 31, 2013

Civil Procedure (Amendment No.7) Rules 2013 (SI 2013/1974)—October 1, 2013

Civil Procedure (Amendment No.8) Rules 2013 (SI 2103/3112)—January 1, 2014

Civil Procedure (Amendment) Rules 2014 (SI 2014/407)—April 1, 6 & 22, 2014

Civil Procedure (Amendment No. 2) Rules 2014 (SI 2014/482)—April 6, 2014

Civil Procedure (Amendment No. 3) Rules 2014 (SI 2014/610)—April 6, 2014

Civil Procedure (Amendment No. 4) Rules 2014 (SI 2014/867)—April 22, 2014

Civil Procedure (Amendment No. 5) Rules 2014 (SI 2014/1233)—June 5, 2014

Civil Procedure (Amendment No. 6) Rules 2014 (SI 2014/2044)—October 1, 2014

4. TRANSITIONAL ARRANGEMENTS IN AMENDING STATUTORY INSTRUMENTS

(b) 2005 to date

Add new paragraphs at end:

12-34   The Civil Procedure (Amendment) Rules 2014 (SI 2014/407) contained (1) a series of amendments to give effect to (and which were consequential upon) the implementation of the single County Court on the coming into force (on April 22, 2014) of provisions in s.17 of, and Sch.9 to, the Crime and Courts Act 2013, (2) a series of amendments (the enforcement amendments), taking effect on April 6, 2014, in particular the insertion of new Parts 83 to 86, to implement Pt 3 of, and Sch.12 to, the Tribunals, Courts and Enforcement Act 2007, and to incorporate into the body of the CPR rules on enforcement contained in Schedules 1 and 2 to the CPR, and to make necessary consequential amendments, (3) amendments (the mediation amendments) to Pt 26 to formalise with effect from April 1, 2014, a scheme for referring money claims to the Small Claims Mediation Service, (4) amendments to r.42.1, r.45.30(2) and r.66.14(2) coming into effect on April 6, 2014, and (5) a rule inserting new r.52.21 requiring the grant of permission by the High Court in respect of appeals from determinations and directions by the Pensions Ombudsman and the Pension Protection Fund Ombudsman filed on or after April 6, 2014. In the statutory instrument transitional provisions (1) affecting the enforcement amendments were contained in r.41(1) to (5), and (2) affecting the mediation amendments in r.41(6) & (7). Rule 3 of the Crime and Courts Act 2013 (Commencement No.10 and Transitional Provision) Orders 2014 (SI 2014/954) stated that any judgment, order, warrant, direction or other act of a county court before April 22, 2014 (except one in relation to proceedings under jurisdiction transferred to the family court established under s.31A of the Matrimonial and Family Proceedings Act 1984, as amended by the 2013 Act, for which separate transitional provision is made) is to have the same effect on or after that date as if it had been a judgment etc of the single County Court.

The Civil Procedure (Amendment No.2) Rules 2014 (SI 2014/482) inserted in Part

84 (Enforcement by Taking Control of Goods) a new Section IV (rr.84.17 to 84.20) providing rules in support of the Certification of Enforcement Agents Regulations 2014 (SI 2014/421) and coming into force on April 6, 2014. Rule 5 of the statutory instrument made transitional provision to cover the effects of rr.84.18 to 84.20 during the period between the date of the coming into effect of the enforcement amendments in SI 2014/407 (see above), i.e. April 6, 2014, and the date of the establishment of the single County Court, i.e. April 22, 2014.

The Civil Procedure (Amendment No.3) Rules 2014 (SI 2014/610) amended Pt 54 (Judicial Review and Statutory Review) with effect from April 6, 2014, by inserting in a second Section new rules (rr.54.21 to 54.24) creating the Planning Court as a specialist list for judicial review claims or statutory challenges involving specified matters made on or after that date. Rule 4(2) of the statutory instrument provides that where a claim issued before April 6, 2014, is transferred to the Planning Court after that date, the new rules apply to the claim from the date of transfer.

The Civil Procedure (Amendment No.4) Rules 2014 (SI 2014/867) came into effect on April 22, 2014, and contained (1) amendments to r.3.12 and r.3.15 altering the scope of proceedings to which costs management rules apply and clarifying circumstances in which the court will make a costs management order (the costs management amendments), (2) amendments to r.81.13 and r.81.18 to enable certain permission applications in contempt proceedings to be dealt with by any High Court judge, (3) amendments to r.66.6 consequential upon the enactment of Pt 81 by SI 2012/2208, (4) amendments to r.83.2 and the insertion of r.83.2A to remedy oversights in enactment of Pt 83 by SI 2014/407, and (5) a series of amendments to numerous provisions consequential upon rules enacted by SI 2014/407 (see above) for the purposes of implementing bailiff and enforcement reform (the enforcement amendments), and the introduction of the single County Court (the County Court amendments). Rule 25 of this statutory instrument contains transitional provisions affecting the costs management amendments (r.25(1)) (subsequently amended by SI 2014/1233, see below), the enforcement amendments (r.25(3) & (4)), and the County Court amendments (r.25(5)).

The Civil Procedure (Amendment No.5) Rules 2014 (SI 2014/1233) came into effect on June 5, 2014, and contained (1) an amendment to r.3.8 (Sanctions have effect unless defaulting party obtains relief) making provision for the extension of certain procedural time limits by party agreement, (2) an amendment to r.54.22 as inserted by SI 2014/610 (see above) to provide for the nomination of specialist planning judges to deal with certain Planning Court claims, and (3) for purposes of clarification, an amendment to the transitional provision in r.25(1) of SI 2014/867 affecting r.3.12(1) (see above). This statutory instrument contains no transitional provision.

The Civil Procedure (Amendment No.6) Rules 2014 (SI 2014/2044) came into effect on October 1, 2014, and contained amendments (1) to Part 35, Part 36 and Part 45 (subject to a transitional provision) to provide for fixed costs in relation to medical reports in relation to certain claims started under the Pre–Action Protocol for Low Value Personal Injury Claims in Road Traffic Accidents, (2) to Part 52 to make separate provision for judicial review appeals from the UpperTribunal and for the providing of transcripts at public expense, (3) to Part 57 to make provision (a) for proceedings commenced under the Inheritance (Provision for Family Dependants) Act 1975 before grant of representation has been obtained, and (b) for application for presumed death etc under the Presumption of Death Act 2013, (4) to Part 65 to make provision for injunctions under the Anti–social Behaviour, Crime and Policing Act 2013 Pt 1, and (5) to Part 83 for purpose of rectifying a practical problem that had arisen in the application of r.83.6. In addition this statutory instrument made some other minor amendments. The transitional provision relating to the amendments made to Parts 35, 36 and 45 (r.14) states that they apply only to soft tissue injury claims under the RTA Protocol where the claim notification form was sent on or after October 1, 2014.

SECTION 13

RIGHTS OF AUDIENCE

G. RIGHT OF AUDIENCE GRANTED BY THE COURT IN RELATION TO THE PROCEEDINGS (SCH.3, PARA.1(2))

4. EXERCISE OF THE DISCRETION

(a) Generally

Before the fourth paragraph (beginning "In Harris v Society") add:

13–17 In *Durkan v Madden* [2013] EWHC 4409 (Ch), September 16, 2013, unrep. (Norris J.), at the start of a hearing for the continuation of a freezing injunction a lay person (X) applied for a right of audience so that he might represent a party (C) in her absence. C had signed an application notice in which the first item of relief sought was the grant of rights of audience to X. The judge said a court must be extremely cautious about granting a right of audience to a lay representative in the absence of the party themselves, and refused the application, principally on the grounds that there was nothing in the evidence to explain the circumstances in which that application notice had come to be signed and there were matters which the judge wished to put to C and explore with her before granting a right of audience to X.

SECTION 14

ALTERNATIVE DISPUTE RESOLUTION

B. ADR IN THE CONTEXT OF THE CPR

1. CASE MANAGEMENT

(a) ADR as integral to our litigation culture

14–4 *Delete last sentence (beginning "He also spoke").*

(c) Voluntary v compulsory/mandatory ADR and case management

In the first paragraph, for "http://www.ucl.ac.uk/laws/judicial–institute/docs/ Twisting__arms__mediation__report__Genn__et__al__1.pdf [accessed July 21, 2014]", substitute:

14–6 *http://www.ucl.ac.uk/laws/judicial–institute/files/ Twisting__arms__mediation__report__Genn__et__al__1.pdf* [accessed July 21, 2014]

Delete the last paragraph and substitute:

See also para.14–9 below, Shirley Shipman, "Compulsory Mediation: The Elephant in the Room" (2011) 30(2) C.J.Q. 63–355, Dr S. Shipman, "Waiver: Canute against the tide?" (2013) 32(4) C.J.Q. 470–492 and Gary Meggitt, "PGF II SA v OMFS Co and compulsory mediation" (2014) C.J.Q.

(d) Active case management in relation to ADR after the introduction of the CPR

In the first paragraph, for the sentence beginning "As the CPR became established", substitute:

14–7 As the CPR became established it was also clear that the courts' initial interpretation (prior to *Halsey*, see below) of the CPR on this issue was that parties could be ordered to use ADR.

(f) Judicial speeches—ADR case management post Halsey—power to direct ADR

Add new paragraph at end:

Mostyn J, in *SM v DAM* [2014] EWHC 537 (Fam) 2014 WL 795215 referred to **14-9** these remarks on *Halsey* by Ward L.J. He thought that, in fact, a stay for "a while" would hardly amount to an order obliging the parties to engage in ADR. He added "For my part I am not sure that the kind of order proposed by Sir Alan in fact requires the Court of Appeal "to review the rule in *Halsey*". I cannot see that it is in fact inconsistent with what was said there, nor in fact inconsistent now with the terms of CPR rule 26.4(2A) whereby the court may, on its own initiative, and whether or not the parties agree, impose a stay on proceedings for a specified period.

(g) Case management and the duty of the parties

After the second sentence (ending "encouraged by the court to do so.") add:

In *Garritt–Critchley v Ronnan* [2014] EWHC 1774 (Ch) (at para.25) the court clearly **14-10** took the view this was a continuing duty, throughout the litigation.

Delete the last sentence (beginning "See further below") and substitute:

See also (a) the remarks with reference to *PGF II SA v OMFS Co* [2013] EWCA Civ 1288 in para.14–7 above and (b) further below.

(h) Case management and cost sanctions

In the seventh paragraph, (after the sentence ending "on the indemnity basis.") add:

Indemnity costs were awarded by way of a sanction in *Garritt–Critchley v Ronnan* **14-11** [2014] EWHC 1774 (Ch).

(i) Case management: facilitation of ADR procedures and criteria for referral to ADR

Delete paragraph 14–12 and substitute:

The overriding objective in the CPR, which is to enable "...the court to deal with **14-12** cases justly and at proportionate cost" (r1.1(1)), requires the court to encourage the use of an ADR procedure, in appropriate cases, and to facilitate the use of such procedure, as one of the elements of active case management (r.1.4(2)(e)). The concept of proportionality reinforces the need for the court to keep the potential of ADR procedures under review whenever it deals with any aspect of case management. It should be noted, when considering case management, that although ADR, and mediation in particular, often leads to settlement of the entire action, there is the potential to use an ADR process to attempt settlement or agreement of discrete issues. This can be particularly useful in multi–party cases; see, for example *Supershield Ltd v Siemens Building Technologies FE Ltd* [2010] EWCA Civ 7 and *Mouchel Ltd v Van Oord (UK) Ltd* 2011 WL 579031. The manner in which the court may facilitate the use of an ADR procedure includes the following:

(i) By ensuring that the opportunity to explore ADR prospects is not prejudiced by the rigours of case management procedures generally. (For example, see *Electrical Waste Recycling Group Ltd v Philips Electronics UK Ltd* [2012] EWHC 38 (Ch) where the court considered how ordering a split trial might impact on the prospects of mediating the matter.)

(ii) By acting as a source of information about professional and commercial bodies providing ADR services (for example, see *http://www.civilmediation.justice.gov.uk/* [accessed July 21, 2014] and paras 14–24 and 14–27 below).

(iii) By verbally encouraging the parties to consider ADR at a hearing or telephone conference, such as a case management conference or a pre–trial review. (see para.14–11).

(iv) By ordering a stay of the whole or part of the proceedings, for mediation or some other ADR procedure, pursuant to the application of the parties or one of them (r.3.1(2)(f) and r.3.3(1) and see para.14–13 below).

(v) By ordering such a stay of its own initiative (r.3.1(2)(f) and r.3.3(1)). An appropriate time to make such an order might be upon perusal of the parties' statements about ADR in their directions questionnaires. (See para.14–13 below.)

(vi) By ordering such a stay upon the written request of a party or of its own initiative when considering completed directions questionnaires (r.26.4). (See also Standard Directions Model Paragraph B05–stay for settlement.doc which provides:

"1) ...

2) The claim is stayed until xxxx, during which period the parties will attempt to settle the matter or to narrow the issues.

3) By 4pm on xxxx the Claimant must notify the court in writing of the outcome of negotiations (without disclosing any matters which remain subject to 'without prejudice' terms) and what, if any, further directions are sought. Failure to comply with this direction or to engage properly in negotiations may result in the application of sanctions. If settlement has been reached, the parties must file a consent order signed by all of them." (See *http://www.justice.gov.uk/courts/procedurerules/ civil/standard–directions/list–of–cases–of–common–occurrence/menu–of–sd–paragraphs B05–ADR.doc* [accessed 21 July, 2013]).

(vii) By ordering the parties to consider ADR (including Mediation) using, for example a direction in the form of Standard Directions Model Paragraph A03–ADR.doc, whether at the time of giving standard directions or otherwise as follows:

"1) ...

2) At all stages the parties must consider settling this litigation by any means of Alternative Dispute Resolution (including Mediation); any party not engaging in any such means proposed by another must serve a witness statement giving reasons within 21 days of that proposal; such witness statement must not be shown to the trial judge until questions of costs arise.

'21 days' can be altered manually.

The words 'and not less than 28 days before trial' can always be added after the word 'proposal' by the managing judge if appropriate. Not necessary for every Order." (See *http://www.justice.gov.uk/courts/procedurerules/ civil/standard–directions/list–of–cases–of–common–occurrence/menu–of–sd–paragraphs A03–ADR.doc* [accessed 15 May, 2013]).

It might be particularly appropriate to consider directions of the type referred to immediately above when considering cost budgets and proportionality during the costs management and case management process. Such directions might be combined with directions designed to facilitate the holding of an immediate mediation. For example, provision could be made for early disclosure of a particular category of documents that would facilitate a mediation prior to full disclosure. See *SM v DAM* [2014] EWHC 537 (Fam) 2014 WL 795215 at para.525.

(viii) By making an order, whether on directions for allocation or a later stage, of the type referred to in the Multi–Track Practice Direction (sometimes referred to as an "Ungley Order"). (29PD4.10(9) and see para.14–13 below.)

(ix) By making an ADR order on the basis of the draft in App.7 to the Admiralty and Commercial Courts Guide (see para.14–22). The draft order includes the following paragraph: "4. The parties shall take such serious steps as they may be advised to resolve their disputes by ADR procedures before the neutral individual or panel so chosen by no later than [*]." See para.14–9 above regarding the issue of the court's power to order parties to take part in a mediation process.

(x) By making an ADR order on the basis of the draft order in App.E to and Section 7 of the Technology and Construction Court Guide (see para.14–22). Although these Guides refer to their particular courts there appears to be no reason why the type of ADR orders made in these courts could not be made, where appropriate, in other courts. Again, see para.14–9 above regarding the issue of the court's power to order parties to take part in a mediation process. See also paras 14–22 and 14–23 below regarding ADR in the Commercial Court and the Technology and Construction Court.

(xi) By arranging, in the Admiralty and Commercial Court or the Technology and Construction Court, for the court to provide Early Neutral Evaluation (see the references to the respective Court Guides in sub–paras (vii) and (viii) immediately above). Further, in the Technology and Construction Court the court can provide a judge to act as a mediator. (See *http://www.justice.gov.uk/downloads/courts/tech–court/tech–con–court–guide.pdf* [accessed 28 April 2013].)

(xii) By, in a case which is suitable to be resolved by an ADR procedure except for one sticking point, ordering the hearing of that point as a preliminary issue with a view to the case then being referred to ADR (see s.8 of the Technology and Construction Court Guide, para.14–22, although, again, there is no reason why the approach taken by the Technology and Construction Court cannot be taken by other courts, where appropriate).

(xiii) By referring a Small Claim to the Small Claims Mediation Service (see para.14–24).

(xiv) By making an appropriate costs order (or advising that such an order might be made in the future) in respect of failure to give adequate consideration to ADR prior to the commencement of proceedings (para.14–21) or during proceedings (see paras 14–11 and 14–17).

Criteria for referral to mediation is given in Guidance on Judicial Referral to Mediation issued to members of the judiciary in 2007: see para.14–28 below. The Guidance deals with the type of cases suitable for mediation and the indicators and counter indicators for referral.

(j) Case management: the stages at which ADR may be encouraged

In the first paragraph, delete the second sentence (beginning "It is dealt with"). **14–13**

In the third paragraph (beginning "The main opportunity"), for "allocation questionnaire", in each place it occurs, substitute:
directions questionnaire

In the fourth paragraph (beginning "Section A of"), for "Allocation Questionnaire", substitute
directions questionnaire

Add at end:
See also *PGF II SA v OMFS Co* [2013] EWCA Civ 1288 at para.35 et seq where Briggs L.J. outlined the desirability of requiring reasons for refusing ADR being put in writing at the time of the refusal.

3. COSTS WHERE ADR DECLINED

Before the seventh paragraph (beginning "For an application"), add as a new paragraph:
See also *National Museums and Galleries On Merseyside (Trustees of) v AEW Architects* **14–17** *and Designers Ltd* [2013] EWHC 3025 (TCC). The court will, however, disregard an offer to mediate which is made subject to an unreasonable pre condition: *R (Royal Free London NHS Foundation Trust) v Secretary of State for the Home Department* [2013] EWHC 4101 (Admin), December 18, 2013, unrep.

In the ninth paragraph (beginning "In two cases"), for "allocation questionnaire", substitute:
directions questionnaire

After the fifteenth paragraph (beginning "This decision was"), add as a new paragraph:
It is not, however, the case that silence in response to an offer to mediate will always attract a costs sanction: see *R (Crawford) v Newcastle Upon Tyne University* [2014] EWHC 1197 (Admin), April 16, 2014, unrep.

In the seventeenth paragraph (for the first sentence beginning "The Court also made"), substitute:
The Court of Appeal in *PGF II SA* also made it clear that a party should put reasons for refusing mediation in writing at the time and endorsed the view of the court below:

...the court should be wary of arguments only raised in retrospect as why a party refused to mediate or as to why it cannot be demonstrated that a mediation would have had a reasonable prospect of success" (Briggs L.J., paragraphs 33–40).

Add new paragraph at end:
In *Garritt–Critchley v Ronnan* [2014] EWHC 1774 (Ch) HHJ Waksman QC sitting as a Judge of the High Court examined and dismissed a series of arguments that a refusal of mediation had been reasonable and awarded indemnity costs by way of

sanction. A costs sanction for unreasonable refusal to mediate was also imposed in *Lakehouse Contracts Ltd v UPR Services Ltd* [2014] EWHC 1223 (Ch).

6. MISCELLANEOUS MATTERS

In the last paragraph, in the last sentence, for "Mann v Mann [2014] EWHC 537" substitute:

14–20 *SM v DAM* [2014] EWHC 537

7. MEDIATION AND EU CROSS–BORDER DISPUTES

Add new paragraph 14–20.5:

14–20.5 An EU Directive on alternative dispute resolution (ADR) for consumer disputes and an EU Regulation on online dispute resolution (ODR) for consumer disputes were adopted by all EU Member States on April 22, 2013. The UK Government has two years in which to transpose the requirements into UK law. The legislation will come into force across the EU in 2015. (ADR Directive: *http://eur–lex.europa.eu/LexUriServ/ LexUriServ.do?uri=OJ:L:2013:165:0063:0079:EN:PDF* ODR Regulation: *http://eur– lex.europa.eu/LexUriServ/LexUriServ.do?uri=OJ:L:2013:165:0001:0012:EN:PDF* [both accessed July 21, 2014]).

C. ADR IN PRE–ACTION PROTOCOLS AND COURT GUIDES

1. ADR IN PROTOCOLS

In the first paragraph, for "para.4.3", substitute:

14–21 para.4.4

In the second paragraph, for "The new para.8", substitute:
Paragraph 8

2. ADR IN COURT GUIDES

In the third bullet point, for "http://www.judiciary.gov.uk/Resources/JCO/Documents/Reports/ rep_comm_wrkg_party_long_trials.pdf", substitute:

14–22 *http://www.judiciary.gov.uk/publications/long–trials–working–party–report/*

D. ADR IN PARTICULAR COURTS

3. COURT OF APPEAL MEDIATION SCHEME (CAMS)

In the first paragraph, for "http://www.justice.gov.uk/guidance/courts–and–tribunals/courts/ court–of–appeal/civil–division/mediation.htm", substitute:

14–25 *http://www.justice.gov.uk/courts/rcj–rolls–building/court–of–appeal/civil–division/mediation*

In the last paragraph, for "http://www.judiciary.gov.uk/media/media–releases/2012/news– release–mediation–pilot–court–of–appeal", substitute:
http://www.judiciary.gov.uk/announcements/news–release–mediation–pilot–court–of–appeal/

SECTION 15

INTERIM REMEDIES

A. INTERIM INJUNCTIONS

2. PRINCIPLES AND GUIDELINES TO BE APPLIED (AMERICAN CYANAMID CO. CASE)

(a) Principles—a serious question to be tried

After the second paragraph, add as a new paragraph:

15–8 The proposition in principle (3) is frequently stressed, particularly by appeal courts.

For example, in *Sukhoruchkin v Van Bekestein* [2014] EWCA Civ 399, March 31, 2014, CA, unrep., Sir Terence Etherton C., referred to relevant authority and stated (at para.32) that it is now well–established as a general principle that, on an application for an interim injunction, the court should not attempt to resolve "critical disputed questions of fact or difficult points of law" on which the claim of either party may ultimately depend, particularly where the point of law "turns on fine questions of fact which are in dispute or are presently obscure".

3. GUIDELINES—ADEQUACY OF DAMAGES AS A REMEDY AND THE BALANCE OF CONVENIENCE

(a) Stage 1—adequacy as a remedy of damages awarded at trial or payable under undertaking

Add at end as a new paragraph:

In *B v D* [2014] EWCA Civ 229, March 6, 2014, CA, unrep., where a dispute arose **15–11** in relation to a contract containing a clause limiting the damages payable in the event of a breach, the contract–breaking party argued that damages were an adequate remedy, and that the contractually capped damages meant that no injunction could be granted in respect of such loss. The Court of Appeal held (i) that it was not only direct financial losses which may be relevant, (ii) that the parties' pre–quantification of recoverable losses were not an agreed price which entitled one party to breach its primary obligations to perform, and (iii) whilst such pre–quantification might affect a claim to recover damages, it did not affect a claim for an injunction to restrain further breaches (whether for an interim period or for the term of the contract), thus designed to avoid a claim to recover damages.

7. STRENGTH OF APPLICANT'S CASE IN FREEZING INJUNCTION CASES

After the second paragraph, add as new paragraphs:

For an explanation of the provenance of the "good arguable case" test, and a **15–23** comparison with the "much better of the argument" test traditionally applied by the English courts when considering whether to order service out of the jurisdiction, with references to relevant authorities, see *Kazakhstan Kagazy Plc v Arip* [2014] EWCA Civ 381, April 2, 2014, CA, unrep., at para.62 et seq per Elias L.J.

The Court of Appeal ought to respect the instincts of experienced commercial judges on the question whether there is a good arguable case, and should only interfere if it is plain that the judge was wrong (*Lakatamia Shipping Company Limited v Nobu Su Limited* [2012] EWCA Civ 1195, July 18, 2012, CA, unrep., at para.27 per Longmore L.J.).

9. UNDERTAKING AS TO DAMAGES

(e) Applicant unable to offer credible undertaking

Before "In Oxy Electric" add:

The position was clarified in *R (Ellson) v London Borough of Greenwich*, [2006] EWHC **15–30** 2379 (Admin), September 25, 2006, unrep. (Burton J.) at [12] to [14] when it was said that, where an impecunious claimant was applying for an injunction, the court would know that, although the claimant was putting on the line all the assets that they had, thus showing how strongly they felt about the claim that they were making, they would not in practice be able to meet the damages. That would be a factor to be taken into account by the court in deciding whether or not to make the order.

(h) Enforcement and assessment

(i) *Application to enforce undertaking*

At the end of the second paragraph add:

At the stage of exercising its discretion whether or not to order an inquiry, the **15–34** court does not ordinarily hear protracted argument on whether the suggested loss will be recoverable. In seeking to persuade the court to order an inquiry, the applicant must adduce credible evidence that he has suffered loss, which was prima facie or arguably caused by the making of the order; assumingthere is such credible evidence, the burden of any contention that the relevant loss would have been suffered anyway passes to the claimant, and an inquiry will be ordered (*Malhotra v Malhotra* [2014] EWHC 113 (Comm), January 31, 2014, unrep. (Blair J.)).

(v) *Measure of damages*

Delete paragraph 15–38 and substitute:

15–38   On an inquiry as to damages, the measure of damages is not at large such that the court can punish a claimant who wrongfully obtained the injunction. The issue is whether the party subject to the injunction can show that he has suffered loss as a result of the injunction and, if so, what that loss is. In *F. Hoffmann–La Roche & Co A.G. v Secretary of State for Trade and Industry* [1975] A.C. 295, HL, on the basis of *Smith v Day* (1882) 21 Ch D 421, CA), Lord Diplock expressed the view (at p.361) that quantification of compensation under a cross–undertaking should be on the basis of a breach of a notional contract between the parties to the effect that the injunctor would not prevent the injunctee from doing the injuncted acts (see also *Cheltenham and Gloucester Building Society v Ricketts* [1993] 1 W.L.R. 1545; [1993] 4 All E.R. 276 at 285, CA, per Neill L.J.).

After a series of first instance decisions had expressed doubts about the so–called contractual basis of assessment, the question was addressed by the Court of Appeal in *Abbey Forwarding Ltd v Hone* [2014] EWCA Civ 711, May 23, 2014, CA, unrep. The Court held (1) (applying *Schlesinger v Bedford* (1893) 9 TLR 370, per Lindley L.J.) that the remote consequences of obtaining an injunction are not to be taken into account in assessing damages: only damages which naturally flow from the injunction are recoverable; (2) Lord Diplock's dictum in *F. Hoffmann–La Roche & Co A.G. v Secretary of State for Trade and Industry* [1975] A.C. 295, HL, at p.361 reflects the law as to such recoverability; but (3) that the analogy with contract must allow for "logical and sensible adjustments" in appropriate cases, such as, for example, that a claimant might have to accept a greater risk of losses incurred by a defendant in the period between the making of an order on an ex parte application and the return date, before the defendant has had the chance to alert the claimant or the court to serious and imminent losses, and before there is any sensible chance to apply to the court for a discharge or variation of the order; (4) the remoteness rules are applied so that the claimant giving the cross–undertaking should have reasonably foreseen loss of the type that was actually suffered, and not the particular loss within that type; (5) in appropriate cases, and where such losses are satisfactorily proved, realistic compensation can be awarded for loss of business opportunities, for business and other disruption (including the adverse effects of the inappropriate policing of the injunction on the injunctees) as well as for upset, stress, and loss of reputation (although the awards for the latter three heads are generally modest).

In *Al–Rawas v Pegasus Energy Ltd* [2008] EWHC 617 (QB), April 8, 2008, unrep. (Jack J.) it was explained that, subject to an exception, the undertakings in the prescribed forms for search and seizure orders and for freezing orders require claimants to accept liability for compensatory damages only. The exception is where the claimant in carrying out a search order acted in breach of its terms or otherwise in a manner inconsistent with his solicitor's duties as an officer of the court. The comments in the judgment about damages for emotional distress not being recoverable must be considered to be overruled by the decision in *Abbey Forwarding Ltd v Hone* [2014] EWCA Civ 711, May 23, 2014, CA, unrep.

At an inquiry as to damages, the question may arise whether the injuncted party failed reasonably to mitigate his loss. It arose in *Al–Rawas v Pegasus Energy Ltd* [2007] EWHC 2427 (QB), October 23, 2007, unrep. (Eady J.) where, for the purpose of avoiding the restrictions imposed by a freezing injunction, the defendants paid US $33m into court, taking out a loan in order to do so. Upon the injunction being discharged, an inquiry as to damages was ordered, and the money in court released. The defendants applied for summary judgment to recover the difference between the interest paid to service the loan and the interest earned whilst the money was in court (US $392,972.79 plus interest). In granting the application the judge rejected the claimant's submission that there were sufficient grounds to suppose that, at trial, the claimants would be able to show on a balance of probabilities that the defendants failed to discharge their obligation to mitigate their loss (it being suggested that there were alternative courses that they could and should have taken).

One of the undertakings in the example forms of freezing and search order is that if the order ceases to have effect (for example, if the respondent provides security, or if the order is discharged) the applicant will immediately take all reasonable steps to inform in writing anyone to whom he has given notice of this order, or who he has reasonable grounds for supposing may act upon this order, that it has ceased to have effect. The burden is thus normally on the person who obtained the injunction. In *Triodos Bank N.V. v Dobbs*, [2005] EWHC 108 (Ch), February 8, 2005, unrep. (Lightman J.), the injuncted party was dilatory in taking the steps required of him to perfect the order discharging the injunction, and had the delay aggravated his losses, his failure in that respect could have amounted to a failure to mitigate his loss.

B. FREEZING INJUNCTIONS

1. INTRODUCTION

Add new paragraph at end:

15–54 A freezing order prohibits the respondent from removing, disposing of, dealing with, or diminishing the value of his "assets", whether or not they are in his own name, and whether they are solely or jointly owned. A respondent is to be regarded as having power to deal with assets if a third party holds or controls the asset in accordance with his direct or indirect instructions. For a discussion of the authorities on what is meant by "assets" in this context, see *JSC BTA Bank v Ablyazov* [2013] EWCA Civ 928, [2014] 1 Lloyd's Rep. 195, CA, where the Court held, allowing the respondent's appeal, that his contractual right to draw down under a loan facility agreement was not an "asset", and his exercise of that right by directing the lender to pay the sum drawn down to a third party did not constitute "disposing of" or "dealing with" an asset.

2. NATURE AND SCOPE OF POWER – GENERALLY

After the first paragraph, add as a new paragraph:

15–55 In giving the lead judgment of the Court of Appeal in *JSC BTA Bank v Ablyazov*, [2013] EWCA Civ 928, [2014] 1 Lloyd's Rep. 195, CA, Beatson L.J. explained (para.34) that there are three legal principles "in play" as to the approach of the court to the exercise of the jurisdiction to make freezing orders; they are (1) that the purpose of such an order is to stop the injuncted defendant dissipating or disposing of property which could be the subject of enforcement if the claimant goes on to win the case it has brought, and not to give the claimant security for his claim (enforcement principle), (2) that the jurisdiction should be exercised in a flexible and adaptable manner so as to be able to deal with new situations and new ways used by "sophisticated and wily operators" to make themselves immune to the courts' orders or deliberately to thwart the effective enforcement of those orders (principle of flexibility), and (3) that, because of the penal consequences of breaching a freezing order and the need of the defendant to know where he, she or it stands, such orders should be clear and unequivocal, and should be strictly construed (principle of strict construction). The first is the primary principle. There is a certain tension between the principles.

3. JURISDICTION

(c) County courts

Add new paragraph at beginning:

15–59 With effect from April 22, 2014, the County Court Remedies Regulations 1991 (as amended) were revoked and replaced by the County Court Remedies Regulations 2014 (SI 2014/982). The 2014 Regulations make no provision for freezing injunctions; consequently, that remedy is no longer prescribed and the County Court has unrestricted jurisdiction to make orders for that form of injunctive relief. An application in the County Court for a freezing order must be made to a Circuit Judge.

5. "DOMESTIC" FREEZING INJUNCTIONS

(b) Assets excepted

(iii) *Legal expenses*

At the end of the second paragraph add:

15-73   It is for the party seeking to pay legal expenses out of frozen funds to persuade the court that it would be just to permit it in all the circumstances; if it is clear that the defendant has assets which are not restrained assets, the court will normally not vary the order to permit payment from frozen funds as it would not be consistent with the underlying purpose of the order (*Fortress Value Recovery Fund I LLC v Blue Skye Special Opportunities Fund LP* [2014] EWHC 551 (Comm), February 4, 2014, unrep. (Andrew Smith J.)).

C. SEARCH ORDERS

4. LEGAL EFFECT OF ORDER

After the third paragraph, add as a new paragraph:

15-92   Where in particular proceedings a search order is made by a claimant (C) for the purpose of preserving material evidence in the form of documents in the possession of the defendant (D), the execution of the order will have the effect of requiring D to deliver up the documents without giving D the opportunity of considering whether he or she would be required, in the progress of the proceedings, to disclose the documents in accordance with the rules as to disclosure in CPR Part 31 or to permit the inspection of them; see further Vol. 1 para.31.6.7 (Disclosure and inspection of documents subject to search order).

APPENDIX 1

COURTS DIRECTORY

APPENDIX 1

List of District Registries

Delete the table and substitute:

AP-7   [Civil Courts Order 2014 (SI 2014/819), as amended]

Name of place	Districts defined by reference to areas served by hearing centres of the County Court
ABERYSTWYTH	Aberystwyth
BARNSLEY	Barnsley
BARNSTAPLE	Barnstaple
BARROW IN FURNESS	Barrow in Furness
BASINGSTOKE	Basingstoke
BATH	Bath Chippenham and Trowbridge
BEDFORD	Bedford
BIRKENHEAD	Birkenhead
BIRMINGHAM (CHANCERY)	Birmingham
BLACKBURN	Blackburn

Name of place	Districts defined by reference to areas served by hearing centres of the County Court
Blackpool	Blackpool
Blackwood	Blackwood
Bolton	Bolton
Boston	Boston
Bournemouth	Bournemouth and Poole
Bradford	Bradford
Brecon	Brecknock
Bridgend	Bridgend Neath and Port Talbot
Brighton	Brighton Lewes
Bristol (Chancery)	Bristol Weston–super–Mare
Burnley	Accrington Burnley
Bury	Bury
Bury St Edmunds	Bury St Edmunds
Caernarfon (Chancery)	Caernarfon Conwy and Colwyn Porthmadog
Cambridge	Cambridge
Canterbury	Canterbury
Cardiff (Chancery)	Cardiff
Carlisle	Carlisle
Carmarthen	Carmarthen Llanelli
Chatham	Medway Dartford
Chelmsford	Chelmsford Hertford
Chester	Chester
Chesterfield	Chesterfield
Chichester	Chichester
Colchester	Colchester and Clacton
Coventry	Banbury Coventry Nuneaton Warwick
Crewe	Crewe
Croydon	Bromley Croydon
Darlington	Darlington
Derby	Buxton Derby
Doncaster	Doncaster Rotherham
Dudley	Dudley
Durham	Durham
Eastbourne	Eastbourne

Name of place	Districts defined by reference to areas served by hearing centres of the County Court
EXETER	Exeter
GLOUCESTER	Gloucester and Cheltenham
GREAT GRIMSBY	Great Grimsby
GUILDFORD	Aldershot and Farnham Guildford Reigate
HALIFAX	Halifax
HARROGATE	Harrogate
HARTLEPOOL	Hartlepool
HASTINGS	Hastings
HAVERFORDWEST	Haverfordwest
HEREFORD	Hereford
HUDDERSFIELD	Huddersfield
IPSWICH	Ipswich
KENDAL	Kendal
KING'S LYNN	King's Lynn
KINGSTON UPON HULL	Kingston upon Hull
LANCASTER	Lancaster
LEEDS (CHANCERY)	Leeds
LEICESTER	Leicester
LINCOLN	Lincoln
LIVERPOOL (CHANCERY)	Liverpool
LLANGEFNI	Llangefni
LUTON	Luton
MACCLESFIELD	Macclesfield
MAIDSTONE	Maidstone
MANCHESTER (CHANCERY)	Altrincham Manchester
MANSFIELD	Mansfield
MARGATE	Thanet
MERTHYR TYDFIL	Merthyr Tydfil
MIDDLESBROUGH	Middlesbrough
MILTON KEYNES	Aylesbury Milton Keynes
Mold (Chancery)	Mold
NEWCASTLE UPON TYNE (CHANCERY)	Morpeth and Berwick Newcastle upon Tyne
NEWPORT (GWENT)	Newport (Gwent)
NEWPORT (ISLE OF WIGHT)	Newport (Isle of Wight)
NORTHAMPTON	Kettering Northampton
NORWICH	Norwich
NOTTINGHAM	Nottingham
OLDHAM	Oldham Tameside
OXFORD	Oxford
PETERBOROUGH	Peterborough

Name of place	Districts defined by reference to areas served by hearing centres of the County Court
PLYMOUTH	Plymouth
PONTYPRIDD	Pontypridd
PORTSMOUTH	Portsmouth
PRESTON (CHANCERY)	Preston
READING	Reading
	Slough
RHYL	Rhyl
ROMFORD	Basildon
	Romford
ST. HELENS	St. Helens
SALISBURY	Salisbury
SCARBOROUGH	Scarborough
SCUNTHORPE	Scunthorpe
SHEFFIELD	Sheffield
SKIPTON	Skipton
SOUTHAMPTON	Southampton
SOUTHEND–ON–SEA	Southend–on–Sea
SOUTH SHIELDS	North Shields
STAFFORD	Stafford
STOCKPORT	Stockport
STOKE ON TRENT	Stoke on Trent
SUNDERLAND	Gateshead
	Sunderland
SWANSEA	Swansea
SWINDON	Swindon
TAUNTON	Taunton
Telford	Telford
TORQUAY	Torquay and Newton Abbot
TRURO	Bodmin
	Truro
TUNBRIDGE WELLS	Tunbridge Wells
WAKEFIELD	Wakefield
WALSALL	Walsall
WARRINGTON	Warrington
WELSHPOOL	Welshpool and Newtown
WEYMOUTH	Weymouth
WIGAN	Wigan
WINCHESTER	Winchester
WOLVERHAMPTON	Wolverhampton
WORCESTER	Worcester
Workington	West Cumbria
WORTHING	Horsham
	Worthing
WREXHAM	Wrexham
YEOVIL	Yeovil
YORK	York

Note

Delete Note and substitute:

AP–8   Table substituted by the Civil Courts Order 2014 (SI 2014/819), with effect from April 22, 2014.

INDEX

LEGAL TAXONOMY
FROM SWEET & MAXWELL

This index has been prepared using Sweet and Maxwell's Legal Taxonomy. Main index entries conform to keywords provided by the Legal Taxonomy except where references to specific documents or non-standard terms (denoted by quotation marks) have been included. These keywords provide a means of identifying similar concepts in other Sweet & Maxwell publications and online services to which keywords from the Legal Taxonomy have been applied. Readers may find some minor differences between terms used in the text and those which appear in the index. Suggestions to *sweetandmaxwell.taxonomy@thomson.com*.

(All references are to paragraph number and all references to material in Volume 2 are enclosed in square parentheses)

Aarhus Convention on Access to Information 1998
costs limits on claims
definitions, 45.41.1
generally, 45.41.1
scope of provision, 45.41.1

Abandonment
taking control of goods, and
'abandoned goods', 84.12.2
evidence, 84.12.3
generally, 84.12 — 84.12.1
statutory provisions, [9A–1280]

Abuse of process
attempts to re–litigate decided issues, 3.4.3.2
other forms, 3.4.3.6
pointless litigation, 3.4.3.4
wasteful litigation, 3.4.3.4

Accelerated possession claims
application of Part, 55.11.2

Acceptance
Part 36 offers
cost consequences, 36.10A

Access
medical records
applications to court, [3F–30]

Access to Justice report
introduction, 1.0.2
possession claims, 55.0.2

Access to Justice Act 1999
see also Funding arrangements

Access to Justice Act 1999—*cont.*
general provisions
appeals, [9A–841] — [9A–848.1]

Accountant General of the Supreme Court
statutory basis, [6A–5] — [6A–5.1]

Accrual
cause of action
contracts, [8–12.1]
generally, [8–5]

Acknowledgment of service
default judgments
conditions, 12.3.1
failure to file
Part 8 claims, 8.4.3
Part 8 claims
failure to file, 8.4.3
procedural guides
Queen's Bench Guide, [1B–24]
TCC claims, [2C–38]

"Act to be done at expense of disobedient party"
generally, 70.2A — 70.2A.1

Addition of parties
expiry of limitation period, after
bankruptcy, 19.5.8
conditions, 19.5.8
death, 19.5.8

Additional claims
Queen's Bench Guide, [1B–39]
small claims track, 27.1.1
TCC claims, [2C–40]

559

INDEX

Appeals (Court of Appeal)

appellant's notices
non–availability of documents,
52CPD.6
service on respondent, 52CPD.7
assignment
statutory basis, [9A–848] —
[9A–848.1]
closed material applications, 82.32
commencement, 52CPD.3 — 52CPD.7
contempt of court
statutory basis, [9B–18] — [9B–19]
determination of applications,
52CPD.15
filing
generally, 52.12.1.2
introduction
jurisdiction, 52.0.12
judicial review, 52.15 — 52.15.7
non–availability of documents,
52CPD.6
permission to appeal
determination of applications,
52CPD.15
Practice Direction
commencement, 52CPD.7
procedure
Queen's Bench Guide, [1B–80]
second appeals
statutory basis, [9B–843] — [9B–844]
service of appellant's notices, 52CPD.7
Upper Tribunal, from
introduction, 52.13.6

Appeals (High Court)

commencement, 52BPD.5
deposit of order, 40.14B — 40.14B.1
Extradition Act 2003, 52DPD.22
Practice Direction
commencement, 52BPD.5
procedure
Queen's Bench Guide, [1B–79]

Appeals (procedure)

appellants' notices
Queen's Bench Guide, [1B–76]
striking out, 52.9
case stated
Queen's Bench Guide, [1B–82]
costs
orders to limit recoverable sums,
52.9A.1
Court of Appeal
filing, 52.12.1.2
Queen's Bench Guide, [1B–80]
second appeals, 52.13.6
court powers
generally, 52.10.7.3
Queen's Bench Guide, [1B–75]
deposit of order, 40.14B — 40.14B.1
disposal by consent
Queen's Bench Guide, [1B–78]
extensions of time (filing)

Appeals (procedure)—cont.

criteria, 52.6.2
grounds for allowing appeal
failure to give reasons, 52.11.5
introduction, 52.11.4
unjust decision, 52.11.4
wrong decision, 52.11.4
imposition of conditions
introduction, 52.9.4
introduction
Court of Appeal, 52.0.12
judicial review
application for permission to appeal,
52.15.1 — 52.15.4
from Upper Tribunal, 52.15A —
52.15A.1
generally, 52.15 — 52.15.7
hearing the respondent, 52.15.5
time limits, 52.15.6
transfer to Upper Tribunal, 52.15.7
orders to limit recoverable sums,
52.9A.1
permission to appeal
imposition of conditions, 52.9
Queen's Bench Guide, [1B–74]
setting aside, 52.9
statutory basis, [9A–841] —
[9A–841.1]
Queen's Bench Guide
appellant's notices, [1B–76]
county court, [1B–79]
Court of Appeal, [1B–80]
court's powers on appeal, [1B–75]
disposal by consent, [1B–78]
generally, [1B–73]
High Court, [1B–79]
permission to appeal, [1B–74]
respondent's notices, [1B–77]
statutory appeals, [1B–81]
respondents' notice
Queen's Bench Guide, [1B–77]
striking out, 52.9
routes of appeal
Queen's Bench Guide, [1B–75]
second appeals
'first appeals', 52.13.2
meaning, 52.13.2
statutory basis, [9B–843] — [9B–844]
Upper Tribunal, from, 52.13.6
statutory appeals
general provisions, 52DPD.4
Queen's Bench Guide, [1B–81]
stay of proceedings
generally, 52.7.1
variation of time for filing
criteria, 52.6.2

Appellants' notices

appeals to Court of Appeal
non–availability of documents,
52CPD.6
service on respondent, 52CPD.7
extensions of time

564

Court documents
closed material applications, and,
82.18
copies, [1B–10]
content of Rule, 5.0.1
editorial introduction, 5.0.2
filing by electronic means
generally, 5.5.1
Practice Direction, 5CPD.10
filing by fax
generally, 5.5.1
Queen's Bench Guide
copies of documents, [1B–10]
sending
generally, 5.5.1
signature
generally, 5.3.1
supply
closed material applications, 82.18
supply from court records
open justice, and, 5.4C.10
party, to a, 5.4B.9
supply from court records to
non–parties
open justice, and, 5.4C.10

Court Funds Rules 2011
application, [6A–20]

Court guides
alternative dispute resolution, and
generally, [14–22]
Queen's Bench, [1B–35]
Queen's Bench Division, [1B–1] —
[1B–114]
Technology and Construction Court,
[2C–35] — [2C–61]

Court of Appeal
appeals to
arbitration, [2E–268]
order for new trial, 52.10.7.3
powers
order new trial, 52.10.7.3

Court officers
County Court
assault, [9A–435] — [9A–436]
responsibilities and liabilities,
[9A–665]
qualifications
list of, [9A–401]

Court records
supply of documents from
party, to a, 5.4B.9

Court rules
Civil Procedure Rule Committee
statutory basis, [9A–738] —
[9A–740.1]

Court rules—*cont.*
County Court, [9A–566] — [9A–566.1]

Court sittings
vacation business
High Court, 39BPD.2

Court users' committees
Technology and Construction Court,
[2C–36]

Courts' powers and duties
automatic striking out
County Court Money Claims Centre,
in, 3.5A — 3.5A.1
generally, 3.5 — 3.5.1
case management
correction of errors, 3.10.3
relief from sanctions, 3.8
setting aside judgment, 3.6 — 3.6A
coercive powers
automatic striking out, 3.5 — 3.5A
striking out, 3.4.10
discretion
place of proceedings, 2.7.1
expert evidence, 35.4
general powers
correction of errors, 3.10.3
generally, 3.1.4
issues
identification, 1.4.5
relief from sanctions
consequence if refused, 3.9.13
generally, 3.9.2
Mitchell v News Group Newspapers
Ltd, 3.9.3 — 3.9.4.4
post–Mitchell decisions, 3.9.5 —
3.9.5.14
procedure, 3.8 — 3.8.1
setting aside judgment, 3.6 — 3.6A
summary judgments
costs, 24.6.7

Crime and Courts Act 2013
general provisions, [9B–1425.1] —
[9B–1431]

"Cross–judgments"
set–off, 40.13A — 40.13A.1

Crown
party, as
County Court, [9A–488] —
[9A–488.1]

Crown proceedings
County Court
parties, [9A–488] — [9A–488.1]
information from judgment debtors,
66.6
third party debt orders, 66.6

Default judgments—*cont.*
default of defence, 12.3.3
costs–only proceedings, 12.9.1
County Court Money Claims Centre,
12.5A — 12.5A.1
default of acknowledgment of service,
in, 12.3.1
default of defence, in
conditions, 12.3.3
Money Claim Online, 7EPD.11
money claims
costs, 12.9.1
Queen's Bench Guide
generally, [1B–27]
setting aside, [1B–28]
setting aside
grounds, 13.3.5
Queen's Bench Guide, [1B–28]

Defences
Commercial Court
contents, [2A–56]
form, [2A–56]
generally, 2A–46]
summaries, [2A–56]
further information, 18.1.2
Queen's Bench Guide, [1B–26]
service
generally, 15.6.1
TCC claims, [2C–40]

Delivery
*see also Warrants of delivery;Writs of
delivery*
Queen's Bench Guide, [1B–85]

Demoted tenancies
jurisdiction of court, [3A–1185] —
[3A–1186]

Demotion claims
commencement, 65.14

Demotion orders
assured tenancies, and, [3A–765] —
[3A–765.1]
secure tenancies, and, [3A–349] —
[3A–350]

Deposits
assured shorthold tenancies
proceedings, [3A–1622] —
[3A–1623]
sanctions for non–compliance,
[3A–1628] — [3A–1629]

Designated money claims
introduction, 70.0.7

Detailed assessment
appeals
court hearing, 47.22.1
commencement
points of dispute, 47.9.2
default costs certificates
setting aside, 47.12.1
points of dispute
general rules, 47.9.2
setting aside default costs certificates
generally, 47.12.1
solicitor and client costs, of
procedure, 46.10.2

Directions
evidence
exclusion of witnesses from court,
32.1.4.3
exclusion of witnesses from court,
32.1.4.3
fast track
agreed, 28.3.4
generally, 28.3.1
variation, 28PD.4
multi–track
variation, 29PD.6
Queen's Bench Guide, [1B–43]

Disclosure
closed material applications, 52.3
County Court
personal injury actions, [9A–506] —
[9A–507]
pre–action, [9A–500] — [9A–501]
statutory basis, [9A–500] — [9A–511]
supplementary provisions, [9A–510]
— [9A–511]
fast track
generally, 28.3.1
mercantile claims, [2B–27]
non–parties
generally, 31.17.1, 31.17.3
statutory basis, [9A–115]
personal injury claims
County Court, [9A–506] — [9A–511]
generally, [9A–115] — [9A–116]
pre–action disclosure
generally, 31.16.1
statutory basis, [9A–110] —
[9A–111], [9A–500] — [9A–501]
Queen's Bench Guide
generally, [1B–49]
pre–action, [1B–17]
statutory basis
personal injury actions, [9A–115] —
[9A–116]
supplementary provisions, [9A–118]
— [9A–119]
TCC claims
cost, [2C–46]
limits, [2C–46]
standard disclosure, [2C–46]
types

Pre–action disclosure—*cont.*

pre–action protocols
  case law, C1A–012.2
procedure, 31.16.1
Queen's Bench Guide, [1B–17]
statutory basis
  SCA 1981, [9A–110] — [9A–119]

Pre–action protocols

alternative dispute resolution
  generally, [14–21]
compliance
  courts role, C1A–010
Construction and Engineering
  Disputes
  editorial notes, C5A–001
disclosure
  pre–action, C1A–012.2
editorial introduction
  compliance, C1A–010
  pre–action disclosure, C1A–012.2
landlord and tenant claims, 56.0.5
low value personal injury claims
  aims, C13–004
  amendments (2014), C13A–010
  contents, C13–001
  definitions, C13–002
  scope, C13–005
  stages of process, C13–007
pre–action disclosure
  case law, C1A–012.2
TCC Claims
  editorial notes, C5A–001
  Guide, [2C–37]

Preliminary issues

TCC claims
  appeals, [2C–43]
  common types, [2C–43]
  general, [2C–43]
  guidelines, [2C–43]
  other types, [2C–43]
  precise wording, [2C–43]
  use as adjunct to ADR, [2C–43]

Presumption of death orders

advertisement of claim
  generally, 57.21 — 57.21.1
  Practice Direction, 57PD.21
case management, 57PD.21
commencement of proceedings, 57.18
declaration of presumed death claims
  advertisement, 57.21 — 57.21.1
  generally, 57.19 — 57.19.1
  notice, 57.20
definitions, 57.17
editorial note, 57.17.1
generally, 57.17
interveners, 57.22 — 57.22.1
notices of claim, 57.20
place of proceedings, 57.18
Practice Direction, 57PD.21

Presumption of death orders—*cont.*

procedure for claims
  generally, 57.19
  Practice Direction, 57PD.21
requirement to provide information
  generally, 57.23
  Practice Direction, 57PD.21
variation order claims
  advertisement, 57.21 — 57.21.1
  generally, 57.19 — 57.19.1
  notice, 57.20

Pre–trial checklists

multi–track
  costs estimates, 29.6.3

Pre–trial reviews

Queen's Bench Guide, [1B–47]
TCC claims
  attendance, [2C–49]
  directions, [2C–49]
  documentation, [2C–49]
  Guide, [2C–39], [2C–49]
  issues, [2C–49]
  timetabling, [2C–49]
  timing, [2C–49]
  trial logistics, [2C–49]

Prevention of Social Housing Fraud Act 2013

general provisions, [3A–1766]

Principal place of business

service
  generally, 6.9.7

Private hearings

closed material applications
  generally, 82.6
  notification, 82.7
  proceedings to be determined, 82.8
contempt of court
  appeal, [9B–18] — [9B–19]
  generally, [9B–15] — [9B–16]
criteria
  interest of justice, 39.2.7.1
  Practice Direction, 39APD.1
  transcripts, 39.2.8

Private sector tenancies

secure tenancies, [3A–503]

Privilege against self incrimination

data protection, [3G–11]

Pro bono work

contact details, 39.7.6
costs (before April 1, 2013)
  statutory provisions, [9B–550] —
    [9B–550.1]